WORKSHOPS IN COMPUTING
Series edited by C. J. van Rijsbergen

Also in this series

14th Information Retrieval Colloquium
Proceedings of the BCS 14th Information
Retrieval Colloquium, University of Lancaster,
13–14 April 1992
Tony McEnery and Chris Paice (Eds.)

Functional Programming, Glasgow 1992
Proceedings of the 1992 Glasgow Workshop on
Functional Programming, Ayr, Scotland,
6–8 July 1992
John Launchbury and Patrick Sansom (Eds.)

Z User Workshop, London 1992
Proceedings of the Seventh Annual Z User
Meeting, London, 14–15 December 1992
J.P. Bowen and J.E. Nicholls (Eds.)

Interfaces to Database Systems (IDS92)
Proceedings of the First International Workshop
on Interfaces to Database Systems,
Glasgow, 1–3 July 1992
Richard Cooper (Ed.)

AI and Cognitive Science '92
University of Limerick, 10–11 September 1992
Kevin Ryan and Richard F.E. Sutcliffe (Eds.)

Theory and Formal Methods 1993
Proceedings of the First Imperial College
Department of Computing Workshop on Theory
and Formal Methods, Isle of Thorns Conference
Centre, Chelwood Gate, Sussex, UK,
29–31 March 1993
Geoffrey Burn, Simon Gay and Mark Ryan (Eds.)

**Algebraic Methodology and Software
Technology (AMAST'93)**
Proceedings of the Third International Conference
on Algebraic Methodology and Software
Technology, University of Twente, Enschede,
The Netherlands, 21–25 June 1993
M. Nivat, C. Rattray, T. Rus and G. Scollo (Eds.)

Logic Program Synthesis and Transformation
Proceedings of LOPSTR 93, International
Workshop on Logic Program Synthesis and
Transformation, Louvain-la-Neuve, Belgium,
7–9 July 1993
Yves Deville (Ed.)

Database Programming Languages (DBPL-4)
Proceedings of the Fourth International
Workshop on Database Programming Languages
– Object Models and Languages, Manhattan, New
York City, USA, 30 August–1 September 1993
Catriel Beeri, Atsushi Ohori and
Dennis E. Shasha (Eds.)

**Music Education: An Artificial Intelligence
Approach**, Proceedings of a Workshop held as
part of AI-ED 93, World Conference on Artificial
Intelligence in Education, Edinburgh, Scotland,
25 August 1993
Matt Smith, Alan Smaill and
Geraint A. Wiggins (Eds.)

Rules in Database Systems
Proceedings of the 1st International Workshop on
Rules in Database Systems, Edinburgh, Scotland,
30 August–1 September 1993
Norman W. Paton and
M. Howard Williams (Eds.)

Semantics of Specification Languages (SoSL)
Proceedings of the International Workshop on
Semantics of Specification Languages, Utrecht,
The Netherlands, 25–27 October 1993
D.J. Andrews, J.F. Groote and
C.A. Middelburg (Eds.)

Security for Object-Oriented Systems
Proceedings of the OOPSLA-93 Conference
Workshop on Security for Object-Oriented
Systems, Washington DC, USA,
26 September 1993
B. Thuraisingham, R. Sandhu and
T.C. Ting (Eds.)

Functional Programming, Glasgow 1993
Proceedings of the 1993 Glasgow Workshop on
Functional Programming, Ayr, Scotland,
5–7 July 1993
John T. O'Donnell and Kevin Hammond (Eds.)

Z User Workshop, Cambridge 1994
Proceedings of the Eighth Z User Meeting,
Cambridge, 29–30 June 1994
J.P. Bowen and J.A. Hall (Eds.)

6th Refinement Workshop
Proceedings of the 6th Refinement Workshop,
organised by BCS-FACS, London,
5–7 January 1994
David Till (Ed.)

**Incompleteness and Uncertainty in
Information Systems**
Proceedings of the SOFTEKS Workshop on
Incompleteness and Uncertainty in Information
Systems, Concordia University, Montreal,
Canada, 8–9 October 1993
V.S. Alagar, S. Bergler and F.Q. Dong (Eds.)

continued on back page...

Wojciech P. Ziarko (Ed.)

Rough Sets, Fuzzy Sets and Knowledge Discovery

Proceedings of the International Workshop on Rough Sets and Knowledge Discovery (RSKD'93), Banff, Alberta, Canada, 12–15 October 1993

Published in collaboration with the
British Computer Society

Springer-Verlag
London Berlin Heidelberg New York
Paris Tokyo Hong Kong
Barcelona Budapest

Wojciech P. Ziarko, MSc, PhD
Department of Computer Science,
University of Regina, Regina,
Saskatchewan, S4S 0A2, Canada

ISBN-13:978-3-540-19885-7   e-ISBN-13:978-1-4471-3238-7
DOI: 10.1007/978-1-4471-3238-7

British Library Cataloguing in Publication Data
A catalogue record for this book is available from the British Library

Typesetting: Camera ready by contributors

34/3830-543210 Printed on acid-free paper

Preface

The objective of this book is two-fold. Firstly, it is aimed at bringing together key research articles concerned with methodologies for knowledge discovery in databases and their applications. Secondly, it also contains articles discussing fundamentals of rough sets and their relationship to fuzzy sets, machine learning, management of uncertainty and systems of logic for formal reasoning about knowledge. Applications of rough sets in different areas such as medicine, logic design, image processing and expert systems are also represented. The articles included in the book are based on selected papers presented at the International Workshop on Rough Sets and Knowledge Discovery held in Banff, Canada in 1993. The primary methodological approach emphasized in the book is the mathematical theory of rough sets, a relatively new branch of mathematics concerned with the modeling and analysis of classification problems with imprecise, uncertain, or incomplete information. The methods of the theory of rough sets have applications in many sub-areas of artificial intelligence including knowledge discovery, machine learning, formal reasoning in the presence of uncertainty, knowledge acquisition, and others. This spectrum of applications is reflected in this book where articles, although centered around knowledge discovery problems, touch a number of related issues. The book is intended to provide an important reference material for students, researchers, and developers working in the areas of knowledge discovery, machine learning, reasoning with uncertainty, adaptive expert systems, and pattern classification.

As editor, I would like to express my sincere thanks to all contributors for their efforts to submit the high quality articles on time and within the specified size and format constraints. The preparation of this book was supported in part by a grant from the Natural Sciences and Engineering Research Council of Canada. The Computer Science Department of the University of Regina has provided all necessary technical facilities and support for the editorial work and rapid communication with contributors. Finally, I would like to thank Ms. Rosie Kemp, the Editorial Assistant for Springer-Verlag, and Mr. Ning Shan for their help in the preparation of this book.

Wojciech Ziarko
University of Regina

Contents

An Overview of Knowledge Discovery in Databases: Recent Progress and Challenges

Gregory Piatetsky-Shapiro

GTE Laboratories, MS 45

40 Sylvan Road

Waltham MA 02154 USA

Abstract

I examine the state of the art in Knowledge Discovery in Databases and review progress in several research areas, including discovery of models, multistrategy discovery systems, and detection of changes and deviations. I describe a number of successful applications and discuss the remaining challenges for further research and application development.

1   Introduction

The first wave of computerization, which began in 1960's, was the automation of routine tasks, such as payroll systems and accounts receivable. This was the beginning step in the creation of the massive business databases we see today. The second wave of computerization, dating from the mid-1970's, was transaction processing, which allowed computers to interactively perform much more complex activities, such as airline reservations or manufacturing control. This need for managing complex transactions and easy data retrieval led to the creation of database management systems. These systems are well suited to extracting information from databases. The massive growth of databases, which began in the 1980's, is beginning to overwhelm the human abilities to analyze data with a few manually composed queries. At the same time the need to understand the data is greater than ever.

This need is answered by the third wave of information processing, which began in the 1990's, and has been called by many names, including knowledge discovery in databases (KDD), data mining, knowledge extraction, pattern processing, and information harvesting. All these stand for the same idea, which is the *nontrivial extraction of implicit, previously unknown, and potentially useful information from data* (Frawley et al 1992). KDD encompasses a number of different technical approaches, such as clustering, data summarization, learning classification rules, deriving dependency (and other) models from data, analyzing changes and deviations, and detecting anomalies (see Matheus et al 1993).

According to Inmon and Osterfelt (1991), the third wave has the potential to eclipse the importance of the first two waves. The importance lies in the competitive advantage from the greatly increased market responsiveness and awareness that results from rapid discovery of patterns in data. Outside of business world, intelligent, automated data analysis is essential in many scientific fields such as astronomy or molecular biology, where the amounts of data already vastly exceed human capabilities to examine it. The relationship between data, information, and knowledge is shown in figure 1.

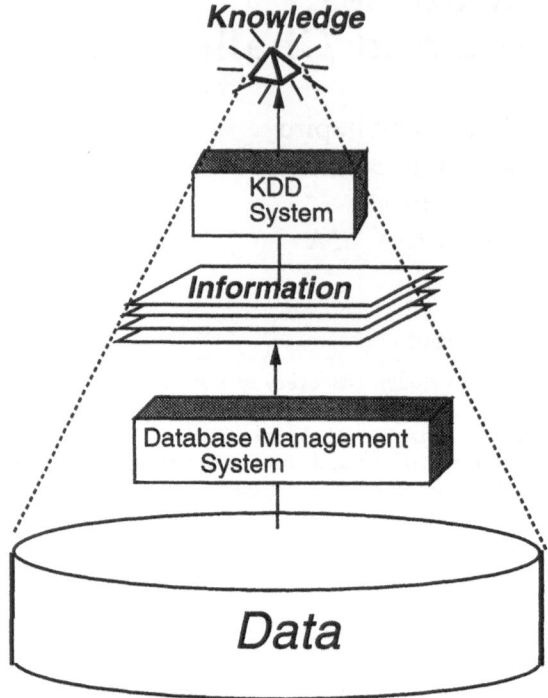

Figure 1: Data, Information, and Knowledge Pyramid

The theory of KDD is of growing interest to researchers in machine learning, statistics, intelligent databases, and knowledge acquisition, as evidenced by the number of recent workshops (Piatetsky-Shapiro 1991a, 1991b, Zytkow 1992, Ziarko 1993, Piatetsky-Shapiro 1993) and special journal issues (Piatetsky-Shapiro 1992, Zytkow 1993, Cercone and Tsuchiya 1993, Piatetsky-Shapiro 1994) devoted to or closely related to discovery in databases. The research progress will be discussed in the following section.

The research in the KDD core area of analysis of large relational databases has matured and is being transferred to applications, which have been reported in many areas of business, government, and science (Piatetsky-Shapiro and Frawley 1991, Inmon and Osterfelt 1991, Parsaye and Chignell 1993). Applications are the focus of section 3.

Finally, a number of challenges stand in the way of successful application development. They are dealt with in section 4.

2 Research Progress

At the 1991 KDD workshop (Piatetsky-Shapiro 1991b) the participants identified a number of research areas important for discovery in databases: Database

Technology and Integration of a Discovery System with a DBMS, Discovery of Models in Data, Integrated and Interactive Systems, Detection of Changes and Deviations, Intelligent Query Answering, and Discovery in Complex Data. Significant progress was made in the first four areas, while little progress has happened in the last two.

2.1 Database Technology and Integration with a DBMS

Since most learning algorithms cannot efficiently handle very large datasets, it is usually necessary to reduce the size of data on which learning is performed. One way is to eliminate irrelevant data using data dependencies. This has been shown (Almuallim and Dietterich 1991) to increase the performance of the classifier methods. Other methods rely on various forms of data sampling. Catlett (1991) used an intelligent sampling approach to make a sublinear algorithm for decision tree induction. His method has been used to efficiently learn decision trees from databases with hundreds of thousands of records.

An important design issue for a discovery system is how to manage its data. The two alternatives are (1) to use an *internal* DBMS or (2) an *external* DBMS. Systems which take the first approach include IMACS (Brachman et al 1993) and Explora (Kloesgen 1992). They pre-load relevant parts of the database and transform it into their internal and presumably more efficient format. This approach generally speeds up processing for small or medium-size databases. However, it limits a system's ability to work with large external databases, and creates the problem of data redundancy.

An *external database* approach, taken in discovery systems such as DBLEARN (Han et al 1993), Spotlight (Anand and Kahn 1992), SKICAT (Fayyad et al 1993), and Health KEFIR (Matheus et al 1994), is to build an interface, usually based on SQL, to a DBMS. This approach has its difficulties, such as dealing with communication problems and having to fit the discovery requests into the Procrustean bed of SQL. Retrieval from an external database may take longer, since in addition to a communication delay, the physical database organization may be sub-optimal for discovery system requests. However, this approach allows handling of large external databases that would not fit in memory and avoids duplicating the code for DBMS operations like joins or aggregations.

I expect the coming technical advances, such as faster hardware and communications, in-memory database management, SQL servers, and forthcoming standards for improved SQL, to make the external database approach more attractive.

2.2 Discovery of Models in Data

One of the simplest models is a graph. Graphical models of dependency (also called belief or causal networks) are a powerful knowledge representation mechanism and are the subject of much recent work (e.g. Pearl 1992; Cooper and Herskovitz 1992, Spirtes et al 1993). Significant progress in this field is very encouraging for KDD.

At the KDD-93 workshop (Piatetsky-Shapiro et al 1994) Greg Cooper summarized recent research progress in the discovery of directed probabilistic networks from data: there is a greater understanding of what relationships can be captured from data by directed acyclic graphs (DAGs) and which DAGs are indistinguishable based only on data; new methods have been developed for the discovery of probabilistic networks with measured and possibly unmeasured (latent) variables; these methods have been applied to real data with promising results. Major improvements needed for applications to real databases include better computational efficiency, integration of different methods (especially those dealing with discrete and continuous variables), and estimating the confidence and the stability of the output.

Another field whose recent progress is very promising for KDD is the Inductive Logic Programming (ILP), which can be thought of as discovering logical models in data. ILP is an important paradigm that goes beyond the attribute-value relations, which are the limit of what can be learned by most current machine learning methods, to the more general language of first-order relations. The field has developed rapidly in recent years (Muggleton 1992), and now offers relatively sophisticated algorithms and methods for handling a variety of discovery problems. ILP methods have been used for deriving qualitative models in physics and numerous other areas (Lavrač and Džeroski 1993). In one particularly successful experiment in prediction of protein secondary structure, not only was the ILP method better in terms of predictive accuracy than alternative published methods, but, perhaps more significantly, it yielded new domain knowledge.

The major challenges in applying ILP to KDD are in handling noisy probabilistic concepts and in improving the efficiency to deal with very large databases.

Rough set methodology, described elsewhere in this book, develops models of a different type. Rough sets help to classify the data using the approximation space and lower and upper approximations of a set. Rough sets can be used for inducing from data the best description of the subset of interest, representing uncertain knowledge, identifying data dependencies, and using the discovered patterns to make inferences. Several interesting applications of rough sets to data mining are described elsewhere in this volume (e.g. Hu et al 1994).

2.3 Integrated and Interactive Discovery Systems

These two approaches are closely related, since multi-method, integrated discovery systems frequently rely on human expertise to select the next discovery method, and interactive systems frequently offer a choice of multiple discovery algorithms.

Several recent comparisons of different learning and discovery algorithms have showed that different methods are superior for different types of problems (Brodley 1993) – no single method is best across a range of problems. As a result, there is a movement to multistrategy learning methods, especially for classification, which apply a number of different methods to the *same* task and select rules from the best method. I will call such integration *surface-level*. This is an area of very active research interest, with recent progress reported in (Michalski & Tecuci, 1993).

A deeper level of integration is reached by combination of different discovery methods applied to different tasks, e.g. a decision-tree builder and a dependency network generator. While there are some initial attempts to do it, this task remains very difficult.

Several recent multistrategy data mining systems integrate the different discovery methods by relying upon the user to select the appropriate discovery method. These systems include IMACS (Brachman et al 1993), KDW (Piatetsky-Shapiro and Matheus 1992), and RECON (Kerber 1994). They offer a user a choice of many different methods of data analysis, including standard statistics, decision trees, data summarization, and visualization. Such systems are suitable for sophisticated users who understand the data and the particulars of various methods and for whom the discovery is a multi-step process.

Interactive discovery systems can also tap the major recent advances in the fields of data visualization and multimedia interfaces. So far there have been only limited attempts (Grinstein et al 1992) to do this.

2.4 Detection of Changes and Deviations

Every new monthly or quarterly update of a large database raises the question of "what's new". For many large business databases it is no longer feasible to answer this question by manually submitting SQL queries – for such databases there is a crying need for automatic methods for detecting changes. Focus on changes and deviations has an additional benefit of separating interesting patterns from the trivial ones (such as `patient=pregnant` $\rightarrow$ `sex=female`). Since the trivial patterns do not change, they are not detected by the system.

Several deviation detection systems have been implemented and are in actual use, including Coverstory (Schmitz et al 1990), Spotlight, and Health KEFIR. These systems share the following similar design.

The relevant data can be thought of as a multidimensional space. The system's knowledge base defines a hierarchy of interesting subsets in that space (e.g. surgical patients for Health KEFIR), dimensions for further breakdown of these subsets (e.g. medical procedure type), and functions or measures that can be applied to a subset (e.g. average length of stay). An event is defined as a change in a measure between a current value and a previous or normative value. The interestingness of an event is computed based on the impact of the deviation on the bottom line, the statistical significance of the deviation, and other parameters.

Using this knowledge base, the discovery system performs an automatic drill-down of the data along multiple dimensions to identify the most interesting events. Some events, where possible, are linked to and explained via other events. The final output is usually a written report, generated using natural language and business graphics.

The next step after finding "what's new", is to answer the follow-up question "so what?". Since each detected event is a potential problem, the user wants to know how to correct it. Thus, the next step is to augment a deviation detection system with an expert system that can recommend useful actions, as is done in Health KEFIR. This is a open problem and a topic of further research.

2.5 Other Areas

Intelligent Query Answering. Here efforts have been made in two main directions: logical inference of intensional results (Imielinski 1987), which infer the summary of the extensional query answer, and approximate query answers

(Motro 1988), which attempt to find items similar to those requested. The problems remain very difficult and no major advances have been made.

Discovery in Text, Complex Data, and Knowledge Bases. This task remains very difficult with only a few notable efforts (Shen 1992). Perhaps, the situation will change when large knowledge bases, such as those developed by CYC (Lenat and Guha 1991) will achieve a critical mass.

3 Applications

Applications of data mining have been reported in astronomy, supermarket sales analysis, health care, stock market, direct marketing, insurance fraud detection, manufacturing, software analysis, and other areas. The most successful applications appeared in the areas of greatest need, where the databases are so large that manual analysis is impossible. Below we describe some of the most successful applications.

SKICAT (Fayyad et al 1993) is an automated system for analyzing large-scale sky surveys. The multi-terabyte size of the database ruled out a manual approach to image classification. The system used a number of innovative machine learning methods to recognize objects at least one magnitude fainter in resolution than was previously possible while achieving an accuracy of about 94%. This work is noteworthy as a real application of machine learning to a difficult problem with results that are being used by scientists on a regular basis.

Spotlight is a commercial system developed by A.C. Nielsen for identifying and reporting on trends and exceptional events in the extremely large supermarket sales databases. An innovative feature of Spotlight was the automatic explanation of relationships between key events. Spotlight is in use in many sites. Coverstory is a similar system developed by IRI. Recently Spotlight was extended into an Opportunity Explorer (Anand and Kahn 1993), a more general tool for developing interactive, hypertextual reports using knowledge discovery templates which convert a large data space into concise, inter-linked information frames. It is marketed to help sales analysts and product managers of consumer packaged goods companies develop better sales strategies.

Texas Instruments (Saxena 1993) developed a system for fault isolation during semiconductor manufacturing using automated discovery from wafer tracking databases. Based on prior manual analysis of such databases, classes of queries to the database as well as patterns in the responses to these queries that are useful for fault isolation were identified. Diagnosis is accomplished by automating the query generation and the detection of potentially useful patterns. A prototype system was implemented and tested on real data, finding both known and previously unknown faults.

While most of the above applications used unique, custom-developed tools, future application development will be facilitated by the large number of commercially available tools, both generic tools for operations like classification and deviation detection, and application-specific tools for vertical markets like retail sales and financial data analysis.

4 Challenges

Insufficient statistical awareness: Some KDD experiments are performed without sufficient awareness of statistical theory. The classical example of this problem is testing N independent patterns for deviation from the norm, each test having a significance of α. Then, $N\alpha$ patterns are likely to pass the test purely due to chance. Eliminating such "random" discoveries requires statistical controls, such as Bonferroni adjustments (Harris 1985), which in the above example means reducing the significance level for each test to α/N, in order to assign the final discovery the significance of α. Other ways to eliminate chance discoveries include randomized testing procedures (Jensen 1991).

Overabundance of patterns: As many pioneers of KDD have found, even with proper statistics, it is all too easy to find many statistically significant patterns which are either obvious, redundant, or useless. A common approach to reducing the number of obvious "discoveries" (such as only women have pregnancies), is to focus on changes, since "obvious" patterns will not change. Redundant discoveries can be eliminated by rule refinement methods (Major 1993, Kloesgen 1993), or by using some findings to explain others. The more difficult task of separating the important patterns from the useless requires domain knowledge. A general heuristic here is that rules and patterns are important to the degree they can lead to a useful action. This suggests a decision-theoretic framing of the problem of evaluating the usefulness of discovered patterns. The *utility* of a particular pattern should not be measured in isolation, but instead evaluated in the context of set of possible actions.

Integration with Existing Systems: Even if a perfect discovery systems is built, it needs to be integrated with other existing hardware/software systems to be useful. As expert system developers discovered years earlier, usually only a small part of the deployed system is new technology – the rest is interfacing and system integration, mundane but critical steps in moving from the prototype stage to deployment.

Privacy vs Discovery: Discovery in social or business data may raise a number of legal, ethical, and privacy issues. In 1990, Lotus was planning to introduce a CD-ROM with data on more than 100 million American households. A stormy protest led to the withdrawal of this product (Rosenberg 1992). Recent conferences on Computers, Freedom, and Privacy have also increased the awareness about issues of privacy and data ownership.

Versatility vs Autonomy: Most discovery systems developed so far fall into three broad groups with respect to their versatility and autonomy (see figure 2). The first group contains multistrategy systems, such as IMACS, KDW, and RECON, which offer the user a choice of many different methods of data analysis, including standard statistics, decision trees, data summarization, and visualization. These systems view discovery as a multi-step process and rely on the user for the selection of the next step. These systems are suitable only for sophisticated users.

The second group contains systems which have only one generic type of discovery method. Systems in this group include Explora, Opportunity Explorer, and several commercially available data mining tools. These systems have higher autonomy but lower versatility than the first group.

Finally, there are systems like SKICAT, Spotlight, CoverStory, Health KE-FIR, which combine a single discovery method with a built-in application-

8

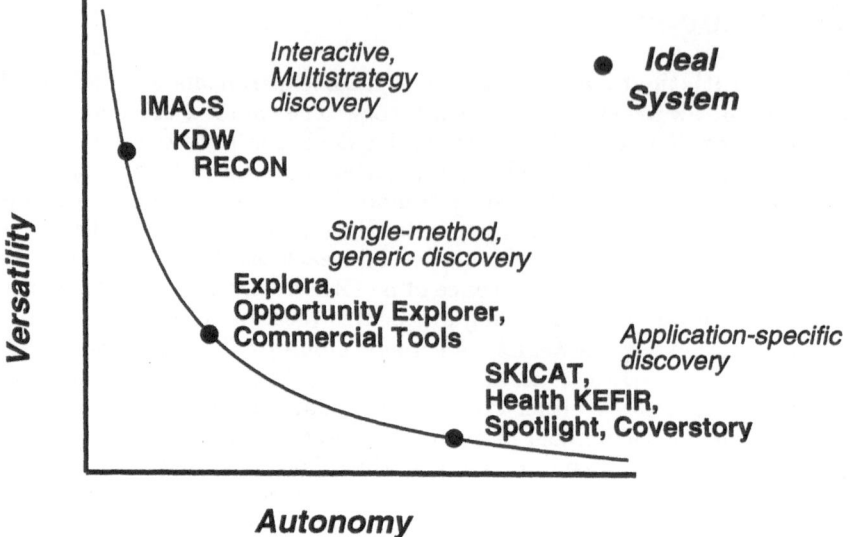

Figure 2: Autonomy versus Versatility in KDD Systems

specific knowledge. The built-in knowledge and high autonomy of such systems made them more acceptable to end-users than the other two types.

Ultimately, there should be an *ideal* system which would combine multiple discovery methods with a high degree of autonomy. Such ideal system would constitute a real breakthrough in the quest towards powerful discovery tools.

Acknowledgments: I am grateful to Chris Matheus, Bud Frawley, Padhraic Smyth, and Sam Uthurusamy for their comments. I thank Shri Goyal and Bill Griffin for their support.

5   References

H. Almuallim and T. Dietterich, 1991. Learning with Many Irrelevant Features. In Proceedings of AAAI-91, 547-552. Menlo Park, Calif: AAAI.

T. Anand and G. Kahn 1992. SPOTLIGHT: A Data Explanation System. Proceedings of CAIA-92. Washington, D.C.: IEEE Computer Society.

T. Anand and G. Kahn, 1993. Opportunity Explorer: Navigating Large Databases Using Knowledge Discovery Templates. In Proceedings of KDD-93 workshop. AAAI Press.

R. Brachman, P. Selfridge, L. Terveen, B. Altman, F. Halper, T. Kirk, A. Lazar, D. McGuiness, L. Resnick, and A. Borgida, 1993. Integrated Support for Data Archaeology. In Proceedings of KDD-93 workshop. AAAI Press.

C. Brodley, 1993. Addressing the Selective Superiority Problem: Automatic Algorithm/Model Class Selection, In Proc. of 10th Machine Learning Conference, 17–24. Morgan Kaufmann.

J. Catlett, 1991. Megainduction: A Test Flight. In Proc. of 8th Machine Learning Conference, 596–599. Morgan Kaufmann.

N. Cercone and M. Tsuchiya, 1993. Editors, Special Issue on Learning and Discovery in Databases, *IEEE Transactions on Knowledge and Data Engineering* 5(6).

G. Cooper and E. Herskovits, 1992. A Bayesian Method for the Induction of Probabilistic Networks from Data. *Machine Learning* 9(4), 309–348.

U. Fayyad, N. Weir, and S. Djorgovski 1993. Automated Analysis of a Large-Scale Sky Survey: The SKICAT System, in Proceedings of KDD-93 Workshop. AAAI Press.

W. Frawley, G. Piatetsky-Shapiro, and C. Matheus, 1992. Knowledge Discovery in Databases: An Overview. *AI Magazine*, Fall issue.

G. Grinstein, J. Sieg, S. Smith, M. Williams, 1992. Visualization for Knowledge Discovery, *Int. J. of Intelligent Systems* 7:7, Sep.

J. Han, Y. Cai, and N. Cercone, 1993. Data-driven discovery on quantitative rules in relational databases. *IEEE Transactions on Knowledge and Data Engineering* 5(1).

R. Harris, 1985. *A Primer of Multivariate Statistics*, Academic Press.

X. Hu, N. Cercone, J. Han, 1994. An Attribute-oriented Rough Set Approach for Knowledge Discovery in Databases, elsewhere in this volume.

T. Imielinski, 1987. Intelligent Query Answering in Rule-Based Systems, *J. Logic Programming*, 4, 229–257.

D. Jensen, 1991. Knowledge discovery through induction with randomization testing, in *Proceedings of the 1991 AAAI KDD Workshop*, G. Piatetsky-Shapiro (ed.), AAAI, Anaheim, CA, pp. 148–159.

W. H. Inmon and S. Osterfelt, 1991. *Understanding Data Pattern Processing: the key to Competitive Advantage*. QED Technical Publishing Group, Wellesley, MA.

R. Kerber, B. Livezey, E. Simoudis, 1994. Recon: A Framework for Database Mining, submitted for publication.

W. Kloesgen, 1992. Problems for Knowledge Discovery in Databases and their treatment in the Statistics Interpreter EXPLORA, *Int. J. of Intelligent Systems* 7:7, Sep.

W. Klosgen, 1993. Some Implementation Aspects of a Discovery System, In Proceedings of KDD-93 workshop. AAAI Press.

N. Lavrač and S. Džeroski, 1993. *Inductive Logic Programming: Techniques and Applications*. Ellis Horwood, Chichester.

D. Lenat and R. Guha, 1991. *Building Large Knowledge-Based Systems*. Reading, MA: Addison-Wesley.

J. Major and J. Mangano, 1993. Selecting Among Rules Induced from a Hurricane Database, In Proceedings of KDD-93 workshop. AAAI Press.

C. Matheus, P. Chan, G. Piatetsky-Shapiro, 1993. Systems for Knowledge Discovery in Databases, *IEEE Transactions on Knowledge and Data Engineering* 5(6).

C. Matheus, G. Piatetsky-Shapiro, and D. McNeill, 1994. Key Findings Reporter for Analysis of Health Care Information, submitted for publication.

R. Michalski and G. Tecuci, 1993. Editors, *Machine Learning: A Multistrategy Approach*, Volume IV. Morgan Kaufmann.

A. Motro, 1988. VAGUE: a user interface to relational databases that permits vague queries, *ACM Transactions on Office Information Systems*, 6(3) 187–214.

S. Muggleton, 1992. *Inductive Logic Programming*. Academic Press, London.

J. Pearl, 1992. Probabilistic Reasoning in Intelligent Systems: Networks of plausible inference, 2nd ed. San Mateo, Calif.: Morgan Kaufmann.

G. Piatetsky-Shapiro, 1991a. Report on IJCAI-89 workshop on Knowledge Discovery in Databases, *AI Magazine*, January.

G. Piatetsky-Shapiro, 1991b. Report on AAAI-91 workshop on Knowledge Discovery in Databases, *IEEE Expert*, October.

G. Piatetsky-Shapiro and W. Frawley, 1991. Editors, *Knowledge Discovery in Databases*, Cambridge, Mass.: AAAI/MIT Press.

G. Piatetsky-Shapiro, 1992. Editor, Special issue on Knowledge Discovery in Databases and KnowledgeBases, *International J. of Intelligent Systems* 7:7, Sep.

G. Piatetsky-Shapiro and C. Matheus, 1992. Knowledge Discovery Workbench for Exploring Business Databases, *International J. of Intelligent Systems* 7:7, Sep.

G. Piatetsky-Shapiro, 1993. Editor, KDD-93: Proceedings of AAAI-93 workshop on Knowledge Discovery in Databases, AAAI Press.

G. Piatetsky-Shapiro, 1994. Editor, Special issue on Knowledge Discovery in Databases, *J. of Intelligent Information Systems* 3(4), Dec.

G. Piatetsky-Shapiro, C. Matheus, P. Smyth, R. Uthurusamy, 1994. KDD-93: Progress and Challenges in Knowledge Discovery in Databases, workshop report. Submitted to AI Magazine.

K. Parsaye and M. Chignell, 1993. *Intelligent Database Tools & Applications*. NY: John Wiley.

M. Rosenberg, 1992. Protecting Privacy, Inside Risks column, *Communications of ACM*, 35(4), p. 164.

S. Saxena, 1993. Fault Isolation during Semiconductor Manufacturing using Automated Discovery from Wafer Tracking Databases, Proc. of Ninth Conf. on AI Applications, IEEE, pp. 313–320.

Schmitz, J., Armstrong, G., and Little, J. D. C. 1990. CoverStory - Automated news finding in marketing. In *DSS Transactions*, Linda Volino (Ed.), The Institute of Management Sciences, Providence, RI. 46-54.

W. M. Shen, 1992. Discovering Regularities from Knowledge Bases, *Int. J. of Intelligent Systems* 7:7, Sep.

P. Spirtes, C. Glymour, R. Scheines, 1993. *Causation, Prediction, and Search*, Lecture Notes in Statistics, Springer-Verlag.

W. Ziarko, 1993. Editor, Proceedings of the Int. Workshop on Rough Sets and Knowledge Discovery, Banff, Canada.

J. Zytkow, 1992. Editor. Proceedings of the Machine Discovery Workshop, Aberdeen, Scotland, July.

J. Zytkow, 1993. Editor. Special Issue on Machine Discovery, *Machine Learning* 12(1-3).

Rough Sets and Knowledge Discovery: An Overview

Wojciech Ziarko

Computer Science Department

University of Regina

Regina, Saskatchewan, Canada S4S 0A2

1 Rough Sets

The primary methodological framework to study classification problems with imprecise or incomplete information in this book is the theory of rough sets. The theory was originally introduced by Pawlak[1]. The uniqueness as well as the complementary character of rough set theory to other approaches for dealing with imprecise, noisy, or incomplete information such as fuzzy set theory[4], or theory of evidence[5] was recognized by mathematicians and researchers working on mathematical foundations of Computer Science. Currently, there are over 800 publications in this area, including two books and an annual workshop. The rough sets model is used as a departure point to study formal reasoning with uncertain information[6-8], machine learning, knowledge discovery[9-13, 20], and representation and reasoning about imprecise knowledge[6]. The theory of rough sets has been applied in numerous domains such as, for example, analysis of clinical data and medical diagnosis[14], information retrieval[15], control algorithm acquisition and process control[16], analysis of complex chemical compounds[17], structural engineering[18], market analysis[12], and others[9].

The use of rough sets framework as a research tool has a number of advantages. First, the theory of rough sets provides a collection of mathematical techniques to deal, with full mathematical rigour, with data classification problems, particularly when data are noisy, incomplete or imprecise. Secondly, the rough set theory includes a formal model of knowledge defined as a family of indiscernibility relations so that the knowledge has a clearly defined mathematical sense and can be analyzed and manipulated using mathematical techniques.

The key idea in the rough sets approach stems from the observation that imprecise representation of data helps uncover data regularities. The question is how much imprecision should be allowed without loss of essential information which is understood here as an ability to discern, fully or partially, a concept or a class of concepts. The quality of the information is measured in the framework of rough sets by using the notions of lower and upper set approximation[1]. To maximally reduce the degree of precision, the idea of "reduct"[1] is used which allows for discernibility-preserving elimination of irrelevant information. After finding "reducts" for each concept, the maximally imprecise, that is with easily determinable patterns, representation of data is obtained. Based on such a representation, general rules characterizing each concept can be computed[34]. The computation of the rules can be reduced to the problem of finding prime implicants of a Boolean function called indiscernibility function[26,44]. Also, the degree of functional dependency between attributes can be computed by using the idea of set lower bound[34]. The subsequent computation of relative reducts[34] allows one to find all alternative groups of attributes which are non-redundant and preserve the dependency level. This kind of a feature is particularly useful for knowledge discovery applications of this methodology[25].

2 Knowledge Discovery

Knowledge discovery in databases is a relatively new, rapidly growing research and application direction stemming from earlier research in database theory, machine learning, statistics, rough sets theory, and other areas. The central question in knowledge discovery research is how to turn information, expressed in terms of stored data, into knowledge expressed in terms of generalized statements, or rules about some characteristics, or relationships occurring in data. A great deal of knowledge can be extracted from data without using any sophisticated techniques, for example by reading the contents of an individual employee record, one can acquire some knowledge about the employee's personal characteristics. However, large amounts of knowledge are "hidden" in the database in the form of relationships among data items. For instance, the general relationship between employee's age, sex, and salary of an information system may not be easily visible and its analysis may require the usage of some statistical techniques. Some other interesting relationships occurring in the database may assume the form of functional, or partial functional dependencies and their discovery analysis and characterization may involve methods of rough sets theory, or some other techniques such as rule or decision tree induction, regression analysis, etc. In fact, most of the really new and interesting knowledge is "buried" in databases and is usually not available due to lack of proper tools. Although statistical methods have been used for decades to extract some additional information about data, their usage and validity of results are limited to rather large data collections satisfying very specific assumptions regarding the probability distributions. Consequently, there is a real need for techniques and tools which would complement statistical methods in the task of acquiring an extra dimension of knowledge from data. In particular, the availability of high speed processors makes it possible to look into the structure of inter-data relationships, to search for the optimal characterization of such relationships, or to find some interesting data anomalies, for example, for the purpose of database fraud detection.

Due to the young age of the knowledge discovery research there is not much common language or terminology linking researchers and practitioners working in this field. Nevertheless, progress have been made during recent years within individual approaches to knowledge discovery[35], such as rough sets[1], concept hierarchy[2], decision tree and rule induction, inductive logic programming, and others[3]. Also, progress has been also achieved in developing methods for reasoning about discovered knowledge. The knowledge extracted from data may be often incomplete or imprecise with the predicates about the properties or relationships of the data set not always having definite truth values. This kind of knowledge requires novel reasoning techniques to expand on basic facts obtained from data.

A number of prototype discovery systems were built in the recent years.

They can be broadly categorized as data-driven and theory-driven systems. The typical representative of the latter class is system AM[19] which was able to discover a number of mathematical concepts based on an initial set of theory concepts and search heuristics. Some systems are combinations of theory and data-driven models. An example system from this class is RX[20] which was used to discover causal relationships from large clinical database. RX contains a large medical knowledge base which is applied to derive a hypothesis to be tested in the database. Data-driven systems are the major part among existing discovery systems and related research. Many systems of this kind have been used for discovery of algebraic models and/or classification rules. The typical approach is to employ data-driven heuristics to direct a search through the space of the theoretical terms and numerical laws. The best known system in this category is system BACON[21], designed to produce algebraic equations that describe numerical data. The best known achievement of BACON was the rediscovery of Kepler's laws. An extension of the idea of BACON is FAHREN-HEIT[22] which has been successfully applied to the development of empirical equations from results of chemical experiments. Other better known systems from this class are IDS[23], ABACUS[7], and GALILEO[25]. Many approaches are aimed at discovering decision trees. Systems such as ID-3 and its derivatives[19,27], CART[27], employ statistical techniques to control classification decision tree generation. Another group of systems discovers classification rules which do not form a decision tree, for example, APACS[26] (based on statistical techniques), LERS1[10] and DATALOGIC[23] (based on rough set theory). System DBLEARN integrates a relational database with an extended SQL with built-in capability to discover rules[2]. The verification of the discovered rules in terms of their general validity and their relevance or "interestingness" level is another research problem[34]. Statistical techniques have been proposed for rule validation[31] and interestingness criteria are being developed to select the potentially most useful rules[34]. The identification of data anomalies, i.e. of potentially interesting data values or relationships are also an important research direction within knowledge discovery field[3]. A large class of approaches is concerned with discovering data dependencies, both functional and probabilistic[32]. Rough sets and rule induction techniques are used for discovering functional dependencies, whereas Variable Precision Rough Sets[30,33] and statistical techniques, sometimes integrated with symbolic learning are being applied for discovering weaker probabilistic dependencies.

References

[1] Pawlak, Z. *Rough Sets - Theoretical Aspects of Reasoning about Data*, Kluwer, 1991.

[2] J. Han, Y. Cai, N. Cercone, *Knowledge Discovery in Databases: An Attribute-Oriented Approach*, Proc. of the 18th VLDB Conference, Vancouver, B.C., Canada, 1992, pp. 335-350.

[3] Piatetsky-Shapiro, G. (ed.) *Proc. of AAAI-93 Workshop on Knowledge Discovery in Databases*, Washington, D.C., 1993.

[4] Pawlak, Z. *Rough Sets - A New Approach to Vagueness*, in Fuzzy Logic for Management of Uncertainty (ed. L.A. Zadeh and J. Kacprzyk), Wiley and Sons, New York 1992.

[5] Skowron, A., Grzymala-Busse, J. *From Rough Set Theory to Evidence Theory*, In Advances in the Dempster-Shafer Theory of Evidence, John Wiley & Sons, Inc., 1993.

[6] Rasiowa, H. *Rough Concepts and Multiple-Valued Logic*, Proc. of 16th Intl. Symp. on Multiple-Valued Logic, Computer Society Press, 1986.

[7] Orlowska, E. et al. *DAL-a logic for Data Analysis*, Theoretical Computer Science 36, 1985.

[8] Wasilewska, A. *Syntactic Procedures in Information Systems*, J. of Man-Machine Studies, 30, 1989, 273-285.

[9] Ziarko, W. (ed). *Proc. Intl. Workshop on Rough Sets and Knowledge Discovery*, Banff, 1993.

[10] Grzymala-Busse, J. *An Overview of the LERS1 Learning System*, Proc. of the 2nd Intl. Conf. on Engineering Applications of AI, Tullahoma, 1989, 838-844.

[11] Wasilewska, A. et al. *Interactive Inductive Learning*, J. of Man-Machine Studies, Vol. 38, 1993, 147-167.

[12] Ziarko, W., Golan R. and Edwards, D. *An Application of Datalogic/R Knowledge Discovery Tool to Identify Strong Predictive Rules in Stock Market Data*, Proceedings of AAAI Workshop on Knowledge Discovery in Databases, Washington, D.C., 1993, pp. 89-101.

[13] Ziarko, W. and Shan, N. *A Rough Set-Based Method for Computing All Minimal Deterministic Rules in Attribute-Value Systems*, Computational Intelligence: An International Journal, to appear, U. of R. Tech. Report CS-93-02.

[14] Slowinski, K. *Rough Sets Approach to Analysis of Data from Peritoneal Lavage in Acute Pancreatitis*, Medical Informatics. 13, 1988, no. 3, 143-159.

[15] Gupta, S. *Rough Sets and Information Retrieval*, 11th Intl. Conf. on Inf. Retrieval, 1988.

[16] Mrozek, A. *Rough Sets and Dependency Analysis*, J. of Man- Machine Studies, 30, 4, 1989, 448-457.

[17] Krysinski, J. *Rough Sets Approach to the Analysis of the Structure-Activity Relationship of Quaternary Imidazolium Compounds*, Arzneimittel-Forschung 40(II), 1990, 795-799.

[18] Arciszewski, T., Ziarko, W. *Inductive Learning in Civil Engineering: Rough Sets Approach*, Microcomputers and Civil Engineering. Vol. 5, no. 1, 1990.

[19] Michalski, R. et. al. (eds.) *Machine Learning: An Artificial Intelligence Approach*, vol. 1-2, Morgan Kaufmann, 1983, 1986.

[20] Blum, R. *Discovery and Representation of Casual Relationships*, Springer Verlag, 1982.

[21] Langley, P. *Data-Driven Discovery of Physical Laws*, Cognitive Science, 5, 1981, 31-54.

[22] Zytkow, J. et al. *Automated Discovery in Chemistry Laboratory*, Proc. of 8th National Conference on AI, The AAAI Press, 1990, 889-894.

[23] Nordhausen, B. *An Integrated Approach to Empirical Discovery*, In Computational Models of Discovery and Theory Formation, Morgan Kaufmann, 1990.

[24] Falkenheiner, B. et al. *Integrating Quantitative and Qualitative Discovery: The ABACUS System*, Machine Learning, 1, 1986, 367-401.

[25] Zytkow, J. *Deriving Basic Laws by Analysis of Processes and Equations*, In Computational Models of Discovery and Theory Formation, Morgan Kaufmann, 1990.

[26] Chan, K. et al. *Automatic Construction of Expert Systems from Data - A Statistical Approach*, In Proc. of IJCAI-1989 Workshop on Knowledge Discovery in Databases, 1989, 37-48.

[27] Weiss, S. et al. *Computer Systems that Learn*, Morgan Kaufman, 1991.

[28] Szladow, A. *Mining the Knowledge in Databases*, PC AI, Jan./Feb. 1993.

[29] Szladow, A., Ziarko, W. *Rough Sets: Working with Imperfect Data*, AI Expert, July 1993, 36-41.

[30] Ziarko, W. *Variable Precision Rough Sets Model*, Journal ofComputer and Systems Sciences, vol. 46, no. 1, 1993, 39-59.

[31] Piatetsky-Shapiro, G. *Discovery, Analysis, and Presentation of Strong Rules*, In Piatetsky-Shapiro, G. Frawley, W. (eds). Knowledge Discovery in Databases, AAAI/MIT Press, 1991, pp.229-248.

[32] Schlimmer, J.V. *Using Learned Dependencies to Automatically Construct Sufficient and Feasible Editing Views*, Proceeding of AAAI Workshop on Knowledge Discovery in Databases, Washington D.C., 1993, pp.186-196.

[33] Katzberg, J. and Ziarko, W. *Variable Precision Rough Sets with Asymmetric Bounds*, in this volume.

[34] Major, J. and Mangano, J. *Selecting Among Rules Induced from a Hurricane Database*, Proceeding of AAAI Workshop on Knowledge Discovery in Databases, Washington D.C., 1993, pp.28-41.

[35] Piatesky-Shapiro, G. *An Overview of Knowledge Discovery in Databases: Recent Progress and Challanges*, in this volume.

Search for Concepts and Dependencies in Databases

Rokia Missaoui

Robert Godin

Département de Mathématiques et d'Informatique

Université du Québec à Montréal

Montréal, Canada, H3C 3P8

Abstract

In addition to being a technique for classifying objects and defining concepts from data, the concept lattice may be exploited to discover relationships among descriptors or attributes. This paper addresses the problem of generating implication rules, and shows that the lattice is an interesting framework for functional dependency generation and checking.

1 Introduction

Recent work in the field of databases shows an increasing interest in knowledge discovery from data [1, 7, 9]. The basic motivations for such an interest are: (i) in many organizations, databases are very huge information mines that can be usefully exploited to discover concepts, patterns and relationships, (ii) the discovered knowledge may be efficiently used for many purposes such as business decision making, database schema refinement, integrity enforcement, semantic query optimization, and intelligent query handling.

The main purpose of this paper is to present algorithms for generating implication rules and functional dependencies from the concept lattice structure of a binary relation. The remainder of this abstract is organized as follows. In the next section we give a background on the concept lattice theory and provide in Section 3 algorithms for implication rule and functional dependency generation. Finally, a brief discussion on further refinements is proposed.

2 Background

2.1 The concept lattice

From the context $(\mathcal{O}, \mathcal{D}, \mathcal{R})$ describing a set $\mathcal{O}$ of objects, a set $\mathcal{D}$ of descriptors (properties) and a binary relation $\mathcal{R}$ (Table 2.1) between $\mathcal{O}$ and $\mathcal{D}$, there is a unique ordered set which describes the inherent lattice structure defining natural groupings and relationships among the objects and their descriptors (Figure 2.2). This structure is known as a concept lattice [2, 11] or Galois lattice [4]. The notation $x\mathcal{R}x'$ is used to express the fact that an element x from $\mathcal{O}$ is related to an element x' from $\mathcal{D}$. Each element of the lattice $\mathcal{L}$ derived from the context $(\mathcal{O}, \mathcal{D}, \mathcal{R})$ [11] is a couple, noted (X, X'), composed of an object set X of the power set $\mathcal{P}(\mathcal{O})$ and a property set $X' \in \mathcal{P}(\mathcal{D})$. Each couple must be complete with respect to $\mathcal{R}$, i.e., the next two properties hold:

(i) $X' = f(X)$ where $f(X) = \{x' \in \mathcal{D} \mid \forall x \in X, x\mathcal{R}x'\}$.

(ii) $X = f'(X')$ where $f'(X') = \{x \in \mathcal{O} \mid \forall x' \in X', x\mathcal{R}x'\}$.

Moreover, the following partial order must hold.

Given $C_1 = (X_1, X_1')$ and $C_2 = (X_2, X_2')$, $C_1 \leq C_2 \Leftrightarrow X_1' \subset X_2'$. The partial order is used to generate the graph in the following way: there is an edge from C_1 to C_2 if $C_1 < C_2$ and there is no other element C_3 in the lattice such that $C_1 < C_3 < C_2$. The graph is usually called a Hasse diagram and the precedent order means that C_1 is parent of C_2. Given, $\mathcal{C}$, a set of elements from the lattice $\mathcal{L}$, $inf(\mathcal{C})$ and $sup(\mathcal{C})$ will denote respectively the infimum and the supremum of the elements in $\mathcal{C}$.

Table 2.1 An example.

Objects	Attributes				
	F	R	E	M	S
Tiger	f_1	r_1	e_1	m_1	s_1
Horse	f_2	r_1	e_3	m_1	s_1
Sheep	f_2	r_1	e_3	m_1	s_0
Penguin	f_3	r_2	e_1	m_0	s_1
Frog	f_3	r_2	e_1	m_0	s_2
Rat	f_1	r_1	e_2	m_1	s_1

In the above relation, the attributes and their values have the following meaning:

$F=$ Feet; $f_1=$claw, $f_2=$hoof, $f_3=$web.

$R=$Ears; $r_1=$ external, $r_2=$ middle.

$E=$Eats; $e_1=$ meat, $e_2=$ grain, $e_3=$grass.

$M=$Gives milk; $m_0=$ no milk, $m_1=$milk.

$S=$Swims; $s_0=$unable, $s_1=$able, $s_2=$well.

2.2 Implication rules and functional dependencies

In the following we use P, Q, X', Y', and Z' to denote sets of properties, while we use X, Y, and Z to name either sets of objects (see Algorithm 3.1) or sets of attributes (see the last two algorithms). An elementary property p_i can be expressed by $a_i(x) = V_{ij}$, where $a_i(x)$ is a predicate for the attribute A_i and V_{ij} is the value of the attribute A_i for a given object x. For example, $feet(x) = "f_3"$ is a predicate about webbed animals that we shall write simply as $f_3(x)$ or as f_3.

Definition 1. A *conjunctive* implication rule for *descriptors* (IRD) is an implication rule of the form $P \Rightarrow Q$ where P and Q are subsets of $\mathcal{D}$ [4]. A context $(\mathcal{O}, \mathcal{D}, \mathcal{R})$ satisfies the IRD $P \Rightarrow Q$ if for every object x in $\mathcal{O}$, whenever x is described by P it has also properties Q, i.e.,

$$f(x) \supseteq P \implies f(x) \supseteq Q$$

Proposition 1. $P \Rightarrow Q$ *is a conjunctive* IRD $\Leftrightarrow [[(Z, Z') = inf\{(X, X') \in \mathcal{L} \mid P \subset X' \text{ and } X \neq \emptyset\}] \Rightarrow Q \subset Z']$. $\qquad\square$

Definition 2. A context $(\mathcal{O}, \mathcal{D}, \mathcal{R})$ satisfies the FD $X \rightarrow Y$ [6] if for every pair of tuples t_1 and t_2 in $\mathcal{R}$, $t_1[X] = t_2[X] \Rightarrow t_1[Y] = t_2[Y]$. The well-known inference axioms for FDs also apply to IRDs.

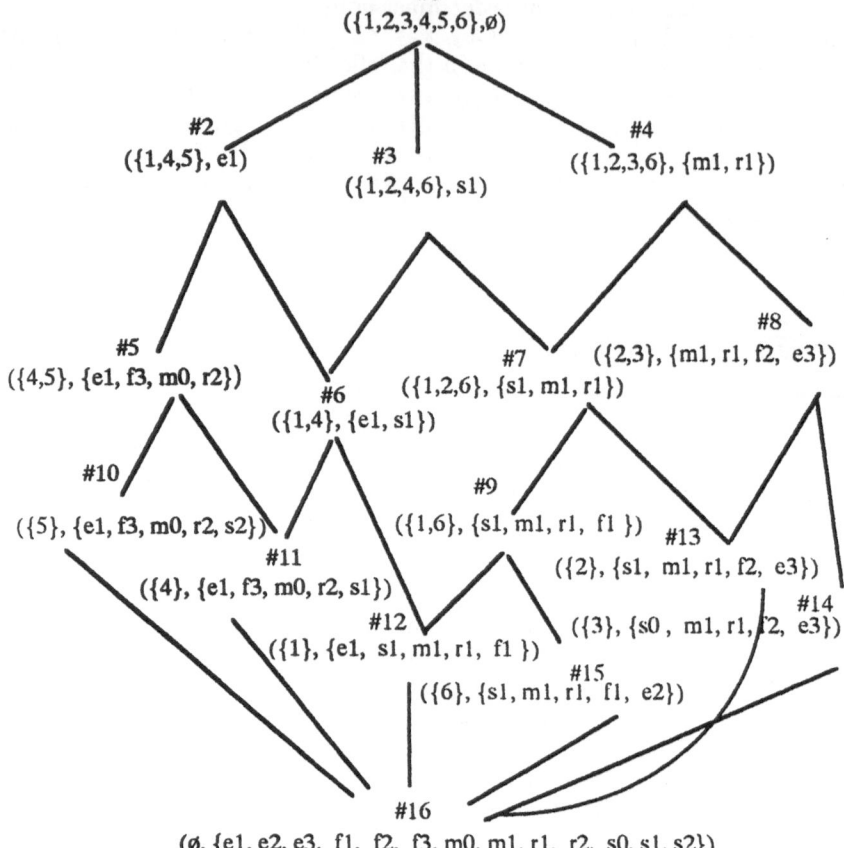

Figure 2.2 The Concept lattice.

3 Rule and functional dependency generation

3.1 Generation of implication rules

Algorithm 3.1 computes a complete set of IRDs from an already built lattice. In [4], we propose an algorithm that incrementally builds the lattice and computes the set of rules in one shot.

Algorithm 3.1

Input: A lattice $\mathcal{L}$.

Output: A set Σ of conjunctive IRDs: $P \Rightarrow Q$ (not necessarily reduced), and the array $Rules[1 \cdots \|\mathcal{L}\|]$, where an element $Rules[H]$ represents IRDs associated with the node H.

Function *GenerateRulesForNode(N = (X, X'))*

begin

$\Delta := \emptyset$;

If $X \neq \emptyset$ and $\|X'\| > 1$ **then** /* discard some trivial rules such as $P \Rightarrow \emptyset$ */

    For each non empty set $P \in \{\mathcal{P}(X') - X'\}$ in ascending $\|P\|$ **do**

        If $\not\exists\, M = (Y, Y')$ parent of N such that $P \subseteq Y'$ **then**

            If $\not\exists\, P' \Rightarrow Q \in \Delta$ such that $P' \subset P$ **then**

                $\Delta := \Delta \cup \{P \Rightarrow X' - P\}$

            endIf

        endIf

    endFor

endIf

return(Δ)

end {*GenerateRulesForNode*}

begin

$\Sigma := \emptyset$; /* the cumulative set of IRDs */

For each node $H = (X, X') \in \mathcal{L}$ in ascending $\|X'\|$ **do**

    begin

    $Rules[H] := GenerateRulesForNode(H)$

    $\Sigma := \Sigma \cup Rules[H]$

    end

endFor

return(Σ)

end

Complexity analysis

If we assume there exists an upper bound K on the number of descriptors per object, i.e. $\|f(\{x\})\| \leq K$, the time complexity of Algorithm 3.1 is $O(\|\mathcal{O}\|)$.

The *If* tests inside the *GenerateRulesFromNode* function help eliminate redundant rules produced by a same node. However, the rules generated by Algorithm 3.1 are not necessarily reduced and non-redundant. Redundancy may occur between rules generated from two different nodes of the lattice, and can be removed using the polynomial time algorithm for nonredundant cover generation [6].

Example. The IRD: $s_2 \Rightarrow f_3 r_2 e_1 m_0$ is generated from node #10 (see Figure 2.2), and can later be reduced to $s_2 \Rightarrow f_3$ using the rule $f_3 \Rightarrow r_2 e_1 m_0$ (from node #5) and the inference axioms (see Table 3.1).

3.2 Generation of functional dependencies

The procedure for choosing which attributes in the binary relation $\mathcal{R}$ should be the left-hand side (LHS) of a functional dependency is in the worst case exponential in the total number of attributes. There are many works in the rough set community [8, 10] and the database area that have dealt with the issue of generating functional dependencies from a binary relation [5]. In the following, we propose two procedures: Algorithm 3.2 which scans the lattice to check if a given FD: $Y \rightarrow Z$ holds with a degree k of accuracy [8, 10], and Algorithm 3.3 which starts from a set of implication rules to generate a set of FDs. It is important to note that the lattice is a good starting point and an appropriate framework for FD generation since only complete couples (nodes of the lattice) are taken into account, and therefore useless (and irrelevant) combinations of attributes (i.e, those that do not represent the LHS of an FD) are discarded.

Algorithm 3.2

Input: Y and Z subsets of attributes, $\|\mathcal{O}\|$, and a lattice $\mathcal{L}$.

Output: "The FD:" $Y \rightarrow Z$ "holds with a degree" k.

begin

Step (1) Collect in the set $PART(Y)$ the extent of the smallest concepts involving all the attributes in Y. In the same way, collect in $PART(Z)$ the extent of the smallest concepts involving all the attributes in Z. $PART(Y)$ and $PART(Z)$ are the partitions of the set $\mathcal{O}$ with respect to the equivalence relations: $IND(Y)$ and $IND(Z)$ respectively [8].

$PART(Y) := \emptyset; \ PART(Z) := \emptyset;$

$POS_Y(Z) := \emptyset; \ /* \ POS_Y(Z)$ is the positive region of Z w.r.t. Y */

$Mark_Y[i] := 0$ and $Mark_Z[i] := 0$ for $i = 1, \ldots, \|\mathcal{L}\|;$

For each node $H = (X, X') \in \mathcal{L}$ in ascending $\|X'\|$ with $X \neq \emptyset$ **do**

    begin

      If $Y \subseteq Attrib(X')$ and $Mark_Y(H) \neq 1$ **then**

        $Mark_Y(N) := 1$ for each descendant N of H

        $PART(Y) := PART(Y) \cup \{X\}$

      endIf

      If $Z \subseteq Attrib(X')$ and $Mark_Z(H) \neq 1$ **then**

        $Mark_Z(N) := 1$ for each descendant N of H

        $PART(Z) := PART(Z) \cup \{X\}$

      endIf

    end

  endFor

Step (2) Compute the positive region of Z w.r.t. Y.

For each element $E \in PART(Y)$ **do**

> **If** $\exists E' \in PART(Z)$ s.t. $E \subseteq E'$ **then**
> $POS_Y(Z) := POS_Y(Z) \cup E$
> **endIf**

endFor

Step (3) Compute the degree k of functional dependency between Y and Z.

$k := \|POS_Y(Z)\|/\|\mathcal{O}\|;$

return(k)

end

Example. The FD: $F \rightarrow R$ holds *totally* $(k = 1)$ since the partition: $PART(F) = \{\{1,6\},\{2,3\},\{4,5\}\}$ is a refinement of $PART(R) = \{\{1,2,3,6\},\{4,5\}\}$. However, $S \rightarrow F$ holds *partially* $(k = 0.33)$ because $PART(S) = \{\{1,2,4,6\},\{3\},\{5\}\}$ is not a full refinement of $PART(F)$. A value for k almost equal to 1 could be an indication that the corresponding FD does not hold for some data.

Algorithm 3.3

Input: A set Σ of conjunctive IRDs of the form $P \Rightarrow Q$ where $Q = P^+ - P$ and P^+ is the closure of P according to Σ.

Output: A set Γ of FDs

begin

Step (1) Partition the set Σ into $\Sigma_1, \ldots, \Sigma_m$ according to the following equivalence relation $\{(P \Rightarrow Q, P' \Rightarrow Q') \in \Sigma * \Sigma \mid Attrib(P) = Attrib(P')\}$, where $Attrib(P)$ represents the set of attributes appearing in the description of P. E.g., $Attrib(F = f_1 \wedge M = m_1) = \{F, M\}$

Step (2) Collect functional dependencies.

$\Gamma := \emptyset$;

For each equivalence class Σ_i **do**

> $\Delta := \emptyset;$
> $Mark[i] := 0$ for $i = 1, \ldots, \|\mathcal{L}\|;$
> **For** each node $H = (X, X') \in \mathcal{L}$ in ascending $\|X'\|$ **do**
>> **If** $Attrib(LHS_i) \subseteq Attrib(X')$ and $Mark(H) \neq 1$ **then**
>> $Mark(N) := 1$ for each descendant N of H
>> $\Delta := \Delta \cup \{Z'\}$ /* Z' is a subset of X' such that $Attrib(Z') = Attrib(LHS_i)$ */
>> **If** $\|Attrib(LHS_i)\| > 1$ **then**

$$\Sigma_i := \Sigma_i \cup \{Z' \Rightarrow X' - Z'\} \text{ /* Add non-reduced IRDs */}$$

endIf

endIf

endFor

If $\|\Sigma_i\| = \|\Delta\|$ and $\cap_{j=1,\|\Sigma_i\|} Attrib(RHS_j) \neq \emptyset$ **then**

$$\Gamma := \Gamma \cup Attrib(LHS_i) \rightarrow \cap_{j=1,\|\Sigma_i\|} Attrib(RHS_j)$$

endIf

endFor

return(Γ)

end

Complexity analysis

The number of iterations of the outer *For* loop is $\|\Sigma\|$ which is $O(\|(\mathcal{O})\|)$ under the assumption of a fixed bound K on the number of descriptors per object. The number of iterations of the inner *For* loop is $\|\mathcal{L}\|$ which is $O(\|(\mathcal{O})\|)$. Therefore, the time complexity of Algorithm 3.3 is $O(\|(\mathcal{O})\|^2)$.

Example. Using the set Σ_6 initially limited to one IRD, and by executing the inner *For* loop of Algorithm 3.3, we get:

$\Sigma_6 = \{r_2e_1 \Rightarrow f_3, r_1e_3 \Rightarrow f_2, r_1e_1 \Rightarrow f_1, r_1e_2 \Rightarrow f_1\}$,

$\Delta = \{r_2e_1, r_1e_3, r_1e_1, r_1e_2\}$.

Since $\|\Sigma_6\| = \|\Delta\|$ and $\cap_{j=1,\|\Sigma_6\|} Attrib(RHS_j) = \{F\}$, we get the FD: $RE \rightarrow F$.

Table 3.1 depicts the set of IRDs and FDs generated from the lattice in Figure 2.2.

Table 3.1 Generating IRDs and FDs.

Equiv. classes Σ_i	Rules and Dependencies		
	Reduced IRDs	Node #	FDs
1	$m_0 \Rightarrow f_3 r_2 e_1$	5	
	$m_1 \Rightarrow r_1$	4	$M \rightarrow R$
2	$r_1 \Rightarrow m_1$	4	
	$r_2 \Rightarrow f_3 e_1 m_0$	5	$R \rightarrow M$
3	$f_1 \Rightarrow m_1 s_1$	9	
	$f_2 \Rightarrow e_3 m_1$	8	
	$f_3 \Rightarrow r_2 e_1 m_0$	5	$F \rightarrow M$
4	$s_0 \Rightarrow f_2$	14	
	$s_2 \Rightarrow f_3$	10	
5	$e_2 \Rightarrow f_1$	15	
	$e_3 \Rightarrow f_2 m_1$	8	
6	$r_1 e_1 \Rightarrow f_1$	12	$RE \rightarrow F$
7	$e_1 m_1 \Rightarrow f_1$	12	$EM \rightarrow F$

4 Conclusion

We have proposed procedures to discover implication rules and functional dependencies from a concept lattice structure. This kind of knowledge is very common in DB applications and may be exploited for many purposes.

Our current research in the area of knowledge discovery includes: (i) generalizing the Galois lattice nodes structure to allow richer knowledge representation schemes such as conceptual graphs, (ii) dealing with complex objects, (iii) and testing the potential of these ideas in different application domains such as software reuse, database design, and intensional query answering.

References

[1] N. Cercone, and M. Tsuchiya, ed. "Special Issue on Learning and Discovery in Knowledge-Based Databases," *Knowledge and Data Engineering*, 5(6),1993.

[2] B.A. Davey and H.A. Priestley, *Introduction to Lattices and Order*, 1990, Cambridge: Cambridge University Press. 248.

[3] R. Godin, R. Missaoui, and H. Alaoui, "Incremental Concept Formation Algorithms Based on Galois (Concept) Lattices," Technical Report, Département de Mathématiques et d'Informatique, Université du Québec à Montréal, 1994. Also submitted for publication.

[4] R. Godin and R. Missaoui, "An Incremental Concept Formation Approach for Learning from Databases," Special Issue on Formal Methods in Databases and Software Engineering, *Theoretical Computer Science*, to appear, 1994.

[5] J. Kivinen and H. Mannila, "Approximate Dependency Inference from Relations," in *4th Int. Conf. on Database Theory*, J. Biskup and R. Hull, (Ed.), 1992, Springer-Verlag Pub.: London, 86-98.

[6] D. Maier, *The theory of Relational Databases*, 1983, Rockville, Md.: Computer Science Press.

[7] S. Muggleton, L. De Raedt, "Inductive Logic Programming: Theory and Methods," submitted to *The Journal of Logic programming*, 1993.

[8] Z. Pawlak, *Rough Sets: Theoretical Aspects of Reasoning about Data*, Kluwer Academic Pub.: Dordrecht/Boston/London, 1992.

[9] Piatetsky-Shapiro, G. and Frawley, W.J., ed. *Knowledge Discovery in Databases*, 1991, AAAI Press / The MIT Press: Menlo Park, Calif. 525.

[10] R. Slowinski, Ed., *Intelligent Decision Support. Handbook of Applications and Advances of the Rough Sets Theory*, Kluwer Academic Pub.: Dordrecht/Boston/London, 1992.

[11] R. Wille, "Knowledge Acquisition by Methods of Formal Concept Analysis," in *Data Analysis, Learning Symbolic and Numeric Knowledge*, E. Diday, (Ed.), 1989, Nova Science Pub.: New York, 365-380.

Rough Sets and Concept Lattices

G. Deon Oosthuizen*

Department of Computer Science, Stanford University
Stanford, California CA94305, USA

Abstract

A Concept lattice is a special kind of lattice, the explicit representation
of which can be viewed as a semantic network with special properties.
Concept lattices have been applied to Machine Learning as well as to the
uncovering of the underlying structure in discrete-valued data. They also
embody the cladistic approach to classification. This paper describes how
the use of a concept lattice as representation model is related to the rough
set approach to data analysis and how operations of rough set theory can
be implemented using a concept lattice.

1   Introduction

In the course of the human endeavour to gain insight from large data bases,
the uncovering of dependence and causality has been studied by many people.
The use of graphs to model dependence and causality in data has been shown
to have several advantages [12]. It provides a vivid and concise account of the
relations between the variables in the universe of discourse.

In this paper we consider the use of a special kind of data structure for
the distillation of knowledge from data: a formal lattice. Although Wille [15]
introduced the notion of a *concept lattice*, the particular organization of data
described here also corresponds to the so-called *cladistic* approach to classification used by biologists and linguists for some time [5]. In fact, the underlying
principle referred to as the *duality of intension and extension* had already been
noted by Aristotle [14] and refers to the inverse relation between the number
of properties required to define a concept and the number of entities to which
the concept applies. This paper briefly explains how a concept lattice can be
applied to discover regularities in data, i.e. to learn rules. It then informally
describes how concept lattices relate to rough set theory, explaining that a concept lattice constitutes a representation model for the implementation of rough
set operators.

We first describe how a concept lattice is constructed, how dependence
relationships and rules are derived and, finally, its relation to rough set theory.

2   Concept Lattices

Since we are concerned with the graphical representation of a formal lattice
(referred to as a Hasse diagram) we provide a graph theoretical description for
it. A lattice is a directed acyclic graph with an additional constraint: every pair

---

*On leave from the University of Pretoria, Pretoria, 0001, South Africa.

of nodes in the graph has a unique nearest common descendent - or *meet* - and a unique nearest common ancestor - their *join*. (In the formal mathematical definition these are referred to as *greatest lower bounds* and *least upper bounds* respectively.)

The lattices discussed here are of a special kind, called *concept lattices* [15] [7], which have the following additional properties:

- Apart from the nodes adjacent to the universal node (at the top) and the NULL node at the bottom, no nodes in the graph have exactly one parent or exactly one child.

- No node has a parent (i.e. no node is directly linked to another node) to which it is also indirectly linked by means of a path that goes via one or more other nodes.

Concept lattices have also been referred to as Galois lattices in the literature [2].

In the current application of concept lattices, we treat them as semantic networks, reflecting entity-attribute relationships. For this reason the universal node (at the top) which ensures that all pairs of nodes in a lattice have joins and the NULL node (at the bottom) which ensures that all pairs of nodes have meets, are omitted. Consequently, every pair of nodes in the current lattices has a unique meet or no meet, as well as a unique join or no join. This is merely an implementation measure, however, and has no impact on the fundamental properties of the lattices. Thus, the concept lattices described here consist of a set **A** of nodes with no parents, called *attributes*, a set **E** of nodes with no children, called *entities*, and a set **I** of nodes in between, called *internal nodes*.

A lattice is constructed using discrete-valued entities as input, i.e. entities consisting of vectors of discrete attribute-values (like a record in a database). The graph is constructed by creating a node (an element of **E**) for each entity, and connecting it to each of its attributes by means of upward pointing arcs, whilst ensuring that the graph remains a lattice, i.e. ensuring that each pair of attributes or internal nodes has a unique meet - if this condition is met, all pairs of nodes automatically have unique joins. During this process, the elements of **I** are created between the bottom and top rows [1]. It can be shown that a given set of entities gives rise to a unique lattice.

Each node in **I** relates a unique subset of **E** to a unique subset of **A**. Intuitively, the elements of **I** can be regarded as sets of entities that have attributes in common. With each node, we associate a value referred to as its *strength*, reflecting the number of entities below it in the graph. The strength of a node could also be interpreted as the size of the set (or class) denoted by the node, i.e. the number of entities which have the attributes above the node in common. We shall henceforth refer to the attributes above a given node as attributes *spanned* by the node, and to the entities below it as entities *covered* by it.

In the worst case, the number of nodes in the lattice increases exponentially with the number of attributes per entity. However, as we will explain later, the lattices can be pruned to prevent this. The computational complexity of constructing a pruned lattice can be kept at a level less than $O(n^3)$, where

---

[1] The manner in which this is accomplished is not relevant to the topic of this paper. Algorithms are described in [8][1].

n is the number of attributes per entity. The work described here has been implemented in a system called GRAND [8] as well as an analysis tool called DATA-MAP [10].

Let us consider an example. Fig. 1 shows a lattice generated from the data shown in Table 1. (For the sake of simplicity, some nodes have been omitted in fig. 1.) It depicts underground sample information regarding rock samples collected for laboratory analysis. The irregularity of the structure is due to the fact that the lattice structure is not complete, i.e. it does not contain an internal node for every possible combination of attributes, but only for the fraction of the combinations which actually occurred in the data. The second reason why the structure is irregular, is that fig. 1 displays an n-dimensional structure, where n is the number of attributes, in two dimensions.

Entity no.	Size	Colour	Shape	Contains Heavy Metals	Structure
E1	small	brown	regular	yes	hard
E2	large	brown	irregular	no	brittle
E3	large	yellow	regular	yes	hard
E4	small	black	regular	no	brittle
E5	large	black	regular	yes	brittle
E6	large	brown	regular	yes	hard
E7	large	black	irregular	no	brittle
E8	small	brown	irregular	no	brittle
E9	large	brown	irregular	yes	brittle

Table 1.

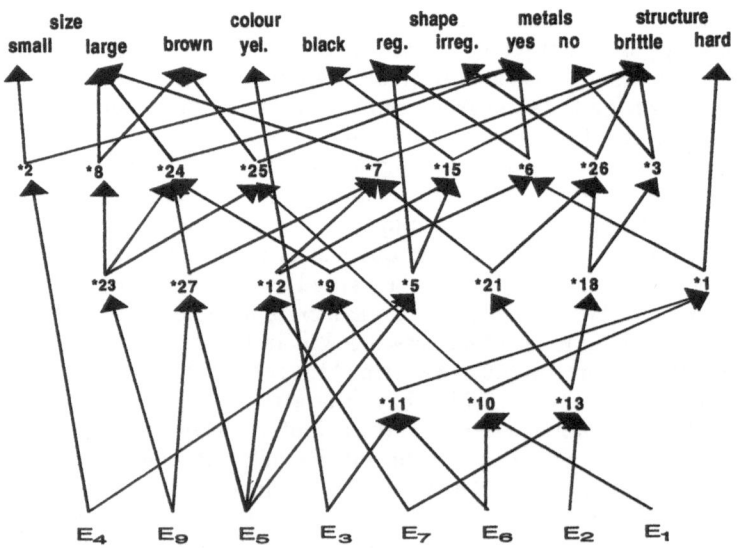

Fig. 1

3 Derivation of Dependence Relations

In this section we explain how relationships between attributes are derived from the lattice structure.

The elements of **A** can be regarded as variables. The strengths of the nodes indicate the number of times a variable had the value TRUE. Thus, it serves as a frequency count, and by using it in combination with the value N - the total number of entities seen thus far - it provides us with an estimate of the prior probability for each element of **A** (or reliable prior probabilities if N is large enough).

We mentioned before that an internal node represents a unique class of entities which have a unique set of attributes in common. ¿From a knowledge representation point of view it denotes a *concept*. The attributes it spans constitute its *intension* and the entities it covers constitute its *extension*. As in the case of the attributes, the internal nodes can be regarded as boolean variables which can be TRUE or FALSE, and their strengths can be used in a similar way to compute estimates of prior probability for them.

Thus, the estimate of prior probability (EP) of an internal node w,

$$EP(w) = strength(w)/N,$$

where strength(w) is the strength of w and N is the total number of entities seen.

Let us consider a node $w \in \mathbf{I}$ which spans two attributes, i.e. both its parents are recorded variables, a and b, say. Since any two nodes in a lattice have a unique meet, an entity has attributes a and b if and only if w is true, i.e. it belongs to the class a *and* the class b if it is in the class w.

The formula for conditional probability states that

$$p(b|a) = p(b,a)/p(a)$$

where $p(b,a)$ is the probability of b *and* a being true. Thus, the relationship between two attributes a and b can be expressed as

$$\begin{aligned} EP(a|b) &= EP(a,b)/EP(b) \\ &= EP(w)/EP(b) \\ &= (strength(w)/N) / (strength(b)/N) \\ &= strength(w)/strength(b) \end{aligned} \tag{1}$$

where w is the meet of a and b, indicated by meet(a,b), and N is the total number of entities inserted into the lattice, as before (see fig. 2a).

Now, since every two nodes in a lattice have a unique meet x, and x and any third node y would also have a unique meet z, it follows that any number of nodes greater than two also have a unique meet. Consequently, equation (1) above can be extended to include more than two observed variables. Thus, for any $b_i \in \mathbf{A}$, i=1..n

$$EP(b|a_1, a_2, ... a_n) = strength(w)/strength(v) \tag{2}$$

where $v = $ meet$(a_1, a_2, ... a_n)$, $w = $ meet(b,v) and n is a positive integer less than the total number of attributes recorded in the system (see fig. 2b).

A special case occurs when a is spanned by the meet of $a_1..a_n$, i.e. by v, in which case $w = v$, and $EP(b|a_1...a_n) = 1$. If a and v do not have a meet, $EP(b|a_1, a_2, ... a_n) = 0$.

Finally, the above equation also holds for *any* set of nodes in the lattice, i.e. not just for attributes, but also for internal nodes that do or do not span each other.

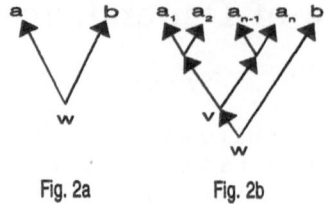

Fig. 2a   Fig. 2b

Nodes near the bottom of the lattice denote small sets of entities which do not provide adequate support to justify inference. They are often generated as a result of statistical noise or erroneous coincidences between attributes. Such nodes are removed from the lattice in order to ensure the statistical justifiability of the inferences defined above.

The procedure of removing such nodes is referred to as *pruning*. For the purposes of pruning, the members of **E** are regarded as nodes denoting patterns that occurred once only, and they are, therefore, also removed. Pruning is, however, restricted to nodes that can be removed without affecting the defining properties of the lattice. This means that pruning is limited to nodes at the bottom of the lattice and the immediate parents of nodes at the bottom that have at most two parents (the proof for this can be found in [7]). Initially, only the members of **E** are eligible for pruning, but after they have been removed, a new layer of nodes are 'exposed', and so on.

The above equations form the basis for defining the following inference procedure on a concept lattice [9]. The *downward closure* of a node includes the node and all the nodes below it, i.e. all the nodes it covers. Similarly, its *upward closure* includes the nodes spanned by it.

Inference is conducted as follows. The meet v of a given set of attributes Q is located and the upward closure of v is computed. If v spans any attributes u_i in addition to those in Q, then u_i ($i=1,2,...$) are inferred. If the elements of Q do not have a meet, we determine if a subset of Q has a meet v' which spans additional attributes - these additional features would be inferred. Also, each child of v spans at least one additional attribute that can be inferred probabilistically (using equation (2)).

Thus, the lattice itself can be used as the basis of inference. Alternatively, explicit rules can be extracted and used for inference. In this manner many rules can be derived from the lattice.

4 Relation to Rough Set Theory

The rough sets approach to data analysis hinges on two basic concepts, namely the *lower* and *upper approximations* of a set, referring to two approximate characterizations of a set which include
- the elements that are without doubt included in the set

- the elements that have at least one attribute which make them eligible for being members of the set (resp.).

The lower and upper approximations are defined in terms of equivalence classes defined over the entities in the universe of discourse, denoted by sets of attribute-values.

Now, it is interesting to note that each of the nodes in the lattice denotes an equivalence class: in Section 3 we explained that each node in **I** denotes a set of entities that has the attributes spanned by the node in common. This means that the lower approximation of a set can be obtained by computing the downward closure of the meet of the attributes in the set-description [2]. The upper approximation is the union of the downward closures of the attributes themselves.

As we explained in section 3, each of the nodes in **I** denotes a rule. Thus, the lattice uncovers *all* the rules that can be generated to describe (or summarize) the known information. This is similar to what has been done in the rough set theory-based system LERS, described elsewhere in this volume [4]. The reader can verify that all the different *covers* employed in the LERS system are contained in the lattice. The strengths of the internal nodes used during inference reflect the number of examples described by the rule and can be used to compute, for example, the upper or lower *quality of approximation* - the latter is based on the EP of the meet involved - and the *rough measure* [3] - which corresponds to the EP of the concept inferred given the attributes provided.

GRAND learns incrementally, similar to the rough set approach described by [13]. Furthermore, apart from learning rules from examples, handcrafted rules (background theory) can be added to the lattice and are dynamically integrated into the system. This is accomplished by first disregarding the distinction between the left- and right hand side of a rule and inserting it as a conjunction of attributes into the lattice just as entities are being inserted, with the only difference that a strength higher than one is assigned to it (i.e. it is treated as if the same entity is entered ten times, say, into the lattice). If the right hand side of the rule inserted contains more than one attributes, the right hand side is then inserted on its own, without the left hand side, increasing its strength as well. The transformation procedure automatically ensures that invalid inferences are inhibited.

The lattice also provides an optimally integrated semantic network-like view of the relationships between the attributes. In other words, it embeds the rules in a structure which is more informative than a 'flat' list of rules.

GRAND was developed with the explicit intention of doing machine learning, i.e. to extend inference beyond the given dataset (the training set). As a result, it employs (domain theory-based) heuristics and pruning in order to handle noisy and incomplete data. In such environments, it is important not to *overfit* the data. Overfitting of data occurs when the rule set fits the given data set so well that it implicitly captures the errors that are present in the data. This stands in contrast to, what Grzymala-Busse calls the "knowledge acquisition approach to building the rule base" which "should induce all potential rules that can be induced".

Fundamentally, however, GRAND is based on the same principles as rough

---

[2]If the attributes do not have a meet, subsets of them would have meets. The lower approximation is then obtained by computing the union of the downward closures of these meets.

set-based systems for knowledge discovery, and the differences lie primarily on the implementation level, i.e. in the data structures employed to store information and the heuristics employed to manipulate it. Kent [6] made an attempt to formalize the relation between rough set theory and formal concept analysis.

5 Conclusion

In this paper we described how a concept lattice can be used to discover dependencies in data. We showed that the lattice structure together with its closure operations provides a platform for the application of rough set theory. Pawlak [11] made the following interesting remark regarding rough sets: "whether an element belongs to a set or not is not an objective property of the elements but depends on our knowledge of it". The relationship between elements and sets, based on the knowledge about the elements (their attributes), forms the basis of the lattice structure and gives expression to this statement.

The current method uncovers dependencies between attribute values. Determination of dependencies between (non-boolean) attributes in the context of database normalization has been described elsewhere [8].

Acknowledgements
I am indebted to Nils Nilsson for providing me with a stimulating environment and to the Foundation for Research Development for supporting the research financially.

References

[1] C. Carpineto, G. Romano: GALOIS: An order-theoretic approach to conceptual clustering. Proceedings of the International Machine Learning Conference, Amherst, 1993, pp.33-40.

[2] R. Godin, R. Missauoui, A. Hassan: Learning Algorithms using a Galois Lattice Structure. Proceedings of 1991 IEEE International Conference on Tools for AI, San Jose, pp.22-29.

[3] J.W. Grzymala-Busse: ESEP An Epert System for Environmental Protection. In this volume.

[4] D.M. Grzymala-Busse, J.W. Grzymala-Busse: Comparison of Machine Learning and Knowledge Acquisition Methods of Rule Induction Based on Rough Sets. In this volume.

[5] H.M. Hoenigswald, L.F. Wiener: Biological Metaphor and Cladistic Classification: An Interdisciplinary Perspective. University of Pensylvania Press, Philadelphia, 1987.

[6] R.E. Kent: Rough Concept Analysis. In this volume.

[7] G.D. Oosthuizen: The Use of a Lattice in Knowledge Processing. Unpublished Ph.D. dissertation, Strathclyde University, Glasgow, 1988.

[8] G.D. Oosthuizen: Lattice-Based Knowledge Discovery. In Proceedings of AAAI-91 Knowledge Discovery in Databases Workshop, Anaheim, 1991, pp.221-235.

[9] G.D. Oosthuizen, D.R. McGregor: Induction through Knowledge Base Normalisation. In Proceedings of ECAI-88, Pitman Publishing, 1988, pp. 396-401.

[10] G.D. Oosthuizen, F.J. Venter: Using A Lattice for Visual Analysis of Categorical Data. In: G. Grinstein, H. Levkowitz (Eds.) Proceedings of IFIP WG5.10 Workshop on Perceptual Issues in Visualization, Springer-Verlag, 1994.

[11] Z. Pawlak: Rough Sets: Theoretical aspects of Reasoning about Data. Kluwer Academic Publishers, 1991.

[12] J. Pearl: Probabilistic Reasoning in Intelligent Systems: Networks of Plausible Inference. Morgan Kaufmann, 1988.

[13] N. Shan, W. Ziarko: An Incremental Learning Algorithm for Constructing Decision Rules, Proceedings of International Conference on Rough Sets and Knowledge discovery Bannf, 1993 (This volume).

[14] J.F. Sowa: Conceptual Structures: Information Processing in Mind and Machine. Addison-Wesley, 1984.

[15] R. Wille: Restructuring Lattice Theory: An Approach Based on Hierarchies of Concepts. In I.Rival (Ed.) Ordered Sets. Reidel, Dordrecht - Boston, 1982, p. 445-470.

Human-Computer Interfaces:
DBLEARN and SystemX

Nick Cercone
University of Regina
Regina, Saskatchewan

Paul McFetridge, Jiawei Han and Fred Popowich
Simon Fraser University
Burnaby, British Columbia

Abstract
Two systems developed over the past several years for easy accessing of information from relational databases, DBLEARN and SystemX, are described. We
explain their architectural characteristics, providing pointers to appropriate references for specific details. Examples given to illustrate the usefulness of these
systems are drawn from databases in use with Rogers Cablesystems and the
Natural Sciences and Engineering Research Council of Canada (NSERC).[*]

1 Introduction

For many years the natural language group at Simon Fraser University has been
engaged in a project entitled "Assessing Information with Ordinary Language" which has
found its realization in several versions of SystemX. The initial SystemX natural language
interface prototypes (English to SQL translation systems) were modularly designed utilizing proven technology [1, 2], for example, extended augmented transition network gram-
mars (ATNs). The design of the interface thus served as an umbrella project for new ideas
and technologies to be incorporated [3, 4], as a testbed for various techniques espoused by
our graduate students and visitors [5, 6, 7, 8], and for experimenting with nonstandard or
not yet completely specified theories [9, 10].

DBLEARN, our database learning program consisting of *background knowledge,* a
learning language, and *learning procedure*, was implemented and described in detail [11,
12, 13]. DBLEARN performs attribute-oriented induction on database relations to discover database knowledge including characteristic rules and discrimination rules from
relational databases. Characteristic rules are assertions which characterize the concept satisfied by all of the data in the database and discrimination rules are assertions which dis-
criminate concepts of one class from other classes. Advances in the theory took us in the
direction of an attribute-oriented *rough set* approach for knowledge discovery in databases
[14] in order to refine earlier *data mining* capabilities of DBLEARN.

We describe SystemX and DBLEARN and provide examples of both systems from
several relational databases in use in Canada. We explain and speculate future plans for
these systems and report our consideration to combine them into one package.

2 SystemX

At Roger's Cablesystems Ltd., executive Vice President for customer service Ted
Hotzak enters the following into his computer terminal, *"Give me the Western region out-*

[*]The authors are members of the Institute for Robotics and Intelligent Systems (IRIS) and wish to
acknowledge the support of the Networks of Centres of Excellence Program of the Government of
Canada, the Natural Sciences and Engineering Research Council, and the participation of PRE-
CARN Associates Inc. We are grateful to Canadian Cable Labs Fund for their financial assistance.

age log for June". Within seconds SystemX presents him with a neatly formatted table (or graph) of the data retrieved from Rogers' relational database. Ted could have said, *"What's the outage log for the Western region for June?"*, or *"Tell me the June regional outage log for the West."* or *"Find the Western outages for June."*, etc. SystemX can determine that whichever phrase Ted uses, he means the same thing. Such flexibility in *parsing*, applying the logical rules of grammar to determine meaning, is nontrivial. SystemX's parsing techniques are described below. After parsing, SystemX reformulates the question in SQL (structured query language) and data is extracted for presentation from Roger's large central database.

The problem described above is one of a large number of difficult problems of understanding natural language. Understanding a natural language is a remarkable achievement; fortunately, a natural language/database interface is simpler to comprehend. Although one ultimately encounters comparable problems, the domain of discourse, and thereby the context, is highly constrained by the database schema. General analysis of language phenomena and the ambiguity inherent in natural language understanding is limited; however, complexities arise when building natural language capabilities into such interfaces, consider the myriad examples given in [15, 16].

We chose the Head Driven Phrase Structure [HPSG] grammar [9] approach, which uses *unification* [17] as its primary control mechanism. HPSG is part of a tradition which expresses grammatical knowledge in the lexicon rather than in rules.* Our current implementation of HPSG [18] contains only seven grammar rules; extending the coverage of the grammar consists of building the lexicon, not in adding more rules.†

In unification-based formalisms, like HPSG, information is organized in *attribute value matrices* (AVMs) which consist of a collection of *attributes* (feature names) which may have simple atoms or complex AVMs as their values. AVMs are used to encode syntactic and semantic information. Consider the AVM depicted in Figure 1(a); it contains attributes for *company name*, *location*, and *parent_company*. The first two of these features have simple values, while the *parent_company* feature takes an AVM as its value. The values within an AVM need not be completely specified, as reflected in the appearance of variables within the AVM illustrated in Figure 1(b).

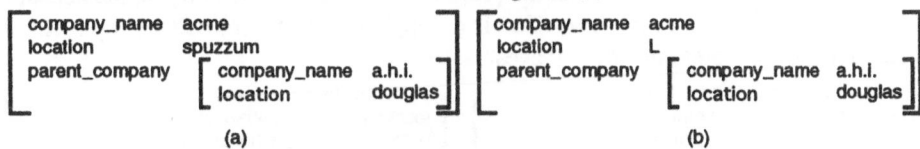

(a)   (b)

Figure 1. Two attribute value matrices.

We will adopt the convention that tokens starting with uppercase letters correspond to variables. When a single variable occurs in two locations, it indicates that the values of the

---

* HPSG is not a theory of syntax, but a theory of the sign, by which its developers mean a theory of the relation between sound and meaning. Attention has been paid to how semantics fits the theory. Although we have not implemented the semantics outlined in [9], the fact that there is a clear place for semantics in the theory has facilitated incorporation of a semantics for database representation.

† This lexicalist tradition seems amenable to a natural language interface which strives for portability among application domains. Attaching an interface to a new domain requires a long period of customization during which the lexicon, the grammar and the semantics must be developed to accommodate expressions unique to the domain. The lexicalist tradition focuses customization on the lexicon, the area we targeted as customizable.

34

two attributes are the same (even if the specific value is unknown). So the information contained in the above AVM can be paraphrased as "the company named acme, whose parent company is a.h.i, has the same location as its parent company".

Unification is an operation that can be defined over AVMs. Given two feature structures, the unification of the two AVMs is an AVM that contains all the information of each of the initial AVMs, and nothing more. If the two initial AVMs contain information which is mutually incompatible, then the unification is said to fail. For example, the unification of the AVMs in Figures 1(a) & 1(b) fails, since the AVM in Figure 1(a) specifies two different values for the *location* of the company and its parent company, while that in Figure 1(b) requires the locations to be the same. However, consider the *unifiable* AVM as shown in Figure 2.

$$\begin{bmatrix} \text{location} & \text{spuzzum} \\ \text{owner} & \text{john\_smith} \end{bmatrix}$$

Figure 2. Unifying AVM.

This AVM will unify with the Figure 1(a) AVM or with the Figure 1(b) AVM, yielding the AVMs shown in Figures 3(a) and 3(b) respectively. Observe that the pair of unifying AVMs need not contain the same features; *owner* is not in either of the first two AVMs, but when either of these is unified with the last AVM, the resulting AVM will contain the owner information. Furthermore, the order of the attributes in the AVM is not relevant.

Representations of the type described above are incrementally constructed as queries are parsed. As words and phrases are combined into larger phrases, the representations associated with each constituent are combined. In the simplest cases, the process by which they are combined is unification. For example, in the phrase **the outages for June [1]** the representation of "outages" contributes an AVM which specifies a table and a set of columns from that table. The representation of "June" contributes a matrix which specifies a column and its value (the database representation of "June") but does not specify a table because many of the tables in the domain contain the column represented by "June". The preposition "for" does not have a database representation. Thus, the representation of "for June" (the unification of the representations of "for" and "June") is the representation of "June". The representation of the entire phrase in [1] is created by unifying the constituents "outages" and "for June". The effect is to supply a value for the column representing dates in the table represented by "outages".

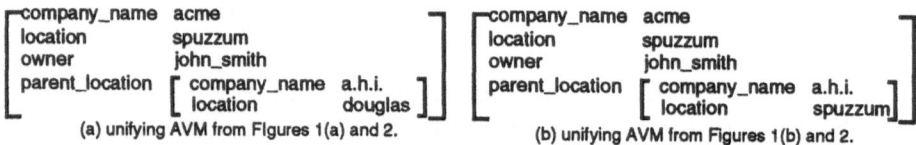

(a) unifying AVM from Figures 1(a) and 2.   (b) unifying AVM from Figures 1(b) and 2.

Figure 3. Unifying AVMs.

Phrase [1] illustrates cases in which adjunct modifiers further specify restrictions on a particular table in the database. In a relational database this is not sufficient, as it is often necessary to construct virtual relations by joins on different tables. For example, in the Rogers Cablesystems database locations are represented by numeric codes. As is the case for dates, location codes appear in many tables in the database. However, the description of each code resides in a table which is joined with any table containing a location code. Thus, in the phrase **the Vancouver outages for June [2]** the term "Vancouver" contributes an AVM representing a column in the table containing descriptions of locations.

Notice that because the AVM representing "Vancouver" specifies a table, it cannot unify with that representing "outages", the AVM for which also specifies a table, one different from that specified by "Vancouver". Instead, the representation of the phrase will contain two tables, the join between them represented by identical variables in the columns on which they are joined. The AVM built up in this manner for [2] is presented in Figure 4. The join is indicated by identical variables prefixed with "@" in the *location-code* columns. In this and subsequent AVMs, NIL is a special "unnamed" variable used when the value is unknown but is required in the output. Multiple occurrences of NIL do not denote the same value unlike conventional variables.

The column on which tables are joined is determined dynamically by the module *pathfinder* described in [8]. This facility determines for any set of columns the minimal path through the database which will join the set into a virtual relation. This module eliminates the need for customizing joins.*

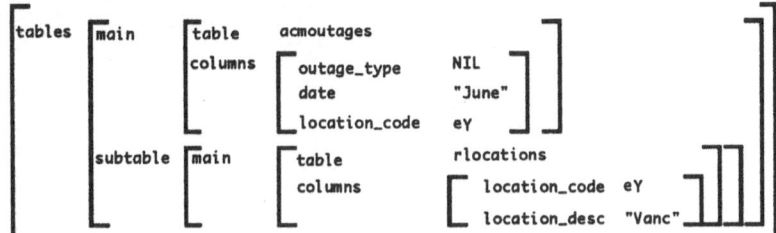

Figure 4. Semantic representation of *the Vancouver outages for June*.

Translating from English to SQL

The overall organization of SystemX is depicted in Figure 5. We have focussed on the HPSG parser above, amalgamating the information it requires with the relations and tables specified in the database system.

---

* In cases, the meaning of a complex phrase is not a simple composition of the meaning of its parts. The phrase "trouble call ratio" from the Rogers' database, requires information in several tables. However, when asking for the "trouble call ratio total", not only is a different table required, but different columns as well; furthermore, a join is unnecessary. Unification of AVMs associated with each of the constituents will not be able to produce the information structure needed. Unification, by definition, incorporates all of the information of the initial structures: unification never throws information away. In arriving at a solution to this problem, we noticed that the only information from the AVM for "trouble call ratio" used in the AVM for "trouble call ratio total" is servcgrp_code = 30. Within HPSG, it is possible for a word like "total" to *examine* the AVM that it is to be combined with (in our case, the AVM for "trouble call ratio") and extract specific information. Based on this scrutiny, HPSG can then determine what the AVM for the complex phrase should look like. So the AVM associated with "trouble call ratio total" can be obtained from the AVM for "total". The AVM for "trouble call ratio" thus does not play a direct role in determining the AVM for the complex phrase; it contributes only the information that "total" selects from it. This case is handled by a feature of the AVM which states that it has *priority* over another AVM in unification. [A related mechanism exists by which an AVM can specify *default* information. Thus, when a default AVM is unified with some other AVM, it is the information from the other AVM that is used, which differs from default unification and overriding as usually discussed in unification-based formalisms, [19]. Default unification merges part of one AVM with another in such a way that incompatibilities between different AVMs are avoided; default unification never fails.] When we specify an AVM to have priority, it overrides all of the information from the other AVM. Other mechanisms are used to extract the relevant information from the *overridden* AVM. In cases where both AVMs are specified as having priority, unification may fail. Examples of compositionally as in "Vancouver outages" and noncompositionality as in "trouble call ratio total" are prevalent in the Rogers database. They serve to illustrate that principles of natural language interface design must be sufficiently robust to handle accidental properties of the database schema.

36

We illustrate one of several stages in the English to SQL translation process by an example.[*] The example input to the parser is *"the vancouver unscheduled outages."* Since all input is interpreted to be a request for the tabular display of the most recent data in the database (unless specified), this phrase is unambiguous.

Figure 6 illustrates various stages in the process of translating the semantic output of the parser into SQL. The first stage shown is that of the semantic substructure for the sign representing the input generated by the HPSG parser. This structure is then translated into our internal logical form [LF] which makes explicit which database objects and operations are required to retrieve the data specified by the input. At this stage defaults are added. In this example, the specification that the latest data available is required, has been added. Finally the LF representation is translated to SQL. The SQL is enhanced to display the output in as *user-friendly* a manner as possible. Figure 6 concludes with the display of the data corresponding to the systems's input interpretation.

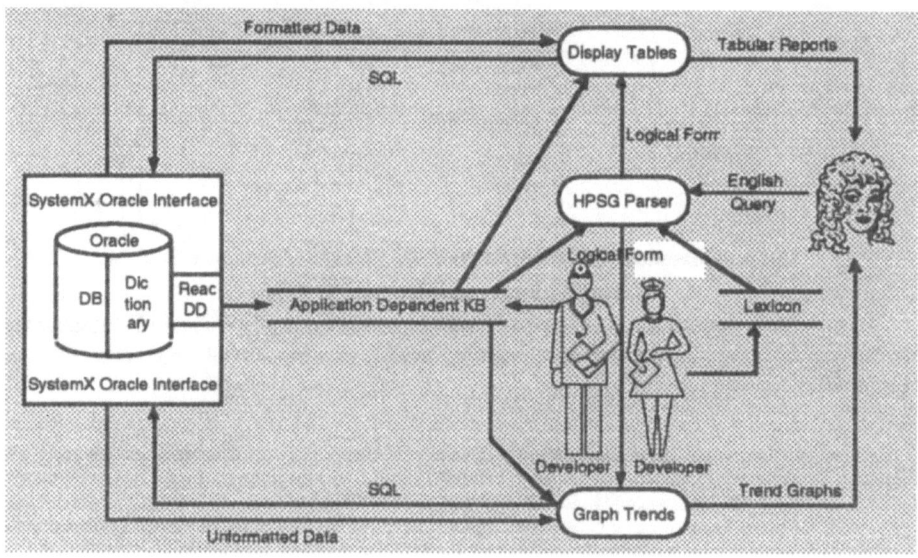

Figure 5. Overall Organization of SystemX.

3   Introduction to DBLEARN

An attribute-oriented induction method has been developed for knowledge discovery in databases. This method integrates the machine learning paradigm, particularly the learning-from-examples technique, with set-oriented database operations and extracts generalized data from actual data in databases. An attribute-oriented concept tree ascension technique is applied in generalization, which substantially reduces the computational complexity of database learning processes. Different kinds of knowledge rules, including characteristic rules, discrimination rules, quantitative rules, and data evolution regularities can be discovered efficiently using the attribute-oriented approach. Learning can also be performed with databases containing noisy data and exceptional cases using database statistics. Furthermore, the rules discovered can be used to query database knowledge,

---

[*] run on a Sun Microsystems sparcstation using SUN Common Lisp and the Oracle relational database management system.

answer cooperative queries, and facilitate semantic query optimization. A prototype database learning system, DBLEARN, has been constructed for experimentation.

```
WHAT NEXT? > the vancouver scheduled outages

Parsing Completed.

WHAT NEXT? > Display semantics

((TABLES
    ((MAIN
        ((TABLE ACMSREL NIL)
            (COLUMNS ((S_DATE NIL NIL)  (LOCATION 2700 NIL)
                                        (OUTAGE_CODE 10 NIL)
                                        (OUTAGES NIL NIL))
                    NIL))
        NIL)
        (SUBTABLES NIL NIL))
    NIL)
    (FUNCTION NIL NIL)
    (REFERENT NIL NIL)
    (TYPES
        ((DTYPE ((SUB ((SUPER OUTGS NIL)) NIL) (SUPER DMNS NIL))
                NIL)
        (FTYPE ((SUB ((SUB ((SUPER ESET NIL)) NIL) (SUPER PIVOT NIL))
                    NIL)
                (SUPER NONMOD NIL))
            NIL))
    NIL))

WHAT NEXT? > Display Logical Form

(((SETX X30
        (SETX X32
            (AND
                (RELATION ACMSREL
                        (OUTAGES OUTAGE_CODE LOCATION S_DATE)
                        (X32 '10 '2700 X30)
                        (= = =))
                    (MAX X30((SETX X31 (RELATION ACMSREL (S_DATE) (X31) (=)))))))))))

WHAT NEXT? > Display SQL

SELECT A.S_DATE Date , A.OUTAGES # of Outages
    FROM ACMSREL A
    WHERE A.OUTAGE_CODE = 10
        AND A.LOCATION = 2700
        AND A.S_DATE = (SELECT MAX(DISTINCT B.S_DATE) FROM ACMSREL B)
    ORDER BY A.S_DATE

WHAT NEXT? > Consult Oracle

Date       # of Outages
---------- ------------
31-AUG-92       36

1 row(s) selected
```

Figure 6. Stages in the translation of the semantic output of the parser.

We presented the general idea of basic attribute-oriented induction in detail elsewhere, [11, 12, 13]. Basic attribute-oriented induction, in which generalization is performed attribute by attribute using attribute removal and concept tree ascension[*], is specified in Algorithm 1.

Algorithm 1. Basic attribute-oriented induction in relational databases.
Input: (i) A relational database, (ii) a concept hierarchy table, and (iii) the learning task, and optionally, (iv) the preferred concept hierarchies, and (v) the preferred form to express learning results.
Output. A characteristic rule learned from the database.
Method. Basic attribute-oriented induction consists of the following four steps:
Step 1. Collection of the task-relevant data.
Step 2. Basic attribute-oriented induction.
Step 3. Simplification of the generalized relation, and
Step 4. Transformation of the final relation into a logical rule.

Notice that the basic attribute-oriented induction (Step 2) is performed as follows.

---

[*] We utilize 7 strategies actually: (1) generalization on smallest decomposable components; (2) attribute removal; (3) concept tree ascension; (4) "vote" propagation; (5) attribute threshold control; (6) generalization threshold control; and (7) rule transformation.

38

```
begin for each attribute Aᵢ (1<i<n, the # of attributes) in the generalized relation do
      while  number_of_distinct_values_in_Aᵢ > generalization_threshold do
      begin
          if no higher level concept in the concept hierarchy table for Aᵢ
          then remove Aᵢ
          else substitute for the values of Aᵢ's by its corresponding minimal
                     generalized concept;
          merge identical tuples
      end
      while  #_of_tuples_in_generalized_relation > generalization_threshold do
          selectively generalize some attributes and merge identical tuples
end. {Basic attribute-oriented induction}
```

Suppose we wish to learn characteristic rules for graduate students relevant to attributes Major, Birth-Place, and GPA using a conceptual hierarchy developed for academic databases. The learning task is presented to DBLEARN as

> **in relation** Student
> **learn characteristic rule for** Status = "graduate"
> **in relevance to** Name, Major, Birth_Place, GPA

After applying appropriate strategies (generalization on the smallest decomposable components, attribute removal, concept tree ascension, etc.), DBLEARN would produce:

$\forall$x graduate(x) → {Birth_Place(x)∈Canada ∧ GPA(x)∈excellent} [75%] |

{Major(x)∈science ∧ Birth_Place(x)∈foreign ∧ GPA(x)∈good} [25%].

4   Examples: NSERC Grants Information System (NGIS)

The NSERC Grants Information System (NGIS) for 1991 was used for some of our experiments.[*] The central table in the database is made up of rows each of which describes an award by NSERC to a researcher. The values constituting each row (i.e., the columns constituting the table) specify the different properties of the award, including the name of the recipient, the amount of the award and so on. In the schema diagram below,[†] Figure 7, nodes representing the properties of awards are represented by nodes linked to the "Award" node.

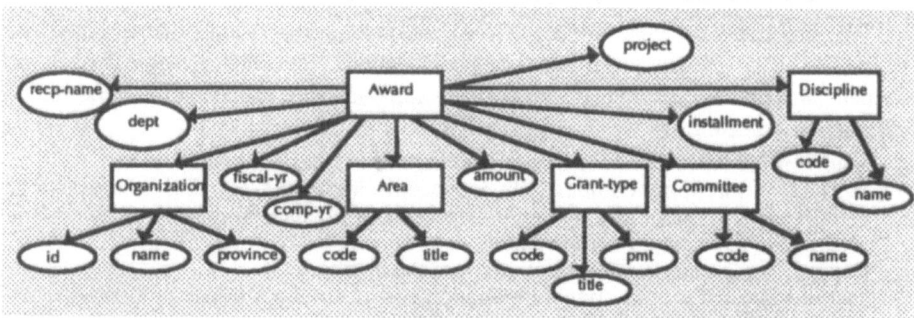

Figure 7. Schema diagram for NSERC Grants Information System.

---

[*] We reproduced its database in Oracle and Sybase, preserving the relations inherent in the original implementation and ran tests on them with SystemX and DBLEARN. The NGIS consists of a database of information about grants awarded by NSERC, and a menu-based interface. The central table in the database had 10,087 tuples with 11 attributes. It is intended to be used by individuals in "universities, government agencies and industry ... to search for grants that are of particular interest"[p.2, Grants Info. System manual, NSERC, 1992].

[†] In the schema diagram, tables are specified by rectangular nodes.

There are a number of subsidiary tables which record details about some of the properties of awards, (e.g., the province of the organization in which the recipient is to carry out the research). Most subsidiary tables are used simply to associate (English and French) phrases describing the entity to a code denoting a particular entity.

While the NGIS provides "easy and effective" access, it is limited since access to certain information (particularly information involving the comparison of data of the same domain) requires significant user time and effort whereas a natural language interface can provide ready access to this information. The NGIS is limited in its usability by the lack of an ad-hoc query capability. While the menu-based interface does permit access to all of the data contained in the database in one form or another, it places much of the burden on the user to derive the information (s)he is seeking. For example, suppose a user wishes to know the answer to the following question:

"What types of grants were received by SFU Computing Science?"

The best way to access this information via the existing interface is to request a search on University ("SFU") and Department ("Computing Science") and then page through set of awards that are returned, one at a time, noting the different grant types represented. If an ad hoc query capability was available, the system could return immediately the simple list the user desires. There are many examples of this type of situation, e.g., "Which universities won major equipment grants?", "Which departments won grants for research into expert systems?" and so on. The NGIS user required to put time and effort into extracting the information from the response and also (s)he is forced to wait while the system retrieves, calculates and formats the noise which obscures it from immediate view.

Experiments with the Natural Language Interface (SystemX)

The following examples were generated using SystemX and illustrates its most basic mode of operation.

```
>Enter sentence to be parsed:
what types of grants were received by sfu computing science in 1990
>Parsing Completed.

((SETX X1
        (RELATION AWARD
                (GRANT_CODE FISCAL_YR ORG_CODE DEPT)
                (X1 '1990 '1030 "COMPUTING SCIENCE")
                (= = = =))))

SELECT DISTINCT B.GRANT_TITLE
FROM AWARD A, GRANT_TYPE B
   WHERE A.FISCAL_YR = 1990
     AND A.ORG_CODE = 1030
     AND UPPER(A.DEPT) = 'COMPUTING SCIENCE'
     AND A.GRANT_CODE = B.GRANT_CODE

>Consulting Oracle.
what types of grants were received by sfu computing science in 1990

GRANT_TITLE
----------------------
Individual Operating
Infrastructure
Microelectronics Fund

3 row(s) selected

?New query
>Enter sentence to be parsed:
which universities won grants for expert systems research in 1990
>Parsing Completed.
```

```
SELECT DISTINCT B.ORG_NAME
   FROM AWARD A, ORGANIZATION B
    WHERE A.AREA_CODE = 865
      AND A.COMP_YR = 1990
      AND A.ORG_CODE = B.ORG_CODE
```

>Consulting Oracle.
which universities won grants for expert systems research in 1990

ORG_NAME

Acadia
Alberta
British Columbia
Calgary
Carleton
Guelph
Laval
McMaster
Regina
Ryerson Polytech. Inst.
Simon Fraser
Toronto
Victoria
cole Polytechnique

14 row(s) selected

Experiments with the Database Mining Program (DBLEARN)

DBLEARN is an experimental database learning system which consists of *background knowledge*, a *database learning language* (an extension to SQL), and a *learning procedure*. Background knowledge in DBLEARN is represented by concept hierarchies, in which the most general concept is the null description (described by a reserved word "ANY"), and the most specific concepts correspond to the specific values of attributes in the database.

Example1. One possible concept hierarchy table for the attribute "province" of NGIS database is shown directly below, where A < B indicates that B is a generalization of A.

```
{British Columbia} < B.C.
{Alberta, Saskatchewan, Manitoba} < Prairies
{Ontario} < Ont.
{Quebec} < Queb.
{New Brunswick, Nova Scotia, Newfoundland, PEI} < Maritime
{B.C., Prairies, Ont., Queb., Maritime, Other in Canada} < Canada
{Canada, Outside Canada} < ANY
```

Example2. One possible concept hierarchy table for the attribute "disc_code" of NGIS database is shown directly below, where A < B indicates that B is a generalization of A.

```
{23000 ~ 23499} < Hardware
{23500 ~ 23999} < System Organization
{24000 ~ 24499} < Software
{24500 ~ 25499} < Theory
{25500 ~ 25999} < Database Systems
{26000 ~ 26499} < AI
{26500 ~ 26999} < Computing Methods
{0~ 22999, 27000} < Other Disciplines
{Hardware, System Organization, Software, Theory, Database Systems,
   AI, Computing Methods} < Computing Science
{Computing Science, Other Disciplines} < ANY
```

Example 3. Suppose we wish to learn rules characterizing the computer science discipline with respect to attributes *province*, *grant_code*, and *amount*. The learning task is represented in DBLEARN as follows.

```
in relation award
learn characteristic rule for disc_code = "Computer_Science"
where grant_code = "Operating_Grants"
in relevance to amount, province, count()*, prop(amount)*
```

Result of query:

Amount	Geography	# Grants	% Amount
0-20Ks	B.C.	7.4%	4.7%
0-20Ks	Prairies	8.3%	5.4%
0-20Ks	Quebec	13.8%	8.7%
0-20Ks	Ontario	24.5%	15.7%
0-20Ks	Maritime		
20Ks-40Ks	B.C.	5.3%	7%
20Ks-40Ks	Prairies	5.3%	6.6%
20Ks-40Ks	Quebec	5.1%	7%
20Ks-40Ks	Ontario	12.9%	16%
20Ks-40Ks	Maritime	1%	1.3%
40Ks-60Ks	B.C.	1.2%	3.1%
40Ks-60Ks	Prairies	0.2%	0.4%
40Ks-60Ks	Quebec	1%	2.5%
40Ks-60Ks	Ontario	5.1%	11.5%
60Ks-	B.C.	0.2%	0.6%
60Ks-	Prairies	0.4%	1.6%
60Ks-	Quebec	0.2%	0.6%
60Ks-	Ontario	1.2%	4.5%
Total:	**$10,196,692**	**100%**	**100%**

Running time: 27 seconds.

*Notes: count() and prop() are two built-in functions which return the number of original tuples covered by a generalized tuple in the final result and the proportion of the specified attribute respectively. Experiments were conducted on a Sun Sparcstation 1 against a Sybase version of the NGIS database.

Suppose we wish to qualify further the request illustrated above with respect to AI. The learning task is represented in DBLEARN as follows.

```
in relation award
learn characteristic rule for disc_code = "Computer_Science"
where disc_code = "AI" and grant_code = "Operating_Grants"
in relevance to disc_code, amount, province, count(), prop(amount)
```

Disc.	Amount	Geography	# Grants	% Amount
AI	0-20Ks	B.C.	5.6%	4.1%
AI	0-20Ks	Prairies	15.5%	10.3%
AI	0-20Ks	Quebec	14.1%	9%
AI	0-20Ks	Ontario	25.3%	17.8%
AI	0-20Ks	Maritime	2.8%	1%
AI	20Ks-40Ks	B.C.	12.7%	16.3%
AI	20Ks-40Ks	Prairies	5.6%	6.2%
AI	20Ks-40Ks	Ontario	9.8%	13%
AI	20Ks-40Ks	Maritime	1.4%	1.7%
AI	40Ks-60Ks	B.C.	1.4%	4%
AI	40Ks-60Ks	Ontario	4.2%	11.3%
AI	60Ks-	Quebec	1.4%	4.2%
Total:	**$1,464,250**		**99.8%**	**98.9%**

Running time: 21 seconds.

Suppose we wish to qualify the initial request illustrated above with respect to subdisciplines with no regard for geography. The learning task is represented in DBLEARN as follows.

```
in relation award
learn characteristic rule for disc_code = "Computer_Science"
where grant_code = "Operating_Grants"
in relevance to disc_code, amount, count(), prop(amount)
```

Result of query:

Discipline	Amount	# Grants	% Amount
Hardware	0-20Ks	8.5%	5.7%
Hardware	20Ks-40Ks	2.9%	3.7%
Hardware	40Ks-60Ks	0.6%	1.3%
Hardware	60Ks-	0.2%	0.7%
System_Organization	0-20Ks	5.3%	3.4%
System_Organization	20Ks-40Ks	3.6%	4.5%
System_Organization	40Ks		
System_Organization	60Ks-	0.6%	2.4%
Software	0-20Ks	7.8%	4.4%
Software	20Ks-40Ks	3.9%	5.4%
Software	40Ks-60Ks	1%	2.5%
Software	60Ks-	0.2%	0.7%
Theory	0-20Ks	19.7%	11.8%
Theory	20Ks-40Ks	10.3%	13.6%
Theory	40Ks-60Ks	2.7%	6%
Theory	60Ks-	0.8%	2.7%
Database_sys	0-20Ks	6.6%	3.6%
Database_sys	20Ks-40Ks	1.3%	1.5%
Database_sys	40Ks-60Ks	1%	2.3%
AI	0-20Ks	9.2%	6.1%
AI	20Ks-40Ks	4.3%	5.3%
AI	40Ks-60Ks	0.9%	2.1%
AI	60Ks-	0.2%	0.6%
Computing_Methods	0-20Ks	3.5%	2.2%
Computing_Methods	20Ks-40Ks	3.5%	4.5%
Computing_Methods	40Ks-60Ks	0.8%	1.7%
Total:	$10,196,692	100%	100%

Running time: 145 seconds.

5 Concluding Remarks

We discussed natural language interfaces briefly and presented SystemX, our prototype next generation interface. We illustrated one problem we encounter frequently, nominal compounds, and explain how the general HPSG parsing theory handles it with relative ease and further explain that we have adopted this parsing methodology in SystemX.

We explained our attribute-oriented approach for knowledge discovery in databases. Our approach applies an attribute-oriented concept tree ascension technique in generalization which integrates the machine learning methodology with set-oriented database operations and extracts generalized data from actual data in databases. Different knowledge rules, including characteristic rules, discrimination rules, quantitative rules, and data evolution regularities can be discovered efficiently using the attributed-oriented approach.

Finally we presented some examples to illustrate SystemX and DBLEARN in action, querying NSERC's NGIS. Obviously much work remains to be done, nonetheless we anticipate that our approach will provide a promising methodology for future success, especially when constructing information systems for appropriate use for executives and decision makers.

References

[1] Cercone, N., Hall, G., Joseph, S., Kao, M., Luk, W., McFetridge, P., & McCalla, G. (1990) Natural Language Interfaces: Introducing SystemX. **Advances in AI in Software Engineering.** T. Oren (ed), JAI Press, Greenwich, Conn., 169-250.

[2] McFetridge, P., Hall, G., Cercone, N., & Luk, W. (1988) System X: a portable natural language interface, *7th CSCSI/SCEIO*, Edmonton, Alberta, 30-38.

[3] McFetridge, P., & Cercone, N. (1991) Installing an HPSG Parser in a Modular Natural Language Interface, **Computational Intelligence III**, N. Holland, Amsterdam, 169-178.

[4] McFetridge, P., Hall, G., & Cercone, N. (1988) Knowledge acquisition in System X: a natural language interface, *International Computer Science Conf.*, Hong Kong, 604-610.

[5] Cercone, N., Joseph, S., Kao, M., Luk, W., & McCalla, G. (1991) A Knowledge-Based Approach to Providing Quality Responses from and Eliminating Unnecessary Database Accesses to Relational Databases with Natural Language Interfaces. **Advances in Computing in the Humanities.** E. Nissan (ed), JAI Press, Greenwich, Conn. (to appear).

[6] Strzalkowski, T. & Cercone, N. (1989) Non Singular Concepts in Nat. Lang. Discourse. *Comp. Linguistics 15(4)*, 171-187.

[7] Kao, M., Cercone, N., & Luk, W.S. (1988) Providing Quality Responses with Natural Language Interfaces: the Null Value Problem. *IEEE Transactions on Software Engineering, 14(7) July*, 959-984.

[8] Hall, G., Luk, W., & Cercone, N. (1988) A solution to the MAP problem in natural language interface construction, *International Computer Science Conference*, Hong Kong, 351-359.

[9] Pollard, C. and Sag, I. (1987). Information-based Syntax and Semantics: Fundamentals. Stanford: CSLI.

[10] Shieber, S. (1986). An Introduction to Unification-Based Approaches to Grammar. Stanford: CSLI.

[11] Han, J., Cai, Y., & Cercone, N. (1992) Data Driven Discovery of Quantitative Rules in Relational Databases. *IEEE Transactions on Knowledge and Data Engineering 5(2)*.

[12] Cai, Y., Cercone, N., & Han, J. (1991) Attribute Oriented Induction in Relational Databases, in G. P. Shapiro (ed.) **Knowledge Discovery in Databases**, AAAI Press, 213-228.

[13] Han, J., Cai, Y., & Cercone, N. (1992) Knowledge Discovery in Databases: An Attribute-Oriented Approach, *Proc. of the 18th VLDB Conference*, Vancouver, Canada.

[14] Hu, X., Cercone, N., and Han, J. (1993) An Attribute-Oriented Rough Set Approach for Knowledge Discovery in Databases, *International Workshop On Rough Sets And Knowledge Discovery (RSKD-93)*, Banff, 79-94.

[15] Cercone, N, and McCalla, G. (1986) Accessing Knowledge Through Natural Language. Invited chapter for M.Yovits 25th Anniversary Issue **Advances in Computers** series, Academic Press, 1-99.

[16] Perrault, R., and Grosz, B. (1986) Natural Language Interfaces, *Annual Review of Computer Science 1*, Annual Reviews Inc., Palo Alto, California, 47-82.

[17] Knight, K.(1989) Unification: A multidisciplinary survey, *ACM Computing Surveys*, 21(1).

[18] Popowich, F., P. McFetridge, D. Fass and G. Hall. (1992). Processing Complex Noun Phrases in a Natural Language Interface to a Statistical Database. *14th International Conference on Computational Linguistics*. Nantes, France, 46-52.

[19] Bouma, G. (1992) Feature Structures and Nonmonotonicity. *Computational Linguistics* 18(2), 183-203.

A Heuristic for Evaluating Databases for Knowledge Discovery with DBLEARN

David Fudger*
Information Systems Department, City of Regina
Regina, Sask., Canada S4P 3C8
fudger@cs.uregina.ca

Howard J. Hamilton[†]
Department of Computer Science, University of Regina
Regina, Sask., Canada S4S 0A2
hamilton@cs.uregina.ca

Abstract

We propose a heuristic method for choosing databases for attempting knowledge discovery. The DBLEARN knowledge-discovery program uses an attribute-oriented inductive-inference method to discover potentially significant relations in a database. A concept forest defines the possible generalizations that DBLEARN can make for a database. The concept forest consists of trees, each of which represents a concept hierarchy for one attribute. We propose that the potential for discovery in a database be estimated by examining the complexity of its concept forest. One measure which has proven useful is the based on the depths and heights of all the interior nodes in their trees. Higher values for this measure indicate more complex concept forests, and thus, we believe, more potential for discovery. Given several databases and their concept forests, we rank them according to a heuristic measure, and recommend that DBLEARN be applied to those with the highest values.

1 Introduction

We propose a heuristic method for evaluating a relational database with regard to DBLEARN's potential for knowledge discovery in that database. *Knowledge discovery* is the nontrivial extraction of implicit, previously unknown, and potentially useful information from data [2]. DBLEARN is a knowledge-discovery system that summarizes information in a database based on a user-defined concept hierarchy for each attribute [1, 5, 6]. Our heuristic method is based on estimating the complexity of the concept hierarchies using a heuristic measure. A preliminary version of this paper appeared in [4].

---

*Current address: Information System Department, Brick Warehouse Corp., 11411 - 170 Street, Edmonton, Alberta, Canada.

†Supported by Natural Sciences Engineering Research Council of Canada (NSERC) Research Grant OPG0121504.

DBLEARN and other knowledge-discovery systems are being developed to address the rapid accumulation of computer-readable data [2]. DBLEARN combines the learning-from-examples paradigm from Machine Learning with database operations to extract knowledge from existing databases. It uses an attribute-oriented inductive-inference method [1] to summarize data in a database according to concept hierarchies for the attributes. The concept hierarchy for an attribute provides a tree which can be ascended until an appropriate level of generality is found. DBLEARN has been applied in controlled settings on several databases, including the NSERC Grant-Information Database [5] and the City of Regina water-meter database [3].

The three inputs needed for DBLEARN are:

1. *Base Data*: the unconditioned data present in a database;

2. *Learning Task*: specification of a subset of the base data and parameters on learning; and

3. *Concept Hierarchies*: expert-supplied domain knowledge about potential generalizations.

Typically the strategy for automatically analyzing a database with DBLEARN consists of the following steps: identify a target database, devise concept hierarchies for this database, and then generalize the data (based on the concept hierarchies) in the hopes of identifying new and useful information. The generalization method used is *attribute-oriented inductive inference*, whereby specific data values in tuples are repeatedly replaced by more general values, giving a reduced set of distinct tuples, until the threshold number of tuples is reached. The *tuple threshold* (or *table threshold*) is specified as part of the learning task. As implemented in the DBLEARN program, this generalization method requires large amounts of memory and processor time for a large database. This strategy for knowledge discovery from databases works well if:

1. a specific database has been identified or the database is to be chosen from a small set of databases, and

2. the DBLEARN program can interface with the database package (e.g., Sybase) of the database.

Often organizations have many data stores varying in structure, size and proprietary environments. Some organizations do not have the resources to analyze their databases in a random order. This paper proposes a heuristic method for measuring the complexity of the concept hierarchies for a set of databases and ranking the corresponding databases according to their potential for discovery. This heuristic has been implemented as a computer program that, given a list of the names of files (each containing the concept hierarchies for one database), produces a ranked list of the databases and their scores according to a selected measure. The ranked list indicates the order in which the databases should be analyzed to maximize the chance of making interesting discoveries soon.

The remainder of this paper is organized as follows. In Section 2 we describe concept hierarchies, and in Section 3 we describe our intuitions about evaluating the complexity of concept hierarchies. In Section 4 we present the evaluation procedure and analyze a heuristic measure for evaluating concept hierarchies. Finally, we draw conclusions in Section 5.

2   Concept Hierarchies

A *concept hierarchy* is a collection of generalization relations for an attribute in a database. Following [1], we define a *generalization relation* to be a relation between an exhaustive set of attribute values and a single higher-level, more-general value. A generalization relation can be represented by $\{A_1, ..., A_k\} \subset B$, which indicates that B is a generalization of each A_i, for $1 \leq i \leq k$. All concept hierarchies for a database are obtained from domain experts and stored together in a *concept hierarchy table* (also called a *concept hierarchy file*). For example, a concept hierarchy table for a university's enrolled student data might include the following generalization relations:

$$\{\text{Chem220}, \text{Chem240}, \text{Chem300}, \text{Chem400}\} \subset \text{Chemistry}$$
$$\{\text{Mathematics}, \text{Chemistry}, \text{Biology}, \text{Physics}\} \subset \text{Science}$$
$$\{\text{English}, \text{French}, \text{Philosophy}, \text{Sociology}\} \subset \text{Arts}$$
$$\{\text{Arts}, \text{Science}\} \subset \text{Course}$$
$$\{\text{1st year}, \text{2nd year}, \text{3rd year}, \text{4th year}\} \subset \text{Undergraduate}$$
$$\{\text{Masters}, \text{PhD}\} \subset \text{Graduate}$$
$$\{\text{Undergraduate}, \text{Graduate}\} \subset \text{Student}$$

Each line describes one generalization relation. The first four lines describe the Course concept hierarchy and the last three lines describe the Student concept hierarchy.

A convenient way to think of a concept hierarchy for an attribute is as a tree whose arcs (links) have all been reversed. In a tree, all arcs go from the root node towards the leaf nodes, but in a concept hierarchy, all arcs go from the "leaf nodes" toward the "root node" (the single sink of the directed acyclic graph). To simplify presentation, we refer to a concept hierarchy as a type of tree and we ignore the reversal of the links. Also, we refer to the set of concept hierarchies for a database as a *concept forest*. The attribute values in the database correspond to the leaf nodes of the tree. Concept hierarchies for one or more attributes in the database are required by DBLEARN if any generalization is to be performed.

Concept hierarchies are essential to DBLEARN's generalization process. DBLEARN first builds a table of relevant data from a database. Each attribute is generalized by ascending a specific tree until the distinct number of values for that attribute is less than the user-specified *attribute threshold*. After all attributes have been generalized, duplicate tuples are removed and the attributes with the most distinct values are generalized further until the number of tuples is less than or equal to the user-specified tuple threshold. The remaining tuples are called the *final generalized relation*. When generalization stops, DBLEARN can be said to have a set of active nodes in each of the concept hierarchies, where an *active node* is a node corresponding to a generalized attribute value that appears in at least one of the tuples in the final generalized relation. For example, the final generalized relation might contain the following (generalized) tuples

Chemistry	Undergraduate	14%
Chemistry	Graduate	2%

(where the final column identifies the percentage of the original tuples summarized in this generalized tuple). Here, Chemistry is an active node in the Course concept hierarchy and Undergraduate and Graduate are both active nodes in the Student concept hierarchy. Chem220, Chem240, Chem300 and Chem400 are **not** active nodes in the Course concept hierarchy because generalization has proceeded to the ancestor of these nodes. For more details on the method used in DBLEARN, see [5, 7].

3 Complexity of Concept Hierarchies

Let us consider the relationship between the concept hierarchies and the potential for DBLEARN to find interesting results. If more concept hierarchies are present, DBLEARN has more opportunities to perform generalizations. Also, a more complex tree affords more nodes that may be active and thus may be mentioned in the conclusions. As well, an active node that is farther from the leaf nodes is conceptually farther from the base values for the attribute. Finally, an active node that is farther from the root node allows more specific results to be stated; more specific results are less likely to be "platitudes," i.e., general statements about general classes. For all these reasons, if the concept hierarchies are more complex, more interesting results are likely to be found.

Let us consider measures of complexity for concept hierarchies. A single concept hierarchy can be regarded as a tree. No generally accepted measure of the complexity of a tree is used in the data structures literature. Two obvious candidates are:

- the number of nodes, and

- the depth of the tree, i.e., the length of the longest branch.

One example for each of these measures will be sufficient to illustrate why neither is suitable for our application.

First, consider a wide, shallow concept hierarchy, i.e., a tree with many nodes but with all nodes at depth 1, such as that shown in Figure 1(a). We define the *depth of a node* such that the depth of the root node is 0, the depth of a direct descendant of the root node is 1, and so on. Here all base values generalize to the same value (A, corresponding to ANY). Regardless of how many nodes are present at depth 1, no interesting conclusions can be formed by DBLEARN, since any generalization will simply refer to ANY value. We regard any generalization to the root node as uninteresting because it indicates that the values of the attribute are simply being ignored.

Next, consider a deep tree with few children for each node, such as that shown in Figure 1(b). In this case there are few base values (only J and K in fact) and many levels of the tree with only one child for each parent. A generalization up either branch of this tree (other than the final generalization to A) does not produce any true generalization, since each higher value actually corresponds to the same number of base values. From this example, we see that any linear chain in a tree is uninteresting and should be compressed.

Next we turn to some less obvious examples. Figures 2 and 3 show the concept forests for two databases. Concept forest CF1 has 8 attributes (i.e., 8 separate trees), a maximum depth of 4, a total of 27 nodes, and 15 leaf nodes.

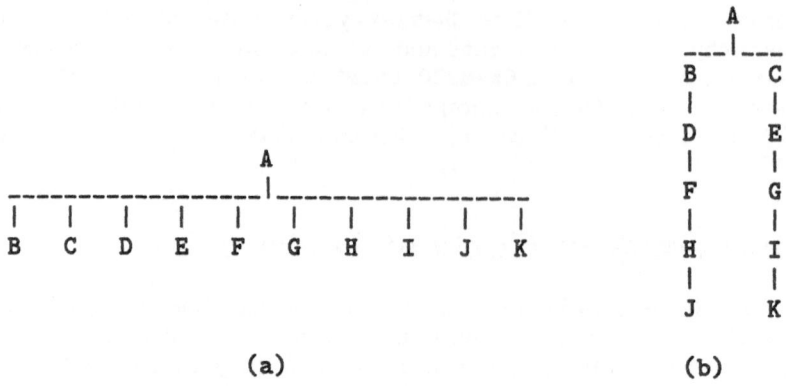

Figure 1: Concept Hierarchies: (a) CH1, (b) CH2

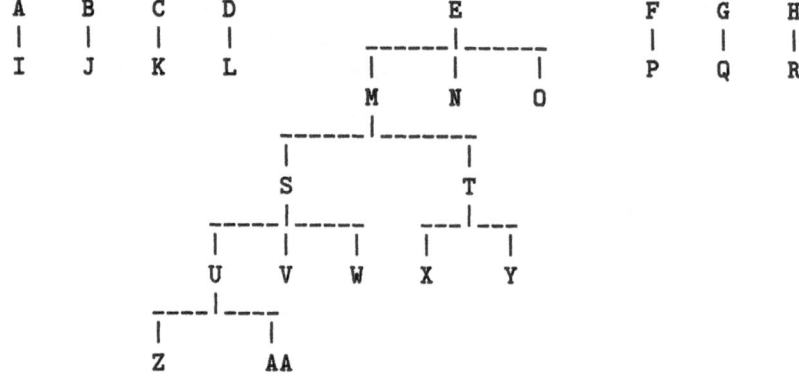

Figure 2: Concept Forest CF1

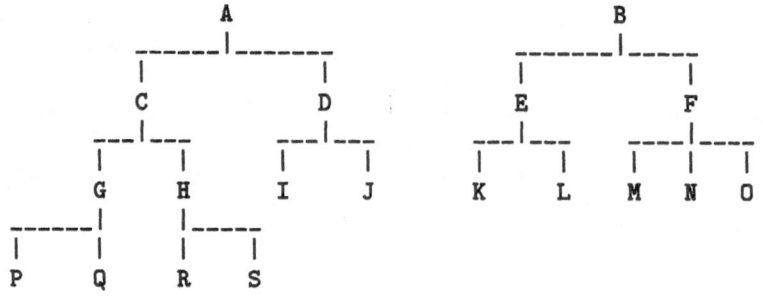

Figure 3: Concept Forest CF2

Concept forest CF2 has 2 attributes, a maximum depth of 3, a total of 19 nodes, and 12 leaf nodes. Although CF1 is larger in all these aspects, CF2 seems to provide more complicated domain knowledge than CF1.

Since the leaf nodes represent the base values of the attribute, they do not provide opportunities for drawing interesting conclusions. The base values are present in the database, and any conclusion mentioning them is not based on "nontrivial extraction" and does not represent "implicit knowledge," as are required for knowledge discovery. Conclusions regarding the base values can be drawn using standard database **count** queries.

Since neither the root node nor the leaf nodes allow interesting results to be found, attention should be restricted to the other nodes. An *interior node* is a node that is neither the root node nor a leaf node. Concept forest CF1 has 4 interior nodes (M, S, T, U), while concept forest CF2 has 6 interior nodes (C, D, E, F, G, H).

In the next section, we describe a measure for evaluating the relative complexities of concept forests based on the ideas introduced in this section.

4   Evaluation Procedure and Heuristics

The following procedure is used for measuring the complexity of a concept forest.

1. Augment each concept hierarchy for an attribute until it is complete. A *complete concept hierarchy* includes generalizations for all possible values for the attribute. The augmentation may be accomplished best by adding an OTHER node as a default for any unexpected values.

2. Arrange each concept hierarchy in tree form, with ANY as the root of each tree.

3. Delete any node (other than the root) that has only one child and then make the child into a new child of the grandparent. This removes linear chains.

4. If the root node has only one child, remove the child, and make the grandchildren (if any) into children of the root.

5. Determine the complexity of the concept forest using the measure discussed below.

Let f be a concept forest consisting of k concept hierarchies (trees) $t_1, \ldots t_k$, with depths $d_1, \ldots, d_k$ respectively. Measure m_1 is calculated based on the number of interior nodes weighted by their depth and height in their tree. The *height* of a node in a tree is the **minimum** distance of that node from the nearest leaf node. The height of a leaf is 0, and the height of any nonleaf node is 1 more than the minimum height of any of its children. (This definition of *height* differs from the standard definition used in the data structures where the height of a non-leaf node is 1 more than the *maximum* height of any of its children.) We define:

$$m_1(f) = \sum_{t \in f} \sum_{i \in t} (d_i + h_i),$$

node i	d_i	h_i	total
M	1	2	3
S	2	1	3
T	2	1	3
U	3	1	4
Total			13

(a)

node i	d_i	h_i	total
C	1	2	3
D	1	1	2
E	1	1	2
F	1	1	2
G	2	1	3
H	2	1	3
Total			15

(b)

Table 1: Evaluation of Measure m_1 on (a) CF1 and (b) CF2

where d_i is the depth of node i in tree t and h_i is the height of node i. Higher values for $m_1(f)$ indicate more complex concept hierarchies.

For example, as shown in Table 1(a), measure m_1 evaluates to 13 on concept forest CF1 (see Figure 2), where the only interior nodes are M, S, T, and U. Also, as shown in Table 1(b), measure m_1 evaluates to 15 on concept forest CF2 (see Figure 3). Here, m_1 ranks CF2 as more complex than CF1 and suggests that DBLEARN would be more likely to make interesting discoveries in the database corresponding to CF2 than in the database corresponding to CF1.

5 Conclusions

DBLEARN relies heavily on the concept hierarchies to provide new knowledge based on the existing data. If the tree structure is short and simple, the data will generalize very quickly from many tuples to fewer than the tuple threshold, but few new and interesting discoveries will be made. This was demonstrated using small examples. If there are more distinct values to generalize to, the attribute-oriented inductive-inference method used by DBLEARN produces results with more specific values. By paying attention to the number of concept hierarchies, the number of interior nodes in these hierarchies, and the depth and height of each of these interior nodes, a measure of complexity was designed for concept hierarchies.

There are several reasons to use the measure described in this paper. First, the size of a concept hierarchy is very small compared to the size of a database. This allows for a very fast cursory analysis of the potential for knowledge discovery before DBLEARN is applied to the databases.

Secondly, as it exists today, DBLEARN must be ported to any proprietary platform where it is to be run, which may involve changes to DBLEARN to deal with a different operating system or a different database environment. The heuristic procedure proposed in this paper can be performed easily using a concept hierarchy file before any porting of DBLEARN is done. As well, m_1 could conceivably be applied to a paper description of the concept hierarchies for a database. The results of the heuristic procedure could be used to determine if porting DBLEARN to a new environment would be worth the effort.

Thirdly, the heuristic procedure could be used during the design of the concept hierarchies to guide the designers to more useful concept hierarchies. For example, if the heuristic procedure gives a low score to a concept forest, the domain experts should be consulted to try and refine the concept hierarchy further. However, aiming for a high score according to our procedure cannot replace the need for the concept hierarchy to describe useful relationships in the domain.

Finally, and perhaps most importantly, the measure described here can be used to direct the knowledge discovery process among many databases. DBLEARN requires a large amount of memory space and can take several hours to analyze a relatively small database. Using our heuristic procedure, we can rank many databases by the level of complexity in their concept hierarchies, and then direct DBLEARN to the most likely candidates for discovery. This is especially useful when complete analysis of only a few databases is possible.

In ongoing work we are applying the heuristic described in this paper to a wide variety of academic and commercial databases.

References

[1] Y.D. Cai, N. Cercone, and J. Han. Attribute-oriented induction in relational databases. In *Knowledge Discovery in Databases*, pages 213–228. AAAI/MIT Press, Cambridge, MA, 1991.

[2] W.J. Frawley, G. Piatetsky-Shapiro, and C.J. Metheus. Knowledge discovery in databases: An overview. *AI Magazine*, 13(3):57–70, 1992.

[3] D. Fudger. Knowledge discovery in large databases: DBLEARN applied to a large commerical database. Department of Computer Science, University of Regina, Regina, Sask., April 1993.

[4] D. Fudger and H.J. Hamilton. Heuristic evaluation of databases for knowledge discovery with DBLEARN. In *RSKD'93: International Workshop on Rough Sets and Knowledge Discovery*, pages 29–39, Banff, Canada, October 1993.

[5] J. Han, Y.D. Cai, and N. Cercone. Knowledge discovery in databases: An attribute-oriented approach. In *Proc. of 18th Int'l Conf. on Very Large Data Bases*, Vancouver, August 1992.

[6] J. Han, Y.D. Cai, and N. Cercone. Data-driven discovery of quantitative rules in relational databases. *IEEE Trans. on Knowledge and Data Engineering*, 5(1):29–40, February 1993.

[7] Y. Huang and Yandong Cai. A tutorial on the DBLEARN system. School of Computing Science, Simon Fraser University, Burnaby, B.C., Canada, 1993.

KNOWLEDGE RECOGNITION, ROUGH SETS, AND FORMAL CONCEPT LATTICES

Walter A. Sedelow, Jr.   Sally Yeates Sedelow
University of Arkansas at Little Rock
Little Rock, Arkansas U.S.A.

As we have recently emphasized elsewhere (W. A. Sedelow & S. Y. Sedelow, 1993b), Knowledge Delivery globally at least compares with Health Care Delivery in social importance--which is to say that internationally it is one of the salient social problems of the present day. At this Conference we are concerned, by way of current and prospective interactions between research and researchers in the domains of Knowledge Discovery and of Rough Sets, to make technical contributions to the alleviation of that problem. Knowledge, it goes without saying, always has been in shorter supply than needed; but now the deficit in available, delivered knowledge has become an overriding concern around the world, in no small measure owing to the disarray in human lives occasioned by widespread disruption in more or less traditional and systemic relationships (W. A. Sedelow & S. Y. Sedelow, 1993a), thereby creating a necessity for working through to solution more problems in less time than ever previously has been required of the human species.

Although we celebrate Thomas Aquinas and Gottfried Leibniz in part for the remarkable comprehensiveness of their familiarity with the intellectual capital of scholarship transitted to them by means of manuscripts, scriptoria, books, and libraries, even those unique paragons of knowledgeability did not know all that was known, even in the West--much less in other cultural traditions, (despite such significant and impressive exceptions to that non-knowledge as Leibniz's acquaintanceship with the elaboration of a binary number system in China). Nonetheless, in their 'world' it was assumed that the route to knowledge primarily was by means of retrieval, a notion strongly reinforced by the long dominance of the wrong-headed assumption of innateness of ideas. It really remained for those of us in the latter half of the current century to conclude--in effect, by practice, if not always in a principled way--that often a knowledge generator system was more economic than a knowledge retrieval system, even when relevant knowledge (sometimes) might be or already was available somewhere. The sheer magnitude of growth in science, scientists, and scientific output mightily facilitated such a (sometimes unthinking) episodic shift in orientation to generation rather than retrieval; and that oscillation in orientation was further enhanced by, unfortunately, the greater ease (with now larger clusterings of scientists in any one specialty in any one place) of falling into the 'NIH' or Not-Invented-Here [and, hence, not of salient interest] Syndrome, currently widespread, even with the availability of advanced information retrieval capabilities at minor as well as major scientific research foci. So, it may be said, just when knowledge is most badly needed, we often find, inter alia, an at least tacit tendency to ignore accomplishment already on deposit in the bank of human knowledge in favor of comparatively ab initio fresh starts--all without organized attention to relative cost and other dimensionalities involved in not drawing on the species' 'bank account' of already achieved knowing. [As to the scale and significance of that social-cost-accounting omission, one is reminded of the U.S. failure in the Kennedy era to consider the comparative implications of undertaking space exploration instrumentationally rather than with humans--or, even more fundamentally, whether it made sense to invest so massively in space exploration and its associated (prospective) military adventurisms under the circumstances of accumulated unsolved and massive terrestial problems, especially when those problems were combined with a rapid diminution of necessary solutional resources.]

Per contra, one of the few highly visible, and necessarily inherently contrarian, expositions as to the desirability of utilizing Knowledge Discovery by way of Knowledge Recognition within existing published scholarship is in the work of Don Swanson, the physicist and information scientist at The University of Chicago.

Our own research group's interest in mobilizing the resources of Rough Sets for a more effective Knowledge Recognition capability is part of a still larger research enterprise, and network of associated research efforts, which we acronymically denominate SSA [pronounced 'Say'], standing for Symbol Systems Access (W. A. Sedelow & S. Y. Sedelow, 1992a). The central thrust is studies in how to enhance human access (with as little interference as possible from limitations in one's knowledge of multiple languages) to (i) the accomplishments [via retrieval] and (ii) the potentialities [via generation (D. M. Armstrong, 1989)] of languages of all sorts (whether spoken, logico-mathematical, iconic, cinematographic, etc., and whether or not hyper-medial), and with special attention to what already is instantiated in those languages, as with published science and schlarship. Time doesn't allow the recapitulation here of the accomplishments on this front cited elsewhere of Ronald Rousseau, K. D. Shearer (1986), and others; but because of its prospective importance for the general theme of this Conference we will mention the recent grant to Professor Shearer for exploring the generation of what we call Shearer Maps--mappings of the location (as in libraries, whether electronic or traditional) of knowledge by type (as to, e.g., the scientific literature on nephrology in Portuguese), as well as, subsequently, mappings of the resources (teachers, computer communication networks [CCNs], terminals, librarians and information specialists, and the like) for accessing such stored (but spatially differentially distributed) 'intellectual capital.' With the probable (and only somewhat technology-driven) partial deinstitutionalization of education--or, more accurately, learning--such aspects of Symbol Systems Accessibility may come to seem much more important to social policy makers, parents, students, school boards, and others, than such currently forefront (and related) issues as efforts toward the equalization of per capita funds for school districts; mutatis mutandis, the same considerations may come to obtain with reference to 'post-secondary' (i.e., university) education/learning, R&D labs, etc. (W. A. Sedelow, 1968).

A major, albeit largely latent, issue here is the optimization of Knowledge Representations (KRs)--optimization, on the one side, vis-a-vis (i) the human central nervous system/brain (W. A. Sedelow, 1991), and, on the other, vis-a-vis (ii a) specific knowledge content to be represented and, also, (ii b) available representational resources (e.g., quill pens, Windows environments, Backus-Naur notation). It would be, of course, a massive petitio to assume in advance of genuinely scientific investigation that the (knowledge-representational) form in which, say, a scientific or technological assertion or treatise was initially expressed is by even any one alone of these associated criteria roughly sub-optimal to an appropriate degree. For the moment, setting aside the problem of what we do not (yet) know as to how the brain processes (P. B. Churchland & T. J. Sejnowski, 1992), and so attending at this point only to the other optimization front, it may be said that even history-of-ideas attention to the hermeneutics of scientific prose--as with unnecessary, and technically undesirable, assumptional content brought into, say, Darwin's writings in consequence of specifics of the dialoging with his father--may provide useful insight as to improvements in the formulation of models, theorems, and the like. More comprehensively, W. A. Sedelow's Expert System TEST-bed (The Expert System Test-bed) approach is meant to make that process of optimization vastly more organized and systematic, concerning itself as it does with optimization as to a large and systematic set of dimensionalities (W. A. Sedelow, 1988).

It has been said that, had the calculus been utilized in the expression of pre-Keynesian economic theory, the entire content of it could have been put together during the course of a long English country-house weekend; without doubt, Rough Sets, Fuzzy Sets, Formal Concept Lattices (S. Y. Sedelow & W. A. Sedelow, 1992), and other notational and logical stratagems also are going to contribute mightily to avoiding wasted time, as well as avoiding awkwardness, inconsistency, unwarranted 'certainty,' and incompleteness, when it comes to expressing Well-Formed Formulae (wffs), or other modalities of representing knowledge. Within Expert Systems (ES) research (W. A. Sedelow & S. Y. Sedelow, 1994) the increasing recognition that (i) unnecessary assumptions and (ii) system metaknowledge representations are the strategically most promising facets to attend to in improving existing ES points to a situation in ES where a version of the Canadian McLuhan's notion that the medium of expression (e.g., in our terms, KR) is central ["The medium is the message."] also obtains.

Specifically apropos Rough Sets, it is notable that as to Knowledge Discovery their multi-valued-logic character means that they are sensitive isomorphism detectors, and across disparate domains--where without them structural parallelisms in models from diverse disciplines, especially when the knowledge in them is necessarily imprecise, might well go [probably would go?] undetected.

Through the KR clarification they provide, Rough Sets, by means of their abstracting and simplifying of structure, are a major resource for discovering, or recognizing, certain essentials of knowledge already stored in knowledge bases; with the additional assistance of machine learning techniques utilizing Rough Sets--as with J. W. Grzymala-Busse's 'Learning by Examples using Rough Sets' [LERS] programs (J. W. Grzymala-Busse, 1990; J. W. Grzymala-Busse & S. Mithal, 1990)--it is possible to still further compress data and instance space. In our own Whole-Language-Scale Semantic Space research the advantage of using LERS already is manifest (J. W. Grzymala-Busse & Soe Than, 1993); and inasmuch as one goal of our research is to discover the knowledge already (tacitly) embedded in conceptual thesauri such as Roget's, and then to use such whole-language thesauri as a basis for simplifying the construction ('domain-transcendence') and interaction of varied ESs, it must be evident that for us the role of Rough Sets in knowledge recognition (i.e., knowledge [re]discovery by pattern recognition), knowledge consolidation, knowledge generalization, knowledge encoding or representation, and, hence, in knowledge delivery is crucial. Knowledge recognition is essentially dependent on the establishment of sense comparabilities, irrespective of their lexical expression; means for making possible automatically such determinations of sense comparability.

With the rapid spread of InterNet and related technology in the United States and abroad (W. A. Sedelow & S. Y. Sedelow, 1993b), including immensely heightened multi-media and hypermedia transmission capability (currently primarily being driven by optical fiber technology, but consider also packet broadcast satellite communication prospects, as with The University of Hawaii ALOHA Net [W. A. Sedelow & S. Y. Sedelow, 1992b]), the importance of recognizing, retrieving, reorganizing, repackaging, and re-using extant knowledge--whether in data bases or knowledge bases--can only grow in importance, as is certainly implied by 'Gore II.' In fact already it is the case that in, for example, medicine techniques for the functional merger of existing and prospective ESs are of practical importance, even at a single site (i.e., a medical center, such as Physicians & Surgeons in New York City). For such purposes, much less for the reanalysis and meta-analysis of earlier research, Rough Sets are important in enabling us to achieve a consistency-driven necessary harmonization of levels of (un)certainty in the information bases involved, while our basic studies in whole-language semantic space imply a means of automatically transiting from any one ES to any other.

At the moment we ourselves are also engaged in the early phase of a research project intended to illuminate and make mutually useful and complementary the models employed in different systematicity disciplines, such as control theory, cybernetics, ecology, general systems research, and others; necessarily, a central question therein is the discovery of structural similarities (if not isomorphisms) across models, which, owing to divergences in technical lexicons and KR preferences among different academic disciplines, otherwise likely would remain masked and thus not as mutually beneficial as can be the case when Rough similarities in their structure are made manifest thanks to the use of Rough Sets.

Resultant Rough Set simplifications in models can produce results conformal with Occam's shaving (or 'razor') and Newton's stinginess (or 'parsimony'); consequently they contribute to increased elegance of expression and, further, then, to greater intellectual (gedanken-experimental) manipulability--all of course highly beneficial in trying to model so as to solve problems in complex, highly multidimensional and highly parametric domains, precisely the point from which this paper started.

Before turning to an exposition of some of our specific accomplishments, in part contingent upon the already achieved demonstration within our research group of the isomorphicity obtaining as between Formal Concept Lattices and Rough Sets, as well as with Bryan Model graphs, there are two related matters to which we would like to draw attention here, one historical, the other futuristic. Historically, it is a matter of no small interest that that great pioneer in the theory of signs and semiotics, C. S. Peirce (J. Brent, 1993), made much of the significance of 'abduction' in the generation of new knowledge, arguing, as you will remember, that the function of the representation of existing knowledge was not only to sum it up, but also (in doing so) to facilitate the discovery of new knowledge by, then, well-informed guess-work (i.e., surmises or hypothesis formation or 'insight' enabled by familiarity with the summation of prior relevant knowledge, "chance thus [abductively] favoring the prepared mind"). So, with Peirce, we have a theorist who sees knowledge discovery as both--and somewhat simultaneously--a knowledge retrieval activity to discover what already is known (if sometimes only latently) and also (through the same process) a knowledge generating activity by means of the process of abduction. As to the future, at the 1993 International Conference on Computing & Information (ICCI), held in Sudbury, Ontario in late May, Lotfi Zadeh on the occasion of his keynote address confirmed what was announced sometime ago: that in Japan design efforts are in train for producing a general purpose computer optimized for the processing of Fuzziness in varied forms, what Professor Zadeh calls 'soft computing' (contra: 'crisp computing'); (en passant he also indicated that within a year or two approximately half the Motorola chip production will be of Fuzzy chips; [But how many Rough chips are in production now? By 1995 how many are likely to be? Is Poland taking a lead in utilizing its advantage as a Roughness manufacturing site?]). Thus, one wonders whether it also would not be timely to begin the design of general purpose and special purpose hardware optimized for Roughness in varied forms, for enhancing 'flexible computing' as opposed to 'rigid'(?) [i.e., exclusively mathematically-analytic, determinate, or two-valued....] computing.

A sharp focus for some of our current research efforts has to do with the KR modalities (such as Rough Sets and Formal Concept Lattices) especially well-suited to presenting the in-lines (high-resolution, fine granularity distinctions) as well as the outlines of the semantic space (W. A. Sedelow & S. Y. Sedelow, 1987) created by the lexical repertory (S. Y. Sedelow & W. A. Sedelow, 1986a), along with its combinatoric constraints, of any given language at any given time. Although our initial explorations at whole-language scale so far have been confined to English, that new, systemic approach to semantics also is important--in addition to its

Knowledge Discovery potential which is the primary target for our attention here--for machine translation (MT) applications as well as otherwise (e.g., totally electronically mediated communication, including automatic interpretive telephony; building ESs domain-transcendentally), so that we may be enabled to do analyses of semantic space mapping problems between various pairs or more of languages, preferably using an interlingua (W. A. Sedelow & S. Y. Sedelow, 1993a). To that end we have accomplished some preliminary studies of English versus Chinese semantic space (S. Y. Sedelow, 1987), as well as data gathering for some fine-grained sample tests with reference to English versus German. For both theoretical and practical reasons we also are interested in the possibility of constructing--somewhat after the manner of the ethnoscience efforts incorporated within the Human Relations Area Files--a universal lexicon matrix within which to locate automatically the individual semantic-resource items of any language. The Knowledge Discovery and SSA importance of such a capability for locating, with the aid of RS pattern-matching, banked knowledge irrespective of the language within which it is encoded becomes increasingly evident as the electronic library ceases to be only visionary.

Robert Kent having demonstrated the isomorphism of Rough Sets with Formal Conceptual Lattices, as well as with the Robert Bryan graph-theoretic model of an abstract conceptual thesaurus, it became especially apparent that there was an attractive synergism between the research activity of the formal concept lattice theoreticians in the Allgemeine Algebra Gruppe, Fachbereich Mathematik, Technische Hochschule Darmstadt, led by Rudolf Wille, concerned to represent concepts as "units of thought," and our studies of associative conceptual dictionaries (thesauri). We are enabled to represent more effectively than had been possible with the Bryan model deep and extensive partial ordering relationships among the terms in a whole-language thesaurus, while for Darmstadt the scale and specific character of our work creates attractive large challenges for applying their nested line diagrams (Haase) and the formal mathematics underlying them. Given as well the Grzymala-Busse software for data and instance space reduction with reference to a whole-language thesaurus by utilizing Rough Sets when employing machine learning, we now have a potent armamentarium for coping with the massive knowledge modelling problems implied by a thesaurus with hundreds of thousands of individual entries.

Briefly as to Concept Lattices (Concept Analysis), in his basic paper, "Concept Lattices and Conceptual Knowledge Systems" (1990), Wille begins with the primitive notion of a formal context as a triple (G,M,I) where G and M are sets while I is a binary relation between G and M, i.e., $I \subseteq G \times M$ (elements of G are objects and the elements of M are attributes). Therefore gIm may be read as the object g has the attribute m. Derivation operators, represented by "prime" notation, are defined for the subsets $X \subseteq G$ and $Y \subseteq M$ as follows:

$$X: \rightarrow X' := \{m \varepsilon M \ gIm \ \text{for all} \ g \varepsilon X\}$$

$$Y:\rightarrow Y' := \{g\varepsilon G \ g\text{Im for all } m\varepsilon Y\}$$

These operators form a Galois connection between the power sets of G and M which can be expressed by the following conditions indicating a natural "duality" between objects and attributes:

(1) $X_1 \subseteq X_2$ implies $X'_2 \subseteq X'_1$ for $X_1, X_2 \subseteq G$;

(1') $Y_1 \subseteq Y_2$ implies $Y'_2 \subseteq Y'_1$ for $Y_1, Y_2 \subseteq M$;

(2) $X \subseteq X''$ and $X' = X'''$ for $X \subseteq G$;

(2') $Y \subseteq Y''$ and $Y' = Y'''$ for $Y \subseteq M$;

(3) $(U \ X_t)' = \cap X'_t$ for $X_t \subseteq G$ (tεT);
    tεT   tεT

(3') $(U \ Y)' = \cap Y'_t$ for $Y_t \subseteq M$ (tεT) (Wille, pp. 1-2).
    tεT   tεT

Now with reference to success in applying the Rough Sets approach--isomorphic with the above Formal Concept Lattices--the research of Jerzy Grzymala-Busse, with assistance from his doctoral student Soe Than, is central. We have been studying intensely the relationality among senses of the word 'over' for some time, notably thanks to the efforts of our former graduate student and present research group colleague L. John Old (1993). 'Over' was one word selected for special attention in part owing to the fact that an earlier publication by Claudia Brugman and George Lakoff (1988) had reported on the extensive study they had devoted to that term. Old formalized the analysis of the term 'over,' and also placed the Lakoff-Brugman effort in a comparative context by means of adding to the 'over' data base the numerous sense entries for the term in The Oxford English Dictionary, as well as information extracted from Roget's International Thesaurus--which we have been modelling and otherwise studying computationally for some years.

Building on those antecedents, Professor Grzymala-Busse and Dr. Soe Than have just published in a Psychonomic Society journal "Data Compression in Machine Learning Applied to Natural Language" (1993), a paper given in the 'Symposium on Natural Language Computing: New Developments,' which was devoted to a discussion of various facets of our research and chaired by W. A. Sedelow for the 1992 annual meeting of The Society for Computers in Psychology (SCiP). With their LERS algorithm and programs--Learning by Examples Using Rough Sets--they demonstrated how to achieve such groupings of entries, attributes, and attribute values as to achieve compression, with resultant changes in the machine learning rules in consequence of that data compression. A major goal of the paper, which was successfully reached, was to demonstrate the utility of this Rough Sets approach for the study of the semantic space of an entire language. In that small-scale but exemplary instance the decision table file consisted in four hundred entries.

Standing explicity behind the approach taken was the early basic work of Zdzislaw Pawlak (1982), as well as his more recent RS medical application study with K. and R. Slowinski. The cited earlier study by Grzymala-Busse, as well as a previous joint study done by him with Soe Than (1992), also were built on in accomplishing the present results. The SCiP paper impressively places terms in correct positions within the conceptual thesaurus by achieving a concept description inductively--the goal being "to describe all positive examples from the concept and none of the negative examples," with the description expressed in a set of rules or a decision tree.

Similarly, with Formal Concept Analysis objects (such as individual words) are jointly characterized with their attributes as forming concepts. Hence the basis for the isomorphicity between these two approaches to this major problem of how to achieve the crucial accomplishment of Knowledge Discovery by way of concept recognition. The successes reported on here are of course very heartening with reference to the use of RS in conjunction with whole-language semantic space modelling as a means to discover relevant knowledge units already available in published literature.

[This research is supported by Grant #IRI-9114068, U. S. National Science Foundation, Knowledge Models and Cognitive Systems Program.]

Bibliography

Armstrong, D.M. 1989. A Combinatorial Theory of Possibility. Cambridge: Cambridge University Press.

Brent, Joseph. 1993. Charles Sanders Peirce. Bloomington: University of Indiana Press.

Brugman, Claudia, and George Lakoff. 1988. "Cognitive Topology and Lexical Networks," in S. Small, G. Cottrell, and M. Tanenhaus, eds., Lexical Ambiguity Resolution, Palo Alto: Morgan Kaufmann, 477-508.

Churchland, Patricia S., and Terrence J. Sejnowski. 1992. The Computational Brain. Cambridge: MIT Press.

Grzymala-Busse, J.W. 1990. "On the Reduction of Instance Space in Learning from Examples," Proceedings, Methodologies for Intelligent Systems, 5, 388-395. Elsevier.

Grzymala-Busse, J.W., and Sachin Mithal. 1990. "A Comparison of Four Tests for Attribute Dependency in the LEM and LERS Systems for Learning from Examples," Proceedings, Third International Conference on Industrial and Engineering Applications of Artificial Intelligence & Expert Systems, Vol. II:949-958. ACM.

Grzymala-Busse, Jerzy W., and Soe Than. 1993. "Data Compression in Machine Learning Applied to Natural Language," Behavioral Research Methods, Instrumentation,and Computers, 25:2, 318-321.

Old, John. 1993. "Image Schemas and Lexicons: A Comparison Between Lexical Networks," Proceedings, Fifth Midwest Artificial Intelligence and Congitive Science Society Conference, ed. Thomas Ahlswede, Central Michigan University.

Pawlak, Zdzislaw. 1982. "Rough Sets," International Journal of Information and Computer Science. 11:341-356.

Sedelow, Sally Yeates. 1987. "An Interlingual Communication Support System (ICSS) Example Re Chinese/English Classroom Instruction," Proceedings, Methods III, International Conference on Foreign Language Teaching, University of Northern Iowa, Cedar Falls, 115-120.

Sedelow, Sally Yeates, and Walter A. Sedelow, Jr. 1986a. "The Lexicon in the Background," Winfred Lehmann, ed., Computers and Translation, I:2, 73-81.

Sedelow, Sally Yeates, and Walter A. Sedelow, Jr. 1992. "Recent Model-Based and Model-Related Studies of a Large-Scale Lexical Resource," Proceedings, COLING-92 [14th Biennial Conference for The International Committee on Computational Linguistics; Nantes], 1223-1227.

Sedelow, Walter A., Jr. 1968. "History as Language," Computer Studies in the Humanities and Verbal Behavior, 1 (4).

Sedelow, Walter A., Jr. 1991. "Human Computing in a Neurosciences Perspective: Implications for MT [Machine Translation] in Europe, Proceedings, 15th Annual European Studies Conference; University of Nebraska/Omaha; 336-339.

Sedelow, Walter A., Jr. 1988. "Knowledge Retrieval from Domain-Transcendent Expert Systems: I. Some Concepts from Cognitive Robotics," Proceedings, 51st Annual Meeting of the American Society for Information Science, 25: 205-208.

Sedelow, Walter A., Jr. 1992. "Petri Nets for Coordinating Studies Across University and National Boundaries in the Pacific Region," Proceedings, Pacific Telecommunications Conference, ed. Lofstrom and Wedemeyer, Pacific Telecommunications Council, Honolulu; 258-265.

Sedelow, Walter A., Jr. and Sally Yeates Sedelow. 1992a. "Artificial Intelligence, A New Tack," Proceedings, Martha Evens, ed., Fourth Midwest Artificial Intelligence and Cognitive Science Society Conference, Illinois Institute of Technology, 122-130.

Sedelow, Walter A., Jr. and Sally Yeates Sedelow. 1994. "Graph Theory, Set Theory, and Order Theory in Semantic Space Analysis for Use in Knowledge Representation," Proceedings, World Congress on Expert Systems '94 [Estoril/Lisbon]. (In Press.)

Sedelow, Walter A., Jr. and Sally Yeates Sedelow. 1993a. "Interlinguae," _ Proceedings, International Conference on Computing and Information [Sudbury, Ontario], IEEE Press. (In Press.)

Sedelow, Walter A., Jr. and Sally Yeates Sedelow. 1993b. "Multicultural/Multilingual Electronically-Mediated Communication." [1993 Conference on Computing for the Social Sciences: "Grand Challenges for the Social Sciences." National Center for Supercomputing Applications, University of Illinois].

Sedelow, Walter A., Jr. and Sally Yeates Sedelow. 1987. "Semantic Space," Winfred Lehmann, ed., Computers and Translation, 2: 231-242.

Shearer, Kenneth D. 1986. "The Geolinguistics of Information: English vis-a-vis Other Major Languages," International Library Review, 18: 223-230.

Wille, R. 1990. Concept Lattices and Conceptual Knowledge Systems. Preprint Nr. 1340, Darmstadt: Technische Hochschule.

Quantifying Uncertainty of Knowledge Discovered From Databases

Y. Xiang

S.K.M. Wong

N. Cercone

Department of Computer Science, University of Regina

Regina, Saskatchewan, Canada S4S 0A2

Abstract

This paper focuses on the application of rough set constructs to inductive learning from a database. A design guideline is suggested, which provides users the option to choose appropriate attributes, for the construction of classification rules. Error probabilities for the resultant rule are derived. A classification rule can be further generalized using concept hierarchies. The condition for preventing overgeneralization is derived. Moreover, given a constraint, an algorithm for generating a rule with minimal error probability is proposed.

1 Introduction

The rapidly growing size and number of databases, and the realization that intelligently analyzed data is a valuable resource have generated increasing demands for knowledge discovery in databases [2].

In this paper, we assume data are represented by a relational database in which information about individual objects in a domain is represented by a set of tuples of attribute values. Adopting the view of 'learning by examples' in AI, we may regard a database as a set of training examples. The objective of learning is to produce a classification rule in a disjunctive normal form (DNF) for a particular concept or class. A learned rule can be generated using the vocabulary of attributes. We shall call the set of selected attributes a *basis set* [3], and call the learning process *induction using attributes*. The rule from induction using attributes can be further generalized using a concept hierarchy for each individual attribute. The rule is then represented in a higher level language and is more compact. We shall call this generalization process *induction by hierarchy*.

Given a basis set A' of attributes, a user may be interested only in a subset which is then used to create the rule. Given this restriction, we can generate the rule using a minimum subset $A \subset A'$ of attributes. Such minimal subset may not be unique. We will discuss a design guideline based on rough sets [6] to provide users with different options.

Once a rule is generated by a learning system, a user may wish to know how reliable the rule is. We will show how error probabilities can be estimated for each component of the rule and for the rule as a whole.

Induction by hierarchy produces generalized rules. However, this induction process may overgeneralize and thus increase the classification error of the resultant rule. In this paper, we derive a condition for induction by hierarchy, which guarantees that no additional error is introduced.

In complex domains, the number of conjuncts in the resultant rule may be large. A user may want to limit the number of conjuncts involved. We discuss how to produce a rule which satisfies such a restriction and minimizes the classification error.

In complex domains, there are often exceptions to general principles. For example, most birds fly but penguin as a bird does not. Each such exception will form a conjunct in a DNF rule. Sometimes, the user is interested in only the general principles. An error bound can be used to prune those conjuncts which corresponds to exceptions. We will show how to generate a rule whose classification error is below a given threshold such that it includes minimal exceptions.

Our approach is based on the rough set theory [6] which provides a sound theoretical framework for knowledge discovery in databases.

2 Terminology

2.1 Basic Notions of Rough Sets

Let U be the *universe* of discourse, and let R be an equivalence relation on U. The pair $Z = (U, R)$ is called an *approximation space*. If $x, y \in U$ and $(x, y) \in R$, x and y are said to be *indistinguishable* in Z. Each equivalence classe of the relation R is called an *elementary set* in Z. A finite union of elementary sets in Z is called a *composed definable set* or simply *composed set* in Z.

Let X be a subset of U. The least composed set in Z containing X is called *upper approximation* of X in Z, denoted by $\overline{Apr}(X)$; the greatest composed set in Z contained in X is called the *lower approximation* of X in Z, denoted by $\underline{Apr}(X)$. The set $Bnd(X) = \overline{Apr}(X) - \underline{Apr}(X)$ is called the *boundary* of X in Z.

2.2 A Database as Learning Examples

Let Y be a domain of objects. Let $C \subset Y$ be a class of objects. We define a function $c : Y \rightarrow \{0, 1\}$ by the following rule: for each $y \in Y$, $c(y) = 1$ if $y \in C$, and $c(y) = 0$ if $y \notin C$. Let $S \subset Y$ be a finite set of sample objects. Let $A' = \{A_1, \ldots, A_n\}$ be a set of attributes, and let $V' = \{V_1, \ldots, V_n\}$ be the domains of these attributes. Let T' be the Cartesian product: $T' = V_1 \times \ldots \times V_n$. Let $f : Y \rightarrow T'$ be an one-to-one function such that each object $y \in Y$ is assigned to a tuple $t' \in T'$ $(f(x) = f(y)) \Rightarrow (x = y)$. The function f assigns each object to a *unique* tuple. This is the case in most database implementations where duplication is removed.

Let $D' = f[S]$ and $E' = f[C]$ be the images of S and C under f, respectively. D' represents a database of tuples as learning examples. $E' \cap D'$ is the set of positive examples of the class C, and $D' - E'$ is the set of negative examples. Throughout this paper, we will call an object $y \in S$ a *sample*, and call its value $f(y) = t' \in T'$ an *example tuple*.

3   Superfluous Attributes

Given positive examples $D' \cap E'$ and negative examples $D' - E'$, our task is to generate a classification rule for C such that, given the representation $t' \in T'$ of an object $y \in Y$, the membership of y in C can be determined with minimal error.

We could describe the rule based on the entire set A' of attributes. However, for many practical reasons, we often use only a subset of attributes of A' to generate the classification rule. One reason is because we know some attributes have no dependence relation with the class to be described. For example, social insurance numbers do not help to distinguish a patient with tuberculosis from one without. Another reason may be because it is not appropriate to use some attributes in the classification task. For example, to exact a rule for selecting good employees, we may not want to include attributes sex and race in the rule. This restriction of attributes can be easily performed by using a *projection* operation in relational databases. The option of specifying a desired set of attributes should be given to the user of a learning system. The removal of a subset B of attributes represents a *conceptual bias* [3] of the learning process.

We formalize the projection in the following: Let $B \subset A'$ be a proper subset of A'. A *projection* of the function f to the set of attributes $A = A' - B$ is defined as $g : U \rightarrow T$ where $T = V_{j_1} \times \ldots \times V_{j_m}$ and V_{j_i} is the domain of $A_{j_i} \in A$. We use $t = g(u)$ to denote the projected tuple obtained under g. Note that, unlike f, g is not one-to-one. Multiple objects in Y can be mapped into the same tuple by g.

After the attributes have been restricted to a subset in the above manner, it is often possible to further reduce the subset without increasing the classification error of the resultant rule. This involves the notion of *reduct* [8, 11] in the rough set theory.

Let g be the projection of f, $D = g[S]$ be the set of learning examples described by the set of attributes $A = A' - B$, and $E = g[C] \cap D$ be the set of positive training examples described by A. Following the notion in Section 2.1, let D be the universe, and let the equivalence relation $R(A)$ be defined as follows: $(r, t) \in R(A)$ iff for every $\Lambda \in A$, $r_\Lambda = t_\Lambda$ where r_Λ is the value of the attribute Λ in the tuple r. An attribute $\Lambda \in A$ is *superfluous* in A if $R(A) = R(A - \{\Lambda\})$; otherwise Λ is *indispensable* in A. If all attributes of A are indispensable in A, then A is *orthogonal*. A subset $W \subseteq A$ is a *reduct* of A iff W is orthogonal and $R(W) = R(A)$.

Since a reduct does not change the equivalence relation R, given a set $X \subseteq D$, none of $\overline{Apr}(X)$, $\underline{Apr}(X)$, or $Bnd(X)$ will change. This implies that the accuracy of classification relative to X does not change if we use a reduct as the basis set. The advantage of using a reduct rather than the original set A of attributes is that we have a more concise classification rule.

Given a set of examples D and the set A of attributes, there may exist more than one reduct. It would be useful for a learning system to provide all the reducts to the user, and to proceed with the subsequent learning task using the reduct selected by the user. The user may select the reduct with minimum cardinality, or the one which makes the most sense to him.

To compute a reduct, we remove an arbitrarily chosen attribute, say A_1, from the basis set A. We then check if all the elementary sets are unchanged. If so, we proceed with A_2, otherwise, we put A_1 back and proceed with A_2.

We go through all the attributes in A in this fashion. The attributes left at the end constitute a reduct.

However, although a single reduct can be computed relatively easily, the general problem of finding all reducts is NP-hard [10, 11].

4 Error Probability Estimation in Induction Using a Reduct

Given the set D of examples and the set $E \subset D$ of positive examples, D can be partitioned into $Neg(E) = D - \overline{Apr}(E)$ which is a set of negative examples, $Pos(E) = \underline{Apr}(E)$ which is a set of positive examples, and $Bnd(E)$ which is a set of mixed positive and negative examples. In the following discussion, we will omit the variable E for brevity, and simply write Neg, Pos and Bnd.

Since all tuples in an elementary set are indistinguishable, we shall use $s[t]$ to denote the elementary set of a tuple t.

Throughout this paper, we assume that the set of examples D is truly a representative of the class C in the universe of interests.

Assumption 4.1 *Let Y be a domain and let D be a set of examples. Let the number of positive examples in an elementary set $s[t]$ be $n_+[t] \geq 0$ and the number of negative examples be $n_-[t] \geq 0$. The examples in D satisfy the following properties:*

1. **Completeness** *For every object $x \in Y$, there is a sample $y \in Y$ such that $g(x) = g(y)$.*

2. **Proportion** *For every elementary set $s[t]$ in D and every object $y \in Y$,*

$$p(c(y) = 1|g(y) = t) = n_+[t]/(n_+[t] + n_-[t]).$$

3. **Miniworld** *For every elementary set $s[t]$ in D and every object $y \in Y$,*

$$p(g(y) = t) = (n_+[t] + n_-[t])/Card(D).$$

In the following, we construct a classification rule for the class C expressed in terms of a disjunctive normal form:

$$\forall y \in Y((class(y) = 1) \Longleftrightarrow (t_1 \vee \ldots \vee t_n)),$$

where each $t_i \in D$ is a tuple (conjunct) corresponding to an elementary set, and $class(y) = 1$ means that the object y is classified by the rule as a member of the class C.

Proposition 4.1 *Let t be a tuple in an elementary set $s[t] \subset Pos$. If $g(y) = t$ for $y \in Y$, then $c(y) = 1$.*

Proof:

Suppose $g(y) = t$, and $c(y) = 0$ which means $y \notin C$. Since $g(y) = t$, $s[t]$ must be either a subset of Neg or Bnd. This contradicts the assumption $s[t] \subset Pos$. □

Based on Proposition 4.1, for each t such that $s[t] \subset Pos$, we include t as a conjunct in the classification rule. We label the conjunct with an error probability:

$$p(c(y) \neq 1 | g(y) = t) = 0$$

which means that if the new tuple $g(y)$ matches t, we can conclude $c(y) = 1$ with certainty.

For each elementary set $s[t] \subset Bnd$, we include t as a conjunct in the classification rule if $n_+[t] \geq n_-[t]$. We label it with an error probability:

$$p(c(y) \neq 1 | g(y) = t) = n_-[t]/(n_+[t] + n_-[t])$$

which means that if the new tuple $g(y)$ matches t, we can conclude $c(y) = 1$ with probability $1 - p(c(y) \neq 1 | g(y) = t)$. This is justified by the following Proposition.

Proposition 4.2 *Let t be a tuple such that $s[t] \subset Bnd$ and $n_+[t] \geq n_-[t]$). If $g(y) = t$ for $y \in Y$, then*

$$p(c(y) = 1 | g(y) = t) = n_+[t]/(n_+[t] + n_-[t]) \geq p(c(y) = 0 | g(y) = t)$$

Proof:

By Assumption 4.1 and the given condition,

$$p(c(y) = 1 | g(y) = t) = n_+[t]/(n_+[t] + n_-[t]) \geq 0.5.$$

Therefore, $p(c(y) = 0 | g(y) = t) = 1 - p(c(y) = 1 | g(y) = t) = n_-[t]/(n_+[t] + n_-[t]) \leq 0.5.$ □

The above proposition states that, to minimize the chance of error, if $n_+[t] \geq n_-[t]$, we should conclude $class(y) = 1$; otherwise conclude $class(y) = 0$ (by not firing the rule).

The error probability of the classification rule as a whole is determined by the following Proposition.

Proposition 4.3 *The probability of false-positive error of the classification rule is*

$$p(class(y) = 1 \wedge c(y) = 0) = \frac{\sum_{g(y) \in Bnd(E) \wedge n_+[g(y)] \geq n_-[g(y)]} n_-[g(y)]}{Card(D)}.$$

The probability of false-negative error of the classification rule is

$$p(class(y) = 0 \wedge c(y) = 1) = \frac{\sum_{g(y) \in Bnd(E) \wedge n_+[g(y)] < n_-[g(y)]} n_+[g(y)]}{Card(D)}.$$

The error probability of the classification rule as a whole is

$$p(class(y) \neq c(y))$$
$$= p(class(y) = 1 \wedge c(y) = 0) + p(class(y) = 0 \wedge c(y) = 1).$$

We summarize the above discussion by the following Algorithm for the construction of a classification rule.

Algorithm 4.1 (Construct)

Input: A set $Z \subset D$ of distinct tuples, where D is the set of all examples.
Output: A classification rule in DNF.

BEGIN
    Initialize List to empty list
    FOR each $t \in Z$ such that $s[t] \subset Pos$ DO
        Label t with $p(c(y) \neq 1|g(y) = t) = 0$
        Add t with its label to List
    END FOR
    FOR each $t \in Z$ such that $s[t] \subset Bnd$ and $n_+[t] \geq n_-[t]$ DO
        Label t with $p(c(y) \neq 1|g(y) = t) = n_-[t]/(n_+[t] + n_-[t])$
        Add t with its label to List
    END FOR
    Construct the classification rule
        $\forall y \in Y((class(y) = 1) \Leftrightarrow (t_1 \lor \ldots \lor t_n))$
        where $t_i, \ldots, t_n$ are all the tuples in List
    Label the rule with $p(class(y) \neq c(y))$ as determined by Proposition 4.3.
END

The error probability used to label the individual conjunct in a rule can be used for *posterior* decision-making. For example, after a patient's symptom matches a conjunct, the error probability labeling the conjunct tells the doctor the chance of misdiagnosis.

The overall error probability labeling the entire rule can be used for *prior* decision-making. Suppose two learning systems have learned the same concept from different sets of examples possibly using different attribute descriptions. If we must commit to one of the systems for future classifications, the overall error probabilities of the two systems help us to make a choice. For example, if we are to select one of two family doctors, we would prefer the one with lower overall rate of misdiagnosis.

The overall error probability may also be used to limit the number of conjuncts contained in a rule. We will discuss this issue in the next section.

5   Restriction on the Number of Conjuncts

In order to increase the efficiency of a classification rule (less space to store and less time to apply), the user may impose a restriction on the number of conjuncts, subject to the minimization of error probability. To meet such a requirement, we can rank the conjuncts in a rule by their contribution to the overall error probability.

The removal of a conjunct from a rule increases only the false-positive error but not the false-negative error. In particular, the removal of a conjunct t_i will add n_{+i} to and subtract n_{-j} from the numerator of the error probability, where n_{+i} and n_{-j} are the number of positive examples and negative examples in $s[t_i]$, respectively. That is, the net increase to the numerator is $n_{+i} - n_{-i}$. Therefore, to find a conjunct whose removal causes minimal increase of error probability, we need only to select the one with minimal $n_{+i} - n_{-i}$. These observations lead to the following Algorithm and Proposition.

Algorithm 5.1 (SortConjuncts)

Input: A list I of conjuncts $t_1, \ldots, t_m$, the number of positive examples in each elementary set $n_{+1}, \ldots, n_{+m}$, and the number of negative examples in each elementary set $n_{-1}, \ldots, n_{-m}$.

Output: The list O of conjuncts such that the removal of a conjunct from the end of the list causes minimal increase of error probability.

BEGIN
        Initialize O to an empty list
        WHILE $I \neq \phi$ DO
                Find t in I with maximal $n_+ - n_-$
                Remove t from I and place it at the end of O
        END WHILE
END

Proposition 5.1 *Given a list of n conjuncts in a classification rule, and $m < n$ as an additional restriction on the number of conjuncts, Algorithm 5.1 sorts n conjuncts such that retaining the first m conjuncts in the list minimizes the increase of error probability.*

6   Removal of Exceptions

In many applications, the general principle is associated with some exceptions. For example, a bird is one that flies, but penguin is an exception to the flying principle. Each exception will necessarily produce a conjunct in the classification rule. The above example would produce a rule with two conjuncts: (x is a bird) $\iff$ (x flies or x is a penguin). Sometimes we would like to remove such exceptions from the rule. This entails relaxing the error probability. The task presented to the learning system is then the following: given a threshold for error probability, find the minimal subset of conjuncts that satisfies the threshold.

The sorted list of conjuncts by Algorithm 5.1 can be used for this task. We may remove as many conjuncts as necessary subject to the threshold. At each step we remove the conjunct whose removal causes minimal increase of the overall error probability. The last conjunct in the sorted list is such a conjunct.

Algorithm 6.1 (RemoveExceptions)

Input: A list I of m conjuncts $t_1, \ldots, t_m$ sorted by Algorithm 5.1, and an error probability threshold P.

Output: The list O which contains the minimal set of conjuncts such that the error probability of the rule constructed from O is less than or equal to P.

BEGIN
        Initialize p to the error probability of the rule obtained from I
        If $p > P$, print an error message and exit
        Initialize Last to null
        Initialize O to I
        WHILE $p \leq P$ DO

Remove Last from O
Assign the last conjunct in O to Last
Compute the error probability p of the rule
obtained from O − {Last}

  END WHILE
END

7 Induction by Concept Hierarchy

One of the characteristics of knowledge discovery in databases is that the discovered knowledge is represented in a high-level language [2]. This aspect of knowledge discovery is different from learning in neural networks.

We consider here an externally provided generalization hierarchy [5] in which different levels of generalization are organized into a tree called a *concept-tree* [1].

Definition 7.1 *Let Λ be an attribute with domain Δ. Let Γ be a rooted balanced [1] directed tree. Γ is a* **concept tree** *for an attribute Λ if the following conditions hold:*

1. *The leaves of Γ are labeled by the elements in Δ.*

2. *The set of leaves are partitioned and leaves in each partition are connected to a common parent node labeled by the partition.*

3. *The parent nodes of leaves are further partitioned and nodes in each partition is connected to a common parent node labeled by the partition. This process continues until all nodes at a level form a single partition. Their common parent, the root, is labeled by 'any'.*

In a concept tree, each node is identified with a unique label. Thus we will use terms *node* and *label* interchangeably. Figure 1 gives an example of a concept tree for attribute Birth-Place.

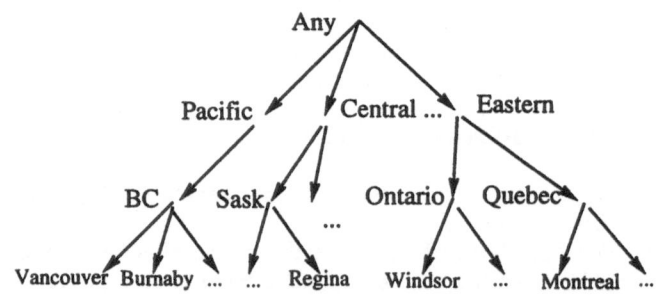

Figure 1: A concept tree for attribute BirthPlace

In induction by concept hierarchy, we consider the issue of substituting the attribute values of some tuples by a more general concept: their ancestor label

---

[1] We consider here balanced trees whose leaves have identical height.

in the concept tree. This will extend the domain of each attribute to include all concepts in the corresponding concept tree. Note that the values in the *extended domain* will no longer be exclusive any more. We call a tuple resulting from such a substitution a *generalized tuple*.

Definition 7.2 *Let* Λ *be an attribute with its concept tree* Γ. *Let a and b be two labels in* Γ. *Labels a and b are* **compatible** *if either (1) a = b, or (2) one of them is a descendent of the other. Otherwise, a and b are said to be* **incompatible**.

For example, in Figure 1, *Vancouver* and *BC* are compatible, but *Vancouver* and *Victoria* are incompatible, so are *Vancouver* and *Ontario*.

Definition 7.3 *Let r and t be two tuples. Let* Λ *be an attribute. Tuples r and t are* **compatible** *if all the values of corresponding attributes of r and t are compatible; r and t are* **incompatible** *at only* Λ *if all the values of corresponding attributes of r and t are compatible except the values for* Λ.

For example, for a tuple schema *(BirthPlace, Position)*, tuples *(Vancouver, assit-prof)* and *(BC, assit-prof)* are compatible; *(Vancouver, assit-prof)* and *(Victoria, assit-prof)* are incompatible at only *BirthPlace*.

Definition 7.4 *A set L of tuples in a database is a* **full sibling** *with respect to an attribute* Λ *and its corresponding concept tree* Γ, *if for every pair of tuples* $r, t \in L$, *(1) r and t are incompatible at only* Λ, *(2)* r_Λ *and* t_Λ *have a common parent node w in* Γ, *and (3) the children of w are exhausted in L. The node w is called the* **parent** *of the full sibling with respect to* Λ.

For example, for the tuple schema *(BirthPlace, Position)*, tuples *(Vancouver, assit-prof)* and *(Victoria, assit-prof)* are siblings, but *(Vancouver, assit-prof)* and *(Ontario, assit-prof)* are not siblings. Tuples *(Vancouver, assit-prof),..., (Victoria, assit-prof)* form a full sibling, but, if any one tuple is missing, the rest are no longer a full sibling.

Definition 7.5 *Let* Λ *be an attribute with its concept tree* Γ. *Let w be a label for a non-leaf node in* Γ. *Let L be a set of tuples. The substitution of w for the values of* Λ *in each* $r \in L$ *is a* **proper induction** *if*

1. *L is a full sibling with respect to* Λ,

2. *w is the parent of the full sibling with respect to* Λ,

3. $L \subseteq Pos$;

otherwise, the substitution is a **strict overgeneralization**.

For example, if the positive examples for *Professor* include the following full sibling with respect to *BirthPlace*, {*(Vancouver, assit-prof),..., (Victoria, assit-prof)*} , then the substitution of *Vancouver, ..., Victoria* by *BC* is a proper induction. As another example, suppose we have two tuples for classifying a preferred electronic appliance: 'Type=TV and Size=big' and 'Type=portable calculator and Size=small'. The concept tree for Size has only three nodes: a root 'any' and two leaves 'big' and 'small'. Substitution of 'big' and 'small' by 'any' for the attribute 'Size' causes a strict overgeneralization. Now 'Type=TV and Size=small' is classified as a preferred appliance which is not intended by the original example tuples.

Overgeneralization may or may not cause classification error. In the above example, if there is a small TV in our object domain, in which case, $L \cap Neg \neq \phi$, the overgeneralization will cause classification error. On the other hand, if there is no small TV in our object domain, in which case, $L \cap Neg = \phi$, the overgeneralization does not cause any error. This shows that, if we restrict to the object domain from which the samples are drawn, overgeneralization is not equivalent to the increase of error probability. However, overgeneralization *is* equivalent to the increase of error probability with an extended object domain, e.g., a domain including a small TV. A detailed discussion of this issue is beyond the scope of this paper.

Proposition 7.1 *A proper induction does not change the error probability of the resultant classification rule.*

Proof:

We refer the three conditions in Definition 7.5 as conditions 1, 2 and 3. Suppose the three conditions hold. After substitution, a new tuple z will be generated to replace the corresponding full sibling L in the classification rule. Because of conditions 1 and 2, every tuple $t \in Pos \cap L$ is compatible with z and will fire the conjunct correctly. Because of conditions 1, 2, and 3, no tuple $t \in Neg \cup Bnd$ is compatible with z, and t cannot incorrectly fire the conjunct. Since neither new false-positive nor false-negative error are introduced by the proper induction, the error probability remains the same. $\square$

Recall that Algorithm 4.1 labels each conjunct of the rule as well as the entire rule with error probabilities. Proposition 7.1 shows that the error probability of the entire rule remains the same. By Definition 7.5, the only conjuncts that are changed during a proper induction are from Pos, and their error probabilities are zero. The conjuncts generalized from them have the identical zero error probability. Each conjunct from Bnd should not be changed and their error probabilities also remain the same.

8 Remarks

In this paper, we apply the rough set theory and probability concepts to inductive learning from databases. Under the assumption of representative set of examples, we derive the error probabilities for components of a classification rule as well as for the rule as a whole. We derive the result for induction using attributes, and show the condition under which further induction can be performed without increasing the error probabilities.

Our work are closely related to several other work in the area of knowledge discovery in databases: Ziarko [11] discussed the application of reducts in inductive learning in databases. Cai, Cercone and Han [1] and Han, Cai, and Cercone [4] developed an attribute-oriented approach for inductive learning in databases using concept trees, and implemented in an experiment database learning system, DBLEARN. Our work extends theirs and attempts to provide a theoretical basis for knowledge discovery in databases. Pawlak, Wong and

Ziarko [7] discussed similar decision rules in Section 4. However, they did not provide the error probabilities explicitly.

There are cases where the representative assumption on examples is not practical. In these cases, our estimation provides a lower bound for the error probability. We plan to implement and test our results in the next version of DBLEARN.

Acknowledgements

The authors are members of the Institute for Robotics and Intelligent Systems (IRIS) and wish to acknowledge the support of the Networks of Centres of Excellence Program of the Government of Canada, the Natural Sciences and Engineering Research Council, and the participation of PRECARN Associates Inc. We are grateful to Canadian Cable Labs Fund for their financial assistance.

References

[1] Y. Cai, N. Cercone, and J. Han, "Learning in relational databases: an attribute-oriented approach", *Computational Intelligence*, 7, 119-132, 1991.

[2] W.J. Frawley, G. Piatetsky-Shapiro, and C.J. Matheus, "Knowledge discovery in databases: An overview", in *Knowledge Discovery in Databases*, eds., G. Piatetsky-Sapiro and W.J. Frawley, AAAI/MIT, 1-27, 1991.

[3] M.R. Genesereth and N.J. Nilsson, *Logical Foundations of Artificial Intelligence*, Morgan Kaufmann, 1987.

[4] J. Han, Y. Cai, and N. Cercone, "Data-driven discovery of quantitative rules in relational databases", *IEEE Trans. on Knowledge and Data Engineering*, 5 (1): 29-40, 1993.

[5] D. Haussler, "Bias, version spaces and Valiant's learning framework", *Proc. 4th International Workshop on Machine Learning*, Irvine, CA, 324-336, 1987.

[6] Z. Pawlak, "Rough sets", International Journal of Computer and Information Sciences, 11 (5): 341-356, 1982.

[7] Z. Pawlak, S.K.M. Wong and W. Ziarko, "Rough sets: probabilistic versus deterministic approach", *International Journal of Man-Machine Studies*, 29: 81-95, 1988.

[8] Z. Pawlak, "Anatomy of conflicts", *ICS Research Report 11/92*, Warsaw University of Technology, Warsaw, May, 1992.

[9] J.R. Quinlan, "Learning efficient classification procedures and their application to chess end games", in *Machine Learning: An Artificial Intelligence Approach*, Vol.1, Morgan Kaufmann, 463-482, 1983.

[10] S.K.M. Wong and W. Ziarko, "On optimal decision rules in decision tables", *Bulletin of Polish Academy of Sciences*, 33 (11-12): 693-696, 1985.

[11] W. Ziarko, "The discovery, analysis, and representation of data dependencies in database", in *Knowledge Discovery in Databases*, eds., G. Piatetsky-Sapiro and W.J. Frawley, AAAI/MIT, 195-209, 1991.

Temporal Rules Discovery using Datalogic/R+ with Stock Market Data

Robert Golan

Department of Computer Science, University of Regina
Regina, SK, S4S 0A2, Canada

Donald Edwards

First Marathon Securities
Regina, SK, S4S 0A2, Canada

Abstract

A methodology for the discovery of temporal rules in stock market data is presented. The two types of temporal rules defined are snapshot and aggregate. Snapshot temporal rules are formulated by associating a current decision attribute instance to the relevant past condition attribute instances. Aggregate temporal rules are formulated by associating a current decision attribute instance to the total change of relevant past condition attribute instances. Any chronologically based data can be disretized in this manner to produce snapshot and aggregate temporal rules. The knowledge discovery tool, Datalogic/R+, was used from Reduct Systems which applies the concepts of Rough Set Theory for pattern recognition in data. Monthly stock market data through the 80's representing 120 cases containing 32 stock and economic indicators are analyzed. The main objective is to discover relationships with a company's stock price change to stock and economic indicators over a time lapse of six months. Relationships were derived by the discovery of snapshot and aggregate temporal rules. The temporal rules discovered are consistent and confirm one another.

1 Introduction

The discovery of temporal rules is a real boon to aid in the predictability of various events within reason. Reasonability is dependent on the data accessability and the capability of discovering data patterns. Many events are interpreted as chaotic especially if there isn't enough data for pattern recognition. Even the most complex events may be predictable by current learning system tools. Advances in the predictability of stock market trends are being researched through the use of neural networks[2][3][4]. It is evident that by using the rough set approach to knowledge discovery one can successfully discover strong rules in stock market data as indicated by Ziarko, Golan, Edwards[1]. The original rough sets model was introduced by Pawlak[7]. The emphasis of this paper is on the methodology of discovering temporal rules for the ongoing pursuit of stock market predictability. In what follows are additional results of an on-going research project on the application of knowledge discovery methods which takes advantage of the variable precision model of rough sets (VPRS) proposed by Ziarko[9][10] to discover relationships over time.

2 Background Information

The Registered Retirement Savings Plan(RRSP) is an incentive program for Canadians to save for their retirement. The incentive is tax breaks. Many Canadians are investing in portfolios which include equity funds which have investment managers managing the fund. Other Canadians are controlling the investing themselves through self directed RRSPs. With this abundance of money for investment purposes, stock market awareness is important to many Canadians who have put their RRSP's in equity funds. Stock market investment techniques were defined before the adage of high tech. These investment techniques can be defined into the 3 areas: Fundamental, Random Walks, and Technical. Fundamental techniques set an intrinsic value to a stock. If a stock is well below it's intrinsic value then this is and indicator to buy. The sale of the stock needs to be anticipated as the stock gets closer to it's intrinsic value. Intrinsic values are based on many principles which may include dividend history, past earnings, prices, Gross Domestic Product(GDP), company profits. The polymetric, value line, and value scan reports use this technique for investment management purposes. Random walk techniques believe in the buy and hold technique over a long period of time. Random walks imply that the market will eventually go up and that it is non predictable. Technical techniques believe that the timing of the sale and purchase is important and that relationships amongst the market indicators exist. Three types of trends defined by Charles Dow are minor, intermediate, and major. Charles felt the major bear and bull market trends are predictable, but the minor and intermediate trends are not. These types of techniques include such analysis as charting, odd lot indexing, and the Barron Confidence Index. Computers using AI are being used to predict the minor and intermediate trends within the market. These tools can also be classified as technical techniques. Fuzzy sets[5], neural nets, genetic algorithms[6], and rough sets are all techniques which are being researched for stock market analysis.

3 Temporal Rule Discovery Problem

The problem is to apply knowledge discovery (KD) techniques to identitify temporal rules from stock and economic data. By temporal rules we mean discovered relationships going back in time reflecting common repetitive patterns occurring in the data. These are strong rules which are not necessarily precise or deterministic, but can be fractional probabilities of the predicted outcome as mentioned in [1]. As reported by Piatetsky-Shapiro in [8], strong rules have a high number of supporting cases supporting the rule generated. A close approximation of a true fact existing in a domain of interest is supported by a higher probability of supporting cases over a random subset of all feasible combinations of data. If the data is in chronological order the data can be modified to process snapshot and aggregate temporal rules. Discovering temporal rule relationships will also support the relationships discovered with the data table in current time. In fact, similar relationships should show up through time. Verification of these rules is done by the domain expert, the broker. Rules contradicting the brokers experience can be analyzed to determine which part of the data is producing these noise rules.

4 Data Collection

The Toronto Stock Exchange(TSE) is used for our analysis. Two types of data are collected. The first type of data is the company stock closing prices for the month. Initially Dow Jones Online was accessed for the Canadian companies data. This data only went back one year, but good historical data existed for American companies. Five companies were chosen which represented some of the major industries. These were top performing companies selected from the Financial Post Fortune 100 magazine. The Investment Corporation was contacted to get the stocks closing prices. The five companies selected are Loblaws, Imperial Oil, Bank of Montreal, Bell Canada, and Northern Telecom. The second type of data is the stock and economic indicators. Most of this data is non-existent on Dow Jones Online. Stats Canada data is used for the stock and economic indicators. The stock indicators included the TSE, DOW, S&P, PE, and 7 of the 14 major industry indexes. The economic indicators include: M1; GDP in current and constant prices; non-farm GDP; industrial production in constant prices; wages and salaries as per unit of output; total labour income; corporate profits before taxs; labour force total; government expenditures on goods and services; non-residential fixed investment; housing starts; car sales; exports and imports; interest rates; treasury bills; bonds; US dollar value; unemployment; and inflation. Some of the data is in a quarterly format. This data is repeated 3 times representing 3 months. The companies represent the decision variable. The stock and economic indicators represent the conditions. To analyze this data to the previous months conditions, the data table is duplicated through Lotus and shifted down one row. For the analysis of the conditions 2 months ago the data table is copied again and shifted down 2 rows. This is repeated until the 6 months is represented in time. Time analysis of the data over the six months doesn't come into effect until the 6th row of data. In order to look at the full temporal effects starting at January of 1980, the data needs to be accumulated starting from July of 1979.

5 Discretization

Discretization is the key to generating the two types of temporal rules for analysis. Discretization is the process by which a set of values are grouped together into a range symbol. As indicated in [1], Lotus macros are used to discretize values which are not already in a percentage change format. This includes the company and stock indicators along with some of the economic indicators. These values are discretized by replacing the raw values recorded for a given month with range symbols representing the percentage change of the current values relative to the value recorded in the previous month. This is the basis for generating snapshot temporal rules once the data tables are repeated by the above method with an elapsed time period of 6 months. Aggregate temporal rules are generated by a different discretization approach. The total percentage change over a elapsed time period covering 6 months is discretized. The discretization going back the first month are similar for both the snapshot and aggregate methods. Changes start occurring in the discretization process once the analysis of the data goes back more then one month since the total change over the months are discretized for the aggregate method. An example of the discretization method recommended by the expert for assignment of the range symbols is as follows:

```
Range Symbol    % Difference
        2:      10% to 15%
        1:      5% to 10%
        0:      0% to 5%
       -1:      -5% to 0%
       -2:      -10% to -5%
```

The ranges for the above index are -40 to 40. For example, a 18change according to the index will produce the symbol 3. An ascii file of the disretized values are prepared for import into DATALOGIC/R+. Importing the ascii data needs each variable defined with a name, type, and length.

6 Optimization

Rule precision and roughness are the two important optimization parameters needing adjustments before generating rules in DATALOGIC/R+. Rule precision sets the percentage of identical cases tolerated when associated with a particular decision value. The decision value represented by a range symbol is the company's stock price change. The identical cases are the recurring data patterns which are made up of the selected condition values representing the stock and economic indicators. These are sets which exist in the boundary region since sets which exist in the lower approximation would have all their identical cases represented by a single decision value. Sets which exist in the boundary region have identical cases which exist in other sets which are associated with other decision values. Weak rules can be pruned by setting the rule precision threshold. Our threshold is set to .55 which means at least 55% of the cases must be related to a particular decision value before the rule is generated. Roughness pertains to the granularity of the grid lines. Sets are sliced into a finer granularity when the roughness parameter is set low. This leads to many exact rules which are not supported by very many cases. As pointed out by Ziarko, Golan, and Edwards in [1] a low roughness setting will lead to weak rules which are in contradiction to the experts experience. When the roughness parameter is set high, generalized rules are produced with many supporting cases which lead to strong rules as indicated by Piatesky-Shaprio in [8]. The roughness is set at .93 for our analysis.

7 Analysis

The analysis is broken up into the two sections of discovered snapshot and aggregate rules for the Bank of Montreal. Similiar results were obtained with the other companies analyszed. In the presented rules the "p" indicator represents probability and the "c" indicator represents the number of supporting cases. The following are the results:

```
Discovered Snapshot Temporal Rules
Bank of Montreal rises by 5% when: (p=75) (c=32)
        -financial index drops or rises by 10%.
        -2 months ago the paper index changed between -40% and 10%.
Bank of Montreal rises by 10% to 15% when: (p=100) (c=4)
        -2 months ago gold:
            -dropped more then 20% or
            -rose more then 10%.
        -4 months ago the M1 was between 6% and 17%.
        -5 months ago the Gross Domestic Product at current prices
            -was between -5% and 2%.


Discovered Aggregate Temporal Rules
Bank of Montreal rises by 5% when: (p=79.2) (c=24)
        -financial index drops or rises by 10%.
        -over the last 4 months:
            -corporate profits were between 1% and 24%.
Bank of Montreal rises by 10% to 15% when: (p=75) (c=4)
        -over the last 2 months gold:
            -dropped more then 20% or
            -rose more then 10%.
        -car sales drop below -8%.
```

8 Reporting

The previous rules are interpreted for the expert, the broker, as follows:

```
Bank of Montreal
This stock drops up 5% when: (p=.78,c=.59)
        -the financial index drops from 10% to 20%.
```

```
This rule is derived from the generated Datalogic rule:
        Decision ::    Bankmon ==> -1
            1  |  |  |  (-2 <= Finance <= -1)
```

As described above, probabilities and cases are listed later on in the rule report under the topic of rule strength. Also listed with rule strength is each supporting case which is used to derive the rule. This is a very powerful feature which gives the ability to pinpoint the raw data rows which support the rule. This is great for discovering noises in data which may look like rules. One can verify that the data is valid for rules which exist in the lower approximation where p=1.0 and a low number of supporting cases exist. For temporal data it helps to determine whether the supporting cases are evenly distributed throughout time. If cases are bunched together during a certain time period which does not agree with the expert's experience then external factors during that time period could be investigated. For example an election or an earthquake may have caused this random noise to occur. Another asset to the reporting is the ability to determine attribute strength as follows:

```
Decision: Bankmon ==> 0
==========================
Attribute Max. Loc. Str
Finan          0.81
Corpro         0.32
```

Knowing the attribute strength of the conditions matched with the decision variable helps in understanding the implied relationships. This is valuable if a cost is associated with the condition attribute. The cost of an attribute is justifiable if the importance of the attribute is high.

9 Verification

This section presents comments of our expert, an experienced stock broker, Mr. Donald Edwards regarding the temporal relationships discovered.

> " There is no doubt that the analysis complete to date has discovered some logical relationships. Stocks known as interest sensitive show a relationship to changes in interest rates. All stocks that have been analyzed to date show a relationship to its own index.
>
> I also find the fact that the two forms of analysis "snapshot" and "aggregate" seem to consistently confirm one another. To me this helps validate the program.
>
> While the rules and relationships are interesting, they still need more work to become reliable. While I can understand these rules they are not yet refined enough to become part of a decision-making process. I can, however, see the potential of this in the not too distant future. "

10 Conclusions and Future Research Directions

As indicated by the expert, valid relationships were discovered by the temporal rules generated by DATALOGIC/R+ confirming the previous results indicated by Ziarko, Golan, and Edwards in [1]. The methodology of discovering both snapshot and aggregate temporal rules adds to the credibility of DATALOGIC/R+ for consistent rule generation.

In general, temporal rules when compared to rules generated in current time are weaker rules with lower probabilities and fewer supporting cases. This brings up the question of how strong a rule needs to be in order to be reasonably certain that it is generally correct. Currently it's the experts experiences which are paramount for rule validation.

As indicated in [1] quantity and quality of the data and the discretization
methods are crucial to generating stronger rules. It is evident that DATA-
LOGIC/R+ is capable of handling noisy and erroneous data while still generating decent rules indicating common market relationships. Better discretization
methods are especially needed for market indicators which have the discretization granularity too fine. Another range variable index which may lead to more
interesting results is as follows:

```
+2 - Upward Jump
+1 - Upward Trend
 0 - No Change
-1 - Downward Trend
-2 - Downward Jump
```

The above entails establishing the raw data ranges with the proper range symbols according to the experts knowledge of the relevant indicators.

As indicated by Piatetsky-Shapiro in [8] discretization of ordered and interval domains need consideration. Range and equality rules are important for rule
analysis. Range rules consisting of condition indicators(attributes) which cross
the up and down trend boundaries are difficult to interpret. Multi-valued decision variables which cross the trend boundaries need to be eliminated. Equality
rules are useful for the interpretation of reoccurring precise events.

In conclusion, as indicated by the expert more work is needed before this research can be applied to the decision making processes of a broker or investment
manager for commercial applications. The objective of using a methodology
for discovering valid temporal rules is achieved. The first steps to this ongoing pursuit of knowledge discovery for market analysis and prediction looks
promising. The search continues.

References

[1] Ziarko, W. and Golan, R. and Edwards, D. An Application of Datalogic/R
Knowledge Discovery Tool to Identify Strong Predictive Rules in Stock
Market Data. AAAI-93 Workshop on Knowledge Discovery in Databases.

[2] Chinetti, D. and Garden, F. and Rossignoli, C. A Neural Network Model
for Stock Market Prediction. The 2nd International Conference on AI Applications on Wall Street. April 19, 1993.

[3] Barr, D. and Mani, G. Neural Networks in Investment Management: Multiple Uses. The 2nd International Conference on AI Applications on Wall
Street. April 19, 1993.

[4] Cassetti, M. A Neural Network System for Reliable Trading Signals. The
2nd International Conference on AI Applications on Wall Street. April 19,
1993.

[5] Hiemstra, Y. Tactical Asset Allocation Using Fuzzy Logic and Mean-
Variance Optimization. The 2nd International Conference of AI Applications on Wall Street. April 19, 1993.

[6] Gargano, M and Chamoun, P, and von Kleeck, D. Using Genetic Algorithms to Solve Financial Portfolio Problems Related to Optimal Allocation, Portfolio Insurance, and Performance Predication. The 2nd International Conference of AI Applications on Wall Street. April 19, 1993.

[7] Pawlak, Z. Rough Sets: Theoretical Aspects of Reasoning About Data. Kluwer Academic Publishers, Dordrecht, The Netherlands, 1991.

[8] Piatetsky-Shapiro, G. Discovery of Strong Rules in Databases. Proc. of IJCAI-89 Workshop on Knowledge Discovery in Databases, 264-274

[9] Ziarko, W. Variable Precision Rough Sets Model. Journal of Computer and Systems Sciences. Volume 46, no 1, 1993, pp 39-59.

[10] Ziarko, W. Analysis of Uncertain Information in the Framework of Variable Precision Rough Sets. Foundations of Computing and Decision Sciences. Volume 18, no 3-4, 1993, pp 381-396.

A System Architecture
for Database Mining Applications

Vijay V. Raghavan[1] Hayri Sever[1] Jitender S. Deogun[2]

University of Southwestern Louisiana[1]
Lafayette, LA 70504, USA

University of Nebraska[2]
Lincoln, NE, 68588, USA

Abstract

The problem of enhancing a database management system (DBMS) to support mining applications is twofold. First DBMSs of today have limited functionality for supporting mining applications. Second scaling traditional knowledge discovery techniques for large data sets is not straightforward. We propose a mining kernel that could be incorporated into future DBMSs. The mining kernel provides a common knowledge base encapsulated by a complete set of knowledge management operators such that interactive modules for database mining applications can be built on top of it. The novelty of our approach is to study how the concept-based retrieval, relevance feedback, and information dissemination techniques used in intelligent information retrieval systems relate to each other and to apply the result of this study to the database mining problem.

1 Introduction

Following rapid advances in computer technology, it has been feasible to extend database systems into new application areas. One such application that is likely to get considerable attention in the near future is database mining [1,2,3]. The goal of database mining is to discover valuable information from a very large database that is hidden in the data and a user is unaware of this before discovery. The kinds of database mining queries that we are specifically interested in are classification, hypothesis testing, and association.

We believe that knowledge discovery is one of the areas of interest shared by both database and information retrieval research communities. One of the current research issues in Intelligent Information Retrieval Systems (IIRSs) is to equip IIRS with following capabilities [4,5,6,7]:

i. Retrieval based on the presence or absence of descriptors or keywords in a desired combination,
ii. Retrieval based on learning the characterization of relevant documents through user feedback,
iii. Categorization of text based on preselected concepts or topical areas,
iv. Automatic extraction of concepts or facts from text, and
v. Concept-based retrieval of text.

Although, at present time, practically no text retrieval aims to provide all of these functions, there is a great deal of commonality among the functional components of information retrieval, concept-based retrieval and fact extraction systems. For example, the relevance feedback techniques needed in retrieval systems to characterize a user's concept of relevance can also provide a mechanism for deriving characterization of the class of documents each element of which contains a fact of interest. Similarly, the process of concept structuring based on relationship among concepts is important for both concept-based retrieval as well as fact extraction.

Our research is directed towards the idea of organizing accumulated knowledge for use by future queries, which will substantially reduce the time needed for searching existing knowledge and in generating new knowledge. Our approach is to design and implement a kernel consisting of a set of constructs encapsulated by primitive operations to create, maintain and manipulate the knowledge. These mining operations developed will be orthogonal to each other and complete enough to allow a user to build interfaces on top of the kernel. This design choice is motivated by the fact that a concept based system is an area of investigation in its own right; that is, it is not affected by particular data analysis methods if a common knowledge base is used. This is in contrast to EXIS [8] which makes the assumption that knowledge discovery is based on some specific methods. Our approach is similar to INLEN system [9], which clearly differentiates Knowledge Management Operators (KMOs) from Knowledge Generation Operators (KGOs); however, it organizes the KMOs around KGOs.

This paper is organized as follows. In Section 2, we describe the types of mining queries in which we are interested. The notion of a concept, and concept hierarchy as persistent knowledge are discussed in Section 3. In Section 4, a brief outline of our extended DBMS architecture for database mining applications is developed. Concluding remarks are provided in Section 5.

2 The Database Mining Queries

Let A be the set of attributes for that relation. In database mining, we use rules to specify how the value of an attribute of interest or the class label of a tuple is determined by the values of other attributes. Rules are also used to specify functional dependencies among attributes. A rule may be associated with a confidence factor. Each attribute $a \in A$ in the antecedent part of a rule is called a *condition* attribute. There exists only one attribute at the consequent part of that rule, and it is called a *decision* attribute. If a decision attribute is an element of A then it is said to be *persistent;* otherwise it is *nonpersistent.* We are interested in three kinds of mining queries as shown below.

i. *Association*: Given a value of a persistent decision attribute and a set of condition attributes, generate a rule that can be used to determine how values of certain condition attributes are associated with the given value of the decision attribute. For that kind of query, a user may also omit to give the set of condition attributes if he or she wishes to do so.

ii. *Hypothesis testing*: Given a decision rule and its confidence factor, test if it is validated by the tuples in the population. The confidence factor is assumed to constitute a lower boundary for the validation process of a hypothesis.

iii. *Classification*: Upon the specification of positive and negative samples with respect to a nonpersistent decision attribute (i.e., a classification label), determine the potential condition attributes and/or generate a decision rule.

A rule can be labeled as a dynamic or a static rule depending on the nature of the established relationship. For example, if we state that "a desktop is a personal computer," then it is a static rule and thus is not affected by the change of database population. However, if we have a rule such as: "if a customer buys a personal computer, then it is a desktop with 0.6 certainty," then this rule depends on the database population at a given time. Hence, the DBMS should offer some facilities (e.g., daemon processes for if-condition-then-fire triggers) to support dynamic rules.

3 The Representation and Organization of Concepts

We have used the language of predicate logic to represent concepts and a reader not familiar with basic notations of this mathematical discipline may refer to [10]. Let W be a vocabulary. For each symbol $t \in W$, we assume there is an integer $\delta(t)$ called the *degree of t*. For t a function symbol, $\delta(t) \geq 0$, while for t a relation symbol, $\delta(t) > 0$. In W, the symbols r, v, and g (with or without subscript) are reserved for relations, constants, and functions, respectively. We call a relation symbol whose degree is 1 an attribute symbol. We reserve the subscripted symbols c, p and d in W for attributes. Every atomic W-formula is supposed to stand for a relation, and we denote it by a capital case of corresponding relation symbol. The projection of a relation R onto the components 1,2,.., k is denoted by $\pi_{1,2,...,k}(R)$, where $k \leq \delta(r)$.

Views are crucial in the provision of logical data independence and also represent a form of data security. Hence, ideally, a mining component integrated with a DBMS must facilitate the specification of a user context that is consistent with the user's view. In this paper, we consider, however, a global context; that is, a W-sentence in the language is interpreted using entire database population.

3.1 Notions of a Concept

A *basic concept* corresponds to either a subset of attribute values or a subset of tuples. We obtain a *derived concept* by applying association, classification, or generalization to the existing concept(s). For example, in Table 1, "corel_draw" is a basic concept obtained by grouping all versions of Corel Draw Package in the domain of the attribute PNAME. Similarly "graphics" is a derived concept whose domain is the set of print_shop, harvard_graphic, and corel_draw.

```
software I hardware → product
operating_system I user_environment I application → software
accounting I spread_sheet I education I database I graphics → application
accessories I peripherals I personal_computer → hardware
PTYPE(window) → user_environment
PNAME[window/3.1 I window/3.0] → PTYPE(window)
PTYPE[harvard_graphic I print_shop I corel_draw] → graphics
PNAME[corel_draw/3.0 I corel_draw/3.1] → PTYPE(corel_draw)
PTYPE[ms_dos_system I macintosh] → personal_computer
PNAME[286PC I 386PC I 486PC] → ms_dos_system
```

**Table 1. A partial concept hierarchy from the perspective of
generalization of the computer products**

First, we specify the association query for a relation symbol $r \in W$, in predicate logic by the formula as shown below:

$$\forall(x_1, x_2, .., x_{k-1}) \ \exists(x_k, certainty\_factor)[\ r_{1,k-1}(x_1, x_2, ..., x_{k-1}) \Rightarrow$$
$$d(x_k) \ \& \ certainty\_factor = g(x_1, x_2, .., x_{k-1}, x_k)],$$

where $k \le \delta(r)$, $D = \pi_k(R)$, and $R_{1,k-1} = \pi_{1,2,...,k-1}(R)$.

We are not usually interested in all possible interpretations of the formula given above. Hence, we define the association query by using following notation:

$$c_1(v_1) \ \& \ c_2(v_2) \ \& \ ... \ \& \ c_{k-1}(v_{k-1}) \ \xrightarrow{r} \ d(v_{concept}), \ certainty\_factor,$$

It means that the values of condition attributes of the relation R functionally determine the value of the decision attribute of the relation R with some certainty factor. Using rough set theory, we may assign a value to the certainty factor or eliminate superfluous condition attributes.

The second way to derive a concept is a classification method. We specify the classification query in predicate logic by the formula as shown below:

$$\forall(x_1, x_2, .., x_k) \ [(p_1(x_1) \ \& \ p_2(x_2) \ \& \ ... \ \& \ p_k(x_k)) \Rightarrow$$
$$dummy(v_{concept}, \ g(x_1, x_2, .., x_k))].$$

We say that the values of patterns are related to $v_{concept}$ with some value of confidence factor returned by the classification function g. The concept learned by this method is indeed dynamic. From time to time, a decision may be made to incorporate a dynamic concept into the concept hierarchy. In that case we drop the tag of "dummy" from the concept and interpret it as a relation symbol.

A generalization, the last method to derive a concept, groups some sub-concepts into a more abstract concept. and its notation is defined as "$v_{sub-concept} \rightarrow v_{concept}$." If either sub-concept or concept is drawn from the domain of an attribute, then it is surrounded by brackets following the attribute name. For the sake of simplicity, we combine sub-concepts by disjunction if they generalize to the same concept. Table 1 contains a partial list of generalization rules drawn from the domain of PNAME, product names, PTYPE, product types, and some other derived concepts. These rules are constructed for a hypothetical warehouse that sells computer hardware and software products by mail order.

We explained what a concept is and how to derive a new concept. As a final note, the type of a concept can be either basic or derived. The status of a concept is persistent if it is associated with an attribute's domain; nonpersistent otherwise. In the next subsection, we present two essential structures used for organizing the concepts. First one, a concept-set, contains the description of concepts, and second one, a concept hierarchy, holds the relationships between concepts.

3.2 Organization of the Concepts

A concept-set contains the concepts and their description. A description gives various information depending on a concept's type and its status. For example, If the concept is a basic concept, then the description keeps the set of corresponding values. For a derived concept, we keep the type of the rule and related information (e.g., access path to the classification function if the classification rule is used). Similarly, if a concept is persistent, then the name of the attribute associated with that concept is kept in the description. To access a concept in the concept-set, the name of the concept is used. A synonym list, which keeps a set of equivalent concepts, is used to provide alternative access paths to a concept. For example in Table 1, the concept "drawing" is a synonym for "graphics".

A concept hierarchy is a weighted AND/OR polytree (i.e., singly connected graph) and is used to define relationships between concepts. In a polytree, OR arcs are used to generalize a concept, and AND arcs are used to either classify or associate a concept to other concepts. The value of a weight between two nodes gives confidence factor for the corresponding relationship. Every leaf and intermediate node of the graph correspond to a basic and a derived concept, respectively. We introduce the notion of *perspective* that gives the type of a link established between concepts.

The concept hierarchy can be viewed from three perspectives, which are association, classification, and generalization. If we had treated all concepts without any perspective, then the semantic power of our mining model would have been reduced to the power of syntactically driven models. For example suppose we have two derived concepts: "PTYPE(486PC) $\xrightarrow{\text{sale}}$ PTYPE(window),0.9" and "PTYPE[window] $\rightarrow$ user_environment." Then, without having any knowledge of their perspective, there is nothing in the model to avoid from making the inference of "PTYPE(486PC) $\rightarrow$ user_environment, 0.9." The reflection of a perspective on the concept hierarchy gives a tree whose root is possibly a dummy node. The rules or restrictions applicable to all members of a perspective (e.g., if the propagation of confidence factors is allowed) is kept in the description of the perspective. The perspective of generalization allows, however, us to detect either association rules or classification rules that are closely related.

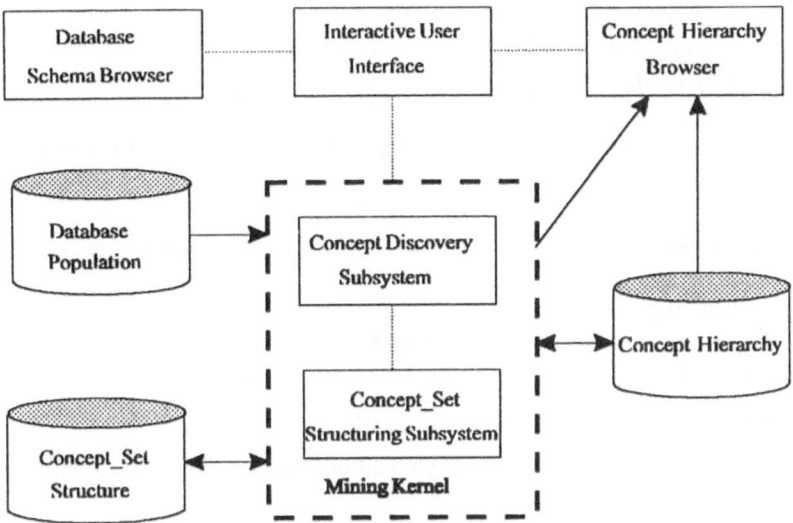

Figure 1. A block diagram of mining system architecture

4 The System Architecture

The idea of a concept is central to our system. On the basis of this idea, the notions of a concept-set and concept-set structure are defined. The various functional modules are then described by specifying what kinds of operations need to be performed with respect to concepts and concept-set structures. As it can be seen in Figure 1, the mining system consists of two major subsystems: mining kernel and interactive user interface. This two-level design paradigm provides a common concept-base structure and user interface to various mining methods and makes the mining system customizable. The user controls the concepts either directly through interactive user interface or implicitly through query language interface of the DBMS.

4.1 Mining Kernel

This kernel system provides primitive operations related to the management and manipulation of concepts. As mentioned before a concept can be specified either by generalization or association, and more than one rule can be associated to a concept. The relationship between database functions and mining kernel depends on how they are coupled. We are currently investigating pros and cons of different coupling choices.

4.1.1 Concept Discovery Subsystem

This subsystem provides operations to be used for discovering (or deriving) a rule with respect to a concept. The functionality of operations is listed below:

- Dropping concept(s) from the condition part of a concept's rule,
- Joining concept(s) to the condition part of a concept's rule,
- Adding a value to the basic concept,
- Finding a distance between two concepts,
- Generating the concept hierarchy for the set of concepts within a particular perspective,
- Constructing a rule for a concept,
- Proposing relevant domains (i.e., either attribute or relation names) for a concept,
- Deleting a rule of the concept,
- Accessing a particular rule of a concept, and
- Testing a hypothesis.

4.1.2 Concept-Set Structuring Subsystem

This subsystem is responsible for the management of concepts. The functionality of the operations can be listed as
- Realizing dictionary operations for a concept (and synonyms),
- Making a non-persistent concept persistent,
- Accessing description fields of a concept,
- Moving forward/backward from a concept in the concept hierarchy for given perspective,
- Creating or revoking a view.

4.2 Interactive User Interface

Interactive user interface provides browsers and an interactive query language for mining applications in terms of primitive operations defined in the mining kernel. The concept hierarchy browser offers following features. With respect to a persistent concept, it retrieves the associated rule(s) and then navigate the concept hierarchy. With respect to a dynamic concept, one can select concept(s) in the concept hierarchy that are "close" and browse the condition attributes involved in the associated rules.

5 Conclusion

In this paper, we develop a system architecture that emphasizes functions of a database system that are essential for data mining queries. Our work on user oriented clustering [11] and on organizing of concepts discovered through past interactions with users [12], in the context of text retrieval systems, provides us the motivation for our proposal. In particular, we provide subsystems to organize persistent concepts into a hierarchy and to enable users to perform a variety of operations on the concept-set structure. As a result, our approach can support discovery of knowledge through co-operation among a group of users. In addition, our approach offers opportunities for concept discovery phase to be made more efficient since the process can begin with the rule associated with a similar concept already in the hierarchy.

Our eventual goal is to integrate such functionality with currently available DBMS software. Although we have not specifically discussed how the proposed subsystems would impact design principles of the future DBMSs, we currently favor the choice of embedding them into a DBMS package because of the need to use trigger facilities and to access status information, such as authorization privileges, of the DBMS. This design choice can offer important benefits. For example, mining queries are strictly read-oriented long running transactions. Since we deal with classification of the data, in most cases, it is unnecessary and even harmful to exclude other transactions from write accesses to the data to which a mining query has acquired a read lock (or vice-versa). The tradeoff is here the performance of the system versus possible amount of classification error. If error tolerance, say ε, is known in advance, then we can use $\varepsilon\_$serializibity protocol instead of the traditional one.

References

[1] Agrawal R., Ghosh S., Imielinski T., Iyer B., and Swami B. An Interval Classifier for Database Mining Applications. In: Proc. of the 18th VLDB conf., Vancouver, British Columbia, Canada 1992, pp 560-573.

[2] Krishnamurty R and Imielinski T. Research Directions in Knowledge Discovery. SIGMOD RECORD 1991; 20: 76-78.

[3] Shapiro D. G. and Frawley W. J. (Editors). Knowledge Discovery in Databases. AAAI/MIT Press, Cambridge, 1991.

[4] Belkin N. J. and Croft W. B. Information Filtering and Information Retrieval: Two Sides of the Same Coin. Comm. of ACM 1992; 35:29-39.

[5] Deogun J. S. and Raghavan V. V. Description of the UNL/USL System used for MUC-3. In: Proc. of DARPA's 3rd Message Understanding Conference (MUC-3). Morgan-Kauffmann Pub., San Diego, 1991, pp. 234-242.

[6] Hayes P. and Weinstein S. CONSTRUE/TIS: a system for content-based indexing of a database of news stories. Second Annual Conf. on Innovative Applications of Artificial Intelligence, 1990.

[7] McCune B. P., Tong R. M., Dean J. S., and Shapiro D. G. RUBRIC: A system for rule-based information retrieval. IEEE Trans. Software Engineering 1985; SE-11:939-945.

[8] Yasdi R. Learning Classification Rules from Database in the Context of Knowledge Acquisition and Representation. IEEE Trans. Knowl. Data Eng. 1991; 3:293-306.

[9] Kaufman K. A., Michalski R. S., and Kerschberg L. Mining for Knowledge in Databases: Goals and General Description of the INLEN System. Knowledge Discovery in Databases. AAA/MIT, Cambridge, MA, 1991.

[10] Davis M. D. and Weyuker E. J. Computability, Complexity, and Languages. Academic Press, New York, 1983.

[11] Bhatia S. K., Deogun J. S. and Raghavan V. V. Automatic Rule-Base Generation for User-oriented Information Retrieval. In: Proc. of the Fifth Int'l. Symposium on Methodologies for Intelligent Systems. Knoxville,1990, pp 118-125.

[12] Zhang Y., Raghavan V. V. and Deogun J. S. An Object-Oriented Modeling of History of Optimal Retrievals. In: Proc. of the 14th Int'l. ACM-SIGIR Conf. on Research and Development in Information Retrieval. Chicago, Oct 1991, pp. 241-250.

An Attribute-Oriented Rough Set Approach for Knowledge Discovery in Databases *

Xiaohua Hu

Department of Computer Science, University of Regina
Regina, Sask., Canada S4S 0A2

Nick Cercone

Department of Computer Science, University of Regina
Regina, Sask., Canada S4S 0A2

Jiawei Han

School of Computing Science, Simon Fraser University
Burnaby, B.C., Canada V5A 1S6

Abstract

In this paper we present an attribute-oriented rough set approach for knowledge discovery in databases. The method integrates machine learning paradigm, especially learning-from-examples techniques, with rough-set techniques. An attribute-oriented concept tree ascension technique is first applied in generalization, which substantially reduces the computational complexity of database learning processes. Then the cause-effect relationship among the attributes in the database is analyzed using rough set techniques and the unimportant or irrelevant attributes are eliminated. Thus concise and strong rules with little or no redundant information can be learned efficiently. Our study shows that attribute-oriented induction combined with the rough set technique provides an efficient and effective mechanism for knowledge discovery in database systems.

1 Introduction

Knowledge discovery is the extraction of implicit, useful information from data. Knowledge discovery in databases is a form of machine learning which discovers interesting knowledge from databases and represents the knowledge in a high-level language. The growth in the size and number of existing databases far

---

*The authors are members of the Institute for Robotics and Intelligent Systems (IRIS) and wish to acknowledge the support of the Networks of Centres of Excellence Program of the Government of Canada, the Natural Sciences and Engineering Research Council, and the participation of PRECARN Associates Inc.

exceeds human's ability to analyze this data, which creates both a need and an opportunity to extract knowledge from databases.

In our previous studies [1], an attribute-oriented induction approach has been developed for discovering knowledge in relational databases. Our previous attribute-oriented induction method did not analyze data dependency relationships among attributes, and thus the rules so generated may not be concise and strong since they may contain some redundant information or unnecessary constraints. Thus, a technique is needed to perform comprehensive analysis of properties of the generalized data prior to the generation of rules. On the other hand, the rough set technique introduced by [3] provides the necessary tools to analyze the set of attributes globally but may not be feasible to apply to a large database directly because of its computational complexity, which is NP-hard [5]. The two approaches are apparently different. But in both methods, objects are assumed to be characterized by attributes and attribute values. Our study finds out that there is a close connection between attribute-oriented induction and rough set approach. A natural approach would combine the advantages of both techniques. In this paper, a new method for knowledge discovery is proposed, which generalizes the data by performing attribute-oriented induction and then applies the rough set techniques to the generalized relation to find data dependency among the generalized attributes and choose the best minimal attribute set to represent the final generalized relation. Finally, the final generalized relation is transformed into the logical rule form.

The paper is organized as follow. In Section 2, the rough set theory and information system is introduced. The principle and algorithm for learning from database is presented in Section 3. In Section 4, a comparison with other knowledge discovery method is discussed and the concluding remarks are in Section 5.

2 Principal Concepts of Rough Set

2.1 Information System (IS)

By an **IS** S, we mean that $S = \{U, A, V\}$, where U is a finite set of object, $U = \{x_1, x_2, ..., x_n\}$, A is a finite set of attributes, the attributes in A are further classified into disjoint *condition* attributes C and *decision* attributes D, $A = C \cup D$, $V = \bigcup_{p \in A} V_p$ and V_p is a *domain* of attribute p.

Let $P \subset A$, $x_i, x_j \in U$, we define a binary relation $\tilde{P}$, called an *indiscernibility relation*, as follow: $\tilde{P} = \{(x_i, x_j) \in U \times U : for\ every\ p \in P\ p(x_i) = p(x_j)\}$. We say that x_i and x_j are indiscernible by set of attributes P in S iff $p(x_i) = p(x_j)$ for every $p \in P$. $\tilde{P}$ is an equivalence relation on U for every $P \subset A$. Equivalence classes of relation $\tilde{P}$ are called P-elementary sets in S.

For an **IS** $S = \{U, A, V\}$, and $IND \subset A$ is an equivalent relation (*indiscernibility relation*), an order pair $AS = (U, IND)$ is called an *approximation space*. For any element x_i of U, the equivalence class of x_i in relation IND is represented as $[x_i]_{IND}$. Equivalence class of IND is called *elementary set in A* because it represents the smallest discernible groups of objects. Any finite union of elementary sets in AS is called a *definable set in AS*.

Let $X \subset U$, the lower approximation of X in AS is $\underline{IND}X = \{x_i \in U | [x_i]_{IND} \subset X\}$, the upper approximation of X in AS is $\overline{IND}X = \{x_i \in U | [x_i]_{IND} \cap X \neq \emptyset\}$. $\underline{IND}X$ is the union of all those elementary sets each of which is contained by X. For any $x_i \in \underline{IND}X$, it is certain that it belongs to X. $\overline{IND}X$ is the union of those elementary sets each of which has a non-empty intersection with X. For any $x_i \in \overline{IND}X$, we can only say that x_i is possible to belong to X.

2.2 Core and Reducts of Attributes

Core and reduct are the two fundamental concepts of rough set. A reduct is the essential part of an **IS** which can discern all objects discernible by the original **IS**. A core is the common parts of all reducts.

Let $S = \{U, A, V\}$ be an **IS**, $A = C \cup D$ and $B \subset C$, we define a positive region B in $IND(D)$, $POS_B(D)$, as $POS_B(D) = \cup\{\underline{B}X : X \in IND(D)\}$. The positive region $POS_B(D)$ includes all objects in U which can be classified into classes of $IND(D)$ without error just based on the classification information in $IND(B)$.

Definition 2.1 An attribute $p \in B$ is superfluous in B with respect to D if $POS_B(D) = POS_{B-\{p\}}(D)$, otherwise p is indispensable in B with respect to D.

If an attribute is superfluous in an **IS**, it can be removed from the **IS** without changing the dependency relationship of the original system. While an indispensable attribute carries the essential information about objects of the information system. It should be kept if you do not want to change the dependency relationship of the original system.

Definition 2.2 The set of all indispensable attributes in C with respect to D is called the core of C. $CORE(C,D) = \{a \in C : POS_C(D) \neq POS_{C-\{a\}}(D)\}$.

Definition 2.3 $B \subset C$ is defined as reduct in S if B is independent with respect to D and $POS_C(D) = POS_B(D)$

Definition 2.4 A **discernibility matrix** of P in S, $M(P) = \{m_{i,j}\}_{n \times n}$ is defined as

$$(m_{i,j}) = \{q \in P : p(x_i, q) \neq p(x_j, q)\} \; for \; i, \; j = 1, 2, \ldots, n.$$

The entry $m_{i,j}$ is the set of all attributes which discern objects x_i, x_j. $M(P)$ is symmetric, we only need to compute the entries m_{ij} for $1 \leq j < i \leq n$.

Using the discernibility matrix, one can easily see that to test whether $P' \subset P$ is the reduct of P, it is enough to check whether $P' \cap m \neq \emptyset$ for any nonempty entry m in $M(P)$. That means, reduct is the minimal subset of attributes that discerns all objects discernible by the whole set of attributes.

For each pair of objects $x_i, x_j \in$ U, a subset of attributes $\delta(x_i, x_j) \subset P$ is attached. $\delta(x_i, x_j)$ is the set of attributes that distinguish the object x_i, x_j. Also, for each attribute $q \in P$, a binary variable $\tilde{q}$ is associated, the definition *discernibility function* is defined as follows.

Definition 2.5. The **discernibility function f(P)** is

$$f(P) = \prod_{(x_i, x_j) \in U \times U} \sum \delta(x_i, x_j)$$

where $\sum \delta(x_i, x_j)$ is the boolean sum of all boolean variable assigned to the set of attributes δ_{x_i, x_j}.

Theorem [4] All constituents in the disjunctive normal form of the function f(P) are all the reducts of P.

In many applications, classes are determined by a small number of attributes and sometimes even by one attribute, rather than by minor differences in all of the attributes in the databases. There are different standards based on different preferences and applications. For example, the best minimal subset of attributes can be chosen based on a combined value of lower spareness and low complexity [1]. In [5], several approaches were proposed. In our algorithm, we adopt the approach which chooses the reduct with the least number of combination of values of its attributes.

3 Principles and Algorithms for Learning in Relational Databases

Rough set theory has been successful in many areas, such as knowledge-based system in medical diagnosis, machine learning and industry [5]. In this section, a new algorithm DBROUGH is presented which is feasible to be used in databases to derive knowledge rules. The method integrates generalization and reduction and provides a simple, efficient and effective way to extract knowledge from databases. To simplify our discussion, the following assumptions are made in our study.

Assumption 1: A database stores a large amount of information-rich and relatively reliable data.

Assumption 2: A knowledge discovery process is initiated by a user's learning request.

Assumption 3: Generalized rules are expressed in terms of high level concepts.

Assumption 4: Background knowledge is generally available for knowledge discovery process.

Our method is performed in three steps: First, an attribute-oriented concept tree ascending technique is applied to the task-relevant data relation, which removes some undesirable attributes [1] and generalizes the concepts of desirable attribute to a certain level based on the conceptual bias and the tuple threshold values. Then the rough set technique is applied to analyze the data dependency of the attribute and find the best minimal reduct. Finally, rule-extraction is performed on the reduced relation, which generates concise, expressive and strong rules.

Example 3.1 Suppose we have a collection of Japanese and America cars with the attributes as **plate#**, **Make_model**, type of fuel system (**fuel**), engine displacement (**disp**), **weight**, number of cylinders (**cyl**), **power**, presence of turbocharge (**t**), compression ratio (**comp**), transmitter (**tran**) and **m** depicted in Table 1 and the concept hierarchy table for the car relation in Figure 1.

{Honda_civic, Honda_acura,..., Honda_accord} $\subset$ Honda
{Toyota_tercel,...,Toyota_camry} $\subset$ Toyota

Plate#	Make-Model	fuel	disp	weight	cyl	Power	t	comp	tran	m
BCT89	Ford escort	EFI	Med	876	6	High	y	high	auto	m
UI89P	Dodge shadow	EFI	Med	1100	6	High	n	medium	manu	m
P0967	Ford festival	EFI	Med	1589	6	High	n	high	manu	m
LKIPO	Chevrolet corvette	EFI	Med	987	6	high	n	medium	manu	m
IUTY5	Dodge stealth	EFI	Med	1096	6	High	n	high	manu	m
ERTW3	Ford probe	EFI	Med	867	6	High	n	medi	manu	m
TYUR4	Ford mustang	EFI	Med	1197	6	High	n	high	manu	m
0987U	Dodge daytona	EFI	Med	798	6	High	y	high	manu	h
9876	Chrysler Le B	EFI	Med	1056	4	Medi	n	medium	manu	m
UYTHG	Dodge sprite	EFI	Med	1557	6	High	n	medium	manu	l
OPLSA	Honda civic	2-BBL	Sma	786	4	Low	n	high	manu	h
KMN89	Ford escort	2-BBL	Sma	1098	4	Low	n	high	manu	m
LKOPL	Ford temple	2-BBL	Sma	1187	4	Medi	n	high	auto	m
WEQ54	Toyota corolla	EFI	Sma	1023	4	Low	n	high	manu	h
PLMNH	Mazda 323	EFI	Med	698	4	Medi	n	medium	manu	h
QAS45	Dodge Dayton	EFI	Med	1123	4	Medi	n	medium	manu	m
PLMJH	Honda prelude	EFI	Sma	1094	4	High	y	high	manu	h
DSA32	Toyota Paso	2-BBL	Sma	1023	4	Low	n	medium	manu	h
GHF6U	Chevrolet corsica	EFI	Med	980	4	High	y	medium	manu	m
KNM87	Chevrolet beretta	EFI	Med	1600	6	High	n	medium	auto	l
IKLO9	Chevrolet cavalier1	EFI	Med	1002	6	High	n	medium	auto	m
IKHTY	Chrysler Le b	EFI	Med	1098	4	High	n	medium	auto	m
OPL87	Mazda 626	EFI	Sma	1039	4	Medi	n	high	manu	h
UYT34	Chevrolet corsic	EFI	Sma	980	4	Medi	n	high	manu	h
UYTBN	Chevrolet Lumina	EFI	Sma	1000	4	Medi	n	high	manu	m

Table 1: Car Relation.

{Mazda_323, Mazda_626,..., Mazda_939} ⊂ Mazda
{Toyota , Honda , ..., Mazda } ⊂ Japan(Car)
{Ford_escort, Ford_probe,..., Ford_taurus } ⊂ Ford
{Chevrolet_corvette, Chevrolet_camaro,...,Chevrolet_corsica } ⊂ Chevrolet
{Dodge_stealth, Dodge_daytona,..., Dodge_dynasty } ⊂ Dodge
{Ford, Dodge, ..., Chevrolet } ⊂ USA(Car)
{Japan(Car), ..., USA(Car)} ⊂ Any(Make_model)
{0..800} ⊂ Light
{801..1200} ⊂ Medium
{1201..1600} ⊂ Heavy
{Low, Medium, High} ⊂ Any(Weight)
Figure 1: A concept hierarchy table.

The process is demonstrated using Example 3.1.

A large data relation usually contains a huge set of distinct attribute values. To obtain a simple and concise scheme and derive decision rules for each class, we should first generalize the primitive data instances to higher level concepts. This is realized by an attribute-oriented generalization [1] on the task-relevant relation. The first attribute, "Plate#", is the key of the relation. The key value is distinct for each tuple in the relation. If there is no higher level concept provided for such an attribute in the concept tree, the values of the attribute cannot be generalized, and they should be removed in the generalization. Also, other candidate key attributes or nonkey attributes can be eliminated under a similar condition. We then examine the remaining attributes.

By examining the values attribute-by-attribute and substituting the values in each attribute by their higher level concepts in the corresponding concept tree, e.g., from *Mazda 323* to *Mazda*, 798 (weight of car) to *light*, the relation is generalized. In general, we have

Strategy 1: *Attribute-oriented generalization*

The generalization is performed on each attribute by removing the attribute if there is a large set of distinct values for the attribute and no higher-level concept hierarchy available, or by ascending the concept tree (i.e., substituting the values of the attribute in each tuple by its corresponding higher level concept) otherwise.

As a result of generalization, different objects may be generalized to equivalent ones where two (generalized) objects are **equivalent** if they have the same corresponding attribute values without considering a special internal attribute **vote**, which registers the number of tuples in the initial working relation that are generalized to the tuple in the current resulting relation. The *vote* accumulated in the generalized relation incorporates quantitative information in the learning process.

Strategy 2: *Vote propagation*

The value of the vote of a tuple should be carried to its corresponding generalized tuple, and the vote should be accumulated when merging equivalent tuples in generalization.

Notice that it is often necessary for some attribute values to be generalized by climbing up a concept tree several times in order to derive a simple class scheme. To control the generalization process and integrate it with the classification process, it is necessary to provide a class threshold value, which is the upper bound on the number of classes to be partitioned. Then the generalization can be repeatedly performed on an attribute (*without examining other attributes*) until the number of distinct values is under the specified threshold value. For instance, if the threshold value is set to three in this example (because there are only three distinct values for the decision attribute *mileage*), the concepts in the attribute "Make_Model" should be generalized two levels (*Mazda 323 to Mazda then to Japanese car*). In general, we have

Strategy 3: *Threshold control on generalized relations*

If the number of tuples of a generalized relation is larger than the generalization threshold value, further generalization on the relation should be performed.

Since different attribute values can be substituted by the higher level concepts in the generalization process, a set of tuples may be generalized to the same generalized tuples in the generalized relation, the size of the generalized relation is reduced. After the generalization procedure, Table 2 is obtained.

Taking "mileage" as the decision attribute, we examine how to compute the reduct of the condition attributes

Strategy 4: *Minimal subset of attributes and choose the desired one*

we can compute all the reducts of attributes with decision attribute "mileage" and other attributes as conditions. Five of the reducts are listed below.

(1) Make_model, fuel, disp, weight (2) Cyl, fuel, comp, power, weight (3) Make_model, fuel, comp, power, weight, (4) Make_model, cyl, fuel, power, weight, (5) Make_model, cyl, fuel, comp, weight.

Each of these minimal subset can be chosen to represent the original relation without losing essential information when we want to determine which are the

Make_Model	fuel	disp	weight	cyl	Power	t	comp	tran	mileage	vote
USA	EFI	Med	Medium	6	High	y	high	manu	medium	1
USA	EFI	Med	Medium	6	High	n	medium	manu	medium	3
USA	EFI	Med	Medium	6	High	n	medium	auto	medium	1
USA	EFI	Med	Medium	6	Medi	n	Medium	manu	medium	1
USA	EFI	Med	Medium	6	High	n	high	manu	medium	2
USA	EFI	Med	Light	4	High	y	high	manu	high	1
USA	EFI	Sma	Medium	4	Medi	n	high	manu	high	1
USA	EFI	Med	Medium	6	High	n	high	manu	medium	2
USA	EFI	Med	Heavy	6	High	y	high	auto	low	1
USA	EFI	Med	Medium	6	Medi	n	medium	manu	medium	1
USA	EFI	Med	Heavy	6	High	n	medium	manu	low	1
Japan	2-BBL	Sma	Light	4	Low	n	high	manu	high	1
USA	2-BBL	Sma	Medium	4	Medi	n	high	auto	medium	1
Japan	EFI	Sma	Medium	4	Low	n	high	manu	high	1
Japan	EFI	Med	Light	4	Medi	n	medium	manu	high	1
USA	2-BBL	Med	Medium	4	Medi	n	medium	manu	medium	1
Japan	EFI	Sma	Medium	4	High	y	high	auto	high	1
Japan	2-BBL	Sma	Medium	4	Low	n	medium	manu	high	1
USA	EFI	Med	Medium	4	High	y	medium	manu	medium	1
USA	EFI	Med	Medium	6	High	n	medium	manu	medium	1
Japan	EFI	Sma	Medium	4	Medi	n	high	auto	high	1

Table 2: The Car Relation After Generalization.

Make_model	fuel	disp	weight	mileage	vote
USA	EFI	Medium	Medium	medium	13
USA	2-BBL	Medium	Medium	medium	1
USA	2-BBL	Small	Medium	medium	1
USA	EFI	Medium	Heavy	low	2
USA	EFI	Medium	Light	high	1
USA	EFI	Small	medium	high	1
Japan	2-BBL	Small	Light	high	1
Japan	EFI	Small	Medium	high	3
Japan	EFI	Small	Light	high	1
Japan	2-BBL	Small	Medium	high	1

Table 3: Reduced Table for Car Relation

real factors that affect the mileage of a car. Based on our criteria, we choose set (1) because it has only 10 combinations of attribute values and produce the reduction relation for the original relation as shown in Table 3.

Strategy 5: *Combining similar tuples*

In the same class, two tuples can be combined into one if the values of condition attributes differ in only one attribute. If the data values appearing in the merged tuples cover all the possible values of the attribute in the corresponding generalization hierarchy, then this attribute should be dropped from the tuple. For example, the first and the second tuples in Table 3 differ only in *fuel*. Then they can be combined into *(USA, {EFL,2-BBL}, Medium, Medium, medium)*, which can be further simplified to *(USA, , Medium, Medium, medium)*. After examine the distribution of the values for each attribute, the reduced table is further simplified to Table 4.

Strategy 6: *Rule transformation*

Transformation of the tuples in the reduced relation into logical rules.

The value of *vote* is the number of cases in the original relation that support

Make-model	fuel	disp	weight	mileage	vote
USA		Medium	Medium	medium	14
USA	2-BBL		Medium	medium	2
USA	EFI	Medium	Heavy	low	2
USA	EFI	Medium	Light	high	1
USA	EFI	Small	Medium	high	1
Japan		Small	Light,Medium	high	6

Table 4: Reduced Table for Car Relation after Combination

each given rule. Since the tuples in the original relation may be distributed along the full spectrum of the possible values. Without using quantitative information, it is impossible to obtain a meaningful set of rules for such kind of data. We would not trust a rule based on just a few cases. However, using the quantitative information, various kinds of techniques can be developed to extract meaningful rules. A simple method is introduced here.

The method treats the tuples which occur rarely in the reduction relation as exceptional or noise case and filters them out before the rule-generalization. This is accomplished by calculating the *frequency ratio* for each tuple and filtering out the *exceptional* tuples using the *noise filter threshold*.

Definition 3.1 *The* **frequency ratio** *is the ratio of the tuple vote value versus the summation of the vote in the reduction relation, that is, (where n is the number of tuples in the reduction relation)*

$$r_{frequency} = vote\_of\_the\_tuple / \sum_{i=1}^{n}(vote\_of\_tuple_i)$$

The **noise filter threshold** is a small percentage number which is used to filter out those tuples in the reduction relation with a very low frequency ratio (i.e., below the specified noise filter threshold).

Suppose the *noise filter threshold* is set to 5%. The noise filtering operation is performed as follows. If the frequency ratio of a tuple is less than 5%, then the tuple is cleared, otherwise the tuple is transformed to a logical rule.

(1) *if* (Make_model=USA(car)) & (disp=Medium) & (weight=Medium)
    then (mileage=medium)
(2) *if* (Make_model=USA(car)) & (fuel=2-BBL) & (weight=Medium)
    then (mileage=medium)
(3) *if* (Make_model=Japan(car)) & (disp=Small) & (weight=Light ∪ Medium)
    then (mileage=high)
(4) *if* (Make_model=USA(car)) & (fuel=EFL) & (disp=Medium) & (Weight=Heavy)
    then (mileage=low)

In summary, we present the algorithm below:

Algorithm. DBROUGH–An Attribute-Oriented Rough Set Knowledge Discovery Algorithm in Databases
Input. (i) A set of task-relevant data R (assume that they are obtained by a relation query and are stored in a relation table), a relation of arity n with a set of attributes A_i ($1 \leq i \leq n$); (ii) a set of concept hierarchies, H_i, where H_i

is a hierarchy on the generalized attribute A_i, if available; (iii) the threshold value T, and (iv) decision attribute name.

Output. A set of decision rules.

Method

    Step 1. *Attribute-oriented induction.*

/* Suppose d_i is the number of distinct values in attributes A_i */.

begin

for each attribute A_i ($1 \leq i \leq n$) of R **do** {

while $T \leq d_i$ **do**

if there is no higher level concepts of A_i **then** remove A_i;

else substitute the values by its corresponding minimal generalized concept; }

eliminate redundant tuples and register the number of identical tuples in *vote*.

    end *attribute-oriented induction*

    Step 2. *find the desired minimal subset of attributes*

    begin

construct the discernibility matrix $M(R)$ and discernibility function $f(R)$, simplify $f(R)$.

select the desired reduct from f(R) based on the criteria.

    end

    Step 3. *Reduce the generalized relation using the reduct of the attributes and combine the similar tuples.*

    Step 4. *Transform the tuples in the reduced relations into decision rules.*

4 Discussion & Conclusion

The algorithms presented in this paper are based on the research work in [1] and influenced by the ideas presented in [5]. Our algorithms adopt the attribute-oriented conceptual ascension technique combined with the rough set technique; attribute-oriented induction provides a simple and efficient way for the generalization process and rough set provides an effective tool to find out the reduction form of the generalized relation. The major difference of our approach from others is attribute-oriented vs. tuple-oriented induction. The former techniques perform generalization, attribute by attribute, while the latter, tuple by tuple. The two approaches involve significantly different search spaces.

Our algorithm use rough set to analyze the attribute dependency and choose the reduct form of the best minimal subset for rule generalization. Our method eliminates undesirable attributes in the generalization process and removes irrelevant attributes in the reduction process. The rules generated are concise, expressive and strong because it is in the most generalized form. Besides, with concept generalization, the derived rules are represented in higher level abstraction.

Based on our previous implementation of the database learning system DBLEARN [1] which performs attribute-oriented generalization to extract knowledge rules in relational database, we are currently working on the implementation and testing of the DBROUGH for the large database environment. We plan to test it on a real large database: Research Grants Information System of Natural Science and Engineering Research Council of Canada and hope to report our results in the future.

References

[1] J. Han, Y.Cai, N. Cercone, Knowledge Discovery in Databases: An Attribute-Oriented Approach, *Proceeding of the 18th VLDB Conference*, Vancouver , B.C., Canada, pp. 340-355, 1992.

[2] R.S. Michalski, A Theory and Methodology of Inductive Learning, *in Machine Learning: An Artificial Intelligence Approach, Vol. 1.* Michalski et. al. (eds), Morgan Kaufmann, 1983, pp 41-82.

[3] Zdzislaw Pawlak, Rough sets, *International Journal of Information and Computer Science* (1982) 11(5), 341-356

[4] Zdzislaw Pawlak, Anathomy of Conflicts, *ICS Research Report 11/92*, Warsaw University of Technology, Nowowiejska 15/19, 00-665, Warsaw, Poland, 1992.

[5] Wojciech Ziarko, The Discovery, Analysis, and Representation of Data Dependency in Databases, in *Knowledge Discovery in Databases* G. Piatetsky-Shapiro and W. J. Frawlwy,(eds), Menlo Park, CA: AAAI/MIT, 1991, 213-228.

A Rough Set Model for Relational Databases

Theresa Beaubouef   Frederick E. Petry
Center for Intelligent and Knowledge-Based Systems, Tulane University
New Orleans, LA 70118   USA

1 Introduction

In recent years it has become increasingly necessary to capture information on uncertainty, imprecision, and ambiguity along with precise values in databases. Fuzzy set theory has been established as a useful tool for representing imprecision and grades of membership. It has also been integrated with the relational database model and proven to be an excellent mechanism for expressing relationships among attribute values and imprecision in querying [1].

More recently, the theory of rough sets [2] has been gaining acceptance, especially as a tool for knowledge discovery [3] in databases. Rough sets theory is also based on a strong mathematical foundation, but captures the notion of indiscernibility or ambiguity instead of a "fuzzy" type of imprecision.

The ability of rough sets to capture indiscernibility and to define sets by lower and upper approximations led to the design of the rough relational database model. This model incorporates all the essential features of the rough set theory into the basic relational database to provide a model which improves on the standard relational model [4] by greater recall and greater flexibility for the querier. The major differences between the two models, along with several important properties of the rough relational database are discussed. Important definitions are presented and properties and usefulness of the model illustrated through the use of a geographical information system example.

2 The Rough Relational Database Model

The rough relational database model, like the standard relational database model, represents data as a collection of *relations* containing *tuples*. These relations are sets. The tuples of a relation, its elements, are unordered and nonduplicated. A tuple t_i takes the form $(d_{i1}, d_{i2}, ..., d_{im})$, where d_{ij} is a *domain value* of a particular *domain set* D_j. In the ordinary relational database, $d_{ij} \in D_j$. In the rough relational database, however, $d_{ij} \subseteq D_j$, and although d_{ij} does not have to be a singleton, $d_{ij} \neq \emptyset$. Let 2^{D_i} denote any non-null member of the powerset of D_i.

Definition. A *rough relation R* is a subset of $2^{D_1} \times 2^{D_2} \times \cdots \times 2^{D_m}$.

For a specific relation, R, membership is determined semantically.

This research was supported in part by the Louisiana Board of Regents Fellowships--
     Tulane, LAQSF(1990-95)-GF-13.

Definition. A *rough tuple* t is a member of both R and $2^{D_1} \times 2^{D_2} \times \cdots \times 2^{D_m}$. If t_i is some arbitrary tuple, then $t_i = (d_{i1}, d_{i2}, ..., d_{im})$ where $d_{ij} \subseteq D_j$.

Definition. An *interpretation* $\alpha = (a_1, a_2, ..., a_m)$ of a rough tuple $t_i = (d_{i1}, d_{i2}, ..., d_{im})$ is any value assignment such that $a_j \in d_{ij}$ for all j.

The interpretation space is the cross product $D_1 \times D_2 \times \cdots \times D_m$, but is limited for a given relation R to the set of those tuples which are valid according to the underlying semantics of R. In an ordinary relational database, because domain values are atomic, there is only one possible interpretation for each tuple t_i, the tuple itself. In the rough relational database, this is not always the case.

Let $[d_{xy}]$ denote the equivalence class including d_{xy}.

Definition. Tuples $t_i = (d_{i1}, d_{i2}, ..., d_{im})$ and $t_k = (d_{k1}, d_{k2}, ..., d_{km})$ are *redundant* if $[d_{ij}] = [d_{kj}]$ for all $j = 1, ..., m$.

In rough relations, there are no redundant tuples. The merging process used in relational database operations removes duplicate tuples since duplicates are not allowed in sets, the structure upon which the relational model is based. However, it is possible for more than one tuple to have the same interpretation.

DOMAIN	VALUE	IND
FEATURE	MARSH	00149
FEATURE	WETLAND	00149
FEATURE	BEACH	89754
FEATURE	COAST	89754
FEATURE	SAND	89754
FEATURE	ROAD	11122
FEATURE	URBAN	33333
FEATURE	LAKE	22444
FEATURE	SEA	22444
FEATURE	RIVER	22444
FEATURE	GRASS	00055
FEATURE	PASTURE	00055
FEATURE	MEADOW	00055
FEATURE	FOREST	00788
FEATURE	WOODS	00788
FEATURE	JUNGLE	00788
COUNTRY	US	00067
COUNTRY	USA	00067
COUNTRY	BELIZE	44667
COUNTRY	BRITISH HONDURAS	44667
COUNTRY	MEXICO	99779
COUNTRY	INT	85632

Figure 1. *INDISCERNIBILITY*

Indiscernibility may be represented in the rough relational database by an additional ordinary relation, having as its tuples all possible values d_{ij} for every D_j, paired with an arbitrary indiscernibility identifier which is unique for every equivalence class. This indiscernibility relation is an integral part of the rough relational database. All database retrieval operations implicitly access the indiscernibility relation in addition to the rough relations named in the query.

Consider the following example. A geographical information system assumes that the earth is subdivided into areas of uniform size called subregions. For a given subregion, data from maps, image processing, and/or ground truth observations may be available. This data includes such facts as the country or countries in which the subregion is located and land classification information.

In feature extraction and other land classification, it may not be possible or even desirable to distinguish between closely-related classes. For example, it may be necessary to identify water areas, but not necessary to discern salt water from fresh water. Salt water and fresh water are then considered to be *indiscernible*.

When data is the result of multiple sources, another type of indiscernibility is possible. An attribute may contain different values with identical connotations, and should therefore be considered indiscernible. The indiscernibility relation of the rough sets theory classes is ideally suited to such situations. The example indiscernibility relation in Figure 1 defines the following set of equivalence classes:

{[MARSH, WETLAND], [BEACH, COAST, SAND], [ROAD], [URBAN], [RIVER, LAKE, SEA],
[GRASS, PASTURE, MEADOW], [FOREST, WOODS, JUNGLE],
[US, USA], [BELIZE, BRITISH HONDURAS], [MEXICO], [INT]}.

The sample relation *SUBREGIONS* (Figure 2) contains the country and feature information for each subregion which is uniquely identified by the attribute ID. It is a rough relation having all tuples in its lower approximation. The non-first normal form of relations in the rough relational database is evident in this relation, where multiple values of an attribute within a tuple are denoted by enclosure within { }. For simplicity of notation, the set brackets are omitted from singletons.

ID	COUNTRY	FEATURE
U123	US	{MARSH, LAKE}
U124	US	MARSH
U125	USA	{MARSH, PASTURE, RIVER}
U126	US	{FOREST, RIVER}
U147	US	{SAND, ROAD, URBAN}
U157	{US, MEXICO}	{SAND, ROAD}
M007	MEXICO	{SAND, ROAD}
M008	MEXICO	BEACH
M009	MEXICO	SAND
C039	BELIZE	JUNGLE
C040	{BELIZE, INT}	{JUNGLE, COAST, SEA}

Figure 2. *SUBREGIONS*

Because a subregion may contain any number of land or water features, the system should allow entries of the FEATURE attribute to contain more than one value. Consider the subregion identified as U123, for example. This region contains both MARSH and LAKE areas and is located in the US. Multiple values for the COUNTRY attribute arise whenever a subregion spans political boundaries.

In order to utilize the notion of indiscernibility, the interpretation of a query in the ordinary relational database must be modified. Every domain value d_{ij} specified within a clause of a query, including variable names, is translated into the equivalence class $[d_{ij}]$ of which the value is a member. For example, the query to return the IDs of those subregions containing wetland areas is interpreted as

select [X.ID]			U123
from SUBREGIONS	resulting in	$\Longrightarrow$	U124
where FEATURE = ["WETLAND"],			U125.

In this example [X.ID] produces the same results as would X.ID because for this particular application, the attribute ID is the primary key which means that every value of ID must be unique. Therefore, each ID belongs to its own equivalence class. However, suppose one wanted to retrieve the countries of subregions having a "WETLAND" feature. In this case, the indiscernibility makes a difference, and the value returned would be "[US]" instead of both "US" and "USA".

In addition to indiscernibility, the rough relational database must incorporate lower and upper approximations into the querying in order to retrieve a rough set. A query to return the names of subregions with a country of "MEXICO" and a land feature "SAND", for example,

			M008
select X.ID	yields	$\Longrightarrow$	M009
from SUBREGIONS			(U157)
where COUNTRY = "MEXICO" and FEATURE = "SAND",			(M007).

where parentheses represent elements of the boundary region of the rough set result.

3 Rough Relational Operators

There are two basic types of relational operators. The first type arises from the fact that relations are sets of tuples. Therefore, operations which can be applied to sets also apply to relations. Some examples are *set difference*, *union*, and *intersection*. Operators which do not come from set theory, but which are useful for retrieval of relational data are *select*, *project*, and *join*.

In the rough relational database, relations are rough sets as opposed to ordinary sets. Therefore, new rough operators (-, ∪, ∩, ,σ, π, ⋈), which are comparable to the standard relational operators, must be developed for the rough relational database. Moreover, a mechanism must exist within the database to mark tuples of a rough relation as belonging to the lower or upper approximation of that rough relation. Because the definitions for the rough relational operators which follow are independent of any implementation details, only issues related to the determination of the approximation area to which a tuple belongs will be discussed.

The definitions for set operations on rough relations are comparable to those defined in the standard relational model. These binary operations require that the argument relations be "union compatible". Relations $X(A_1, A_2, ..., A_n)$ and $Y(B_1, B_2, ..., B_n)$ are union compatible if they have the same number of attributes in their relation schemas and if domain(A_i) = domain(B_i) for all i = 1, n.

DIFFERENCE. The rough relational difference operator is a binary operator that returns those elements of the first rough relation which are not contained in the second rough relation. Let X and Y be two union compatible rough relations.

Definition. The *rough difference*, X - Y, between X and Y is a rough relation T where

$$\underline{R}T = \{t \in \underline{R}X \mid t \notin \underline{R}Y\} \text{ and } \overline{R}T = \{t \in \overline{R}X \mid t \notin \overline{R}Y\}.$$

The lower approximation of T = X - Y contains those tuples belonging to the lower approximation of X which are not redundant with a tuple in the lower approximation of Y. The upper approximation of the rough relation T contains those tuples in the upper approximation of X which are not redundant in the upper approximation of Y.

UNION. Let X and Y be two union compatible rough relations.

Definition. The *rough union* of X and Y, X ∪ Y is a rough relation T where

$$\underline{R}T = \{t \in \underline{R}X \cup \underline{R}Y\} \text{ and } \overline{R}T = \{t \in \overline{R}X \cup \overline{R}Y\}.$$

The lower approximation of the resulting rough relation T contains those tuples which are a member of either or both of the lower approximations of X and Y, and the upper approximation of T contains tuples which belong to either or both of the upper approximations of X and Y.

INTERSECTION. Rough intersection is defined similarly.

Definition. The *rough intersection* of X and Y, X ∩ Y is a rough relation T where

$$\underline{R}T = \{t \in \underline{R}X \cap \underline{R}Y\} \text{ and } \overline{R}T = \{t \in \overline{R}X \cap \overline{R}Y\}.$$

In rough intersection, tuples are compared based on redundancy rather than equality of attribute values. The lower approximation of the T contains those tuples of the lower approximation of X which have corresponding redundant tuples in the lower approximation of Y, and the upper approximation of T contains tuples of the upper approximation of X which have redundant tuples in the upper approximation of Y.

Other rough relational database operators, which are analogous to select, project, and join for the ordinary relational database are also defined. Refer to [5] for formal definitions for these operators in the ordinary relational database.

SELECTION. The select operator for the rough relational database model, σ, is a unary operator which takes a rough relation X as its argument and returns a rough relation containing a subset of the tuples of X, selected on the basis of values for a specified attribute. The operation $\sigma_{A=a}(X)$, for example, would return those tuples in X where attribute A is equal to the value a, or more precisely, the value [a].

Let R be a relation schema, X a rough relation on that schema, A an attribute in R, and a = {a$_i$} where a$_i$,b$_j$ ∈ dom(A). $\cup_x$ means "the union over all x".

Definition. The *rough selection*, $\sigma_{A=a}(X)$, of tuples from X is a rough relation Y having the same schema as X and for a$_i$ ∈ a, b$_j$ ∈ t(A)

$$\underline{R}Y = \{t \in X \mid \cup_i [a_i] = \cup_j [b_j]\} \text{ and } \overline{R}Y = \{t \in X \mid \cup_i [a_i] \subset \cup_j [b_j]\}.$$

The lower approximation of Y = $\sigma_{A=a}(X)$ contains tuples having a value of attribute A which is indiscernible from the members of a. The upper approximation contains tuples where the members of a are a subset of the values of attribute A.

PROJECTION. Project is a unary operator which takes a relation as its argument and returns a relation which contains a subset of the columns of the original relation. Let X be a rough relation with schema A, and let B be a subset of A. The rough projection of X onto B is a relation Y obtained by omitting the columns of X which correspond to attributes in A - B, and removing redundant tuples.

Definition. The *rough projection* of X onto B, $\pi_B(X)$, is a relation Y with schema Y(B) where Y(B) = {t(B) | t ∈ X}.

When comparing tuples for redundancy, if both belong to the lower approximation or both belong to the upper approximation, either can be deleted. In the case that one tuple is from the lower and the other from the upper approximation, the tuple from the lower approximation should be retained.

COUNTRY	MAPPER
US	{USGS, NG}
MEXICO	MAP1
BELIZE	BELMAP
INT	{USGS, NG, DBDB5, MARINE-MAPPER}
({US, MEXICO}	{USGS, MAP1, NG, ETOPO5})

Figure 3. *MAP-INFO*

JOIN. The join operator is a binary operator which takes related tuples from two relations and combines them into single tuples of the resulting relation. It uses common attributes to combine the two relations into one, usually larger, relation. Let $X(A_1, A_2, ..., A_m)$ and $Y(B_1, B_2, ..., B_n)$ be rough relations with m and n attributes, respectively, and AB = C, the schema of the resulting rough relation T.

Definition. The *rough join*, $X \bowtie_{<JOIN\ COND>} Y$, of two relations X and Y, is a relation $T(C_1, C_2, ..., C_{m+n})$ where

$$T = \{t \mid \exists\, t_X \in X, t_Y \in Y \text{ for } t_X = t(A), t_Y = t(B)\}, \text{ and where}$$
$$t_X(A \cap B) = t_Y(A \cap B), \text{ for } \underline{R}T$$
$$t_X(A \cap B) \subseteq t_Y(A \cap B) \text{ or } t_Y(A \cap B) \subseteq t_X(A \cap B), \text{ for } \overline{R}T$$

<JOIN COND> is a conjunction of one or more conditions of the form **A = B.**

ID	COUNTRY	FEATURE
U123	US	{MARSH, LAKE}
U130	USA	{FOREST, GRASS}
U136	US	WOODS
({U123, U124}	US	{MARSH, LAKE, GRASS})

Figure 4. *US-SUBREGIONS*

If insufficient data is available for a particular subregion of interest, it may be necessary to try to locate additional information from another source for entry into the database. This can be accomplished by JOINing the *MAP-INFO* relation (Figure 3) with the relation of interest. The values for the attribute COUNTRY[1] were taken from the rough relation *US-SUBREGIONS* shown in Figure 4 and values for the attribute COUNTRY[2] from *MAP-INFO*. In ordinary relational databases, the values for these two like attributes are identical, so one of the columns is typically projected out. It is evident from this example that values within the two COUNTRY columns are not identical, and therefore, one should not automatically project out one of the columns without careful consideration.

$$T = \text{US-SUBREGIONS} \bowtie_{\text{COUNTRY = COUNTRY}} \text{MAP-INFO} \text{ yields}$$

ID	COUNTRY[1]	FEATURE	COUNTRY[2]	MAPPER
U123	US	{MARSH,LAKE}	US	{USGS,NG}
U130	USA	{FOREST,GRASS}	US	{USGS,NG}
U136	US	WOODS	US	{USGS,NG}
({U123,U124} US		{MARSH,LAKE,GRASS}	US	{USGS,NG})
(U123	US	{MARSH,LAKE}	{US,MEXICO}	{USGS,MAP1,NG,ETOPO5})
(U130	USA	{FOREST,GRASS}	{US,MEXICO}	{USGS,MAP1,NG,ETOPO5})
(U136	US	WOODS	{US,MEXICO}	{USGS,MAP1,NG,ETOPO5})
({U123,U124} US		{MARSH,LAKE,GRASS}	{US,MEXICO}	{USGS,MAP1,NG,ETOPO5})

□

4 Properties of Rough Relational Operators

There are many properties of the relational algebra, most of which deal with equivalence of results of various combinations of operations. Many properties remain valid when the model is extended to incorporate rough sets as the structure upon which relations are based. The closure property, for example, states that any operations applied to relations result in another relation. In the rough relational database, the result of applying any of the previously defined rough relational operators to one or more rough relations is also a rough relation. This follows from the definitions presented, where rough relations result from the defined operators.

Another interesting property is the distribution of the select operator over the Boolean set operators. This property states that for an operator γ, where $\gamma \in \{\cup, \cap, -\}$, and two relations X and Y, $\sigma_{A=a}(X \gamma Y) = \sigma_{A=a}(X) \gamma \sigma_{A=a}(Y)$.

PROOF: Let $\gamma = \cap$.

$\sigma_{A=a}(X \cap Y)$

$= \sigma_{A=a}(T)$ where

$\underline{R}T = \{t \mid t \in \underline{R}X \text{ and } t \in \underline{R}Y\}$ and $\overline{R}T = \{t \mid t \in \overline{R}X \text{ and } t \in \overline{R}Y\}$

$= T'$ where

$\underline{R}T' = \{t' \in \{t \mid t \in \underline{R}X \text{ and } t \in \underline{R}Y\} \mid \bigcup_i [a_i] = \bigcup_j [b_j]\}, a_i \in a, b_j \in t'(A)$

$\overline{R}T' = \{t' \in \{t \mid t \in \overline{R}X \text{ and } t \in \overline{R}Y\} \mid \bigcup_i [a_i] \subseteq \bigcup_j [b_j]\}, a_i \in a, b_j \in t'(A)$

$= Q$ where

$\underline{R}Q = \{t \mid t \in X \text{ and } \bigcup_i [a_i] = \bigcup_j [b_j]\} \cap \{t \mid t \in Y \text{ and } \bigcup_i [a_i] = \bigcup_j [b_j]\}$

$\overline{R}Q = \{t \mid t \in X \text{ and } \bigcup_i [a_i] \subseteq \bigcup_j [b_j]\} \cap \{t \mid t \in Y \text{ and } \bigcup_i [a_i] \subseteq \bigcup_j [b_j]\}$

$= \sigma_{A=a}(\{t \mid t \in X\}) \cap \sigma_{A=a}(\{t \mid t \in Y\})$

$= \sigma_{A=a}(X) \cap \sigma_{A=a}(Y)$

□

A property of the rough projection operator is that for a string of projections upon a relation Y having schema R, where $X_1 \subseteq X_2 \subseteq \cdots \subseteq X_n \subseteq R$, only the outermost projection operator is necessary: $\pi X_1(\pi X_2(\cdots (\pi X_n(Y)) \cdots)) = \pi X_1(Y)$.

The operations on both sides of the equality produce relations which are equal in the sense that every tuple in one rough relation has a corresponding tuple in the other rough relation such that the tuples are indiscernible. Every tuple of one relation is redundant with one and only one tuple of the other relation.

5 Conclusion

The rough operators defined in this paper operate upon a rough relation to result in another rough relation. Within these operations, it is often necessary to determine to which approximation area a resulting tuple belongs. These specifications, included with the definition, are not arbitrary, but should follow some convention. In this model, tuples known to belong to a lower approximation take precedence over redundant tuples from an upper approximation. When tuples result from the joining of tuples, only those tuples where all the joined parts are from lower approximations belong to the lower approximation of the resulting rough relation. All others are assigned to the upper approximation. This reasoning follows the conventions for calculating uncertainty as can be found in database models such as [6].

Support for the set values in relations as shown in the rough relational database model is easily provided for by non-first normal form extensions to the relational model which have been developed in the past [7]. In addition, the basic features of rough sets, including the notions of indiscernibility and lower and upper approximations are integrated into the relational model in such a way that important properties of rough sets theory also apply to the rough relational database.

References

1. Buckles, B.P. and F.E. Petry. A fuzzy model for relational databases. Journal of Fuzzy Sets and Systems 1982; Vol. 7, No. 3, 213-226.
2. Pawlak, Z. Rough sets. Int. J. Computer and Info. Sciences 1982; 11:341-356.
3. Slowinski, R. A generalization of the indiscernibility relation for rough sets analysis. First International Workshop on Rough Sets, Poland, 1992.
4. Codd, E.F. A relational model of data for large shared data banks. Communications of the ACM 1970; 13:377-387.
5. Maier, D. The Theory of Relational Databases, Computer Science Press, Rockville, MD, 1983.
6. Buckles, B.P. and F.E. Petry. Uncertainty models in information and database systems. Journal of Information Science 1985; 11:77-87.
7. Roth, M.A., H.F. Korth, and D.S. Batory. SQL/NF: A query language for non-1NF databases. Information Systems 1987; 12:99-114.

Data Filtration: A Rough Set Approach

Andrzej Skowron

Institute of Mathematics
Warsaw University
Banacha 2, 02-097 Warsaw, Poland
e-mail: skowron@mimuw.edu.pl

Abstract

We show how to apply some near-to-functional relations between data
to data filtration. A method for searching for new classifiers (features)
is described. It is based on searching for some functions approximating
near-to-functional relations.

1 Introduction

We propose a rough set approach to data filtration extending some ideas developed in such areas as signal filtration or image compression [14] and mathematical morphology [7], [15], [6]. We present a general strategy for filtering data in a given decision table on the basis of discovered local near-to-functional relations between data.

We discuss also a method for searching for classifiers in the set of approximation functions representing some near-to-functional relations between data. This method seems to be a promising tool for automatic extracting of classifiers from decision tables.

2 Rough Set Preliminaries

Information systems [4] are used for representing knowledge. Rough sets have been introduced [4] as a tool to deal with inexact, uncertain or vague knowledge in artificial intelligence applications.

An *information system* is a pair $\mathbb{A} = (U, A)$, where U is a non-empty, finite set of *objects* and A – a non-empty, finite set of *attributes*, i.e. $a : U \to V_a$ for $a \in A$, where V_a is called the *value set* of a. By V we denote the set $\cup \{V_a : a \in A\}$.

Any information system $\mathbb{A} = (U, A)$ and non-empty set $B \subseteq A$ determine a *B-information function*

$$Inf_B^{\mathbb{A}} : U \to \mathbb{P}(B \times \bigcup_{a \in B} V_a)$$

defined by $Inf_B^{\mathbb{A}}(x) = \{(a, a(x)) : a \in B\}$. We write Inf_B instead of $Inf_B^{\mathbb{A}}$ when no confusion arises. The set $\{Inf_B(x) : x \in U\}$ is denoted by $INF(\mathbb{A})|B$.

Elements of $INF(\mathbb{A})|B$ are called *information vectors* of $\mathbb{A}$ restricted to B. The set $INF(\mathbb{A})|A$ will be denoted by $INF(\mathbb{A})$. By $INF(A, V)$ we denote the set of all functions a from U into V satisfying $a(x) \in V_a$ for any $x \in U$ and $a \in A$.

We consider a special case of information systems called decision tables. A *decision table* is an information system of the form $\mathbb{A} = (U, A \cup \{d\})$, where $d \notin A$ is a distinguished attribute called the decision. The elements of A are called *conditions*.

The cardinality of the image $d(U) = \{k : d(s) = k \text{ for some } s \in U\}$ is denoted by $r(d)$. We assume that the set V_d of values of the decision d is equal to $\Theta = \{1, \ldots, r(d)\}$.

Let us observe that the decision d determines a partition $CLASS_\mathbb{A}(d) = \{X_1, \ldots, X_{r(d)}\}$ of the universe U, where $X_k = \{x \in U : d(x) = k\}$ for $1 \leq k \leq r(d)$. The set X_i is called the *i-th decision class of* $\mathbb{A}$.

Let $\mathbb{A} = (U, A)$ be an information system. With every subset of attributes $B \subseteq A$, an equivalence relation, denoted by $IND_\mathbb{A}(B)$ (or $IND(B)$) called the *B-indiscernibility relation*, is associated and it is defined by

$$IND(B) = \{(s, s') \in U^2 : \text{ for every } a \in B, a(s) = a(s')\}$$

Objects s, s' satisfying the relation $IND(B)$ are indiscernible by attributes from B.

If $\mathbb{A} = (U, A)$ is an information system, $B \subseteq A$ is a set of attributes and $X \subseteq U$ is a set of objects, then the sets

$$\{s \in U : [s]_B \subseteq X\} \quad \text{and} \quad \{s \in U : [s]_B \cap X \neq \emptyset\}$$

are called the *B-lower* and the *B-upper approximation* of X in $\mathbb{A}$, and they are denoted by $\underline{B}X$ and $\overline{B}X$, respectively.

The set $BN_B(X) = \overline{B}X - \underline{B}X$ will be called the *B-boundary* of X. When $B = A$ we also write $BN_\mathbb{A}(X)$ instead of $BN_A(X)$.

Sets which are unions of some classes of the indiscernibility relation $IND(B)$ are called *definable* by B (or, *B-definable*, in short). A set X is thus B-definable iff $\overline{B}X = \underline{B}X$. Some subsets (categories) of objects in an information system cannot be exactly expressed by employing available attributes but they can be defined *roughly*.

If $\mathbb{A} = (U, A \cup \{d\})$ is a decision table and $B \subseteq A$, then we define a function $\partial_B : U \to \mathbb{P}(\{1, \ldots, r(d)\})$, called *the B-generalized decision in* $\mathbb{A}$, by

$$\partial_B(x) = \{i : \exists x' \in U(x' IND(B)x \text{ and } d(x) = i)\} .$$

The A-generalized decision ∂_A in $\mathbb{A}$ is called the generalized decision in $\mathbb{A}$.

A decision table $\mathbb{A}$ is called *consistent (deterministic)* if $|(\partial_A(x)| = 1$ for any $x \in U$, otherwise $\mathbb{A}$ is *inconsistent (non-deterministic)*.

Now we recall the definition of decision rules. Let $\mathbb{A} = (U, A \cup \{d\})$ be a decision table and let $V = \bigcup\{V_a : a \in A\} \cup V_d$.

The atomic formulas over $B \subseteq A \cup \{d\}$ and V are expressions of the form $a = v$, called *descriptors* over B and V, where $a \in B$ and $v \in V_a$. The set $\mathbb{F}(B, V)$ of formulas over B and V is the least set containing all atomic formulas over B and V and closed with respect to the classical propositional connectives $\vee$ (disjunction), $\wedge$ (conjunction), and $\neg$ (negation).

Let $\tau \in \mathbb{F}(B,V)$. Then by $\tau_{\mathbb{A}}$ we denote the meaning of τ in a decision table $\mathbb{A}$, i.e. the set of all objects in U with property τ, defined inductively as follows:

1. if τ is of the form $a = v$ then $\tau_{\mathbb{A}} = \{x \in U : a(x) = v\}$;

2. $(\tau \wedge \tau')_{\mathbb{A}} = \tau_{\mathbb{A}} \cap \tau'_{\mathbb{A}}; \; (\tau \vee \tau')_{\mathbb{A}} = \tau_{\mathbb{A}} \cup \tau'_{\mathbb{A}}; \; (\neg \tau)_{\mathbb{A}} = U - \tau_{\mathbb{A}}$

The set $\mathbb{F}(A,V)$ is called the set of *conditional formulas of* $\mathbb{A}$ and is denoted by $\mathbb{C}(A,V)$.

A *decision rule of* $\mathbb{A}$ is any expression of the form

$$\tau \Rightarrow d = v \quad \text{where} \quad \tau \in \mathbb{C}(A,V) \quad \text{and} \quad v \in V_d.$$

A decision rule $\tau \Rightarrow d = v$ for $\mathbb{A}$ is *true in* $\mathbb{A}$, symbolically $\tau \Rightarrow_{\mathbb{A}} d = v$, iff $\tau_{\mathbb{A}} \subseteq (d = v)_{\mathbb{A}}$; when $\tau_{\mathbb{A}} = (d = v)_{\mathbb{A}}$, we say that the rule is $\mathbb{A}$-*exact*.

If $\mathbb{A} = (U, A \cup \{d\})$ is a decision table, then by $\mathbb{A}_\partial$ we denote the decision table $(U, A \cup \{\partial_A\})$. Let us observe that any decision rule $\tau \Rightarrow \partial_A = \theta$ where $\tau \in \mathbb{C}(A,V)$ and $\emptyset \neq \theta \subseteq V_d$ valid in $\mathbb{A}_\partial$ and having examples in $\mathbb{A}$, i.e. satisfying $\tau_{\mathbb{A}} \neq \emptyset$, determines a distribution of objects satisfying τ among elements of θ. This distribution is defined by

$$\mu_i(\mathbb{A}, \tau, \theta) = \frac{|Y \cap X_i|}{|Y|}, \quad \text{for } i \in \theta$$

where $Y = \tau_{\mathbb{A}}$.

Any decision rule $\tau \Rightarrow \partial_A = \theta$ valid in $\mathbb{A}_\partial$ and having examples in $\mathbb{A}$ with $|\theta| > 1$ is called *non-deterministic*, otherwise it is *deterministic*.

The number $n(\mathbb{A}, \tau, i) = |\tau_{\mathbb{A}} \cap X_i|$ is called the *number of examples supporting* τ *in the i-th decision class* X_i *of* $\mathbb{A}$.

Let us observe that for any formula τ over A and V with $\tau_{\mathbb{A}} \neq \emptyset$ there exists exactly one subset θ_τ of Θ such that $\tau \Rightarrow_{\mathbb{A}} \partial_A = \theta_\tau$ and $\mu_i(\mathbb{A}, \tau, \theta_\tau) > 0$ for any $i \in \theta_\tau$. In the sequel we write $\mu_i(\mathbb{A}, \tau)$ instead of $\mu_i(\mathbb{A}, \tau, \theta_\tau)$.

Some methods for decision rule synthesis from decision tables are presented in [5,11,12].

3 Data Filtration

The aim of this section is to present a basic idea to data filtration in decision tables.

3.1 A General Searching Scheme for Decision Table Filtration Based on Rough Set Approach

A decision table $\mathbb{A}' = (U, A' \cup \{d\})$ *is compatible with* $\mathbb{A} = (U, A \cup \{d\})$ iff $A = \{a_1, \ldots, a_m\}$, $A' = \{a'_1, \ldots, a'_m\}$ and $V_{a'_i} \subseteq V_{a_i}$ for $i = 1, \ldots, m$.

Let $\mathbb{A} = (U, A \cup \{d\})$, $\mathbb{A}' = (U, A' \cup \{d\})$ be decision tables and let $\delta \in (0, 1]$. We say that $\mathbb{A}'$ is a δ-*filtration* of $\mathbb{A}$ iff

(i) $\mathbb{A}'$ is compatible with $\mathbb{A}$

(ii) $\partial_A = \partial_{A'}$

(iii) $|\{[x]_{A'} : [x]_{A'} \subseteq Z_\theta\}| < \delta|\{[x]_A : [x]_A \subseteq Z_\theta\}|$

for any $\theta \subseteq V_d$ with $\emptyset \neq Z_\theta = \partial_A^{-1}(\theta)$.

We can also consider another version of this definition with condition (ii) substituted by a weaker condition specifying that ∂_A and $\partial_{A'}$ should be sufficiently close with respect to some distance function.

Let k be a real number from the interval $(0, 1]$. Let $\mathbb{A} = (U, A \cup \{d\})$ be a decision table and let τ be a formula over A and V. If $\alpha = \{(a_1, v_1), \dots, (a_m, v_m)\}$ then $\bigwedge \alpha$ denotes the formula $a_1 = v_1 \wedge \dots \wedge a_m = v_m$. If τ is a formula over A and V then by $\mathbb{A}_\tau$ we denote the restriction of $\mathbb{A}$ to the set of all objects from U satisfying τ, i.e. $\mathbb{A}_\tau = (\tau_\mathbb{A}, A \cup \{d\})$. By $T(\mathbb{A}, \tau, k)$ we denote the conjunction of the following conditions:

(i) $\tau_\mathbb{A} \neq \emptyset$

(ii) for any $\alpha \in INF(\mathbb{A}_\tau)$:

  (*) $\max_i \mu_i(\mathbb{A}, \bigwedge \alpha \wedge \tau) > k$

and

  (**) there exists exactly one i_o with the following property:
  $\mu_{i_o}(\mathbb{A}, \bigwedge \alpha \wedge \tau) = \max_i \mu_i(\mathbb{A}, \bigwedge \alpha \wedge \tau)$.

Conditions (*) and (**) imply that exactly one of distribution coefficients $\mu_i(\mathbb{A}, \bigwedge \alpha \wedge \tau)$ $(i \in \theta)$ exceeds the *threshold* k.

Let $\mathbb{A} = (U, A \cup \{d\})$ be a decision table and let δ be a reduction coefficient. We present a general procedure **F** for searching for a filtration of $\mathbb{A}$, where k is a fixed threshold and l is a positive integer, called *the critical level of examples*.

STEP 1. For any $a \in A' \subseteq A$, where A' is a randomly chosen sample set of conditions, apply the methods for decision rule synthesis (see [5],[11],[12]) to the decision table $\mathbb{A}_a = (U, (A - A') \cup \{a\})$. The output of this step is a set of decision rules of the form:

$$\tau \Rightarrow \partial_{A-A'} = \theta_\tau$$

where $\partial_{A-A'}$ is the generalized decision corresponding to the condition $a \in A'$ and τ is a formula over $A - A'$ and V. Now some strategies should be applied to get from these decision rules a "global" decision rule for a

$$\tau_o \Rightarrow \partial_{A-A'} = \theta$$

such that $T(\mathbb{A}_a, \tau_o, k)$ holds and $\max_i n(\mathbb{A}_a, \bigwedge \alpha \wedge \tau_o, i) > l$ for $\alpha \in INF((\mathbb{A}_a)_{\tau_o})|B$, where B is the set of conditions occuring in τ_o and $(A_o)_{\tau_o}$ is the restriction of A_o to the set of objects satisfying τ_o.

STEP 2. The approximation functions (defined in Section 3.2) are built from the global decision rules for conditions in $\mathbb{A}$. In this way we obtain a set $\mathcal{F}$ of approximation functions.

STEP 3. We apply some approximation functions from $\mathcal{F}$ to $\mathbb{A}$ (using some strategies, see Section 3.3) and in this way a new decision table $\mathbb{A}'$ is constructed.

STEP 4. **If** $\mathbb{A}'$ is a δ-filtration of $\mathbb{A}$ **then** stop **else** go to STEP1 substituting $\mathbb{A}$ by $\mathbb{A}'$ if $\mathbb{A}'$ is a δ'-filtration of $\mathbb{A}$ with $\delta' < 1$.

There are several problems to be solved when the above method is to be implemented. Among them are:

1. **The sampling problem:** How to choose A' in STEP 1?
   The random choice of A' (proposed in STEP 1) may not be sufficient. Basing on properties of reducts [10], [12] some methods for the proper choice of A' can be developed . One can also apply some analogies from mathematical morphology [1], [7] which have been used in building the so called analytical morphology [6] (see Section 3.4). Here we would only like to add, by analogy with the mathematical morphology operations of erosion and dilation, that a subset $A"$ of $A - A'$ can randomly chosen as a new subset of A after re-entering STEP 1, where A' is the previously chosen subset of A. We shall now look for decision rules

$$\tau \Rightarrow \partial_{A'} = \theta_\tau$$

   where τ is over A' and V and $\partial_{A'}$ is the generalized decision corresponding to a condition $a \in A"$.

2. **Generation of approximation functions for decision rules** (see Section 3.2).

3. **The conflict problem.** This problem occurs when one wants to apply the parallel strategy of STEP 3. We discuss this problem in Section 3.3.

4. **Application of approximation functions.** The problem is related to the question how to choose a proper subset of approximation functions from $\mathcal{F}$ and in which order to apply them to get the best filtration of $\mathbb{A}$.

In the above procedure **F** two strategies can be distinguished. The first one, S , produces from the actual decision table $\mathbb{A}$ for any $a \in A'$ a sequence of decision rules of the following form:

$$\tau_1 \longrightarrow \partial_{A-\{a\}} = \theta_1, \dots, \tau_p \longrightarrow \partial_{A-\{a\}} = \theta_p$$

satisfying $T(\mathbb{A}, \tau_i, k)$ for $i =, \dots, p$.

The rules are used to generate approximation functions by the second strategy H. The strategy H produces from the above sequences a new sequence

$$(s_1, \dots, s_r)$$

where s_i is a set of non-conflicting (see Section 3.3) decision rules of the form $\tau \longrightarrow \partial_{A-\{a\}} = \theta$ for some $a \in A$, $\theta \subseteq V_d$ and a formula τ over $A - \{a\}$ and V. The approximation functions corresponding to the decision rules from s_i are chosen by H for simultaneous application to $\mathbb{A}$ in the i-the step of transformation of the actual decision table $\mathbb{A}$.

Thus our procedure **F** has parameters S, H, $\mathbb{A}$, δ (by assumption l and k are fixed). The proper values for k and l should be chosen by making experiments with $\mathbb{A}$.

Now we can formulate a general version of two filtration problems.

FILTRATION PROBLEM :

Input: $\mathbb{A}$, and $\delta \in [0,1] \cap Q$, where Q is the set of rational numbers

Output: Strategies S and H such that a δ-filtration of $\mathbb{A}$ is returned after calling **F** with parameters $S, H, \mathbb{A}$ and δ, if such strategies exist

OPTIMAL FILTRATION PROBLEM :

Input: $\mathbb{A}$

Output: $inf\{\delta \in Q :$ there exist strategies S and H such that a δ-filtration of $\mathbb{A}$ is returned after calling **F** with parameters $S, H, \mathbb{A}$ and $\delta\}$

We cannot expect the solutions S and H for the above filtration problems to be of polynomial time complexity with respect to the size of $\mathbb{A}$ and δ , because the strategies S and H are based e.g. on procedures for decision rule generation and these procedures are based on reduct set generation [10]. Nevertheless, one can build efficient heuristics for solving the filtration problems for practical applications.

3.2 Approximation Functions for Non-Deterministic Decision Rules

In this section we show a method for generating a family of functions approximating non-deterministic decision rules.

For any decision table $\mathbb{A} = (U, A \cup \{d\})$, formula τ over A and V and a threshold k satisfying the condition $T(\mathbb{A}, \tau, k)$ we can define a τ-*approximation function in $\mathbb{A}$ with a threshold k*

$$F(\mathbb{A}, \tau, k) : INF(\mathbb{A}_\tau)|B \rightarrow INF(\{d\}, V)$$

by setting $F(\mathbb{A}, \tau, k)(\alpha) = \{(d, i_o)\}$ for any $\alpha \in INF(\mathbb{A}_\tau)|B$, where $\mu_{i_o}(\mathbb{A}, \bigwedge \alpha \wedge \tau) = max\{\mu_i(\mathbb{A}, \bigwedge \alpha \wedge \tau) : i \in \theta_\tau\}$ and B is the set of conditions from A occuring in τ.

We apply the above construction to decision tables derived from a given decision table $\mathbb{A} = (U, A \cup \{d\})$. These decision tables are of the form $\mathbb{B} = (U, B \cup \{c\})$ and they are constructed from information systems $\mathbb{B} = (U, B \cup C)$, where $B, C \subseteq A$ and $B \cap C = \emptyset$, by representing C by means of one decision attribute c. We denote by $code_C$ (or, $code$, in short) a fixed (one-to-one) coding function for information vectors, restricted to C in V_c, and define c by $c(x) = code_C(\{(a, a(x)) : a \in C\})$ for any $x \in U$. For a given threshold k we consider decision tables $\mathbb{B} = (U, B \cup \{c\})$ with the property that there exists a formula τ over B and V such that $T(\mathbb{B}, \tau, k)$ holds. These tables correspond to near-to-functional relations in data table $\mathbb{A}$ by which term we understand that only one decision is pointed out with a strength exceeding the threshold k. Observe that by assumption we have $INF(\mathbb{B}_\tau)|B = INF(\mathbb{A}_\tau)|B$.

Let l be a positive integer called the *critical level of examples*. We denote by $\mathcal{F}(\mathbb{A}, k, l)$ the family of all functions of the form $F(\mathbb{B}, \tau, k)$ such that $(T(\mathbb{B}, \tau, k)$ holds and) $\max_i n(\mathbb{B}, \tau, i) > l$. By $\mathcal{F}(\mathbb{A}, l)$ (or, $\mathcal{F}(\mathbb{A})$, in short) we denote the union of the family $\{\mathcal{F}(\mathbb{A}, k, l) : 0 < k \leq 1\}$.

Let us observe that any function $F(\mathbb{B}, \tau, k)$ produces from a decision table $\mathbb{A} = (U, A \cup \{d\})$ with $A = \{a_1, \ldots, a_m\}$ a new decision table $\mathbb{A}' = (U, A' \cup \{d\})$ with $A' = \{a_1', \ldots, a_m'\}$ defined by $\{(c, code_C\{(a_i', a_i'(x)) : a_i \in C\})\} = F(\mathbb{B}, \tau, k)(Inf_B^{\mathbb{A}}(x))$ and $a_i'(x) = a_i(x)$ when $a_i \notin C$, for any $x \in \tau_\mathbb{B}$. If $x \in U - \tau_\mathbb{B}$ then $a_i'(x) = a_i(x)$ for any i.

3.3   The Conflict Problem

Let us assume that a set $\mathcal{F}$ of approximation functions of $\mathbb{A}$ is given. Now we would like to transform rows in the decision table in parallel, i.e. by simultaneous application of functions chosen from $\mathcal{F}$ on the basis of some strategies. In this case it is necessary to solve the conflict problem due to the form of functions in $\mathcal{F}$.

Let $\mathcal{F}$ be a given set of approximation functions and let $c \in A$. Let $\mathcal{F}(c)$ be the set of all functions from $\mathcal{F}$ with counter domains equal to $INF(\{c\}, V)$. We say that $\mathcal{F}(c)$ *is conflicting in* $\mathbb{A}$ iff there exists $x \in U$ and $f, f' \in \mathcal{F}(c)$ such that

$$f(Inf_B(x)) \neq f'(Inf_{B'}(x))$$

where $f : INF(\mathbb{A}_\tau)|B \to INF(\{c\}, V)$

$\qquad f' : INF(\mathbb{A}_{\tau'})|B' \to INF(\{c\}, V)$ for some τ, τ'.

We say that $\mathcal{F}$ is *conflicting* in $\mathbb{A}$ iff $\mathcal{F}(c)$ is conflicting in $\mathbb{A}$ for some $c \in A$.

If the value set of c is ordered, then one of the possibilities to resolve the conflict caused by $\mathcal{F}(c)$ is to take a randomly chosen value from the interval $[min, max]$ as the new value of c for a given $x \in U$, where min and max are the minimum and maximum of the values of functions from $\mathcal{F}(c)$ at x. This is an analogy to morphological operations [1] which in analytical form modify geometrical objects according to min and max functions. This will be explained in Section 3.4.

Another strategy to resolve the conflict caused by $\mathcal{F}(c)$ is to define the new value of c for a given $x \in U$ as the value of an approximation function corresponding to a formula $\tau(\mathcal{F}, c)$ representing in some sense the influence of all elements of $\mathcal{F}(c)$ on c and built from some formulas defining conflicting functions from $\mathcal{F}(c)$. Such a formula can be found among disjunctions and conjunctions of formulas defining conflicting functions from $\mathcal{F}(c)$.

The main constraint in searching for a conflict resolving function

$$f : INF(\mathbb{A}_\tau)|B \to INF(\{c\}, V)$$

is the necessity to preserve:

1. the classification of objects by $\mathbb{A}$ and $\mathbb{A}'$ where $\mathbb{A}'$ is obtained from $\mathbb{A}$ by applying f, i.e. $\partial_A = \partial_{A'}$;

2. $\max_i n(\mathbb{A}, \bigwedge \alpha \wedge \tau, i) > l$ for $\alpha \in INF(\mathbb{A}_\tau)|B$, where B is the set of conditions occuring in τ and l is the critical level of examples.

3.4 Analytical Morphology

The problems of conflict resolution among approximation functions and of new approximation function generation can be approached by following some analogies with mathematical morphology [1], [7].

In the binary case of mathematical morphology [1] objects are subsets of an either Euclidean or digital space E. In order to obtain analytical formulas for morphological operations let us represent objects by binary vectors, i.e. we assume $V = \{0,1\}$. Let $A = \{a_1, \ldots, a_m\}$. The filtering of an object x is done by selecting a structuring element $b \subseteq \{1, \ldots, m\}$ and by defining basic operations of *erosion*

$$e : INF(A,V) \rightarrow INF(A,V)$$

by

$$e(\{(a_1,v_1), \ldots, (a_m,v_m)\}) = \{(a_1,v_1'), \ldots, (a_m,v_m')\}$$

where $\quad v_i' = 1$ iff $(i \oplus b) \cap \{1, \ldots, m\} \subseteq \{j : v_j = 1\}$, i.e

$$v_i' = min\{v_j : j \in i \oplus b\}.$$

and *dilation*

$$d : INF(A,V) \rightarrow INF(A,V)$$

by

$$d\{(a_1,v_1), \ldots, (a_m,v_m)\}) = \{(a_1,v_1'), \ldots, (a_m,v_m')\}$$

where $\quad v_i' = 1$ iff $i \in j \oplus b$ for some j with $v_j = 1$, i.e

$$v_i' = max\{v_j : i \in j \oplus b\}.$$

These operations can be composed, e.g. *the opening of x* is defined by $o(x) = d(e(x))$ and the *closing of x* by $c(x) = e(d(x))$. The above operations can be expressed in an analytical form:

$$o(\{(a_1,v_1), \ldots, (a_m,v_m)\}) = \{(a_1,v_1'), \ldots, (a_m,v_m')\}$$

where $v_i' = max\{min\{v_k : k \in j \oplus b\} : i \in j \oplus b\}$ and

$$c(\{(a_1,v_1), \ldots, (a_m,v_m)\}) = \{(a_1,v_1'), \ldots, (a_m,v_m')\}$$

where $v_i' = min\{max\{v_k : j \in k \oplus b\} : j \in i \oplus b\}$.

We can consider any approximation function $F(\mathbb{B}, \tau, k) : INF(\mathbb{A}_\tau)|B \rightarrow INF(\{c\}, V)$ as a partial function from $INF(A,V)$ into $INF(C,V)$ with the domain $INF(\mathbb{A}_\tau)|B$ on which the partial function coincides with $F(\mathbb{B}, \tau, k)$.

The following general idea can be derived from the above definitions. An analytical form of morphology for a family $\mathcal{F}$ consists of the sets $\mathcal{N}(C)$ and $\mathcal{M}(B)$ where

$$\mathcal{N}(C) = \{B : \exists F \in \mathcal{F}(F : INF(B,V) \rightarrow INF(C,V))\}$$

$$\mathcal{M}(B) = \{C : \exists F \in \mathcal{F}(F : INF(B,V) \rightarrow INF(C,V))\}$$

and mappings of *analytical erosion e_C and dilation d_B*:

$$e_C : \Pi\{INF(B,V) : B \in \mathcal{N}(C)\} \rightarrow INF(C,V)$$

$$d_B : \Pi\{INF(C,V) : C \in \mathcal{M}(B)\} \rightarrow INF(B,V)$$

In classical mathematical morphology mappings of erosion and dilation may be regarded as negotiations among conflicting influences of points from a neighborhood on its center (erosion) or influences of centers of neighborhoods containing a point on this point (dilation). In analytical morphology these mappings negotiate among conflicting influences of sets of conditions expressed by approximation functions from $\mathcal{F}$. In analytical morphology opening and closing operations [6] can also be defined. Analytical morphology gives some tools for data filtration in case of data without an a priori knowledge of their inherent structure.

3.5 Searching for Classifiers in the Set of Functions Approximating Decision Rules

The search for new features (classifiers) [2],[3],[9] which yield a better classification of objects or help to express laws encoded in experimental data is one of the main goals of knowledge discovery [8] and machine learning [2],[3]. In this section we present a searching method for new classifiers. The method is based on an application of approximation functions introduced above.

We have applied approximation functions for data filtration in decision tables. It can be observed that these functions can also be applied to searching for new classifiers (features). Below we describe the main idea related to this application of approximation functions.

We want to search for approximation functions of the form

$$F : INF(\mathbb{A}_\tau)|B \rightarrow INF(C,V)$$

with the following property: if $F(u) = v$, where u and v are pieces of information about a classified object, then there is strong evidence (measured by threshold k) that the object belongs to a distinguished set of decision classes. If it is possible to discover this kind of approximation function, then we can add as to the decision table a new condition (feature, classifier) i.e. the binary attribute a_F defined by

$$a_F(x) = 1 \ \text{ iff } \ F(\{(a,a(x)) : a \in B\}) = \{(a,a(x)) : a \in C\}.$$

By discovering several classifiers of the above form which distinguish a particular set of decision classes with sufficiently large evidence (related to the value of the threshold k) we expect to get an efficient classification mechanism.

The proposed method for searching for new classifiers based on discovery of approximation functions, can be implemented as procedure for automatic generation of new classifiers based on approximation functions.

Conclusions

Two presented above methods, namely

(i) data filtration based on near-to-functional relations among data;

(ii) searching for new classifiers in the set of functions approximating the above-mentioned near-to-functional relations;

seem to have some special value in the process of law extraction from experimental data. We are working on implementation of these methods. Initial tests on implemented methods support our claim.

Acknowledgments. The author would like to thank dr Lech Polkowski for his valuable remarks and joint work on the part of the paper related to analytical morphology.

References

[1] Giardina, C.R. and Dougherty, E.R.: Morphological methods in image and signal processing, Prentice-Hall 1988.

[2] Kodratoff, Y. and Michalski, R.: Machine Learning. An Artificial Intelligence Approach, vol.3, Morgan Kaufmann 1990.

[3] [3] Michalski, R., Carbonell, J.C., and Mitchell, T.M. : Machine Learning. An Artificial Intelligence Approach, vol.1, Tioga Pub. Comp., Palo Alto 1983, vol.2, Morgan Kaufmann 1986.

[4] Pawlak, Z.: Theoretical Aspects of Reasoning about Data, Kluwer 1991.

[5] Pawlak, Z. and Skowron, A.: A rough set approach to decision rules generation, Warsaw University of Technology, ICS Research Report 23/93, Proc. of the IJCAI'93 Workshop: The Management of Uncertainty in AI, Chambery Savoie, France 1993.

[6] Polkowski, L and Skowron, A.: Analytical morphology: Morphology for decision tables, Warsaw University of Technology, ICS Research Report 41/93.

[7] Serra, J.: Image Analysis and Mathematical Morphology, Academic Press 1982.

[8] Shrager, J. and Langley, P. (eds.) : Computational Models of Scientific Discovery and Theory Formation, Morgan Kaufmann 1990.

[9] Skowron, A. and Stepaniuk, J.: Searching for classifiers, Proc. First World Conference on the Fundamentals of Artificial Intelligence, 1-5 July 1991, Paris, Angkor, eds. M. de Glas, D.Gabbay, 447-460

[10] Skowron, A. and Rauszer, C.: The Discernibility Matrices and Functions in Information Systems, in: Intelligent Decision Support - Handbook of Applications and Advances of the Rough Sets Theory, ed. R.Slowinski, Kluwer 1992, 331-362.

[11] Skowron, A.: Boolean Reasoning for Decision Rules Generation, Proc. of the 7th International Symposium, ISMIS'93, Trondheim, Norway, June 1993, Lecture Notes in Artificial Intelligence vol.689, Springer-Verlag 1993, 295-305.

[12] Skowron, A.: A synthesis of decision rules: Applications of discernibility matrix properties, Proc. of the Workshop Intelligent Information Systems, Augustów (Poland), 7-11 June, 1993.

[13] Slowiński, R.(ed.): Intelligent Decision Support: Handbook of Applications and Advances of the Rough Sets Theory, Kluwer 1992.

[14] Storer, J.A.: Data Compression: Methods and Theory, Computer Science Press 1988.

[15] Yamada, H., Yamamoto, K. and Hosokawa, K.: Directional mathematical morphology and reformalized Hough transformation for the analysis of topographic maps, IEEE Transactions on Patern Analysis and Machine Intelligence 15(4), 1993, 380-387.

Automated Discovery of Empirical Laws in a Science Laboratory

Jan M. Żytkow

Computer Science Department
Wichita State University
Wichita, KS 67260-0083

zytkow@wise.cs.twsu.edu

1 Main Directions of Machine Discovery

Machine discoverers can be briefly defined as computer systems that autonomously pursue knowledge. The research in machine discovery has been growing in two main directions: (1) automated scientific discovery and (2) knowledge discovery in databases. The latter is focused on data which are fixed, prearranged and typically sparse. Because data available in databases are different from data which can be obtained by an experimental scientist, both the search techniques and the results of knowledge discovery in databases differ from those of automated scientific discovery. Results in knowledge discovery in databases have been described in several collections of papers, typically conference proceedings, edited by Piatetsky-Shapiro (1991, 1993), Piatetsky-Shapiro & Frawley (1991), Zytkow (1992), Ras (1993), Ziarko (1993), and many other papers.

Automated scientific discovery is concerned with reconstruction of discovery mechanisms in natural sciences such as physics, chemistry and biology. It is also concerned with the construction of new discovery mechanisms. Many of the recent results can be found in collections edited by Shrager & Langley (1990), Edwards (1993) and Zytkow (1992, 1993). This research can be further split into discovery of empirical laws and discovery of hidden structure.

In this paper we will focus on automated discovery of empirical laws by a system which includes a robotic component so that it can empirically investigate the real world to develop theories. In preparation, we will briefly discuss insights coming from different disciplines, we will clarify the notion of discoverer's autonomy and argue that empirical laws are the most fundamental form of knowledge.

2 Knowledge Discovery Research Communities

Machine discovery benefits from methods developed in various domains. In this section we will briefly describe both contributions and limitations of these communities, contrasting them with machine discovery.

2.1 Machine Learning

Research in machine learning concentrates on concept learning in inductive
and analytical contexts. The results are concept definitions expressed as rules,
decision trees, clusters, and recently by concept lattices. Machine learning
contributed many methods for concept learning, innovative evaluation methods and experience in empirical comparisons of various methods for concept
learning. The main weaknesses are limited focus, user dependence, and overde-
pendence on a small number of fixed data, which sometimes borders on data
worshipping.

2.2 Rough Sets

Here the focus and results are similar to machine learning. The major strengths
are treatment of vague data and a theoretically innovative and practically useful model of data in terms of upper and lower closures, complementing the
notions of error and fuzziness. The main weakness is limited focus on knowledge expressed by concepts defined by rules and trees. A major progress will
be achieved when the rough approach will be generalized to relational and
numerical terms.

2.3 Databases

Data mining and data dredging are terms coming from database community.
They describe a limited search for knowledge, dependent on the interaction with
the user, and limited in scope. The use of database management techniques and
experience with large datasets are the major strengths, while the main weakness
is lack of large scale search and little statistics applied in the evaluation.

2.4 Statistics

Statistics offers a wealth of data analysis methods and well developed theories
for the evaluation of results. The main forms of knowledge are equations,
contingency tables, correlations, histograms, and the like. The strength lies in
a broad scope of available inferences of knowledge of many types, and practically
useful treatment of error. The weaknesses include concentration on individual
pieces of knowledge and on single steps in the statistical inference process,
neglect of hypothesis generation and of large scale search for knowledge, and
lack of representation of large bodies of knowledge.

2.5 Machine Discovery

In contrast, machine discovery offers combination of many discovery steps, automated search over large hypotheses spaces, and representation of larger bodies
of knowledge by knowledge networks. The major weakness is that the results
are still spread thin over a large research area, so that practical applications
are limited.

3 Autonomy of Discoverer

Throughout history, human discoverers did not rely on external authority while making their discoveries, or else they would not be discoverers. They sought new knowledge by applying their own choices of discovery techniques and evaluation criteria. The long term goal of machine discovery is to reach similar cognitive autonomy in computer agents.

After many years of research on machine learning, it becomes clear that to efficiently acquire knowledge, an agent must be far more active and autonomous than our current learning systems. A good learner must have a broad understanding of what is knowledge. It must also know how to link new piece of knowledge to the knowledge already possessed. Such links are typically missing in the instruction. These skills are developed in the field of machine discovery, through systems which link together many cognitive tasks.

Through our machine learning and discovery research we are coming to an appreciation of the autonomous absorption of knowledge by a good learner. Human learners need surprisingly little instruction. It becomes increasingly reasonable to claim that good learners are discoverers; hence understanding the discovery process is fundamental for understanding learning. There must be profound reasons why we are discoverers. Certainly we were discoverers before we became learners. Otherwise we would not discover the meaning of the pointing gesture by which, as infants, we are taught the meaning of our first words. Most of our early knowledge must be discovered rather than learned. Discovery must be even more dominant in animals, which lack two basic carriers of learning: language and culture.

To be useful in our research on computer made discoveries, the notion of autonomy requires clarification. Suppose that agent A discovers piece of knowledge K which is already known to others, as is often the case with our machine discoverers. Agent A can still be considered a discoverer of K, if A did not know K earlier and if A not only proposed K, but also demonstrated that K is true. did not get hints about K from external authorities. Since all details of the software are available for inspection, it is relatively easy to trace the external guidance received by a machine discoverer. It is true that existing machine discoverers lack autonomy in many ways. They would not reach success in making discoveries if we humans did not provide help by setting system parameters, selecting search strategies, preparing input data, and providing them with empirical setup with which to experiment. These breaches in autonomy do not disqualify machine discoverers, however, because they are also characteristic of even the greatest human discoverers, who use mainly the existing methods and make only small steps beyond their inherited background of knowledge and method.

An agent becomes more autonomous as it is able to make more choices, satisfy more values and investigate a broader range of goals. Overcoming each of the individual limitations is a big challenge for machine discovery. The mere accumulation of solutions in the form of new system components, however, does not suffice. The components must be strongly integrated, so that many discovery steps can be performed in succession without external intervention, leading to even greater autonomy. The accumulation of discovery steps and the use of feedback between them become an even bigger challenge. But it provides motivation and opportunity for asking the right research questions that will stimulate the growth of autonomy. It also creates the perspective necessary for the reconstruction of the scientific evaluation. A single cognitive step rarely permits a sound judgment about the results. A combination of steps provides more informed reasons for acceptance.

4 Knowledge in Concepts and Regularities

The relationships between different forms of knowledge have not received sufficient consideration. Before we concentrate on discovery of empirical laws, we would like to explain why we pay less attention to discovery of concepts and concept hierarchies (taxonomies), which is the dominant focus of research in machine learning. Let us consider differences between concepts, taxonomies, and regularities (law-like knowledge) in the context of discovery from data matrices (also called relational tables in databases, and collections of examples in the machine learning research) which have been used for a long time by many research communities to seek different kinds of knowledge. We argue that concepts and taxonomies are a limited form of knowledge, compared to regularities.

4.1 Concept Learning and Concept Discovery

In technical terms of logic, concepts are predicates which include free variables. Concepts are neither true nor false. They name objects, properties or patterns, but they are not statements. Truth values can be assigned to statements, which use concepts and which have all variables bound by quantifiers, either in explicit or implicit way. Statements are claims about the world. With the exception of tautologies, true and universally quantified statements are typically called laws or regularities.

A proven model of concept discovery comes from science. Among an unlimited number of concepts that can be proposed, science uses a very limited number, choosing them based on the generality, utility, and accuracy of laws in which they occur. Concepts can be viewed as investments which produce payoff when they allow us to express regularities and laws. Better investments, that is, better concepts are recognized by more knowledge and knowledge of greater generality that they permit to express. Concept discovery in science is justified by feedback from knowledge. In machine discovery we also use the same feedback (Langley, Simon, Bradshaw, & Zytkow, 1987; Nordhausen & Langley, 1993; Shen, 1993; Zytkow 1991), which is notably weak in machine learning.

Concept learning from examples can be viewed as a very limited discovery of regularities. The learner seeks the best definition of the target class in terms of other attributes. Such a definition has a truth value. If true, it shares many features of regularities, for instance, it can be used to predict class membership. The target class, however, is externally defined and a learner searches only for a class definition. In contrast, a discoverer can propose various target attributes, and search for regularities for each. A discoverer will see more value in the target concept when it occurs in many regularities, especially when they are more general. While a learner may not understand the reasons for a concept's worth, a discoverer should, because the focus on regularities gives it a good foundation for the autonomous judgement of concepts.

4.2 Clustering and Taxonomy Formation as Limited Discovery

Clustering is a step towards autonomy in concept learning. Here the task is more open, aimed at autonomous creation of classes. Given a data matrix, clustering seeks to divide all records into classes and to find a description of each class. When the cluster generation is guided by predictivity of clusters (Fisher, 1987), the resultant cluster hierarchies may demonstrate predictive power. This occurs when regularities are present in the data. In addition to knowledge that is contained in concept definitions, additional knowledge is implicit in a cluster hierarchy when it is exhaustive and disjoint. However, knowledge included in a taxonomy falls into the category of monadic logic; membership criterion for each class is represented by a one place predicate, while relations between descriptors for each class and between classes is represented by equivalences and implications between such predicates. Knowledge represented by monadic predicates is, of course, very limited.

4.3 Regularities and Clusters

Regularities are poorly represented by clusters. For instance, a simple proportionality between attributes x and y must be approximated by many clusters, while a simple equation $y = ax$ is more appropriate. The same criticism applies also to discrete numerical data and to non-numerical data. In contradistinction to clustering, the main goal of many discovery systems is to find regularities in the data. In those systems, new concept construction has only a limited, instrumental role in the search for regularities. A regularity does not separate existing objects into classes, but it specifies a pattern obeyed by all objects, distinguishing events that are possible from impossible. Regularities are poorly represented by clusters. To reach satisfactory predictivity, many classes may be needed, even when all data follow one pattern. So even if clustering is a limited form of discovery, the global regularities as such are overlooked, while their combinations are captured locally by clusters.

In conclusion, regularities (laws) are the basic form of knowledge and must be the primary target of discovery. Other forms of knowledge such as concepts and concept hierarchies are justified by laws and can be inferred from them, but not the other way.

5 Anatomy of Discoverer

The goal of modern empirical sciences, such as physics and chemistry, is to develop theories of elementary interactions in the world, and mechanisms to combine those simple interactions to models of complex physical systems. In modern science, the path to serious discovery leads through many steps. We will now present the emerging theoretical framework for machine discovery, focused on reconstruction of the empirical scientific method. Given the limited space, we will keep our presentation at the level of the main goals.

Long experience of machine discovery leads to a vision of an automated discoverer that consist of a few basic building blocks: (1) empirical semantics, (2) experimentation strategies, (3) theory formation from data, (4) recognition of the unknown on which to focus further research, (5) identification of similar patterns (needed before theory formation), (6) theory decomposition into knowledge about elementary interactions.

Different combinations of these blocks have been explored in systems such as LIVE (Shen, 1993), DIDO (Scott & Markovitch, 1993), and FAHRENHEIT (Zytkow & Zhu, 1991). Induction, which has been often considered the key element of discovery, is a part of (3), as one of many skills needed in the process. Many elements of the scientific discovery method are still missing. Empirical inquiry requires experimentation on physical systems. In machine discovery little has been done to understand the design of experiment setup. Rajamoney (1993) considered situations in which two competing theories $T1$ and $T2$ cannot be distinguished by experiments on a particular physical setup S. His system redesigns S to permit crucial experiments that distinguish between $T1$ and $T2$. Other empirical discovery systems, however, take an experiment setup as a given.

Notoriously underdeveloped is reasoning about theories including relationships among theories and theory transformations. Although model construction has been extensively studied in artificial intelligence, hardly anything useful has been done on scientific model construction.

5.1 Empirical Semantics

Empirical discoverers make experiments by the combined application of manipulators and sensors. Examples of manipulators are hand, gripper, buret, or heater. Examples of sensors are eye, camera, balance, or thermometer. Manipulators and sensors are applied to the experiment setup, creating states desired by the scientist and watching the natural responses of the setup.

Software necessary for real-world experiments includes device drivers, that is programs which control the available sensors and manipulators. But meaningful to the discovery process are not individual operations of device drivers, but their combinations, prescribed by operational definitions of scientific concepts (Bridgman, 1927; Carnap, 1936; Zytkow, 1982). Operational definitions are algorithms expressed in terms of elementary actions of sensors and manipulators, by which scientifically meaningful magnitudes are set or measured. A typical operational definition uses many actions by manipulators and many readings of sensors. To yield accurate and repeatable results, each operational definition must be adjusted to the details of the investigated empirical setup (Zytkow, Zhu & Zembowicz, 1992). Shen's (1993) definitions of intrinsic properties also combine statements about sensors and manipulators.

5.2 Empirical Theory Formation Task

After devices are linked to an empirical setup S, and operational procedures are developed to produce accurate and repeatable results, we can abstract from empirical semantics, and represent S by a multi-dimensional space $\mathcal{E}$, defined as a Cartesian product of possible values of all parameters that can be controlled or measured in S. Experiments are the only way for obtaining information about $\mathcal{E}$, through data which they generate, representable in $\mathcal{E}$.

The discovery task in $\mathcal{E}$ is to generate as complete and adequate a theory of $\mathcal{E}$ as possible, including regularities between control variables and dependent variables, and boundary conditions for each regularity. The theory should be empirically as adequate as possible, preferably within empirical error. The task can also include detection of patterns in the dependent variables, such as maxima and discontinuities, and regularities for parameters of those patterns.

5.3 Experimentation Strategies

An autonomous explorer must assume control over the values of all independent variables in $\mathcal{E}$ and can measure the physical response in terms of values of dependent variables. Each experiment consists of selecting a set of values for all independent variables, and in collecting the values of all dependent variables.

Experiments are typically organized in sequences, different for goals such as induction of empirical equations, verification, or detection of the scope of applications of a given equation (Langley et.al. 1987; Kulkarni & Simon, 1987; Koehn & Zytkow, 1986). Shen (1993) considers another experimentation strategy, driven by the need for pieces of knowledge required in problem solving. In BACON and FAHRENHEIT, generalization requires recursively organized sequences of experiments.

5.4 Theory Formation Mechanism

We will now consider formation of a complete empirical theory of a multi-dimensional space $\mathcal{E}$. The tasks involved in this process include discovery of regularities and other patterns in two variables, identification of similar patterns in preparation for their generalization, recursive generalization of patterns to further dimensions, discovery of regularity boundaries, data partitioning in preparation for discovery of regularities in each partition, and recognition of areas in which patterns have not been found. We will now discuss each of these tasks and their combinations.

Finding the regularities between one control variable and one dependent variable is an important scientific goal, and a subgoal to many others. Such regularities, typically empirical equations, have been used in discovery systems by Gerwin (1974), Langley et al. (1987), Falkenhainer & Michalski (1986), Nordhausen & Langley (1990a), Kokar (1986), Wu & Wang (1989), Wong (1991), Zembowicz & Zytkow (1992), Moulet (1992,1992a), Schaffer (1993), Dzeroski & Todorovski (1993), Cheng & Simon (1992), and others.

Quantitative discovery systems traditionally focused on regularities in the form of equations, whereas scientists are often interested in other patterns, such as maxima, minima, discontinuities, and the like. The maxima can, for instance, indicate various chemical species, whereby maximum location indicates the type of ion, while the maximum height indicates the concentration (Zytkow, Zhu, & Hussam, 1990). Discontinuities may indicate phase changes, leading to the boundary conditions on regularities. Zytkow & Zhu (1991) show how different types of patterns can be represented by similar frame structures and generalized recursively by a common mechanism.

When an equation Q has been found for a sequence of data, new goals are to find the limits of Q's application and to generalize Q to another control variable. When the former goal is successful, that is, when the boundaries for application of Q have been found, this leads to the goals of finding regularities beyond the boundaries, which are goals of the same type as finding the first regularity. Generalization, in turn, is typically conducted by recursively invoking the goals of data collection and equation fitting (Langley et al, 1987; Nordhausen & Langley, 1990, 1993; Koehn & Zytkow, 1986).

If an equation which fits the data cannot be found, the data can be decomposed into smaller fragments and the equation finding goal can be invoked for each fragment separately. Useful data partitioning can be accomplished by detection of maxima, minima, discontinuities, and other special points detected in the data (Falkenhainer & Michalski, 1986; Rao & Lu, 1992; Zytkow et al. 1990, 1992). If no regularity can be found, a data set can be treated as a regularity in the form of a lookup table used for interpolation.

5.5 Identification of Similar Patterns

When patterns are generalized, it is important to put together those patterns which have the same meaning. They are typically more similar than patterns with different meaning. Grouping the corresponding patterns is a precondition for search for meaningful regularities among them (Zytkow, Zhu & Hussam, 1990).

5.6 Recognition of Unknown

Discoverers always seek the unknown. They examine the world around them, and ask: what are the boundaries that separate the known from the unknown? Then they cross the boundaries to explore the new areas beyond them. Machine discoverers can use the same strategy (Scott & Markovitch, 1993; Shen, 1993; Zytkow & Zhu, 1993).

Discovery goals correspond to the limitations of knowledge, typically to areas in $\mathcal{E}$ which have not been explored, the boundaries which have not been found, generalizations which have not been made, and the like. Not every knowledge representation mechanism makes it easy to find the unknown. Increasingly, discovery systems use graphs to represent relationships between the incrementally discovered pieces of knowledge, and they use frame-like structures to represent knowledge contained in individual nodes in the graphs (Scott & Markovitch, 1993; Nordhausen & Langley, 1990, 1993). A knowledge graph can model the topology of laws and their boundaries in the space $\mathcal{E}$ (Zytkow & Zhu, 1991, 1993).

The graph which represents the current state of knowledge can be examined at any given time to find its limitations, which then become new goals for future discovery. We can call this approach a knowledge-driven goal generation. Each state of knowledge can be transcended in different directions, so that the goal generator typically creates many goals and should be followed by the goal selector.

A big advantage of our knowledge representation lies in separating knowledge, goals and discovery methods from each other. The mechanisms for goal generation, selection of the next goal, and selection of the method to approach the goal, can be independent. Other discoverers, using the same knowledge graph, can select different goals and apply new methods. This creates a situation similar to real science, making machine discoverers more flexible and improving the efficiency of their exploration.

5.7 Discovery of Elementary Interactions

Thus far we have concentrated on the goal of finding a network of empirical equations to describe the space of many empirical variables over a fixed physical system. The next important goal, leads from the equations to elementary interactions that occur in the investigated system. Scientists interpret the equations so that their component terms obtain physical meaning, for instance the momentum or kinetic energy of each individual object in the physical system. Equation transformations leading to such interpretations form a search space explored by Zytkow (1990).

6 Conclusion

In the last decade, machine discovery developed into advanced research area. We outlined the most developed, implemented and tested elements of the search for empirical laws, and we described their combinations. Limited space permitted only a sketchy presentation. Details are available in the references.

We cannot claim finality of any solutions. Each of the elements of the scientific method will require extensive refinements. We can expect perennial problems with real data. Nevertheless, further development of machine discovery will not only help us to understand science but also will provide tools which will be very useful to empirical scientists.

References

Bridgman, P.W. 1927. The Logic of Modern Physics.

Carnap, R. 1936. Testability and Meaning, Philosophy of Science, Vol.3.

Cheng, P.C. & Simon, H.A. 1992. The Right Representation for Discovery: Finding the Conservation of Momentum. in: Sleeman & Edwards eds. Proc. of Ninth Intern. Conference on Machine Learning, 62-71.

Dzeroski, S. & Todorovski, L. 1993. Discovering Dynamics, Proc. of 10th International Conference on Machine Learning, 97-103

Edwards, P. ed. 1993. Working Notes MLNet Workshop on Machine Discovery. Blanes, Spain, Sep.23.

Falkenhainer, B.C. & Michalski, R.S. 1986. Integrating quantitative and qualitative discovery: The ABACUS system. Machine Learning, Vol.1, 367-401.

Gerwin, D.G. 1974. Information processing, data inferences, and scientific generalization, Behav.Sci. 19, 314-325.

Gordon, A. 1992. Informal Qualitative Models in Scientific Discovery. in: Żytkow J. ed. Proc. of ML-92 Workshop on Machine Discovery, Aberdeen, UK, July 4, 98-102.

Karp, P. 1990. Hypothesis Formation as Design. in: J.Shrager & P. Langley eds. Computational Models of Scientific Discovery and Theory Formation, Morgan Kaufmann Publishers, San Mateo, CA, 275-317.

Koehn, B. & Żytkow, J.M. 1986. Experimenting and Theorizing in Theory Formation. in: Ras Z. & Zemankova M. eds. Proc. of the International Symposium on Methodologies for Intelligent Systems. ACM SIGART Press, 296-307.

Kokar, M.M. 1986. Determining Arguments of Invariant Functional Descriptions, Machine Learning, 1, 403-422.

Kulkarni, D., & Simon, H.A. 1987. The Processes of Scientific Discovery: The Strategy of Experimentation, Cognitive Science, 12, 139-175.

Langley, P., Simon, H.A., Bradshaw, G.L. & Żytkow, J.M. 1987. Scientific Discovery: Computational Explorations of the Creative Processes. Cambridge, MA: The MIT Press.

Metaxas, S. 1993. The Prediction of Physical Properties with CRITON. In: Edwards P. ed. Working Notes, MLnet Workshop on Machine Discovery, Blanes, Spain Sep.23, 61-65.

Moulet, M. 1992. A symbolic algorithm for computing coefficients' accuracy in regression, in: Sleeman D. & Edwards P. eds. Proc. of Ninth Intern. Conference on Machine Learning.

Moulet, M. 1992a. ARC.2: Linear Regression In ABACUS, in: Żytkow J. ed. Proc. of ML-92 Workshop on Machine Discovery, Aberdeen, UK, July 4, 137-146.

Nordhausen, B., & Langley, P. 1990. An Integrated Approach to Empirical Discovery. in: J.Shrager & P. Langley eds. Computational Models of Scientific Discovery and Theory Formation. Morgan Kaufmann Publishers, San Mateo, CA. 97-128.

Nordhausen, B., & Langley, P. 1990a. A Robust Approach to Numeric Discovery, Proc. of Seventh International Conference on Machine Learning, Palo Alto, CA: Morgan Kaufmann. 411-418.

Nordhausen, B. & Langley, P. 1993. An Integrated Framework for Empirical Discovery, Machine Learning, 12, 17-47.

Piatetsky-Shapiro, G. ed. 1991. Proc. of AAAI-93 Workshop on Knowledge Discovery in Databases.

Piatetsky-Shapiro, G. ed. 1993. Proc. of AAAI-93 Workshop on Knowledge Discovery in Databases.

Piatetsky-Shapiro, G. & Frawley, W. eds. 1991. Knowledge Discovery in Databases, The AAAI Press, Menlo Park, CA.

Rajamoney, S.A. 1993. The Design of Discrimination Experiments. Machine Learning, 12, 185-203.

Rao, R.B. & Lu S.C. 1992. Learning Engineering Models with the Minimum Description Length Principle, Proc. of Tenth National Conference on Artificial Intelligence, 717-722.

Ras, Z. ed. 1993. Journal for Intelligent Information Systems, Vol.2.

Schaffer, C. 1993 Bivariate Scientific Function Finding in a Sampled, Real-Data Testbed. Machine Learning, 12, 167-183.

Scott, P.D & Markovitch, S. 1993. Experience Selection and Problem Choice in an Exploratory Learning System. Machine Learning 12, 49-68.

Shen, W. 1993. Discovery as Autonomous Learning from the Environment. Machine Learning, 12, 143-165.

Shrager, J., & Langley, P. eds. 1990. Computational Models of Scientific Discovery and Theory Formation, Morgan Kaufmann Publishers, San Mateo, CA.

Sleeman, D.H., Stacey, M.K., Edwards, P., & Gray, N.A.B. 1989. An Architecture for Theory-Driven Scientific Discovery, in: Morik K. ed. Proc. of 4th European Working Session on Learning, 11-23.

Wong, P. 1991. Machine Discovery of Function Forms, PhD dissertation, Univ. of Waterloo.

Wu, Y. & Wang, S. 1989. Discovering Knowledge from Observational Data, in: Piatetsky-Shapiro, G. ed. Knowledge Discovery in Databases, Proc. of IJCAI-89 Workshop, Detroit, MI, 369-377.

Zembowicz R. & Żytkow, J.M. 1992. Discovery of Equations: Experimental Evaluation of Convergence. Proc. of 10th National Conference on Artificial Intelligence, The AAAI Press, 70-75.

Ziarko, W. ed. 1993. Proc. of the Intern. Workshop on Rough Sets and Knowledge Discovery, Banff, Oct.12-15.

Żytkow, J.M. 1982. An Interpretation of a Concept in Science by a Set of Operational Procedures, in: Krajewski, W. ed. Polish Essays in the Philosophy of the Natural Sciences, D. Reidel Publishing Company, 169-185.

Żytkow, J.M. 1990. Deriving Basic Laws by Analysis of Processes and Equations, in: Langley, P., & Shrager J. eds. Computational Models of Scientific Discovery and Theory Formation, Morgan Kaufmann, San Mateo:CA, 129-156.

Żytkow J.M. ed. 1992. Proc. of ML-92 Workshop on Machine Discovery, Aberdeen, UK, July 4.

Żytkow, J.M. ed. 1993. Machine Learning, 12.

Żytkow, J.M., Zhu, J. 1991. Automated Empirical Discovery in a Numerical Space, in: Proc. of Third Annual Chinese Machine Learning Workshop, July 15-19, Harbin Institute of Technology, 1-11.

Żytkow, J.M. & Zhu, J. 1993. Experimentation Guided by a Knowledge Graph, in: Shen W. ed. Proc. of AAAI-93 Workshop on Learning Action Models, 23-27.

Żytkow, J.M., Zhu, J. & Hussam, A. 1990. Automated Discovery in a Chemistry Laboratory, Proc. of AAAI-90, AAAI Press, 889-894.

Żytkow, J.M., Zhu, J., & Zembowicz, R. 1992. Operational Definition Refinement: A Discovery Process, Proc. of 10th National Conference on Artificial Intelligence, AAAI Press, 76-81.

Hard and Soft Sets

Zdzislaw Pawlak

Institute of Computer Science

Warsaw University of Technology

ul. Nowowiejska 15/19, 00 665 Warsaw, Poland

Motto: "Apart from the known and the unknown, what else is there?"
Harold Pinter in The Homecoming

In this paper I would like to make some remarks on the concept of a set in the context of some recent developments concerning vagueness, imprecision and uncertainty.

It is well know that the concept of a set in the Cantor's setting has several disadvantages. The most important ones are antinomies. Besides, Cantor's approach is not taking into account neither the *uncertainty* of being an element of a given set nor the *multiplicities* of elements.

One of the most discussed and attracting attention of logicians and philosophers questions is the problem of antinomies. The antinomies problem is connected with the concept of the "set of all sets", which is inherently embedded in the Cantor's concept of a infinite set. There are at least two well known solutions to this problem, the axiomatic set theory of Zermelo and Fraenkel and the class theory of Whithead and Russell. It is worthwhile to mention in this context the mereology developed by Lesniewski and the alternative set theory created by Vopenka, both meant as escapes from the Cantor's set theory. I will refrain from the discussion of these problems here since there are rather of philosophical than practical significance.

The two remaining problems, i.e. multiplicity and uncertainty of elements, concern not only infinite but also finite sets. They have not been studied very extensively by mathematicians since they are not of essential significance to mathematical problems tackled by the set theory, and are addressed rather by researches wrestling with applications. We are going to give some remarks on these problems here, for they are of greatest importance to many applications, in particular in Artificial Intelligence. Both, the uncertainty and the multiplicity problems refer to *membership* of elements in *multiset* and *fuzzy set* theory, respectively.

In Cantor's theory, set is defined uniquely by its elements, i.e. in order to define a set we have to point out its elements. In other words, any element of the universe is either in or outside the set under consideration, i.e. the membership function of the set can assume exactly one of two values 0 or 1, for non-member and member of the set respectively.

Many applications require multisets. In a multiset, i.e. set having multiple elements, elements may occur more then once. This is, however, not allowed in the "ordinary" set theory. For example the collection of elements $\{1, 1, 1, 2, 2, 3, 4, 4\}$ is not a set according to Cantor's set theory, since every element in this theory may occur in the set only once. Consequently the membership (characteristic) function of a multiset assumes non negative integer values.

Another aspect of membership problem was considered by Zadeh[11], who proposed that the characteristic function may assume values from the closed interval $[0, 1]$, thus introducing partial membership of elements in the set. In this setting, an element may belong in the set upto a certain degree, which is supposed to capture our uncertainty about its membership. This is, of course again in contradiction with the Cantor's set theory, which requires full membership.

Both, the multiset and fuzzy set theory were recently axiomatized in an elegant, unified way by Blizard[1].

Let us note that both membership problems address various questions. The multi-membership concerns multiplicities of elements in a set, whereas fuzzy-membership refers to the uncertainty of being a member of the set.

The membership problem can be generally formulated by defining for each kind of sets proper membership function $\mu_{(X)}(x)$. For the classical sets the range of the membership function is the set $\{0, 1\}$; for fuzzy sets the range is the closed interval $[0,1]$, and for the multisets the range is the set of nonnegative integers $\{0, 1, 2, \ldots\}$.

One can also consider sets with characteristic function having the range $[0, +\infty)$, i.e. all nonnegative reals. This kind of sets, considered by Blizard cf. [2] may be called *multi-fuzzy sets*. We can give the following interpretation of this kind of membership function: the integer part $E(\mu_X(x))$ of $\mu_X(x)$ denotes the multiplicity of x in X, whereas $\mu_X(x) - E(\mu_X(x))$ means the value of fuzzy membership of x, e.g. $\mu_X(x) = 2.3$ means that there are two elements x in the set X, belonging to X in the degree 0.3.

Some authors considered multisets with negative multiplicity[3], which leads to membership function with integers as its range. Let us call this kind of sets Blizard's sets. A motivation for negative membership can be the following[9]. Suppose there are n experts who vote, whether an element x belongs to the set X, or not. One can define a membership function, which represents result of voting, as shown below:

$$\mu_X(x) = \sum_{i=1}^{n} \mu_X^i(x)/n,$$

where $\mu_X^i(x) \in \{-1, +1\}$

meaning that if $\mu_X^i(x) = -1$, then x does not belong to X according to expert i and if $\mu_X^i(x) = +1$, then x does belong to X according to expert i. Obviously

$-1 \leq \mu_X(x) \leq 1.$

Finally, from the formal point of view it seems natural to consider quite general concept of a set for which the whole real axis $(-\infty, +\infty)$ can be assumed to be the range of the membership function.

The above considerations can be summarized as follows:

i) $\mu_X(x) \in \{0, 1\}$ - Cantor's sets

ii) $\mu_X(x) \in [0, 1]$ - fuzzy sets

iii) $\mu_X(x) \in \{0, 1, 2, \ldots\}$ - multisets

iv) $\mu_X(x) \in [0, +\infty)$ - multi-fuzzy sets

v) $\mu_X(x) \in Z$ - Blizard's sets

vi) $\mu_X(x) \in (-\infty, +\infty)$ - general sets,

where Z denotes the set of integers.

The above discussed concepts of a set share the two following features. Firstly, the membership is the primitive notion of each set theory and secondly, the union and intersection of sets are defined for each kind of the above considered sets by max and min operations on constituent sets, respectively.

Note that in all the above described extensions of Cantor's set theory, in order to express the degree of membership, the existence of integers or real numbers is required before the concept of a set can be defined. This is obviously not the case for Cantor's sets, where the concept of a set is prior to the concept of numbers.

Another philosophy of defining sets is offered by the rough set theory[6,7] where both of the above mentioned features are not valid. Membership is not the primitive concept for rough sets. Besides, the memberships for union and intersection of sets cannot be defined by max and min operations on constituents sets, respectively.

The starting point of the rough set theory is the assumption that we have initially some information (knowledge) about elements of the universe, which is not the case in the above discussed concepts of a set. In other words, in the proposed approach we "see" elements of the universe in the context of the available information about them, in contrast to the previously discussed approaches, where elements of the universe are purely abstract objects, and any information about them is not necessary. As a consequence, two different elements can be indiscernible in the context of the information about them, and "seen" as the same. This view is motivated not by philosophical considerations, but by practical requirements.

In order to express the above ideas more precisely, let us give some formal definitions. Information about $x \in U$ is a function $I : U- > 2^U$, such that $x \in I(x)$ for every $x \in U$. We will say that every element $y \in I(x)$ is *indiscernible* from x with respect to the information I. The introduced definition is intended to capture the fact that if we "see" elements of the universe through the information about them then some elements may be "seen" as identical. This leads to the following membership function definition, which is the basis for the rough set theory:

$$\mu_X^I(x) = card(X \cap I(x)/cardI(x).$$

Obviously

$$\mu_X^I(x) \in [0, 1].$$

The above assumed membership function, is used to define two basic operations on sets, which are shown below

$$\underline{I}(X) = \{x \in U : \mu_X^I(x) = 1\},$$

$$\overline{I}(X) = \{x \in U : \mu_X^I(x) > 0\},$$

and called *the I-lower* and *the I-upper approximation* of a X, respectively.

This is to mean that if we "see" the set X through the information I, only the above approximations of X can be "observed". The difference between the upper and the lower approximation, called the *boundary region* of the set, expresses how exactly we "see" the set X through the information I. If the boundary region is the empty set, X can be defined exactly using the information I, and in the opposite case the set X can be defined *roughly (approximately)* only - employing the information I. The former sets are *crisp (exact)*, whereas the later - are *rough (inexact)*, with respect to information I. Consequently, the definition of a set is related to our information (knowledge) about elements of the universe. Moreover, information about elements is the primitive concept necessary to define a set, but not the membership, as in the previous cases. Thus this approach is rather *subjective*.

The indiscernibility relation can be assumed to be equivalence or tolerance relation or can be defined by a distance function in any metric space. For practical reasons, we assume that the information about elements is presented in the form of an attribute-value table, called also an information system.

Formally an *information system* can be seen as a system $S = (U, A)$, where U is the *universe* and A is the set of *attributes*. Each attribute $a \in A$, defines an *information* function $f_a : U- > V_a$, where V_a is the set of *values* of a, called *domain* of the attribute a. Obviously any subset of attributes $B \subseteq A$ defines the equivalence (indiscernibility) relation

$$IND(B) = \{(x,y) \in U_2 : f_a(x) = f_a(y)\}.$$

In the considered case $I(x) = [x]_B$.

The membership function can be expressed now as

$$\mu_X^B(x) = card(X \cap [x])/card[x]_B,$$

where $[x]_B$ denotes the equivalence class of the equivalence relation $IND(B)$ containing the element x. Let us observe that now the membership depends upon knowledge about x expressed by the set of attributes B and is no more a primitive concept. Moreover the union and intersection of rough sets cannot be, in general case, defined by means of max and min operations on memberships of constituent sets, because it would violate the topological properties of rough sets. This definition is valid only when some conditions are satisfied. More details about this kind of membership function can be found in [8,10]. (See also[5]).

Obviously, approximations can be expressed now as

$$\underline{B}X = \{x \in U : [x] \subseteq X\}$$

$$\overline{B}X = \{x \in U : [x] \cap X \neq \emptyset\}.$$

Rough sets can be also seen as a generalization of multisets, in the sense that we can associate with the element x its "multiplicity" in the whole universe defined as $card[x]_B$, which is the number of elements of the equivalence class of the equivalence relation generated by the set of attributes B and containing the element x. Thus, in the rough set approach, instead of identical elements we allow many indiscernible elements in a set. In other words rough set can be seen as a classical set with an indiscernibility relation superimposed on its elements. Hence, multisets can be viewed as a special case of rough sets.

It is also worthwhile to mention in this context that the rough set theory has been axiomatized by Bryniarski[4].

It seems that the time has come to look at all the escapes from the Cantor's set theory in a more general, unified way, which I believe deserve special attention from philosophers, logicians and computer scientists and need joint, general treatment. I propose for all this new developments a name "soft set theory" in opposite to "hard" Cantor's theory. Both theoretical and practical aspects of such an approach should be of equal importance.

Acknowledgements

The author is indebted for critical remarks to Prof. Andrzej Skowron, Prof. Salomon Marcus, Prof. Roman Slowinski and Dr. Wayne D. Blizard.

References

[1] W.D. Blizard, (1989a). Multiset Theory, **Notre Dame Journal of Formal Logic**, 30, pp. 36-66.

[2] W.D. Blizard, (1989b). Real-valued Multisets and Fuzzy Sets, **Fuzzy Sets and Systems**, 33, pp. 77-79.

[3] W.D. Blizard, (1990). Negative Membership, **Notre Dame Journal of Formal Logic**, 31, pp. 346-368.

[4] E. Bryniarski, (1993). Formal Concept of Rough Set (in polish). Ph.D. Dissertation.

[5] Z. Pawlak, S.K.M Wong and W. Ziarko, (1988). Rough Sets: Probabilistic Versus Deterministic Approach, **Int. J. Man-Machine Studies**, 29, pp. 81-95

[6] Z. Pawlak, (1991). Rough Sets - Theoretical Aspects of Reasoning about Data, **Kluwer Academic Publishers.**

[7] Z. Pawlak, (1982). Rough Sets, **Int. J. of Inf. and Comp. Sci.**, 11, 5, pp. 341-356.

[8] Z. Pawlak, (1985). Rough Sets and Fuzzy Sets, **J. of Fuzzy Sets and Systems**, 17, pp.99-102.

[9] Z. Pawlak, (1988). Hard Sets and Soft Sets, **Bull. Pol. Acad. Sci. Tech.**, 36, 1-2, pp. 119-123.

[10] Z. Pawlak, and A. Skowron, (1993). Rough Membership Function: a Tool for Reasoning with Uncertainty. Algebraic Methods in Logic and Computer Science, **Banach Center Publications Vol. 28, Polish Academy of Sciences, Warsaw**, 1993, 135-150.

[11] L. Zadeh, (1965). Fuzzy Sets, **Information and Control** 8, pp.338-353.

Rough Set Analysis of Multi-Attribute Decision Problems

Roman Słowiński

Institute of Computing Science, Technical University of Poznań

60-965 Poznań, Poland

Abstract

Rough set theory answers two basic questions related to multi-attribute decision problems: one about explanation of a decision situation and, another, about prescription of some decisions basing on analysis of a decision situation. In this paper, four classes of multi-attribute decision problems are defined, depending on a structure of their representation, their interpretation and the kind of questions related, as well as the rough set methodology of their analysis are briefly described.

1 Explanation and prescription – central problems of decision analysis

Scientific decision analysis provides various tools for modelling decision situations in view of explaining them or prescribing actions increasing the coherence between the possibilities offered by the situation, and goals and value systems of the agents involved. Both modelling and explanation/prescription stages are also crucial in operations research aiming at elaboration of a systematic and rational approach to modelling and solving complex decision problems [1].

Generally speaking, a *decision problem* involves a set of *objects* (actions, states, competitors, etc.) described or evaluated by a set of *attributes* (criteria, features, issues, etc.) Independently of further interpretation, a decision situation may be represented by a *table* rows of which correspond to objects and columns to attributes; for each pair (object-attribute) there is known a value called *descriptor*. We can also say that the table represents *knowledge* about a decision situation. Typically, one or several *agents* (experts, decision makers, nature, etc.) are also involved in a decision problem. By an agent we understand a person or thing that works to produce a result (observation, decision, evaluation, etc.). The agent may be either identified with an object or an attribute, or may exist "outside" the description of a decision situation. In the former case, a result produced by the agent is a descriptor in the table while in the latter, the whole table may be set up by the agent although he is not represented in the table.

The attributes used to describe objects are build on some elementary features of the objects. They may be *nominal* (also called *categorical* or *qualitive*, e.g. male or female) or *cardinal* (also called *non-nominal* or *quantitative*, e.g. financial ratios or temperature). Although characterization of an object on the component features may be "distributional" (distribution in time or space, or probability distribution), it is usually translated into a unique term (qualitative or quantitative) via a "point-reduction" technique [15]. Another possible quality of an attribute is a *preferential ordering* of its domain. Attributes with domains (finite or not) ordered according to preferences of an agent become *criteria* allowing to compare the objects from particular points of view [4].

An important issue of decision analysis is the kind of questions related to a decision problem. The most general question is probably about *explanation* of a decision situation. Explanation means discovering important facts and dependencies in the table describing a decision situation. A more specific question is about *prescription* of some decisions basing on analysis of information from the table. If this information can be interpreted as *preferential information* of an agent, its analysis tends to synthesis of a *comprehensive preference model* which represents a decision policy of the agent and can be used to support new decisions.

There are two major ways of constructing a comprehensive preference model upon preferential information obtained from an agent involved in the decision process [20]. The first one comes from mathematical decision analysis and consists in building a functional or a relational model [14]. The functional model has been extensively used within the framework of multi-attribute utility theory [6,7]. The relational model has its most widely known representation in the form of an outranking relation [17,18] or a fuzzy relation [5]. Relationship among these models have been established [21] and some criticisms have been made [3].

The second way comes from artificial intelligence and builds up the comprehensive preference model via inductive knowledge acquisition (also called rule induction, inductive learning or learning from examples). The resulting model is a set of *"if ...then ..."* rules or a decision tree [8,13]. This way is motivated by the hypothesis that the comprehensive preference model can be inferred by studying global evaluations made by the agents (decision makers, experts) when presented with a set of representative objects from the problem domain of interest (examples). The appeal of this approach is that the agents are typically more confident exercising their evaluations than explaining them. Neural networks also fall into this category, however, the comprehensive preference model inferred using this approach is encoded in the structure of the neural network and thus it is unknown explicitly [22]. It seems that such a "black box" model is not well-suited to decision aid which seeks to give a convincing prescription.

The information about a decision situation is usually vague because of uncertainty and imprecision coming from many sources (cf. [16]). Vagueness may be caused by *granularity* of representation of the information. Granularity may introduce an ambiguity (inconsistency) to explanation or prescription based on the vague information. For example, if a comprehensive preference model is assessed in the form of production rules, the ambiguity makes that some rules are non-deterministic, i.e. they are not univocally described by means of "granules" of the representation of preferential information.

A formal framework for dealing with granularity of information has been given by *the rough set theory* [9,10]. The rough set theory assumes a representation of the information in a *table* form called *information system*. Rows of this table correspond to *objects* and columns to *attributes*. As was pointed out above, the table is just an appropriate form for description of decision situations. Through the last decade, rough set theory has proved to be a useful tool for analysis of a large class of multi-attribute decision problems (cf. [19]). It answers, in an original way, both the questions of explanation and prescription related to decision situations.

This paper is a shoet version of [12], where the rough set methodology has been characterized for four classes of multi-attrbute decision problems and illustrated by simple practical examples. In the next section the four classes of decision problems are defined and main results of the rough sets analysis are pointed out. The final section groups some conclusions.

2 Definition of decision problems and main results of the rough set analysis

Given an information system S in which a finite set U of objects is described by a finite set Q of multi-valued attributes, we can distinguish three classes of decision problems:

(i) multi-attribute sorting problem,

(ii) multi-attribute, multi-sorting problem,

(iii) multi-attribute description of objects.

The above classification of decision problems overlaps with classification made by Roy [15] where multi-criteria sorting and description problems are also distinguished. However, while our understanding of problem (i) is the same as Roy's understanding of the multi-criteria sorting problem, we differ in the understanding of the multi-attribute description. This shows that the multi-criteria analysis and the rough set analysis represent rather different philosophies of analyzing multi-attribute decision problems.

A key feature differentiating the sorting problems (i) and (ii), and the description problem (iii) is a division of the set of attributes Q into subset C of condition attributes and subset D of decision attributes. Moreover, in the sorting problems, one or several agents are explicitly involved in the decision situation and represented by decision attributes. In multi-attribute description of objects, depending on interpretation of the information system, agents may be represented by objects or by attributes, or they may not be represented neither by objects nor by attributes and exist "outside" the description. Another difference between sorting problems (i) and (ii), and description problem (iii) is that the main question related to the formers is prescription, while to the latters, explanation.

Problem (i) is a classical multi-attribute sorting problem where there is only one decision attribute. It consists in assignment of each object to an appropriate pre-defined category, for instance: acceptance, rejection or request for an additional information. In this case, the rough set approach will be used to analyse a preferential information consisting of sorting examples. The sorting examples may be tutorial examples constructed by an agent or examples of real decisions, or observations, made by him in the past.

Examples of sorting decisions are given in the form of a decision table where objects correspond to examples. Examples are composed of condition and decision parts. The condition part describes an object in terms of condition attributes and the decision part specifies its assignment to one of the categories.

One can expect the following results from the rough set analysis of the decision table:

(a) evaluation of a relevance of particular attributes,[1]

(b) construction of minimal subsets of independent attributes ensuring the same quality of sorting as the whole set, i.e. reducts of the set of attributes,

(c) intersection of those reducts giving a core of attributes which cannot be eliminated without disturbing the ability of approximating the sorting decisions,

(d) elimination of redundant attributes from the decision table,

(e) generation of sorting rules from the reduced decision table; they involve the relevant attributes only and explain a decision policy of the agent (decision maker or expert).

The sorting rules discovered from sorting examples may be used to support new sorting decisions. Specifically, the sorting of a new object can be supported by matching its description to one of the sorting rules (cf. [20]).

Let us stress an important feature of the rough set approach, especially for the sorting problem. The vagueness manifested in the information system is not corrected but the rules produced are categorized into deterministic and non-deterministic (approximate). In the context of sorting, the non-deterministic rules mean that, under the corresponding conditions, it is not possible to assign the objects univocally to classes unless one seeks for some additional information. For example, in the case of selection of candidates to a school on the basis of application packages [11], the two original classes correspond to admission and rejection, respectively. The non-deterministic rules create in this case a third class of candidates: those who are invited to an interview.

Sorting problem (ii) differs from (i) by existence of multiple decision attributes. It means, for instance, that the same set of objects has been sorted by several agents. For the same values of condition attributes, the sorting decision may be different for some agents, so the global preference models (decision policies) can be different for them.

The sorting examples are given in a decision table form where there is more than one decision attribute. Using the rough set approach to analysis of the decision table one can obtain the same results (cf. points (a) to (e)) as for problem (i) but related to particular agents (decision attributes). Besides, one can measure the degree of consistency of the agents with the description of the objects by the set of condition attributes, detect and explain discordant and concordant parts of agents' decision policies, evaluate the grade of conflict among the agents, and construct the preference models (sorting rules) expressed in common terms (condition attributes) in order to facilitate a mutual understanding of the agents.

As was mentioned above, further distinction of decision problems within the multi-attribute description (iii) is possible on the basis of interpretation of the information system.

Specifically, if agents are explicitly represented either by objects or by attributes, we have to deal with:

(iii-α) multi-attribute description of a decision situation.

---

[1] Attributes in points (a) to (e) mean, in fact, condition attributes.

In this case, the attribute-values represent opinions of agents on specific issues of a decision situation. Primary objective of multi-attribute description of a decision situation can be formulated in the language of the rough set philosophy as searching for description of objects of the information system, in terms of a minimal set of attribute-values, that uniquely discerns all the objects.

As in the case of multi-attribute sorting problem (i), the rough set approach offers here several advantages, including (a), (b) and (c). Besides, it is worthwhile to mention that by employing the rough set methodology we get all possible solutions to the problem considered, i.e. all minimal descriptions, each using a different set of attributes. This suggests an optimization of the description, for if we have various possibilities of describing objects, we can ask which is the most useful one with regard to some presumed criteria.

Next important issue that can be tackled using the rough set theory is searching what happens if some attributes (or attribute-values) are not available, i.e. how the description of objects will be affected by missing data.

Last but not least, description of not single objects, but collections of objects (subsets of the universe), in terms of attribute-values can be of interest. It turns out that exact description of collection of objects is not always possible and approximate description is here a must. In this case, the notions of the lower and the upper approximations can be used.

The rough set approach to the description of decision situations seems to be particularly well suited, especially when minimal description in terms of attributes is of primary concern. This is where the rough set theory shows its strength, and in contrast to other theories offers full range of techniques to investigate this kind of situations.

Another important problem that can be tackled by the rough set theory within the multi-attribute description is an analysis of *conflicts* among the agents involved [12].

If agents are not explicitly represented in the information system but exist "outside" the description, we are basically interested in:

(iii - β) discovering dependencies among attributes.

attributes are interpreted as consequences of decisions represented by objects. So, contrary to description problem (iii - α), all attributes (conseqences) are important and cannot be eliminated from the decision situation. Instead, one might be interested in searching for dependencies among consequences, i.e. try to find out how consequences of decisions are interrelated among each other. Using the rough set approach, one is able to discover all minimal functional dependencies among attributes. They often have interpretation of "cause-effect" relationships.

3 Conclusions

The two sorting problems, (i) and (ii), are mainly related with prescription of sorting decisions basing on analysis of sorting examples. We claim that the comprehensive preference model in the form of rules derived from a set of examples may have an advantage over a functional or a relational model because it explains the preferential attitude through relevant and easily understandable facts in terms of significant attributes only. The rules are well-founded by examples and, moreover, inconsistencies manifested in the examples are neither corrected nor aggregated by a single function or relation.

The two problems of description, (iii-α) and (iii-β), are mainly related with explanation of a decision situation. The rough set approach is particulary well suited when minimal description in terms of attribute-values is of primary concern. A minimal description enables a thorough analysis of conflicts which is an important issue of explanation. Finally, if attributes are consequences of some decisions, the rough set analysis permits discovering all minimal elementary dependencies among consequences; in some applications, the dependencies may be interpreted as "cause-effect" relationships.

The rough set approach does not need any additional information like probability in statistics or grade of membership in fuzzy set theory. It accepts both nominal and cardinal attributes, including those whose domains are not ordered. It is also conceptually simple and needs simple algorithms.

References

[1] R.L. Ackoff, M.W. Sasieni, *Fundamentals of Operations Research*. Wiley, New York, 1968.

[2] C.A. Bana e Costa, *Readings in Multiple-Criteria Decision Aid*. Springer -Verlag, Berlin, 1990.

[3] D. Bouyssou, Expected utility theory and decision-aid: a critical survey. In: O. Hagen and F. Wenstop (eds.), *Progress in Utility and Risk Theory*, Reidel, Dordrecht, 1984.

[4] D. Bouyssou, Building criteria: a prerequisite for MCDA. In: [4], pp. 58-80.

[5] D. Dubois, H. Prade, Criteria aggregation and ranking of alternatives in the framework of fuzzy set theory. *TIMS/Studies in Management Sciences* 20 (1984) 209-240.

[6] P.H. Farquahr, A survey of multiattribute utility theory and applications. *TIMS/Studies in Management Science* 6 (1977) 59-89.

[7] R.L. Keeney, H. Raiffa, *Decisions with Multiple Objectives - Preferences and Value Tradeoffs*. Wiley, New York, 1976.

[8] R.S. Michalski, A theory and methodology of inductive learning. *Artificial Intelligence* 20 (1983) 11-116.

[9] Z. Pawlak, Rough Sets. *Int. J. of Information & Computer Sciences* 11 (1982) 341-356.

[10] Z. Pawlak, Rough Sets. Theoretical Aspects of Reasoning about Data. Kluwer Academic Publishers, Dordrecht/Boston/London, 1991.

[11] Z. Pawlak, R. Słowinski, Decision analysis using rough sets. *International Transactions in Operational Research* 1 (1994), to appear.

[12] Z. Pawlak, R. Słowinski, Rough set approach to multi-attribute decision analysis. Research Review, *Europ, J. of Operational Research* (1994), to appear.

[13] M. Roubens, Ph. Vincke, *Preference Modelling*, Springer-Verlag, LNEMS vol. 250, Berlin, 1985.

[14] B. Roy, *Mèthodologie Multicritère d'Aide à la Décision*, Economica, Paris, 1985.

[15] B. Roy, Main sources of inaccurate determination, uncertainty and imprecision in decision models. *Math. & Comput. Modell.* 12 (1989) 1245-1254.

[16] B. Roy, The outranking approach and the foundations of ELECTRE methods. In: [3], pp. 155-183.

[17] B. Roy, D. Bouyssou, *Aide Multicritère à la Décision: Méthodes et Cas* Economica, Paris, 1993.

[18] R. Słowinski, ed., *Intelligent Decision Support. Handbook of applications and Advances of the Rough Sets Theory.* Kluwer Academic Publishers, Dordrecht/Boston/London, 1992.

[19] R. Słowinski, Rough set learning of preferential attitude for multi-criteria decision making. In: J. Komorowski, Z. W. Raś (eds.), *Methodologies for Intelligent Systems*, Lecture Notes in Artificial Intelligence, vol. 689, Springer-Verlag, Berlin, 1993, pp. 642-651.

[20] Ph. Vincke, Basic concepts of preference modelling. In [3], pp. 101-118.

[21] J. Wang, B. Malakooti, A feedforward neural network for multiple criteria decision making. *Computers & Operations Research* 19 (1992) 151-167.

Rough Set Semantics for Non-classical Logics

Ewa Orlowska[*]
Institute of Theoretical and Applied Computer Science
Polish Academy of Sciences

1 Introduction

In the paper a general framework of defining information semantics for nonclassical logics is discussed. Rough sets theory (Pawlak 1992) has been an inspiration for logical investigations aimed at development of logical systems and deduction methods for representing and handling incomplete information and for reasoning in the presence of incompleteness. During the last decade a representation paradigm of rough-set-based information logics and models has received a lot of attention (Orlowska and Pawlak 1984a,b, Orlowska 1985, Farinas del Cerro and Prade 1986, Rasiowa and Skowron 1986, Nakamura 1988, Vakarelov 1988, Dubois and Prade 1992, Rauszer 1992). Information logics are formalisms for representation of and reasoning about data that consist of entities of the following two types: objects and properties of objects. According to the Tarskian tradition semantic structures for formalized languages are abstract relational systems consisting of a nonempty set and a family of relations of a finite arity over this set. In the paper we define a "more concrete", in a sense, semantics provided by a suitable class of information models. In information models we introduce explicitly objects, properties and various relationships between them. Each information model is determined by what is called an information frame, in a similar way as possible world frames (Kripke 1963) determine models. Information frames are generated by nondeterministic information systems (Orlowska and Pawlak 1984a). Completeness of logical systems with respect to classes of information frames is discussed. The notion of informational representability of frames is introduced and investigated.

2 General models

Semantical presentation of nonclassical logics is usually provided in terms of possible world frames. Under possible world interpretation formulas are understood as subsets of a universe of possible worlds, with the intuition that the meaning of a formula is a set of those worlds at which the formula is true. The meaning of formulas built with classical propositional operations of negation (not F), disjunction (F or G), conjunction (F and G) is completely determined by meanings of subformulas of the given formula. The meaning of formulas built with nonclassical operations like temporal operations (sometime in the future F, always in the past F) depends not only on the meaning of subformulas, but also on how the possible worlds at which the subformulas are true are related to each other. For instance, the

---

[*] The mailing address: Azaliowa 29, 04-539 Warsaw, Poland

meaning of formula "sometime in the future F" consists of the worlds such that some of their successors (in the admitted time scale) belong to the set of worlds providing the meaning of F. Propositional operators of that kind are called intensional operators. Rough set-based information logics contain several intensional operations, for example operations corresponding to lower and upper approximation and their generalizations, strong and weak similarity operations, knowledge operators etc.

A great variety of nonclassical logics is defined in terms of classes of frames of the form $K=(W,R)$ where W is a nonempty set of possible worlds and R is a binary relation in W called accessibility relation. For instance, in frames for temporal logic set W consists of moments of time and R is an earlier-later relationship between moments of time. In frames for information logics the accessibility relations are, for example, indiscernibility, similarity, informational inclusion. Frames generate models of propositional languages. Let K be a frame, then by a model generated by K we mean any system $M=(W,R,m)$ such that m is a meaning function that assigns subsets of W to atomic formulas (propositional variables) and is extended in a natural way to all the formulas. For example, set m(For G) is the union of sets m(F) and m(G). An example of meaning of a temporal formula built with an intensional operator is: m(sometime in the future F)=$\{w \in W$: there is $y \in W$ such that $(w,y) \in R$ and $y \in m(F)\}$, where R is an ordering relation in a time scale. In a rough set-based epistemic logic (Orlowska 1989) meaning of formulas built with knowledge operator Know is defined as m(Know F)=$\{w \in W$: for all $y \in W$ if $(w,y) \in R$, then $y \in m(F)$ or for all $z \in W$ it $(w,z) \in R$, then $z \notin m(F)\}$, where R is an indiscernibility relation. In a more general setting a frame is a system (W,R) where R is an n-ary relation in W.

In general, for an intensional propositional Operation the set m(Operation F) providing meaning of the respective formula in a model (W,R,m) is defined in terms of R and m(F). A formula is said to be true in a model M iff m(F)=W, F is true in a frame K iff it is true in every model generated by K, and F is valid iff it is true in all frames. Let a fixed propositional language be given with a set FOR of formulas, and let CL be a class of frames for that language. By a logic of class CL we mean set $L(CL) \subseteq FOR$ of those formulas that are true in every frame from CL.

3 Information models

Let a nondeterministic information system $S=(OB, PROP, f)$ be given, where OB is a nonempty set of objects, PROP is a nonempty set of properties, and f: $OB \rightarrow P(PROP)$ is an information function that assigns subsets of properties to objects. In the original Pawlak's formulation (Pawlak 1981) properties have the form of pairs consisting of an attribute and a set of values of that attribute, the more general formulation admitted in the present paper is due to Vakarelov (1991b).

Given a collection of objects and their properties, a natural question arises whether these properties enable us to discern every object from the remaining ones. If f(o1)=f(o2) for some objects o1, o2, then clearly, they are 'the same' up to the properties provided by the given data. The indiscernibility phenomenon is a consequence of incompleteness of information, we have not enough discriminative resources at our disposal to characterize the given objects precisely and exhaustively. As a consequence, we migh not be able to grasp single objects but only the classes of them such that in each class there are objects that are indiscernible in terms of the given properties. We conclude that one of the manifestations of incompleteness of information is the indiscernibility phenomenon. This type of incompleteness is modelled by means of the indiscernibility relation. We say that objects o1 and o2 are indiscernible whenever sets f(o1), f(o2) of their properties are equal.

The other form of incompleteness appears in data such that with an object there is associated a subset of values of an attribute, and not necessarily a single value. For example, we might not know the age of a person but usually we can estimate it approximately, within a certain range. In such a case the value f(o) of information function f for object o is interpreted as a collective representation of presumed properties of o. These properties are close to each other and cannot be separated on the basis of the available data. This type of incompleteness is reflected by the similarity relation. We say that objects o1 and o2 are similar whenever sets f(o1), f(o2) of their presumed properties have a nonempty intersection. Indiscernibility and similarity are examples of what is called information relations.

By a multiagent information system we mean a system that includes a family of information functions. The functions reflect views of agents, every agent characterizes the given objects in terms of his local resources. For the sake of simplicity in what follows we define information frames determined by single agent systems, it will be easy to see how to generalize the respective notions to capture multiagent case.

To represent data taking into account several types of incompleteness, we need a variety of information relations. We define an information language whose formulas are intended to represent these relations between objects in an information system. Given a system, information relations are defined in terms of sets of properties that are values of the information function. Therefore in the language we admit the syntactic entities that enable us to express these information items explicitly. The language consists of terms and formulas. Let VAROB be a set of object variables, and let 0,1 be constants interpreted as the empty set and a set PROP, respectively. The set TI of information terms is the smallest set including 0, 1 and the atomic terms $f(x)$, where $x \in$ VAROB, and f is a function symbol denoting an information function, and moreover TI is closed with respect to set operations $-, \cap, \cup$ of complement, intersection, and union, respectively. Information terms are intended to represent subsets of properties. Set FORI of information formulas is the smallest set including atomic formulas of the form $t=t'$ and $t \subseteq t'$ for any information terms t, t', and closed with respect to the classical propositional operations $\neg, \wedge, \vee, \rightarrow$ of negation, conjunction, disjunction, and implication, respectively.

Semantics of the information language is determined by an information system $S=(OB, PROP, f)$ and a meaning function m_S that provides meaning to the constants of the language, that is $m_S(0)=\emptyset$, $m_S(1)=PROP$, $m_S(f)=f_S$. Function m_S is extended to a mapping that provides meaning to all the terms, for the sake of simplicity it is denoted by m_S too. Let $t(x_1,...,x_n)$ be a term such that $x_1,...x_n$ are all the variables that occur in t, then $m_S(t):OB^n \rightarrow P(OB)$ is the mapping that assigns subsets of objects to n-tuples of objects. Let $v:VAROB \rightarrow OB$ be a valuation of object variables over (objects of) S, by $m_S(t)(v)$ we denote the value of $m_S(t)$ in the point $(v(x_1),...,v(x_n))$. We say that an information formula is satisfied in system S by valuation v iff the following conditions hold:

S,v sat $t=t'$ iff $m_S(t)(v)=m_S(t')(v)$

S,v sat $t \subseteq t'$ iff $m_S(t)(v) \subseteq m_S(t')(v)$

S,v sat $\neg F$ iff not S,v sat F

S,v sat F∧G iff S,v sat F and S,v sat G

S,v sat F∨G iff S,v sat F or S,v sat G

S,v sat F→G iff not S,v sat F or S,v sat G.

Information formulas define relations between objects. For example, the relations of indiscernibility (IND), similarity (SIM), and informational inclusion (IN) are defined by means of the following information formulas:

IND: $f(x)=f(y)$, SIM: $\neg(f(x) \cap f(y)=0)$, IN: $f(x) \subseteq f(y)$.

Given a system S, and objects a,b from S, we have aINDb iff S,v sat $f(x)=f(y)$, where v is a valuation such that v(x)=a and v(y)=b, and similarly for relations SIM and IN.

By an information frame determined by information system S=(OB,PROP,f) and a formula $F(x_1,...x_n) \in$ FORI, $n \geq 2$, we mean frame

$K_{S,F}=(OB, \{(a_1,...,a_n) \in OB^n$: there is v over S such that $v(x_i)=a_i$,

i=1,...,n, and S,v sat F}).

The class of information frames is then defined as:

INF={$K_{S,F}$: S is an information system and F is a formula from FORI}.

Hence accessibility relation in an information frame is defined in terms of subsets of properties from an information system. Every information frame generates a class of information models such that the respective meaning function assigns subsets of objects from this frame to formulas of the language under consideration.

Information models imitate very closely the form of experimental data in various application areas (Slowinski 1992), and therefore they provide an intended semantics for logical systems which are being developed to support reasoning processes in these domains.

4   Informational representability

We say that a frame K=(W,R) is informationally representable iff there is a frame K'∈ INF such that K is isomorphic to K'. If K' is determined by a system S and a formula F∈ FORI, then we say that K is represented by S with scheme F.

Intuitively, a frame is representable iff its universe can be treated as a set of objects of an information system and its accessibility relation is definable by means of a formula from the information language that is satisfiable in this system. It follows that in a representable frame the accessibility relation can be defined in terms of subsets of properties that are attributed to objects in an information system. Examples of frames that are informationally representable can be found in Vakarelov (1987, 1988, 1991a,b). The techniques employed there for constructing the respective information systems can be treated as an extension of the Stone representation theory (Stone 1936). It seems that non-representable frames will arise, in general, from relational systems whose first order theories do not admit elimination of quantifiers. It is an interesting phenomenon that a power construction which is most often used to define sets of properties in information systems that provide representation of frames, replaces somehow those parts of the definition of accessibility relations that are infinitary in nature.

Proposition 4.1

Let frame K be informationally represented by S with scheme F, and let K' be an information frame determined by S and F. Then for every formula G∈ FOR the following holds: G is true in K iff G is true in K' .

Proposition 4.2

If a logic L is complete with respect to a class CL of frames and if every frame from class CL is informationally representable, then logic L is complete with respect to the class $\{K_{S,F}$: there is $K' \in CL$ such that K' is informationally represented by S with scheme $F\}$ of information frames.

Completeness of a logic with respect to a class of information frames is an argument for its adequacy of being a means for reasoning in an application domain that is modelled by the respective class of information models.

The notions of information frame and informational representability can be extended in a natural way to multiframes of the form $(W, \{R_i: i \in I\})$ with a family of relations in W of a finite rank. To represent multiframes we need a family $\{F_i: i \in I\}$ of formulas from the information language such that if R_i is a n-ary relation then F_i is a formula with n free variables. In fact, most of applied logics admit several intensional operations in their languages, each of which is semantically determined by an accessibility relation. To establish informational representability of the respective frames we have to model all the relationships between accessibility relations in these frames.

A problem of informational representability can be viewed as a variant of the correspondence problem in nonclassical logics (Rodenburg 1986, Van Benthem 1984). It provides also a new perspective to the problem of verisimilitude of theories (Popper 1963), namely we can postulate criteria for comparision of theories based on informational representability of their models, similar to the rough set based criteria proposed in Orlowska (1990).

References

Dubois,D. and Prade,H. (1992) Putting rough sets and fuzzy sets together. In: Slowinski,R. (ed) Intelligent decision support. Kluwer, Dordrecht, 203-232.

Farinas del Cerro,L. and Prade,H. (1986) Rough sets, fuzzy sets and modal logic-Fuzziness in indiscernibility and partial information. In: Di Niola,A., Ventre,A. and Fodor,J. (eds) The mathematics of fuzzy systems. Verlag TUV Rheinland, Koeln, 103-120.

Kripke,S. (1963) Semantical analysis of modal logic I. Zeitschrift fuer Mathematische Logik und Grundlagen der Mathematik 9, 67-96.

Nakamura,A. (1988) Fuzzy rough sets. Notes on Multiple-Valued Logic in Japan 9(8), 1-8.

Orlowska,E. (1985) Logic of nondeterministic information. Studia Logica XLIV, 93-102.

Orlowska,E. (1989) Logic for reasoning about knowledge. Zeitschrift fuer Mathematische Logik und Grundlagen der Mathematik 35, 559-572.

Orlowska,E. (1990) Verisimilitude based on concept analysis. Studia Logica XLIX,307-319.

Orlowska,E. and Pawlak,Z. (1984a) Representation of nondeterministic information. Theoretical Computer Science 29, 27-39.

Orlowska,E. and Pawlak,Z. (1984b) Logical foundations of knowledge representation. ICS PAS Report 537, Warsaw.

Pawlak,Z. (1981) Information systems-theoretical foundations. Information Systems 3, 205-218.

Pawlak,Z. (1992) Rough sets. Kluwer, Dordrecht.

Popper,K. (1963) Conjectures and refutations. Routledge and Kegan, London.

Rasiowa,H. and Skowron,A. (1986) Approximation logic. In: Mathematical methods of specification and synthesis of software systems' 85. Akademie Verlag, Berlin, Band 31, 123-139.

Rauszer,C. (1992) Logic for information systems. Fundamenta Informaticae 16, 371-383.

Rodenburg,P. (1986) Intuitionistic correspondence theory. PhD dissertation, University of Amsterdam.

Slowinski,R. (1992) (ed) Intelligent decision support. Handbook of applications and advances of the rough sets theory. Kluwer, Dordrecht/ Boston/London.

Stone,M. (1936) The theory of representations for Boolean algebras. Transactions of the American Mathematical Society 40, 37-111.

Vakarelov,D. (1987) Abstract characterization of some knowledge representation systems and the logic NIL of nondeterministic information. In: Jorrand,Ph. and Sgurev,V. (eds) Artificial Intelligence II: Methodology, Systems, Applications. Elsevier Science Publishers, Amsterdam, 255-260.

Vakarelov,D. (1988) Modal logics for knowledge representation. Lecture Notes in Computer Science 363, Springer, Berlin/Heidelberg/New York, 257-277.

Vakarelov,D. (1991a) A modal logic for similarity relations in Pawlak knowledge representation systems. Fundamenta Informaticae XV, 61-79.

Vakarelov,D. (1991b) Logical analysis of positive and negative similarity relations in property systems. In: De Glas,M. and Gabbay,D. (eds) Proceedings WOCFAI, 491-499.

Van Benthem,J. (1984) Correspondence theory. In: Gabbay,D. and Guenther,F. (eds) Handbook of Philosophical Logic. Vol II, Reidel, Dordrecht, 167-247.

A Note on Categories of Information Systems

J.A. Pomykala

Institute of Computer Science, Warsaw University of Technology
Warsaw, Poland

E. de Haas

ILLC & Department of Mathematics and Computer Science,
University of Amsterdam, Amsterdam, The Netherlands

1 Introduction

Several notions motivated by the problem of classifying objects according to the values of their attributes were introduced and examined. We mention for example the logical kit of Semadeni [2], the information system of Pawlak [1], the context of Wille [3] and the probably most commonly known and applied relational database model of Codd [7]. From some points of view the above notions are equivalent or inter-translatable (see e.g. Wiweger [4], where the relation among logical kits, information systems and contexts is explained); of course there are important differences among them. In every of the models mentioned we have other classes of questions considered and areas of applications also do not coincide.

Category theory has proved to be useful in so many areas that it should also be possible to apply it in the field of information systems, logical kits, contexts etc.. In fact there exist results for logical kits using category theory, for example showing that this notion can be translated to information systems and contexts, see e.g. Semadeni [2], Wiweger [4]; other results of this kind connected to a similar notion, rough sets, can be found in Bieganska [6], Obtulowicz [5] and Banerjee, Chakraborty [9].

Our starting point will be the notion of *information systems* due to Pawlak. Our aim here is the following: we would like to define some categories related to information systems, which can profit in better understanding of structures associated to these systems. In particular we hope to obtain new insight into indiscernibility of objects, dependence of attributes and problems related to reducing the number of attributes. This note only gives introductory considerations. We suggest that it is worthwhile to develop a theory for the categories introduced in this paper and to find applications for the results obtained. In particular we hope that the tool of category theory can help to analyse situations in which we deal with information systems with incomplete, damaged or lost information. We shall be interested in questions similar to the following: assume we changed some of the values of an information system, how does that fact influence the indiscernibility of objects and the dependence of attributes, or determinant of this information system?

The paper is organized as follows: We start with some basic definitions concerning information systems. Then we introduce some categories for these information systems to outline the approach we take in describing various ways of fiddling with the information contained in an information system. Subsequently we present a theory, based on the notion of natural transformations, in which we can describe nicely and categorically the fiddling with information. We conclude the paper with some remarks.

2   Basic Definitions

The notion of information systems was introduced by Pawlak in [1].

An *information system* is a quadruple $(U, A, (V_a)_{a \in A}, f)$ where U is a set of objects, A stands for a set of attributes, V_a is a set of values for an attribute a, and $f : U \times A \rightarrow \bigcup_{a \in A} V_a$ is a function such that $f(x, a) \in V_a$ for any $x \in U, a \in A$. The function f is called the information function. Shortly the system will be denoted by (U, A, V, f) where $V = \bigcup_{a \in A} V_a$

For every set of attributes $B \subseteq A$ an *indiscernibility relation* $\mathrm{Ind}(B) \subseteq U^2$ is defined in the following way: For every $x, y \in U$ $\mathrm{Ind}(B)xy$ iff $\forall a \in B$ $f(x, a) = f(y, a)$.

We say that the set of attributes B *depends* on the set of attributes C (denoted by $C \rightarrow B$), if $\mathrm{Ind}(C) \subseteq \mathrm{Ind}(B)$.

We also recall that a set of attributes $B \subseteq C$ is a *reduct* of C if $\mathrm{Ind}(B) = \mathrm{Ind}(C)$ and the set B is minimal with respect to inclusion.

3   Categories of Information Systems

In this section we introduce some categories of information systems. The basic definition of such a category is the following: We take as objects information systems and consider morphisms between them. These morphisms preserve the structure of an information system in some way. We consider special kinds of these morphisms, which are related to well known notions in the theory of information systems. In this framework we can reason about information systems with lost or damaged information, by considering the information which is *not* preserved as being lost or damaged.

A particular class of categories is the following: we look at (sub)categories of information systems (U, A, V, f) such that $U = \{x_1, \ldots, x_n\}$, $A = \{a_1, \ldots, a_m\}$ and V are fixed. Now given two information systems $S_1 = (U, A, V_1, f_1)$ and $S_2 = (U, A, V_2, f_2)$, we say that m_p is a *permuting attribute morphism* from S_1 to S_2 iff there exists a permutation $\sigma : \{1, \ldots, m\} \overset{1-1}{\rightarrow} \{1, \ldots, m\}$ such that:

$$\forall i \forall j [f_2(x_i, a_j) = f_1(x_i, a_{\sigma(j)})]$$

Furthermore of course m_p should map U on U, A on A and V_1 on V_2[1]. Sometimes we shall say that m_p is a permutation of columns of the information system and we shall write: $m_p : \{a_1^c, \ldots, a_m^c\} \rightarrow \{a_1^c, \ldots, a_m^c\}$. Of course σ^{-1} gives a dual morphism of m_p.

As a subclass we can also consider morphisms determined by a subset $A_0 \subseteq A$ and permuting morphisms $m_p : A \rightarrow A$ such that $m_p \mid A_0 = \mathrm{Id}_{A_0}$ where Id_{A_0} is the identity on A_0

---

[1] In this special case $V_1 = V_2$ would be sufficient

We call categories with morphisms of the first kind *permuting (attributes) category*. In a similar way a morphism determined by a permutation of objects is defined. This way we obtain a *permuting object category*.

An other type of categories is determined by the information concerning indiscernibility of objects. Let us assume that the set of objects U is fixed and the sets of attributes are arbitrary. Therefore objects in this category are information systems $(U, A, V, f), (U, A', V', f'), (U, A'', V'', f''), \ldots$ etc.. We define morphisms here in the following way:

$$(U, A, V, f) \xrightarrow{m_i} (U, A', V', f') \text{ iff } \text{Ind}(A) = \text{Ind}(A')$$

This category is called the *indiscernibility category*.

We obtain a category with the same objects by adding some more morphisms: $(U, A, V, f) \xrightarrow{m_d} (U, A', V', f')$ iff the set of attributes A depends on the set A' i.e. $\text{Ind}(A) \subseteq \text{Ind}(A')$. A category with these morphisms shall be called *dependency category*. A refinement on this category would be considering, next to identity morphisms, only *strict* dependencies: $m_{ds} : (U, A, V, f) \xrightarrow{m_{ds}} (U, A', V', f')$ iff $\text{Ind}(A) \subset \text{Ind}(A')$.

It would be interesting to consider a category related to another important notion of information systems, namely reducts. Let us observe that we can not define a category with morphisms determined by reducts in an analogous way as above, because in general we shall not have identity morphisms. We may however construct a subcategory, with objects having the property of *independence*, that is for information systems (U, A, V, f) we say they are independent if it is true that for all $B \subseteq A$ it holds that $B \neq A \to \text{Ind}(B) \neq \text{Ind}(A)$. On the other hand it is possible to consider functions $m_r : A \to A'$ such that $A' \subseteq A$ is a reduct of A and we may call m_r a semi-morphism. Here we not always have identity morphisms and there are no nontrivial compositions.

In summary, we have defined the following subcategories of information systems: $\mathbf{IS}_p, \mathbf{IS}_i, \mathbf{IS}_d$ and $\mathbf{IS}_r$ where all the (sub)categories have as their objects information systems $\{(U, A, V, f)|U, A, V \text{ are sets } \& f : U \times A \to V\}$ and as their classes of morphisms respectively M_p, M_i, M_d and M_r where the elements of M_p are morphisms determined by permutations of attributes, elements in M_i are determined by $\text{Ind}(A)$ relations, morphisms in M_d and M_r are defined using respectively dependency relations and reducts. Note that by definition of a category, we have to add identity morphisms to the reduct morphisms to obtain $\mathbf{IS}_r$.

At this point, having defined some basic categories we can start developing the theory. It is not difficult to define the product and the comma category. Some simple functors like a forgetful or an inclusion functor are also easy to obtain. At present we consider natural transformations.

4 Natural Transformations and Information Systems

It is often mentioned (e.g. in Lambek and Scott [8]) that the concept of natural transformations is the key concept that necessitated the invention of category theory. Many objects of interest to mathematicians may be viewed as functors

from small categories to the category of **Sets**. When these functors are seen
as objects of a category and we take as morphisms the natural transformations
between these functors, we obtain a functor category. In order to understand
the structure of a mathematical object like an information system, it is useful
to analyse its description as such a functor, especially because there is much
known about properties of functor categories that have the category **Set** as
their basis. For example, categories of this kind are in general cartesian closed
and have nice behaviour concerning limits and co-limits.

In this section we will construct a functor category for information system.
For reasons of explanation we first build a functor category for a more simple
mathematical object: the nondeterministic information system. The construction of morphisms for the functor category of information systems gives rise to
a general scheme for dealing with special morphisms like the ones we defined
in the previous section. We obtain a framework in which we can reason about
(damaging) information.

Let us consider the following very small category[2] **PreSIS** of figure 1 and
consider the category $\mathbf{Set}_{\mathrm{FinTot}}$ of all finite sets as objects and total functions
as morphisms. Let us consider (arbitrary) functors from **PreSIS** to $\mathbf{Set}_{\mathrm{FinTot}}$.
Such a functor F maps U to some finite set $F(U)$ which we will view as a
set of objects. Similarly F maps A to a finite set $F(A)$ of attributes, V to a
finite set $F(V)$ of values and I to a finite set $F(I)$ of 'information entries'[3].
Furthermore F maps the arrows obj,val,att to respectively the total mappings
$F(\mathrm{obj}) : F(I) \to F(U)$, $F(\mathrm{val}) : F(I) \to F(V)$, $F(\mathrm{att}) : F(I) \to F(A)$. Such
a functor F defines a what we call a *nondeterministic information system*.
A nondeterministic information system is a system for which in general the
information function f_F is nondeterministic (set valued), i.e. for an object there
are several possible values for each of its attributes ($f_F(x, a)$ is a set) or the value
of some of its attribute can be unknown ($f_F(x, a) = \emptyset$). A nondeterministic
information system $S_F = (U_F, A_F, V_F, f_F)$ is given by a functor $F : \mathbf{PreSIS} \to$
$\mathbf{SET}_{\mathrm{FinTot}}$ as follows:

- $\bullet U_F = F(U)$ $\bullet A_F = F(A)$ $\bullet V_F = F(V)$
- $\bullet f_F : U_F \times A_F \to V_F$ such that
  $f_F(x, a) = \{v | \exists i \in F(I)[F(\mathrm{obj})(i) = x \wedge F(\mathrm{att})(i) = a \wedge F(\mathrm{val})(i) = v]$

It is clear that for the information systems S_F we defined above the information function f_F is nondeterministic.

We will construct an abstract and very small category called **SIS** such that
the functor category $\mathbf{Set}_{\mathrm{FinTot}}^{\mathbf{SIS}}$ defines a category of (deterministic and complete) information systems. Consider figure 2. We start (I) with a diagram
containing the objects U, A, V which are abstract entities representing respectively the objects, the attributes and the values of an information system. Then
(II) we add to this diagram the object $U \times A$ and require that the functors map
this object to the *product* of $F(U)$ and $F(A)$, i.e., $F(U \times A) = F(U) \times F(A)$.

---

[2] We did not draw the identity morphisms; the composition of morphisms is the obvious
(and only possible) one.

[3] If we view an information system as a matrix determined by information function $f(u, a)$
we can view the set I of information as entries in this matrix

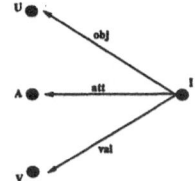

Figure 1: The small category **PreSIS**

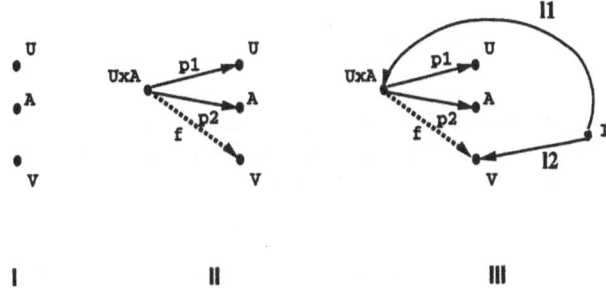

Figure 2: three steps in constructing the category **SIS**

Furthermore we draw an arrow $f : U \times A \to V$ which will be mapped to the information function $F(f) : F(U) \times F(A) \to F(V)$. Subsequently (III) we add object I and require that $F(I)$ is the limit of the sub-diagram[4], consisting of two objects $U \times A$ and V, connected by the arrow f. To complete the diagram we add[5] the compositions obj $= p1(l1)$, att $= p2(l2)$, val $= f(l1) = l2$, rename $h = l_1$ and obtain the very small category **SIS** (See figure 3).

Note that we do not allow arbitrary functors from **SIS** to $\mathbf{Set_{FinTot}}$. We demand functors F to satisfy the conditions $F(U \times A) = F(U) \times F(A)$ and $(F(I), F(l1), F(l2)) = \lim^F_{\to}(U \times A, f, V)$. Observing that a product is also a limit and that $(U \times A, p1, p2)$ and $(I, l1, l2)$ are trivialiter limits in **SIS**, it is sufficient to restrict the functors to be *limit preserving*.

Consider the small category **SIS** of figure 3. Let $F : \mathbf{SIS} \to \mathbf{Set_{FinTot}}$ be a functor in $\mathbf{Set^{SIS}_{FinTot}}$. F defines an information system $S = (U_F, V_F, A_F, f_F)$ in two different ways.

(A) S is determined by F is as follows:

- $U_F = F(U)$, • $V_F = F(V)$, • $A_F = F(A)$, • $f_F = F(f)$

(B) Alternatively, S determined by F as follows:

- $U_F = F(U)$, • $A_F = F(A)$, • $V_F = F(V)$,

---

[4]This sub-diagram is also called the category **2** in the literature of category theory. See for example MacLane [10]

[5]We do not draw the identity morphisms; the composition of morphisms with the identity morphisms is the obvious (and only possible) one.

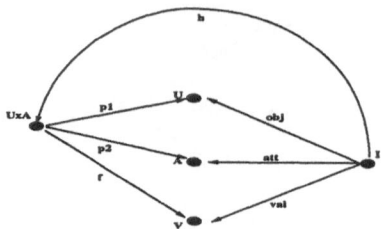

Figure 3: The small category **SIS**

- f_F is given by: $f_F(x,a) = v$ **iff** $\exists i \in F(I)[F(\text{obj}) = x \wedge F(\text{att}) = a \wedge F(\text{val}) = v]$

Proposition 4.1 *Consider the (limit preserving) functors between the categories* **SIS** *and* **Set**$_{\text{FinTot}}$. *These functors define, using either definition A or definition B, precisely the information systems; moreover the definitions of A and B are equivalent.*

proof: We forced $F(U \times A)$ to be the cartesian product of $F(U)$ and $F(A)$. The observation that all the morphisms in **Set**$_{\text{FinTot}}$ are total completes the proof for definition A. From the commutativity of the diagram determined by **SIS** and from the fact that $F(I)$ being a limit forces $F(I)$ to be unique (up to isomorphism), it follows that definitions A and B are equivalent. □

Proposition 4.2 *Considering the category* **Set**$_{\text{FinTot}}^{\text{SIS}}$ *with natural transformations as morphisms we get a (necessary) condition for those natural morphisms. Let $m = (m_U, m_A, m_V)$ be a morphism between two information systems $S_1 = (U_1, A_1, V_1, f_1)$ and $S_2 = (U_2, A_2, V_2, f_2)$ and let $u \in U_1, a \in A_1, v \in V_1$, then m must satisfy:* (*) $\quad m_V(f_1(u,a)) = f_2(m_U(u), m_A(a))$

Proof: directly from the definition of a natural transformation (see e.g. [8]). □

We can characterize the categories of section 3 as subcategories of the functor category we defined above. We will show this for the permuting and the indiscernibility category of information systems. The characterization of these subcategories can be done in a uniform way, and this gives rise to a more general scheme of defining subcategories of information systems. We will put constraints on the natural transformations in some special manner. Actually the condition (*) is due to weakest of constraint on a natural transformation: the constraint of being a natural transformation. One can think of constraints which allow only restricted transformations, formalizing the event of damaging part of the information, or damaging information in some small extent.

Consider the diagram of figure 4. First we characterize the permuting category. Let F, G be functors in **Set**$_{\text{FinTot}}^{\text{SIS}}$ and let $\sigma : F(A) \to F(A)$ be a permutation of the attribute set $F(A)$. In order to have two informations systems related by a permuting morphism, we draw the permutation σ in the diagram

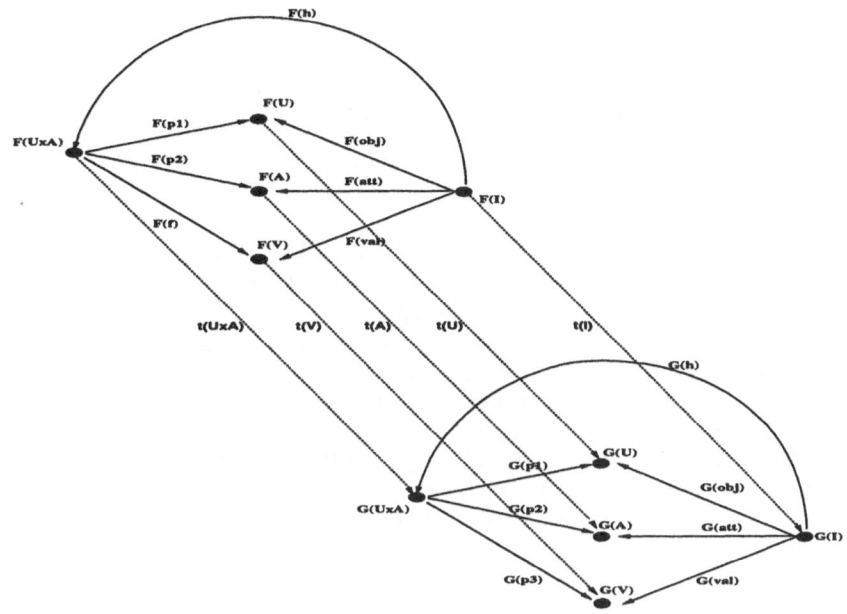

Figure 4: A natural transformation of information systems

of figure 4. This amounts to setting $t(A)$ to σ. Note that in a permuting category the sets of attributes of different information systems are the same, i.e. $G(A) = F(A)$. In order to get a condition on the morphism we have to complete the diagram[6] (i.e. construct the natural transformation t) such that the relevant squares in this diagram commute. We obtain as a side effect a function $t(I) : F(I) \rightarrow G(I)$ giving the change of information. The class of all permuting morphisms consist of all those natural transformations we can construct like above starting with a permutation on the set of attributes.

We can characterize the indiscernibility category in a similar way. Let $\text{Ind}(A)$ be a indiscernibility relation on a a set of objects $F(U)$. Let $r : F(U) \rightarrow F(U)/\text{Ind}(A)$ a function mapping object u to its equivalent class $[u]$. Fix for each equivalent class $c \in U/\text{Ind}(A)$ one representative $u \in F(U)$. Let $r' : F(U) \rightarrow F(U)$ map each object to the representative of its equivalence class. We can construct now an indiscernibility morphism by drawing r' in figure 4 (i.e. $t(U) = r'$) and completing the diagram.

In summary we can characterize classes of morphisms between information systems by completing a diagram of the general scheme of figure 4. Next to characterizing well-known concepts of information systems to this categorical framework - to obtain better insight - , we can take the opposite route and translate well-known concepts of category to the framework of information systems. We will give two motivating examples.

Consider the diagram of figure 5, which is an abbreviation of figure 4.

---

[6]note that in this case $F(A) = G(A), F(U) = G(U), F(U \times A) = G(U \times A), F(V) = G(V)$

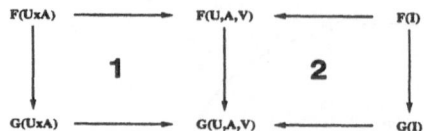

Figure 5: The general framework

Consider the case where $t(X)$ (X is U or A or V) is given and squares 1 and 2 are pullbacks. Then the information system G should be the unique (up to isomorphism) co-limit given by the change $t(X)$. Informally, this amounts to saying that G is the information system that remains after applying the damage $t(X)$ and nothing but the damage $t(X)$ to F.

An other example concerns the characterization of reducts. Consider a category of information systems in which morphisms are draw between two information systems A and B if and only if $\text{Ind}(A) = \text{Ind}(B)$ and $A \supseteq B$ then the reducts of some information systems C are precisely the *terminal objects* in this category, that are connected with C by a morphism.

5 Final Remarks

1. This paper is only a starting point for further investigation.
2. It is interesting to study the representation of information systems categories as a family of functors from other simple structures, e.g. see Wiweger [4].

References

[1] Z. Pawlak, *Information systems - theoretical foundations*; Information systems, 6 (1981), pp. 205-218.

[2] Z. Semadeni, *On classification, logical educational materials, and automata*, Colloq. Math., 31 (1974), pp. 137-153

[3] R. Wille, *Restructuring lattice theory: an approach based on hierarchies of concepts*; in: I. Rival (ed.), *Ordered sets*, Reidel, 1982, p. 445-470.

[4] A. Wiweger, *Knowledge representation systems, Logical Kits, and Contexts*, Bull. Pol. Math. 36(3-4), 1988, pp.99-111.

[5] A. Obtulowicz, *Rough sets and Heyting algebra valued sets*, Bull. Pol. Math. 35(9-10), 1987, pp. 667-673.

[6] T. Bieganska, *Algebraic and categorial aspects of rough sets*, Phd thesis, Warsaw University of Technology, 1990 (in Polish).

[7] E.F. Codd, *A relational model for large shared data banks*; in: Communications of the ACM, vol. 13 1970.

[8] J. Lambek and P.J. Scott, *Introduction to higher order categorical logic*, Cambridge studies in advanced mathematics 7, 1986.

[9] M. Banerjee, M.K. Chakraborty, *A category for rough sets*, preprint, Dept. of pure Math., University of Calcutta, India, 1993.

On Rough Sets in Topological Boolean Algebras

Marek Chuchro

Department of Computer Science and Applied Logic, University of Opole
Opole, Poland

Abstract

We have focused on rough sets in topological Boolean algebras. Our main ideas on rough sets are taken from concepts of Pawlak [4] and certain generalizations of his constructions which were offered by Wiweger [7]. One of the most important results of this note is a characterization of the rough sets determined by regular open and regular closed elements.

1 Introduction

We shall briefly review several basic notions which will be used later.

Definition 1.1 (see [5]) *We say that a set A is a* topological Boolean algebra *with respect to the operations* $\cup$, $\cap$, $-$, *and,* $\mathbf{I}$, *when:*

(i_1) *A is a Boolean algebra with respect to* $\cup$, $\cap$, *and* $-$

(i_2) *If x is in A, then $\mathbf{I}x$ is in A,*

(i_3) *If x is in A, then $\mathbf{I}x \leq x$,*

(i_4) *If x is in A, then $\mathbf{I}\mathbf{I}x = \mathbf{I}x$,*

(i_5) *If x and y are in A, then $\mathbf{I}(x \cap y) = \mathbf{I}x \cap \mathbf{I}y$,*

(i_6) *$\mathbf{I}\mathbf{1} = \mathbf{1}$.*

In other words: a topological Boolean algebra is an abstract algebra, $< A;\ \cup, \cap, -, \mathbf{0}, \mathbf{1}, \mathbf{I} >$ such that $< A;\ \cup, \cap, -, \mathbf{0}, \mathbf{1} >$ is a Boolean algebra, and $\mathbf{I}$ satisfies (i_2)–(i_6).

We shall use in connection with topological Boolean algebras certain terms with which the reader will be familiar from topology.

Let A be a topological Boolean algebra.

Definition 1.2 *By the* closure (interior) *of an element $x \in A$ we mean the element $\mathbf{C}x = -\mathbf{I}{-}x$ ($\mathbf{I}x = -\mathbf{C}{-}x$).*

Definition 1.3 *An element $x \in A$ is said to be* open (closed) *provided $x = \mathbf{I}x$ ($x = \mathbf{C}x$).*

Definition 1.4 *An element $x \in A$ is called* regular open (regular closed)*, if $\mathbf{I}\mathbf{C}x = x$ ($\mathbf{C}\mathbf{I}x = x$).*

Definition 1.5 *By the* boundary *of an element $x \in A$ we mean the element $\mathbf{F}x = \mathbf{C}x - \mathbf{I}x$.*

2 Selected properties of rough sets in topological Boolean algebras

Let A be a topological Boolean algebra and let x, y be elements of A. Let us define the rough equality relation.

Definition 2.1 *The elements x, y are roughly equal ($x \approx y$) if*

$$Ix = Iy \quad and \quad Cx = Cy \ (\ cf. \ [1], [3] \ ).$$

The following conclusion is an immediate consequence of the definition of equality relation.

Conclusion 2.2 *The rough equality relation ($\approx$) is an equivalence relation in A.*

We will call the pair $(A, \approx)$ an *approximation algebra*.

Definition 2.3 *Equivalence classes of the rough equality relation are called rough sets in $(A, \approx)$ ($cf.$ [3], [7]).*

Definition 2.4 *In an approximation algebra $(A, \approx)$, rough sets $[x]_\approx$, which satisfy the condition $Ix = Cx$ are called* exact sets.

Proposition 2.5 *If $x \in A$, then*

$$Cx = ICx \cup Fx, \tag{1}$$

$$Ix = ICx - Fx \tag{2}$$

Proof: (1) $Cx = Ix \cup (Cx - Ix) = Ix \cup Fx \leq ICx \cup Fx \leq Cx$. Hence $Cx = ICx \cup Fx$.

(2) $Cx - Fx = (Ix \cup Fx) - Fx = Ix - Fx = Ix$ (it follows from this that $Ix \cap Fx = 0$). ¿From (1) we have $Ix = Cx - Fx = (ICx \cup Fx) - Fx = ICx - Fx$. Thus the proof is finished.

Proposition 2.6 *If $x \in A$, then*

$$Cx = ICx \cup Fx, \tag{3}$$

$$Ix = CIx - Fx \tag{4}$$

The proof is similiar to that of Proposition 2.5 and will be omitted.

It is also easy to prove the following conclusion:

Conclusion 2.7 *The following conditions are equivalent:*

$$Ix = Iy \ and \ Cx = Cy, \tag{5}$$

$$ICx = ICy \ and \ Fx = Fy, \tag{6}$$

$$CIx = CIy \ and \ Fx = Fy. \tag{7}$$

Let u be any fixed regular open element of A.

Let us take the set $A(u) = \{x \in A: \ x = u \cup z \ \text{and} \ z \leq \mathbf{F}u = \mathbf{C}u - u\}$. We can define an operation $\cup_1$ of addition, and an operation $\cap_1$ of multiplication, and an operation $-_1$ of complementation, in $A(u)$, namely

$$x \cup_1 y = x \cup y,$$

$$x \cap_1 y = x \cap y,$$

if $x = u \cup z$ and $z \leq \mathbf{F}u$ then $-_1 x = u \cup (\mathbf{F}u - z)$

for any $x, y \in A(u)$.

It is not difficult to verify that the following is held:

Theorem 2.8 *The algebra* $< A(u); \ \cup_1, \cap_1, -_1, u, \mathbf{C}u >$ *is a Boolean algebra with the zero element u and the unit element $\mathbf{C}u$.*

The main result of this section is the following:

Theorem 2.9 *Let $(A, \approx)$ be an approximation algebra. If u is any fixed regular open element of A, then*

$$A(u) = [u]_{\approx}.$$

Proof: Firstly we shall prove the following inclusion $A(u) \subseteq [u]_{\approx}$. Assume that $x \in A(u)$. Then $x = u \cup z$ and $z \leq \mathbf{C}u - u$. Hence

$$\mathbf{C}x = \mathbf{C}\,(u \cup z) = \mathbf{C}u. \tag{8}$$

From this we have $\mathbf{I}x = \mathbf{I}\,(u \cup z) \leq \mathbf{IC}\,(u \cup z) \leq \mathbf{IC}u = u = \mathbf{I}u$. This and the fact that $\mathbf{I}u \leq \mathbf{I}x$ imply that

$$\mathbf{I}\,x = \mathbf{I}u. \tag{9}$$

From (8), (9) we have $x \in [u]_{\approx}$. Hence $A(u) \subseteq [u]_{\approx}$.

In order to prove the inclusion $[u]_{\approx} \subseteq A(u)$ assume that $x \in [u]_{\approx}$. Hence $\mathbf{I}x = u$ and $\mathbf{C}x = \mathbf{C}u$. This implies that $u \leq x \leq \mathbf{C}u$. From this we have $\mathbf{F}u = \mathbf{C}u - u = (\mathbf{C}u - x) \cup (x - u)$. Hence $x - u \leq \mathbf{F}u$. This and the fact that $x = u \cup (x - u)$ imply that $x \in A(u)$, which proves that $[u]_{\approx} \subseteq A(u)$. This completes the proof of Theorem 2.9

Let w be any fixed regular closed element of A.

Let us take the set $B(w) = \{y \in A: \ y = w - z \ \text{and} \ z \leq \mathbf{F}w = w - \mathbf{I}w\}$. We can define an operation $\cup_2$ of addition, and an operation $\cap_2$ of multiplication, and an operation $-_2$ of complementation, in B(w), namely

$$x \cup_2 y = x \cup y,$$

$$x \cap_2 y = x \cap y,$$

if $x = w - z$ and $z \leq \mathbf{F}w$ then $-_2 x = w - (\mathbf{F}w - z)$

for any $x, y \in B(w)$.

It is easy to show that the following is held:

Theorem 2.10 *The algebra* $< B(w); \ \cup_2, \cap_2, -_2, \mathbf{I}w, w >$ *is a Boolean algebra with the zero element $\mathbf{I}w$ and the unit element w.*

The next main theorem we establish is the following:

Theorem 2.11 *Let $(A, \approx)$ be an approximation algebra. If w is any fixed regular closed element of A, then*

$$B(w) = [w]_\approx.$$

Proof: Firstly we shall prove the following inclusion $B(w) \subseteq [w]_\approx$. Let us assume, without loss of generality, that $y \in B(w)$. Then $y = w - z$. Since $z \leq w - \mathbf{I}w$, so $-(w - \mathbf{I}w) = -w \cup \mathbf{I}w \leq -z$ and $\mathbf{I}w \leq -z$. Hence $\mathbf{I}w \leq \mathbf{I}{-}z$. This implies that

$$\mathbf{I}y = \mathbf{I}(w - z) = \mathbf{I}(w \cap -z) = \mathbf{I}w \cap \mathbf{I}{-}z = \mathbf{I}w. \tag{10}$$

From this we have $\mathbf{C}y = \mathbf{C}(w - z) \geq \mathbf{C}\mathbf{I}(w - z) = \mathbf{C}\mathbf{I}w = w = \mathbf{C}w$. This and the fact that $\mathbf{C}y \leq \mathbf{C}w$ imply

$$\mathbf{C}y = \mathbf{C}w \tag{11}$$

From (10) and (11) we have $y \in [w]_\approx$. Hence $B(w) \subseteq [w]_\approx$.

In order to prove the inclusion $[w]_\approx \subseteq B(w)$ assume that $y \in [w]_\approx$. Hence $\mathbf{I}y = \mathbf{I}w$ and $\mathbf{C}y = \mathbf{C}w = w$. This implies that $\mathbf{I}w \leq y \leq w$. ¿From this we have $\mathbf{F}w = \mathbf{C}w - \mathbf{I}w = w - \mathbf{I}w = (w - y) \cup (y - \mathbf{I}w)$. Hence $w - y \leq \mathbf{F}w$. This and the fact that $y = w - (w - y)$ imply that $y \in B(w)$, which proves that $[w]_\approx \subseteq B(w)$. The proof of Theorem 2.11 is therefore complete.

¿From Theorems 2.9, 2.11 we obtain:

Fact 2.12 *If $[x]_\approx$ is an exact set, then $[x]_\approx = \{x\}$.*

The author gratefully acknowledges the many helpful suggestions of Professor U. Wybraniec–Skardowska during the preparation of the paper.

References

[1] Bonikowski, Z., A Certain Conception of the Calculus of Rough Sets, **Notre Dame Journal of Formal Logic**, vol. 33, no. 3 (1992), pp. 412–421.

[2] Bryniarski, E., A Calculus of Rough Sets of the First Order, **Bull. Pol. Ac.: Math**, vol. 37 (1989), pp. 71–78.

[3] Chuchro, M., A Certain Conception of Rough Sets in Topological Boolean Algebras, **Bulletin of the Section of Logic**, vol. 22, no. 1 (1993), pp. 9–12, Department of Logic, Lódź University.

[4] Pawlak, Z., Rough Sets: An Algebraic and Topological Approach p. 482, **ICS PAS Report**, Pol. Ac. Sc., Warsaw, 1982.

[5] Rasiowa, H. and Sikorski, R., **The Mathematics of the Metamathematics**, PWN, Warsaw, 1968.

[6] Skowron, A., On Topology in Information Systems, **Bull. Pol. Ac.: Math**, 36 (1988) pp. 447–479.

[7] Wiweger, R., On Topological Rough Sets, **Bull. Pol. Ac.: Math**, vol. 37 (1989), pp. 89–93.

Approximation of Relations

Andrzej Skowron

Institute of Mathematics
Warsaw University
Banacha 2, 02-097 Warsaw, Poland
e-mail: skowron@mimuw.edu.pl

Jaroslaw Stepaniuk

Institute of Computer Science
Technical University of Bialystok
Wiejska 45A, 15-351 Bialystok, Poland
e-mail:jstepan@plbial11.plearn.bitnet

Abstract

We generalize the notion of an approximation space introduced in [3]. In generalized approximation spaces we define the lower and upper set approximations. We illustrate the introduced notions with different types of relation approximation.

1 Introduction

Investigations on relation approximation are well motivated both from theoretical and practical points of view. The equality approximation is fundamental for a generalization of the rough set approach [3] to the case of an indiscernibility relation being based on an approximation of the equality relations in the value sets of attributes rather than on the exact equality relations in these sets. Applications of rough set methods in process control require some good tools for function approximation. Finally, let us also mention some applications of relation approximation to discrete optimization problems [7] where approximations of input-output relations of programs are investigated.

The relation approximation based on the rough set approach is formulated in [3] and investigated in several papers (see e.g.[7]). In this paper we introduce a generalization of approximation spaces formulated in [3] and we also present a generalization of set approximation in these spaces. Our intention is to give a general tool for the investigation of relation approximations.

2 Generalized approximation spaces

In this section we present a generalization of the lower and upper approximations of sets, introduced in [3] and [9]. First we recall the definitions from [3], [9].

An *approximation space* is an ordered pair $\mathbb{R} = (U, IND)$, where U is a nonempty set and $IND \subseteq U \times U$ is an equivalence relation called the *indiscernibility relation*. By $[x]_{IND}$ we denote an equivalence class of the relation IND defined by the object x. The *lower* and *upper* approximations of a set X are defined as follows:

$$\underline{X} = \{x \in U : [x]_{IND} \subseteq X\} \text{ and } \overline{X} = \{x \in U : [x]_{IND} \cap X \neq \emptyset\}$$

respectively.

The *rough membership function* of a set $X \subseteq U$ (in a given approximation space $\mathbb{R}$) is defined [4] as follows:

$$\mu(x, X) = \frac{|X \cap [x]_{IND}|}{|[x]_{IND}|}$$

where $|.|$ denotes set cardinality. Hence we have

$$\underline{X} = \{x \in U : \mu(x, X) = 1\} \text{ and } \overline{X} = \{x \in U : \mu(x, X) > 0\}.$$

Moreover

$\mu(x, X) = 1 \quad \text{iff} \quad [x]_{IND} \subseteq X;$

$\mu(x, X) > 0 \quad \text{iff} \quad [x]_{IND} \cap X \neq \emptyset;$

$\mu(x, X) = 0 \quad \text{iff} \quad [x]_{IND} \cap X = \emptyset.$

The definition of lower and upper approximations of sets has been generalized in [9] by introducing the so called variable precision rough set model. Let β be a real number within the range $0 \leq \beta < 0.5$ and let $f_\beta : [0, 1] \rightarrow [0, 1]$ be a non-decreasing function such that $f_\beta(t) = 0$ iff $0 \leq t \leq \beta$ and $f_\beta(t) = 1$ iff $1 - \beta \leq t \leq 1$. The f_β-*membership function* $\mu(f_\beta)$ can now be defined by

$$\mu(f_\beta)(x, X) = f_\beta(t), \quad \text{where} \quad t = \frac{|X \cap [x]_{IND}|}{|[x]_{IND}|}$$

where $x \in X$ and $X \subseteq U$.

By putting $\beta = 0$ and $f_\beta = id$ we obtain the case considered in [3].

The lower and upper approximations of a set $X \subseteq U$ with respect to the membership function $\mu(f_\beta)$ can be presented in the following form:

$\mathbb{L}(\mu(f_\beta), X) = \{x \in U : \mu(f_\beta)(x, X) = 1\}$ and

$\mathbb{U}(\mu(f_\beta), X) = \{x \in U : \mu(f_\beta)(x, X) > 0\}$, respectively.

Let us observe that the following facts hold:

- if $\mu(f_\beta)(x, X) = 1$, then not necessarily $[x]_{IND} \subseteq X$;

- if $[x]_{IND} \subseteq X$, then $\mu(f_\beta)(x, X) = 1$;

- if $\mu(f_\beta)(x, X) > 0$, then $[x]_{IND} \cap X \neq \emptyset$;

- if $[x]_{IND} \cap X \neq \emptyset$, then not necessarily $\mu(f_\beta)(x, X) > 0$;

- if $\mu(f_\beta)(x, X) = 0$, then not necessarily $[x]_{IND} \cap X = \emptyset$;

- if $[x]_{IND} \cap X = \emptyset$, then $\mu(f_\beta)(x, X) = 0$.

Hence we have:

$$\mathbb{L}(\mu(id), X) \subseteq \mathbb{L}(\mu(f_\beta), X) \text{ and } \mathbb{U}(\mu(id), X) \supseteq \mathbb{U}(\mu(f_\beta), X)$$

for any set X and function f_β satisfying the conditions formulated above.

The membership functions introduced above can be extended to functions from $\mathbb{P}(U) \times \mathbb{P}(U)$ into the interval $[0, 1]$ of reals, namely

$$\nu(f_\beta)(X, Y) = f_\beta(t), \text{ where } t = \frac{|X \cap Y|}{|Y|}$$

for any $X, Y \subseteq U$ and $0 \le \beta < 0.5$. The extension can be treated as a measure of inclusion vagueness. We must decide what conditions should a function, called *inclusion vagueness*

$$\nu : \mathbb{P}(U) \times \mathbb{P}(U) \to [0, 1]$$

satisfy to be an appropriate measure for the degree of inclusion of sets.

Here we only assume *monotonicity* with respect to the second argument, i.e. $\nu(X, Y) \le \nu(X, Z)$ for any $Y \subseteq Z$, where $X, Y, Z \subseteq U$.

One can observe an analogy with fuzzy set theory [1],[8], i.e. that ν is a fuzzy inclusion function. The difference is that we are taking as a primitive notion a function of the above form measuring the degree of set inclusion rather than the degree membership function for objects. The reason is that in general one can only expect to have some partial information about any considered object accessible. In general it is not possible to identify an object having that partial information only. In rough set theory [3] the information $Inf(x)$ about an object x is specified by the vector of attribute values on that object x. This information $Inf(x)$ defines the set $[x]$ of all objects indiscernible with respect to a given set of attributes. Thus we obtain an *uncertainty function* $I : U \to \mathbb{P}(U)$ defined by $I(x) = Inf^{-1}(Inf(x))$ for any $x \in U$ [4],[5]. In general, an *uncertainty function* I on U is any function from U into $\mathbb{P}(U)$ satisfying the condition $x \in I(x)$ for any $x \in U$.

The inclusion vagueness function ν and the uncertainty function I define the *membership function* $\mu(I, \nu)(x, X) = \nu(I(x), X)$, where $x \in U$, $X \subseteq U$.

We would like to add one more condition to the definition of set approximation which arises by analogy with mathematical morphology [6]. This is the notion of a *structural element*. Let I be a given uncertainty function and let $P : I(U) \to \{0, 1\}$. Any set $X \in I(U)$ satisfying $P(X) = 1$ is called a *P-structural element* (in $I(U)$). The function P is called the *structurality function*.

An *approximation space* is a system

$$\mathbb{R} = (U, I, \nu, P)$$

where U is a non-empty set of objects, $\nu : \mathbb{P}(U) \times \mathbb{P}(U) \to [0, 1]$, $I : U \to \mathbb{P}(U)$ $P : I(U) \to \{0, 1\}$ are inclusion vagueness, uncertainty and structurality functions, respectively.

The lower and upper approximations of a set $X \subseteq U$ in $\mathbb{R}$ are defined by:

$$\mathbb{L}(\mathbb{R}, X) = \{x \in U : P(I(x)) = 1 \text{ and } \mu(I, \nu)(y, X) = 1$$
$$\text{for any } y \in \bigcap\{I(z) : x \in I(z)\}$$

and

$$\mathbb{U}(\mathbb{R}, X) = \{x \in U : P(I(x)) = 1 \text{ and } \mu(I, \nu)(y, X) > 0 \text{ for any } y \in I(x)\},$$

respectively.

In the case when I is defined by the indiscernibility relation the above definitions can be written in a simpler form, namely

$$\mathbb{L}(\mathbb{R}, X) = \{x \in U : P(I(x)) = 1 \text{ and } \mu(I, \nu)(x, X) = 1\} \text{ and}$$

$$\mathbb{U}(\mathbb{R}, X) = \{x \in U : P(I(x)) = 1 \text{ and } \mu(I, \nu)(x, X) > 0\},$$

respectively. This holds because in the considered case the following implication is true: if $I(x) \cap I(y) \neq \emptyset$ then $I(x) = I(y)$.

In rough set theory $I(x) = [x]_{IND}$ for any $x \in U$, $\nu(X, Y) = |X \cap Y|/|X|$ for any $X, Y \subseteq U$ and P is the identity on $I(U)$. For variable precision rough set model approach only the inclusion vagueness ν is defined differently, namely

$$\nu(f_\beta)(X, Y) = f_\beta(|X \cap Y|/|X|)$$

where f_β is specified as above.

There is one more aspect of set approximation which we would like to discuss. It concerns information availability for the approximated sets. In [3] sets are represented by listing their elements in an information system. Sets are approximated on the basis of available information about objects. In this case the approximated sets are taken to be exact, which does not hold in general, e.g. we can only have some information about relations which we would like to approximate. We consider the case when information about approximated sets in a given approximation space $\mathbb{R} = (U, I, \nu, P)$ is specified by a *projection function* (from $\mathbb{R}$ into $(\mathbb{R}_1, \ldots, \mathbb{R}_k)$) $J : \mathbb{P}(U) \to \mathbb{P}(U_1 \cup \ldots \cup U_k)$, where $\mathbb{R}_i = (U)_i, I_i, \nu_i, P_i)$ for any $i = 1, \ldots, k$ are approximation spaces and $U_i \cap U_j \neq \emptyset$ for $i \neq j$. If $X \subseteq U$, then the set $J(X) \cap U_i$ is called the (J, i)-*projection* of X.

3   Approximation of relations

In this section we show examples of structurality and inclusion vagueness functions. We also present some relationships between different approximation spaces related by projections. Finally we formulate an optimization problem.

Let $\mathbb{R} = (U, I, \nu, P)$ and $\mathbb{R}_i = (U_i, I_i, \nu_i, P_i)$ for $i = 1, \ldots, k$ be approximation spaces, where $U = U_1 \times \ldots \times U_k$. If $R \subseteq U_1 \times \ldots \times U_k$, then by $\pi_i(R)$ we denote the projection of the k-ary relation R onto the i-th axis i.e.

$$\pi_i(R) = \{x : \exists x_1 \ldots \exists x_{i-1} \exists x_{i+1} \ldots \exists x_k R(x_1, \ldots, x_{i-1}, x, x_{i+1}, \ldots, x_k)\}.$$

Let us consider examples of properties $P(Q_1, \ldots, Q_k, G)$ defining structurality functions. They are described by: $P(Q_1, \ldots, Q_k, G)(I(x)) = 1$ iff

$$Q_1 y_1 \in \pi_1(I(x)) \ldots Q_k y_k \in \pi_k(I(x))(y_1, \ldots, y_k) \in G$$

where $Q_i \in \{\forall, \exists\}$ for $i = 1, \ldots, k$, $G \subseteq U_1 \times \ldots \times U_k$ and $x \in U$.

Applying in the construction of relation approximation the structural elements defined above we choose to consider only those $I(x)$ which have these additional properties $P(Q_1, \ldots, Q_k, G)$.

The definition of the vagueness function ν for relations can be based on different idea than the cardinality of the intersection with a structural element, e.g. for $k = 2$ and a threshold $p(0 < p < 1)$ let us assume $\mu(X, Y) = c$ iff $w/|\pi_1(X)| = c$, where $w = |\{y_1 \in \pi_1(X) : |y_2 \in \pi_2(Y) : (y_1, y_2) \in Y|/|\pi_2(Y)| \geq p\}|$.

In [3] it is assumed that structural elements are of the form $I(x) = I_1(x_1) \times \ldots \times I_k(x_k)$ for $x = (x_1, \ldots, x_k) \in U$ and $I_i(x_i) = [x_i]_{IND_i}$, i.e. the i-th information function is defined by the indiscernibility relation $IND_i \subseteq U_i \times U_i$. In this case I is also defined by the indiscernibility relation. Assuming $\nu = \nu(f_\beta)$ and $P(x) = 1$ for all $x \in U$ we obtain the following equalities [10] for the approximation of a relation R in $\mathbb{R}_o = (U, I, \nu, P)$:

$$\mathbb{L}(\mathbb{R}_o, R) = \{(x_1, \ldots, x_k) \in U : \frac{|R \cap [x_1]_{IND_1} \times \ldots \times [x_k]_{IND_k}|}{|[x_1]_{IND_1} \times \ldots \times [x_k]_{IND_k}|} \geq 1 - \beta\}$$

$$\mathbb{U}(\mathbb{R}_o, R) = \{(x_1, \ldots, x_k) \in U : \frac{|R \cap [x_1]_{IND_1} \times \ldots \times [x_k]_{IND_k}|}{|[x_1]_{IND_1} \times \ldots \times [x_k]_{IND_k}|} > \beta\}.$$

Proposition. *Let* $\mathbb{R} = (U, I, \nu, P)$, $\mathbb{R}' = (U, I, \nu', P)$, $\mathbb{R}_i = (U_i, I_i, \nu_i, P_i)$ *for* $i = 1, \ldots, k$ *be approximation spaces, where* $U = U_1 \times \ldots \times U_k$, I_i *is defined by an indiscernibility relation* $IND_i \subseteq U_i \times U_i$, *i.e.* $I_i(x_i) = [x_i]_{IND_i}$ *for* $x_i \in U_i, I(x) = I_1(x_1) \times \ldots \times I_k(x_k)$ *for* $x = (x_1, \ldots, x_k) \in U$. *We assume also that* $P(I(x)) = P_i(I_i(x_i)) = 1$ *for* $x = (x_1, \ldots, x_k) \in U$, $\nu_i = \nu(f_{\beta_i})$ *for some* $0 \leq \beta_i < 0.5$. *If* J *and* J_X *(where* $\emptyset \neq X \subseteq U$*) are projections of* $\mathbb{R}$ *into* $(\mathbb{R}_1, \ldots, \mathbb{R}_k)$ *defined by* $J(R) \cap U_i = \pi_i(R)$ *and* $J_X(R) \cap U_i = \pi_i(R \cap X)$ *for* $R \subseteq U$ *and*

$$\nu(X, Y) = \min\{\nu_i(J(X) \cap U_i, J(Y) \cap U_i) : 1 \leq i \leq k\}$$

$$\nu'(X, Y) = \min\{\nu_i(J_X(X) \cap U_i, J_X(Y) \cap U_i) : 1 \leq i \leq k\}$$

then

1. ν, ν' *are monotonic with respect to the second argument;*

2. $\mathbb{L}(\mathbb{R}, R) = \{x \in U : |[x_i]_{IND_i} \cap \pi_i(R)|/|[x_i]_{IND_i}| \geq 1 - \beta_i$ *for* $i = 1, \ldots, k\}$;

3. $\mathbb{L}(\mathbb{R}', R) = \{x \in U : |\pi_i(R \cap I(x))|/|[x_i]_{IND_i}| \geq 1 - \beta_i$ *for* $i = 1, \ldots, k\}$;

4. $\mathbb{U}(\mathbb{R}, R) = \{x \in U : |[x_i]_{IND_i} \cap \pi_i(R)|/|[x_i]_{IND_i}| > \beta_i$ *for* $i = 1, \ldots, k\}$;

5. $\mathbb{U}(\mathbb{R}', R) = \{x \in U : |\pi_i(R \cap I(x))|/|[x_i]_{IND_i}| > \beta_i$ *for* $i = 1, \ldots, k\}$;

6. $\mathbb{L}(\mathbb{R}, R) = \times_{i=1}^k \mathbb{L}(\mathbb{R}_i, \pi_i(R))$ *and* $\mathbb{U}(\mathbb{R}, R) = \times_{i=1}^k \mathbb{U}(\mathbb{R}_i, \pi_i(R))$;

7. $\mathbb{L}(\mathbb{R}', R) \subseteq \mathbb{L}(\mathbb{R}, R)$ *and* $\mathbb{U}(\mathbb{R}', R) \subseteq \mathbb{U}(\mathbb{R}, R)$. $\square$

Finally let us formulate an important problem related to relation approximation.

Optimization Problem:

INPUT: approximation spaces $\mathbb{R} = (U, I, \nu, P), \mathbb{R}_i = (U_i, I_i, \nu_i, P_i)$, for $i = 1, \ldots, k$, where $U = U_1 \times \ldots \times U_k$; projection J from $\mathbb{R}$ into $(\mathbb{R}_1, \ldots, \mathbb{R}_k)$; family F of functions from $[0, 1]^k$ into $[0, 1]$.

OUTPUT: $f_{opt} \in F$ such that $S(f_{opt}) = \inf\{S(f) : f \in F\}$, where $S(f) = \sup\{|\mu(X, Y) - f_{opt}(\mu_1(X_1, Y_1), \ldots, \mu_i(X_k, Y_k))| : X, Y \subseteq U\}$, $\mu = \mu(I, \nu)$, $\mu_i = \mu(I_i, \nu_i)$, $X_i = J(X) \cap U_i$, $Y_i = J(Y) \cap U_i$ for $i = 1, \ldots, k$.

Strategies for finding optimal (sub-optimal) solutions for this problem are important for applications of rough set methods in process control area. Results related to this problem will be presented in our next papers.

4 Conclusions

We have proposed the generalizations of approximation space and set approximation as a tool for the investigation of relation approximation. These definitions allow to omit some drawbacks of the classical definitions. We hope that they can be considered as a good starting point for investigations of important problems related to relation approximation, e.g. the optimization problem for controllers design.

References

[1] Dubois D., Prade H. and Yager R.: **Fuzzy Sets for Intelligent Systems**, Morgan Kaufmann, San Mateo 1993.

[2] Pawlak Z. : Rough Relations, Bull. Acad. Polon. Sci, Ser. Tech. Sci. vol. 34 (9-10), 1986, 587-590.

[3] Pawlak Z. : **Rough Sets. Theoretical Aspects of Reasoning about Data**, Kluwer Academic Publishers, Dordrecht 1991.

[4] Pawlak Z., Skowron A. : Rough Membership Functions In: M.Federizzi, J.Kacprzyk and R.R.Yager (eds.): Advances in the Dempster-Shafer Theory of Evidence. New York: John Wiley and Sons (to appear).

[5] Pawlak Z.: Hard and soft sets, Proceedings of the International Workshop on Rough Sets and Knowledge Discovery, Banff, Alberta, Canada, October 12-15, 1993, 107-110.

[6] Serra, J.: **Image Analysis and Mathematical Morphology**, Academic Press, New York - London, 1982.

[7] Skowron A., Stepaniuk J. : Towards an Approximation Theory of Discrete Problems, Fundamenta Informatice 15(2), 1991, 187-208.

[8] Zadeh L: Fuzzy sets, Information and Control 8, 1965, 338-353.

[9] Ziarko W. : Variable Precision Rough Set Model, Journal of Computer and System Sciences, vol. 46 (1), 1993, 39-59.

Variable Precision Rough Sets with Asymmetric Bounds

Jack David Katzberg

Electronic Information Systems Engineering
University of Regina
Regina, Saskatchewan, Canada S4S 0A2

Wojciech Ziarko

Computer Science Department
University of Regina
Regina, Saskatchewan, Canada S4S 0A2

Abstract

A generalization of the original idea of rough sets as introduced by Pawlak is presented. The generalization, called the Variable Precision Rough Sets Model with Asymmetric Bounds, is aimed at modeling data relationships expressed in terms of frequency distribution rather than a full inclusion relation. The model presented is a direct extension of the previous concept, the Variable Precision Rough Sets Model. The properties of the extended model are investigated and compared to the original model.

1 Introduction

This paper presents a methodology for automated pattern analysis. The object is to determine the best variables and data patterns to categorize the data in terms of the likelihood of a given event. It is assumed that the data is available in tabular or data base form. This information is then analyzed to determine the relationship between the variables holding values in specified ranges and the likelihood of the specified event occurring. An approach based on an extension of the Rough Sets [1-3] methodology, called Variable Precision Rough Sets with Asymmetric Bounds, is used to determine the best minimum set of variables and rules to predict which likelihoods will lie within given ranges. This work was motivated by a "pacing" problem in the steel industry. It was necessary to use automated pattern analysis to determine the best variables to categorize the production data in terms of the probability of a delay occurring at the finishing mill. The objective of this work is to determine which variables and what categorization will give good prediction of a delay frequency with reasonable complexity. There are many factors which could be used to predict the likelihood of a delay occurring while processing steel on the finishing mill. If the effect of all these variables is to be determined, then an organized approach is required.

   The variable precision rough set [4] or probabilistic approximate classification methods [5] offer such an organized approach. However, the basic model assumes we are interested in events with probability greater than 0.5. Hopefully, even the largest delay probabilities are much smaller than that. Consequently, the basic definitions must be redefined to make it possible to characterize events whose probabilities fall into any range.

In the rough sets approach, the classification of the data is developed using three regions: the positive region in which an event would occur, the negative region in which an event would not occur, and a boundary region in which an event might occur. The variable precision rough set approach defined the positive and negative regions as areas where the approximate classification with an error rate less than some predefined level is possible. The boundary region then is the area where the classification with an error smaller than some predefined level is not possible. The positive region then became a region where the event occurred most of the time, and the negative region is the region where the event occurred infrequently.

In this paper, we extend this idea to define the negative region as the region where the likelihood of some event is less than some defined lower limit, the positive region as the region where the likelihood of the event is greater than some defined upper limit and the boundary region is the region where the likelihood of the event is between the specified limits. All the likelihoods were less than 0.5 in our steel industry problem. It will be shown that this generalized model inherits all the basic mathematical properties of the original rough set model introduced by Pawlak.

2 Information Tables and Decision Rules

It is assumed the data is available in a table or data base form. Each line or record is a representation of an object called a situation. The situations are formally denoted as a set, the universe $U = \{e_1, e_2, ...e_N\}$. Each situation has a set of attributes, i.e. the fields of a record. This set of attributes, A, may be broken into a set of condition attributes, C, and a set of decision attributes, D, such that $A = C \cup D$. That is, A is the union of C and D. The table so defined is referred to as an Information Table. It is a special case of a Knowledge Representation System (or Information System) whose logical properties have been investigated by many researchers [6,7]. Formally, the Information Table, IT is a quintuple $IT =< U, C, D, V, f >$, where U is a set of situations; C is a set of condition attributes or variables and D is a set of decision attributes or variables; and $f : U \times (C \cup D) \rightarrow V$ is an information function which assigns values of system variables to situations. That is, for every situation, e_i, $f(e_i, a_j)$ is a particular value from the set or range of possible values, a_j, for each j.

We can partition the set of situations in the Information Table into a number of disjoint classes based on any subset Z of the set of attributes A. The classes, or elementary sets, are constructed by the equivalence relation $Q(Z)$ which we define as follows:

Two situations e_i and e_j are indistinguishable or equivalent with respect to Z if $f(e_j, z) = f(e_i, z)$ for all variables z belonging to Z. The set of all situations such that this is true forms an equivalence class (or elementary set), X, which is a subset of U, the set of all situations. For the equivalence relation $Q(Z)$ defined in this way, each of its equivalence classes X is associated with a unique combination of values of variables from Z. That is, each $z \in Z$ has a specified value. This combination of values is referred to as a description of the class

X. The description of the class X is the set of values each variable within Z must take to be associated with a situation in the set X. The description of the class X is denoted by $Des_Z(X) = \wedge_{z \in Z}(z := f(e, z))$, where e is an arbitrary situation from the class X, the symbol, $\wedge$, denotes a logical conjunction of terms and $:=$ is an assignment symbol. The collection of all equivalence classes of the relation $Q(Z)$ will be denoted by Z^*, which is termed a partition.

Let $C^* = \{C_1, C_2, ..., C_I\}$ denote the classification of the set of situations U generated by values of condition variables C. Similarly, let $D^* = \{D_1, D_2, ..., D_J\}$ denote the classification corresponding to the set of decision attributes.

Any subset X of the set of all situations (the universe) U which can be expressed as a union of some classes of the partition C^* is called C-definable set. Each C-definable set is associated with the characteristic description $Desc(X)$ in the form of a logical disjunction of descriptions of its component elementary sets.

A deterministic decision rule occurs when the C-definable set X is included in a class D_K of the partition based on the decision attributes D. The decision rule is normally expressed as a conditional statement $r : Desc(X) \rightarrow Des_D(D_K)$.

That is, a given vector of condition variable values always implies a given vector of decision variable values. The vector of decision variable values may occur in other situations as well. The deterministic decision rule reflects the presence of partial functional dependency between the condition and decision variables in an information table.

To define the notion of a non-deterministic decision rule, let us associate with any C-definable set X, a collection G of those classes from D^* which have non-empty intersections with X. That is, $G(X) = \{D \in D^* : X \cap D \neq \emptyset\}$, where $\emptyset$ is the null set. The non-deterministic decision rule r associated with the class $C \in C^*$ can be defined as the statement

$$r : Des_C(X) \rightarrow \bigvee Des_D(D_j), \qquad D_j \in G(X)$$

where the conclusion part of the rule, the right side is a disjunction of descriptions of all classes of D^* which are contained in $G(X)$. The non-deterministic decision rule reflects the fact that there is more than one outcome possible in response to conditions specified by $Des_C(X)$. The non-deterministic decision rule reflects the presence of partial or statistical dependency among events.

In this paper, we are interested in situations where most or all of the decision rules are non-deterministic and some of the less likely outcomes are important. Such outcomes might be a delay of a given length, the possible discovery of oil, or the concentration of gold in an ore. We are then interested in the likelihood or frequency of a decision variable when predicted by a given vector of condition variables.

3   Variable Dependencies and Likelihoods

Let us define the relative frequency of Y given X to be

$$P(Y|X) = card(X \cap Y)/card(X)$$

where $card(U)$ is the total number of situations under consideration. Rather than knowing if X predicts Y most of the time, we may simply be interested if X changes the frequency of the occurrence of Y significantly.

Let us assume we have some frequency of Y given X, F, that is of interest. It might have some economic impact or other significance. Let us further assume that σ_1 and σ_2 represent a significant increase or decrease in frequency such that if $P(Y|X) > F + \sigma_1$ then one decision will result, or if $P(Y|X) < F - \sigma_2$ then a different decision will be taken. If $P(Y|X)$ is between these limits, either the decision may be uncertain or a third action might be appropriate. In the case of delay frequencies in a steel mill, three different decisions on pacing strategy may result.

As a given situation must either be in the set, Y, or its complement, $-Y$, and as a set and its complement are disjoint, for the set of situations, X, we know $card(X) = card(X \cap Y) + card(X \cap -Y)$. If we divided through by card(X) and reorder, we define

$$c(X,Y) = 1 - \frac{card(X \cap Y)}{card(X)} = \frac{card(X \cap -Y)}{card(X)} = P(-Y|X)$$

The quantity $c(X,Y)$ will be termed the *classification factor*.

In a manner analogous to the variable precision rough sets concept[4], if the frequency of Y given X is above the value of interest, then the classification factor will be below some significant lower value called the lower limit ℓ, i.e.

$$c(X,Y) \leq 1 - (F + \sigma_1) = \ell$$

We will associate this lower range of classification factors with the *relative inclusion* of the set X within Y: $Y \supseteq^\ell X$ if and only if $c(X,Y) \leq \ell$.

Similarly, if the frequency of Y given X is below the value of interest, then the classification factor will be above some significant upper value called the upper limit u, i.e. $c(X,Y) \geq 1 - (F - \sigma_2) = u$.

We will associate this upper range of classification factors with the *relative exclusion* of the set X from Y: $Y \not\supseteq^u X$ if and only if $c(X,Y) \geq u$.

Note that it is only necessary that $0 \leq \ell < u \leq 1$. It is possible for both upper and lower classification factor ranges to be small. Below we present some elementary properties of the relative inclusion/exclusion relations.

Proposition 3.1

If $\ell_2 \geq \ell_1$ then $Y \supseteq^{\ell_1} X \Rightarrow Y \supseteq^{\ell_2} X$.

Proof:

$Y \supseteq^{\ell_1} X$ if and only if $c(X,Y) \leq \ell_1 \leq \ell_2$.

Proposition 3.2

If $u_1 \geq u_2$ then $Y \not\supseteq^{u_1} X \Rightarrow Y \not\supseteq^{u_2} X$.

Proof:

$Y \not\supseteq^{u_1} X$ if and only if $c(X,Y) \geq u_1 \geq u_2$.

Proposition 3.3

If $Y \cap Z = \emptyset$, the null set, then $Y \supseteq^\ell X \Rightarrow Z \not\supseteq^{1-\ell} X$.

Proof:

As the sets Y and Z are disjoint

$card(X) \geq card(X \cap (Y \cup Z)) = card(X \cap Y) + card(X \cap Z)$.

Dividing through by $card(X)$ and using the definition of relative frequency, we find $1 \geq (P(Y|X) + P(Z|X))$. From this we can see $c(X, Z) = (1 - P(Z|X)) \geq P(Y|X)$. The inclusion of X in Y with classification factor ℓ implies $\ell \geq c(X, Y) = 1 - P(Y|X)$; Hence, $c(X, Z) \geq P(Y|X) \geq 1 - \ell$.

Corollary

If $\ell < 1/2$ and $Y \cap Z = \emptyset$, the null set, then $Y \supseteq^{\ell} X \Rightarrow \neg(Z \supseteq^{\ell} X)$.

Proof:

If $\ell < 1/2$ then $1 - \ell > 1/2$ so $c(X, Z) > \ell$.

Proposition 3.4

If $Y \not\supseteq^{u} X$ then $-Y \supseteq^{1-u} X$.

Proof:

Clearly, $P(Y|X) + P(-Y|X) = 1$ which implies $c(X, -Y) = 1 - P(-Y|X) = P(Y|X)$. Since the exclusion of the set X from Y requires $u \leq c(X, Y) = 1 - P(Y|X)$, it follows that $c(X, -Y) = P(Y|X) \leq 1 - u$.

Corollary

If $u > 1/2$, then $Y \not\supseteq^{u} X \Rightarrow \neg(-Y \not\supseteq^{u} X)$.

Proof:

From the assumption $c(X, Y) \geq u > 1/2$. Consequently, $c(X, -Y) = 1 - c(X, Y) < 1/2 < u$.

4   Set Approximations

In this section, in line with ideas presented in Section 3, the basic concept of set approximation [1] is generalized to enable flexible construction of set approximations with varying degrees of approximation accuracy. One of the primary components in this extension is the notion of the approximation space $A = (U, R)$ consisting of a universe of discourse, U, and of the relation, R, on U[1]. The equivalence relation, called an indiscernibility relation, represents a partition of the universe into indiscernibility classes, or elementary sets. The elementary sets are the atomic components of given information representation systems. They correspond to the smallest groups of objects which are distinguishable in terms of the information used to represent them, e.g. in terms of object features and their values. Since objects belonging to an elementary set are perceived as identical, it may not be possible to determine set membership criteria for every subset of the universe, U. The set membership criteria for subsets partially intersecting some elementary sets can, in general be specified only approximately, meaning that a classification error is possible when applying such criteria. However, by analyzing the distribution information in elementary sets, one can derive classification criteria which will guarantee that the classification factor will fall into predefined boundaries. This leads to the following generalization of the concept of rough approximation.

Let us assume that U is finite and let $R^* = \{E_1, E_2, ...E_M\}$ be the collection of equivalence classes of the relation R. As in Section 3, let ℓ and u be two real parameters referred to respectively as a lower limit and an upper limit such that $0 \leq \ell < u \leq 1$. For any subset $Y \subseteq U$ we define the lower approximation of Y as a union of those elementary sets whose degree of overlap with the complement, $-Y$, of Y is not higher than the lower limit, that is

$$\underline{R_\ell}(Y) = \bigcup\{E \in R^* : c(E, Y) \leq \ell\}$$

The lower approximation, or l-positive region characterizes a region in the universe, U, whose classification criteria guarantee that the relative error when using this criteria to classify situations to the subset Y will not be higher than ℓ.

The boundary region of the set Y with respect to the lower and upper limits ℓ and u is the union of those elementary sets for which the degree of overlap with the complement of Y is higher than the lower limit ℓ and lower than the upper limit u. Formally,

$$BNR_{\ell,u}(Y) = \bigcup\{E \in R^* : \ell < c(E, Y) < u\}$$

Objects belonging to the boundary region $BNR_{\ell,u}(Y)$ will be classified into Y with classification factor greater than ℓ, but smaller than u. In practical decision situations, the boundary area represents objects which cannot be classified with sufficiently high confidence (represented by ℓ) into Y and which also cannot be excluded from Y with the required factor (represented by u).

The union of the positive region and of the boundary region is called an upper approximation, i.e.

$$\overline{R_u}(Y) = \bigcup\{E \in R^* : c(E, Y) < u\}$$

The upper approximation is a characterization of objects which cannot be classified with predefined classification factors $1 - u$ as being excluded from Y.

The negative region of the subset, Y, is a union of such elementary classes of relation R whose degree of exclusion from Y is not lower than u, that is,

$$NEGR_u(Y) = \bigcup\{E \in R^* : c(E, Y) \geq u\}$$

The objects from the negative region can be classified as not belonging to Y with the confidence level $1 - u$. This property follows from the following.

Proposition 4.1

For every $Y \subseteq U$, $\underline{R_{1-u}}(-Y) = NEGR_u(Y)$.

Proof:

The proof follows directly from the fact that $c(E, Y) = 1 - c(E, -Y)$, and, consequently, the proposition $c(E, Y) \geq u$ is equivalent to the proposition $c(E, -Y) \leq 1 - u$.

Proposition 4.2

For every $Y \subseteq U$, $BNR_{\ell,u}(Y) = BNR_{1-u,1-\ell}(-Y)$.

Proof:

$BNR_{\ell,u}(Y) = \bigcup\{E \in R^* : \ell < c(E, Y) < u\}$. Note if $\ell < c(E, Y) < u$
then $\ell < 1 - c(E, -Y) < u$ as $C(E, Y) = 1 - C(E, -Y)$
and $\ell - 1 < -c(E, -Y) < u - 1$ or $1 - \ell > c(E, -Y) > 1 - u$. Therefore,
$BNR_{\ell,u}(Y) = \bigcup\{E \in R^* : 1 - u < c(E, -Y) < 1 - \ell\} = BNR_{1-u,1-\ell}(-Y)$

4.1 Relationship to Variable Precision Rough Sets Model

If we let $\ell = \beta$ our relative inclusion relation reduces to $Y \supseteq^\beta X$ if and only if $c(X, Y) \leq \beta$ and our lower approximation becomes

$$\underline{R}_\beta Y = \bigcup \{E \in R^* : c(E, Y) \leq \ell\} = \bigcup \{E \in R^* : Y \supseteq^\beta E\}$$

which corresponds to the VPRS case. However, when we compare the boundary region conditions, we find more severe restrictions are necessary. For our asymmetric rough sets model case $BNR_{\ell,u}(Y) = \bigcup \{E \in R^* : \ell < c(E, Y) < u\}$, while in the VPRS case

$$BNR_\beta(Y) = \bigcup \{E \in R^* : \beta < c(E, Y) < 1 - \beta\}$$

Thus for these regions to correspond we require $u = 1 - \beta = 1 - \ell$.

4.2 Relationship to the Deterministic Rough Sets Model

In this subsection, we review some basic connections between the extended model presented here and the original deterministic model of rough sets [1]. According to the original model, the lower approximation of a subset $X \subseteq U$ in the approximation space (R, U) is defined as

$$\underline{R}(X) = \bigcup \{E \in R^* : E \subseteq X\}$$

The lower approximation of X is a union of elementary classes totally included in X. The upper approximation of X, denoted as $R(X)$, is a union of these elementary classes which have some overlap with X, i.e.

$$\overline{R}(X) = \bigcup \{E \in R^* : E \cap X = \emptyset\}$$

The boundary area of X in the deterministic model is defined as $BNR(X) = R(X) - \underline{R}(X)$, that is, it is a union of such elementary classes which have only partial overlap with the set X. The collection of all elementary classes completely disjoint from the set X is called the negative region of X, denoted $NEGR(X)$:
$NEGR(X) = \bigcup \{E \in R^* : E \cap X = \emptyset\}$
The properties linking the extended model with the deterministic model follow directly from the definitions and are given in the next proposition.

Proposition 4.3
1. $\underline{R}_0(X) = \underline{R}(X)$
2. $\overline{R}_1(X) = \overline{R}(X)$
3. $BNR_{0,1}(X) = BNR(X)$
4. $NEGR_1(X) = NEGR(X)$

In addition to the properties listed in Proposition 4.2 for all $0 \leq \ell < u \leq 1$, the following relationships are satisfied:

Proposition 4.4
1. $\underline{R}_\ell(X) \supseteq \underline{R}(X)$
2. $\overline{R}_u(X) \subseteq \overline{R}(X)$
3. $BNR_{\ell,u} \subseteq BNR(X)$
4. $NEGR_u(X) \supseteq NEGR(X)$

5   Properties of Approximately Specified Sets

In this section, we will investigate the main properties of set approximations as defined in Section 4. The properties are a direct generalization of the properties given in [3] for the deterministic rough sets model and variable precision rough sets model with symmetric bounds [4]. When presenting these properties, we will use the concept of a relative inclusion relation which is an extension of the idea of a majority inclusion relation given in [4]. In the following proposition, we summarize all basic properties of approximate sets.

Proposition 5.1

For every $0 \leq \ell < u \leq 1$ and any subsets $X, Y \subseteq U$, the following relationships are satisfied:

1. (a) $\underline{R_\ell}(X) \subseteq^\ell X$ (b) $\underline{R_\ell}(X) \subseteq \overline{R_u}(X)$
2. (a) $\underline{R_\ell}(\emptyset) = \overline{R_u}(\emptyset) = \emptyset$ (b) $\underline{R_\ell}(U) = \overline{R_u}(U) = U$
3. $\overline{R_u}(X \cup Y) \supseteq^u \overline{R_u}(X) \cup \overline{R_u}(Y)$
4. $\underline{R_\ell}(X \cap Y) \subseteq \underline{R_\ell}(X) \cap \underline{R_\ell}(Y)$
5. $\underline{R_\ell}(X \cup Y) \supseteq \underline{R_\ell}(X) \cup \underline{R_\ell}(Y)$
6. $\overline{R_u}(X \cap Y) \subseteq \overline{R_u}(X) \cap \overline{R_u}(Y)$

Since the approximate inclusion relation is a direct extension of the majority inclusion relation by relaxing the range of permissible values which the parameter β can assume (for the majority inclusion relation β is restricted to the range $[0, 0.5]$), the proofs of the properties $1 - (a)$ and $3 - 6$, are identical to the proofs of similar properties for the variable precision rough sets model [4]. Consequently, in the following proof, we will only demonstrate the new properties which are specific to the rough sets model introduced in this paper.

Proof of the Proposition 5.1:

1-(b) This property follows directly from the definitions of the lower and upper approximations of a set and from the fact that for any elementary set $E \in R^*$ if $c(E, X) \leq \ell$ then $c(E, X) < u$.

2-(a) For $X = \emptyset$, we have $c(E, X) = 1$ for any $E \in R^*$. Since $\ell < u \leq 1$, it follows that $\underline{R_l}\emptyset = \emptyset$ and $\overline{R_u}\emptyset = \emptyset$.

2-(b) For $X = U$, we have $c(E, X) = 0$ for all $E \in R^*$. Since $\ell \geq 0$ and $u > 0$, it follows that $\underline{R_\ell}(U) = U$ and $\overline{R_u}(U) = U$.

6   Quality of Approximation, Discernibility and Dependency

The quality of set approximation, discernibility and attribute dependency are all concepts which indicate how well we can predict outcomes with a given set of variables, and upper and lower classification factors. We use these concepts in minimizing the number of variables, variable ranges and rules. Any non-empty subset X of the universe U can be approximately characterized in terms of its lower and upper approximations. According to the definitions given in section 4.1. $\underline{R_\ell}(X) \subseteq \overline{R_u}(X)$ for any $0 \leq \ell < u \leq 1$.

Consequently, in finite approximation spaces, the ratio, called approximation accuracy

$$\alpha_{\ell,u}(R, X) = \quad card(\underline{R}_\ell(X))/card(\overline{R}_u(X)) \quad if \quad \overline{R}_u(X) \neq \emptyset, \quad and$$
$$\alpha_{\ell,u}(R, X) = \quad 0 \quad otherwise$$

provides a measure of the fit or quality of approximation of the set X. Clearly, $0 \leq \alpha_{\ell,u}(R, X) \leq 1$ for any subset X. In infinite metric spaces the cardinality function ($card$) can be replaced with a generalized measure function representing the size of a set Y.

In a manner similar to VPRS [4], one can also categorize sets with respect to the degree of discernibility achievable with given lower and upper approximation limits. We say that the set X is (ℓ, u)-discernible if its lower approximation is equal to its upper approximation, i.e. if $\underline{R}_\ell(X) = \overline{R}_u(X)$. This kind of discernibility essentially means that, based on the available information, any object of the universe U can be either classified as a member of set X with the classification factor being less than or equal to ℓ, or it can be classified as excluded from X, with a classification factor greater than or equal to u. Clearly, if X is (ℓ, u)-discernible then its boundary is empty, that is $BNR_{\ell,u}(X) = \emptyset$. The approximation accuracy of (ℓ, u)-discernible sets is equal to 1.

Proposition 6.1

If X is discernible for given lower and upper precision limits ℓ, and u, then X is also discernible for any

$$\ell' \geq \ell \quad and \quad u' \leq u \quad such \quad that \quad \ell' < u'.$$

Proof:

Since $BNR_{\ell,u} = \emptyset$, it follows that $\{E \in R^* : \ell < c(E, Y) < u\} = \emptyset$. However, we also have $\{E \in R^* : \ell' < c(E, Y) < u'\} \subseteq \{E \in R^* : \ell < c(E, Y) < u\}$, which means that $BNR_{\ell',u'} = \emptyset$.

Proposition 6.2

If X is not discernible for given lower and upper limits ℓ, and u, then X is also not discernible for any $\ell' \leq \ell$ and $u' \geq u$.

Proof:

The proof follows directly from the fact that

$$\emptyset \neq \{E \in R^* : \ell < c(E, Y) < u\} \subseteq \{E \in R^* : \ell' < c(E, Y) < u'\}.$$

Any set which is not discernible for given precision limits will be called (ℓ, u)-rough. For any (ℓ, u)-rough set not all objects of the universe, U, can be categorized as members, or non-members of the set with predefined classification error limits.

To define the notion of attribute dependency, let Z be a subset of the condition variables, C, inducing the classification $Z^* = \{Z_1, Z_2, ...Z_K\}$ of the situations contained in U. We will also use the symbol Z to denote the equivalence relation corresponding to the partition Z^*. In addition, let $D^* = \{D_1, D_2, ...D_J\}$ be a classification of decisions or outcomes. We will define the degree of dependency between the subset of condition variables, Z, and the decision, D_j, to be $deg_{\ell,u}(Z, D_j) = (card(\underline{Z}_\ell(D_j)) + card(NEGZ_u(D_j)))/card(U)$.

This degree of dependency characterizes our ability to predict an outcome D_j, or its complement $-D_j$ from the accumulated experience recorded in the Information Table. The degree of dependency is the proportion of those situations in the information table which can be uniquely assigned not lower than

$1 - \ell$ likelihood of occurrence of D_j or not lower than u likelihood of occurrence of $-D_j$ (i.e., D_j not occurring).

7 Reduction of Attributes

It is always desirable to reduce the amount of information required to predict an outcome. A reduced number of variables results in a larger number of cases in each category, making the results statistically more meaningful. A reduced number of categories will also make the results of the analysis easier to use and implement. The reduction method is inspired by the idea of a reduct [3]. If we can remove some of the condition variables without affecting the degree of dependency between the subset of condition variables, Z, and the decision, D_j, the remaining condition variables will be termed a reduct for D_j. The reduced number of condition variables means less measurements or observations are required to make a given decision.

To explain in more detail the notion of reduct, let us again assume that Z is a subset of the set of condition variables, C. The subset, Z, is said to be dependent with respect to the decision, D_j, if there exists a proper subset, say X, of Z such that the dependency predicate defined as $\underline{X}_\ell(D_j) = \underline{Z}_\ell(D_j)$ and $NEGX_u(D_j) = NEGZ_u(D_j)$ is satisfied.

Otherwise, Z is regarded as an independent set, or reduct, with respect to D_j. Intuitively, the set of variables, Z, is dependent if we can remove some variables from Z without affecting our ability to predict the outcome D_j with the estimated probability not less than $1 - \ell$, and also without affecting an ability to predict the outcome $-D_j$ with the probability not less than u.

A relative reduct of the set of condition variables will be defined as a maximal independent subset of condition variables. In general, there exists more than one reduct. The computational procedure for finding a single reduct is very straightforward. Each condition attribute is tested by removing it temporarily from the set C. The satisfaction of the dependency predicate is checked. If the predicate is valid then the attribute is marked as being redundant and is permanently deleted from the set of condition attributes, C. This step is repeated until all condition attributes in C have been tested. The final collection of condition attributes contains non-redundant attributes only and preserves the dependency with the decision D_j. The problem of finding all reducts is much more complex. Some solutions to this problem are provided in [8-10,11].

8 Conclusion

A method of predicting the factors which most effect the likelihoods of specified events from tables of data has been presented. The Variable Precision Rough Sets method has been extended to handle problems where the classification factors can take on arbitrary values between zero and one. In particular, we are interested in predicting changes in likelihood when all the likelihoods are fairly small. In these cases both the upper and lower classification factor are above 0.5. In using this method, the data is broken into a limited number of sets based on values of the condition variables. The tables of data are then used to compute a minimum set of variables for predicting the likelihood of the specified event. We do this by computing the dependency of a decision on the condition variable sets and then examining changes in dependency when variables are removed from the set of condition variables. The smallest set of condition variables that does not produce a reduced dependency is termed a reduct. We can then choose the set of variables to be used to predict the event of interest from the reducts.

9 Acknowledgments

The research reported in this paper was supported in part by an operating grant from the Natural Sciences and Engineering Research Council of Canada. Many thanks to Marzena Kryszkiewicz for helpful discussion and suggesting an improved definition of reduct. The help of Paula Katzberg and Lila Wendling when preparing the manuscript is gratefully acknowledged.

References

[1] Pawlak, Z. *Rough Sets*, International Journal of Information and Computer Sciences, 11, 5, (1982). pp. 341-356.

[2] Pawlak, Z. *Rough Classification*, International Journal of Man-Machine Studies, 20, (1984), pp. 469-483.

[3] Pawlak, Z. *Rough Sets - Theoretical Aspects of Reasoning about Data*, Kluwer Academic Publishers, (1991), Book pp. 229.

[4] Ziarko, W. *Variable Precision Rough Sets Model*, Journal of Computer and Systems Sciences, vol. 46. no. 1, 1993, pp. 39-59.

[5] Pawlak, Z., Wong, S.K.M., Ziarko, W. *Rough Sets: Probabilistic versus Deterministic Approach*, International Journal of Man-Machine Studies, vol. 29, 1988, pp. 81-95.

[6] Marek, W., Pawlak, Z. *Rough Sets and Information Systems*, Fundamenta Informaticae, 17, 1, (1984), pp. 105-115.

[7] Orlowska, A., Pawlak, Z. *Expressive Power of Knowledge Representation*, International Journal of Man-Machine Studies, 20, (1984), pp. 458-500.

[8] Wasilewska, A. *Syntactic Decision Procedures in Information Systems*, International Journal of Man- Machine Studies, 30 (1989), pp. 273-285.

[9] Skowron, A., Rauszer, C. *The Discernibility Matrices and Functions in Information Systems*, ICS Research Report 1/91, Technical University of Warsaw 1991, pp. 1-44.

[10] Ziarko, W., Shan, N. *A Rough Set-Based Method for Computing All Minimal Deterministic Rules in Attribute Value Systems*, C.S. Department, University of Regina, Report 2/93.

[11] Kryszkiewicz, M. and Rybinski, H. *Finding Reducts in Composed Information Systems*, in this volume.

Uncertain Reasoning with Interval-Set Algebra

Y.Y. Yao and Xining Li

Department of Mathematical Sciences, Lakehead University

Thunder Bay, Ontario, Canada P7B 5E1

Abstract

An interval set is characterized by a pair of ordinary sets referred to as the lower and upper bounds. The interval-set algebra is different from the rough-set model with respect to the truth functionality of the set-theoretic operations. Based on a generalized version of possible-worlds analysis, we show that the interval-set algebra corresponds to Kleene's three-valued logic K_3. The interval-set algebra is useful in interval-based qualitative and quantitative reasoning.

1   Introduction

Uncertainty seems to be a characteristic feature of many problems involving human intelligence. Our knowledge is usually subject to a degree of uncertainty [4, 11]. This may stem from a lack of information, from the incompleteness or unreliability of the available information, or from our inability to measure precisely a physical quantity. In order to make meaningful judgments, it is important to understand different aspects of uncertainty and devise various ways for its management.

The possible-worlds semantics analysis has been used to interpret various approaches for uncertainty representation and uncertain reasoning, such as propositional logic, probabilistic logic, and fuzzy logic [2, 5, 10, 15, 16]. This framework consists of, for example, a propositional language, a set of possible worlds, and a valuation function that maps each proposition to a truth value with respect to a particular possible world. Through the valuation function, one can map a proposition into a subset of possible worlds in which the proposition is true. The logical operations are therefore interpreted in terms of set-theoretic operations. If one defines a probability or a possibility function on the set of all possible worlds, the ordinary *true-false* semantics for logical sentences is extended to a semantics that allows probabilistic or possibilistic values on sentences. Although some initial work has been done using a *true-unknown-false* semantics instead of the ordinary true-false semantics, there is still a lack of rigorous treatment on a three-valued logic in possible-worlds analysis [2, 15, 17].

The main objective of this paper is to adopt Kleene's three-valued logic system K_3 as an extension of the ordinary logic in possible-worlds analysis [14]. Since Kleene's three-valued logic is truth functional while the rough-set model is not, we will have to add truth functionality to rough-set model [18]. The proposed new model forms an interval-set algebra corresponding to Kleene's system K_3.

Section 2 reviews the key concepts of the interval-set algebra pertinent to our discussion [9, 18]. Section 3 summarizes the possible-worlds analysis approaches, with emphasis on a particular qualitative reasoning approach known as incidence calculus [2]. Based on these results, Section 4 presents a detailed possible-worlds analysis using Kleene's three-valued system $\mathbf{K_3}$, which suggests an uncertain reasoning method with interval-set algebra.

2 Interval-set Algebra

Let U be a finite non-empty set, called the universe or the reference set, and 2^U be its power set. The following subset of 2^U,

$$\mathcal{A} = [A_1, A_2] = \{X \in 2^U \mid A_1 \subseteq X \subseteq A_2, A_1, A_2 \in 2^U\}, \tag{1}$$

is called a closed *interval set*, where $A_1 \subseteq A_2$. The set A_1 is called the lower bound of the interval set and A_2 the upper bound. That is, an interval set is a set of subsets bounded by two particular elements of the Boolean algebra $(2^U, \cap, \cup)$. This interpretation is different from the lower and upper approximations of the rough-set model [12, 13].

Let $\cap, \cup$ and $-$ be the usual set intersection, union and difference defined on 2^U, respectively. We define the following binary operations on interval sets based on the set-theoretic operations on their members. For two interval sets $\mathcal{A} = [A_1, A_2]$ and $\mathcal{B} = [B_1, B_2]$, the interval-set intersection, union and difference are defined as:

$$\begin{aligned}
\mathcal{A} \sqcap \mathcal{B} &= \{X \cap Y \mid X \in \mathcal{A}, Y \in \mathcal{B}\}, \\
\mathcal{A} \sqcup \mathcal{B} &= \{X \cup Y \mid X \in \mathcal{A}, Y \in \mathcal{B}\}, \\
\mathcal{A} \setminus \mathcal{B} &= \{X - Y \mid X \in \mathcal{A}, Y \in \mathcal{B}\}.
\end{aligned} \tag{2}$$

Let $I(2^U)$ denote the set of all closed interval sets. Then the above defined operations are closed on $I(2^U)$, namely, $\mathcal{A} \sqcap \mathcal{B}$, $\mathcal{A} \sqcup \mathcal{B}$ and $\mathcal{A} \setminus \mathcal{B}$ are interval sets. In fact, these interval sets can be explicitly computed by:

$$\begin{aligned}
\mathcal{A} \sqcap \mathcal{B} &= [A_1 \cap B_1, A_2 \cap B_2], \\
\mathcal{A} \sqcup \mathcal{B} &= [A_1 \cup B_1, A_2 \cup B_2], \\
\mathcal{A} \setminus \mathcal{B} &= [A_1 - B_2, A_2 - B_1].
\end{aligned} \tag{3}$$

The interval-set complement $\neg[A_1, A_2]$ of $[A_1, A_2]$ is defined by $[U, U] \setminus [A_1, A_2]$. This is equivalent to $[U - A_2, U - A_1] = [A_2^c, A_1^c]$, where $A^c = U - A$ denote the usual set complement. Clearly, we have $\neg[\emptyset, \emptyset] = [U, U]$ and $\neg[U, U] = [\emptyset, \emptyset]$.

For operations $\sqcap$, $\sqcup$ and $\neg$, the following properties hold: for $\mathcal{A}, \mathcal{B}, \mathcal{C} \in I(2^U)$,

(I1) Idempotent :
$$\mathcal{A} \sqcap \mathcal{A} = \mathcal{A}, \qquad \mathcal{A} \sqcup \mathcal{A} = \mathcal{A};$$

(I2) Commutativity :
$$\mathcal{A} \sqcap \mathcal{B} = \mathcal{B} \sqcap \mathcal{A}, \qquad \mathcal{A} \sqcup \mathcal{B} = \mathcal{B} \sqcup \mathcal{A};$$

(I3) Associativity :
$$\begin{aligned}
(\mathcal{A} \sqcap \mathcal{B}) \sqcap \mathcal{C} &= \mathcal{A} \sqcap (\mathcal{B} \sqcap \mathcal{C}), \\
(\mathcal{A} \sqcup \mathcal{B}) \sqcup \mathcal{C} &= \mathcal{A} \sqcup (\mathcal{B} \sqcup \mathcal{C}),
\end{aligned}$$

(I4)   Distributivity :
$$A \sqcap (B \sqcup C) = (A \sqcap B) \sqcup (A \sqcap C),$$
$$A \sqcup (B \sqcap C) = (A \sqcup B) \sqcap (A \sqcup C);$$

(I5)   Absorption :
$$A \sqcap (A \sqcup B) = A, \qquad A \sqcup (A \sqcap B) = A;$$

(I6)   De Morgan's laws :
$$\neg(A \sqcap B) = \neg A \sqcup \neg B, \qquad \neg(A \sqcup B) = \neg A \sqcap \neg B;$$

(I7)   Double negation law :
$$\neg\neg A = A,$$

(I8) $[U, U]$ and $[\emptyset, \emptyset]$ are the unique identities for interval set intersection and union, that is,
$$A = \mathcal{X} \sqcap A = A \sqcap \mathcal{X} \text{ for all } A \in I(2^U) \iff \mathcal{X} = [U, U],$$
$$A = \mathcal{Y} \sqcup A = A \sqcup \mathcal{Y} \text{ for all } A \in I(2^U) \iff \mathcal{Y} = [\emptyset, \emptyset].$$

These properties may be regarded as the counterparts of the properties of the corresponding set-theoretic operations. However, unlike elementary set theory, for an interval set A, $A \sqcap \neg A$ is not necessarily equal to $[\emptyset, \emptyset]$, $A \sqcup \neg A$ is not necessarily equal to $[U, U]$, and $A \setminus A$ is not necessarily equal to $[\emptyset, \emptyset]$. Nevertheless, the following properties hold:

(I9) $\emptyset \in A \sqcap \neg A, \qquad U \in A \sqcup \neg A, \qquad \emptyset \in A \setminus A.$

Therefore, $I(2^U)$ is a completely distributive lattice but not a Boolean algebra, whereas 2^U is a Boolean algebra [9].

The interval-set algebra can be considered as a qualitative counterpart of the interval-number algebra [1, 8]. The interpretation of an interval set given by equation (1) provides plausible justification for the proposed interval-set operations. Moreover, degenerate interval sets of the form $[A, A]$ are equivalent to ordinary sets. For degenerate interval sets, the proposed operations $\sqcap$, $\sqcup$, $\setminus$, and $\neg$ reduce to the usual set-theoretic operations. Thus, interval-set algebra may be considered as an extension of elementary set algebra.

An interval set $[A_1, A_2]$ is also referred to as a *flou set* [9]. A_1 is called the *sure region*, A_2 the *maximum region*, and $A_2 - A_1$ the *flou region*. From this point of view, the notion of interval sets is similar to that of rough sets [12, 13]. On the other hand, in interval-set algebra, the value of a compound formula can be computed from its components using equation (3), whereas it is impossible to do so in rough set theory. One may consider interval-set algebra as a kind of rough-set model with truth functionality. This makes the interval-set algebra a suitable tool for qualitative reasoning where truth functionality is required.

3   Possible-worlds Semantics of Uncertain Reasoning

Let Φ be a finite non-empty set of propositions of interest. A propositional language formed from Φ is denoted by $L(\Phi)$, which is the smallest set containing the truth values and the members of Φ and is closed under negation ($\sim$), disjunction ($\wedge$), conjunction ($\vee$), and implication ($\rightarrow$). Let W be a non-empty set of possible worlds, which is used to represent states or situations of the system being modeled. Each possible world can be considered as a partial interpretation of some logical formulas in the propositional language $L(\Phi)$. Formally, for a particular possible world w, we define a valuation function $\pi_w : \Phi \longrightarrow \{true, false\}$. If $\pi_w(\phi) = true$, we say that the proposition ϕ is true in the world w, otherwise we say that the proposition is false. According to the semantics of two-valued logic, given two propositions ϕ and ψ, $\phi \wedge \psi$ is true in a world w if and only if both ϕ and ψ are true in w. Similar rules can be used for other logical connectives. Thus, the valuation function π_w can be extended to $L(\Phi)$.

Using valuation functions π_w for all possible worlds, we define another mapping $i : L(\Phi) \longrightarrow 2^W$ as follows:

$$i(\phi) = \{w \in W \mid \pi_w(\phi) = true\}. \tag{4}$$

The set $i(\phi)$ contains those possible worlds in which ϕ is true and can be interpreted as the value of the proposition. Such a valuation of propositions is referred to as an incidence mapping and $i(\phi)$ the incidence of ϕ [2]. An advantage of this framework is that the logical connectives are interpreted using the set-theoretic operations as shown by the following properties of incidence calculus:

$$
\begin{aligned}
i(true) &= W, & (5)\\
i(false) &= \emptyset, & (6)\\
i(\sim \phi) &= W - i(\phi), & (7)\\
i(\phi \wedge \psi) &= i(\phi) \cap i(\psi), & (8)\\
i(\phi \vee \psi) &= i(\phi) \cup i(\psi), & (9)\\
i(\phi \rightarrow \psi) &= (W - i(\phi)) \cup i(\psi). & (10)
\end{aligned}
$$

Equations (5)-(10) indicate that the incidence mapping is truth functional. The incidence of a compound formula can be calculate solely from the incidences of its components.

In practice, we only know the incidences of a subset of all propositions in $L(\Phi)$. Thus, an important task of incidence calculus is to infer the incidences for these propositions whose incidences are not given. In ordinary two-valued logic, the *modus ponens* rule:

$$\frac{\phi \rightarrow \psi, \ \phi}{\psi}, \tag{11}$$

allows us to infer ψ from $\phi \rightarrow \psi$ and ϕ. In the framework incidence calculus, it is impossible to derive the incidence $i(\psi)$ from $i(\phi \rightarrow \psi)$ and $i(\phi)$, using the above *modus ponens* rule. Instead, we may specify bounds within which lies the true incidence $i(\psi)$. Consider a world w in which both $\phi \rightarrow \psi$ and ϕ are true, we can immediately conclude that ψ is also true in w. That is, $w \in i(\phi) \cap i(\phi \rightarrow \psi)$ implies $w \in i(\psi)$. Similarly, if ψ is true in a world w, then $\phi \rightarrow \psi$ is also true in w, namely, $w \in i(\psi)$ implies $w \in i(\phi \rightarrow \psi)$. However, it is impossible to have a world in which both ϕ and $\phi \rightarrow \psi$ are false, such a world is referred to as an inconsistent world. Nilsson proposed a method using binary semantic tree to perform such an analysis [10]. All consistent possible worlds are summarized in the following table:

$\phi \to \psi$	ϕ	ψ
true	*true*	*true*
true	*false*	$\{true, false\}$
false	*true*	*false*

The second row says that if $\phi \to \psi$ is true and ϕ is false in a world w, then ψ can either be true or false in w. According to this table, the best bounds of $i(\psi)$ is the given by the interval set $[i(\phi) \cap i(\phi \to \psi), i(\phi \to \psi)]$, based solely on $i(\phi \to \psi)$ and $i(\phi)$. Therefore, the following modified *modus ponens* rule may be used in incidence calculus:

$$\frac{i(\phi \to \psi), \quad i(\phi)}{i(\phi) \cap i(\phi \to \psi) \subseteq i(\psi) \subseteq i(\phi \to \psi)} \quad . \tag{12}$$

More inference rules using incidence bounds can be found in [2].

The incidence calculus can also be used to carry out quantitative inference. Suppose there is a probability function P_0 defined on the set of possible worlds W. By setting the probability of a proposition as the probability of its incidence, i.e., $P(\phi) = P_0(i(\phi))$, we can immediately perform probabilistic inference [2, 10, 15]. For example, based on the *modus ponens* rule (12), we have:

$$P_0(i(\phi) \cap i(\phi \to \psi)) \leq P_0(i(\psi)) \leq P_0(i(\phi \to \psi)), \tag{13}$$

which can be equivalently expressed as the bounds given by Nilsson [10]:

$$P(\phi \to \psi) + P(\phi) - 1 \leq P(\psi) \leq P(\phi \to \psi). \tag{14}$$

By using a similar technique, incidence calculus can also be used for reasoning with Dempster-Shafer theory of belief functions [3].

4 Interpretation of Three-valued Logic Using Interval-set Algebra

In this section, we extend the possible-worlds semantics for uncertain reasoning using the three-valued logic proposed by Kleene [6, 14].

In Kleene's three-valued logic, denoted by $\mathbf{K}_3$, a proposition is allowed to take a third truth value I, which means that the proposition may in fact be true or false, but it is merely *unknown* or *undeterminable* what its specific truth status may be. This system is characterized by the following truth tables:

ϕ	$\sim \phi$
T	F
I	I
F	T

ψ / ϕ	$\phi \wedge \psi$ $T\ I\ F$	$\phi \vee \psi$ $T\ I\ F$	$\phi \to \psi$ $T\ I\ F$
T	$T\ I\ F$	$T\ T\ T$	$T\ I\ F$
I	$I\ I\ F$	$T\ I\ I$	$T\ I\ I$
F	$F\ F\ F$	$T\ I\ F$	$T\ T\ T$

According to this definition, $\mathbf{K}_3$ satisfies properties similar to (I1)-(I8) of the interval-set algebra. In fact, one can obtain a set of properties for $\mathbf{K}_3$ by replacing interval sets with propositions, $\sqcap$ with $\wedge$, and $\sqcup$ with $\vee$. Thus, the interval-set algebra may provide a possible-worlds based interpretation for $\mathbf{K}_3$ in the same way as the ordinary set theory provides for the two-valued logic. This point is formally explicated below.

For a possible world $w \in W$, we define a mapping $\pi_w : \Phi \longrightarrow \{T, I, F\}$. By $\pi_w(\phi) = T$, we mean that the proposition ϕ is true in the world w, and $\pi_w(\phi) = F$ for case that the proposition is false. The third value $\pi_w(\phi) = I$ indicates that the truth value of ϕ is unknown or undeterminable. Using $\mathbf{K}_3$, one can extend the valuation function to any proposition in $L(\Phi)$. For example, $\pi_w(\phi \wedge \psi) = \pi_w(\phi) \wedge \pi_w(\psi)$. With such an extended valuation function, we define two mappings, $i_* : L(\Phi) \longrightarrow 2^W$ and $i^* : L(\Phi) \longrightarrow 2^W$, as follows:

$$i_*(\phi) = \{w \in W \mid \pi_w(\phi) = T\}, \tag{15}$$
$$i^*(\phi) = \{w \in W \mid \pi_w(\phi) \in \{T, I\}\}. \tag{16}$$

Obviously, we have $i_*(\phi) \subseteq i^*(\phi)$. Hence, $[i_*(\phi), i^*(\phi)]$ forms an interval-set representation of proposition ϕ. The set $i^*(\phi) - i_*(\phi)$ denotes the set of possible worlds in which the truth value of ϕ is unknown or undeterminable, which is similar to the doubtful region in the rough-set theory [12].

With the possible-worlds semantics of $\mathbf{K}_3$, we derive the following correspondence between $\mathbf{K}_3$ logical operations and the interval-set operations:

$$[i_*(\sim \phi), i^*(\sim \phi)] = \neg[i_*(\phi), i^*(\phi)], \tag{17}$$
$$[i_*(\phi \wedge \psi), i^*(\phi \wedge \psi)] = [i_*(\phi), i^*(\phi)] \sqcap [i_*(\psi), i^*(\psi)], \tag{18}$$
$$[i_*(\phi \vee \psi), i^*(\phi \wedge \psi)] = [i_*(\phi), i^*(\phi)] \sqcup [i_*(\psi), i^*(\psi)], \tag{19}$$
$$[i_*(\phi \rightarrow \psi), i^*(\phi \rightarrow \psi)] = \neg[i_*(\phi), i^*(\phi)] \sqcup [i_*(\psi), i^*(\psi)]. \tag{20}$$

With respect to negation, conjunction and disjunction, Kleene's three-valued logic is the same as the three-valued logic $\mathbf{L}_3$ of Lukasiewicz [14]. Hence, the interval-set algebra also provides an interpretation for $\mathbf{L}_3$.

Inference using interval-set algebra (i.e., Kleene's three-valued logic) can be carried out in a similar manner as in incidence calculus. For analyzing consistent possible worlds, we extend Nilsson's binary semantic tree into ternary semantic tree by adding the third truth value I. For the *modus ponens* rule, we derive the following consistent possible worlds:

$\phi \rightarrow \psi$	ϕ	ψ
T	T	T
T	I	T
T	F	$\{T, I, F\}$
I	T	I
I	I	$\{I, F\}$
F	T	F

For example, the second row says that if $\phi \rightarrow \psi$ is true (T) and ϕ is unknown or undeterminable (I) in a world w, according to $\mathbf{K}_3$, it is consistent to assume that ψ is true (T) in w. On the other hand, as indicated by the third row, if $\phi \rightarrow \psi$ is true (T) and ϕ is false (F) in w, then ψ may take any of the three truth values $\{T, I, F\}$. By examining this table carefully, we can see that the interval set $[i^*(\phi) \cap i_*(\phi \to \psi), i^*(\phi \to \psi)]$ is the best possible bounds for interval set $[i_*(\psi), i^*(\psi)]$. Thus, we introduce the following *modus ponens* rule for interval-set algebra:

$$\frac{[i_*(\phi \to \psi), i^*(\phi \to \psi)], \quad [i_*(\phi), i^*(\phi)]}{i^*(\phi) \cap i_*(\phi \to \psi) \subseteq i_*(\psi) \subseteq i^*(\psi) \subseteq i^*(\phi \to \psi)} \quad , \tag{21}$$

which is similar to the one used in incidence calculus.

When a probability function P_0 is defined on the set of all possible worlds W, a proposition ϕ will be associated with a lower probability $P_*(\phi) = P_0(i_*(\phi))$ and a upper probability $P^*(\phi) = P_0(i^*(\phi))$. In other words, an interval probability $[P_*(\phi), P^*(\phi)]$ is used to represent the truth of proposition ϕ. Using the extend *modus ponens* rule (21), we obtain a probabilistic version:

$$\frac{P_*(\phi \to \psi) \le P(\phi \to \psi) \le P^*(\phi \to \psi), \quad P_*(\phi) \le P(\phi) \le P^*(\phi)}{P^*(\phi) + P_*(\phi \to \psi) - 1 \le P_*(\psi) \le P(\psi) \le P^*(\psi) \le P^*(\phi \to \psi)} \quad , \tag{22}$$

which may be regarded as a generalized result of equation (14). This suggests that interval-set algebra may be used to perform interval-probability inference using three-valued logic [7].

5 Conclusion

The standard notion of rough sets does not have the property of truth functionality, which limits its applicability in uncertain reasoning. By imposing this property in rough-set model, we have introduced the interval-set algebra. Moreover, we have presented a straightforward generalization of possible-worlds analysis using Kleene's three-valued logic $\mathbf{K_3}$. An extended *modus ponens* rule has been suggested for interval-set algebra. Our analysis clearly shows that interval-set algebra provides an useful tool for interval-based qualitative and quantitative reasoning.

References

[1] G. Alefeld, and J. Herzberger, *Introduction to Interval Computations*, New York, Academic Press, 1983.

[2] A. Bundy, Incidence calculus: a mechanism for probabilistic reasoning. *Journal of Automated Reasoning*, 1, 263-283, 1985.

[3] F. Correa da Silva, and A. Bundy, On some equivalence relations between incidence calculus and Dempster-Shafer theory of evidence. *Proceedings of 6th International Workshop on Uncertainty in Artificial Intelligence*, 378-383, 1990.

[4] W.B. Gallie, Uncertainty as a philosophical problem. In: C.F. Carter, G.P Meredith, and G.L.S. Shackle, Eds., *Uncertainty and Business Decisions: the Logic, Philosophy and Psychology of Business Decision-making under Uncertainty*, Liverpool University Press, 1957.

[5] J.Y. Halpern, and Y. Moses, A guide to completeness and complexity for modal logics of knowledge and belief. *Artificial Intelligence*, **54**, 319-379, 1992.

[6] S.C. Kleene, *Introduction to Mathematics*, New York, Groningen, 1952.

[7] H.E. Kyburg, *Logical Foundations of Statistical Inference*, Dordrecht, Reidel, 1974.

[8] R.E. Moore, *Interval Analysis*, Englewood Cliffs, New Jersey, Prentice-Hall, 1966.

[9] C.V. Negoiţă, and D.A. Ralescu, *Applications of Fuzzy Sets to Systems Analysis*, Basel, Birkhäuser Verlag, 1975.

[10] N.J. Nilsson, Probabilistic logic. *Artificial Intelligence*, **28**, 71-87, 1986.

[11] S. Parsons, and J. Fox, Qualitative and interval algebras for robust decision making under uncertainty. In: M.G. Singh, and L. Travé-Massuyés, Eds., *Decision Support System and Qualitative Reasoning*, 163-168, New York, North-Holland, 1991.

[12] Z. Pawlak, Rough sets. *International Journal of Computer and Information Sciences*, **11**, 341-356, 1982.

[13] Z. Pawlak, Rough classification. *International Journal of Man-Machine Studies*, **20**, 469-483, 1984.

[14] N. Rescher, *Many-valued Logic*, New York, McGraw-Hill, 1969.

[15] E.H. Ruspini, Approximate reasoning: past, present, future. *Information Sciences*, **57-58**, 297-313, 1991.

[16] E.H. Ruspini, On the semantics of fuzzy logic. *International Journal of Approximate Reasoning*, **5**, 45-88, 1991.

[17] P. Smets, Belief functions (with discussions). In: P. Smets, A. Mamdani, D. Dubois, and H. Prade, Eds., *Non-standard Logics for Automated Reasoning*, New York, Academic Press, 253-285, 1988.

[18] Y.Y. Yao, Interval-set algebra for qualitative knowledge representation. *Proceedings of the Fifth International Conference on Computing and Information*, 370-374, 1993.

On a Logic of Information for Reasoning about Knowledge

Akira Nakamura
Department of Computer Science
Meiji University
Kawasaki, 214
JAPAN

Abstract

This paper discusses on a logic of information for reasoning about various persons' knowledge or time-depending knowledge. The motivation comes from the problem of logical foundations of knowledge representation proposed by Z. Pawlak and E. Orlowska [6], and partially from Orlowska [8]. We consider monadic predicate symbols in this logic. We give its semantics and syntax. Further, we give a deductive system for the logic, and prove the soundness and completeness.

0. Introduction

The problem of knowledge representation has been one of the central topics of *artificial intelligence*. In the pioneering papers [6] and [7], Pawlak and Orlowska discussed theoretical foundations of knowledge representation from a point of view of modal logic. Pawlak [9] introduced a concept of *rough sets*, which leads to the notion of approximations of sets of objects by means of equivalence relations modeling indiscernibility of knowledge. Also, he published an introductory book [10] on rough sets. Orlowska [8] and del Cerro et al. [1] presented a logic of *indiscernibility relations*. Indiscernibility relations are primarily based on equivalence relations and thus the logic of indiscernibility relations corresponds to the modal logic S5. Along this line, in [3] the author developed a logic for fuzzy data analysis which was built by extending indiscernibility relations to the fuzzy case. By the way, knowledge is generally considered as "knowledge of a person". For example, a person a knows that a predicate P(c) is true, but another person b knows that the same predicate P(c) is not true. Hence, it happens that knowledge systems of different persons are not the same.

As a continuous works of previous papers [3]-[5], this paper discusses a logic of information which is based on the above-mentioned rough sets. And an introduction of parameter "person" plays an important role in this paper. According to the concept of the information logic IL in Orlowska and Pawlak [6], we consider monadic predicate symbols in the rough logic. And we give its semantics and present a deductive system for this logic. Further, we prove the soundness and completeness by making use of the technique of tableau method in [11]. Finally, we remark the undecidability of this logic and solvable cases. The undecidability are proved by the same technique as that in [2] and proofs of the solvable cases are based on well-known ones in the usual predicate logic.

1. Preliminaries

In this section, we review definitions of rough sets which are basic concepts of knowledge representation systems. Let us consider a system $S = (OB, AT, \{VAL_a\}_{a \in AT}, f)$, where

OB is a set (not necessarily finite) of objects,

AT is a set (not necessarily finite) of attributes,

VAL_a is a set of values of attribute a for each AT, and VAL is the union of all the sets VAL_a,

and

f is a mapping from OBxAT into VAL.

This system is usually called an *information system*. We define a binary relation R on the set OB as follows:

$$(o_i, o_j) \in R \quad \text{iff} \quad f(o_i, a) = f(o_j, a) \quad \text{for each } a \in AT.$$

Relation R on the set OB is referred to as *indiscernibility* with respect to attributes from the set AT ([9] and [10]). It is easily shown that R is an equivalence relation on the set OB. Speaking more generally, let R be an equivalence relation defined on a set X. Let us denote the equivalence class of x in X in the sense of R by $[x]_R$.

Given a subset S of X and an equivalence relation R, a *lower approximation* $R_*(S)$ and an *upper* one $R^*(S)$ of S with respect to R are defined as follows:

Definition 1.1 Let S be a subset of a given set X and R be an equivalence relation defined on X. $R_*(S)$ and $R^*(S)$ are defined as follows:

$$R_*(S) = \{x \in X \mid [x]_R \subseteq S\}, \qquad R^*(S) = \{x \in X \mid [x]_R \cap S \neq \phi\}. \quad //$$

Then, it is well-known that the R_* and R^* correspond to the modal operations necessity and possibility in the S5 modal system, respectively. We get easily the following facts:

Fact 1.2 (1) $R_*(F) \subseteq F \subseteq R^*(F)$

(2) $R_*(X) = X, \ R_*(\phi) = \phi, \ R^*(X) = X, \ R^*(\phi) = \phi.$

(3) If $F \subseteq G$ then $R_*(F) \subseteq R_*(G)$ and $R^*(F) \subseteq R^*(G)$.

(4) $R^*(R^*(F)) = R^*(F), \ R_*(R_*(F)) = R_*(F),$

(5) $R^*(R_*(F)) = R_*(F), \ R_*(R^*(F)) = R^*(F).$

Fact 1.3 (1) $R^*(F \cap G) \subseteq R^*(F) \cap R^*(G),$

(2) $R^*(F) \cup R^*(G) = R^*(F \cup G),$

(3) $R_*(F) \cap R_*(G) = R_*(F \cap G),$

(4) $R_*(F) \cup R_*(G) \subseteq R_*(F \cup G),$

(5) $R_*(F \cup R^*(G)) = R_*(F) \cup R^*(G),$

(6) $R^*(F \cap R_*(G)) = R^*(F) \cap R_*(G)$,

(7) $R^*(F \cap R^*(G)) = R^*(F) \cap R^*(G)$,

(8) $R_*(F \cup R_*(G)) = R_*(F) \cup R_*(G)$.

As shown in from Fact 1.2, $R_*(F) \subseteq F \subseteq R^*(F)$. If $R_*(F) \subset F \subset R^*(F)$ for a subset F of X, F is a *rough set* . The rough sets are undefinable ones in the given knowledge base.

2. Information logic of knowledge

In this section, we consider a logic of information for reasoning about knowledge mentioned in the preceding section.   Hereafter, this logic is referred to ILK (information logic of knowledge).

First of all, we define the language of logic ILK, namely, a *syntax* of the logic. Expressions of this language are built from the symbols of the following nonempty, at most denumerable, and pairwise disjoint sets:

a set VAROB of *object variables*, denoted by x, y, x_1, y_1, ...,

a set PRED of *monadic predicate letters*, denoted by p, q, p_1, q_1, ...,

a set CONOB of *object constants*, denoted by o, o_1, ...,

a set $\{\neg, \vee, \wedge, \supset, \equiv\}$ of propositional operations of negation, disjunction, conjunction, implication, and equivalence, respectively,

a set $\{\exists, \forall\}$ of quantifiers, called *existential quantifier* and *universal quantifier*, respectively,

a set $\{<>, [\ ]\}$ of *modal operations*, called *possibility* operation and *necessity* operation, respectively,

a set $\{(,)\}$ of parentheses.

The set WFF of well-formed formulas (denoted by wff's) of ILK is the least set satisfying the following conditions:

if $x \in$ VAROB, $o \in$ CONOB, $p \in$ PRED, then $p(x) \in$ WFF and $p(o) \in$ WFF,

if A, B $\in$ WFF, then $\neg$A, A$\vee$B, A$\wedge$B, A$\supset$B, A$\equiv$B $\in$ WFF,

if A $\in$ WFF and $x \in$ VAROB, then $\exists$xA, $\forall$xA $\in$ WFF.

if A $\in$ WFF, then $<>$A, $[\ ]$A $\in$ WFF.

In the above definition, it is noticed that monadic predicate letters correspond to (a, val) where $a \in$ AT and val$\in$ VAL, namely, they correspond to predicates "red (val) in color (a)" or "triangle in shape" , and so on.

As usually we assume that formulas do not contain redundant or overlapping quantifiers. Moreover, we adopt the usual definition of *free* and *bound* variable. An object variable in a wff is said to have a *bound* occurrence if it stands within the scope of a quantifier with the same variable; otherwise it is said to have a *free* occurrence. A wff without free variables is called a *sentence*.

Considering information systems mentioned in §1, a *semantics* of ILK is given as follows:

We take the universe U and a mapping m: CONOB∪PRED → U∪2^U such that

m(o)∈ U and m(p)∈ 2^U. This m is called a *meaning function* over the universe U.

Further, we consider a mapping v: VAROB → U. This v is called a *valuation* over the universe U.

By a model for the logic ILK we mean a system M = (U, m, v, W), where U is a universe and m is a meaning function over U and v is a valuation over U and W is a countably infinite set of persons. Given a model M = (U, m, v, W) and a valuation

v over U, $a \in$ W, we say that a wff A is *satisfied* by v, a in M (denoted by M, v, a ⊨ A) whenever the following conditions are satisfied:

M, v, a ⊨ p(x)   iff   v(x)∈ m(p),

M, v, a ⊨ p(o)   iff   m(o)∈ m(p),

M, v, a ⊨ ¬A   iff   not M, v, a ⊨ A,

M, v, a ⊨ A∨B iff   M, v, a ⊨ A or M, v, a ⊨ B,

M, v, a ⊨ A∧B iff   M, v, a ⊨ A and M, v, a ⊨ B,

M, v, a ⊨ A⊃B iff   M, v, a ⊨ ¬A∨B,

M, v, a ⊨ A≡B   iff   M, v, a ⊨(A⊃B)∧(B⊃A),

M, v, a ⊨ ∃xA iff   there is a o∈ OB such that M, v_0, a ⊨ A,

 M, v, a ⊨ ∀xA iff   for all o∈ OB we have M, v_0, a ⊨ A,

where v_0 is the valuation over U such that v_0(x)=o and v_0(y)=v(y) for y ≠x.

M, v, a ⊨ < >A iff   there is a $b \in$ W such that M, v, b ⊨ A,

M, v, a ⊨ [ ] A iff for all $b \in$ W we have M, v, b ⊨ A.
In this definition, it is noticed that the set W is considered as one equivalence class.

A wff A is said to be *true* in a model M = (U, m, v, W) (denoted by ⊨$_M$ A) iff

for every valuation v over the universe U and every $a \in$ W we have M, v, a ⊨ A
. A wff A is said to be *valid* in the logic ILK (denoted by ⊨ A) iff A is true in every model for ILK. A set T of wff's is said to be true in a model M iff every wff

A∈ T is true in M. A set T is said to be *satisfiable* iff there is a model such that T is true in M. Also, we say that a wff A is a *semantical consequence* of a set T (denoted by T ⊨A) iff for every model M the wff A is true in M whenever T is true in M.

Fact 2.1   (1)   All valid wff's in the usual monadic predicate logic are also valid in ILK.

(2) $\models [\ ]F \supset F$ and $\models F \supset <\ >F$,

(3) $\models [\ ]I \equiv I$, $\models [\ ]O \equiv O$, $\models <\ >I \equiv I$, $\models <\ >O \equiv O$,

(4)   If $\models F \supset G$ then $\models [\ ]F \supset [\ ]G$ and $\models <\ >F \supset <\ >G$,

(5) $\models <\ >(<\ >F) \equiv <\ >F$, $\models <\ >([\ ]F) \equiv [\ ]F$,

(6) $\models [\ ]([\ ]F) \equiv [\ ]F$ $\models [\ ](<\ >F) \equiv <\ >F$

(7) $\models <\ >(F \wedge G) \supset <\ >F) \wedge <\ >G$,

(8) $\models <\ >F \vee <\ >G \equiv <\ >(F \vee G)$,

(9) $\models [\ ]F) \wedge [\ ]G \equiv [\ ](F \wedge G)$,

(10) $\models [\ ]F \vee [\ ]G) \supset [\ ](F \vee G)$,

(11) $\models [\ ](F \vee <\ >G) \equiv [\ ]F \vee <\ >G$,

(12) $\models <\ >(F \wedge [\ ]G) \equiv <\ >F) \wedge [\ ]G$,

(13) $\models <\ >(F \wedge <\ >G) \equiv <\ >F \wedge <\ >G$,

(14) $\models [\ ](F \vee [\ ]G) \equiv [\ ]F \vee [\ ]G$,

where I, O mean $p(x) \vee \neg p(x)$, $p(x) \wedge \neg p(x)$, respectively.

It is notice here that the above (2)-(14) correspond to formulas of Facts 1.2 and 1.3 in a interpretation of $\cup$, $\cap$, $\subseteq$, =, R∗, R* by logical operations $\vee$, $\wedge$, $\supset$, $\equiv$, $[\ ]$, $<\ >$, respectively.

3. Deductive system

In this section, we present an axiomatic system for the logic ILK. We admit the following schemes and inference rules:

Axioms

A1. The axioms of the classical propositional logic.

A2. $\forall x(A \supset B(x)) \supset (A \supset \forall x B(x))$, where x is an object variable not occurring free in A.

A3. $\forall x A(x) \supset A(o)$, $\forall x A(x) \supset A(y)$, where o∈ CONOB and y∈ VAROB and y is free for x in A in the usual sense.

A4. $[\ ](A \supset B) \supset ([\ ]A \supset [\ ]B)$.

A5. $[\ ]A \supset A$.

A6. $<>A \supset [\,]<>A.$

Rules of inference

R1. (Modus Ponens) From A, $A \supset B$ we get B.
R2.1. (Generalization 1) From A, we get $[\,]A$.
R2.2 (Generalization 2) From A, we get $\forall xA$.

In the above axiomatic system, the propositional operations $\vee$, $\wedge$, $\equiv$ and the existential quantifier $\exists$, and possibility operation $<>$ are defined, in the usual way, by means of implication, negation, universal quantifier, necessity operation $[\,]$.

A *derivation* of a wff A from a set T of wff's is defined in the usual way, and this denoted by $T \vdash A$. A wff A is said to be *theorem* or *provable* wff (denoted by $\vdash A$) iff it is derivable merely from the axioms. A set T of wff's is *consistent* iff the formula of the form $A \wedge \neg A$ is not derivable from T. A set T is *inconsistent* iff it is not consistent.

Then, we have the following facts:

Fact 3.1

(1) $\vdash [\,]F \supset F$ and $\vdash F \supset <>F$,

(3) $\vdash [\,]I \equiv I,\ \vdash [\,]O \equiv O,\ \vdash <>I \equiv I,\ \vdash <>O \equiv O,$

(4) If $\vdash F \supset G$ then $\vdash [\,]F \supset [\,]G$ and $\vdash <>F \supset <>G,$

(5) $\vdash <>(<>F) \equiv <>F,\ \vdash <>([\,]F) \equiv [\,]F,$

(6) $\vdash [\,]([\,]F) \equiv [\,]F)\ \vdash [\,](<> F) \equiv <>F.$

(7) $\vdash <>(F \wedge G) \supset <>F) \wedge <>G,$

(8) $\vdash <>F \vee <>G \equiv <>(F \vee G),$

(9) $\vdash [\,]F) \wedge [\,]G \equiv [\,](F \wedge G),$

(10) $\vdash [\,]F \vee [\,]G) \supset [\,](F \vee G),$

(11) $\vdash [\,](F \vee <>G) \equiv [\,]F \vee <>G,$

(12) $\vdash <>(F \wedge [\,]G) \equiv <>F) \wedge [\,]G,$

(13) $\vdash <>(F \wedge <>G) \equiv <>F \wedge <>G,$

(14) $\vdash [\,](F \vee [\,]G) \equiv [\,]F \vee [\,]G,$

(15) $\vdash \forall x[\,]F \supset [\,]\forall xF.$

Proof

Since the axiomatic system of ILK includes the axioms and rules of the modal logic S5 system and also the usual predicate logic, we have the above (1)-(14). In particular, we prove (15) in the well-known method.

We have $\vdash \forall x[\ ]F \supset [\ ]F$ from A3.

Thus, $\vdash < >\forall x[\ ]F \supset < > [\ ]F$, and also from $\vdash < >[\ ]A \equiv [\ ]A$, $\vdash < >\forall x[\ ]F \supset$

F. Therefore, from A2 $\vdash < >\forall x[\ ]F \supset \forall xF$ and $\vdash [\ ]< >\forall x[\ ]F \supset [\ ]\forall xF$.

Hence, $\forall x[\ ]F \supset [\ ]\forall xF$ by making use of $[\ ]< >\forall x[\ ]F \equiv < >\forall x[\ ]F$.   //

The above (15) is called *Barcan Formula* .

Fact 3.2   (1) $\vdash [\ ]\forall xF \equiv \forall x[\ ]F.$

(2) $\vdash < >\exists xF \equiv \exists x< >F.$

(3) $\vdash \exists x[\ ]F \supset [\ ]\exists xF.$

(4) $\vdash < >\forall xF \supset \forall x< >F.$

Proof

The proof of (1) and (2) are easy from the Barcan formula. The (4) comes from (3). Therefore, it is sufficient to show (3). We have $\vdash F \supset \exists xF$ and then $\vdash [\ ]F \supset$ $[\ ]\exists xF$. Hence, making use of A2 we get $\vdash \exists x[\ ]F \supset [\ ]\exists xF.$ //

It should be noticed here that $\vdash \exists x[\ ]F \equiv [\ ]\exists xF$ is not correct and also $\vdash < >\forall xF \equiv \forall x< >F$ does not hold.

Fact 3.3   (1) $\vdash [\ ]\forall x[\ ]F \equiv \forall x[\ ]F.$

(2) $\vdash < >\exists x< >F \equiv \exists x< >F.$

(3) $\vdash [\ ]\forall x< >F \equiv \forall x< >F.$

(4) $\vdash [\ ]\exists x< >F \equiv \exists x< >F.$

(5) $\vdash < >\forall x[\ ]F \equiv \forall x[\ ]F.$

(6) $\vdash < >\exists x[\ ]F \equiv \exists x[\ ]F.$

Proof

(1) and (2) are obvious from Fact 3.2 .   And (5) and (6) come from (4) and (3), respectively.   So, we prove (3) and (4).

(3) $\vdash [\ ]\forall x< >F \supset \forall x< >F$ is obvious from A5. $\vdash \forall x< >F \supset [\ ]\forall x< >F$ is shown as follows:

From A6, $\vdash \forall x< >F \supset \forall x[ ]< >F$. Thus, from (1) of Fact 3.2 $\vdash \forall x< >F \supset$ $[ ]\forall x< >F$.

(4) $\vdash [ ]\exists x< >F \supset \exists x< >F$ is obvious from A5. $\vdash \exists x< >F \supset [ ]\exists x< >F$ is shown as follows: $\vdash \exists x< >F \supset \exists x[ ]< >F$ is obvious. But we have $\vdash \exists x[ ]< >F$ $\supset [ ]\exists x< >F$ from Fact 3.2 (3). So, we get (4). $\qquad$ //

Theorem 3.4 (Soundness theorem)
  (1) $\vdash A$ implies $\models A$.
  (2) $T \vdash A$ implies $T \models A$.
  (3) If T is satisfiable then T is consistent.
Proof
  It is easily shown that the axioms are valid and the rules of inference preserve validity. Therefore, we have this fact. $\qquad$ //

From Theorem 3.4 (1), it is known that our axiomatic system is consistent.

We now prove the completeness of the above system. For this end we discuss a relationship between ILK and the usual predicate logic. Let us denote the set of well-formed formulas of the predicate logic by WFFP. And we consider a mapping φ :

WFF $\rightarrow$ WFFP which is inductively defined as follows:

Let us consider a infinite set of new variables: $w, w_1, w_2, \ldots$, where these variables range over a domain different from the previous variables $x, y, x_1, x_2, \ldots$

(1) $\varphi(p(x)) = p(x, w)$,

(2) $\varphi(\neg A) = \neg\varphi(A)$, $\quad \varphi(A \vee B) = \varphi(A) \vee \varphi(B)$, $\quad \varphi(A \wedge B) = \varphi(A) \wedge \varphi(B)$.

$\quad \varphi(A \supset B) = \varphi(A) \supset \varphi(B)$, $\quad \varphi(A \equiv B) = \varphi(A) \equiv \varphi(B)$.

(3) $\varphi(\forall xF) = \forall x\varphi(F)$, $\qquad \varphi(\exists xF) = \exists x\varphi(F)$.

(4) $\varphi([ ]F) = \forall w_i \varphi(F)$, $\varphi(< >F) = \exists w_j \varphi(F)$. In this case, w_i and w_j are new individual variables which are determined as follows:
  (i) If F does not contain $[ ]$ or $< >$, w is replaced by w_i or w_j , respectively.

  (ii) If F contains $[ ]$ or $< >$ and $\varphi(F)$ contains w, this w is replaced by new variables w_i or w_j , respectively, which are not introduced before.

  (iii) If F contains $[ ]$ or $< >$ and $\varphi(F)$ does not contain w, w_i and w_j are new variables which are not introduced before.

For example,

$\varphi([ ](< >p(x) \vee \neg q(y)) \wedge p(x))$ is $\forall w_2(\exists w_1 p(x, w_1) \vee \neg q(y, w_2)) \wedge p(x, w)$.
It is notice that the above interpretation is based on a concept of the *two-sorted* predicate logic.

In this case, we get the following fact:

Theorem 3.5 (Embedding theorem)

Let A be a wff in ILK. Then, A is valid iff φ(A) is valid in the usual predicate logic.
Proof
   This is shown by considering that the set of new variables correspond to special individual variables in the predicate logic.
   That is, if A is not valid then there is a model M = (U, v, m W) such that

$$M, v, a \models \neg A .$$

Thus, by making use of this model we can construct a model S for the predicate logic such that

$$S \models \varphi(\neg A).$$
The case of "only if" is similarly shown.   //

   Here, we would like to prove the converse of Theorem 3.4, i.e., the completeness theorem.   For the proof of this theorem we use the method of tableau in [11]. We assume that readers are familiar with basic terminologies of tableau method such as tableau rules, trees, closed branches, open branches, and etc. .

Theorem 3.6 (Completeness theorem) $\models$A implies $\vdash$A.
Proof

   Let us assume that A is valid, i.e., $\neg$A is not satisfiable.   For this $\neg$A   we

construct a tableau for $\varphi(\neg A)$.   In this case, we use two sets of parameters, namely, one is the set of ordinal parameters (objects) in the predicate logic and other is the set of parameters for new variables w, w_1, w_2, ...   But the corresponding tableau rules are similar to the usual method.   In this case, from the assumption

there must exist a closed tableau for $\neg$A. Therefore, we can construct a proof of A by tracing upward the tableau. In this tracing, it should be noticed that the trace for parameters correspond to the axioms and rules on the modal operations.
   Thus, we get this theorem.   //

4. Remark
   In this paper, we use W as a set of persons.   If the W means the set of times in linear order, we can build up a logic of temporal information for reasoning about knowledge.   There would be interesting problems related to these logics.   We will discuss the topics in further papers.   Also, the author has results on undecidability and solvable cases of this logic, but this paper limited in space could not include these results.

195

References

[1] L. Farinas del Cerro and E. Orlowska: DAL---A logic for data analysis, *Theoretical Computer Science*, 36, (1985), 251-264, CORRIGENDUM, *Theoretical Computer Science*, 47, (1986), 345.

[2] A. Nakamura: On the undecidability of monadic modal predicate logic, *Zeitschr. f. math. Logik und Grundlagen d. Math.*, 16, (1970), 257-260.

[3] A. Nakamura and J-M. Gao: A logic for fuzzy data analysis, *Fuzzy Sets and Systems*, 39, (1991), 127-132.

[4] A. Nakamura: Topological soft algebra for the S5-modal fuzzy logic, *Proc. of the 21st ISMVL, May 26-29, 1991, Victoria*, 80-84.

[5] A. Nakamura: A logic of imprecise monadic predicates and its relation to the S5-modal fuzzy logic, *Lecture Notes in Computer Science, 548, Symbolic and Quantitative Approaches to Uncertainty*, (Eds. R. Kruse and P. Siegel), (1991), 254-261.

[6] E. Orlowska and Z. Pawlak: Logical foundations of knowledge representation, Part I, *ICS PAS* (Polish Academy of Sciences) *Reports*, 537, 1984.

[7] E. Orlowska: Logic of indiscernibility relation, *Bulletin of the Polish Academy of Sciences, Mathematics*, (1985), 475-485.

[8] E. Orlowska: Logic for reasoning about knowledge, *Zeitschr. f. math. Logik und Grundlagen d. Math.*, 35, (1989), 559-572.

[9] Z. Pawlak: Rough sets, *International J. of Information and Computer Sciences*, 11, (1982), 341-356.

[10] Z. Pawlak: **Rough Sets** - Theoretical aspects of reasoning about data - , Kluwer Academic Pub., Dordrecht, (1991).

[11] R.M. Smullyan: **First-Order Logic**, Springer-Verlag, Berlin, 1968.

Rough Consequence and Rough Algebra

Mohua Banerjee[*] and M. K. Chakraborty
Department of Pure Mathematics
University of Calcutta
35, Ballygunge Circular Road
Calcutta 700 019
India

Abstract

A notion of rough consequence is investigated in detail. Two algebraic structures emerge from the modal system S_5. Properties of these structures, called rough algebras, have been studied. A link between rough consequence and one of the rough algebras is established.

1 Introduction

This research has its roots in our former works on the algebraic and logical aspects of rough set theory and the two fundamental works by Pawlak [1,2,3,4]. Though logical aspects include both the propositional as well as quantificational wings we shall be concerned here only with the former one. The fact that has been apparent in the last few years is that most of the propositional aspects of rough set theory are adequately captured by the modal system S_5. But the derivation procedure in S_5 has had to be enhanced because of the following consideration.

Two sets are roughly equal if and only if they have the same lower and upper approximations [3]. In rough set theory this identification is very important in the sense that the purpose to be served by one such set is hoped to be served (roughly) by the other. In the logic of rough sets, accordingly, one should be deducible from the other. But in S_5 this is not accomplished. This consideration led to the introduction of a new consequence relation, the rough consequence [2], which is capable of deriving, in fact, roughly upper equal formulae [3]. In this work we shall present the notion with some new results. Rough truth, rough validity and rough consistency and their relationship with the notion of rough consequence shall be discussed in some detail in section 3.

Another interesting notion, that of rough algebra, has crept in quite naturally. In the set ($\mathscr{F}$, say) of formulae of S_5, an equivalence relation R can be defined by taking formulae ϕ, φ to be related if and only if $\phi \leftrightarrow \varphi$ is an S_5 - theorem. This corresponds to the fact that ϕ and φ represent the same set in any interpretation.

* Research supported by the Council of Scientific and Industrial Research, New Delhi, India.

The quotient set thus obtained can be developed into a Boolean algebra $\mathcal{R}$ with an interior operator. In [1], we proposed an algebra (we call it $\mathcal{R}_1$ here), a structure on $\mathcal{F}$ that grew along similar lines. It is based on an equivalence relation R_{lu} that is not as strict as R. R_{lu} relates ϕ and φ if and only if they represent roughly equal sets in any interpretation. Incidentally, $\mathcal{R}_1$ gave rise to a new class of algebras that we call topological quasi - Boolean algebras. $\mathcal{R}_1$ and its properties are sketched briefly in section 4. Yet another structure $\mathcal{R}_2$ on $\mathcal{F}$ emerges in this paper. The equivalence relation in this case has an even more relaxed requirement : ϕ and φ need to represent only roughly upper equal sets in any interpretation. $\mathcal{R}_2$ turns out to be a topological Boolean algebra. More importantly, a connection, analogous to that between standard consequence in S_5 and $\mathcal{R}$, is found between rough consequence and $\mathcal{R}_2$. This is also presented in section 4. Both $\mathcal{R}_1$ and $\mathcal{R}_2$ will be called rough algebras.

Section 2 gives the rough set interpretation of S_5 and some results that act as prerequisites for those in the later sections.

2 Rough Set Interpretation of S_5

The modal system S_5 has a language consisting of the propositional variables p, q, r,......; logical symbols $\neg, \rightarrow, \wedge, \vee, \leftrightarrow, L, M$ and parentheses (,) .

The axioms are :
   all PC (Propositional Calculus) theorems and the following modal axioms.

$L(\phi \rightarrow \varphi) \rightarrow (L\phi \rightarrow L\varphi)$.

$L\phi \rightarrow \phi$.

$L\phi \rightarrow LL\phi$.

$M\phi \rightarrow LM\phi$.

The rules are :

Modus Ponens: $\dfrac{\phi, \phi \rightarrow \varphi}{\varphi}$ and

Necessitation: $\dfrac{\phi}{L\phi}$.

$\Gamma \vdash \phi$ stands for 'ϕ is derived from Γ in S_5 '.

Now, given an approximation space $<A, \sim >$, where A is a non-empty set, $\sim$ an equivalence relation on A, a formula ϕ of S_5 may be interpreted as a rough set $<A, \sim.\pi(\phi)>$, $\pi(\phi) \subseteq A$ [5] satisfying the following conditions.

$\pi(\neg \phi) \equiv A \setminus \pi(\phi)$.

$\pi(\phi \rightarrow \varphi) \equiv (A \setminus \pi(\phi)) \cup \pi(\varphi)$.

$\pi\,(\phi\,\wedge\,\phi) \equiv \pi\,(\phi)\cap\pi\,(\phi)$.

$\pi\,(\phi\,\vee\,\phi) \equiv \pi\,(\phi)\cup\pi\,(\phi)$.

$\pi\,(L\phi) \equiv \underline{\pi(\phi)}$ (the lower approximation of $\pi(\phi)$).

$\pi\,(M\phi) \equiv \overline{\pi(\phi)}$ (the upper approximation of $\pi(\phi)$).

A triple $<A, \sim, \pi >$ is called a model for S_5 .

Relative to this interpretation, the system S_5 is both sound and complete, i.e. $\vdash \phi$ if and only if for any of its interpretations $< A, \sim, \pi(\phi) >$, $\pi\,(\phi) = A$.

In rough set theory concepts like lower and upper approximations, rough equality, rough lower and upper equalities play crucial roles. Rough-theoretic assertions involving these concepts are aptly represented by S_5 formulae. The wffs $L\phi \leftrightarrow L\phi$, $M\phi \leftrightarrow M\phi$ and $(L\phi \leftrightarrow L\phi)\wedge(M\phi \leftrightarrow M\phi)$ represent respectively the assertions that sets corresponding to ϕ and ϕ are roughly lower equal, roughly upper equal and roughly equal. We state a few such representations.

Rough-set theoretic assertions :

(a) If ϕ and ϕ are roughly equal then the lower approximations of $\phi\cap\tau$ and $\phi\cap\tau$ are the same for any τ .

(b) If ϕ and ϕ are roughly equal then the upper approximations of $\phi\cup\tau$ and $\phi\cup\tau$ are the same for any τ .

(c) The intersection of the lower approximations of ϕ and ϕ is the same as the lower approximation of the intersection of ϕ and ϕ .

(d) The union of the upper approximations of ϕ and ϕ is the same as the upper approximation of the union of ϕ and ϕ .

(a), (b), (c), (d) are true assertions and their syntactic versions are

(a)' $(\phi\approx\phi) \to (L(\phi\wedge\tau) \leftrightarrow L(\phi\wedge\tau))$, where
$\phi\approx\phi \equiv (L\phi \leftrightarrow L\phi)\wedge(M\phi \leftrightarrow M\phi)$,

(b)' $(\phi\approx\phi) \to (M(\phi\vee\tau) \leftrightarrow M(\phi\vee\tau))$,

(c)' $(L\phi\wedge L\phi) \leftrightarrow L(\phi\wedge\phi)$,

(d)' $(M\phi\vee M\phi) \leftrightarrow M(\phi\vee\phi)$.

In S_5 these wffs can be established as theorems. Some more theorems and metatheorems of S_5 follow. These are not usually given attention to in the standard modal logic texts, but are pertinent in the present context.

Let us denote by $\phi\wedge\phi$ and $\phi\vee\phi$ the wffs

$(\phi\wedge\phi) \vee (\phi\wedge M\phi\wedge M\phi \wedge \neg M(\phi\wedge\phi))$ and

$(\phi\vee\phi) \wedge (\phi\vee L\phi\vee L\phi\vee\neg L(\phi\vee\phi))$ respectively.

Proposition 1. $\vdash \phi\vee\phi \leftrightarrow \neg(\neg\phi\wedge\neg\phi)$.
Proposition 2.

(a) $\vdash M(\phi\wedge\phi) \leftrightarrow M\phi\wedge M\phi$.

(b) $\vdash L(\phi\wedge\phi) \leftrightarrow L\phi\wedge L\phi$.

Dually,

(a)' $\vdash M(\phi \vee \varphi) \leftrightarrow M\phi \vee M\varphi$.

(b)' $\vdash L(\phi \vee \varphi) \leftrightarrow L\phi \vee L\varphi$.

Proof. Completeness of S_5 is used : it is shown that in an arbitrary model $<A, \sim, \pi>$,

(a) $\overline{\pi(\phi \wedge \varphi)} = \overline{\pi(\phi)} \cap \overline{\pi(\varphi)}$ and

(b) $\pi(\phi \wedge \varphi) = \pi(\phi) \cap \pi(\varphi) = \overline{\pi(\phi)} \cap \overline{\pi(\varphi)}$.

To prove (a), let $X \equiv \overline{\pi(\phi)} \cap \overline{\pi(\varphi)} \setminus \pi(\phi) \cap \pi(\varphi)$
$[\overline{\pi(\phi) \cap \pi(\varphi)} \subseteq \overline{\pi(\phi)} \cap \overline{\pi(\varphi)}]$. Now

$$\pi(\phi \wedge \varphi) = (\pi(\phi) \cap \pi(\varphi)) \cup (\pi(\phi) \cap X) \qquad \dots\dots(*)$$

It can be checked that $\overline{\pi(\phi)} \cap X = X$, whence

$$\overline{\pi(\phi \wedge \varphi)} = \overline{\pi(\phi) \cap \pi(\varphi) \cup \pi(\phi) \cap X}$$
$$= \overline{\pi(\phi) \cap \pi(\varphi) \cup X}$$
$$= \overline{\pi(\phi)} \cap \overline{\pi(\varphi)} .$$

For (b), we note that as $\pi(\phi) \cap \pi(\varphi) \subseteq \pi(\phi \wedge \varphi)$,
$\overline{\pi(\phi)} \cap \overline{\pi(\varphi)} \subseteq \pi(\phi \wedge \varphi)$. Now let $x \in \pi(\phi \wedge \varphi)$. It can be proved that

$$\pi(\phi \wedge \varphi) \cap (\pi(\varphi) \cap X) = (\pi(\phi) \cap \pi(\varphi)) \cap X = \emptyset . \text{ So } [x]_{\sim} \subseteq \pi(\phi \wedge \varphi)$$

and $\overline{\pi(\phi \wedge \varphi)} = \overline{\pi(\phi)} \cap \overline{\pi(\varphi)}$ (from (a)) imply that $[x]_{\sim} \cap X = \emptyset$. Then if $x \notin \pi(\phi) \cap \pi(\varphi)$, from (*) and $[x]_{\sim} \subseteq \pi(\phi \wedge \varphi)$, we would have $[x]_{\sim} \cap X \neq \emptyset$ - a contradiction. Thus $\pi(\phi \wedge \varphi) = \pi(\phi) \cap \pi(\varphi)$.

Proofs of (a)' and (b)' use proposition 1, the equivalence theorem of S_5 and (a), (b). $\qquad\qquad\qquad\qquad\qquad\qquad\qquad\qquad\qquad\qquad\qquad\qquad\qquad\quad\square$

Proposition 3. $\vdash \phi \wedge \varphi \leftrightarrow \phi \wedge \varphi$ if and only if $\vdash M\phi \wedge M\varphi \rightarrow M(\phi \wedge \varphi)$.
Dually, $\vdash \phi \vee \varphi \leftrightarrow \phi \vee \varphi$ if and only if $\vdash L(\phi \vee \varphi) \rightarrow L\phi \vee L\varphi$.

Let R be the equivalence relation defined on $\mathscr{F}$, the set of all wffs of S_5 , by

$\phi \, R \, \varphi$ if and only if $\vdash \phi \leftrightarrow \varphi$.

It is well known that $\mathscr{R} \equiv < \mathscr{F}/R , \leq, \wedge, \vee, 0, 1, \neg, L>$ is a topological Boolean algebra , where

$[\phi]_R \leq [\varphi]_R$ if and only if $\vdash \phi \rightarrow \varphi$,

$[\phi]_R \wedge [\varphi]_R \equiv [\phi \wedge \varphi]_R$,

$[\phi]_R \vee [\varphi]_R \equiv [\phi \vee \varphi]_R$,

$\neg [\phi]_R \equiv [\neg \phi]_R$,

$L[\phi]_R \equiv [L\phi]_R$.

$1 = [\phi]_R$, where $\vdash \phi$ and

$0 = [\phi]_R$, where $\vdash \neg \phi$ (i.e. ϕ is an antitheorem).

L is an interior operator on $\mathscr{F}/R$. In addition, if M is the corresponding closure operator on $\mathscr{F}/R$,

$\qquad ML[\phi]_R = L[\phi]_R$, for any $[\phi]_R$ in $\mathscr{F}/R$.

As mentioned in the introduction, two algebraic structures $\mathscr{R}_1$ (with equivalence relation R_{lu}) and $\mathscr{R}_2$ (with equivalence relation R_u) shall be constructed in a similar fashion in section 4. While $\phi \, R \, \phi$ means that $\pi(\phi)$ and $\pi(\phi)$ are the same in any model $< A, \sim, \pi >$. $\phi \, R_{lu} \, \phi$ and $\phi \, R_u \, \phi$ will mean that $\pi(\phi) \cdot \pi(\phi)$ are roughly equal and roughly upper equal respectively in $< A, \sim, \pi >$.

3 Rough Consequence

Definition . Let Γ be a set of wffs of S_5 and ϕ a wff. We write $\Gamma \vdash \phi$ and say that ϕ is a rough consequence of Γ if and only if there is a sequence $\phi_1, \ldots , \phi_n (= \phi)$ of wffs such that each ϕ_i , $i = 1, \ldots , n$ is either
   a theorem of S_5 or
   a member of Γ or
   derived from some of the wffs $\phi_1 \ldots \ldots , \phi_{i-1}$ by one of the following rules.

$\qquad$ (RMP)$_1$: $\quad \phi$

$$\frac{\vdash \phi' \to \phi}{\phi} \qquad \text{where } \vdash M\phi \to M\phi' .$$

$\qquad$ (RMP)$_2$: $\quad \phi' \to \phi$

$$\frac{\vdash \phi}{\phi} \qquad \text{where } \vdash L\phi \to L\phi' .$$

If Γ is empty, we write $\vdash \phi$ and ϕ is called a rough theorem.
The following derived rules can be easily established.

$\qquad$ (DR)$_1$: $\dfrac{\phi}{\phi'} \qquad \text{where } \vdash M\phi \to M\phi' .$

$\qquad$ (DR)$_2$: $\vdash \phi$

$$\frac{\phi' \to \phi}{\phi} \qquad \text{where } \vdash \phi \approx \phi' .$$

Proposition 4. $(RMP)_1$ and $(DR)_1$ are equivalent.

Proposition 5. If $\vdash \phi$ then $\vdash \phi$.

Proposition 6. If $\Gamma \vdash \phi$ then $\Gamma \vdash \phi'$, where $\vdash M \phi \to M \phi'$.

Proposition 7. If $\Gamma \vdash \phi$ then for any φ, $\Gamma \vdash \varphi \to \phi'$, where $\vdash M \phi \to M \phi'$.

Proposition 8. If $\vdash \phi$ then $\Gamma \vdash \phi$, for any Γ .

Proposition 9. If $\vdash M \phi$ then $\vdash \phi$.

The converse of proposition 5 is not true, as shown in the following example.

Example. We consider the wff $\phi \to L\phi$. As $\vdash M (\phi \to L\phi)$, by proposition 9 $\vdash \phi \to L\phi$. That $\nvdash \phi \to L\phi$ is proved by using soundness of S_5.

Proposition 10 (Deduction theorem). If $\Gamma \cup \{\phi\} \vdash \varphi$ then $\Gamma \vdash \phi \to \varphi$.

Proof . The proof is by induction on the number of steps of the derivation of φ from $\Gamma \cup \{\phi\}$.

In case of a one-step derivation the proposition can be proved easily.

Supposing now that the proposition holds for all derivations upto length k, let a derivation $\Gamma \cup \{\phi\} \vdash \varphi$ with exactly $k + 1$ steps be considered.

Case (i). Let φ be obtained by $(RMP)_1$. i.e.

$$\Gamma \cup \{\phi\} \vdash \mu$$

$$\underline{\vdash \mu' \to \varphi}$$

$$\varphi \qquad\qquad \text{where } \vdash M \mu \to M \mu'.$$

Now. by induction hypothesis, $\Gamma \vdash \phi \to \mu$.

Also $\vdash \mu' \to \varphi$ implies $\vdash (\phi \to \mu') \to (\phi \to \varphi)$.

And using $\vdash M\mu \to M\mu'$. we get $\vdash M(\phi \to \mu) \to M(\phi \to \mu')$.

So. by $(RMP)_1$, $\Gamma \vdash \phi \to \varphi$.

Case (ii). Let φ be derived by using $(RMP)_2$. So

$$\Gamma \cup \{\phi\} \vdash \mu' \to \varphi$$

$$\underline{\vdash \mu}$$

$$\varphi \qquad\qquad \text{where } \vdash L \mu \to L \mu'.$$

$\vdash \mu$ and $\vdash L \mu \to L \mu'$ imply $\vdash \mu'$ and hence $\vdash \phi \to \mu'$.

Using induction hypothesis we get

$$\Gamma \vdash \phi \to (\mu' \to \varphi)$$

$$\underline{\vdash (\phi \to (\mu' \to \varphi)) \to ((\phi \to \mu') \to (\phi \to \varphi))}$$

$$(\phi \to \mu') \to (\phi \to \varphi) \qquad\qquad (RMP)_1$$

$$\underline{\vdash \phi \to \mu'}$$
$$\phi \to \varphi \qquad\qquad (RMP)_2$$

So $\Gamma \vdash \phi \to \varphi$. $\qquad\qquad\qquad\qquad\qquad\qquad\qquad$ □

Note. The converse of Deduction theorem does not hold (to be proved later using soundness theorem).

Proposition 11. $\{\phi\} \vdash \phi$ if and only if $\vdash M \phi \to M \phi$.

Proof. The proof is by induction on the length n of derivation of ϕ from $\{\phi\}$.

$n = 1$. Case (i). ϕ is ϕ . Then $\vdash M \phi \to M \phi$.

Case (ii). ϕ is a theorem of S_5. In this subcase, we have the following steps.

$$\vdash M \phi \to (M \phi \to M \phi).$$

$$\vdash \phi$$

$$\vdash M \phi$$

$$\vdash M \phi \to M \phi .$$

Assuming that for $n < k$ the proposition holds, it will now be proved for $n = k$. If ϕ is obtained by $(RMP)_1$, then

$$\{\phi\} \vdash \mu$$

$$\underline{\vdash \mu' \to \phi}$$

$$\phi \qquad\qquad \text{where } \vdash M \mu \to M \mu'.$$

By induction hypothesis, $\vdash M \phi \to M \mu$. So $\vdash M \phi \to M \mu'$.

Also from $\vdash \mu' \to \phi$, one obtains $\vdash M \mu' \to M \phi$. So $\vdash M \phi \to M \phi$.

If ϕ is obtained by $(RMP)_2$, then

$$\{\phi\} \vdash \mu' \to \phi$$

$$\underline{\vdash \mu}$$

$$\phi \qquad\qquad \text{where } \vdash L \mu \to L \mu'.$$

Now by induction hypothesis, $\vdash M \phi \to M (\mu' \to \phi)$. $\vdash M \phi \to (L \mu' \to M \phi)$ and thus $\vdash L \mu' \to (M \phi \to M \phi)$. Using $\vdash L \mu \to L \mu'$, then $\vdash L \mu \to (M \phi \to M \phi)$. Also $\vdash L \mu$. Hence $\vdash M \phi \to M \phi$.

Conversely, let $\vdash M \phi \to M \phi$. Then $\{\phi\} \vdash \phi$ and by $(DR)_2$, $\{\phi\} \vdash \phi$. $\qquad\square$

3.1 A Semantics For Rough Consequence: Rough Truth, Rough Validity

Definition . ϕ is roughly true in a model $<A ,\sim, \pi >$ if and only if $\overline{\pi(\phi)} = A$. ϕ is roughly false in $<A, \sim, \pi >$ if and only if $\underline{\pi(\phi)} = \varnothing$. ϕ is roughly valid if and only if it is roughly true in all models.

Note. A formula may be both roughly true and roughly false, neither roughly true nor roughly false; a true formula is roughly true but not conversely; a false formula is roughly false but not conversely. The notions of rough truth and rough falsity were introduced in [4]. Here the definition of rough falsity is different. Rough validity is a new notion which finds significance in the context of rough consequence. Validity implies rough validity, but not conversely (e.g. the wff p→ Lp, where p is a propositional variable).

Notation. We write $\Gamma \vDash \phi$ if and only if for all models whenever every $\gamma \in \Gamma$ is roughly true then so is ϕ . $\vDash \phi$ then means that ϕ is roughly valid.

Proposition 12 (Soundness theorem). If $\Gamma \vdash \phi$ then $\Gamma \vDash \phi$.

Proposition 13. If $\vdash \phi$ then $\vdash M \phi$.

Observation. Thus for any wff ϕ , $\vdash \phi$ if and only if $\vdash M \phi$.

Proposition 14. The converse of Deduction theorem does not hold.
We prove proposition 14 by citing an example.

Example. For any propositional variable p, $\vdash M(p \rightarrow Lp)$. So $\vdash p \rightarrow Lp$ (proposition 9). But let us consider the model $<A , \sim , \pi >$, where $A \equiv \{x_1, x_2, x_3\}$, there are two $\sim$ - equivalence classes $\{x_1\}$, $\{x_2, x_3\}$ in A and $\pi(p) \equiv \{x_1, x_2\}$. One can easily show that $\{p\} \nvDash Lp$, whence by soundness theorem, $\{p\} \nvdash Lp$.   □

Proposition 15 (Completeness theorem). If $\vDash \phi$ then $\vdash \phi$.

Proof. Using completeness of S_5 , it can be proved that if $\vDash \phi$ then $\vdash M \phi$. Then by proposition 9, $\vdash \phi$.   □

3.2   Rough Consistency

It may be recalled that consistency , syntactically , is defined in S_5 as follows [6].

$\{\phi\}$ is inconsistent if and only if $\vdash \neg \phi$.

$\{\phi_1, ..., \phi_n\}$ is inconsistent if and only if $\vdash \neg (\phi_1 \wedge .... \wedge \phi_n)$.
A set Γ of wffs is inconsistent if and only if there is a finite subset of Γ which is inconsistent.
A set of wffs is consistent if and only if it is not inconsistent.

We now define rough consistency and rough inconsistency.
Definition.   A set Γ of wffs is roughly consistent if and only if $M \Gamma \equiv \{M \gamma : \gamma \in \Gamma\}$ is consistent. A set Γ is roughly inconsistent if and only if $L \Gamma \equiv \{L \gamma : \gamma \in \Gamma\}$ is inconsistent.

Remark. A consistent set is roughly consistent and an inconsistent set is roughly inconsistent, but the converses are not true. As examples we have $\{p, \neg p\}$, which is roughly inconsistent but not inconsistent, and $\{p, M \neg p\}$, which is roughly consistent but not consistent, p being any propositional variable.

However, a single wff ϕ can be proved to be consistent if and only if it is roughly consistent. A set of wffs may be both roughly consistent and roughly inconsistent (e.g. $\{p . \neg p\}$, p is a propositional variable). In respect of consistency , sets $\{\phi_1, \ldots, \phi_n\}$ and $\{\phi_1 \wedge \ldots \wedge \phi_n\}$ are equivalent . But generally, they are distinct in case of rough consistency. For instance, though the set $\{p, \neg p\}$ is roughly consistent, $\{p \wedge \neg p\}$ is not.

The following propositions establish the relationship between the notions of rough consequence and rough consistency.

Proposition 16. If $\Gamma \vdash \phi$ then $\Gamma \cup \{\neg \phi\}$ is roughly inconsistent.

Proof. There are $\gamma_1, \ldots, \gamma_n \in \Gamma$ such that $\{\gamma_1, \ldots, \gamma_n\} \vdash \phi$.
Then by Deduction theorem,

$$\vdash \gamma_1 \rightarrow (\gamma_2 \rightarrow \ldots \rightarrow (\gamma_n \rightarrow \phi) \ldots).$$

So $\vdash \neg \gamma_1 \vee \neg \gamma_2 \vee \ldots \vee \neg \gamma_n \vee \phi$, i.e. $\vdash M(\neg \gamma_1 \vee \neg \gamma_2 \vee \ldots \vee \neg \gamma_n \vee \phi)$ (proposition 13) . i.e. $\vdash \neg (L \gamma_1 \wedge L \gamma_2 \wedge \ldots \wedge L \gamma_n \wedge L \neg \phi)$.
Hence $\Gamma \cup \{\neg \phi\}$ is roughly inconsistent. $\qquad \square$

Proposition 17.

(a) $\vdash \phi$ if and only if $\neg \phi$ is roughly inconsistent.

(b) $\vdash \neg \phi$ if and only if ϕ is roughly inconsistent.

Proposition 18. If $\Gamma \vdash \phi$ for every wff ϕ then Γ is roughly inconsistent.
Proof. For every wff ϕ, $\Gamma \cup \{\neg \phi\}$ is roughly inconsistent (proposition 16).
We take ϕ such that $\vdash \neg \phi$. There is a finite subset Γ' of $\Gamma \cup \{\neg \phi\}$ which is roughly inconsistent.
If $\Gamma' \subseteq \Gamma$, then Γ is roughly inconsistent.

$\Gamma' \neq \{\neg \phi\}$, for in that case $\vdash M \phi$ and $\vdash \neg \phi$ imply that in any model $<A, \sim, \pi >$, $\pi(\phi) = \varnothing$ and $\bar{\pi}(\phi) = A$ - which cannot hold together.

So $\Gamma' \equiv \{\gamma_1, \ldots, \gamma_n, \neg \phi\}$, $\gamma_1, \ldots, \gamma_n \in \Gamma$. Then
$\vdash \neg (L \gamma_1 \wedge \ldots \wedge L \gamma_n \wedge L \neg \phi)$. Also $\vdash \neg \phi$ implies $\vdash L \neg \phi$.
So in any model $<A, \sim, \pi >$,

$$\pi(\gamma_1) \cap \ldots \cap \pi(\gamma_n) \cap \pi(\neg \phi) = \varnothing \text{ and } \pi(\neg \phi) = \ddot{A}.$$

Then $\underline{\pi(\gamma_1) \cap \ldots \cap \pi(\gamma_n)} = \varnothing$, which yields $\vdash \neg (L \gamma_1 \wedge \ldots \wedge L \gamma_n)$.
Hence Γ is roughly inconsistent. $\qquad \square$

Proposition 19. If a finite set Γ of wffs is roughly consistent then there is a model in which each $\gamma \in \Gamma$ is roughly true.
Proof (sketch). Let $\Gamma \equiv \{\gamma_1, \ldots, \gamma_n\}$ .There is a model $<A, \sim, \pi >$ in which $P \equiv \pi(\gamma_1) \cap \ldots \cap \pi(\gamma_n) \neq \varnothing$. We consider $<P, \sim|P, \pi' >$, where $\sim|P$ is the restriction of $\sim$ to P and $\pi'(p) \equiv \pi(p) \cap P$, p is any propositional variable. Using induction, it can be shown that for any wff ϕ, $\pi'(\phi) = \pi(\phi) \cap P$. Let $x \in P$. Then $[x]_{\sim|P} \cap \pi(\gamma_i) \neq \varnothing$, $i = 1, \ldots, n$, so that $[x]_{\sim|P} \cap \pi'(\gamma_i) \neq \varnothing$, $i = 1, \ldots, n$.
Thus $\pi'(\gamma_i) = P$, for each $i = 1, \ldots, n$.

4 Rough Algebras

4.1 Rough Algebra $\mathcal{R}_1$

Definition. We define a binary relation R_{lu} on the set $\mathcal{F}$ of wffs of S_5, viz.

$\phi \, R_{lu} \varphi$ if and only if $\vdash \phi \approx \varphi$, i.e. $\vdash (L \phi \leftrightarrow L \varphi) \wedge (M \phi \leftrightarrow M\varphi)$.

R_{lu} is an equivalence relation.
A partial order $\leq$ can be defined on $\mathcal{F}R_{lu}$ thus :

$[\phi]_{R_{lu}} \leq [\varphi]_{R_{lu}}$ if and only if $\vdash (L\phi \rightarrow L\varphi) \wedge (M\phi \rightarrow M\varphi)$, i.e. $\pi(\phi)$ is roughly

included [3] in $\pi(\varphi)$, in every model $<A, \sim, \pi>$.

All S_5 - theorems constitute an equivalence class 1 and this class is the unit of the poset $< \mathcal{F}R_{lu}, \leq >$; while all S_5 - antitheorems constitute an equivalence class 0 and this class is the zero of the poset $< \mathcal{F}R_{lu}, \leq >$.

We can define next the operations $\neg$, $\wedge$, $\vee$ in $\mathcal{F}R_{lu}$ as follows; $\phi \wedge \varphi$, $\phi \vee \varphi$ are as in section 2.

$\neg \, [\phi]_{R_{lu}} \equiv [\neg \, \phi]_{R_{lu}}$.

$[\phi]_{R_{lu}} \wedge [\varphi]_{R_{lu}} \equiv [\phi \wedge \varphi]_{R_{lu}}$.

$[\phi]_{R_{lu}} \vee [\varphi]_{R_{lu}} \equiv [\phi \vee \varphi]_{R_{lu}}$.

Proposition 20. $< \mathcal{F}R_{lu}, \leq, \wedge, \vee, \neg, 0, 1 >$ is a quasi-Boolean algebra [7].

If $L[\phi]_{R_{lu}}$ is defined as $[L\phi]_{R_{lu}}$ for any $[\phi]_{R_{lu}}$ in $\mathcal{F}R_{lu}$, L turns out to be an interior operator on $\mathcal{F}R_{lu}$. Taking the corresponding closure operator M on $\mathcal{F}R_{lu}$, we find that $ML[\phi]_{R_{lu}} = L[\phi]_{R_{lu}}$, for any $[\phi]_{R_{lu}}$ in $\mathcal{F}R_{lu}$. Thus $\mathcal{R}_1 \equiv < \mathcal{F}R_{lu}, \leq, \wedge, \vee, \neg, 0, 1, L >$ is a new algebraic structure that may be called a topological quasi-Boolean algebra. This has not been investigated much but has possibilities .

The law of contradiction and the law of excluded middle do not hold generally in $\mathcal{R}_1$. The following proposition shows that they hold precisely for those wffs ϕ such that $\pi(\phi)$ is a definable set [3] in any model $<A, \sim, \pi >$.

Proposition 21.

(a)   If $\vdash M \phi \rightarrow L \phi$ then $[\phi]_{R_{lu}} \wedge \neg [\phi]_{R_{lu}} = 0$ and $[\phi]_{R_{lu}} \vee \neg [\phi]_{R_{lu}} = 1$.

(b)   If $\nvdash M \phi \rightarrow L \phi$ then $[\phi]_{R_{lu}} \wedge \neg [\phi]_{R_{lu}} \neq 0$ and $[\phi]_{R_{lu}} \vee \neg [\phi]_{R_{lu}} \neq 1$.

It may be observed that $R \subseteq R_{lu}$. The following proposition gives a necessary and sufficient condition when the R_{lu} - equivalence class of a wff ϕ collapses to its R - equivalence class.

Proposition 22. $[\phi]_R = [\phi]_{R_{lu}}$ if and only if $\vdash M \phi \rightarrow L \phi$, i.e. $\pi(\phi)$ is a definable set in every model $<A, \sim, \pi >$.

4.2   Rough Algebra $\mathcal{R}_2$

Definition. In the set $\mathcal{F}$ of wffs of S_5, let another binary relation R_u be defined by

$\phi\, R_u\, \varphi$ if and only if $\vdash M\,\phi \leftrightarrow M\,\varphi$.

It can be easily seen that R_u is an equivalence relation on $\mathcal{F}$. Further, $R \subseteq R_u$ and for any wff ϕ, $\phi\, R_u M\, \phi$.

Definition. A binary relation $\leq$ is defined on the set $\mathcal{F}R_u$ as follows.

$[\phi]_{R_u} \leq [\varphi]_{R_u}$ if and only if $\vdash M\,\phi \to M\,\varphi$, i.e. $\pi(\phi)$ is roughly upper included [3] in $\pi(\varphi)$, in every model $<A, \sim, \pi>$.

The definition is unambiguous.

Proposition 23. $\leq$ is a partial order on $\mathcal{F}R_u$.

Proposition 24. All wffs ϕ such that $\vdash M\,\phi$ constitute an equivalence class 1 and this class is the unit of the poset $< \mathcal{F}R_u, \leq >$.

Proof.   Let $\phi, \varphi \in \mathcal{F}$ with $\vdash M\,\phi$ and $\vdash M\,\varphi$. Then $\vdash M\,\phi \leftrightarrow M\,\varphi$ and hence $\phi\, R_u\, \varphi$. On the other hand, if $\phi\, R_u\, \varphi$ and $\vdash M\,\phi$, we get $\vdash M\,\varphi$. Also, for any $\mu \in \mathcal{F}, \vdash M\,\mu \to M\,\phi$, if $\vdash M\,\phi$. Thus $[\mu]_{R_u} \leq [\phi]_{R_u}$.   □

Corollary. All S_5 - theorems belong to 1.

Proposition 25. All S_5 - antitheorems constitute an equivalence class 0 and this class is the zero of the poset $< \mathcal{F}R_u, \leq >$.

The proof uses the necessitation rule.

Definition. The following operations are now defined on $\mathcal{F}R_u$.

$\neg\, [\phi]_{R_u} \equiv [\neg\, M\,\phi]_{R_u}$.

$[\phi]_{R_u} \wedge [\varphi]_{R_u} \equiv [\phi \wedge \varphi]_{R_u}$.

$[\phi]_{R_u} \vee [\varphi]_{R_u} \equiv [\phi \vee \varphi]_{R_u}$.

Proposition 26. $\mathcal{R}_2 \equiv < \mathcal{F}R_u, \leq, \wedge, \vee, \neg, 0, 1 >$ is a Boolean algebra.

Proof. From proposition 2 (section 2), $\vdash M\,(\phi \wedge \varphi) \to M\,\phi \wedge M\,\varphi$. So $\vdash M\,(\phi \wedge \varphi) \to M\,\phi$ and $\vdash M\,(\phi \wedge \varphi) \to M\,\varphi$, whence $[\phi]_{R_u} \wedge [\varphi]_{R_u} \leq [\phi]_{R_u}$ and $[\phi]_{R_u} \wedge [\varphi]_{R_u} \leq [\varphi]_{R_u}$. Let $[\mu]_{R_u}$ be any lower bound of $[\phi]_{R_u}, [\varphi]_{R_u}$. Then $\vdash M\,\mu \to M\,\phi, \vdash M\,\mu \to M\,\varphi$. So $\vdash M\,\mu \to (M\,\phi \wedge M\,\varphi)$ and hence $\vdash M\,\mu \to M\,(\phi \wedge \varphi)$, i.e. $[\mu]_{R_u} \leq [\phi \wedge \varphi]_{R_u}$. Thus $[\phi]_{R_u} \wedge [\varphi]_{R_u}$ is the greatest lower bound of $[\phi]_{R_u}$ and $[\varphi]_{R_u}$.

Using the result $\vdash M\,(\phi \vee \varphi) \leftrightarrow M\,\phi \vee M\,\varphi$ (proposition 2), one can also prove that $[\phi]_{R_u} \vee [\varphi]_{R_u}$ is the least upper bound of $[\phi]_{R_u}$ and $[\varphi]_{R_u}$.

We have $\vdash \neg\, M\,\phi \vee M\,\phi$. So $\vdash \neg(\, M\,\phi \wedge M \neg M\,\phi)$, and then $\vdash \neg\, M\,(\phi \wedge \neg M\,\phi)$ (by proposition 2 and equivalence theorem of S_5). Thus $\vdash \neg\,(\phi \wedge \neg M\,\phi)$, which implies $[\phi]_{R_u} \wedge \neg\, [\phi]_{R_u} = [\phi \wedge \neg M\,\phi]_{R_u} = 0$.

It can be shown with the help of proposition 1(section 2) that $\wedge$ and $\vee$ satisfy the De Morgan's laws with respect to $\neg$. This fact helps to establish the dual complementation law, viz.

$[\phi]_{R_u} \vee \neg [\phi]_{R_u} = 1$.

The proof of distributivity of $\wedge$ and $\vee$ is straightforward and uses proposition 2.

$\square$

Moreover, if $C [\phi]_{R_u}$ is defined as $[M \phi]_{R_u}$ for any $[\phi]_{R_u}$ in $\mathscr{A}R_u$, then C is a closure operator on $\mathscr{A}R_u$. In fact, $[M \phi]_{R_u} = [\phi]_{R_u}$. So C is the identity operator, and hence it is an interior operator on $\mathscr{A}R_u$ as well.

It is obvious that $R \subseteq R_{lu} \subseteq R_u$. A result corresponding to proposition 22 that may relate the R_u - equivalence class of a wff ϕ to its R (or R_{lu}) - equivalence class, is yet to be obtained.

Finally, we have the following proposition which links the rough consequence relation $\vdash$ and the rough algebra $\mathscr{R}_2$.

Proposition 27. $\{\phi\} \vdash \varphi$ and $\{\varphi\} \vdash \phi$ if and only if $\phi R_u \varphi$.
The proof follows immediately from proposition 11 (section 3).

References

1. Banerjee Mohua, Chakraborty MK. Rough algebra. Bull Polish Acad Sc (Math); to appear

2. Chakraborty MK, Banerjee Mohua. Rough consequence. Bull Polish Acad Sc (Math); to appear

3. Pawlak Z. Rough sets. Int Jour of Comp and Inf Sci 1982; 11, No. 5: 341-356

4. Pawlak Z. Rough logic. Bull Polish Acad Sc (Technical Sc) 1987; 35, No. 5-6: 253-258

5. Banerjee Mohua, Chakraborty MK. A category for rough sets. Foundations of Computing and Decision Sciences 1993; 18, No. 3-4: 167-180

6. Hughes GE, Cresswell MJ. An introduction to modal logic. Methuen, London, 1972

7. Rasiowa H. An algebraic approach to non- classical logics, North Holland, Amsterdam, 1974

Formal Description of Rough Sets

Edward Bryniarski
Department of Computer Science
and
Applied Logic,
University of Opole
Opole, Poland

Abstract

In the paper we present a formal description of rough sets within the limits of the generalized set theory, which is interpreted in the approximation of set theory. The rough sets are interpreted as an approximations, which are defined by means of the Pawlak's rough sets.

1 Introduction.

My main ideas and intuitions on rough sets are taken from the conception of Prof. Pawlak [1]. At present there are many articles and reports published on rough sets theory and their applications [2].

In the paper we present a formal description of rough sets within the limits of the *generalized set theory*, which is interpreted in the *approximation of set theory*. The rough sets are interpreted as an approximations, which are defined by means of the Pawlak's rough sets. We presented this conception of the rough set in author's doctoral dissertation prepared at the inspiration and under the supervision of Prof. U. Wybraniec-Skardowska - [3].

2 The Generalized Set Theory.

In the process of cognition, some components of the reality or its elements called *the objects of the reality* are distinguished. And any object is called the *class* if the whole of distinguished components of the reality, which point at this object (and are its representative), determine it. If the class of elements of an object determines univocally and in the full sense of the word this object, then we call it *the multiset* (for example Blizard's multisets [4]. The multiset such that its every element determines in one way and only one way one and only one component of this multiset, is called here *the set*.

The theory, which describes the sets in this meaning, is called here *the Generalized Set Theory* (GST).

The primitive concept of GST is the concept of an object. The primitive terms are as follows:

- the functor of "determining an object by an object",

- the predicate of "being of generator",

- the predicate of "inclusion of objects".

Intuitive understanding of the primitive terms is as follows: - the inscription "the object determined by an object s" denotes the identification system of the object s, for example - denotation of a name representing the object s; the object determined by an object s is represented by the object s; the object s is the representative of the object determined by an object s; (usually, we shall understand the object determined by an object s as the object s, when the object s is a directly given object and as abstraction class of *indiscernibility relation* with the representative s when the object s is not a directly given object), - the inscription "an object s is included into an object v" represents the knowledge that an object s determines or assigns an object v (for example, when an object s is a component of an object v), - the inscription "an object s is a generator" represents the knowledge about the fact, that an object s is an elementary object of reality, which determines another object of reality.

2.1 Axioms, definitions and choice theorems

The generalized set theory describes objects according to the following method:

2.1.1

It distinguishes among objects all those objects which are representative fragments of other objects, i.e. those which determine the fragments as identification system.

2.1.2

It distinguishes possibly the most elementary objects which are parts of other objects, and which are called generators.

2.1.3

If elementary objects are not satisfying for unambiguous determination of objects, parts of which they are, then objects (called constructions) which do not submit to determination are also elementary.

2.1.4

It also determines representative fragments of elementary objects.

2.1.5

Description of objects consisting of other objects made with a help of representative fragments of elementary objects is unambiguous and minimal.

Let any distinguished components of the reality, i.e. objects of this reality, satisfy the following ontological postulates:

Postulate 1 *There exist objects, which point at some objects (they are representatives of some objects). For every object there exists one and only one object which is his representative.*

Postulate 2 *Some objects form a whole, which is usually called the reality.*

Postulate 3 *The objects of the reality being some wholes are components of some wholes ... .*

Postulate 4 *It is possible to distinguish an object in reality, which is a component of any whole. There exists one and only one such object. For example, in the physical reality, this object is the emptiness.*

Postulate 5 *Any related with some relations objects may be related with some relations within an object, which is the smallest object included in these objects.*

Postulate 6 *Any properties of objects have only one realization within a minimal object, which has these properties.*

Postulate 7 *Elementary components of objects related by relations may be distinguished as the generators of these objects.*

Postulate 8 *Any object contains other object, when the exterior designation of the first object contains the interior designation of the other object.*

Postulate 9 *There exist objects, which may be identified independently of other objects. These objects are "free" in the reality. We may relate them to other objects according to the postulated properties of the wholes of objects. These wholes have the description consistent with the Zermelo-Fraenkl's theory.*

The definitions and axioms of the generalized set theory are formulated according to the ontological postulates and the method of description of objects presented here.

Let us assume that

Axiom 1 *Any x is the object.*

The axiom 1 "allows" to speak only about objects.

Definition 1 *(set.) We call the set an object included into an object or an object which includes an object.*

Axiom 2 *(the empty set.) There exists exactly one such set in which no set different from it is included and it is included in the set different from it.*

The axiom 2 vouches for correctness of a following definition.

Definition 2 *(the empty set.) The object $\emptyset$ is called here the empty set. The empty set is an object, in which no set different from it is included and it is included in the set different from it.*

Axiom 3 *(inclusion of objects is reflexive and transitive.) Any set is included in itself and if it is also included in another set, and that one is included in a third one, then the first one is included in the third one.*

Axiom 4 (*inclusion of objects is "almost" antisimmetric.*) *If one object is included in a second object different from it, then not all the objects included in the second one are included in the first one.*

Axiom 5 (*universum.*) *There exists exactly one object which includes all the objects including some objects .or all the objects which are determined by some objects.*

This axiom vouches for correctness of the following definition:

Definition 3 (*universum.*) *The object x, which includes all the objects including some objects or all the objects which are represented by some objects, is called here the universum.*

Definition 4 (*construction.*) *The object x is a construction, iff it is a set and is not an unambiguously defined by its generators subset of a set. For example, if we will accept atoms as the most basic component of chemical substances, as their generators, molecules of the substances will be the constructions, since we may obtain molecules of various substances from the same atoms.*

For example: the empty set is not a construction.

Axiom 6 (*representatives.*) *Any generator and any construction is determined by a certain object.*

The further characterization of objects described by the theory GST gives

Axiom 7 (*character of the empty set.*) *The empty set is not any generator and it determines an object different from itself.*

Axiom 8 (*determining generator by set.*) *The object determined by the set is the generator.*

After we have characterized the notions of the generator and of the construction, and the notion of determination of one object by another, we will attempt to formulate the most important definition of the theory GST, namely the definition allowing to answer the question about fragments of reality which should be discerned in the process of cognition to let us unambiguously assign any component of reality with their help:

Definition 5 (*membership.*) *The object x is an element of the object iff there exists such object z, which is determined by the object x and it is a generator of the object y (it is the generator and it generates the object y) or it is a construction.*

Thus the object which has an element is a set.

In other words *elements of the set y are representatives of the generators of the set y and of the constructions of which the set y is composed.*

From the definition 5 of being of an element of set, from the respective axiom, some facts and definitions it follows

Elementary facts

(a) The empty set is an element of the universum,

(b) any set is not an element of the universum iff it is not an element of any set,

(c) any object determines a generator or construction iff it is an element of an object which it determines itself,

(d) any set determining an object is an element of the object which it determines itself,

(e) any set determining some object is an element and at the some time a subset of the universum,

(f) any object which is determined by itself is its element.

Elementary theorems

In the theory GST analogically to the classical set theory, inclusion of sets can be expressed with the help of the predicate of belonging of an element to the set, even more, sets equal to one another, when they have the same elements and the empty set has no elements. Any sets possessing the same elements are identical. In other words: any sets univocally determined by its elements.

Other axioms and definitions

The axiom of "distinguishing" of the classical set theory is not the axiom of the theory GST. However, we accept here, the axiom corresponding to the postulate 6,

Axiom 9 (*distinguishing sets by any formula*) *For any formula possessing one free variable x and for any set x there exists a minimal (in the sense of inclusion) set which includes all the objects determined by the objects satisfying the formula and included in the set x.*

The axiom 9 points out the possibility of existence (within some object) of many sets the elements of which have a given property.

Now we will consider another aspect of the reality description - its hierarchy. The hierarchical structure of reality takes into account

Axiom 10 [*existing of power set.*] *For any set x belonging to the universum there exists exactly one set y, belonging to the universum and minimal (in the sense of inclusion of sets), such that all the subsets of the set x belong to y.*

The axiom 10 vouches for correctness of the definition

Definition 6 (*power set.*) *The family of the subsets of the set x we called a set y belonging to the universum and minimal (in the sense of inclusion of sets), such that all the subsets of the set x belong to y.*

If a set on the higher level in the hierarchy of reality is combined of at least one taking the lower place in the hierarchy, then such property may be defined in the following way:

Definition 7 (*combination of sets.*) *The object x is the combination of some objects iff there exists the set beginning of element of x.*

Describing reality usually we describe its hierarchy within the limits of a certain object distinguished in the description (a kind of reference system). Then the notion of the family of sets becomes important, the notion allowing to consider the sets, which can be combined into other objects within the limits of the distinguished object:

Definition 8 (*family of sets.*) *The set x is family of sets iff there exists the set y belonging to universum U such that x is the subset of the family of all the subset of the set y and at the some time combination of certain sets.*

Let us notice that sets determined by the elements of any set belonging to the universum are connected within the family of all its subsets determined by this set. However combination of these sets may be determined univocally in this way. It means that

Axiom 11 (*existing of elements combination*) *For any nonempty set belonging to the uniwersum there exists exactly one minimal family of sets to which all the sets determined by the elements of such set belong.*

The notion of the *selective choice* of the elements of the set also will be useful in the description of the hierarchy of reality.

Definition 9 (*selective choice.*) *The set x that is the selective choice of the elements of the sets belonging to the set y when it is a minimal (in the sense of inclusion of sets) set which has a nonempty part common with each set belonging to y.*

According to the postulate 5 using the notion of selective choice of the elements of the sets we can assume

Axiom 12 (*of choice.*) *¿From all the disjoint in pairs and nonempty sets of any family, we can choose at the same time the elements constituting a minimal (in the sense of inclusion of set) set possessing elements common with each set of the family. In other words for any family of disjoint and nonempty sets there exists a minimal set possessing an element common with all the sets of the family.*

Let us notice that the axiom of choice does not say that there exists set including only and only one element from each set of the family of disjoint in pairs and nonempty sets - in a certain reality (in a certain model) such set could be simply non-existent, i.e. it could happen that arbitrarily chosen object must always be connected with others.

Exact sets

The basic problem which is related to the selective choice of elements from sets is the constructability of the sets consisting only of the element chosen from particular sets one at a time. Such sets satisfy the postulate 9 and their elements will be considered here as the so called *exact* sets and objects.

Definition 10 (*exact object.*) *The exact object is such object which not being its own element determines one-element generator - the singleton.*

Definition 11 (*exact set.*) *An object x will be called here an exact set iff (a1) only exact elements belong to x; (a2) for any element belonging to x the element x includes a set composed of all the remaining elements of x, and (a3) x is the empty set or there exists an element of x such that none of its element belong to x.*

As we will show further, the sets described by the Zermelo-Fraenkel's set theory can be interpreted as the exact sets.

The following axiom says about how the exact sets are placed in the universum

Axiom 13 (*exact sets*) *For any exact set belonging to the universum the family of all its subsets is an exact set. The largest (in the sense of inclusion of sets) exact set is included in any set. For any two exact sets there exists an exact set consisting only of the elements belonging to one ore the other set, or for any two exact set belonging to the universum and containing these sets.*

The exact set consisting only of the elements of the exact set x or of the exact set y is called here the *joint* of the sets x, y.

We already know the hierarchy of sets estimated in the universum by the families of all the subsets of universum. It seems reasonable to assume that the hierarchy of sets can be also estimated for the exact sets. According to the postulate 9 this hierarchy will be estimated in the same way as in the theory of Zermelo-Fraenkel. In order to do it, first we will introduce the definition of the successor of an exact set.

The axiom *of infinity* for exact sets can be formulated in the theory of Zermelo-Fraenkel.

Rough sets

From the elementary theorems and definition 5 of the element of the set it follows that any set is univocally determined by the generators and constructions included in it. In the case of an exact set it is also univocally determined by exactly all its elements. However, if two or more elements belong to some of generators and constructions in a certain set, which is not its element, then this set can not be determined univocally by exactly all its elements. We can do it only "approximately" with exactitude to one chosen representatives of these generators or constructions. Because of this we will call such set a *rough set*. Obviously, when the set is its own element it determines itself and any determination of it, and so approximate determination has no sense. Keeping this in mind, let us accept the following definition of a rough set:

Definition 12 (*rough set*) *A set, which is not its own element and is not exact, will be called here a rough set.*

Now we give the important theorems and facts which characterize the rough sets.

Any object is a rough set, if it is not its own element and is a construction.

Any object is a rough set, if it is not its own element and is not such that at least two elements belonging to it and first or second element determines it.

Any object is a rough set, if it is not its own element and at least two different objects such that first or second belonging to it determine it.

Any object is a rough set iff it is not its element and there exists its subset which is a rough set.

Any object is a rough set, if it is not its own element and there exists an object which has an element belonging to it and which determines it.

Any set is a rough set, if it determines different from it and not being its own element object, which has different from this set element.

Any object not being its own element and which has not an element not being its own element is a rough set.

Any different from the empty set object determining an object, the subset of which it is, and not being its own element is a rough set.

Any rough set determining some object is different from this object.

Any object being the family of all the subsets of some set and not being its own element and such that it has an element not being a set is a rough set.

Basic objects

In the following part of this paper we will show certain generalization of Pawlak's method [1] of approximation of sets.

Definition 13 (*mereological object.*) *Any object is a mereological object iff this object is its own element.*

Any object which is determined by itself is a mereological object.

Axiom 14 *Any set is a mereological object, if only and only these objects belonging to it belong to its some subset which is a mereological object.*

Any set is an exact set or a rough set or a mereological object.

If every object determines some object, then the universum is a mereological object.

Definition 14 (*simple object.*) *Any object is a simple object if it is not a mereological object and if it is the only object which determines an object different from itself.*

Any exact object determines a simple object.

Any object is not a simple object, iff it is not a mereological object and if its every element belongs to some simple object which is different from it and included in it.

Definition 15 (*basic object.*) *Any object is a basic object iff it is a set and all its elements are elements of some mereological object or simple object included in it.*

Any exact object determines a basic object.
An exact set is a basic object.

Definition 16 (*lower approach object.*) *The object x is the lower approach of the object y iff x is the empty set or x is an object included in the basic object y.*

Definition 17 (*upper approach object.*) *The object x is the upper approach of the object y iff the object x is the lower approach of the object y and x is a basic object which includes some nonempty subset y such that it is not included in any object being lower approach of the object y, and x is a minimal (in the sense of inclusion of sets) basic object.*

Definition 18 (*extensionality approach.*) *If for two sets any object is the lower approach of the first set iff it is the lower approach of the second set and if it is the upper approach of the first set iff it is the upper approach of the second set, then these sets are identical.*

Any object is the lower approach of the basic object iff it is the upper approach of the basic object.

Any object is the lower approach of the exact set iff it is the upper approach of the exact set.

2.2 Metatheses.

In author's doctoral dissertation it is shown that

Theory GST is consistent

and that when we interpret the abstract sets as exact sets, which are the elements of an exact sets, the axioms of Zermelo-Fraenkel's set theory are the theorems of theory GST, i.e.

The Zerm'elo-Fraenkel's set theory has interpretation
in theory GST

It is possible to say that

WITHIN THE LIMITS OF GST THEORY
ALMOST WHOLE CONTEMPORARY MATHEMATICS
MAY BE INTRODUCED.

References

[1] Z. Pawlak, Rough Sets, Int. J. Inform. Comp. Sci., 11, 1982, p. 672-683.

[2] Z. Pawlak, Rough Sets, Theoretical Aspects of Reasoning about Data, Kluwer, Dordrecht 1992.

[3] E. Bryniarski, Formalna koncepcja zbiorów przybliżonych (Formal Conception of Rough Sets), the doctoral dissertation prepared under the supervision of Prof. Urszula Wybraniec Skardowska at University of Wrocław, June 1993.

[4] W. D. Blizard, Multiset Theory, Notre Dame Journal of Formal Logic, vol. 30, Number 1, winter 1989, p. 36-66.

Rough Sets: A Special Case of Interval Structures

S.K.M. Wong and Xiaopin Nie

University or College

Department of Computer Science, University of Regina

Regina, Saskatchewan, Canada S4S 0A2

Abstract

The relationship between two different frameworks for representing uncertain information, rough sets and *interval structures*, is discussed in this paper. It is shown that the notion of rough sets is a special case of interval structures which provide a more general framework for modeling uncertainty.

1 Introduction

In decision making, we often find ourselves in a state of uncertainty. This might stem from the incompleteness or unreliability of the information at our disposal. To make decisions under such circumstances, we must use an appropriate structure to represent uncertain information [1, 2].

Pawlak [3] introduced the notion of rough sets, which characterizes an ordinary set by a pair of lower and upper approximations. The lower approximation is a subset containing the objects definitely belonging to the set, whereas the upper approximation is a superset containing the objects possibly belonging to the set. One can derive classification rules for a particular concept from these approximations.

Another non-numeric framework for representing uncertain information, *interval structures*, was introduced by Wong, Wang and Yao [5]. Interval structures are defined by a pair of mappings from one Boolean algebra to another. This pair of mappings must satisfy certain axioms.

In this paper, we study the relationship between rough-sets and interval structures. We will show that interval structures provide a more general framework for representing uncertain information than the rough-sets model.

This paper is organized as follows. For completeness, the basic definitions of rough sets are summarized in Section 2. The notion of interval structures is introduced in Section 3. In Section 4, we study the relationship between rough sets and interval structures.

2 Rough Sets

Let $\Theta = \{\theta_1, \theta_2, ..., \theta_n\}$ be a finite set (representing a universe of interest) and let R be an equivalence relation on Θ. The pair $Apr = (\Theta, R)$ is called an *approximation space*. The equivalence classes of R are referred to as *elementary sets* in *Apr*. The empty set $\emptyset$ is also an elementary set. Any finite union of elementary sets is called a *definable* set in the approximation space.

The equivalence relation R partitions the universe Θ into a number of disjoint subsets, $[\omega_1]_R, [\omega_2]_R, ..., [\omega_m]_R$, where $[\omega_i]_R$ denotes an equivalence class of R labeled by *description* ω_i. Let Ω be the set of descriptions, i.e., $\Omega = \{\omega_1, \omega_2, ..., \omega_m\}$. Let $A \subseteq \Theta$ represent a *concept*. The *lower approximation* of A, written $\underline{Apr}(A)$, is the greatest definable set contained in A, i.e.,

$$\underline{Apr}(A) = \bigcup_{[\omega_i]_R \subseteq A} [\omega_i]_R,$$

Whereas the *upper approximation* of A, written $\overline{Apr}(A)$, is the least definable set containing A, i.e.,

$$\overline{Apr}(A) = \bigcup_{[\omega_i]_R \cap A \neq \emptyset} [\omega_i]_R.$$

A concept A is definable in *Apr* if $\underline{Apr}(A) = \overline{Apr}(A)$; A is said to be roughly definable if $\underline{Apr}(A) \neq \emptyset$ and $\overline{Apr}(A) \neq \Theta$. We call the pair $(\underline{Apr}(A), \overline{Apr}(A))$ the *rough sets* of A in the approximation space $Apr = (\Theta, R)$. The lower and upper approximations $\underline{Apr}$ and $\overline{Apr}$ are mappings from 2^Θ to 2^Θ.

For any concept $A \subseteq \Theta$, we can construct two kinds of *classification rules* as follows:

$$\left(\underline{r}(A) = \bigcup_{[\omega_i]_R \subseteq A} \{\omega_i\} \right) \rightarrow A \quad \text{and} \quad \left(\overline{r}(A) = \bigcup_{[\omega_i]_R \cap A \neq \emptyset} \{\omega_i\} \right) \rightsquigarrow A.$$

Whenever the description of an object belongs to $\underline{r}(A)$, the object is *definitely* in A. We call $\underline{r}(A) \rightarrow A$ the *deterministic* rule for A in *Apr*. We refer to $\overline{r}(A) \rightsquigarrow A$ as the *non-deterministic* rule for A because whenever the description of an object belongs to $\overline{r}(A)$, the object is *possibly* in A. Note that $\underline{r}$ and $\overline{r}$ are mappings from 2^Θ to 2^Ω.

Consider a knowledge representation system, $S = (\Theta, \mathcal{A}, V, f)$, where Θ is a set of objects; $\mathcal{A}$ is a set of attributes; $V = \cup_{a \in \mathcal{A}} V_a$ is a set of attribute values, where V_a is the domain of attribute $a \in \mathcal{A}$; $f : \Theta \times \mathcal{A} \rightarrow V$ is an information function such that $f(\theta, a) \in V_a$ for every $\theta \in \Theta$ and $a \in \mathcal{A}$. It is clear that such a knowledge system S only provides partial information about the perceived reality. Thus, the available information may not be sufficient to characterize some *concepts* exactly. The following example demonstrates the usefulness of rough sets for modeling uncertainty.

Example 1: A knowledge representation system $S = (\Theta, \mathcal{A}, V, f)$ can be conveniently represented by a table. In Table 1, the knowledge we have is about a group of students, $\Theta = \{John, Mike, Dean, Allan, Blaine, Simon, Philip, Peter, Jason, Susan\}$. Each student is described by the set of attributes $\mathcal{A} = \{HEIGHT, EYES, HAIR\}$, with attribute values $V_{HEIGHT} = \{short, medium, tall\}$, $V_{EYES} = \{blue, brown\}$ and $V_{HAIR} = \{black, brown, red, blond\}$. From the information function defined by Table 1, we can construct an equivalence relation R on Θ:

$$\theta_i R \theta_j \iff f(\theta_i, a) = f(\theta_j, a), \forall a \in \mathcal{A}.$$

Θ	HEIGHT	EYES	HAIR
John	*medium*	*blue*	*black*
Mike	*tall*	*brown*	*brown*
Dean	*tall*	*brown*	*brown*
Allan	*medium*	*brown*	*red*
Blaine	*medium*	*brown*	*red*
Simon	*short*	*blue*	*brown*
Philip	*tall*	*brown*	*brown*
Peter	*short*	*blue*	*brown*
Jason	*short*	*blue*	*blond*
Susan	*medium*	*blue*	*black*

Table 1: A knowledge system S=(Θ, A, V, f).

We obtain the following equivalence classes of R:

$$
\begin{aligned}
[\omega_1]_R &= [HEIGHT = medium, EYES = blue, HAIR = black] \\
&= \{John, Susan\}, \\
[\omega_2]_R &= [HEIGHT = tall, EYES = brown, HAIR = brown] \\
&= \{Mike, Dean, Philip\}, \\
[\omega_3]_R &= [HEIGHT = medium, EYES = brown, HAIR = red] \\
&= \{Allan, Blaine\}, \\
[\omega_4]_R &= [HEIGHT = short, EYES = blue, HAIR = brown] \\
&= \{Simon, Peter\}, \\
[\omega_5]_R &= [HEIGHT = short, EYES = blue, HAIR = blond] \\
&= \{Jason\}.
\end{aligned}
$$

These equivalence classes are depicted in Figure 1.

Consider two concepts $A_1 = \{John, Susan, Mike, Dean, Philip\}$, and $A_2 = \{John, Mike, Allan, Blaine\}$. Clearly, concept A_1 is definable in the approximation space $Apr = (\Theta, R)$, since

$$\underline{Apr}(A_1) = \overline{Apr}(A_1) = [\omega_1]_R \cup [\omega_2]_R,$$

and the classification rule for A_1 is given by:

$$(\underline{r}(A_1) = \overline{r}(A_1) = \{\omega_1, \omega_2\}) \to A_1.$$

Concept A_2 is roughly definable as

$$\underline{Apr}(A_2) = [\omega_3]_R, \qquad \overline{Apr}(A_2) = [\omega_1]_R \cup [\omega_2]_R \cup [\omega_3]_R,$$

and the classification rules for A_2 are:

$$(\underline{r}(A_2) = \{\omega_3\}) \to A_2 \quad \text{and} \quad (\overline{r}(A_2) = \{\omega_1, \omega_2, \omega_3\}) \rightsquigarrow A_2. \quad \square$$

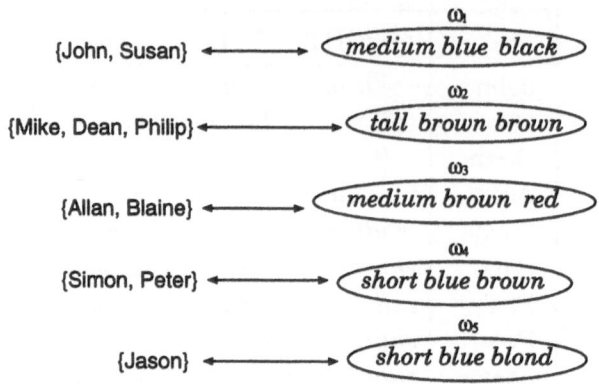

Figure 1: The equivalence classes of R induced by the knowledge system in Table 1. (Each equivalence class is uniquely labeled by a description.)

3 Interval Structures

Consider two arbitrary finite sets $\Theta = \{\theta_1, \theta_2, ..., \theta_n\}$ and $\Omega = \{\omega_1, \omega_2, ..., \omega_m\}$. The *interval structures* $(\underline{F}, \overline{F})$ are defined as a pair of mappings from 2^Θ to 2^Ω, $\underline{F} : 2^\Theta \to 2^\Omega$ and $\overline{F} : 2^\Theta \to 2^\Omega$, where the *lower* mapping $\underline{F}$ satisfies the following axioms: for any subsets $A, B \in 2^\Theta$,

(L1) $\underline{F}(\emptyset) = \emptyset$,
(L2) $\underline{F}(\Theta) = \Omega$,
(L3) $\underline{F}(A \cap B) = \underline{F}(A) \cap \underline{F}(B)$

and the *upper* mapping is defined by $\overline{F}(A) = \neg \underline{F}(\neg A) = \Omega - \underline{F}(\neg A) = \Omega - \underline{F}(\Theta - A)$. One can easily show that the upper mapping $\overline{F}$ satisfies:

(U1) $\overline{F}(\emptyset) = \emptyset$,
(U2) $\overline{F}(\Theta) = \Omega$,
(U3) $\overline{F}(A \cup B) = \overline{F}(A) \cup \overline{F}(B)$.

Conversely, given a upper mapping $\overline{F}$ satisfying properties (U1)-(U3), one can construct from the relationship $\underline{F}(A) = \neg\overline{F}(\neg A)$ the corresponding lower mapping $\underline{F}$ satisfying axioms (L1)-(L3).

It should be noted that a pair of interval structures $(\underline{F}, \overline{F})$ also satisfy the following properties:

(P1) $\underline{F}(A \cup B) \supseteq \underline{F}(A) \cup \underline{F}(B)$,
(P2) $\overline{F}(A \cap B) \subseteq \overline{F}(A) \cap \overline{F}(B)$,
(P3) $A \supseteq B \Longrightarrow (\underline{F}(A) \supseteq \underline{F}(B), \overline{F}(A) \supseteq \overline{F}(B))$.

We can equivalently define a pair of interval structures $(\underline{F}, \overline{F})$ by a *basic set assignment*, $j_F : 2^\Theta \to 2^\Omega$, which satisfies: for any $A, B \in 2^\Theta$,

(A1) $j_F(\emptyset) = \emptyset$,
(A2) $\bigcup_{A \in 2^\Theta} j_F(A) = \Omega$,

(A3) $A \neq B \Longrightarrow (j_F(A) \cap j_F(B) = \emptyset)$.

An element $A \in 2^\Theta$ with $j_F(A) \neq \emptyset$ is called a *focal set*. Based on a given j_F, the corresponding interval structures can be expressed as: for any $A \in 2^\Theta$,

$$\underline{F}(A) = \bigcup_{B \subseteq A} j_F(B), \quad \overline{F}(A) = \bigcup_{A \cap B \neq \emptyset} j_F(B).$$

Conversely, from a pair of interval structures $(\underline{F}, \overline{F})$, one can construct the corresponding basic set assignment j_F by: for any $A \in 2^\Theta$,

$$j_F(A) = \underline{F}(A) - (\bigcup_{B \subset A} \underline{F}(B)).$$

Theorem 1. [5] Let $\underline{F}$ and $\overline{F}$ be two mappings from 2^Θ to 2^Ω. The pair $(\underline{F}, \overline{F})$ are interval structures if and only if there exists a basic set assignment, $j_F : 2^\Theta \to 2^\Omega$, such that: for any $A, B \in 2^\Theta$,

$$\underline{F}(A) = \bigcup_{B \subseteq A} j_F(B), \quad \overline{F}(A) = \bigcup_{A \cap B \neq \emptyset} j_F(B).$$

Let Θ and Ω represent two universes of interest. Here we want to analyze the relationship between a pair of interval structures and a *relation* $C \subseteq \Theta \times \Omega$ [4]. An element $\theta \in \Theta$ is said to be *compatible* with an element $\omega \in \Omega$, written $_\theta C_\omega$, if θ is *semantically* related to ω. Without loss of generality, we may assume for any $\theta \in \Theta$, there exists an $\omega \in \Omega$ such that $_\theta C_\omega$, and vice versa. The physical interpretation of Θ and Ω, and the relationship between these two sets depend very much on the available knowledge and the domain of application.

First, we want to show that from any relation $C \subseteq \Theta \times \Omega$, one can construct a pair of interval structures characterized by C. A relation C between Θ and Ω can be equivalently defined by a mapping, $\gamma_c : \Omega \to 2^\Theta$: for any $\omega \in \Omega$,

$$_\theta C_\omega \iff \theta \in \gamma_c(\omega).$$

Such a mapping γ_c induces a function, $\Gamma : 2^\Omega \to 2^\Theta$: for any $X \in 2^\Omega$,

$$\Gamma(X) = \bigcup_{\omega \in X} \gamma_c(\omega).$$

Note that Γ is not necessarily an onto mapping, i.e., not every subset of Θ has a *pre-image* in 2^Ω. Therefore, it may not be possible to define an inverse of Γ for every subset of Θ. Nevertheless, one can define a lower inverse mapping $\underline{\Gamma^{-1}} : 2^\Theta \to 2^\Omega$ and an upper inverse mapping $\overline{\Gamma^{-1}} : 2^\Theta \to 2^\Omega$ as follows: for any $A \in 2^\Theta$,

$$\underline{\Gamma^{-1}}(A) = \{\omega \in \Omega | \gamma_c(\omega) \subseteq A\}, \quad \overline{\Gamma^{-1}}(A) = \{\omega \in \Omega | \gamma_c(\omega) \cap A \neq \emptyset\}.$$

For an arbitrary subset $A \in 2^\Theta$, the set $\underline{\Gamma^{-1}}(A)$ consists of all the elements in Ω compatible with only those elements in A, while the set $\overline{\Gamma^{-1}}(A)$ consists of all the elements in Ω compatible with at least one element in A. In general, the lower and upper pre-images are not necessarily the same. If we regard information being transferred from Ω to Θ, or if our objective is to characterize the subsets of Θ by the subsets of Ω, the lower pre-image $\underline{\Gamma^{-1}}(A)$ can be interpreted as the *pessimistic* estimation, and the upper pre-image $\overline{\Gamma^{-1}}(A)$ as the *optimistic* estimation of A. That is, the true pre-image of A lies in the interval $[\underline{\Gamma^{-1}}(A), \overline{\Gamma^{-1}}(A)]$. It can be easily verified that the pair of mappings $(\underline{\Gamma}^{-1}, \overline{\Gamma}^{-1})$ from 2^Θ to 2^Ω are indeed a pair of interval structures induced by the relation $\mathcal{C} \subseteq \Theta \times \Omega$.

Conversely, any interval structures $(\underline{F}, \overline{F})$ induce a relation $\mathcal{C} \subseteq \Theta \times \Omega$ as follows. By Theorem 1, one can construct a basic set assignment j_F from a given pair of interval structures $(\underline{F}, \overline{F})$. From this j_F, a relation $\mathcal{C}$ between Θ and Ω can be defined as: for any $A \in 2^\Theta$,

$$\theta \mathcal{C}_\omega \iff \theta \in A \text{ and } \omega \in j_F(A).$$

As mentioned earlier, any relation $\mathcal{C}$ can be equivalently represented by a mapping, $\gamma_c : \Omega \to 2^\Theta$, defined by:

$$\theta \mathcal{C}_\omega \iff \theta \in \gamma_c(\omega).$$

Thus, the original basic set assignment j_F can be expressed as: for any $A \in 2^\Theta$,

$$j_F(A) = \{\omega \in \Omega | \gamma_c(\omega) = A\}.$$

Let us summarize the observations by the following theorem.

Theorem 2. Let $\underline{F}$ and $\overline{F}$ be two mappings from 2^Θ to 2^Ω. The pair $(\underline{F}, \overline{F})$ are a pair of interval structures if and only if there exists a relation $\mathcal{C} \subseteq \Theta \times \Omega$ such that for any $A, B \in 2^\Theta$,

$$\underline{F}(A) = \bigcup_{B \subseteq A} j_F(B), \quad \overline{F}(A) = \bigcup_{A \cap B \neq \emptyset} j_F(B),$$

where $j_F(A) = \{\omega \in \Omega | \gamma_c(\omega) = A\}$.

4 Rough Sets: A Special Case of Interval Structures

In this section, we show that the notion of rough sets is a special case of the notion of interval structures.

In an approximation space $Apr = (\Theta, R)$, the equivalence relation R partitions the universe Θ into m disjoint subsets, $[\omega_1]_R, [\omega_2]_R, ..., [\omega_m]_R$, where $[\omega_i]_R$ is an equivalence class of R labeled by *description* ω_i. Let $\Omega = \{\omega_1, \omega_2, ..., \omega_m\}$ denote the set of descriptions. The relationship between Θ and Ω can be explicitly stated in terms of a binary relation $\mathcal{C} \subseteq \Theta \times \Omega$ defined by: for any $\theta_i \in \Theta$ and $\omega_j \in \Omega$,

$$\theta_i \mathcal{C}_{\omega_j} \iff \theta_i \in [\omega_j]_R.$$

By definition, the above relation is a *function*, namely, $\mathcal{C} : \Theta \to \Omega$ (graphically illustrated in Figure 1(a)). In general, however, $\mathcal{C}$ is a *binary relation* (graphically illustrated in Figure 1(b)). Moreover, the equivalence relation R is the composite CC^{-1}, i.e., $R = CC^{-1}$, where C is now a function and C^{-1} is the inverse of C. It should be noted that for an arbitrary relation C, the composite CC^{-1} is not necessarily an equivalence relation. In general, CC^{-1} is a compatibility relation (i.e., a reflexive and symmetric relation).

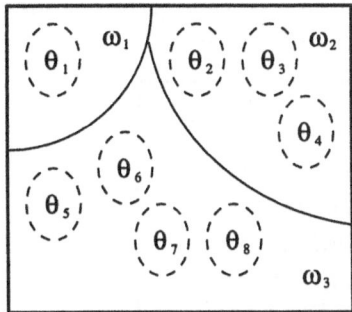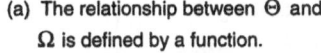 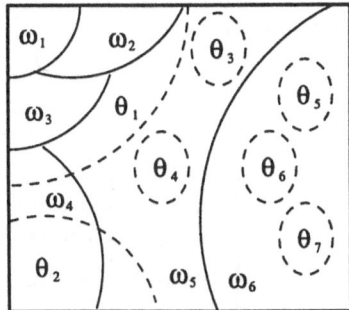

(a) The relationship between Θ and Ω is defined by a function.

(b) The relationship between Θ and Ω is defined by a relation

Figure 1: Graphical Representations of the Relationship Between Θ and Ω.

By Theorem 2, we can construct a pair of interval structures $(\underline{F'}, \overline{F'})$, i.e., a pair of mappings, $\underline{F'} : 2^\Theta \to 2^\Theta$ and $\overline{F'} : 2^\Theta \to 2^\Theta$, from the equivalence relation R of a given approximation space $Apr = (\Theta, R)$: for any $A \in 2^\Theta$,

$$\underline{F'}(A) = \bigcup_{B \subseteq A} j_{F'}(B), \quad \overline{F'}(A) = \bigcup_{B \cap A \neq \emptyset} j_{F'}(B).$$

The basic set assignment of the interval structures $(\underline{F'}, \overline{F'})$, $j_{F'} : 2^\Theta \to 2^\Theta$, is defined by:

$$j_{F'}(B) = j_{F'}([\omega_i]_R) = \{\theta_j \in [\omega_i]_R | \gamma_R(\omega_i) = [\omega_i]_R\} = [\omega_i]_R,$$

i.e., the equivalence classes $[\omega_i]_R$ of R are in fact the focal sets of $j_{F'}$. Thus, we immediately obtain: for any $A \in 2^\Theta$,

$$\underline{F'}(A) = \bigcup_{[\omega_i]_R \subseteq A} [\omega_i]_R = \underline{Apr}(A), \quad \overline{F'}(A) = \bigcup_{[\omega_i]_R \cap A \neq \emptyset} [\omega_i]_R = \overline{Apr}(A).$$

Likewise, we obtain from Theorem 2 the following interval structures $(\underline{r'}, \overline{r'})$ for the classification rules: for any $A \in 2^\Theta$,

$$\left(\underline{r'}(A) = \bigcup_{B \subseteq A} j_{r'}(B) \right) \to A, \quad \left(\overline{r'}(A) = \bigcup_{B \cap A \neq \emptyset} j_{r'}(B) \right) \rightsquigarrow A,$$

where the basic set assignment, $j_{r'} : 2^\Theta \to 2^\Omega$, is defined by:

$$j_{r'}(B) = j_{r'}([\omega_i]_R) = \{\omega_i \in \Omega | \gamma_R(\omega_i) = [\omega_i]_R\}.$$

That is, the equivalence classes $[\omega_i]_R$ of R are the focal sets of $j_{r'}$. Hence,

$$\left(\underline{r}'(A) = \bigcup_{[\omega_i]_R \subseteq A} \{\omega_i\}\right) \to A, \quad \left(\overline{r}'(A) = \bigcup_{[\omega_i]_R \cap A \neq \emptyset} \{\omega_i\}\right) \rightsquigarrow A.$$

The above results clearly demonstrate that the *constructs* of rough sets introduced in Section 2 are special cases of interval structures.

Θ	COLOR	SIZE	FLYING
Duck	*brown*	*big*	*yes*
Duck	*brown*	*medium*	*no*
Duck	*black*	*medium*	*yes*
Seagull	*white*	*medium*	*yes*
Seagull	*grey*	*medium*	*yes*
Pigeon	*white*	*medium*	*yes*
Sparrow	*brown*	*small*	*yes*
Crow	*black*	*medium*	*yes*

Table 2: A generalized knowledge system.

Example 2: Let us consider two different kinds of knowledge representation systems. In Table 1, a group of students in Θ may be described by the same set of attribute values (the same description $\omega_i \in \Omega$), but no student can be described by more than one ω_i. That is, the relationship between Θ and Ω is defined by a function $\mathcal{C} : \Theta \to \Omega$. This is exactly the basic assumption made in the knowledge system $S = (\Theta, \mathcal{A}, V, f)$ used in the rough-sets approach. This restriction seems to be reasonable in many applications.

However, for some universe of interest Θ, it may no longer be valid to assume a functional relationship between Θ and Ω in a generalized knowledge system (see Table 2). The relationship between Θ and Ω is in fact a multivalued mapping. In this example, *Duck* is characterized by three different descriptions: $\{brown, big, yes\}$, $\{brown, medium, no\}$ and $\{black, medium, yes\}$; and *Seagull* by two descriptions: $\{white, medium, yes\}$ and $\{grey, medium, yes\}$. Clearly, the relationship between Θ and Ω in this case is specified by a *relation* rather than by a *function*. This situation can not be conveniently modeled by the standard rough-sets approach, but it can be easily described by the following interval structures $(\underline{F}, \overline{F})$.

In the knowledge system represented by Table 2, we have $\Theta = \{\theta_1, \theta_2, \theta_3, \theta_4, \theta_5\} = \{Duck, Seagull, Pigeon, Sparrow, Crow\}$ and $\Omega = \{\omega_1, \omega_2, \omega_3, \omega_4, \omega_5, \omega_6\}$, where

$$\omega_1 = \{COLOR = brown, SIZE = big, FLYING = yes\},$$
$$\omega_2 = \{COLOR = brown, SIZE = medium, FLYING = no\},$$
$$\omega_3 = \{COLOR = black, SIZE = medium, FLYING = yes\},$$
$$\omega_4 = \{COLOR = white, SIZE = medium, FLYING = yes\},$$
$$\omega_5 = \{COLOR = grey, SIZE = medium, FLYING = yes\},$$

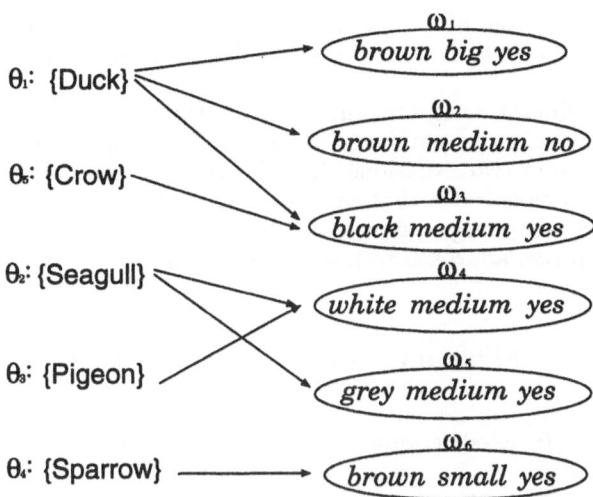

Figure 2: The compatibility relation between Θ and Ω induced
by the generalized knowledge system in Table 2.

$$\omega_6 = \{COLOR = brown, SIZE = small, FLYING = yes\}.$$

From Table 2, the following relation $\mathcal{C}$ between Θ and Ω is inferred (as shown in Figure 2):

$$\theta_1 \mathcal{C} \omega_1, \quad \theta_1 \mathcal{C} \omega_2, \quad \theta_1 \mathcal{C} \omega_3, \quad \theta_2 \mathcal{C} \omega_4, \quad \theta_2 \mathcal{C} \omega_5, \quad \theta_3 \mathcal{C} \omega_4, \quad \theta_4 \mathcal{C} \omega_6, \quad \theta_5 \mathcal{C} \omega_3,$$

which is equivalent to the mapping, $\gamma_c : \Omega \to 2^{\Theta}$:

$$\begin{aligned} \gamma_c(\omega_1) &= \{\theta_1\}, & \gamma_c(\omega_2) &= \{\theta_1\}, & \gamma_c(\omega_3) &= \{\theta_1, \theta_5\}, \\ \gamma_c(\omega_4) &= \{\theta_2, \theta_3\}, & \gamma_c(\omega_5) &= \{\theta_2\}, & \gamma_c(\omega_6) &= \{\theta_4\}. \end{aligned}$$

Based on Theorem 2, the basic set assignment $j_F : 2^{\Theta} \to 2^{\Omega}$ is defined by:

$$\begin{aligned} j_F(\{\theta_1\}) &= \{\omega_1, \omega_2\}, & j_F(\{\theta_2\}) &= \{\omega_5\}, & j_F(\{\theta_4\}) &= \{\omega_6\}, \\ j_F(\{\theta_1, \theta_5\}) &= \{\omega_3\}, & j_F(\{\theta_2, \theta_3\}) &= \{\omega_4\}. \end{aligned}$$

Suppose we are interested in a concept A represented by:

$$A = \{\theta_2, \theta_4\} = \{Seagull, Sparrow\}.$$

From Theorem 2, we obtain the following classification rules for A:

$$\left(\underline{F}(A) = \bigcup_{B \subseteq A} j_F(B) = \{\omega_5, \omega_6\} \right) \to A,$$

$$\left(\overline{F}(A) = \bigcup_{B \cap A \neq \emptyset} j_F(B) = \{\omega_4, \omega_5, \omega_6\} \right) \rightsquigarrow A.$$

Note that only one of *Seagull*'s descriptions ω_5 is contained in the lower mapping of A. This result is different from that obtained from the rough-sets model. □

To further illustrate the difference between the notions of rough sets and interval structures, consider a universe Θ having $\Theta = \{slippery,\ good\ for\ skiing\}$, and Ω consisting of two situations: $\Omega = \{heavy\ rain,\ heavy\ snow\}$. This example clearly demonstrates that in general the relationship between Θ and Ω is a multivalued mapping as shown in Figure 3. Obviously, we can not use the standard rough-sets approach to model such a case.

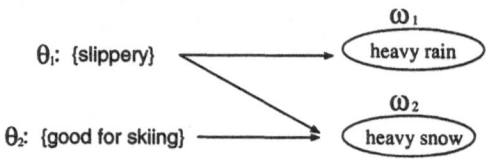

Figure 3. Another example of a multivalued mapping between Θ and Ω.

5 Conclusion

We have shown in this paper that interval structures are the underlying framework of many uncertainty measures. In particular, the rough-sets model is a special case of interval structures. Interval structures therefore provide a more general framework for modeling uncertainty.

References

[1] A. Bundy, Correctness criteria of some algorithms for uncertain reasoning using incidence calculus, **Journal of Automated Reasoning,** vol.2, 109-126, 1986.

[2] F. Correa de Silva and A. Bundy, On some equivalence relations between incidence calculus and Dempster-Shafer theory of evidence, **Proceedings of 6th International Workshop on Uncertainty in Artificial Intelligence,** 109-126, Cambridge, MA, 1990.

[3] Z. Pawlak, Rough classification, **International Journal of Man-Machine Studies.** vol.11, 341-356, 1984.

[4] G. Shafer, Belief functions and possibility measures, **Analysis of Fuzzy Information,** vol.1, 51-84, 1986.

[5] S.K.M. Wong, L.S. Wang and Y.Y. Yao, Interval structures: a framework for representing uncertain information, **Proceedings of the Eighth Conference on Uncertainty in Artificial Intelligence,** 336-343, Ed. by D. Dubois, M. P. Wellman, B. D. Ambrosio and P. Smets, Morgan Kaufmann, 1992.

A Pure Logic-algebraic Analysis of Rough Top and Rough Bottom Equalities

Piero Pagliani

Research Group on Learning and Communication Models

Education Centre, ITALSIEL-FINSIEL

La Rustica, Via F. Depero 24, 00155 Roma, Italy

Abstract

The paper presents an analysis of rough sets, rough top equality and rough bottom equality by means of pure logic-algebraic operations. Namely given an Approximation Space A, we can represent the induced rough sets structure as a particular Nelson algebra $N(A)$ with a weak negation and a strong negation; in its turn $N(A)$ can be viewed as a particular Heyting algebra equipped by its own pseudocomplementation. The relationships among these operations of negation reveal to fulfil some very peculiar properties that are able to provide the logic framework within which we can systematically deduce all the properties of rough (top, bottom) equalities.

1 Introduction

Given an Approximation Space in the sense of Pawlak and the related notion of rough sets (see [14]), some natural problems arise such as how to characterize rough top or rough bottom equalities and how to recognize rough top or rough bottom equalities among the equivalence relations on the powerset $\wp(U)$ of the universe U of the Approximation Space. The resolution of these problems have been applied in several fields such as black-boxes analysis and dependences analysis (see [7], [8]). In [5] a solution to the above characterization and recognition problems has been provided. Nevertheless it is possible to algebraically support these solutions applying the connection between rough sets theory and the theory of Nelson algebras exhibited in [11]. In this framework we will show that the algebraic operations allow to characterize rough top and rough bottom equalities in pure logic-algebraic terms. More precisely given an Approximation Space A, we can interpret the induced rough sets structure as a particular Nelson algebra $N(A)$; thereafter we are able to exploit very peculiar relationships among the "internal" weak and strong negations of A (that are two negations acting on $N(A)$ qua a Nelson algebra) and the "external" pseudocomplementation (that is a negation acting on $N(A)$ qua a Heyting algebra) in order to characterize the rough top equality and the rough bottom equality. Since the used logic-algebraic operations are easily implementable (see [9]), it turns out that the approach here presented is also of practical interest.

2 Approximation Spaces, Rough Sets and logic-algebraic structures

Let us consider an abstract approach to Approximation Spaces (see [8]):

1. Let U be a finite set.
   Consider the Boolean algebra $\mathbf{B}(U) = (\wp(U), \cup, \cap, \neg, \emptyset, U)$ where $\neg$ is the set-theoretical complement.
   Any subalgebra $\mathbf{A} = (A, \cup, \cap, \neg, \emptyset, U)$ with $A \subseteq \wp(U)$ is called *Approximation Space*.

2. The elements of the set $Atom(\mathbf{A})$ of the atoms of $\mathbf{A}$ are called *elementary sets*. Since they are disjoint and their union is U, $Atom(\mathbf{A})$ is the family of the equivalence classes of an equivalence relation R.

3. For any $X \in \wp(U)$, the set $(uR)(X) = \bigcup\{A' \in Atom(\mathbf{A}): A' \cap X \neq \emptyset\}$ is called *upper approximation* of X (w.r.t. the relation R).

4. For any $X \in \wp(U)$, the set $(lR)(X) = \bigcup\{A' \in Atom(\mathbf{A}): A' \subseteq X\}$ is called *lower approximation* of X (w.r.t. the relation R).

5. Two sets $X, Y \in \wp(U)$ are called *rough top equal* (w.r.t. R), $X \approx Y$, iff $(uR)(X) = (uR)(Y)$.

6. Two sets $X, Y \in \wp(U)$ are called *rough bottom equal* (w.r.t. R), $X \simeq Y$, iff $(lR)(X) = (lR)(Y)$.

7. Two sets $X, Y \in \wp(U)$ are called *rough equal* (w.r.t. R), $X \approx pY$, iff $X \simeq Y$ and $X \approx Y$.

8. A set $X \in \wp(U)$ is called *definable* (in the Approximation Space $\mathbf{A}$) iff $X = (lR)(X) = (uR)(X)$.

9. Let us consider $\mathbf{A}$ as the frame of open subset of a topological space $< U, \mathbf{A} >$. By $\mathcal{I}$ and $\mathcal{C}$ we shall denote the interior and, respectively, closure operators of Kuratowski induced by $\mathbf{A}$. Moreover if $X \in \wp(U)$ by $\mathcal{E}(X)$ we shall denote the open set $\neg\mathcal{C}(X)$. Since $\mathbf{A}$ is a Boolean algebra, any element of $\mathbf{A}$ is clopen (closed and open).

10. If $x \in A$, by $\uparrow x$ we intend the set $\{x' \in A : x' \geq x\}$. $\uparrow x$ is a filter on $\mathbf{A}$.

If $X \in \wp(U)$, then by $card(X)$ we shall intend the cardinality of X.

Lemma 2.1 *For any Approximation Space $\mathbf{A}$ on an universe U, $\forall X \in \wp(U)$,*
1. $\mathcal{C}(X) = \bigcap\{A' \subseteq A : A' \supseteq X\}$;
2. $\mathcal{I}(X) = \bigcup\{A' \subseteq A : A' \subseteq X\}$;
3. $\mathcal{C}(X) = (uR)(\bar{X})$;
4. $\mathcal{I}(X) = (lR)(X)$;
5. *if X is definable then $\mathcal{I}(X) \cup \mathcal{E}(X) = U$.*

Proof. Immediate.

11. Definition: THE "ROUGH SET" APPLICATION.

Let us define the following application (see [11]:

$r : \wp(U) \longmapsto A \times A : r(X) = < \mathcal{I}(X), \mathcal{E}(X) >$.

For any $X \in \wp(U)$, the ordered pair $r(X)$ is said (disjunctive representation of) a *Rough Set*. The definition is legitimated by the following Lemma:

Lemma 2.2 *For any* $X, Y \in \wp(U), X \approx pY$ *iff* $r(X) = r(Y)$.

By **Imr** we shall intend the image of $\wp(U)$ by r.

12. Let it be $S = \bigcup \{X \in Atom(\mathbf{A}) : card(X) = 1\}$. By definition of $\mathbf{A}$, $S \in A$. Let us then consider the filter $\uparrow S$ generated by S in $\mathbf{A}$. For $X, Y \in A$, we set $X \Theta Y$ iff $\exists Z \in \uparrow S$ s.t. $X \cap Z = Z \cap Y$. Then Θ is a (Boolean) congruence on $\mathbf{A}$.

Let us now define the map:

13. $N_\Theta : A \longmapsto A \times A : N_\Theta(A) = \{< X_1, X_2 > : X_1 \cap X_2 = \emptyset \text{ and } X_1 \cup X_2 \Theta U\}$

Lemma 2.3 *1. The structure* $\mathbf{N}_\Theta(\mathbf{A}) = (N_\Theta(A), \wedge, \vee, \rightarrow, \neg, \sim, 0, 1)$ *with the operations defined as follows*

(a) $1 = < U, \emptyset >; 0 = < \emptyset, U >;$
(a) $< X_1, X_2 > \wedge < Y_1, Y_2 > = < X_1 \cap Y_1, X_2 \cup Y_2 >;$
(b) $< X_1, X_2 > \vee < Y_1, Y_2 > = < X_1 \cup Y_1, X_2 \cap Y_2 >;$
(c) $< X_1, X_2 > \rightarrow < Y_1, Y_2 > = < \neg X_1 \cup Y_1, X_1 \cap Y_2 >;$
(d) $\sim < X_1, X_2 > = < X_2, X_1 >;$
(e) $\neg < X_1, X_2 > = < \neg X_1, X_1 > = < X_1, X_2 > \rightarrow < \emptyset, U >;$
(where $\cup, \cap, \neg,$ *applied inside the ordered pairs are the operations of* $\mathbf{A}$*),*
is a Nelson algebra.

2. For any Approximation Space $\mathbf{A}$, $\mathbf{N}_\Theta(\mathbf{A}) = \mathbf{Imr}$.

Proof: see [17] for 3.3.1 and [11] for 2.3.2

(Nelson algebras are named *Quasi-Pseudo Boolean algebras* in [16]).

We define also the following additional operation for any $X, Y \in N_\Theta(A)$:

(f) $X \Rightarrow Y = (X \rightarrow Y)(\sim Y \rightarrow \sim X)$.

Moreover, since $\mathbf{A}$ is a Boolean algebra, $\mathbf{N}_\Theta(\mathbf{A})$ is a *semi-simple* Nelson algebra and the following equation is uniformly true:

14. $a \vee \neg a = 1$

In what follows, by $a, b, ..., 1, 0$ we shall denote the ordered pairs $< A_1, A_2 >$, $< B_1, B_2 >, ..., < U, \emptyset >$ and, respectively, $< \emptyset, U >$ belonging to $N_\Theta(A)$, with A_1, A_2, B_1, B_2, U and $\emptyset$ belonging to $A \subseteq \wp(U)$. $\mathbf{N}_\Theta(\mathbf{A})$ is the application of the operator $\mathbf{N}_\Theta$ of Sendlewski to the Boolean algebra $\mathbf{A}$ (see [17] and [11]).

Lemma 2.4 *1. The relation* $\preceq$ *defined by* $a \preceq b$ *iff* $a \rightarrow b = 1$ *is a preorder on* $N_\Theta(A)$.

2. The relation $\leq$ *defined by* $a \leq b$ *iff* $a \Rightarrow b = 1$ *is a partial order on* $N_\Theta(A)$.

3. $a \leq b$ *iff* $a \cap b = a$ *iff* $a \cup b = b$ *iff* $A_1 \subseteq B_1$ *and* $B_2 \subseteq A_2$.

Let us note now that for $\beth \in \{\rightarrow, \Rightarrow\}$ the following adjunction property does not hold for arbitrary $a, b \in N_\Theta(A)$: $a \cap c \leq b$ iff $c \leq a \beth b$. That is, $\rightarrow$ and $\Rightarrow$ are not defined by the lattice order $\leq$.

Let us then define an operation $\supset$ fulfilling the above adjunction property for any a, b and c belonging to $N_\Theta(A)$, that is:

15. $a \leq b$ iff $c \leq a \supset b$

Lemma 2.5 *(OF EXISTENCE OF THE ELEMENT $a \supset b$) : $\forall a$, $b \in N_\Theta(A)$, the element $a \supset b$ is always defined.*

Proof: Since $(N_\Theta(A), \cap, \cup, 0, 1)$ is a distributive finite lattice, it is a Heyting algebra. It follows that the relative pseudocomplementation $\supset$ is always defined.

Since we established that the element $a \supset b$ is always defined, we can try to characterize it.

Lemma 2.6 (OF CHARACTERIZATION OF THE ELEMENT $a \supset b$) :
$\forall a, b \in N_\Theta(A) : a \supset b = (\neg a \cap \neg \sim b) \cup \sim \neg \sim a \cup b$.

Proof: In order to fulfil the adjunction property, $a \supset b$ must be an element $< C_1, C_2 >$ s.t.
(a) C_2 is the $\subseteq$ -least element, X, of **A** s.t. $X \cup A_2 \supseteq B_2$, while
(b) C_1 must be the $\subseteq$-greatest element Y of **A** s.t. $Y \cap A_1 \supseteq B_1$, and $X \cap Y = \emptyset$.
We claim that $C_2 = B_2 \cap \neg A_2$. In fact, in view of the first requirement, $B_2 \cap \neg A_2$
is the least element X s.t. $X \cup A_2 \supseteq B_2$. Now, in view of the disjunction
condition and the requirement of maximization of C_1 , $B_2 \cap \neg A_2$ is the best
solution for C_2. Now, the greatest element Y of **A** s.t. $Y \cap A_1 \subseteq B_1$ is
$\neg A_1 \cup B_1$ but in order to get the disjointness condition we have to subtract C_2
from it obtaining $(\neg A_1 \cup B_1) \cap \neg (B_2 \cap \neg A_2)$. Let us then develop this Boolean
polynomial: $(\neg A_1 \cup B_1) \cap \neg (B_2 \cap \neg A_2) = (\neg A_1 \cup B_1) \cap \neg (\neg B_2 \cup A_2) =$
$= (\neg A_1 \cap (\neg B_2 \cup A_2)) \cup (B_1 \cap (\neg B_2 \cup A_2)) =$
$= (\neg A_1 \cap \neg B_2) \cup (\neg A_1 \cap A_2) \cup (B_1 \cap \neg B_2) \cup (B_1 \cap A_2) =$
$= (\neg A_1 \cap \neg B_2) \cup A_2 \cup B_1 \cup (B_1 \cap A_2)$ but since $(A_2 \cup B_1) \supseteq (B_1 \cap A_2)$ the last
expression reduces to $(\neg A_1 \cap \neg B_2) \cup A_2 \cup B_1$.
Hence we have:
(*) $C_1 = (\neg A_1 \cap \neg B_2) \cup (A_2 \cup B_1)$;
(**) $C_2 = B_2 \cap \neg A_2$.
It follows that $< C_1, C_2 >$ is the *sup* in $N_\Theta(\mathbf{A})$ of two elements d and e s.t.
$D_1 \cup E_1 = (\neg A_1 \cap \neg B_2) \cup (A_2 \cup B_1)$ and $D_2 \cap E_2 = B_2 \cap \neg A_2$.
Again, d is the *inf* in $N_\Theta(\mathbf{A})$ of two elements d' and d'' s.t. $D'_1 \cap D''_1 =$
$\neg A_1 \cap \neg B_2$ and $(D'_2 \cup D''_2) \cap E_2 = D_2 \cap E_2 = B_2 \cap \neg A_2$, while e is the *sup* of
two elements e' and e'' s.t. $E'_1 \cup E''_1 = A_2 \cup B_1$ and $(E'_2 \cap E''_2) \cap (D'_2 \cup D''_2) =$
$(E'_2 \cap E''_2) \cap D_2 =$
$= D_2 \cap E_2 = B_2 \cap \neg A_2$.
We are to find out a solution with minimal structural complexity. We claim
that $d' = \neg < A_1, A_2 >, d'' = \neg \sim < B_1, B_2 >$, $e' = \sim \neg \sim < A_1, A_2 >$ and
$e'' = < B_1, B_2 >$.
In fact on the one hand we have: $\neg < A_1, A_2 > \wedge \neg \sim < B_1, B_2 > =$
$= \neg < \neg A_1, A_1 > \wedge \neg \sim < \neg B_2, B_2 > = < \neg A_1 \cap \neg B_2, A_1 \cup B_2 >$.
On the other hand: $\sim \neg \sim < A_1, A_2 > \vee < B_1, B_2 > =$
$= < A_2, \neg A_2 > \vee < B_1, B_2 > = < A_2 \cup B_1, B_2 \cap \neg A_2 >$.
But $< \neg A_1 \cap \neg B_2, A_1 \cup B_2 > \vee < A_2 \cup B_1, B_2 \cap \neg A_2 > =$
(***) $< (\neg A_1 \cap \neg B_2) \cup (A_2 \cup B_1), (A_1 \cup B_2) \cap (B_2 \cap \neg A_2) >$.
Since $(A_1 \cup B_2) \geq B_2 \leq (B_2 \cap \neg A_2), (A_1 \cup B_2) \cap (B_2 \cap \neg A_2) = (B_2 \cap \neg A_2)$.
Hence (***) becomes $< (\neg A_1 \cap \neg B_2) \cup (A_2 \cup B_1), B_2 \cap \neg A_2 >$ as required by
(*) and (**).

Lemma 2.7 (Corollary) : $\forall a \in N_\Theta(\mathbf{A}), a \supset 0 = \sim \neg \sim a$.

The operator $\sim \neg \sim$ was introduced in [2] and [15], and analyzed within the framework of Nelson algebras in [11]. We shall denote it by the symbol $\div$. From the above discussion it follows that $\supset$ is the relative-pseudocomplementation and $\div$ the pseudocomplementation in the lattice $N_\Theta(A)$ qua a Heyting algebra.

It is worth noticing that the operation $\supset$ is the residuation operation introduced by Moisil in Łukasiewicz algebras, by means of the endomorphisms ϕ_1, ϕ_2, ϕ_1^- and ϕ_2^- (see [3]): it suffices to make the following translation: $\phi_1 = \neg\neg$, $\phi_2 = \div\div$; $\phi_1^- = \sim \neg\neg$ and $\phi_2^- = \sim \div\div$.

Now we shall study the role of the operator $\div$ in characterizing rough top equalities.

3 Double negations and Definability in Information Systems

In the following, given r and an element $a \in N_\Theta(A)$, if $a = r(X)$ for an uniquely determined $X \in \wp(U)$, then by $r^{-1}(a)$ we shall denote X itself.

1. We shall say that an element $a \in N_\Theta(A)$ is *exact* iff $A_1 \cup A_2 = U$.

Lemma 3.1 : $\forall a \in N_\Theta(A)$,
1. a is exact iff $a \vee \sim a = 1$.
2. If a is exact then $r^{-1}(a)$ is a definable subset of U.
3. $\div a$ is exact.
4. $\neg a$ is exact.
5. a is exact iff $\sim a$ is exact.

Proof: trivially from the definitions 2.8 and 3.1 and the following equations: $\div a = \sim \neg \sim < A_1, A_2 > = < A_2, \neg A_2 >; \neg < A_1, A_2 > = < \neg A_1, A_1 >$ and since $A_i \vee \neg A_i = U$ for $1 \le i \le 2$ (from 2.14).

Let us now state a few definitions and a General Lemma that will provide the general algebraic framework of the succeeding results:

Definition

2. By $[a]_{\widetilde{\approx}}$ we shall denote the equivalence class of a modulo the relation: $a \approx b$ iff $\div\div a = \div\div b$.
3. By $[a]_{\simeq}$ we shall denote the equivalence class of a modulo the relation: $a \simeq b$ iff $\neg\neg a = \neg\neg b$.
4. By $[a]_{\sim\widetilde{\approx}}$ we shall denote the equivalence class of a modulo the relation: $a \sim\approx b$ iff $\sim a \approx \sim b$.
5. By $[a]_{\sim\simeq}$ we shall denote the equivalence class of a modulo the relation: $a \sim\simeq b$ iff $\sim a \simeq \sim b$.

In the following Lemma, we put in evidence, using brackets, the operators constructed by means of the various sorts of complementation.

Lemma 3.2 GENERAL LEMMA: $\forall a \in N_\Theta(A)$,
0. $a = b$ iff $\sim a = \sim b$.
1. $\sim (\div)a = (\neg) \sim a = \div\div a$.
2. $\sim (\neg)a = (\div) \sim a = \neg\neg a$.
3. $\sim (\div\div)a = (\neg\neg) \sim a = \div a$.
4. $\sim (\neg\neg)a = (\div\div) \sim a = \neg a$.
5. $a \simeq b$ iff $\neg a = \neg b$.

6. $a \approx b$ *iff* $\div a = \div b$.
7. $a \approx b$ *iff* $a \sim\simeq b$.
8. $a \simeq b$ *iff* $a \sim\approx b$.
9. $\div\div a$ *is the greatest element of* $\mathbf{N_\Theta(A)}$ *in the class* $[a]_{\approx}$.
10. $\neg\neg a$ *is the least element of* $\mathbf{N_\Theta(A)}$ *in the class* $[a]_{\simeq}$.
11. $a \simeq b$ *iff* $a \to b = b \to a = 1$.
12. $\approx b$ *iff* $\sim a \to\sim b =\sim b \to\sim a = 1$.

Proof: (0) trivially from 2.8.2; (1)-(4) by easy calculation.
(5) $a \simeq b$ iff $\neg\neg a = \neg\neg b$ (by 3.3) iff $\sim \neg\neg a =\sim \neg\neg b$ (by 0) iff $\neg a = \neg b$ (from 4). (6) similar.
(7) $a \approx b$ iff $\div a = \div b$ (from 6) iff $\sim \div a =\sim \div b$ (from 0) iff $\neg \sim a = \neg \sim b$ (by 1) iff $\sim a \simeq\sim b$ (from 5) iff $a \sim\simeq b$ (by 4). (8) similar.
(9) trivial from the shape of $\div\div a$ and the definition of the ordering $\leq$.
(10) similar. (11)$a \simeq b$ iff $\neg\neg a = \neg\neg b$ iff $< A_1, \neg A_1 >=< B_1, \neg \bar{B}_1 >$ iff $A_1 = A_1$(iff $\neg A_1 = \neg B_1$).

Lemma 3.3 $\forall X \subseteq U$ *s.t.* $r(X) = a \in \mathbf{N_\Theta(A)}$,
1. $r^{-1}(\neg a)$ *is the greatest definable set* Y *s.t.* $\mathcal{I}(X) \cap Y = \emptyset$.
2. $r^{-1}(\neg\neg a)$ *is the greatest definable set* Y *s.t.* $Y \subseteq X$.
3. $r^{-1}(\div a)$ *is the greatest definable set* Y *s.t.* $\mathcal{C}(X) \cap Y = \emptyset$.
4. $r^{-1}(\div\div a)$ *is the least definable set* Y *s.t.* $X \subseteq Y$.

Proof: (1) by 3.1.4, $\neg a$ is an exact element of $\mathbf{N_\Theta(A)}$.
Moreover $\neg a =< -\mathcal{I}(X), \mathcal{I}(X) >$. Hence if $Y = r^{-1}(\neg a)$ then $\mathcal{I}(Y) = -\mathcal{I}(X)$. But from 3.1.2 Y is definable, thus $Y = \mathcal{I}(Y) = -\mathcal{I}(X)$.
(2) by 3.1.4, $\neg\neg a$ is an exact element in $\mathbf{N_\Theta(A)}$. By 3.2.10 and 3.2.11, $r^{-1}(\neg\neg a)$ is a subset Y s.t. $\mathcal{I}(X) = \mathcal{I}(Y)$. Since Y is definable we have $\mathcal{I}(X) = \mathcal{I}(Y) = Y$ and the result follows immediately.
(3) by 3.1.3 $\div a$ is an exact element in $\mathbf{N_\Theta(A)}$. $\div a =< \mathcal{E}(X), \mathcal{C}(X) >$. It follows that if $Y = r^{-1}(\div a)$ then $\mathcal{I}(Y) = \mathcal{E}(X) = -\mathcal{C}(X)$. Since Y is definable, $\mathcal{I}(Y) = -\mathcal{C}(X)$.
(4) from 3.2.9 and 3.2.12, $r^{-1}(\div\div a)$ is a subset Y s.t. $-\mathcal{C}(X) = -\mathcal{C}(Y)$. Then $\mathcal{C}(X) = \mathcal{C}(Y)$ and since Y is definable from 3.1.2, we have $\mathcal{C}(X) = \mathcal{C}(Y) = Y$ and the result follows.

It is worth noticing the duality of the pairs $<\approx, \sim\approx >$ and $<\simeq, \sim\simeq>$ in terms of closure/internal in the pair $<\approx, \simeq>$ in terms of greatest/least. This duality reflects faithfully, from an algebraic point of view, the duality expressed in [5], par. 7.

Proposition 3.1 ALGEBRAIC CHARACTERIZATION OF ROUGH TOP EQUALITY
For any Approximation Space **A** *on an universe* U: $\forall X, Y \subseteq U$, *the following statements are equivalent:*
1. $X \approx Y$.
2. $\div\div r(X) = \div\div r(Y)$.
3. $\neg \div r(X) = \neg \div r(Y)$.
4. $\neg \sim r(X) = \neg \sim r(Y)$.
5. $\sim \div r(X) =\sim \div r(Y)$.
6. $\div r(X) = \div r(Y)$.

Since statement 3.4.4 has the least structural complexity we could adopt this formulation as standard algebraic characterization of rough top equality.

Proposition 3.2 ALGEBRAIC CHARACTERIZATION OF ROUGH BOTTOM EQUAL-
ITY *For any Approximation Space* **A** *on an universe* U: $\forall X, Y \subseteq U$ *the following
statements are equivalent:*
1. $X \simeq Y$.
2. $\neg\neg r(X) = \neg\neg r(Y)$.
3. $\sim \neg r(X) = \sim \neg r(Y)$.
4. $\neg r(X) = \neg r(Y)$.

4 Algebraic characterization of the properties of Rough Top and Rough-Bottom Equalities

Now we shall derive from the above results the well-known properties of rough
top and rough bottom equalities (see [5], [6]).

Lemma 4.1 *For any Approximation Space* **A** *on an universe* U:
1. $\div\div r$ *is a 0-1 homomorphism from the semilattice* $< \wp(U), \cup >$ *to the semilattice* $< N_\Theta(A), \vee >$.
2. $\neg\neg r$ *is a 0-1 homomorphism from the semilattice* $< \wp(U), \cap >$ *to the semilattice* $< N_\Theta(A), \wedge >$.

Proof: (1): (a) $\div\div r(\emptyset) = \div\div < \emptyset, U >=< \emptyset, U >$;
(b) $\div\div r(U) = \div\div < U, \emptyset >=< U, \emptyset >$;
(c) $\div\div r(X\cup Y) = \div\div < \mathcal{I}(X\cup Y), -\mathcal{C}(X\cup Y) >=< \mathcal{C}(X\cup Y), -\mathcal{C}(X\cup Y) >=$
$=< \mathcal{C}(X)\cup\mathcal{C}(Y), -\mathcal{C}(X)\cap -\mathcal{C}(Y) >=< \mathcal{C}(X), -\mathcal{C}(X) > \vee < \mathcal{C}(Y), -\mathcal{C}(Y) >=$
$\div\div < \mathcal{I}(X), -\mathcal{C}(X) > \vee \div\div < \mathcal{I}(Y), -\mathcal{C}(Y) >= \div\div r(X) \vee \div\div r(Y)$.
(2): by dual reasoning.

Lemma 4.2 *For any Approximation Space* **A** *on an universe* U:
1. $\forall X, Y \in \wp(U)$, *if* $X \subseteq Y$ *then* $r(X) \leq r(Y)$ *in* $N_\Theta(\mathbf{A})$.
2. $\forall a, b \in N_\Theta(\mathbf{A})$, *if* b *is exact and* $a \leq b$, *then* $r^{-1}(a) \leq r^{-1}(b)$.

Proof: (1): immediate from the definition of r (or from the above Lemma and
2.4.3).
(2): Let it be $a = r(X), b = r(Y)$. If $a \leq b$ then I(X)$\subseteq \mathcal{I}(Y)$ and $-\mathcal{C}(Y) \subseteq$
$-\mathcal{C}(X)$; thus $\mathcal{C}(X) \subseteq \mathcal{C}(Y)$. Either $\mathcal{I}(X) \subset X \subset \mathcal{C}(X)$ or X is definable:
$\mathcal{I}(X) = X = \mathcal{C}(X)$. In both cases $X \subseteq \mathcal{C}(Y)$ and since Y is definable for
hypothesis, we get $X \subseteq \mathcal{C}(Y) = Y$.

Lemma 4.3 *For any Approximation Space* **A** *on an universe* U, *the mapping*
$r^{-1} \div\div r : \wp(U) \longmapsto \wp(U)$ *(equivalently,* $r^{-1} \neg \div r$ *or* $r^{-1} \neg \sim r$ *or* $r^{-1} \sim r$*) is
a topological closure operator on* $\wp(U)$.

Proof: It is a standard result that in any Heyting algebra the double pseudocomplementation is a closure operation (that is, increasing, idempotent and
monotonic) (see for instance [1]). But $\div$ is the pseudocomplementation of
$N_\Theta(\mathbf{A})$ qua a Heyting algebra with partial order $\leq$; since $\div\div x$ is exact for all
$x \in N_\Theta(\mathbf{A})$, in view of Lemma 4.2 we have that $r^{-1} \div\div r$ is a closure operator
on $< \wp(U), \subseteq >$.
From Lemma 4.1.1, $r^{-1} \div\div r$ is also topological (as a matter of fact, $r^{-1} \div\div r(X)$
is the unique element Y of $\wp(U)$ s.t. $Y = \mathcal{C}(X)$).

Lemma 4.4 *For any Approximation Space* **A** *on an universe* U *the mapping* $r^{-1} \neg\neg r : \wp(U) \longmapsto \wp(U)$ *(equivalently, $r^{-1} \sim \neg r$ or $r^{-1} \neg \div r$) is a topological internal operator on* $\wp(U)$.

Proof: let us denote by $\mathbf{N_\Theta(A)}^d$ the dual ordered lattice of $\mathbf{N_\Theta(A)}$ and let us denote by $\div^d$ the pseudocomplementation in $\mathbf{N_\Theta(A)}^d$. From Lemma 3.2, $\forall a \in \mathbf{N_\Theta(A)}$, $\neg\neg a = \div^d \div^d a$. It follows from Lemma 4.3 that $\neg\neg$ is an internal operator in $\mathbf{N_\Theta(A)}$. Thus from Lemma 4.1.2 we get the result (as a matter of fact, $r^{-1}\neg\neg r$ is the unique element Y of $\wp(U)$ s.t. $Y = \mathcal{I}(X)$).
The above results must not be confused with the following interesting properties of $\div\div$ and $\neg\neg$.

Lemma 4.5 $\div\div$ *and* $\neg\neg$ *are operators in the lattice* $\mathbf{N_\Theta(A)}$:
1. $\div\div$ *distributes over* $\vee$;
2. $\div\div$ *distributes over* $\wedge$;
3. $\neg\neg$ *distributes over* $\vee$;
4. $\neg\neg$ *distributes over* $\wedge$.

Proof: (1): we have to prove that $\div\div(a \vee b) = \div\div a \vee \div\div b$:
$\div\div(a \vee b) =< \neg(A_2 \cap B_2), A_2 \cap B_2 >=< \neg A_2 \cup \neg B_2, A_2 \cap B_2 >=< \neg A_2, A_2 >$
$\vee < \neg B_2, B_2 >$.
(2): is similar; (3) from (2) and the duality principle of the proof of Lemma 4.4
(4): from 1 and the duality principle of the proof of Lemma 4.4.

Lemma 4.6 *Let* **A** *be an Approximation Space on an universe* U. *Then*
1. *the equivalence relation* $\approx$ *on* $\wp(U)$ *is a congruence on the semilattice* $< \wp(U), \cup >$.
2. *the equivalence relation* $\simeq$ *on* $\wp(U)$ *is a congruence on the semilattice* $< \wp(U), \cap >$.

Proof: Consider the pre-images $\Gamma(a) = (\div\div r)^{-1}(a)$ and $\Delta(a) = (\neg\neg r)^{-1}(a)$ of the homomorphisms $\div\div r$ and $\neg\neg r$ of Lemma 4.1. $\Gamma(a), \Delta(a) \subseteq \wp(U)$ and they differ from $\emptyset$ iff a is an exact element in $\mathbf{N_\Theta(A)}$. By standard results in lattice theory we have that for any $a \in \mathbf{N_\Theta(A)}$ $\Gamma(a)$ is a congruence class w.r.t. the operation $\cup$ and $\Delta(a)$ is a congruence class w.r.t. the operation $\cap$.

Let us now prove the other characteristic property of rough top (bottom) equalities.

Proposition 4.1 *Let* **A** *be an Approximation Space on an universe* U. *Let us denote by* $G(A) = \{r^{-1}\neg\neg r(X) : X \in \wp(U)\}$.
Then $\mathbf{G(A)} =< G(A), \cap, \cup, \neg, \emptyset, U >$ *is a Boolean subalgebra of* $\mathbf{B}(U)$.

Proof: since $\mathbf{N_\Theta(A)}$ is a Nelson algebra, we can define on it the equivalence relation
(a) $a \equiv b$ iff $a \to b \wedge b \to a = 1$. But from Lemma 3.2.11 we have immediately:
(b) $a \equiv b$ iff $a \simeq b$ iff $\neg\neg a = \neg\neg b$.
The quotient structure $\mathbf{N_\Theta(A)}/_{\equiv} =< \{[x]_{\equiv} : x \in \mathbf{N_\Theta(A)}\}, \vee, \wedge, \neg, 0, 1 >$ is an algebra, since $\equiv$ is a congruence for the operations $\vee, \wedge, \neg, 0, 1$ (see [17]). Moreover $\mathbf{N_\Theta(A)}/_{\equiv} \cong \{G(A)$ (by taking $\neg\neg a$ as the representative of $[a]_{\equiv}$, for any $[a]_{\equiv} \in \mathbf{N_\Theta(A)}$, and considering the pre-image $r^{-1}\neg\neg a$). We have at once that $\mathbf{G(A)} \cong \mathbf{A}$: in fact from a general result on Nelson algebras we know that

$\mathbf{N}_\Theta(\mathbf{A})/_\equiv \cong \mathbf{A}$ (see [17]).

A deeper insight shows that since $C = \{\neg\neg x : x \in \mathbf{N}_\Theta(\mathbf{A})\}$ is the centre of $\mathbf{N}_\Theta(\mathbf{A})$, then r maps bijectively A on C; it follows that $A = r^{-1}(C) = G(A)$ (from a different point of view, we can consider $r^{-1}\neg\neg r$ as a retraction of A in $\wp(U)$).

Proposition 4.2 *Let* **A** *be an Approximation Space on an universe* U. *Let us denote by* $F(A) = \{r^{-1} \div \div r(X) : X \in \wp(U)\}$.
Then $\mathbf{F(A)} = < F(A), \vee, \wedge, \neg, \emptyset, U >$ *is a Boolean subalgebra of* $\mathbf{B}(U)$.

Proof: Consider the equivalence $a \sim_\equiv b$ iff $\sim a \rightarrow \sim b \wedge \sim b \rightarrow \sim a = 1$. From Lemma 3.2.6 we have that $a \sim_\equiv b$ iff $a \approx b$ iff $\div a = \div b$.
By 3.2.3, $\div r(Y) = \neg\neg \sim r(Y)$ so we can use the equivalence relation $\sim_\equiv$ instead of $\equiv$ and repeat the same reasoning of the preceding Lemma.

With a proof analogous to that one of [5] we can obtain the reverse implications and the well-known Lemmas of characterization for rough top equalities and rough bottom equalities stated in the aforementioned paper.

EXAMPLE:
Let it be $U = \{a, b, c\}$ and $\mathbf{A} = \{\{a\}, \{b, c\}, \{a, b, c\}, \emptyset\}$. Let us consider for instance the subset $\{b\} : r(\{b\}) = < \emptyset, \{a\} > = r(\{c\})$. We have now:
(*): $\neg\neg r(\{b\}) = < \emptyset, \{a, b, c\} > = \neg\neg r(\{c\}) = \neg\neg r(\emptyset)$. Thus $\{b\} \simeq \{c\} \simeq \emptyset$ and $r^{-1}\neg\neg r(\{b\}) = r^{-1}\neg\neg r(\{c\}) = r^{-1}\neg\neg r(\emptyset) = \emptyset$.
In facts, $\mathcal{I}(\{b\}) = \mathcal{I}(\{c\}) = \mathcal{I}(\emptyset) = \emptyset$.
Moreover from (*) we have $(\neg\neg r)^{-1}(< \emptyset, \{a, b, c\} >) = \{\{b\}, \{c\}, \emptyset\}$ that is a $\cap$-semilattice. On the other hand,
(**): $\div \div r(\{b\}) = \div \div < \emptyset, \{a\} > = < \{b, c\}, \{a\} > = \div \div r(\{c\}) = r(\{b, c\})$.
Thus $\{b\} \approx \{c\} \approx \emptyset$ and $r^{-1}\div\div r(\{b\}) = r^{-1}\div\div r(\{c\}) = r^{-1}\div(\{b, c\}) = \{b, c\}$.
Indeed we can verify that $\mathcal{C}(\{b\}) = \mathcal{C}(\{c\}) = \mathcal{C}(\{b, c\}) = \{b, c\}$.
From (**) we have $(\div \div r)^{-1}(< \{b, c\}, \{a\} >) = \{\{b\}, \{c\}, \{b, c\}\}$ that is a $\cup$-semilattice.

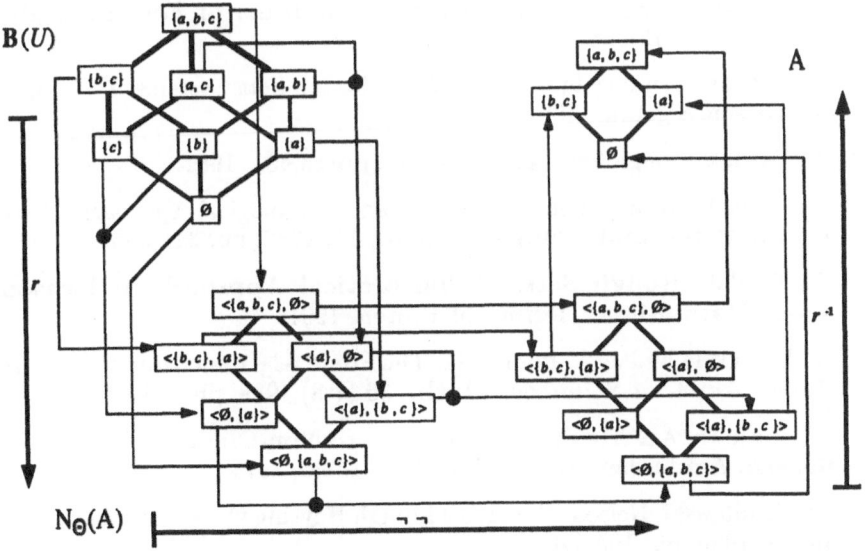

References

[1] G. Gierz, K. H. Hofmann, K. Keimel, J. D. Lawson, M. Mislove and D. Scott, **A compendium of continuous lattices**, Springer Verlag, 1980.

[2] T. B. Iwinski, Rough Orders and Rough Concepts, **Bull. Polish Acad. of Sciences, Math.**, 37 (3-4), 1988, pp. 187-192.

[3] V. Boicescu, A. Filipoiu, G. Georgescu and S. Rudeanu, **Łukasiewicz-Moisil Algebras**, North-Holland, Amsterdam-New York-Oxford-Tokio. 1991.

[4] M. Novotny and Z. Pawlak, On representation of rough sets by means of information systems. **Fund. Inform.**, 6, 1983, pp. 189-296.

[5] M. Novotny and Z. Pawlak, Characterization of Rough Top Equalities and Rough Bottom Equalities, **Bull. Polish Acad. of Sciences, Math.**, 33 (1-2), 1985, pp. 91-97.

[6] M. Novotny and Z. Pawlak, On Rough Equalities, **Bull. Polish Acad. of Sciences, Math.**, 33 (1-2), 1985, pp. 99-104.

[7] M. Novotny and Z. Pawlak, Black box analysis and Rough Top Equalities, **Bull. Polish Acad. of Science.**, Math., 33 (1-2), 1985, pp. 105-113.

[8] M. Novotny and Z. Pawlak, Algebraic Theory of Independence in Information Systems, **Fund. Inform.**, 14, 1991, pp. 454-476.

[9] P.Pagliani, A computer oriented representation of Modal Spaces and Pseudo Boolean Algebras with application to a system of non-deterministic information, **Internal Report PAG/2**, Universita' di Milano, Ist. Scienza dell'Informazione. 1986.

[10] P. Pagliani, Some remarks on Special Lattices and related constructive logics with strong negation, **Notre Dame Jour. of Formal Logic**, 31 (4),1990, pp. 515-528.

[11] P. Pagliani, An Algebraic Analysis on Rough Sets Systems, I: Rough Sets and Nelson Algebras, 1992 (to appear).

[12] Z. Pawlak, Rough Sets, **ICS PAS Reports**,431, 1981.

[13] Z. Pawlak, Rough Sets. Algebraic and Topological approach, **Intern. Journ. of Inf. and Comp. Sciences**, 11, 1982, pp. 341-366.

[14] Z. Pawlak, **Rough Sets: A Theoretical Approach to Reasoning about Data.** Kluwer, Dordrecht-Boston, 1991.

[15] J. Pomykała and J. A. Pomykała, The Stone Algebra of Rough Sets, **Bull. Polish Acad. of Sciences, Math.**, 36 (7-8),1988, pp 495-508.

[16] H. Rasiowa, **An Algebraic Approach to Non Classical Logics**, North-Holland, Amsterdam-New York-Oxford-Tokio, 1974.

[17] A. Sendlewski, Nelson Algebras Through Heyting Ones: I. **Studia Logica**, 49 (1), 1990, pp. 105-126.

A Novel Approach to the Minimal Cover Problem

Piotr Sapiecha

University of Warsaw

Department of Mathematics

Poland

Abstract

Approximation algorithms for the Minimal Cover Problem (MCP) are presented in this paper. Contrary to the greedy approximation algorithm for MCP [Jo-74], [Lo-75], [Co-92], novel approaches to MCP are based on the simulated annealing (SA) and genetic algorithms (GA). The main difference between the existing technique and the new method is that the former algorithm gives one solution whereas the latter algorithms improves simultaneously several solutions. This property is important, particularly in the context of the problem of dependence relation of attributes in information systems [Pa-82], [Sk-92].

1 Introduction

The MCP is a classical combinatorial optimization problem belonging to NP–hard class. Numerous real–world situations can be modeled by MCP, for instance airline crew scheduling, truck delivery, resource allocation, circuit design, and fault tolerant computing. MCP is also the main problem of knowledge reduction in information systems as shown in reference [Sk-92]. For these reasons, an effort was made to explore the MCP and to represent it in such a way as to enable the application of genetic algorithm for its solution.

2 Definition of MCP

According to the paper [Sa-93], MCP can be represented in the following way:

DEFINITION (The Minimal Cover Problem):

Given: The boolean matrix $M = M[i,j]$, where $i = 1, \ldots, n$; $j = 1, \ldots, m$ and $M[i,j] \in \{0,1\}$ for each pair $\{i,j\}$.

Problem: Find a minimal cover set C (in the sense of minimal cardinality) of rows of matrix M such that for all columns j ranging from 1 to m always exists an element $M[i,j] \in C$ which is equal 1.

3 New Approach to MCP

An approach to MCP proposed in this work is based on a new representation. The MCP can be rewritten as follows:

DEFINITION (MCP):

Given: The boolean matrix, the same like presented previously.

Problem: Maximize function F, where for each $C \subseteq \{1, \ldots, n\}$, $F(C)$ is equal to:

  (a) the number of the columns which are covered by C, if C does not cover the set of all columns;

  (b) $m + (n - (\text{cardinality of } C))$, otherwise.

Example 1: Let M be represented in following way:

	c_1	c_2	c_3	c_4	c_5
r_1	1	0	0	1	1
r_2	0	1	1	1	0
r_3	0	1	0	1	0
r_4	1	1	1	0	1
r_5	0	0	0	0	0
r_6	0	1	0	1	1

We can compute function F values for several subsets:

$$\left.\begin{array}{l} F(\{r_1\}) = 3 \\ F(\{r_5\}) = 0 \\ F(\{r_4\}) = 4 \\ F(\{r_1, r_5\}) = 3 \end{array}\right\} \quad \text{case (a)}$$

$$\left.\begin{array}{l} F(\{r_1, r_4, r_5\}) = 8 \\ F(\{r_1, r_4\}) = 9 \\ F(\{r_3, r_4\}) = 9 \end{array}\right\} \quad \text{case (b)}$$

where the function F reaches its maximum in the sets $\{r_1, r_4\}, \{r_3, r_4\}$.

4 Preprocessing

First of all, before starting SA or GA for MCP, it is possible to reduce input data in polynomial time. In many cases this procedure gives a satisfactory results, however the degree of reduction depends on the type of data. This reduction procedure is described in the reference [Sy-83].

5 Simulated Annealing Algorithm and Genetic Algorithm

Simulated annealing is a randomization algorithm for approximate solution of combinatorial optimization problems. The background of the SA technique comes from an analogy between two different fields, namely the simulation of the annealing process of solids and the combinatorial optimization problems. An outline of the SA algorithm is shown below:

```
procedure SA ;
begin
    initialize ;
    T:=0 ;
    repeat
        repeat
            perturb (config.i → config.j, ΔC_ij) ;
            if ΔC_ij < 0 then accept else
                if exp(−ΔC_ij/C_T) > random [0, 1)
                then accept ;
            if accept then UPDATE (config.j)
        until equilibrium is approached sufficiently closely
        C_{T+1} := f(C_T) ;
        T:= T+1
    until stop criterion = true (system is 'frozen')
end.
```

Genetic algorithms are search algorithms based on the mechanics of natural selection and natural genetic. They combine survival of the fittest among string structures with a structured, yet randomized information exchange. In each generation, a new set of artificial creatures (strings) is created using pieces (building blocks) of the fittest members of the older generation. Though randomized, genetic algorithms are no simple random walk. They efficiently exploit historical information to speculate on new search directions with expected improved performance. The outline of the genetic algorithm is shown below:

```
procedure GA ;
begin
    initialize population P(0) ;
    evaluate P(0) ;
    T:=1 ;
    repeat
        select P(T) from P(T-1) ;
        recombine P(T) ;
        evaluate P(T) ;
    until (termination condition) ;
end.
```

To apply SA or GA to a combinatorial optimization problem it is necessary to adequately define the configuration space and consensus function for SA. In addition, for GA the population and fitness functions should be defined. This construction for MCP will be explained in the next part in this paper. The detailed description of SA and GA and correctness proof of these algorithms are presented in the books [Ak-89], [La-87], [Go-82], [Da-87].

6   Coding for SA & GA

Let us consider coding for SA, where a hypercube $\{0,1\}^n$ is a configuration space. For every $r \in \{0,1\}^n$ and $i \in \{1,\ldots,n\}$, $r[i]$ has the following simple interpretation:

$$r[i] = \begin{cases} 1 & \text{it means that row number } i \text{ belongs} \\ & \text{to the cover set } C \subseteq \{1, \ldots, n\} \\ 0 & \text{otherwise} \end{cases}$$

Additionally, the consensus function is given by the function F:

$$CONS(r) := F(C),$$

where C is a cover set corresponding to r.

Example 2: According to example 1:

$$CONS((1,0,0,0,1,0)) := F(\{r_1, r_5\}) = 3,$$
$$CONS((0,0,1,1,0,0)) := F(\{r_3, r_4\}) = 9.$$

A similar situation exists in the case of GA. A set of some boolean vectors from hypercube $\{0,1\}^n$ should be chosen as a population of strings. The interpretation of vector $x \in \{0,1\}^n$ is the same. Moreover, the fitness function is also given by the function F.

7 Experimental Results

The described algorithms have been implemented in the program APPROX. The procedures were tested on different examples of random data, in particular data on which greedy method works ineffectively [Jo-74], [Lo-75], [La-87]. The results are considered satisfactory. In many cases the obtained approximated results have approached or even reached the optimal solutions.

8 Conclusions

Two approximation algorithms for MCP are presented in this paper. In comparison to the well known greedy approximation algorithm, the proposed methods provide improved solutions. Among other applications, the algorithms can be applied to study the dependence relation of attributes in information systems.

9 Acknowledgments

I am very much indebted to my Ph. D. thesis supervisor Professor A. Skowron for several helpful comments and suggestions and also to my student I. Machel for preparing APPROX program.

References

[Ak-89] E.H.L. Aarts, J.H.M. Korst "Simulated Annealing and Boltzmann Machines" John Wiley & Sons 1989.

[Co-92] T.H. Cormen, C.E. Leiserson, R.L. Riverst "Introduction to Algorithms" MIT Press 1992.

[Da-87] Ed. by L. Davis "Genetic Algorithms and Simulated Annealing" Pitman, Morgan Kaufmann 1987.

[Go-82] D. Goldberg "Genetic Algorithms in Search, Optimization, and Machine Learning" Addison–Wesley 1982.

[Jo-74] D.S. Johnson "Approximation Algorithms for Combinatorial Problems" Journal of Computer and System Science 9, 1974.

[La-87] P.J.M. Laarhoven, E.H.L. Aarts "Simulated Annealing Theory and Application" Kluwer, Dordrecht Netherlands 1987.

[Lo-75] L. Lovasz "On the radio of optimal integeral and fractional cover" Discrete Math. 13, 1975.

[Mo-92] R. Motwani "Approximation Algorithms" (lecture notes) Stanford University 1991/1992.

[Pa-82] Z. Pawlak "Rough Sets" International Journal of Computer and Information Science, vol. 11, No. 5, 1982.

[Sa-93] P. Sapiecha "An Approximation Algorithm for Minimal Reduct Problem" Proc. of the First Workshop on Rough Set Theory. Poland 1992; and also in Foundations of Computing and Decision Science vol. 18, No. 3/4, 1993.

[Sk-92] A. Skowron, C. Rauszer "The Discernibility Matrices and Functions in Information Systems" Handbook of Applications and Advances of the Rough Set Theory, ed. Slowinski R., Kluwer 1992.

[Sy-83] M. Syslo, N. Deo, J. Kowalik "Discrete optimization algorithms with Pascal programs" Englewood Cliffs, NJ; Prentice Hall, 1983.

[Zi-91] V. Zissimopoulos, V.Th. Paschos, F. Pekergin "On the approximation of NP–complete problems by using the Boltzmann Machine method: The cases of some covering and packing problems" IEEE Trans on Comp. vol. 40, No. 12, December 1991.

Algebraic Structures of Rough Sets

Zbigniew Bonikowski

Department of Computer Science and Applied Logic, University of Opole
Opole, Poland

1 Preliminaries

This paper deals with some algebraic and set-theoretical properties of rough sets. Our considerations are based on the original conception of rough sets formulated by Pawlak [4, 5]. Let U be any fixed non-empty set traditionally called the *universe* and let R be an equivalence relation on U. The pair $\mathcal{A} = (U, R)$ is called the *approximation space*. We will call the equivalence classes of the relation R the *elementary sets*. We denote the family of elementary sets by U/R. We assume that the empty set is also an elementary set. Every union of elementary sets will be called a *composed set*. We denote the family of composed sets by $ComR$. We can characterize each set $X \subseteq U$ using the composed sets [5].

Definition 1.1 *Let X be any subset of U.*

(a) *The* lower approximation of X *is the set*

$$\underline{X} = \bigcup \{Y : Y \subseteq X \ \wedge \ Y \in U/R\}.$$

(b) *The* upper approximation of X *is the set*

$$\overline{X} = \bigcup \{Y : Y \cap X \neq \emptyset \wedge Y \in U/R\}.$$

There exist subsets of X, which have an identical lower approximation or upper approximation, as set X [4].

Definition 1.2 *Let X be any subset of U.*

(a) *The set Y is called the* upper sample of X *iff $Y \subseteq X$ and $\overline{Y} = \overline{X}$.*

(b) *The set Y is called the* minimal upper sample of X *iff Y is the upper sample of X and there is no upper sample Z of X such that $Z \subset Y$.*

Let us define the rough inclusion relation and the rough equality relation on $P(U)$.

Definition 1.3 *The set X is roughly included in Y ($X \subseteq_R Y$) iff $\underline{X} \subseteq \underline{Y}$ and $\overline{X} \subseteq \overline{Y}$.*

Definition 1.4 *The sets X, Y are* roughly equal *($X \approx Y$) iff $\underline{X} = \underline{Y}$ and $\overline{X} = \overline{Y}$.*

The rough equality relation is an equivalence relation in $P(U)$. We will call equivalence classes of the rough equality relation the *rough sets*. The rough sets determined by composed sets will be called the *exact sets*. Let us notice that an exact set is a one-element set composed only of a composed set determining this exact set.

2   An algebra of rough sets

Let $\mathcal{A} = (U, R)$ be the approximation space and $P(U)/\approx$ be the family of rough sets. Let us introduce inclusion relation of rough sets. Let $[\; X\;]_{\approx}$, $[\; Y\;]_{\approx}$ be any rough sets.

Definition 2.1 *(inclusion relation of rough sets)*

$$[\; X\;]_{\approx} \leq_{\approx} [\; Y\;]_{\approx} \Leftrightarrow X \subseteq_R Y.$$

Theorem 2.2 *The ordered pair $(P(U)/\approx, \leq_{\approx})$ is a partially ordered set, where every pair of rough sets possesses an infimum and a supremum.*

¿From above theorem it follows that for any rough sets $[\; X\;]_{\approx}$, $[\; Y\;]_{\approx}$ we can define an operation $\cup_{\approx}$ of rough addition and an operation $\cap_{\approx}$ of rough multiplication as a supremum and an infimum of set $\{\; [\; X\;]_{\approx}, [\; Y\;]_{\approx}\; \}$, respectively.

Definition 2.3 *Let $[\; X\;]_{\approx}$, $[\; Y\;]_{\approx}$ be any rough sets.*

(a) *(rough intersection)*

$$[\; X\;]_{\approx} \cap_{\approx} [\; Y\;]_{\approx} = [\; \underline{X} \cap \underline{Y} \cup P\;]_{\approx}, \textit{where } P \textit{ is a minimal upper}$$
$$\textit{sample of set } \overline{X} \cap \overline{Y}.$$

(b) *(rough union)*

$$[\; X\;]_{\approx} \cup_{\approx} [\; Y\;]_{\approx} = [\; \underline{X} \cup \underline{Y} \cup P\;]_{\approx}, \textit{where } P \textit{ is a minimal upper}$$
$$\textit{sample of set } \overline{X} \cup \overline{Y}.$$

Let us introduce an operation of exterior complement and an operation of interior complement [6].

Definition 2.4 *Let $[\; X\;]_{\approx}$ be any rough set.*

(a) *(exterior complement)*

$$[\; X\;]_{\approx}^{\;ex} = [\; (\overline{X})'\;]_{\approx}.$$

(b) *(interior complement)*

$$[\; X\;]_{\approx}^{\;in} = [\; (\underline{X})'\;]_{\approx}.$$

244

Theorem 2.5 *The algebra* $\mathcal{R}_{\approx} = (P(U)/\approx, \cap_{\approx}, \cup_{\approx}, ^{ex}, [\ \emptyset\ ]_{\approx}, [\ U\ ]_{\approx})$ *is the complete atomic Stone algebra, where atoms are determined by proper subsets of the elementary sets or by the one-element elementary sets.*

The above theorem was proved in [1] for set U as finite set. Similar theorem was proved by Pomykała [6].

Theorem 2.6 *The pseudocomplement of the rough set* $[\ X\ ]_{\approx}$ *is the complement of this rough set iff the rough set* $[\ X\ ]_{\approx}$ *is an exact set.*

Theorem 2.7 *The algebra* $\mathcal{E} = (ComR/\approx, \cap_{\approx}, \cup_{\approx}, ', [\ \emptyset\ ]_{\approx}, [\ U\ ]_{\approx})$ *is the complete atomic Boolean algebra. Atoms of this algebra are determined by the elementary sets.*

The algebra of exact sets is also the center of the Stone algebra of rough sets [3].

If the relation R determines the partition of set U into one-element equivalence classes, then the algebra of rough sets R is the Boolean algebra. It is isomorphic with the Boolean algebra of subset of set U by the Stone Representation Theorem (see e.g. [7]).

3 Algebras of lower rough sets and upper rough sets

Pawlak has formulated also the notions of the lower rough set and the upper rough set [5].

Definition 3.1 *Let X, Y be any subsets of U.*

(a) *(lower equality relation)*
  The sets X, Y are bottom roughly equal ($X \approx Y$) iff $\underline{X} = \underline{Y}$.

(b) *(upper equality relation)*
  The sets X, Y are top roughly equal ($X \simeq Y$) iff $\overline{X} = \overline{Y}$.

The lower equality relation and the upper equality relation are equivalence relations. The equivalence classes of the lower equality relation are called the *lower rough sets*. The equivalence classes of the upper equality relation are called the *upper rough sets*.

Definition 3.2 (a) *(inclusion relation of lower rough sets)*

$$[\ X\ ]_{\approx} \leq_{\approx} [\ Y\ ]_{\approx} \Leftrightarrow \underline{X} \subseteq \underline{Y}.$$

(b) *(inclusion relation of upper rough sets)*

$$[\ X\ ]_{\simeq} \leq_{\simeq} [\ Y\ ]_{\simeq} \Leftrightarrow \overline{X} \subseteq \overline{Y}.$$

The above inclusion relations are the partially ordering relations. We define operations of lower rough union, lower rough intersection, exterior complement and interior complement in the family of lower rough sets in the same way as the respective operations in the family of rough sets.

Definition 3.3 *Let* $[\ X\ ]_{\underset{\sim}{\approx}}$, $[\ Y\ ]_{\underset{\sim}{\approx}}$ *be any lower rough sets.*

(a) *(lower rough intersection)*

$$[\ X\ ]_{\underset{\sim}{\approx}} \cap_{\underset{\sim}{\approx}} [\ Y\ ]_{\underset{\sim}{\approx}} = [\ \underline{X} \cap \underline{Y} \cup P\ ]_{\underset{\sim}{\approx}}, \quad \text{where } P \text{ is a minimal upper}$$
sample of set $\overline{X} \cap \overline{Y}$.

(b) *(lower rough union)*

$$[\ X\ ]_{\underset{\sim}{\approx}} \cup_{\underset{\sim}{\approx}} [\ Y\ ]_{\underset{\sim}{\approx}} = [\ \underline{X} \cup \underline{Y} \cup P\ ]_{\underset{\sim}{\approx}}, \quad \text{where } P \text{ is a minimal upper}$$
sample of set $\overline{X} \cup \overline{Y}$.

(c) *(exterior complement)*

$$[\ X\ ]_{\underset{\sim}{\approx}}^{ex} = [\ (\overline{X})'\ ]_{\underset{\sim}{\approx}}.$$

(d) *(interior complement)*

$$[\ X\ ]_{\underset{\sim}{\approx}}^{in} = [\ (\underline{X})'\ ]_{\underset{\sim}{\approx}}.$$

Theorem 3.4 *The algebra* $\mathcal{R}_{\underset{\sim}{\approx}} = (P(U)/\approx, \cap_{\underset{\sim}{\approx}}, \cup_{\underset{\sim}{\approx}}, ^{in}, [\ \emptyset\ ]_{\underset{\sim}{\approx}}, [\ U\ ]_{\underset{\sim}{\approx}})$ *is the complete atomic Boolean algebra, where atoms are determined by the elementary sets.*

We can define operations of upper rough union, upper rough intersection, exterior complement and interior complement in the family of upper rough sets as above.

Definition 3.5 *Let* $[\ X\ ]_{\sim}$, $[\ Y\ ]_{\sim}$ *be any upper rough sets.*

(a) *(upper rough intersection)*

$$[\ X\ ]_{\sim} \cap_{\sim} [\ Y\ ]_{\sim} = [\ \underline{X} \cap \underline{Y} \cup P\ ]_{\sim}, \quad \text{where } P \text{ is a minimal upper}$$
sample of set $\overline{X} \cap \overline{Y}$.

(b) *(upper rough union)*

$$[\ X\ ]_{\sim} \cup_{\sim} [\ Y\ ]_{\sim} = [\ \underline{X} \cup \underline{Y} \cup P\ ]_{\sim}, \quad \text{where } P \text{ is a minimal upper}$$
sample of set $\overline{X} \cup \overline{Y}$.

(c) *(exterior complement)*

$$[\ X\ ]_{\sim}^{ex} = [\ (\overline{X})'\ ]_{\sim}.$$

(d) *(interior complement)*

$$[\ X\ ]_{\sim}^{in} = [\ (\underline{X})'\ ]_{\sim}.$$

Theorem 3.6 *The algebra* $\mathcal{R}_{\sim} = (P(U)/\simeq, \cap_{\sim}, \cup_{\sim}, ^{ex}, [\ \emptyset\ ]_{\sim}, [\ U\ ]_{\sim})$ *is the complete atomic Boolean algebra, where atoms are determined by the elementary sets.*

4 Rough element of rough set

It is natural to try to define a notion of the rough element of the rough set so as the rough membership relation will have similar properties as the membership relation. Let us notice that if x is an element of Y then $\{x\}$ is an atom included in X. By analogy a set Y is a rough element of $[\ X\ ]_{\approx}$ if the rough set $[\ X\ ]_{\approx}$ is an atom included in $[\ X\ ]_{\approx}$. Therefore I formulated the following definition.

Definition 4.1 *A set $Y \subset U$ is a proper rough element of the rough set $[\ X\ ]_{\approx}$ (symbolically $Y \underline{\in}_{\approx} [\ X\ ]_{\approx}$) iff the following conditions hold:*

1. $Y \neq \emptyset$,

2. $[\ Y\ ]_{\approx} \leq_{\approx} [\ X\ ]_{\approx}$,

3. there is no $Z \neq \emptyset$ such that $[\ Z\ ]_{\approx} \leq_{\approx} [\ Y\ ]_{\approx}$ and $[\ Z\ ]_{\approx} \neq [\ Y\ ]_{\approx}$.

One can easily prove the following lemmas.

Lemma 4.2 $[\ X\ ]_{\approx} = [\ Y\ ]_{\approx} \Rightarrow \forall Z \in P(U)\, (Z \underline{\in}_{\approx} [\ X\ ]_{\approx} \Leftrightarrow Z \underline{\in}_{\approx} [\ Y\ ]_{\approx})$.

Lemma 4.3 *Let $[\ X\ ]_{\approx}, [\ Y\ ]_{\approx}$ be any exact sets. Then it holds:*

$$\forall Z \in P(U)\, (Z \underline{\in}_{\approx} [\ X\ ]_{\approx} \Leftrightarrow Z \underline{\in}_{\approx} [\ Y\ ]_{\approx}) \Rightarrow [\ X\ ]_{\approx} = [\ Y\ ]_{\approx}$$

The above lemmas imply

Theorem 4.4 *The principle of extensionality for the proper rough membership relation holds in the family of exact sets:*

$$[\ X\ ]_{\approx} = [\ Y\ ]_{\approx} \Leftrightarrow \forall Z \in P(U)\, (Z \underline{\in}_{\approx} [\ X\ ]_{\approx} \Leftrightarrow Z \underline{\in}_{\approx} [\ Y\ ]_{\approx}).$$

The principle of extensionality does not hold in the family of rough sets, because the sets $[\ X\ ]_{\approx}$ and $[\ \overline{X}\ ]_{\approx}$ are different sets, though they have the same proper rough elements. Let us notice, that if Y is a proper rough element of rough set $[\ X\ ]_{\approx}$, then either Y is a proper subset of the elementary set included in $\overline{X}$ or Y is the one-element elementary set included in $\underline{X}$.

It appears that the definition of a proper rough element is too strong. Now we will extend this notion.

Definition 4.5 *A set $Y \subset U$ is a rough element of the rough set $[\ X\ ]_{\approx}$ (symbolically $Y \in_{\approx} [\ X\ ]_{\approx}$) iff the following conditions hold:*

1. $Y \neq \emptyset$,

2. $[\ Y\ ]_{\approx} \leq_{\approx} [\ X\ ]_{\approx}$,

3. $\exists Z \in U/R\ \ \overline{Y} = Z$.

More general definition of this notion was formulated by Bryniarski [2].

Any rough element of rough set $[\ X\ ]_{\approx}$ is either a proper subset of the elementary set included in $\overline{X}$ or elementary set included in $\underline{X}$. Every proper rough element is a rough element but not vice versa. Every rough element is a proper rough element if the relation R determines the partition of U into one-element equivalence classes.

Theorem 4.6 *The principle of extensionality for the rough membership relation holds in the family of rough sets:*

$$[\ X\ ]_{\approx} = [\ Y\ ]_{\approx} \Leftrightarrow \forall Z \in P(U)\,(Z{\in}_{\approx}[\ X\ ]_{\approx} \Leftrightarrow Z{\in}_{\approx}[\ Y\ ]_{\approx}$$

Theorem 4.7 *Let* $[\ X\ ]_{\approx}$ *,* $[\ Y\ ]_{\approx}$ *be any rough sets and let* $Z \in P(U)$. *Then*

(a) $Z{\in}_{\approx}[\ X\ ]_{\approx} \cup_{\approx} [\ Y\ ]_{\approx} \Leftrightarrow Z{\in}_{\approx}[\ X\ ]_{\approx} \vee Z{\in}_{\approx}[\ Y\ ]_{\approx},$

(b) $Z{\in}_{\approx}[\ X\ ]_{\approx} \cap_{\approx} [\ Y\ ]_{\approx} \Leftrightarrow Z{\in}_{\approx}[\ X\ ]_{\approx} \wedge Z{\in}_{\approx}[\ Y\ ]_{\approx}.$

Let $[\ X\ ]_{\approx}$ be any rough set. We denote the set of all rough elements of set $[\ X\ ]_{\approx}$ by $EL(X)$.

Theorem 4.8 $[\ X\ ]_{\approx} = \bigcup_{\approx z \in EL(X)} [\ Z\ ]_{\approx}.$

The above theorem is corresponding to the conclusion, that any set is the union of the singletons, whose elements are elements of this set. However this analogy is not complete. In brief difference is following. Every element of set X is, one can say, "indispensable". For any element of set X the union of the singletons, whose elements are elements of this set, which are different from this element, is not equal to X. In the case of rough sets this remark is not true. The solution of this problem will be a subject of another paper.

5 Acknowledgment

I would like to thank my supervisor, Professor Urszula Wybraniec-Skardowska for much help and guidance.

References

[1] Z. Bonikowski, A Certain Conception of the Calculus of Rough Sets, **Notre Dame Journal of Formal Logic**, vol.33 (1992), pp.412-421.

[2] E. Bryniarski, A calculus of rough sets of the first order, **Bull.Pol.Ac.: Math.**, vol.37 (1989), pp.71-78.

[3] M. Gehrke, E. Walker, On the Structures of Rough Sets, **Bull.Pol.Ac.: Math.**, vol.40 (1992), pp.235-245.

[4] Z. Pawlak, **Information systems. Theoretical foundations.**, WNT, Warszawa, 1983 (in Polish).

[5] Z. Pawlak, **Rough Sets. Theoretical Aspects of Reasoning about Data.**, Kluwer Academic Publisher, Dordrecht, 1991.

[6] J. Pomykała, J.A. Pomykała, The Stone Algebra of Rough Sets, **Bull. Pol.Ac.:Math.**, vol.36 (1988), pp.495-508.

[7] H. Rasiowa, R. Sikorski, **The Mathematics of Metamathematics**, PWN, Warszawa, 1970.

Rough Concept Analysis

Robert E. Kent

University of Arkansas at Little Rock

Little Rock, Arkansas, U.S.A.

Abstract

The theory introduced, presented and developed in this paper, is concerned with Rough Concept Analysis. This theory is a synthesis of the theory of Rough Sets pioneered by Zdzislaw Pawlak [5] with the theory of Formal Concept Analysis pioneered by Rudolf Wille [6]. The central notion in this paper of a *rough formal concept* combines in a natural fashion the notion of a rough set with the notion of a formal concept — to use a slogan: "rough set + formal concept = rough formal concept". A related paper [3] using distributed constraints provides a synthesis of the two important data modeling techniques: conceptual scaling of Formal Concept Analysis, and Entity-Relationship database modeling. A follow-up paper [2] will extend rough concept analysis from formal contexts to distributed constraints.

1 The RS-FCA Community

The theory of Rough Sets initiated by Zdzislaw Pawlak [5] is used to model imprecise or incomplete knowledge and approximate classification. The theory of Formal Concept Analysis initiated by Rudolf Wille [6] is used for data modeling, analysis and interpretation, and also for knowledge representation and knowledge discovery via the special technique of attribute exploration or the more general technique of concept exploration. Rough Sets and Formal Concept Analysis have much in common, both in terms of goals and methodologies. Various analogies ($\cong$) and identities ($\equiv$) between notions from Rough Sets and Formal Concept Analysis are listed here.

Rough Sets		Formal Concept Analysis
approximation space [5]	$\equiv$	formal context morphism
indexed collection of subsets	$\equiv$	formal context [6]
—	$\equiv$	concept lattice
information system	$\equiv$	many-valued formal context [3]
discretization attribute-value pairing subranging complementation $\vdots$	$\cong$	interpretation via constraints [1, 2, 3] (special case: conceptual scaling)
certain rule	$\equiv$	implication
possible rule	$\equiv$	certain rule with dichotomic scaling
rough measure of rule	$\cong$	rough measure of implication $U \overset{k}{\Rightarrow} V$ when $\frac{\lvert U' \cap V' \rvert}{\lvert U' \rvert} = k$ partial implication

Rough Sets works directly with information systems ≡ many-valued formal contexts, and only implicitly with a derived structure (a formal context) containing attribute-value pairs, whereas Formal Concept Analysis has an explicit transformation [many-valued formal context ⇒ (ordinary) formal context] called conceptual scaling, which is regarded to be an act of interpretation.

2 Rough Formal Contexts

This paper introduces the new theory of Rough Concept Analysis, which is a synthesis of Rough Sets and Formal Concept Analysis.

An *approximation space* is a pair $\langle G, E \rangle$, where G is a set of *objects* or *entities* and E is an equivalence relation on G called an *indiscernibility relation*. A *formal context* is a triple $\langle G, M, I \rangle$ consisting of a set of *objects* G, a set of *attributes* M, and a binary *incidence* relation $I \subseteq G \times M$ between G and M, where gIm asserts that "object g *has* attribute m" for any object $g \in G$ and attribute $m \in M$. In this paper a formal context is viewed as an attribute-indexed collection of subsets of objects. A *formal concept* of a given formal context will consist of an extent/intent pair (A, B) where the intent $B = A'_I \stackrel{\text{df}}{=} \{m \in M \mid gIm \text{ for all } g \in A\} = \bigcap_{g \in A} gI \subseteq M$ contains precisely those attributes shared by all objects in the extent A, and vice-versa, the extent $A = B'_I \stackrel{\text{df}}{=} \{g \in G \mid gIm \text{ for all } m \in B\} = \bigcap_{m \in B} Im \subseteq G$ contains precisely those objects sharing all attributes in the intent B. The collection of all concepts is ordered by generalization-specialization. Concepts with the generalization-specialization ordering form a complete lattice $\mathcal{B}\langle G, M, I \rangle$ called the *concept lattice* of $\langle G, M, I \rangle$.

Let $\langle G, E \rangle$ be any approximation space on objects G and let $\langle G, M, I \rangle$ be any formal context between the same objects and some set of attributes M. An attribute $m \in M$ is a *definable attribute* when its extent $Im \subseteq G$ is a definable subset of objects w.r.t. the indiscernibility relation E. A *definable formal context* is a context all of whose attributes are definable. For any formal context $\langle G, M, I \rangle$ we wish to approximate I in terms of definable contexts. We use two notions for this: an upper approximation of possibility and a lower approximation of necessity. These two *contextual* approximations provide upper and lower *conceptual* approximations for concepts in $\mathcal{B}\langle G, M, I \rangle$ (see Section 3).

[Upper E-approximation] The upper E-approximation of I, denoted by $\overline{I}^E$, is defined element-wise: for each attribute $m \in M$, the extent of m in the upper approximation $\overline{I}^E$ is the upper approximation of its extent in I, $\overline{I}^E m \stackrel{\text{df}}{=} \overline{Im}^E = \{g \mid [g]_E \cap Im \neq \emptyset\}$. The upper approximation of I is the least definable context containing I. The extent of a subset of attributes $B \subseteq M$ with respect to the upper E-approximation is $B'_{\overline{I}^E} = \bigcap_{m \in B} \overline{I}^E m = \bigcap_{m \in B} \overline{Im}^E \supseteq \overline{\bigcap_{m \in B} Im}^E = \overline{B'_I}^E$ (see the important discussion below about choices).

[Lower E-approximation] The lower E-approximation of I, denoted by $\underline{I}_E$, is also defined element-wise: for each attribute $m \in M$, the extent of m in the lower approximation $\underline{I}_E$ is the lower approximation of its extent in I, $\underline{I_E}m \stackrel{\mathrm{df}}{=} \underline{Im_E} = \{g \mid [g]_E \subseteq Im\}$. The lower approximation of I is the greatest definable context contained in I. The extent of a subset of attributes $B \subseteq M$ with respect to the lower E-approximation is $B'_{\underline{I_E}} = \bigcap_{m \in B} \underline{I_E}m = \bigcap_{m \in B} \underline{Im_E} = \bigcap_{m \in B} \underline{Im}_E = \underline{B'_{I_E}}$.

There will be some controversy concerning which definition is better for the upper approximation of a formal context (an attribute-indexed collection of subsets of objects). The choices are as follows.

1. The stricter choice $\overline{B'_I}^E = \overline{\bigcap_{m \in B} Im}^E = \bigcup\{[g] \mid [g] \cap (\bigcap_{m \in B} Im) \neq \emptyset\}$ includes only those equivalence classes which contain an element of the extent intersection.

2. The freer choice $B'_{\overline{I}_E} = \bigcap_{m \in B} \overline{Im}^E = \bigcap_{m \in B} (\bigcup\{[g] \mid [g] \cap Im \neq \emptyset\})$ additionally includes those equivalence classes which contain elements in each individual extent, but do not contain an element in the combined extent intersection.

In this and the follow-up paper [2] we have chosen the freer definition, partly for better mathematical tractability, partly because it corresponds to direct existential image of contexts from formal concept analysis, and partly because it by itself has a valid semantics.

For any object $g \in G$ and any subset $B \subseteq M$, we say that g *certainly has* all attributes in B when $g \in B'_{\underline{I_E}} = \underline{B'_{I_E}}$, and that g *possibly has* all attributes in B when $g \in B'_{\overline{I}_E} \supseteq \overline{B'_I}^E$. There are three ordering relations for contexts: the *upper* (Smyth) *order* $I \leq^u J$ iff $\overline{I}^E \subseteq \overline{J}^E$, the *lower* (Hoare) *order* $I \leq^l J$ iff $\underline{I_E} \subseteq \underline{J_E}$, and the *rough* (Milner) *order* $I \leq J$ iff $I \leq^l J$ and $I \leq^u J$ iff $\underline{I_E} \subseteq \underline{J_E}$ and $\overline{I}^E \subseteq \overline{J}^E$. Two contexts $\langle G, M, I \rangle$ and $\langle G, M, J \rangle$ of G-objects and M-attributes are E-*roughly equal*, denoted by $I \equiv J$, when both $I \leq J$ and $J \leq I$. The rough order $\leq$ is only a preorder: it is reflexive and transitive, but it is not necessarily antisymmetric. To make the rough order into a partial order and to change rough equality into true equality, we must "quotient out" by rough equality. A *rough formal context* in $\langle G, E \rangle$ is a collection of roughly equal formal contexts of G-objects and M-attributes; or, equivalently, a rough context is a collection of formal contexts of G-objects and M-attributes which have the same upper and lower approximation contexts. Any quadruple $\langle G, E, M, I \rangle$, consisting of a formal context $\langle G, M, I \rangle$ and an approximation space $\langle G, E \rangle$ on its set of objects, is regarded to be the rough formal context consisting of all contexts roughly equal to I.

3 Rough Formal Concepts

In this section we define the notions of "approximation" and "rough equality" with respect to formal concepts.

Let $\langle G, E \rangle$ be any approximation space on objects G and let $\langle G, M, I \rangle$ be any formal context between the same objects and some set of attributes M. A formal concept $(A, B) \in \mathcal{B}\langle G, M, I \rangle$ is a *definable concept* when its extent $A \subseteq$

G is a definable subset of objects w.r.t. indiscernibility relation E. All concepts of a definable formal context are definable formal concepts. Let $\langle G, M, I \rangle$ be any formal context with an approximation space $\langle G, E \rangle$ on objects. We wish to approximate concepts in $\mathcal{B}\langle G, M, I \rangle$ in terms of E-definable concepts. We do this *externally* in terms of concepts of the upper and lower approximation contexts of I — two E-definable formal contexts. Just as for subsets and contexts, we use two notions for approximating concepts.

[**Upper E-approximation**] The *upper E-approximation* of a concept $(A, B) \in \mathcal{B}\langle G, M, I \rangle$ is the concept $\overline{(A, B)}^E \in \mathcal{B}\langle G, M, \overline{I}^E \rangle$ defined by $\overline{(A, B)}^E = (B'_{\overline{I}^E}, B''_{\overline{I}^E})$. The upper E-approximation assignment map is a monotonic function $\overline{(\,)}^E$, which assigns concepts in the upper approximation concept lattice $\mathcal{B}\langle G, M, \overline{I}^E \rangle$ to concepts in $\mathcal{B}\langle G, M, I \rangle$.

[**Lower E-approximation**] The *lower E-approximation* of a concept $(A, B) \in \mathcal{B}\langle G, M, I \rangle$ is the concept $\underline{(A, B)}_E \in \mathcal{B}\langle G, M, \underline{I}_E \rangle$ defined by $\underline{(A, B)}_E = (B'_{\underline{I}_E}, B''_{\underline{I}_E})$. The lower E-approximation assignment map is a monotonic function $\underline{(\,)}_E$, which assigns concepts in the lower approximation concept lattice $\mathcal{B}\langle G, M, \underline{I}_E \rangle$ to concepts in $\mathcal{B}\langle G, M, I \rangle$.

Upper approximation assignment is left adjoint to a lower-join operator $\overline{(\,)}^E \dashv \bigvee_E$ defined by $\bigvee_E(A, B) \overset{df}{=} \bigvee\{(A_1, B_1) \in \mathcal{B}\langle G, M, I \rangle \mid A_1 \subseteq A\}$ for all concepts $(A, B) \in \mathcal{B}\langle G, M, \overline{I}^E \rangle$. Hence, upper approximation assignment is a join-preserving monotonic function. Lower approximation assignment is right adjoint to an upper-meet operator $\bigwedge_E \dashv \underline{(\,)}_E$ defined by $\bigwedge_E(A, B) \overset{df}{=} \bigwedge\{(A_1, B_1) \in \mathcal{B}\langle G, M, I \rangle \mid A \subseteq A_1\}$ for all concepts $(A, B) \in \mathcal{B}\langle G, M, \underline{I}^E \rangle$. Hence, lower approximation assignment is a meet-preserving monotonic function.

Just as for subsets and contexts, there are three ordering relations for concepts: for any two formal concepts $C_1 = (A_1, B_1)$ and $C_2 = (A_2, B_2)$, the *upper (Smyth) order* $C_1 \leq^u C_2$ iff $\overline{C_1}^E \subseteq \overline{C_2}^E$, the *lower (Hoare) order* $C_1 \leq^l C_2$ iff $\underline{C_1}_E \subseteq \underline{C_2}_E$, and the *rough (Milner) order* $C_1 \leq C_2$ iff $C_1 \leq^l C_2$ and $C_1 \leq^u C_2$ iff $\underline{C_1}_E \subseteq \underline{C_2}_E$ and $\overline{C_1}^E \subseteq \overline{C_2}^E$. Two concepts C_1 and C_2 of a formal context $\langle G, M, I \rangle$ are *E-roughly equal*, denoted by $C_1 \equiv C_2$, when both $C_1 \leq C_2$ and $C_2 \leq C_1$. Again the rough order $\leq$ is only a preorder. To make the rough order into a partial order and to change rough equality into true equality, we must "quotient out" by rough equality. A *rough concept* of a formal context $\langle G, M, I \rangle$ with approximation space $\langle G, E \rangle$ is a collection of roughly equal concepts; or, equivalently, a rough concept is a collection of concepts which have the same upper and lower conceptual approximations. Rough concepts for E-definable contexts are crisp, since concepts of E-definable contexts are roughly equal iff they are precisely equal.

4   Example

In Table 1 is an example of a formal context called the Living context. This formal context is concerned with a simple ecological description of some living

incidence relation									
	nw	lw	ll	nc	2lg	1lg	mo	lb	sk
Le	x	x					x		
Br	x	x					x	x	
Fr	x	x	x				x	x	
Dg	x		x				x	x	x
SW	x	x		x		x			
Rd	x	x	x	x		x			
Bn	x		x	x	x				
Mz	x		x	x		x			

object set	
Le	Leech
Br	Bream
Fr	Frog
Dg	Dog
SW	Spike-Weed
Rd	Reed
Bn	Bean
Mz	Maize

attribute set	
nw	needs water
lw	lives in water
ll	lives on land
nc	needs chlorophyll
2lg	2 leaf germination
1lg	1 leaf germination
mo	is motile
lb	has limbs
sk	suckles young

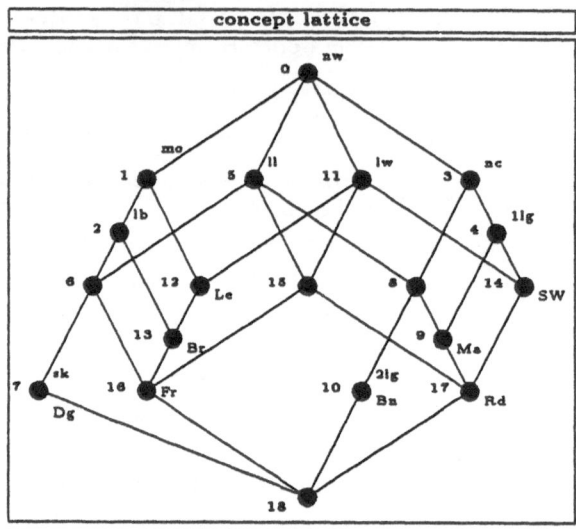

concept lattice

Table 1: the **Living formal context and its concept lattice**

organisms. Although somewhat simplistic, it is quite useful for illustrative purposes. This was one of several formal contexts presented in a seminar by Rudolf Wille at the University of Arkansas in 1992. It was originally taken from an Hungarian children's television show. We provide a rough conceptual analysis of the Living context in this paper. Table 1 also contains the concept lattice for the Living context. The 19 formal concepts of the Living context $\{B_0, B_1, \ldots, B_{18}\}$ represented by indices in Table 1, include the top formal concept B_0 representing "all Living organisms", the bottom formal concept B_{18} with "no Living organisms", and formal concepts such as B_6 representing "limbed land organisms" whose intent consists of the attributes "needs water", "is motile", "has limbs" and "lives on land", and whose extent consists of the organisms "Dog" and "Frog".

$$\{\{\text{Leech}, \text{Bream}, \text{Frog}\}, \{\text{Dog}\}, \{\text{Spike-Weed}, \text{Reed}\}, \{\text{Bean}, \text{Maize}\}\} \quad (1)$$

Partition 1 is an example of an indiscernibility relation which forms an approximation space on the objects of the Living context in Table 1. This indiscernibility relation is determined by the two conditions "lives in water" and

upper approximation									
$\overline{I}^E$	nw	lw	ll	nc	2lg	1lg	mo	lb	sk
Le	x	x	x				x	x	
Br	x	x	x				x	x	
Fr	x	x	x				x	x	
Dg	x		x				x	x	x
SW	x	x	x	x		x			
Rd	x	x	x	x		x			
Bn	x		x	x	x	x			
Mz	x		x	x	x	x			

lower approximation									
$\underline{I}_E$	nw	lw	ll	nc	2lg	1lg	mo	lb	sk
Le	x	x					x		
Br	x	x					x		
Fr	x	x					x		
Dg	x		x				x	x	x
SW	x	x		x		x			
Rd	x	x		x		x			
Bn	x		x	x					
Mz	x		x	x					

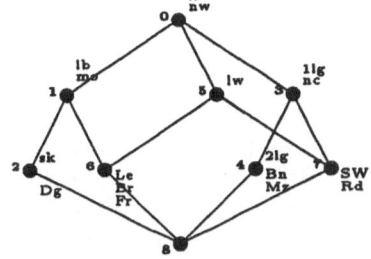 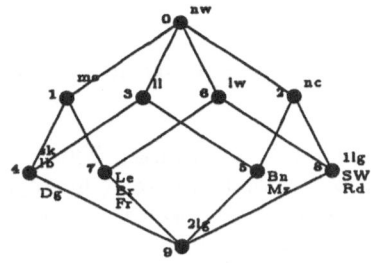

Table 2: the upper and lower approximations of the Living formal context

"needs chlorophyll" — for example, {Bean, Maize} are those Living organisms which do not "live in water" but do "need chlorophyll". The upper and lower approximation contexts with respect to this indiscernibility relation, are displayed in Table 2. Note that the attributes "needs water", "lives in water", "needs chlorophyll", "is motile", and "suckles young" are all definable attributes. Clearly, mutually indiscernible objects are equivalent in the two approximation tables in Table 2, and can be replaced by their equivalence class, [Fr] = {Leech, Bream, Frog}, [Dg] = {Dog}, [Rd] = {Spike-Weed, Reed}, and [Bn] = {Bean, Maize}. The concept lattices for the two approximation contexts of Table 2 are also displayed there.

In Table 3 we list the two assignment maps: the upper approximation conceptual assignment and the lower approximation conceptual assignment. These define two conceptual indiscernibility relations — the conceptual indiscernibility of possibility defined as the kernel of the upper approximation conceptual assignment, and the conceptual indiscernibility of necessity defined as the kernel of the lower approximation conceptual assignment. In Table 3 we use the notation $\overline{B}_i$ for concepts in the upper approximation concept lattice, and we use the notation $\underline{B}_i$ for concepts in the lower approximation concept lattice. Rough equality is the meet of the possibility and necessity conceptual indiscernibility relations. The only distinct roughly equal concepts are

$$B_2 \equiv B_6 \quad \text{and} \quad B_{13} \equiv B_{16}.$$

Consider the concept "limbed animals", which is indexed by B_2 in the original context, where it has extent "Bream", "Frog" and "Dog" (a "Bream" is a European fresh-water fish related to the Carp), and intent "needs water", "is

254

upper approximation assignment		
indiscernibility of possibility		
$\{B_0, B_5\}$	$\mapsto$	$\overline{B}_0$
$\{B_1, B_2, B_6\}$	$\mapsto$	$\overline{B}_1$
$\{B_7\}$	$\mapsto$	$\overline{B}_2$
$\{B_3, B_4, B_8, B_9\}$	$\mapsto$	$\overline{B}_3$
$\{B_{10}\}$	$\mapsto$	$\overline{B}_4$
$\{B_{11}, B_{15}\}$	$\mapsto$	$\overline{B}_5$
$\{B_{12}, B_{13}, B_{16}\}$	$\mapsto$	$\overline{B}_6$
$\{B_{14}, B_{17}\}$	$\mapsto$	$\overline{B}_7$
$\{B_{18}\}$	$\mapsto$	$\overline{B}_8$

lower approximation assignment		
indiscernibility of necessity		
$\{B_0\}$	$\mapsto$	$\underline{B}_0$
$\{B_1\}$	$\mapsto$	$\underline{B}_1$
$\{B_3\}$	$\mapsto$	$\underline{B}_2$
$\{B_5\}$	$\mapsto$	$\underline{B}_3$
$\{B_2, B_6, B_7\}$	$\mapsto$	$\underline{B}_4$
$\{B_8\}$	$\mapsto$	$\underline{B}_5$
$\{B_{11}\}$	$\mapsto$	$\underline{B}_6$
$\{B_{12}\}$	$\mapsto$	$\underline{B}_7$
$\{B_4, B_{14}\}$	$\mapsto$	$\underline{B}_8$
$\{B_9, B_{10}, B_{13}, B_{15}, B_{17}, B_{18}, B_{19}\}$	$\mapsto$	$\underline{B}_9$

Table 3: **approximation assignments & conceptual indiscernibility**

motile" and "has limbs". This concept is indexed by $\overline{B}_1$ in the upper approximation context, where it has extent "Leech", "Bream", "Frog" and "Dog", and intent "needs water", "lives on land", "is motile" and "has limbs". This concept gains the object "Leech" in the upper approximation context, since "Leech" and "Frog" being indiscernibly equivalent, the object "Leech" possibly "has limbs" there. This concept gains the attribute "lives on land" in the upper approximation context, since the implication "has limbs" implies "lives on land" holds there. This concept is indexed by $\underline{B}_4$ in the lower approximation context, where it has extent only the object "Dog", and intent "needs water", "lives on land", "is motile", "has limbs" and "suckles young". This concept loses the objects "Bream" and "Frog" in the lower approximation context, since "Leech" and "Bream" being indiscernibly equivalent, the object "Bream" does not necessarily (certainly) "have limbs" (same for "Frog"). This concept gains the attributes "lives on land" and "suckles young" in the lower approximation context, since the implications "has limbs" implies "lives on land" and "has limbs" implies "suckles young" hold there.

In the crisp Living context of Table 1 the concept "limbed animals which live on land" indexed by B_6 is more specialized than the concept "limbed animals" indexed by B_2, and is distinguished from B_2 by the characteristic "lives on land". Since "Bream" is a fish and does not live on land, in the lower approximation context where "Bream" and "Frog" are indiscernible, it is not necessary (certain) that a "Frog" is a land dwelling organism. In this context "lives on land" is implied by "has limbs", and is no longer a distinguishing characteristic. Although "lives on land" serves as a distinguishing attribute for concepts B_2 and B_6 in the crisp Living context of Table 1, it no longer does in the rough setting of indiscernibility relation 1. By the same token, although the "lives on land" attribute distinguishes the object "Frog" from the objects "Leech" and "Bream" in the crisp Living context of Table 1, it cannot in the rough setting of indiscernibility relation 1 where these three objects are indiscernible.

Summary

This paper has introduced the new theory of Rough Concept Analysis, which is a synthesis of Rough Sets and Formal Concept Analysis. Rough Concept Analysis, which studies the rough approximation of conceptual structures, provides an "approximation theory" for knowledge representation and knowledge discovery. The notions of upper and lower approximations were extended from subsets of objects to formal contexts, which are viewed here as attribute-indexed collections of subsets of objects. Upper and lower formal approximation contexts were used to provide external notions of upper and lower approximation for formal concepts. Since these conceptual approximations were shown to be join and meet-preserving monotonic functions between concept lattices, a notion of rough conceptual join can be defined via upper approximation and a notion of rough conceptual meet can be defined via lower approximation. All of these notions were illustrated by a simple example concerning the ecology of Living organisms.

Data modeling with distributed constraints extends the notion of conceptual scaling in Formal Concept Analysis by combining it with notions from Entity-Relationship database modeling [1, 3]. Formal contexts have been shown to be special cases of distributed constraints (namely, single-sorted distributed constraints), whereas distributed constraints are interpretable via the notion of satisfaction in terms of formal contexts. In this model, formal concepts correspond to database relations, and conceptual meet corresponds to natural join. In the follow-up paper [2], I will develop contextual approximation in terms of contextual flow along description functions. Using this approach I will extend upper and lower approximation from formal contexts to distributed constraints. Then, rough formal concepts will correspond to rough database relations, and rough conceptual meet will correspond to rough natural join.

References

[1] R. Kent and J. Brady, "Formal Concept Analysis with Many-Sorted Attributes", *Proceedings of the 5th International Conference on Computing and Information*, Sudbury, Ontario, Canada, 1993.

[2] R. Kent, "Rough Concept Analysis with Constraints". An extension of the current paper, to be submitted for publication in the journal *Fundamenta Informaticae*, North Holland, Amsterdam.

[3] R. Kent and F. Vogt and R. Wille, "Data Modeling with Constraints" (unpublished). This paper is based upon a series of lectures given by the first author to the Research Group in Formal Concept Analysis at the Technische Hochschule in Darmstadt, Germany, in the summer of 1993, when the first author was on a guest researchership there.

[4] J. Lambek, "The Mathematics of Sentence Structure", *American Mathematical Monthly* 1958, vol. 65.

[5] Z. Pawlak, "Rough Sets", *International Journal of Information and Computer Science* 1982, vol. 11, pp. 341–356.

[6] R. Wille, "Restructuring Lattice Theory: An Approach Based on Hierarchies of Concepts", *Ordered Sets*, I. Rival ed., pp. 445–470, Reidel, Dordrecht-Boston, 1982.

Rough Approximate Operators: Axiomatic Rough Set Theory

T. Y. Lin

Mathematics and Computer Science Department
San Jose State University
San Jose, California 95192, U.S.A

Qing Liu

Department of Computer Science
Jiangxi University
NanChang, Jiangxi
P. R. China

Abstract

In rough set theory, the upper and lower approximations are defined in terms of equivalence relation. In this paper, the reverse problem is considered. Let H and L are two abstract operators acting on the power set of U, the universe of discourse. If the two operators satisfy six axioms, then there is an equivalence relation defined on U such that H(X) and L(X) are precisely the upper and lower approximations. The six axioms are adopted from the axioms of Kuratowski's closure operator. The proof is an easy application of point set topology. Similar results (five axioms) are also obtained for neighborhood systems (a generalized rough set theory) which are based on Frechet (V)spaces. The results can be viewed as a beginning of an axiomatic rough set theory.

1 Introduction

Pawlak introduced the notion of rough sets via equivalence relation. He derived many interesting properties of upper and lower approximation. In this paper, we are interested in the reverse problem. Namely, can we characterize the notion of rough sets in terms of those properties? Let U be the universe of discourse. Assume that there is a pair of abstract rough operators, which assigns every subset X of U a pair (H(X), L(X)) of subsets such that the pair satisfies some of those "equations and inequalities" in Sec 2.3 of [10]. Then the question is: Is there an equivalence relation on U such that H(X) and L(X) are the upper and lower approximations of Pawlak. In this paper, we answer the question affirmatively. The axioms are adopted from the axioms of Kuratowski's closure (and interior) operators [1].

2   Rough Sets

A binary relation is an equivalence relation iff it is reflexive, symmetric and transitive. Every equivalence relation determines a partition and vice versa. Let U be the universe of discourse. Let R be a given equivalence relation over U. The collection of all the equivalence classes is a set, it is called quotient set and denoted by U/R. There is a natural projection from U to U/R.

$$NQ : U \longrightarrow U/R.$$

defined by $NQ(u) = [u]$, where [u] is the equivalence class containing u.

For each X, we associate two subsets, upper and lower approximation:

L_APP(X)={u : [u] is a subset of X }
U_APP(X)= {u : [u] and X has non-empty intersection }

3   Frechet Spaces and Approximation

In modern mathematics, mathematicians generalize the concept of "distance" into the "neighborhood systems", and created the theory of topological space. There, the notion of "neighborhood" is the basic primitive of the whole theory. In his book, Sierpenski introduced a notion, called Frechet (V)space [12]. A Frechet (V)space is a space in which every point has a neighborhood system without any further axioms; in topological spaces, further axioms on the neighborhood systems are required (see [1]). Frechet (V)spaces are more general than topological spaces. However, we will, by abuse of language, refer to both as spaces; their meaning should be clear from the context. We should point out here that the notion of rough sets also gives rise to a topology on U [10], [5]. The topology , called Pawlak topology, is induced from an equivalence relation. In applications, we may need more general type of topology than Pawlak topology. The notion of neighborhood systems are introduced from other circumstances, nevertheless, it can be viewed as a generalized rough set theory [2], [3], [4], [5]. Intuitively neighborhood systems handle the notion of "close to", "analogous to", or "approximate to". Such notion usually is not a transitive relation. For example, San Jose is "close to" Palo Alto, and Palo Alto is "close to" San Francisco. However, San Jose is **not** "close to" San Francisco. In general, approximation is not an equivalence relation, so we often need some notion which is more general than rough sets.

Definition 3.1. A Frechet (V)space U is a set of elements, in which every element is assigned a neighborhood system without any further requirements [12]. Let $p \in U$. A neighborhood, denoted by N(p), of p is a subset of U, which contains the point p. A neighborhood system of p is a non- empty family of neighborhoods of p (the family could be a singleton). The family of all such neighborhood systems determines(and vice versa) a Frechet (V)topology for U. We will call this family the **Frechet topology,** F-topology, or simply topology of U when the context is clear.

Proposition 3.2. A topological space is a Frechet space, but not vice versa.

In the theory of topological spaces, one can define open sets in terms of neighborhood systems. Similar situation holds for Frechet space too. A set X is open if every point in X has a neighborhood that is contained in X. The complement of an open set is a closed set. We refer the readers to [12] for all the details.

Let U be a F-space or topological space, and X be a subset of U. Then, lower approximation of X in U is defined as

L_APP[X]= { p: there is an $N(p) \subseteq X$ } = interior of X

and the upper(higher)approximation of X in A is defined as

U_APP[X]= { p: $N(p) \cap X \neq \emptyset$ (emptyset) for every N(p)} = closure of X

Next, we will consider the interaction between rough sets and Frechet space.

4 Rough Operators and their Generalization

Let U be the universe of discourse. Let $C(X) = U \sim X$, the complement of X. Let P(U) be the power set of U. Let H and L be two mappings $P(U) \longrightarrow P(U)$. The two mappins, H and L, will be called rough approximate operators if H and L satisfy the following axioms:

(1) $H(\emptyset) = \emptyset$;   (1') $L(\emptyset) = \emptyset$;
(2) $H(X) \supseteq X$;   (2') $L(X) \subseteq X$;
(3) $H(X \cup Y)=H(X) \cup H(Y)$;   (3') $L(X \cap Y)=L(X) \cap L(Y)$;
(4) $H(X) = H(H(X))$;   (4') $L(X) = LL(X)$;
(5) $H(C(X)) = C(L(X))$;   (5') $L(C(X)) = C(HX))$;
(6) $H(X) = L(H(X))$;   (6') $L(X) = H(LX)$.

H is called the upper(higher) rough operator, and L the lower rough operator. Note that (5) or (5') can be treated as a definition for L or H respectively. So we may use the operator H or L alone.

(1") $H(\emptyset) = \emptyset$;
(2") $L(X) \subseteq X$;
(3") $H(X \cup Y)=H(X) \cup H(Y)$;
(4") $L(X) = L(L(X))$;
(5") $L(C(X)) = C(H(X))$;
(6") $L(X) = H(L(X))$

We note that (2') implies (1'). (2) can be derived from (2') and (5'). (3) implies (3'). (4) can be derived from (4') and (5'). (6) can be derived by (6') and (5'). So we obtained six axioms. These axioms will be called **Rough Set Axioms.** The pair of operators, H and L, will be called **Axiomatic Rough Set Theory** on U.

Theorem. For the pair of rough operators

$$X \longrightarrow (H(X), L(X))$$

which satisfy the axioms (1") through (6"), there is an equivalence relation such that

$$H(X) = U\_APP(X) \text{ and } L(X) = L\_APP(X).$$

Proof:Observe that the upper rough operator H satisfy Kuratowski's closure axiom [1], pp.43. So H defines a topology on U such that H(X) is the closure of X. The axiom (5) tells us that L is the interior operator of this topology. By (6), $L(X) = H(L(X))$, so L(X) is a closed set. Thus in this topology open sets are also closed, and vice versa. Next, let us consider the connected components. Each component is a closed set, and hence it is also open. So the set of connected components forms a decomposition of U. The decomposition induces an equivalence relation on U, and the collection of equivalence classes forms the base of this topology. So H(X), and L(X) is the upper and lower approximation of this equivalence relation. In other words,

$$H(X) = U\_APP(X) \text{ and } L(X) = L\_APP(X).$$

Q.E.D.

If (3) is reduced to a weaker form, namely

$$(3') \ H(X) \cup H(Y) \subseteq H(X \cup Y)$$

then the upper rough operators, denoted by GH and GL, will be called generalized rough operators. We will show below that GH defines a neighborhood system, or equivalently, a Frechet (V) space [12].

Theorem. For the pair of generalized rough operators

$$X \longrightarrow (GH(X), GL(X))$$

which satisfy the axiom (1) (2), (3'), and (4) through (6), there is a neighborhood system such that

$$GH(X) = U\_APP(X) = \text{the closure of } X \text{ and}$$
$$GL(X) = L\_APP(X) = \text{the interior of } X.$$

Proof: There is a Kuratowski type theorem for Frechet (V)space [12], pp 8. So the Axioms (1), (2), (3'), (4) for GH define a Frechet space on U such that GH(X) is the closure of Frechet space. By (6), it is clear that GL(X) is the interior point of X. This completes the proof.

5 Conclusion

Rough set theory has been axiomatized by abstract operators. The axiomatization will increase the applicability of rough set theory. In applications, the information about the indiscernibility relation is often unavailable. We are considering to extend the abstract operators to the predicates (of first-order logic calculus). Such consideration will lead us to a new formal formulation of "rough reasoning". (e.g., [9]). We will report our new findings in the near future.

260

References

[1] John Kelly, (1955), *General Topology*, Van Nostrand.

[2] T.Y. Lin and S. Bairamian, (1987), *Neighborhood systems and Goal Queries*, Manuscript, California State University, Northridge.

[3] T. Y. Lin, (1988), *Neighborhood Systems and Relational Database*, Proceedings of CSC '88.

[4] T. Y. Lin, (1989), *Neighborhood Systems and Approximation in Database and Knowledge Base Systems*, Proceedings of the Fourth International Symposium on Methodologies of Intelligent Systems, Poster Session.

[5] T. Y. Lin, Qing Liu, K. J. Huang and W. Chen, (1990), *Rough Sets, Neighborhood Systems and Approximation*, Fifth International Symposium on Methodologies of Intelligent Systems, Selected Papers.

[6] Qing Liu and K.J. Huang, T.Y. Lin, (1990), *A Model of Topological Reasoning Expert System with Application to an Expert System for Computer-Aided Diagnosis and Treatment in Acupuncture and Moxibustion*, International Symposium on Expert Systems and Neural Network Theory and Application.

[7] T.Y. Lin, (1992), *A topological and Fuzzy Rough Sets, Intelligent Decision Support*, Kluwer Academic Publishers, Boston, Chapter 5, Part II. edited by Slowinski.

[8] T. Y. Lin and Quing Liu, (1993), *Rough Logic and Its applicaitons*.

[9] E. Orlowska, (1989), *Logic for reasoning about knowledge*, Zeitschrift fuer Mathematik 35, 559-572.

[10] Z. Pawlak, (1982), *Rough sets, Basic Notions*, Institute Comp.Sci.Polish Acad. Sci. rep. # 431, Warsaw, 1981, Also in Int. J. Computer and Information Sci. 11, 341-356.

[11] Z. Pawlak, (1991), *Rough sets, Theoretical Aspects of Reasoning about Data*, Kluwer Acdemic Publishers.

[12] Sierpenski, (1956), *General Topology*, University of Torranto Press.

Finding Reducts in Composed Information Systems

Marzena Kryszkiewicz

Institute of Computer Science, Warsaw University of Technology,
Nowowiejska 15/19, 00-665 Warsaw, Poland

Henryk Rybinski

Institute of Computer Science, Warsaw University of Technology,
Nowowiejska 15/19, 00-665 Warsaw, Poland

Abstract

A set-theoretical approach to finding reducts of composed information systems is presented. It is shown how the search space can be represented in form of a pair of boundaries. It is also shown, how reducts of composing information systems can be used to reduce the search space of the composed system. Presented solutions are implied directly from the properties of composed monotonic Boolean functions.

1   Introduction

The Rough Sets approach [8] has been conceived as a tool to conceptualize, organize and analyze various types of data, in particular, to deal with inexact, uncertain or vague knowledge in applications related to Artificial Intelligence. Over the period of last ten years the rough sets have been intensively studied and developed (see for example [8, 9, 1, 6, 7, 14, 15]), and by now many practical applications have been implemented based on Rough Sets Theory [5, 18]. More applications are reported in the books [10, 16].

The Pawlak's information system may be viewed as a "knowledge base" which is represented by examples. It is inductive by means that it provides tools for inducing general knowledge from the set of examples. A basic problem related to practical applications of the rough sets based knowledge representation systems (shortly RSKRS) is whether the whole set of attributes is really necessary to represent a given partition of the knowledge, and if not, how to determine the simplified and still sufficient knowledge representation equivalent to the original. Significant results in this area have been achieved by [15], where the methods of reducing the knowledge were studied. The problem of reducing the RSKRS (known as finding reducts) is transformable to the problem of finding minimal disjunctive normal form of a monotonic Boolean function.

The paper deals with the problem of finding reduced RSKRS in case when a number of knowledge representation systems is given and we want to integrate them into one RSKRS. The algorithm of finding the reducts is based on some properties of monotonic Boolean functions.

2   Information systems

Let us start with introducing basic notions dealing with information systems.

Basic notions

Information system is a pair $S = (\mathcal{O}, U)$, where
    U - is a non-empty, finite set of *attributes*,
    $\mathcal{O}$ - is a non-empty, finite set of *objects* described by the set of attributes U.

V_a will denote the *domain* of an attribute a.

Function $v_a : \mathcal{O} \to V_a$, assigns a value of the attribute $a \in A$ to every object from $\mathcal{O}$.

With any subset of attributes $A \subseteq U$ we associate a binary *indiscernibility relation IND(A)*, defined as follows:

$$IND(A) = \{(X, Y) \in \mathcal{O} * \mathcal{O} | a \in A, v_a(X) = v_a(Y)\}.$$

¿From the definition of *IND* we have:

i) $IND(A)$ is an equivalence relation,

ii) $IND(A) = \bigcap_{a \in A} IND(\{a\}).$

The family of all equivalence classes of the relation $IND(A)$ will be denoted by $U/IND(A)$.

An attribute $a \in A$ is called *superfluous* in A, if $IND(A) = IND(A \setminus \{a\})$, otherwise a is *indispensable* in A.

If all attributes $a \in A$ are indispensable in A, then A is called *orthogonal*.

A subset $A' \subseteq A$ is a *reduct* of A, iff A' is orthogonal and $IND(A) = IND(A')$. In other words reduct is a minimal subset of attributes that discerns all objects discernible by the whole set of attributes.

The set of all indispensable attributes in A will be called the *core* of A, and will be denoted $CORE(A)$.

We recall here an important relationship between the core and reducts:

$$CORE(A) = \bigcap_{R \in RED(A)} R,$$

where $RED(A)$ is the family of all reducts of A.

Now we introduce two notions of a difference between objects and a discernibility function that helps to express several properties and to construct efficient algorithms related to information systems, e.g. generation of core and reducts.

The measure of difference between two objects, let us say $X, Y \in \mathcal{O}$, for the set A of attributes, will be expressed by the *distance function* $\delta_A(X, Y)$:

$$\delta_A(X, Y) = \{a \in A | v_a(X) \neq v_a(Y)\}.$$

One can prove that $a \in CORE(A)$, if and only if there exist two objects which have the same value for each attribute from A except a. This statement may be expressed by means of distance between two objects:

Proposition 2.1 [15]

$$CORE(A) = \{a \in \delta_A(X, Y) | X, Y \in \mathcal{O}, card(\delta_A(X, Y)) = 1\}.$$

Below we introduce a Boolean function which we call *discernibility function* and denote by Δ. First, to each attribute $a \in A$ we assign a Boolean variable "a". Then, provided $\delta_A(X, Y) \neq \emptyset$, to the function $\delta_A(X, Y) = \{a_1, \dots, a_k\}$ we assign a Boolean function $a_1 \vee \dots \vee a_k$ which for simplicity we denote by $\Sigma \delta_A(X, Y)$. To $\delta_A(X, Y) = \emptyset$ we assign the Boolean constant 1. Finally, we define the (boolean) *discernibility function* $\Delta(A)$ as the formula:

$$\Delta(A) = \prod_{(X,Y) \in \mathcal{O}*\mathcal{O}} \Sigma \delta_A(X, Y).$$

Before discussing some properties of $\Delta(A)$, we recall general notions and theorems related to Boolean functions:

- a Boolean expression E is in *normal form* (*nf*), if E is composed only from Boolean variables and constants linked by operators of disjunction and conjunction;

- a Boolean expression E is in *conjunctive normal form* (*cnf*), if E is a conjunction of a number of disjuncts;

- a Boolean expression E is in *disjunctive normal form* (*dnf*), if E is a disjunction of a number of constituents, each of which is a conjunction;

- a Boolean expression E is in *minimal disjunctive normal form* (*mdnf*) if E is a *dnf*-formula that contains the least number of disjunction constituents;

- $MDNF(f)$ will denote *mdnf*-form of the function f.

Theorem 2.1 [2, 4]
A Boolean function f is non-decreasing, iff there exists nf-formula that describes f.

Theorem 2.2
Given non-decreasing Boolean functions f, g, we state that the function $h = f \wedge g$ satisfies
i) h is a non-decreasing Boolean function,
ii) $MDNF(h) = MDNF(MDNF(f) \wedge MDNF(g))$.

Let us define relative-absorption operator, $ABSREL$, on two formulas: f in cnf-form and g being a single constituent formula, as follows:
$ABSREL(f,g) = $ the formula constructed from f by removing all disjuncts absorbed by some variable from g.

Theorem 2.3
If f is a single constituent formula and $h = f \wedge g$, then
i) $MDNF(f) = f$,
ii) $MDNF(h) = MDNF(f \wedge MDNF(ABSREL(g, f)))$.

One can easily see that $\Delta(A)$ is in nf-form, and as such, it is non-decreasing (according to Theorem 2.1).

The following proposition establishes an important relationship between the minimal disjunctive normal form of the function $\Delta(A)$ and the set of all reducts of A.

Proposition 2.2 [15]
There exists an isomorphic mapping between all conjuncts in $MDNF(\Delta(A))$ and all reducts $RED(A)$.
Let us define

$$single_s(\delta_A(X, Y)) = \textbf{if } card(\delta_A(X, Y)) = 1 \textbf{ then } \delta_A(X, Y) \textbf{ else } \emptyset;$$

$$\overline{single}_s(\delta_A(X, Y)) = \textbf{if } card(\delta_A(X, Y)) = 1 \textbf{ then } \emptyset \textbf{ else } \delta_A(X, Y).$$

Now we can present $\Delta(A)$ as a conjunction of two functions:

$$\Delta(A) = Single(\Delta(A)) \wedge \overline{Single}(\Delta(A)), \text{ where}$$
$$Single(\Delta(A)) = \prod_{(X,Y) \in \mathcal{O} * \mathcal{O}} \Sigma single_s(\delta(X, Y)),$$
$$\overline{Single}(\Delta(A)) = \prod_{(X,Y) \in \mathcal{O} * \mathcal{O}} \Sigma \overline{single}_s(\delta_A(X, Y)).$$

It is obvious that $Single(\Delta(A))$ is a Boolean expression that corresponds to $CORE(A)$.

Theorem 2.2 allows us to compute minima of $\Delta(A)$ according to the equation below:
$$MDNF(\Delta(A)) = MDNF(MDNF(Single(\Delta(A))) \wedge MDNF(\overline{Single}(\Delta(A)))).$$

The problem of determining $MDNF(\Delta(A))$ (and, by this, finding all reducts of A) may be reduced to determining the formula:

$$MDNF(Single(\Delta(A)) \wedge MDNF(ABSREL(\overline{Single}(\Delta(A)), Single(\Delta(A))))).$$

3 Set-theoretical approach to the problem of finding reducts

To find all reducts of A we can (1) apply traditional method that transforms the initial formula to $MDNF(\Delta(A))$ using the absorption law or (2) we can invoke the algorithm [3] seeking for minimal solutions $MDNF(\Delta(A))$ in the search space $\mathcal{P}(\mathcal{U})$ in a depth-first manner.

In the paper we will concentrate on the latter approach. It is based on algebraic operations on family sets determining reducible search space. To this end, we will often consider the function $f_s : \mathcal{P}(U) \rightarrow B$, $U = \{a_1, \ldots, a_n\}$, instead of the function $f : B^n \rightarrow B$. A subscript s indicates that the argument of f_s is a set.

Let $m : \mathcal{P}(U) \rightarrow B^n$ denote isomorphic mapping such that

$$\forall A \in \mathcal{P}(U), \forall X \in B^n, a_i \in A \text{ iff } X_i = 1. \quad (3.1)$$

We assume that there is the following relationship beetwen f_s and f:

$$f_s(A) = f(X) \text{ if } X = m(A).$$

In the sequel, we also assume that any function f considered is non-decreasing (so f_s is also non-decreasing) and $f(1) = 1$ ($f_s(U) = 1$).

$\mathcal{MINS}(f_s)$ will denote now the family set that corresponds to $MDNF(f)$.

3.1 Set-theoretical notions

It is proved in [13] that a search space of a monotonic function $f_s : \mathcal{P}(U) \rightarrow B$ is of special type (which we call *fence*) and can be uniquely determined by a pair of subfamilies called *boundaries*. Among various boundaries there exists a unique *proper* pair of boundaries which are minimal family sets determining a given search space. Usually the cardinalities of the proper boundaries are significantly less than the cardinality of the lattice, which relaxes memory requirements. The algorithm presented in [3] operates on the proper boundaries instead of the whole initial search space. The boundaries are transformed in such a way that they always reduce the search space, restricting it only to those elements, for which the function values are yet unknown. So, instead of searching through the whole space, the algorithm performs manipulations on the boundaries, which consists of just elementary set-theoretical operations [12, 3]. The time cost of the algorithm is $O(k * n^2)$, where k is the number of all minimal solutions and $n = card(U)$.

Below the notions mentioned above are described more formally.

Definition 3.1 A family $\mathcal{F}$ in the lattice $\mathcal{P}(U)$ is a *fence* iff
$$\forall X \in \mathcal{P}(U), (\exists B, T \in \mathcal{F}, B \subseteq X \subseteq T) \Rightarrow X \in \mathcal{F} \qquad \square$$

One can note that for a fence $\mathcal{F}$ there exists at least one pair of families $\mathcal{B}$ and $\mathcal{T}$ such that
i) $\forall B \in \mathcal{B}, T \in \mathcal{T}, X \in \mathcal{P}(U), (B \subseteq X \subseteq T \Rightarrow X \in \mathcal{F})$
ii) $\forall X \in \mathcal{P}(U), (X \in \mathcal{F} \Rightarrow \exists B \in \mathcal{B}, T \in \mathcal{T}, B \subseteq X \subseteq T)$

Given a fence $\mathcal{F}$, families $\mathcal{B}$ and $\mathcal{T}$ satisfying the above conditions are called respectively *lower* and *upper* boundaries of $\mathcal{F}$. Any fence $\mathcal{F}$ is uniquely determined by its boundaries, therefore we will also write $\mathcal{F} = [\mathcal{B}, \mathcal{T}]$.

Among different pairs of boundaries there exists a pair of boundaries the cardinalities of which are minimal. Such pair of boundaries will be called *proper*.

Let $\mathcal{MIS}(\mathcal{F})$ mean a set of all the minimal elements in the family set $\mathcal{F}$ and $\mathcal{MAS}(F)$ - a set of all the maximal elements in $\mathcal{F}$.

The boundaries $\mathcal{B}$, $\mathcal{T}$ of the fence $\mathcal{F}$ are proper iff
$\mathcal{B} = \mathcal{MIS}(\mathcal{F})$ and $\mathcal{T} = \mathcal{MAS}(\mathcal{F})$.

It is obvious that $[\{\emptyset\}, \{U\}]$ are proper boundaries of $\mathcal{F} = \mathcal{P}(U)$.

3.2 Search space of conjunction of monotonic Booleon functions

Let $h_s : \mathcal{P}(U) \to B$ be an equivalent function to the function $h = f \wedge g$, where f, g - non-decreasing Boolean functions.

Now, let us reformulate Theorems 3.2 and 3.3 by means of set-theoretical notions:
Theorem 3.1

$$\mathcal{MINS}(h_s) = \mathcal{MIS}(\{Z | Z = X \cup Y, X \in \mathcal{MINS}(f_s), Y \in \mathcal{MINS}(g_s)\}).$$

Theorem 3.2
If f is a single constituent formula then
i) $card(\mathcal{MINS}(f_s)) = 1$,
ii) $\mathcal{MINS}(h_s) = \mathcal{MIS}(\{Z | Z = X \cup Y, X \in \mathcal{MINS}(fs),$
$$Y \in \mathcal{MINS}(ABSREL_s(g, f))\}).$$

Theorems 3.1, 3.2 show us how to compute $\mathcal{MINS}(h_s)$ if $\mathcal{MINS}(f_s)$ and $\mathcal{MINS}(g_s)$ are already computed. In such a case there is no need to look for minima in the search space.

Let us consider another case, when we only know minima of one of the two factor functions of h_s, let us say $\mathcal{MINS}(f_s)$, and still want to get to know the minima of h_s . Of course, we can start computing $\mathcal{MINS}(h_s)$ with the whole lattice $[\{\emptyset\}, \{U\}]$. However, if we are not really concerned about the minima of function g_s, we can directly look for $\mathcal{MINS}(h_s)$ in the search space $S = [\mathcal{MINS}(f_s), \{U\}]$. This is because $f_s(X) = 0$ for every $X \in \mathcal{P}(U) \setminus S$ and thus $h_s(X) = 0$, regardless of the function value $g_s(X)$.

All values returned by function f_s in S are equal to 1. Hence $h_s(X) = g_s(X)$ for all arguments $X \in S$. In other words, it is sufficient to compute only the values of g_s in S, while seeking for $\mathcal{MINS}(h_s)$.

The theorem below reflects our observations:

Theorem 3.3
Let $S = [\mathcal{MINS}(f_s), \{U\}]$. Then
i) $\mathcal{MINS}(h_s) \subseteq S$,
ii) $\mathcal{MINS}(h_s) = \mathcal{MINS}(g_s|_S)$,
where $g_s|_S$ is such a function that $g_s|_S(X) = g_s(X)$, for every $X \in S$.

3.3 Finding reducts

According to Proposition 2.2 there is an isomorphic mapping between all conjuncts in $\mathcal{MDNF}(\Delta(A))$ and all reducts $RED(A)$. Let us note that the function m (as in eq.3.1) is the required mapping and $RED(A) = \mathcal{MINS}(\Delta_s(A))$. Therefore, $RED(A)$ of an information system $S = (\mathcal{O}, U)$, $A \subseteq U$, may be found as $\mathcal{MINS}(\Delta_s(A))$ by searching through the whole space $[\{\emptyset\}, \{A\}]$. However, $\Delta(A)$ may be seen as the composition of $Single(\Delta(A))$ and $\overline{Single}(\Delta(A))$. Let us note that $\mathcal{MINS}(Single_s(\Delta(A))) = \{CORE(A)\}$. In such a case, the initial search space can be reduced to $S = [\{CORE(A)\}, \{A\}]$ and instead of $\Delta_s(A)$, the function $\overline{Single}_s(\Delta(A))$ (or the reduced function $ABSREL_s(\overline{Single}(\Delta(A)), Single(\Delta(A)))$) may be evaluated (see Theorems 3.2-3.3).

4 Composition of information systems

Specification of the problem

Now we are ready to raise our problem. Given information systems $S_1 = (\mathcal{O}_1, U_1)$ and $S_2 = (\mathcal{O}_2, U_2)$, and all their reducts $RED_1(A)$ and $RED_2(A)$, where $A \subseteq U_1$ and $A \subseteq U_2$, find reducts $RED(A)$ of the information system $S = (\mathcal{O}_1 \cup \mathcal{O}_2, U_1 \cup U_2)$. For the sake of simplicity, without loss of generality, we assume, that $A = U_1 = U_2$.

Let $\Delta_1(A)$, $\Delta_2(A)$ - be discernibility functions of S_1 and S_2 respectively. Thus:

$$\Delta_1(A) = \prod_{(X,Y) \in \mathcal{O}_1 * \mathcal{O}_1} \Sigma \delta_A(X, Y),$$

$$\Delta_2(A) = \prod_{(X,Y) \in \mathcal{O}_2 * \mathcal{O}_2} \Sigma \delta_A(X,Y).$$

Then $\Delta(A)$, as discernibility function of S, may be described by the Boolean formula:

$$\Delta(A) = \prod_{(X,Y) \cup \mathcal{O}_1 \cup \mathcal{O}_2 * \mathcal{O}_1 \cup \mathcal{O}_2} \Sigma \delta_A(X,Y) =$$

$$= \prod_{(X,Y) \in \mathcal{O}_1 * \mathcal{O}_1} \Sigma \delta_A(X,Y) \wedge \prod_{(X,Y) \in \mathcal{O}_2 * \mathcal{O}_2} \Sigma \delta_A(X,Y) \wedge$$

$$\prod_{(X,Y) \in \mathcal{O}_1 * \mathcal{O}_2} \Sigma \delta_A(X,Y) =$$

$$= \Delta_1(A) \wedge \Delta_2(A) \wedge \prod_{(X,Y) \in \mathcal{O}_1 * \mathcal{O}_2} \Sigma \delta_A(X,Y).$$

Let

$$\Delta_{1-2}(A) = \prod_{(X,Y) \in \mathcal{O}_1 * \mathcal{O}_2} \Sigma \delta_A(X,Y).$$

So, $\Delta(A) = (\Delta_1(A) \wedge \Delta_2(A)) \wedge \Delta_{1-2}(A)$.

Let us recall, that according to Proposition 2.2 we have
$RED_1(A) = \mathcal{MINS}(\Delta_{1s}(A))$ and $RED_2(A) = \mathcal{MINS}(\Delta_{2s}(A))$.

On the basis of Theorem 3.1 we can easily compute $\mathcal{MINS}((\Delta_1(A) \wedge \Delta_2(A))_s)$:

$$\mathcal{MINS}((\Delta_1(A) \wedge \Delta_2(A))_s) = \mathcal{MIS}(\{Z | Z = X \cup Y, \ X \in RED_1(A), \\ Y \in RED_2(A)\}).$$

Theorem 3.3 allows us to state that

1. all the minima of the function $\Delta_s(A)$ can be found in the search space
$S = [\mathcal{MINS}((\Delta_1(A) \wedge \Delta_2(A))_s), \{A\}]$,

2. in the search process of $\mathcal{MINS}(\Delta_s(A))$ in S, one can evaluate function $\Delta_{1-2s}(A)$ instead of more complex function $\Delta_s(A)$.

The search space for finding $\mathcal{MINS}(\Delta_s(A))$ may be even more restricted (and by this the search time decreased) if we notice that
$\Delta_{1-2}(A) = Single(\Delta_{1-2}(A)) \wedge \overline{Single}(\Delta_{1-2}(A))$.
So, $\Delta(A) = ((\Delta_1(A) \wedge \Delta_2(A)) \wedge Single(\Delta_{1-2}(A))) \wedge \overline{Single}(\Delta_{1-2}(A))$.

We have from Theorem 3.2:
$\mathcal{MINS}(((\Delta_1(A) \wedge \Delta_2(A)) \wedge Single(\Delta_{1-2}(A)))_s) =$
$\quad \mathcal{MINS}(\{Z | Z = X \cup Y, X \in Single_s(\Delta_{1-2}(A)),$
$\quad Y \in \mathcal{MINS}(ABSREL_s(\Delta_1(A) \wedge \Delta_2(A), Single(\Delta_{1-2}(A))))\}).$

Finally, using Theorem 3.2-3.3 we can conclude:

1. all the minima of the function $\Delta(A)$ one can find in the search space $\mathcal{S} = [\mathcal{MINS}(((\Delta_1(A) \wedge \Delta_2(A)) \wedge Single(\Delta_{1-2}(A)))_s), \{A\}]$,

2. in the search process of $\mathcal{MINS}(\Delta_s(A))$ in $\mathcal{S}$, the algorithm may evaluate function $\overline{Single}(\Delta_{1-2s}(A))$ (or the reduced function $ABSREL_s(\overline{Single}(\Delta_{1-2}(A)), Single(\Delta_{1-2}(A))))$ instead of $\Delta_s(A)$.

5 Examples

Example 5.1

Let us consider the information system $\mathcal{S} = (\mathcal{O}, U)$, where $U = \{a, b, c, d, e, f\}$ and objects $\mathcal{O}$ are described in Table 5.1. Each row represents information (values of attributes) on one object $O \in \mathcal{O}$.

U	a	b	c	d	e	f
1	-1	1	1	1	1	0
2	1	0	-1	-1	-1	1
3	1	-1	-1	-1	0	1
4	0	-1	-1	0	-1	1
5	1	-1	-1	-1	-1	0
6	0	1	-1	0	1	1

Table 5.1

Let $A = \{a, b, c, d, e\}$. In Table 5.2 we place appropriate $\delta_A(X, Y)$, for every $X, Y \in \mathcal{O}$.

U	1	2	3	4	5	6
1						
2	a,b,c,d,e					
3	a,b,c,d,e	b,e				
4	a,b,c,d,e	a,b,d	a,d,e			
5	a,b,c,d,e	b	e	a,d		
6	a,c,d	a,b,d,e	a,b,d,e	b,e	a,b,d,e	

Table 5.2

Then:
$$\Delta(A) = (a \vee b \vee c \vee d \vee e)(a \vee c \vee d)(b \vee e)(a \vee b \vee d)b(a \vee b \vee d \vee e)(a \vee d \vee e)e(a \vee d).$$
Thus:
$$MDNF(\Delta(A)) = abe + bde$$
and hence
$$\mathcal{MINS}(\Delta_s(A)) = RED(\Delta(A)) = \{\{a, b, e\}, \{b, d, e\}\}.$$

The above minima were found in the search space $[\{\emptyset\}, \{A\}]$.

According to Theorem 3.3, since $\Delta(A) = Single(\Delta(A)) \wedge \overline{Single}(\Delta(A))$ and $Single(\Delta(A)) = be$ (and by this $CORE(A) = \{b, e\}$) we can restrict the search space to $S = [\{\{b, e\}\}, \{A\}]$ and evaluate the function

$\overline{Single}(\Delta(A)) =$
$(a \vee b \vee c \vee d \vee e)(a \vee c \vee d)(b \vee e)(a \vee b \vee d)(a \vee b \vee d \vee e)(a \vee d \vee e)(a \vee d)$

or better the reduced function

$$ABSREL(\overline{Single}(\Delta(A)), Single(\Delta(A))) = (a \vee c \vee d)(a \vee d)).$$

instead of the function $\Delta(A)$.

Hence $\mathcal{MINS}(\Delta_s(A)) = \mathcal{MINS}(\overline{Single}_s(\Delta(A))|s) = \{\{a, b, e\}, \{b, d, e\}\}$.

Example 5.2

For the information system $S = (\mathcal{O}, U)$ as presented in the previous example we consider now two arbitrary information subsystems: $S_1 = (\mathcal{O}_1, U)$ and $S_2 = (\mathcal{O}_2, U)$, such that $\mathcal{O}_1 \cup \mathcal{O}_2 = \mathcal{O}$. Tables 5.3 and 5.4 represent S_1 and S_2 respectively. To receive the reducts of the information system S we use now the reducts of the information subsystems S_1 and S_2.

U	a	b	c	d	e	f
1	-1	1	1	1	1	0
2	1	0	-1	-1	-1	1
3	1	-1	-1	-1	0	1

Table 5.3

U	a	b	c	d	e	f
4	0	-1	-1	0	-1	1
5	1	-1	-1	-1	-1	0
6	0	1	-1	0	1	1

Table 5.4

In Tables 5.5, 5.6 we provide the appropriate values of the discernibility function $\delta_A(X, Y)$ between objects described in S_1 and S_2 respectively. Table 5.7 contains the values of $\delta_A(X, Y)$, where $X \in \mathcal{O}_1$ and $Y \in \mathcal{O}_2$.

U	1	2	3
1			
2	a,b,c,d,e		
3	a,b,c,d,e	b,e	

Table 5.5

U	4	5	6
4			
5	a,d		
6	b,e	a,b,d,e	

Table 5.6

U	1	2	3
4	a,b,c,d,e	a,b,d	a,d,e
5	a,b,c,d,e	b	e
6	a,c,d	a b,d,e	a,b,d,e

Table 5.7

$\Delta_1(A) = (a \vee b \vee c \vee d \vee e)(b \vee e),$
$\Delta_2(A) = (a \vee d)(b \vee e)(a \vee b \vee d \vee e),$
$\Delta_{1-2}(A) = (a \vee b \vee c \vee d \vee e)(a \vee c \vee d)(a \vee b \vee d)b(a \vee b \vee d \vee e)(a \vee d \vee e)e.$

$MDNF(\Delta_1(A)) = b \vee e$ thus $RED_1(A) = \{\{b\}, \{e\}\},$
$MDNF(\Delta_2(A)) = ab \vee ae \vee bd \vee de$ thus $RED_2(A) = \{\{a, b\}, \{a, e\}, \{b, d\},$
                                                             $\{d, e\}\}.$

Finally,

$\mathcal{MINS}((\Delta_1(A) \wedge \Delta_2(A))_s) =$
$\quad = \mathcal{MIS}(\{\{a, b\}, \{b, d\}, \{b, d, e\}, \{a, b, e\}, \{d, e\}\}) =$
$\quad = \{\{a, b\}, \{b, d\}, \{d, e\}\}.$

In order to find $\mathcal{MINS}(\Delta_s(A))$, the algorithm may be run that performs some evaluation of $\Delta_{1-2}(A)$ for arguments from the search space
$\mathcal{S} = [\{\{a, b\}, \{b, d\}, \{d, e\}\}, \{A\}].$

As a result we achieve: $\mathcal{MINS}(\Delta_s(A)) = RED(A) = \{\{a, b, e\}, \{b, d, e\}\}.$

A faster way of finding $\mathcal{MINS}(\Delta_s(A))$, when $RED_1(A)$ and $RED_2(A)$ are already known, is as follows:
$Single(\Delta_{1-2}(A)) = be.$ Hence $\mathcal{MINS}(Single_s(\Delta_{1-2}(A))) = \{b, e\}.$
$\overline{Single}(\Delta_{1-2}(A)) = (a \vee b \vee c \vee d \vee e)(a \vee c \vee d)(a \vee b \vee d)(a \vee b \vee d \vee e)(a \vee d \vee e).$
$ABSREL(\overline{Single}_{1-2}(\Delta(A)), Single_{1-2}(\Delta(A))) = (a \vee c \vee d).$

So,
$\mathcal{MINS}(((\Delta_1(A) \wedge \Delta_2(A)) \wedge Single(\Delta_{1-2}(A)))_s) =$
$\quad = \mathcal{MINS}(\{Z | Z = \{b, e\} \cup Y, Y \in \{\{\{a, b\}, \{b, d\}, \{d, e\}\}) =$
$\quad = \{\{a, b, e\}, \{b, d, e\}\}.$

From Theorems 3.2-3.3 we have:

1. all the minima of the function $\Delta(A)$ can be found in the search space
$\mathcal{S} = [\{\{a, b, e\}, \{b, d, e\}\}, \{A\}],$

2. in the search process of $\mathcal{MINS}(\Delta_s(A))$ in S, the algorithm may evaluate function $(a \wedge c \wedge d)$ instead of $\Delta(A)$.

Finally,

$$\mathcal{MINS}(\Delta_s(A)) = \mathcal{MINS}(\overline{Single}(\Delta_{1-2s}(A))|_S) = \{\{a,b,e\},\{b,d,e\}\}.$$

6   Conclusions

A non-standard method of finding minimal disjunctive normal form of the Boolean function was proposed. The presented algorithm searches for all minima through the reduced search space S in such a way that S never indicates elements for which the function value is known or can be deduced when applying properties of monotonic Boolean functions. The search space is represented effectively by means of boundaries. The narrowing of S is performed by means of algebraic operations on boundaries.

Having considered properties of a discernibility function of information system and discernibility functions of its subsystems, we were able to point out how reducts of subsystems might be used in seeking for reducts of the whole information system. Conclusions are implied directly from properties of composed monotonic Boolean functions.

References

[1] J. Grzymala-Busse, On the Reduction of Knowledge Representation Systems, **Proc. of the 6-th International Workshop on Expert Systems and their Applications**, Avignon, France, April 28-30, 463-478

[2] B. Korzan, Basic notions of graph theory and networks, Methods and Applications (The book in Polish), WNT, Warsaw, 1978

[3] M. Kryszkiewicz, H. Rybinski, An Algorithm Searching for Minimal Acceptable Solutions of a Monotonic Boolean Function, **Archiwum Informatyki Stosowanej i Teoretycznej**, 1992

[4] C. Lee Samuel, Modern Switching Theory and Digital Design, Prentice-Hall, Inc., Englewood Cliffs, New Jersey, 1978

[5] A. Mrozek, Rough Sets and Some Aspects of Expert Systems Realization, **Proc. 7-th Internat. Workshop on Expert Systems and their Applications**, Avignon, France, 597-611

[6] E. Orlowska, Z. Pawlak, Expressive Power of Knowledge Representation Systems, **International Journal of Man-Machine Studies**, vol.20, 485-500, 1984

[7] E. Orlowska, Z. Pawlak, Representation of Nondeterministic Information, **Theoretical Computer Science**, vol.29, 27-39, 1984

[8] Z. Pawlak, Information Systems - Theoretical Foundations, **Information Systems**, vol.6, 205-218, 1981

[9] Z. Pawlak, Rough Sets, **International Journal of Information and Computer Science**, vol.11, 344-356, 1982

[10] Z.Pawlak, Rough Sets, Theoretical Aspects of Reasoning about Data, Kluwer Academic Publishers, v. 9, 1991

[11] E.N. Reingold, J. Nievergelt, Deo N. Combinatorial Algorithms. Theory and Practice, Prentice-Hall (1977)

[12] S. Romanski, Operations on Families of Sets for Exhaustive Search, Given a Monotonic Boolean Function, **Proc. 3rd Int'l Conf. on Data and Knowledge Bases**, Jerusalem, Israel, June 28-30, 1988

[13] S. Romanski, An Algorithm Searching for the Minima of Monotonic Boolean Function and its Applications, Ph.D. Thesis, Warsaw University of Technology, 1989

[14] A. Skowron, An Approach to Synthesis of Decision Algorithms in Interaction with Knowledge Bases and Environment. An Example Bases on Some Glaucoma Processes (in cooperation with Medical Center in Warsaw), manuscript pp. 1-173, Warsaw. 1990

[15] A. Skowron, C. Rauszer, The Discernibility Matrices and Functions in Information Systems, Institute of Computer Science Reports, 1/91, Warsaw University of Technology, 1991

[16] R. Slowinski, Intelligent Decision Support, **Handbook of Applications and Advances of the Rough Sets Theory**, Kluwer Academic Publishers, v.11, 1992

[17] R.E. Tarjan, Depth first search and linear graph algorithms, **SIAM J.Comput** 1972 1, 146-160

[18] W. Ziarko, Acquisition of Design Knowledge from Examples, **Math., Comput. Modeling**, vol.10, 551-554

PRIMEROSE:
Probabilistic Rule Induction Method Based on Rough Set Theory

Shusaku Tsumoto and Hiroshi Tanaka

Department of Informational Medicine

Medical Research Institute,Tokyo Medical and Dental University

1-5-45 Yushima, Bunkyo-ku Tokyo 113 Japan

TEL: +81-3-3813-6111 (6159) FAX: +81-3-5684-3618

E-mail:{tsumoto, tanaka}@tmd.ac.jp

Abstract

Automated knowledge acquisition is an important research issue in machine learning. There have been proposed several methods of inductive learning, such as ID3 family and AQ family. These methods are applied to discover meaningful knowledge from large database, and their usefulness is in some aspects ensured. However, in most of the cases, their methods are of deterministic nature, and reliability of the acquired knowledge is not evaluated statistically, which makes these methods ineffective when applied to the domain of essentially probabilistic nature, such as medical one. Extending concepts of rough set theory to probabilistic domain, we introduce a new approach to knowledge acquisition, which induces probabilistic rules based on rough set theory(PRIMEROSE) and develop a program that extracts rules for an expert system from clinical database, using this method. The results show that the derived rules almost correspond to those of medical experts.

1 Introduction

One of the most important problems in developing expert systems is knowledge acquisition from experts. While there have been developed a lot of knowledge acquisition tools to simplify this process, it is still difficult to automate this process. In order to resolve this problem, many methods of inductive learning, such as induction of decision trees [1, 10], AQ method [7, 8] and rough set theory [9], are introduced and applied to discover knowledge from large database, and their usefulness is in some part ensured. However, their methods are of the deterministic nature, and, in most of the cases, the acquired knowledge is not evaluated statistically. Therefore they are not applicable in their present form to probabilistic domain, such as medical domain.

Extending the concepts of rough set theory to probabilistic domain, we introduce a new approach to knowledge acquisition, which we call Probabilistic Rule Induction MEthod based on ROugh SEt theory(PRIMEROSE) and develop a program that is based on this method to extract rules for an expert system from clinical database. It is applied to three medical domains:

headache and facial pain, where one of the authors previously developed an expert system,called RHINOS(Rule-based Headache and facial pain INformation Organizing System), meningitis, and cerebrovascular diseases. The results show that the derived rules almost correspond to those of medical experts.

The paper is organized as follows: in section 2, we mention about some problems of original rough set model. Section 3 presents our new method, PRIMEROSE for induction of RHINOS-type rules. Section 4 gives experimental results. Finally, in section 5, we mention about Ziarko's related work, Variable Precision Rough Set Model.

2 Problems of Consistent Rules based on Rough Sets

Rough set theory clarifies set-theoretic characteristics of the classes over combinatorial patterns of the attributes. These characteristics of rough set theory are precisely discussed in [9, 11, 13].

However, there are also the following problems when we apply the method to inductive learning for real-world domain: 1) When the numbers of samples or attributes are huge, computational cost is very high. 2) This method does not provide statistical evaluation of the derived rules. That is, we cannot evaluate bias, or the degrees of overfitting of the induced rules. Moreover, this method does not give how to evaluate *a priori* probability of the classes, while experts know this kind of knowledge, such as the frequency of each disease. It is also critical information for diagnosis. 3)In the original work, rules are induced only when an indiscernible set is a subset of positive region. However, it is too strict in real world, especially in probabilistic domain. In fact, it is possible that these positive regions might be too narrow. Therefore when we apply rough set theory to automated knowledge acquisition, the following extensions are required: 1) For rule induction, it is insufficient to consider only the rules covering positive region. We have to focus also on the possible region. A positive region is thought to be a specific subset of a possible region. 2) We need introduce some measures to evaluate statistical characteristics. In the next section, we introduce a new program for automated knowledge acquisition which adds the above two features to the basic rough set theory.

3 PRIMEROSE

3.1 Definition of Probabilistic Rules

We extend the definition of consistent rules to probabilistic domain. For this purpose, we use the definition of inclusive rules which Matsumura[5] introduce for the development of a medical expert system, RHINOS(Rule-based Headache and facial pain INformation Organizing System). This inclusive rule is formulated in terms of rough set theory as follows:

Definition 1 (Definition of Probabilistic Rules) *Let R_i be an equivalence relation and D denotes a set whose elements belong to one class and which is a subset of U. A probabilistic rule of D is defined as a tuple, $< D, R_i, SI(R_i, D),$ $CI(R_i, D) >$ where R_i, SI, and CI are defined as follows.*

R_i is a conditional part of a class D and defined as:

$$R_i \quad s.t. \quad [x]_{R_i} \bigcap D \neq \phi$$

SI and CI are defined as:

$$SI(R_i, D) = \frac{card\ \{([x]_{R_i} \cap D) \bigcup ([x]_{R_i}^c \cap D^c)\}}{card\ \{[x]_{R_i} \bigcup [x]_{R_i}^c\}}$$

$$CI(R_i, D) = \frac{card\ \{([x]_{R_i} \cap D) \bigcup ([x]_{R_i}^c \cap D^c)\}}{card\ \{D \bigcup D^c\}}$$

where D^c or $[x]_{R_i}^c$ consists of unobserved future cases of a class X or those which satisfies R_i, respectively. □

A total rule of D is given by $R = \bigvee_i R_i$, and then total CI(tCI) is defined as: $tCI(R, D) = CI(\bigvee_i R_i, D)$. In the following subsection, we discuss about an extension of reduction and the estimation of SI and CI. Since SI and CI include unobserved cases, it is necessary to estimate these measures only from training samples. For this estimation, we introduce cross-validation method.

3.2 SI and CI Estimation

If unobserved cases are expected to be much larger than training samples, then the above formulae can be approximated as follows:

$$SI(R_i, D) \approx \frac{card\ [x]_{R_i}^c \cap D^c}{card\ [x]_{R_i}^c}$$

$$CI(R_i, D) \approx \frac{card\ [x]_{R_i}^c \cap D^c}{card\ D^c}$$

Note that SI is approximately equal to the accuracy of classification for unobserved cases. Since the above formulae include unobserved cases, we are forced to estimate these measures from the training samples. For this purpose, we introduce cross-validation method to generate "pseudo-unobserved" cases from these samples as shown in the next subsection.

3.3 Cross-Validation Method

Cross-validation method for error estimation is performed as follows: first, the whole training samples $\mathcal{L}$ are split into V blocks: $\{\mathcal{L}_1, \mathcal{L}_2, \cdots, \mathcal{L}_V\}$. Second, repeat for V times the procedure in which we induce rules from the training samples $\mathcal{L} - \mathcal{L}_i (i = 1, \cdots, V)$ and examine the error rate err_i of the rules using $\mathcal{L}_i$ as test samples. Finally, we derive the whole error rate err by averaging err_i over i, that is, $err = \sum_{i=1}^{V} err_i / V$ (this method is called V-fold cross-validation). Therefore we can use this method for estimation of CI and SI by replacing the calculation of err by that of CI and SI, and by regarding test samples as unobserved cases.

The main problems of cross-validation are how to choose the value of V and high variability of estimates, or large mean squared errors of the cross-validation

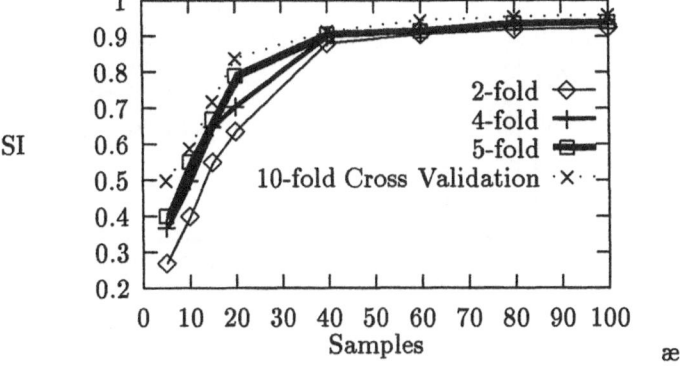

Figure 1: Relation between Accuracy(SI),Training Samples, and Fold

estimates. For the first problem, as the value of V increases, estimates get closer to apparent ones and the variance grows to be smaller. Here we show the result of an experiment in Figure 1 which illustrates the former phenomenon. We use 100 cases of headache as training samples and perform the cross-validation 100 times, and compare the average and the variance of accuracy(averaged SI) and CI. Both of them approach to one as the number of fold increases. On the contrary, the variances decrease. Therefore the choice of V depends on our strategy. If it is desirable to avoid the overestimation of SI and CI, we can safely choose 2-fold cross-validation, whose estimators are asymptotically equal to predictive estimators for completely new pattern of data as shown in [2, 3]. However, variabilities tend to be higher in this case. To reduce this disadvantage, recently, repeated cross-validation method is introduced[1, 12]. In this method, cross-validation methods are executed repeatedly(safely, 100 times), and estimates are averaged over all the trials. Figure 2 illustrates this advantage. In this figure, we plot the relation between the standard deviation of error rates and the number of trials using the above same training samples. Above 100 trials, each variance is almost stable. For precise information about these problems and methods, please refer to [1, 12]. Since our strategy is to avoid the over estimation and the high variabilities, we adopt repeated 2-fold cross-validation method in this paper.

3.4 Cluster-based Reduction of Knowledge

In this subsection, we extend the concept of reduction to probabilistic domain. Instead of consistency-based reduction, we delete an attribute when the deletion does not make SI change. First, we define a primitive cluster.

Definition 2 (a Primitive Cluster) *Let the set of whole attributes denote* $E = \{a_k\}$, *whose cardinality is equal to p. And let* $|R_i|$ *denote the number of*

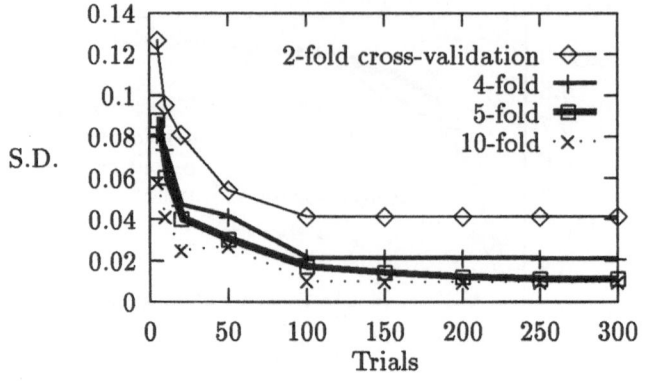

Figure 2: Comparison of standard deviation(S.D.) of error rate(SI)

the attributes included in the relation R_i. A primitive cluster is defined as:

$$Prim_{R_i}(X) = \bigcap_{k}^{p}[x]_{[a_k=v_k]} = [x]_{R_i}$$

such that $|R_i| = p$ and $[x]_{R_i} \cap X \neq \phi$ where v_i denotes the value of an attribute "a_i" □

We also define the partial order of relation R_i. Let $A(R_i)$ denote the set whose elements are the attributes included in R_i. If $A(R_i) \subseteq A(R_j)$, then we represent this relation as $R_i \preceq R_j$.

Using these notations, we define cluster-based reduction method as follows:

Definition 3 (Cluster-based Reduction of Knowledge)
*If an attribute **a** is satisfied with the following equation:*

$$Poss_{R_i-\{a\}}(X) = Poss_{R_i}(X) = Prim_R(X) \quad (R_i \preceq R, |R| = p)$$

then we say that **a** is dispensable in R_i, and **a** can be deleted from R_i. □

This knowledge reduction technique deletes dependent variables which does not change the possible region. That is, the possible region of each relation is invariant over this process, which means that we fix the probabilistic nature of the indiscernible set. We discuss the advantage of this method in Section 6. Note that this definition includes deterministic cases where SI is always equal to one. That is, an indiscernible set of a rule whose SI is equal to one corresponds to the positive region of a class.

3.5 Algorithm for PRIMEROSE

Algorithms for rule induction can be derived by embedding rough set theory concept into the algorithms discussed in Section 2. An algorithm for induction of inclusive rules is described as follows:

1)Using all attributes, calculate all equivalent relation $\{R_i\}$ which covers all of the training samples, that is, calculate $\{R_i | \bigcup[x]_{R_i} = U\}$.

2)For each class D_j, collect all the equivalent relation R_i such that $[x]_{R_i} \cap D_j \neq \phi$. For each combination, calculate its possible region.

3)Calculate $SI(R_i, D_j)$.

4)Apply probabilistic reduction of knowledge to each relation R_i until SI is changed(Minimize the components of each relation). If several candidates of minimization are derived, connect each with disjunction.

5)Collect all the rules, perform the cross-validation method to estimate utCI for each D_j.

4 Results

We develop a system for PRIMEROSE and implement it in a program of Prolog. PRIMEROSE are applied to headache(RHINOS's domain), meningitis, and cerebrovascular diseases, whose precise information is given in Table 1. These data are incomplete, and include many inconsistencies. Experimental results

Table 1: Information of Databases

Domain	Samples	Classes	Attributes
headache	232	10	20
meningitis	198	3	25
CVD	261	6	27

are shown in Table 2. For estimation of SI and CI,we use repeated 2-fold cross-validation(100 trials). In each row of CART,we assign the numbers of leaves to the column of those of rules, and the numbers of nodes to the column of those of conditions. The results of CART are those after pruning.

5 Related Works

We extend rough set theory into probabilistic domain, and introduce a new approach to acquire knowledge which is almost equal to that of medical experts. This kind of learning method is useful in the case where each rule can be constructed as a set of manifestations. In this section, we discuss about the differences between PRIMEROSE and Ziarko's Variable Precision Rough Set model.

Variable Precision Rough Set Model(VPRS) is a probabilistic generalization of rough set model which Ziarko independently introduces[14]. Using this model, Katzberg and Ziarko apply this model to the field of the steel industry[4].

This model focuses on boundary region which cannot be classified by original rough set model. Ziarko introduces **precision** β and allows for some degree of misclassification in the largely correct classification. This means that the elements of boundary region nearer to the positive region are included in the

Table 2: Experimental Results

Domain	Method	Rules	Conditions	Accuracy	Experts' Accuracy
headache	CART	11	40	72.5%	95%
(116/116)	AQ15	19	38	62.4%	
	PRIMEROSE	25	70	89.6%	
meningitis	CART	9	25	74%	99%
(100/98)	AQ15	14	26	75%	
	PRIMEROSE	20	55	85%	
CVD	CART	13	47	72.6%	90%
(137/124)	AQ15	12	26	71.0%	
	PRIMEROSE	15	35	82.5%	

(A/B) denotes (Training samples/Test samples).

β-lower approximation $\underline{R}^{\beta} X$. Therefore VPRS also uses our possible region for rule induction, although our model is based on primitive cluster, which appears in training samples.

Interestingly, although defined region is probabilistic, this generalized model inherits all basic mathematical properties of the original model. Hence VPRS complements the rough set model as a methodological tool for rule induction in probabilistic domain.

However, this model left one problem unsolved. Although precision is pre-defined, the induced results may not reflect "real" precision level. For example, we induce rules from training samples by precision $\beta = 0.1$. Then the accuracy of rules is also derived by this precision level. However, when we get some new samples, the accuracy will be higher than this level. So it is desirable to estimate the bias of precision. For this purpose, our repeated cross-validation method may be used. Such kind of estimation is also important problems in probabilistic rule induction.

6 Conclusion

We introduce a new approach to knowledge acquisition, PRIMEROSE, and develop a program based on this method to extract rules for an expert system from clinical database. It is applied to three medical domains. The results show that the derived rules almost correspond to those of the medical experts. We are studying formulation of our approach in terms of matroid theory. In future work, we will introduce some common framework of machine learning methods based on matroid theory and rough set theory.

Acknowledgements

The authors would like to thank Wojciech Ziarko and Nitin Indurkhya for giving them some comments on the manuscript. This research is supported by Grants-in-Aid for Scientific Research No.04229105 from the Ministry of Education,

Science and Culture in Japan.

References

[1] Breiman, L., Freidman, J., Olshen, R., and Stone, C., *Classification And Regression Trees.* Belmont, CA: Wadsworth International Group, 1984.

[2] Efron, B., Estimating the error rate of a prediction rule: improvement on cross validation. *J. Amer. Statist. Assoc.* **78**, 316-331, 1983.

[3] Efron, B., How biased is the apparent error rate of a prediction rule ? *J. Amer. Statist. Assoc.* **82**, 171-200, 1986.

[4] Katzberg, J.D. and Ziarko, W. Variable Precision Rough Sets with Asymmetric Bounds, *Proceedings of RSKD-93,*in this issue.

[5] Matsumura, Y., et al., Consultation system for diagnoses of headache and facial pain: RHINOS, *Medical Informatics*, **11**, 145-157, 1986.

[6] McLachlan, G.J., *Discriminant Analysis and Statistical Pattern Recognition,* John Wiley and Sons, New York, 1992.

[7] Michalski, R.S., A Theory and Methodology of Machine Learning. Michalski, R.S., Carbonell, J.G. and Mitchell, T.M., *Machine Learning - An Artificial Intelligence Approach*, Morgan Kaufmann, Palo Alto, CA, 1983.

[8] Michalski, R.S., et al. The Multi-Purpose Incremental Learning System AQ15 and its Testing Application to Three Medical Domains, in: *Proceedings of AAAI-86*, 1041-1045, AAAI Press, Palo Alto, CA, 1986.

[9] Pawlak, Z., *Rough Sets*, Kluwer Academic Publishers, 1991.

[10] Quinlan, J.R., Induction of decision trees, *Machine Learning*, **1**, 81-106, 1986.

[11] Slowinski, K. et al., Rough sets approach to analysis of data from peritoneal lavage in acute pancreatitis, *Medical Informatics*, **13**, 143-159, 1988.

[12] Walker, M.G. and Olshen, R.A., Probability Estimation for Biomedical Classification Problems. *Proceedings of SCAMC-92*, McGrawHill, New York, 1992.

[13] Ziarko, W., The Discovery, Analysis, and Representation of Data Dependencies in Databases, in:*Knowledge Discovery in Database*, Morgan Kaufmann, Palo Alto, CA, pp.195-209, 1991.

[14] Ziarko, W., Variable Precision Rough Set Model, *Journal of Computer and System Sciences*, **46**, 39-59, 1993.

Comparison of Machine Learning and Knowledge Acquisition Methods of Rule Induction Based on Rough Sets

Dobroslawa M. Grzymala-Busse and Jerzy W. Grzymala-Busse
Department of Electrical Engineering and Computer Science, University of Kansas
Lawrence, KS 66045, U. S. A.

Abstract

The main objective of this work is to evaluate the usefulness of the machine learning approach to knowledge acquisition. A series of experiments was done to check the quality of rule sets induced by the LERS system, which has four options; two of them represent the machine learning approach and the remaining two represent the knowledge acquisition approach. The six real-life data sets were modified to simulate incomplete knowledge. As a result it is clear that machine learning options performed much worse than knowledge acquisition options.

The final conclusion is that machine learning methods used so far for rule induction in knowledge acquisition should be replaced by other methods of rule induction that will generate complete sets of rules. Knowledge acquisition options of LERS are examples of such appropriate ways of inducing rules for building knowledge bases.

1 Introduction

One of the most important and difficult steps of the process of building an expert system is *knowledge acquisition* [1, 2, 3]. It is the responsibility of the *knowledge engineer* to acquire and organize the knowledge in such a way that the knowledge base is as complete and effective as possible. The sources of knowledge are experts, books, personal experience, data bases, and so on. The most popular technique of knowledge acquisition is still based on an interview of the human domain expert by the knowledge engineer. The key to knowledge acquisition by interviewing is the interaction between the knowledge engineer and the human expert. As a result of interviewing, the knowledge engineer produces *rules* in the form **if then**, first in plain English, later on in the form accepted by a computer program. Rules are elementary units of knowledge. Rules are stored in the knowledge base, called a *rule base*. The corresponding expert system is called *ruled-based expert system*.

The way an expert system performs depends mostly on the quality of its knowledge base. The knowledge base is of high quality if it can still come up with a decision even though values of only some attributes are given, i.e., when available information is incomplete.

In order to simplify interviewing, which is manual, expensive, potentially incorrect, and time-consuming, a variety of computerized methods have been developed [4]. Among them are interactive and learning-based techniques. The former is represented by techniques that help the knowledge engineer in building the knowledge base, while the latter is a fully automated method of building the knowledge base by *machine learning* [1, 5, 6]. In recent years the mainstream of machine learning has been inductive learning. Inductive learning may be categorized as *learning from examples* and *learning from observation*. Learning from examples is practically the only method of machine learning used in expert systems [7]. For the sake of simplicity, in the rest of the paper learning from examples will be called machine learning. Machine learning represents a specific method of building the knowledge base. It provides the knowledge base only with sufficient knowledge, while knowledge acquisition looks for a full spectrum of knowledge. In terms of rule-based systems, it means that machine learning is focused on inducing a sufficient number of rules, while the knowledge acquisition approach to building the rule base should induce all potential rules that can be induced. Hence, we distinguish the machine learning approach and the knowledge acquisition approach in rule induction. There exist machine learning systems that induce some redundant rules [8], but these systems still represent the machine learning approach.

Although it seems obvious that expert systems using rule sets induced by machine learning methods should not perform well because many potential rules that could be induced from the original data are missing, so far no comparative research has been done to document that machine learning methods used for knowledge acquisition are far from perfect. Research in this direction was the main objective of this work.

In this paper two options of LERS are used as examples of machine learning methods. The choice of LERS as a machine learning system is irrelevant to the objective of this research since any machine learning method induces a rule set that is a subset of all potential rules hidden in the original data set. The selection of the rule set by a machine learning method depends on the specific bias of the method.

2 The LERS System

The fundamental goal of learning from examples lies in inducing rules or decision trees from examples. The set of examples is presented by a *decision table*, exemplified by Table 1. Each example in the decision table is characterized by *attributes* and a *decision*. The following parameters are attributes: Solar_Energy, ENSO_Index, Volcanic_Activity, Residual_CO2, while Temperature is the decision.

The system LERS (Learning from Examples based on Rough Sets) consists of options of machine learning from examples and two options of knowledge acquisition [9]. Machine learning options are LEM1 and LEM2. They produce a sufficient set of rules to cover all examples in the decision table. Knowledge acquisition options are called All Global Coverings and All Rules. Both of them usually produce much bigger sets of rules from the input data given by a decision table.

LERS is able to deal with uncertainty in the input decision table as well. The main cause of uncertainty is missing values of attributes or inconsistent examples.

Table   1

Year	Solar_ Energy	ENSO_ Index	Volcanic_ Activity	Residual_ CO2	Temperature
1990	70..120	-0.75..1.5	70..100	1.5..2	medium
1989	70..120	-0.75..1.5	40..70	1.5..2	low
1988	20..70	-3..-0.75	40..70	1..1.5	high
1987	20..70	-3..-0.75	70..100	0.5..1	high
1986	70..120	-0.75..1.5	40..70	1.5..2	medium
1985	20..70	-0.75..1.5	40..70	1..1.5	low
1984	20..70	-0.75..1.5	70..100	1..1.5	low
1983	20..70	-3..-0.75	70..100	1.5..2	high
1982	70..120	-0.75..1.5	70..100	0.5..1	medium

Missing attribute values are due to lack of information or result from the situation where we do not care what the attribute value is. Rough set theory, introduced in the early 1980's [10], is especially useful for dealing with inconsistencies. This approach to uncertainty does not need any preliminary or additional information about data.

First LERS tests the input data for consistency. If data are inconsistent then lower and upper approximations of each concept are computed [9]. Now the user has an option to choose between two machine learning options and two knowledge acquisition options. If a machine learning option is used then the system induces a single minimal discriminant description for each concept. If a knowledge acquisition option is applied a complete set of rules is induced. In both cases local and global approaches may be chosen.

In the case of local options of LERS the system induces certain and possible rules from lower and upper approximation for each concept respectively.

In the case of global options of LERS new partitions on the set U are computed. Say that the original decision table described k concepts, i.e., decision has k values. Then $2k$ new partitions on U, called *substitutional partitions*, are created. Each substitutional partition has exactly two blocks, the first block is either lower or upper approximation of the concept, the second block is the complement of the first block. Substitutional partitions computed from lower approximations are called *lower substitutional partitions*; substitutional partitions computed from upper approximations are called *upper substitutional partitions*. Decisions, corresponding to lower and upper partitions, are called *lower* and *upper substitutional decisions*.

2.1   LEM1 (Single Global Covering Method)

A single global covering method using procedure LEM1 allows the system LERS to compute minimal discriminant description of the concept. This procedure employs the following ideas [9].

Let A denote the set of all attributes and let d denote a lower or upper substitutional decision. A *global covering* of $\{d\}$ is a subset P of A such that $\{d\}$

depends on *P* and *P* is minimal in *A*. LEM1 computes first a global covering of {*d*} and then computes rules using linear dropping conditions [9].

For the decision table from Table 1, LEM1 induced the following certain rules:

(Solar_Energy, 70..120) & (Volcanic_Activity, 70..100) -> (Temperature, medium),
(ENSO_Index, −0.75..1.5) & (Solar_Energy, 20..70) -> (Temperature, low),
(ENSO_Index, −3..−0.75) -> (Temperature, high),

and the following possible rules:

(Solar_Energy, 70..120) -> (Temperature, medium),
(ENSO_Index, −0.75..1.5) & (Volcanic_Activity, 40..70) -> (Temperature, low),
(ENSO_Index, −0.75..1.5) & (Solar_Energy, 20..70) -> (Temperature, low),
(ENSO_Index, −3..−0.75) -> (Temperature, high).

2.2 LEM2 (Single Local Covering Method)

The single local covering method, called LEM2, represents the machine learning approach. The rules generated are minimal because they do not induce unnecessary conditions. The following ideas are employed for LEM2. Let *B* be a lower or upper approximation of a concept represented by a decision-value pair (*d*, *w*). Set B *depends on a set* T of attribute-value pairs if and only if

$$\emptyset \neq \bigcap_{(q,\,v)\in T} [(q,\,v)] \subseteq B,$$

where [(*q*, *v*)] is the set of all examples that for attribute *q* have value *q*. Let $\mathbb{T}$ be a non-empty collection of non-empty sets of attribute-value pairs. Then $\mathbb{T}$ is a *local covering of B* if and only if the following conditions are satisfied:

(1) for each member *T* of $\mathbb{T}$, *B* depends on *T* and *T* is minimal,

(2) $\bigcup_{T\in\mathbb{T}} [T] = B$, and

(3) $\mathbb{T}$ is minimal, i.e., $\mathbb{T}$ has the smallest possible number of members.

The algorithm LEM2 is based on computing a single local covering for each of the concepts from the decision table.

For the decision table presented in Table 1, the set of all induced rules is presented below. Certain rules, induced by LEM2, are

(Solar_Energy, 70..120) & (Volcanic_Activity, 70..100) -> (Temperature, medium),
(Residual_CO2, 1..1.5) & (ENSO_Index, −0.75..1.5) -> (Temperature, low),
(ENSO_Index, −3..−0.75) -> (Temperature, high),

and possible rules are

(Solar_Energy, 70..120) -> (Temperature, medium),
(ENSO_Index, −0.75..1.5) & (Volcanic_Activity, 40..70) -> (Temperature, low),
(Residual_CO2, 1..1.5) & (Volcanic_Activity, 70..100) -> (Temperature, low),
(ENSO_Index, −3..−0.75) -> (Temperature, high).

2.3 All Global Coverings Method

All Global Coverings method represents the knowledge acquisition approach to rule induction. First the set ℝ of all global coverings for every lower and upper substitutional partition of {*d*}* is discovered and next by using the exponential dropping condition [9], rules are induced.

For the decision table presented in Table 1, certain rules induced by All Global Coverings option of the system LERS are:

(Solar_Energy, 70..120) & (Volcanic_Activity, 70..100) -> (Temperature, medium),
(ENSO_Index, –0.75..1.5) & (Residual_CO2, 0.5..1) -> (Temperature, medium),
(ENSO_Index, –0.75..1.5) & (Volcanic_Activity, 70..100) &
(Residual_CO2, 1.5..2) -> (Temperature, medium),
(Solar_Energy, 20..70) & (ENSO_Index, –0.75..1.5) -> (Temperature, low),
(ENSO_Index, –0.75..1.5) & (Residual_CO2, 1..1.5) -> (Temperature, low),
(ENSO_Index, –3..–0.75) -> (Temperature, high),

and possible rules are

(Solar_Energy, 70..120) -> (Temperature, medium),
(ENSO_Index, –0.75..1.5) & (Residual_CO2, 1.5..2) -> (Temperature, medium),
(ENSO_Index, –0.75..1.5) & (Residual_CO2, 0.5..1) -> (Temperature, medium),
(Solar_Energy, 20..70) & (ENSO_Index, –0.75..1.5) -> (Temperature, low),
(Solar_Energy, 70..120) & (Volcanic_Activity, 40..70) -> (Temperature, low),
(ENSO_Index, –0.75..1.5) & (Volcanic_Activity, 40..70) -> (Temperature, low),
(ENSO_Index, –0.75..1.5) & (Residual_CO2, 1..1.5) -> (Temperature, low),
(Volcanic_Activity, 40..70) & (Residual_CO2, 1.5..2) -> (Temperature, low),
(Volcanic_Activity, 70..100) & (Residual_CO2, 1..1.5) -> (Temperature, low),
(ENSO_Index, –3..–0.75) -> (Temperature, high).

2.4 All Rules Method

All Rules method is another knowledge acquisition approach to rule induction. All rules that can be induced from decision table are actually induced. For every concept, represented by a decision-value pair, the lower and upper approximations are computed. Then rules are induced directly from the decision tables, where the original decision is replaced by lower and upper substitutional decisions. Thus, for each rule, the number of conditions is equal to the number of attributes. But final form of induced rules is minimal due to dropping condition process that is used as the last step of the algorithm. For the decision table presented in Table 1, the set of all induced rules is presented below. Certain rules, induced by All Rules option of the system LERS are

(Residual_CO2, 0.5..1) & (ENSO_Index, –0.75..1.5) -> (Temperature, medium),
(Residual_CO2, 0.5..1) & (Solar_Energy, 70..120) -> (Temperature, medium),
(Solar_Energy, 70..120) & (Volcanic_Activity, 70..100) -> (Temperature, medium),
(Residual_CO2, 1.5..2) & (ENSO_Index, –0.75..1.5) &
(Volcanic_Activity, 70..100) -> (Temperature, medium),

(Residual_CO2, 1..1.5) & (ENSO_Index, −0.75..1.5) -> (Temperature, low),
(Residual_CO2, 1..1.5) & (Volcanic_Activity, 70..100) -> (Temperature, low),
(ENSO_Index, −0.75..1.5) & (Solar_Energy, 20..70) -> (Temperature, low),
(ENSO_Index, −3..−0.75) -> (Temperature, high),
(Residual_CO2, 0.5..1) & (Solar_Energy, 20..70) -> (Temperature, high),
(Residual_CO2, 1.5..2) & (Solar_Energy, 20..70) -> (Temperature, high),

and possible rules are

(Solar_Energy, 70..120) -> (Temperature, medium),
(Residual_CO2, 1.5..2) & (ENSO_Index, −0.75..1.5) -> (Temperature, medium),
(Residual_CO2, 0.5..1) & (ENSO_Index, −0.75..1.5) -> (Temperature, medium),
(Residual_CO2, 1.5..2) & (Volcanic_Activity, 40..70) -> (Temperature, medium),
(Residual_CO2, 1..1.5) & (ENSO_Index, −0.75..1.5) -> (Temperature, low),
(Residual_CO2, 1.5..2) & (Volcanic_Activity, 40..70) -> (Temperature, low),
(Residual_CO2, 1..1.5) & (Volcanic_Activity, 70..100) -> (Temperature, low),
(ENSO_Index, −0.75..1.5) & (Solar_Energy, 20..70) -> (Temperature, low),
(ENSO_Index, −0.75..1.5) & (Volcanic_Activity, 40..70) -> (Temperature, low),
(Solar_Energy, 70..120) & (Volcanic_Activity, 40..70) -> (Temperature, low),
(ENSO_Index, −3..−0.75) -> (Temperature, high),
(Residual_CO2, 0.5..1) & (Solar_Energy, 20..70) -> (Temperature, high),
(Residual_CO2, 1.5..2) & (Solar_Energy, 20..70) -> (Temperature, high).

3   Experiments

Six real-life data sets were used for experiments. The data set BANK was created at
the New York University School of Business. Data were collected in 1968 and
present either bankrupt or non-bankrupt firms. The data sets BREAST (breast
cancer), LYMPHOGRAPHY, and TUMOR (primary tumor) were obtained from the
Institute of Oncology of the University Medical Center at Lubljana, Slovenia. The
data set HOUSE represents 1984 United States Congressional Voting Records. The
data set SOYA (also called *small soybean data*) was donated to the machine learning
community by R. M. Michalski (Illinois University).

Our experiments, done on the computers VAX 9000 under VMS and DEC 5000
under UNIX, were designed to check usefulness of rule sets induced by different
options of LERS for applications in the expert system area.

In practice expert systems are forced to make decisions under uncertainty. We
tested how expert systems performance will differ when decisions are made under
incomplete information. That means that values of some attributes are not given.
It was simulated here by checking rule sets, induced from the same input data, by all
four methods, against modified data sets. The modification was accomplished by
deleting from the original data set one single attribute ($x = 1$), two attributes ($x = 2$),
and three attributes ($x = 3$).

In case $x = 1$ every single attribute was deleted from the original data set, one
attribute at a time. In this way for the original data set n new modified data sets
were created, where n is the number of attributes.

In case $x = 2$ every combination of two attributes was deleted (thus, for the

Table   2

	x	LEM1	LEM2	All Global Coverings	All Rules
BANK	1	24.54	24.54	23.64	7.58
	2	50.61	50.61	49.70	25.30
	3	74.39	74.39	73.93	53.33
BREAST	1	24.12	25.17	9.26	4.25
	2	45.46	48.60	23.07	12.58
	3	63.10	67.48	40.77	24.83
HOUSE	1	10.08	9.51	0.54	0.51
	2	20.79	19.39	1.60	1.38
	3	32.52	29.43	3.43	2.77
LYMPHOGRAPHY	1	6.83	10.70	0	0
	2	17.88	22.13	0.009	0.009
	3	26.70	32.30	0.057	0.057
SOYA	1	4.07	3.46	0	0
	2	7.95	6.79	0	0
	3	11.50	10.00	0	0
TUMOR	1	21.48	24.68	5.67	3.57
	2	38.77	43.38	11.88	7.96
	3	52.67	57.59	18.82	13.39

original data set $n * (n - 1)/2$ new modified data sets were created).

In case $x = 3$, a number of triples of attributes, selected randomly, were deleted from the original data set. For each such triple a new modified data set was created. For practical reasons, the total number of modified data sets was kept below 600.

Each of the rule sets induced from the input data set was checked against a modified data set. This was done by Rule Checker, which is a special tool of LERS. Table 2 presents error rates for all experiments.

4   Conclusions

The main, general objective for this work was to study how to improve a knowledge base that is a part of an expert system. Performance of an expert system depends to a great degree on the quality of its knowledge base. Thus it is crucial that the quality of the knowledge base be high. The most important issue is that the knowledge contained in the knowledge base be as complete as possible.

The practical objective of this work was to compare the quality of rule sets obtained using the machine learning approach with those obtained by the knowledge acquisition approach, having expert system application in mind.

Although the main objective of this work seems to be apparent, it should be noted that so far no research has been done to show that the machine learning approach, used for knowledge acquisition, is far from perfect. In current practice, the commercial systems of machine learning used in knowledge acquisition are mostly based on machine learning algorithm ID3 that induces only a small sufficient set of rules like LEM1 or LEM2.

In terms of LERS the most complete rule set is induced by the All Rules option. The original hypothesis was that the quality of rules induced by this option should be the highest. Rule sets induced by the All Global Coverings option should follow the lead. Rule sets induced by machine learning options LEM1 and LEM2 are the least complete and therefore should be of lower quality.

As follows from Table 2, the results of our experiments fully confirmed this hypothesis. It is clear that the smallest error rate is associated with rule sets induced by the All Rules option of LERS. Rule sets induced by the All Global Coverings option of LERS are worse in terms of error rate than those induced by All Rules and better than those induced by machine learning options LEM1 and LEM2.

The final conclusion is that machine learning methods used so far for rule induction in knowledge acquisition should be replaced by other methods that will generate complete sets of rules. Options All Global Coverings and All Rules are examples of such appropriate ways of inducing rules for building knowledge bases.

References

1. Addis T. R., Kodratoff Y., Lopez de Mantaras R., Morik K., and Plaza E. Panel: Four stances on knowledge acquisition and machine learning. In: Proceedings of the European Working Session on Learning—EWSL-91, Porto, Portugal, March 6–8, 1991, pp. 514–533.
2. Grzymala-Busse J. W. Managing Uncertainty in Expert Systems. Kluwer Academic Publishers, Dordrecht, The Netherlands, 1991.
3. Weiss S. M. and Kulikowski C. A. Computer Systems That Learn: Classification and Prediction Methods from Statistics, Neural Nets, Machine Learning, and Expert Systems. Morgan Kaufmann Publishers, San Mateo, California, 1990.
4. Boose J. H. A survey of knowledge acquisition techniques and tools. Knowledge Acquisition, 1989; 1:3–37.
5. MacDonald A. B. and Witten I. H. A framework for knowledge acquisition through techniques of concept learning. IEEE Trans. on Systems, Man, and Cybernetics, 1989; 19:499–512.
6. Shalin V. L., Wisniewski E. J., and Levi K. R. A formal analysis of machine learning systems for knowledge acquisition. Int. J. Man-Machine Studies, 1988; 29:429–446.
7. Buchanan B. G. Can machine learning offer anything to expert systems? Machine Learning, 1989; 4:251–254.
8. Gams M., Drobnic M., and Petkovsek M. Learning from examples—a uniform view. Int. J. Man-Machine Studies, 1991; 34:49–68.
9. Grzymala-Busse J. W. LERS—A system for learning from examples based on rough sets. In: Slowinski R. (ed.), Intelligent Decision Support Handbook of Applications and Advances of the Rough Sets Theory. Kluwer Academic Publishers, Dordrecht, The Netherlands, 1992, pp. 3–18.
10. Pawlak Z. Rough sets. International Journal Computer and Information Sciences, 1982; 11:341–356.

AQ, Rough Sets, and Matroid Theory

Shusaku Tsumoto and Hiroshi Tanaka
Department of Informational Medicine
Medical Research Institute,Tokyo Medical and Dental University
1-5-45 Yushima, Bunkyo-ku Tokyo 113 Japan
TEL: +81-3-3813-6111 (6159) FAX: +81-3-5684-3618
E-mail:{tsumoto, tanaka}@tmd.ac.jp

Abstract

In order to acquire knowledge from database, there have been proposed several methods of inductive learning, such as ID3 family and AQ family. These methods are applied to discover meaningful knowledge from large database, and their usefulness is ensured. However,since there has been no formal approach proposed to treat these methods, efficiency of each method is only compared empirically. In this paper, we introduce matroid theory and rough sets to construct a common framework for empirical machine learning methods which induce knowledge from databases whose patterns are described as the combination of attribute-value pairs. Combination of the concepts of rough sets and matroid theory gives us an excellent framework and enables us to understand the differences and the similarities of these methods clearly. Using this framework, we compare three methods, AQ, Pawlak's Consistent Rules. The results shows that they generate bases of Matroid from attribute-value space and that their solutions are optimal to the classification of the training samples.

1 Introduction

1.1 Motivation

In order to acquire knowledge from database, there have been proposed several methods of inductive learning, such as ID3 family[2, 5] and AQ family[1, 3]. These methods are applied to discover meaningful knowledge from large database, and their usefulness is ensured. However,since there has been no formal approach proposed to treat these methods, efficiency of each method is compared by using real-world databases[1, 2], such as medical databases. These results suggests some differences between these methods. However, sometimes these differences may depend on applied domain, so general discussion is left unsolved.

In this paper, we introduce matroid theory[7, 8] and rough sets[4] to construct a common framework for empirical machine learning methods which induce knowledge from attribute-value pattern database. Combination of the concepts of rough sets and matroid theory gives us an excellent framework and enables us to understand the differences of these methods clearly. Using this framework, we compare three methods: AQ, Pawlak's Consistent Rules[4] and we obtain four interesting conclusions from our approach. First, AQ and Pawlak's method are equivalent to the greedy algorithm for finding bases of Matroid from space spanned by attribute-value pairs. Second, a matroid defined by AQ method(AQ matroid) is a dual matroid of one defined by Pawlak's method[4](Pawlak's matroid). Third, according to the computational complexity of the greedy algorithm, the efficiency of both methods depends on the number of attributes, especially, independent variables. Finally, the induced results are optimal to the training samples if and only if the conditions on independence are hold. So if adding some new examples make independent attributes change their nature into dependent ones, the condition of deriving optimal solution is violated.

The paper is organized as follows: in section 2 and 3, we briefly discuss AQ and Pawlak's method respectively. In section 4, the elementary concepts of matroid theory are introduced,and several characteristics are discussed. Section 5 presents comparison between AQ matroid and Pawlak's matroid. In section 6, we discuss about optimal solutions given by the greedy algorithm. Finally, in section 7, we conclude the results of this paper.

1.2 Notation and Some Assumptions

In this paper, due to the limitation of the space, we only focus on inducing method of stars in AQ, reduction method in Rough Set Theory, and splitting method in ID3, and we do not consider about generalization[3], truncation[1] and pruning[2, 5]. These methods are also formalized by matroid theory if we strengthen our original matroid model, defined as below, by providing some additional concepts. And, moreover, we also have to omit the proofs of the theorems because of the space limitation. For further information, readers could refer to [4, 6, 7].

Below in this subsection, we mention about the following three notations used in this paper. First, for simplicity, we deal with classification of two classes, one of which is supported by a set of positive examples, denoted by D and the other of which is by a set of negative examples, $U - D$. And the former class is assumed to be composed of some small clusters, denoted by D_j, that is , $D = \cup_j D_j$. Second, we regard an attribute-value pair as an **elementary equivalence relation** as defined in rough sets[4]. We denote the combination of an attribute-value pairs, which is called *the complex of selectors* in terms of AQ theory, by an equivalence relation, R. A set of elements which supports R, which is called a *partial star* in AQ, is referred to as an **indiscernible set**, denoted by $[x]_R$. Finally, we define partial order of equivalence as follows:

Definition 1 (Partial Order of Equivalence Relation)
Let $A(R_i)$ denote the set whose elements are the attribute-value pairs included in R_i. If $A(R_i) \subseteq A(R_j)$, then we represent this relation as:

$$R_i \preceq R_j.$$

For example, let R_i represent a conjunctive formula, such as $a \wedge b \wedge c$, where a, b, c are elementary equivalence relations. Then $A(R_i)$ is equal to $\{a, b, c\}$. If we use the notation of Michalski's APC(Annotated Predicate Calculus)[3], R_i can be represented as, say $[a = 1]\&[b = 1]\&[c = 1]$, then $A(R_i)$ is equal to a set of selectors, $\{[a = 1], [b = 1], [c = 1]\}$.

2 AQ method

AQ is an inductive learning system based on incremental STAR algorithm[3]. This algorithm selects one "seed" from positive examples and starts from one "selector"(attribute-value pair) contained in this "seed" example. It adds selectors incrementally until the "complexes" (conjunction of attributes) explain only positive examples. Since many complexes can satisfy these positive examples, AQ finds the most preferred one, according to a flexible extra-logical criterion.

It would be worth noting that the complexes supported only by positive examples corresponds to the lower approximation, or the positive region in rough set theory [4]. That is, the rules induced by AQ is equivalent to consistent rules defined by Pawlak when constructive generalization rules[3] are not used. As a matter of fact, AQ's star algorithm without constructive generalization can be reformulated by the concepts of rough sets. For example, a bounded star denoted by $G(e|U - D, m)$ in Michalski's notation is equal to $G = \{R_i | [x]_{R_i} = D_j\}$, such that $|G| = m$ where $|G|$ denotes the cardinality of G. This star is composed of many complexes, which is ordered by LEF_i, lexicographic evaluation functional, which is defined as the following pair:$< (-negcov, \tau_1), (poscov, \tau_2) >$ where $negcov$ and $poscov$ are numbers of negative and positive examples, respectively, covered by an expression in the star,and where τ_1 and τ_2 are tolerance threshold for criterion $poscov, negcov$ ($\tau \in [0..100\%]$). This algorithm shows that AQ method is a kind of greedy algorithm which finds independent variables using selectors which are equivalent to equivalence relation in terms of rough sets. This characteristic is discussed in section 5.

3 Pawlak's Consistent Rules

Based on the concepts of rough sets, Pawlak[4] introduces *Reduction of Knowledge*, which is a method to examine the independencies of the attributes iteratively and extract the minimum indispensable part of equivalence relations. For the limitation of the space, we only mention about the definition of *consistent rules* and their knowledge reduction. For further details, readers could refer to [4].

Definition 2 (Definition of a consistent rule) *Let R_j be an equivalence relation and D be a set of samples which belongs to a target concept. $R_j \Rightarrow D$ is called a consistent rule when $Posi_{R_j}(D)$ is given by:*

$$Posi_{R_j}(D) = D_k = [x]_{R_j} \subseteq D.$$

Definition 3 (Reduction of Knowledge) *If an attribute a is satisfied with the following equation:*

$$Posi_{R-\{a\}}(D) = Posi_R(D),$$

then we say that a is dispensable in R, and a can be deleted from R.

If we use some weight function for efficiency, this algorithm is also a kind of greedy algorithm which finds independent variables. However, while AQ is based on incremental addition of equivalence relations, Pawlak's method is based on incremental removal of dependent equivalence relations. This characteristic is also discussed in section 5.

4 Matroid Theory

4.1 Definition of a Matroid

Matroid theory abstracts the important characteristics of matrix theory and graph theory, firstly developed by Whitney[8] in the thirties of this century. The advantages of introducing matroid theory is the following: 1)Since matroid theory abstracts graphical structure, this shows the characteristics of formal structure in graph clearly. 2)Since a matroid is defined by the axioms of independent sets, it makes the definition of independent structure clear. 3)Duality is one of the most important structure in matroid theory, and by this definition we can treat relation between dependency and independency rigorously. 4)The greedy algorithm is one of the algorithms for acquiring an optimal base of a matroid. This algorithm is studied in detail, so we can use these well-established results in our problem.

Although there are many interesting and attractive characteristics of matroid theory, for the limitation of space, we only discuss about duality, and the greedy algorithm. For further information, readers might refer to [7].

First, we begin with definition of a matroid. A matroid is defined as an independent space which satisfies the following axioms:

Definition 4 (Definition of a Matroid) *The pair $M(E, \mathcal{J})$ is called a matroid(or an independence space),if*

1) E is a finite set,
2)$\emptyset \in \mathcal{J} \subset 2^E$,
3)$X \in \mathcal{J}, Y \subset X \Rightarrow Y \in \mathcal{J}$,
4) $X, Y \in \mathcal{J}, card(X) = card(Y) + 1 \Rightarrow (\exists a \in X - Y)(Y \cup \{a\}) \in \mathcal{J}$.

If $X \in \mathcal{J}$, it is called **independent**, *otherwise X is called* **dependent**. □

One of the most important characteristic of matroid theory is that this theory refers to the notion of independence using the set-theoretical scheme. As shown in [4], we also consider the independence of the attributes in terms of rough sets,which uses the set-theoretical framework. Therefore our definition of independence can be also partially discussed using matroid theory, which is discussed later.

4.2 Duality

Another important characteristic is duality. While this concept was firstly introduced in graph theory, a deeper understanding of the notion of the duality in graph theory can be obtained by examining matroid structure. Definition of duality is as follows:

Definition 5 (Duality)
If $M = (E, \mathcal{J})$, is a matroid with a set of bases β, then the matroid with a set

*of elements E, and a set of bases $\beta^* = \{E - B | B \in \beta\}$ is termed the **dual** of M and is denoted by M^*.* □

¿From this definition, it can be easily shown that $(M^*)^* = M$, and M and thus M^* are referred to a **dual matroid pair**. And we have the following theorem:

Theorem 1 (Relation between M and M^*) *If M is a matroid, then M^* is a matroid.* □

4.3 the Greedy Algorithm

Since it is important to calculate a base of a matroid in practice, several methods are proposed. In these methods, we focus on the greedy algorithm. This algorithm can be formulated as follows:

Definition 6 (the Greedy Algorithm) *Let B be a variable to store the calculated base of a matroid, and E denote the whole set of attributes. We define the Greedy Algorithm to calculate a base of a matroid as follows:*

1.$B \leftarrow \phi$
2.Calculate "priority queue" Q using weight function of E.
3.If B is a base of $M(E, \mathcal{J})$ then stop. Else go to 4.
4.$e \leftarrow first(Q)$, which has a minimum weight in Q.
5. If $B \cup \{e\} \in \mathcal{J}$ then $B \leftarrow B \cup \{e\}$. goto 2. □

This algorithm searches one solution which is optimal in terms of one weight function. Note that a matroid may have many bases. The base derived by the greedy algorithm is optimal to some **predefined** weight function. Hence if we cannot derive a suitable weight function we cannot get such an optimal base. In the following, we assume that we can define a good weight function for the greedy algorithm. For example, we can use *information gain* as defined in [2, 5] for such function. For further discussion about weight function, readers could refer to [6].

Under this assumption, this algorithm has the following characteristics:

Theorem 2 (Computational Complexity) *The complexity of the greedy algorithm is*

$$\mathcal{O}(mf(\rho(M)) + m \log m)$$

where $\rho(M)$ is equal to a rank of matroid M,m is equal to the number of the elements in the matroid, $|E|$, f represents a function of computational complexity of an independent test, which is the procedure to test whether the obtained set is independent, and is called independent test oracle. □

Theorem 3 (Optimal Solution by the Greedy Algorithm)
The optimal solution is derived by this algorithm if and only if a subset of the attributes satisfies the axioms of the matroid. □

This theorem is very important when we discuss about optimal solution of learning algorithms. This point is discussed in section 7.

5 AQ matroid and Pawlak's Matroid

Here we show that our "rough sets" reformulation of AQ algorithm is equivalent to the greedy algorithm for calculating bases of a matroid and that the derived bases are dual to those derived by Pawlak's reduction method.

5.1 AQ matroid

Under the above assumption we can constitute a matroid of AQ method, which we call *AQ matroid* as follows:

Theorem 4 (AQ matroid) *Let B denote the base of a matroid such that $IND(B) = D_k$. If we define an independent set $\mathcal{J}(D_k)$ as $\{A(R_j)\}$ which satisfies the following conditions:*

1) $R_j \preceq B$,
2) $[x]_B \subseteq [x]_{R_j}$,
3) $\forall R_i$ s.t. $R_i \prec R_j \preceq B$, $D_j = [x]_B \subseteq [x]_{R_j} \subset [x]_{R_i}$,

where the equality holds only if $R_j = B$. then this set satisfies the definition of a matroid. We call this type of matroid, $M(E, \mathcal{J}(D_k)), AQ$ matroid. $\square$

The first condition means that a base is a maximal independent set and each relation forms a subset of this base. And the second condition is the characteristic which satisfies all of these equivalence relations. Finally, the third condition denotes the relationship between the equivalence relations: Any relation R_i which forms a subset of $A(R_j)$ must satisfy $[x]_{R_j} \subset [x]_{R_i}$. Note that these conditions reflects the conditional part of AQ algorithm. For example, let a and b elementary equivalence relations, and let $IND(a)$ and $IND(b)$ be equal to $\{1,2,3\}$ and $\{2,3,5\}$. If the set which supports a target concept is $D = \{2\}$, then $D \subset [x]_{a \wedge b} (= \{2,3\}) \subset [x]_a (= \{1,2,3\})$. Hence $\{a\}$, $\{b\}$ and $\{a, b\}$ belong to the independent sets for the target concept. It is also notable that each D_k has exactly one independent set $\mathcal{J}(D_k)$. Therefore the whole AQ algorithm is equivalent to the greedy algorithm for acquiring a set of bases of AQ matroid, denoted by $\{\mathcal{J}(D_k)\}$. Furthermore, since the independent test depends on the calculus of indiscernible sets, is less than $\mathcal{O}(\rho(M) * n^2)$ where n denotes a sample size, the computational complexity is given as follows:

Theorem 5 (Computational Complexity of AQ algorithm)
Assume that we do not use constructive generalization. Then the complexity of AQ algorithm is less than

$$\mathcal{O}(mn^2 \rho(M)) + m \log m)$$

where $\rho(M)$ is equal to a rank of matroid M, m is equal to the number of the elements in the matroid, $|E|$. $\square$

Hence the computational complexity of AQ depends mainly on the number of the elements of a matroid, since it increases exponentially as the number of the attribute-value pairs grows large.

5.2 Pawlak's Matroid

On the other hand, since $\rho(M)$ is the number of independent variables, $m - \rho(M)$ is equal to the number of dependent variables. From the concepts of the matroid theory, if we define an dependent set $\mathcal{I}$ as shown below, then $M(E,\mathcal{I})$ satisfies the condition of the dual matroid of $M(E,\mathcal{J})$,and we call $M(E,\mathcal{I})$ Pawlak's matroid.

Theorem 6 (Pawlak matroid)
Let B denote the base of a matroid such that $IND(B) = D_k$. If we define an independent set $\mathcal{I}(D_k)$ as $\{A(R_j)\}$ which satisfies the following conditions:

1) $B \prec R_j$,
2) $[x]_B = [x]_{R_j}$,
3) $\forall R_i$ s.t. $B \prec R_i \preceq R_j$, $D_k = [x]_B = [x]_{R_j} = [x]_{R_i}$,

then $M(E,\mathcal{I}(D_k))$ is a dual matroid of $M(E,\mathcal{J}(D_k))$, and we call $M(E,\mathcal{I}(D_k))$ Pawlak's matroid. □

The first condition means that a base is a maximal independent set and each relation forms a superset of this base. And the second condition is the characteristic which satisfies all of these equivalence relations. Finally, the third condition denotes the relationship between the equivalence relations: Any relation R_i which forms a subset of $A(R_j)$ must satisfy $[x]_{R_i} \subset [x]_{R_j}$. Note that these conditions reflects the conditional part of reduction method. For example, let R_1 and R_2 elementary equivalence relations.

Let $A(R_1) = \{a,b,c,d\}$, $A(R_2) = \{a,b,c\}$, $A(B) = \{b,c\}$. And let all of these indiscernible sets be equal to $\{2,3\}$. Then since $[x]_B = [x]_{R_2} = [x]_{R_1}$, both of a and d are dependent on B. So $\{a\}$ and $\{d\}$ are the elements of Pawlak's matroid.

Therefore the algorithm of Pawlak's method is formally equivalent to the algorithm for the dual matroid of AQ matroid, and the computational complexity of Pawlak's method is less than $\mathcal{O}((p - \rho(M)) * (n^2 + 2n) + m \log m)$. Hence, we get the following theorem.

Theorem 7 (Computational Complexity of Pawlak's method)
The complexity of the Pawlak's method is less than

$$\mathcal{O}(mn^2(p - \rho(M))) + m \log m$$

where p is a total number of attributes, $\rho(M)$ is equal to a rank of matroid M, and m is equal to the number of the elements in the matroid,$|E|$. □

¿From these consideration, if $\rho(M)$ is small, AQ algorithm performs better than Pawlak's one under our assumption.

6 Optimal Solution

In this section, we briefly mention about the characteristics of optimal solutions. For further discussion, readers could refer to [6].

As mentioned above, Theorem 3 tells us that an optimal solution is obtained only when training samples satisfies the conditions of AQ matroid. However, this assumption is very strict as shown in Theorem 4. In practice, it is often violated by new additional training samples. For example, when in the old training samples, $R_i \prec R_j$ implies $[x]_{R_j} \subset [x]_{R_i}$, additional samples causes the latter relation to be $[x]_{R_j} = [x]_{R_i}$. In other words, additional samples causes independent variables to be dependent. In this case, the former derived solution is no longer optimal.

7 Conclusion

In this paper, we combine the concepts of matroid theory with those of rough sets, which gives us an excellent framework and enables us to understand the differences of AQ, Pawlak's method clearly. Using this framework, we obtain four interesting conclusions from our approach. First, AQ and Pawlak's method are equivalent to the greedy algorithm for finding bases of matroids when predefined weight function is given. Second, AQ matroids are dual to Pawlak matroids. Third, the efficiency of AQ and Pawlak's method depends on the number of attributes, especially, independent variables. Finally, the induced results are optimal to the classification of training samples.

Acknowledgements

The authors would like to thank Zdzislaw Pawlak, Andrzej Skowron and Nitin Indurkhya for giving insightful comments on the manuscript. This research is supported by Grants-in-Aid for Scientific Research No.04229105 from the Ministry of Education, Science and Culture, Japan.

References

[1] Bergadano, F., Matwin, S., Michalski, R.S. and Zhang, J. Learning Two-Tiered Descriptions of Flexible Concepts: The POSEIDON System, *Machine Learning*, **8**, 5-43, 1992.

[2] Breiman, L., Freidman, J., Olshen, R. and Stone, C. *Classification And Regression Trees*. Belmont, CA: Wadsworth International Group, 1984.

[3] Michalski, R.S. A Theory and Methodology of Machine Learning. Michalski, R.S., Carbonell, J.G. and Mitchell, T.M., *Machine Learning - An Artificial Intelligence Approach*, 83-134, Morgan Kaufmann, CA, 1983.

[4] Pawlak, Z. *Rough Sets*, Kluwer Academic Publishers, Dordrecht, 1991.

[5] Quinlan, J.R. Induction of decision trees, *Machine Learning*, **1**, 81-106, 1986.

[6] Tsumoto, S. and Tanaka, H. Comparing inductive learning methods in the framework of the combination of rough set theory and matroid theory. TMD-IM-TR-94-001, *to appear*, 1994.

[7] Welsh, D.J.A. *Matroid Theory*, Academic Press, London, 1976.

[8] Whitney, H. On the abstract properties of linear dependence, *Am. J. Math.*, **57**, 509-533, 1935.

Rough Classifiers

Andrzej Lenarcik
Zdzisław Piasta
Kielce University of Technology,
25–314 Kielce, Poland

Abstract

A rough classifier inspired by concepts of the rough set theory is defined. A method of the rough classifier generation in the case of continuous condition attributes is presented. The method is illustrated with two real classification problems. The results are compared with those obtained for statistical discriminant classifiers.

1 Introduction

The paper is concerned with a classification problem which consists in predicting the class of an object using some measurements made on it. Our studies were inspired by the question if the classifier based on the ideas of the rough set theory [1] may be used for classifying objects from outside the information system. So far our research is limited to the problem with continuous condition attributes and one discrete decision attribute. To use in this case the rough set approach in its classical form, certain coding of condition attributes is needed. In the paper [2] we presented a method of discretization of condition attributes space. The method was based on maximizing the predictive properties of the information system in the stage of coding, but it turned out to be useful also in the elimination of redundant attributes and in decision algorithm generation [3].

In this paper a formal definition of a rough classifier is given. We present an efficient algorithm of the rough classifier generation, which can be used for analysis of large information systems thanks to the modification of our earlier method of condition attributes coding. The rough classifiers preserve all positive aspects of the decision algorithms generated in the rough set theory.

2 Rough Classifier Generation

Let us denote by $\mathcal{R}$ the set of real numbers. The Cartesian product $\mathcal{R}^m$ we call the continuous condition attribute space. Let S_1, $S_2, \ldots, S_k$ be a family of disjoint and measurable subsets of $\mathcal{R}^m$. Each S_i is labeled by the particular decision j_i $(i = 1, 2, \ldots, k)$ from the domain $V_d = \{1, 2, \ldots, l\}$ of the decision attribute d. This assignment can be expressed in the form of decision rules

$$\textbf{if } x \in S_i, \quad \textbf{then } d = j_i, \quad i = 1, \ldots, k. \tag{1}$$

The subset S_i is the domain of the i–th rule.

By a classifier we mean the set of all decision rules. If $S_1 \cup S_2 \cup \ldots S_k = \mathcal{R}^m$, then we say that the classifier is complete.

A classifier construction is based on an information about finite set U of objects. This information is expressed in terms of points

$$(x_\nu^{(1)}, x_\nu^{(2)}, \ldots, x_\nu^{(m)}, j_\nu) \in \mathcal{R}^m \times V_d, \quad \nu = 1, \ldots, N, \tag{2}$$

where N is the number of objects. The set of points (2) reflects our past experience and is called a learning sample.

By a rough classifier we mean the classifier which consists of the rules

$$\textbf{if } x^{(1)} \in \Delta_i^{(1)}, x^{(2)} \in \Delta_i^{(2)}, \ldots, x^{(m)} \in \Delta_i^{(m)}, \textbf{then } d = j_i \in V_d, \tag{3}$$

where $\Delta_i^{(1)}, \Delta_i^{(2)}, \ldots, \Delta_i^{(m)}$ are intervals in $\mathcal{R}$, and $i = 1, 2, \ldots, k$.

The number of rules in (3) is not given in advance, but is naturally limited by the general requirement that the rules should be confirmed by the learning objects.

The process of the rough classifier generation has to be proceeded by specification of its four elements. These elements will be discussed in detail further. They are the following:

- a primary coding of each continuous condition attribute $x^{(q)}$, which is induced by a sequence of intermediate values $a_1^{(q)} < a_2^{(q)} < \ldots < a_{n_q-1}^{(q)}$, $q = 1, \ldots, m$, where n_q is the number of levels for the coded attribute,

- a partition criterion $\mathcal{K}(S_1, \ldots, S_k)$, which takes on a unique positive value for each particular partition $S_1, S_2, \ldots, S_k$ of $\mathcal{R}^m$, and gives greater value for better partition,

- a procedure of the assigning values of decision attribute to elements of the partition,

- an auxiliary criterion $\mathcal{H}(S_1, \ldots, S_k)$ for additional reduction of the number of decision rules.

Specification of the above-mentioned elements gives the unique rough classifier. The rough classifier generation is a stepwise procedure.

In the **first stage** redundant intermediate values in the primary coding are removed. This elimination process is based on the partition criterion $\mathcal{K}$, because each set of intermediate values determines a certain partition[1] of the space $\mathcal{R}^m$. Each time we eliminate the intermediate value which results in the greatest increase in the value of the used criterion $\mathcal{K}$. The process stops when further elimination that leads to an increase in the value of $\mathcal{K}$ is impossible.

The **second stage** consists of the joining of neighboring elements of the obtained partition. In each step of the joining algorithm a list of permissible joints is determined. A joint is permissible if the resulting subset, obtained by attaching to the particular element of the partition the same-side neighboring elements, is the m-dimensional interval. Each time we perform the permissible joint which results in the greatest increase in the value of the used criterion $\mathcal{K}$.

---

[1] Elements of this partition are the m-dimensional intervals of the form

$S = \Delta_{\alpha_1}^{(1)} \times \ldots \times \Delta_{\alpha_m}^{(m)}$ $\quad \alpha_q \in \{1, \ldots, n_q\}, q \in \{1, \ldots, m\}$,

where $\Delta_1^{(q)} = (-\infty; a_1^{(q)}), \Delta_2^{(q)} = \langle a_1^{(q)}; a_2^{(q)} \rangle, \ldots, \Delta_{n_q}^{(q)} = \langle a_{n_q-1}^{(q)}; +\infty), \quad q \in \{1, \ldots, m\}$.

The process stops when further joining that leads to an increase in the value of $\mathcal{K}$ is impossible.

In the **third stage** each element of the obtained partition is labeled by the particular value of the decision attribute d, according to the selected procedure.

In the **fourth stage** we can decrease the number of rules using the more liberal auxiliary criterion $\mathcal{H}$, because the subsets labeled by the same value of d can have some permissible joints not performed earlier. This procedure has no effect on the classification properties of the decision algorithm.

3 Criteria of the Condition Attribute Space Partition

3.1 Classification Concept in the Rough Set Theory

In this section we give some basic concepts of the rough set theory [1]. The construction of the partition criteria, presented further in this paper, is founded on these concepts. Only as a formality, we make a modification in the definition of an information function and of an information system.

Let U be a finite set of objects, and $Q = \{q_1, \ldots, q_s\}$ be a finite set of attributes which characterize these objects. A particular assignment of the values of attributes to objects is realized by the information function $\rho = (\rho_{q_1}, \ldots, \rho_{q_s}) : U \to V$, where $V = V_{q_1} \times \ldots \times V_{q_s}$ is the product of the attribute domains. Let us note that $\rho_q(u) \in V_q$ for $u \in U$ and $q \in Q$.

The 4-tuple $\mathcal{J} = (U, Q, V, \rho)$ is called an information system. Each subset P of the set of attributes provides a certain equivalence relation. We say that objects u and w are P–indiscernible if $\rho_q(u) = \rho_q(w)$ for all attributes $q \in P$. That means that information about objects u and w respective to all attributes $q \in P$ is identical. We denote by $P^*_{\mathcal{J}} = \{X_1, \ldots, X_h\}$ the set of equivalence classes of the above–defined relation related to the system $\mathcal{J}$. We always omit the index $\mathcal{J}$ if this does not lead to confusion. P^* is a partition of the set of objects U.

Now, if $Y \subset U$ is an arbitrary subset of the set of objects, we can define its P–lower approximation $\underline{P}_Y$ as the sum of the equivalence classes X_i from P^* which are totally included in Y. P–upper approximation $\overline{P}^Y$ of Y is the sum of all the equivalence classes X_i which have a non–empty intersection with Y. Clearly, $\underline{P}_Y$ is the subset of $\overline{P}^Y$. A ratio of the cardinality of the difference $\overline{P}^Y \setminus \underline{P}_Y$ to the number of all objects in U informs us to what extent the set Y may be described by the information provided by attributes $q \in P$. The most desirable value of this ratio is zero. It occurs when the set Y is the sum of the equivalence classes of P^*. Then we say that Y is P^*–measurable.

In practice, we consider two disjoint sets of attributes: the set of condition attributes C which describes objects, and the set of decision attributes D. The rough set theory allows us to investigate to what extent the values of decision attributes may by determined by the knowledge of the values of the condition attributes in the particular information system. The degree of accuracy of this determination depends on the accuracy of the approximation of the classes from $D^* = \{Y_1, \ldots, Y_l\}$ by the classes from $C^* = \{X_1, \ldots, X_h\}$. Inclusions of the type $X_i \subset Y_j$ are particularly desirable. Inclusions of this type allow us to conclude that the values of the condition attributes corresponding to the class X_i are related in a deterministic way with the values of decision attributes that correspond to the class Y_j.[2] Relationships between the values of condition attributes and the values of decision attributes are expressed in the form of decision rules. A decision algorithm is defined as the set of decision rules.

3.2 Condition Attributes Coding Problem

As we mentioned in the introduction, we are considering the case of the continuous condition attributes and one discrete decision attribute. An application of the rough set theory to an information system of this type needs an assumption of a method of the condition attributes coding. We choose the maximizing of predictive properties of the information system as the criterion of the condition attributes coding. Below, we explain what we mean by 'good predictive properties'.

Using concepts presented in section 3.1, the learning sample (2) may be treated as the information system $\mathcal{J} = (U, Q, V, \rho)$, where

- $U = \{u_1, \ldots, u_N\}$ is the N-elemental set of the objects described by the learning sample,

- $Q = C \cup D$, where $C = \{1, \ldots, m\}$ is the set of the continuous condition attributes and $D = \{d\}$ is the one-elemental set of decision attributes,

- $V = \mathcal{R}^m \times V_d$,

- $\rho = (\rho_1, \ldots, \rho_m, \rho_d)$ is the information function such that $\rho(u_\nu) = (x_\nu^{(1)}, \ldots, x_\nu^{(m)}, j_\nu) \in V$, $\nu = 1, \ldots, N$.

Let a family of sets

$$S_1, S_2, \ldots, S_k \tag{4}$$

be an arbitrary partition of $\mathcal{R}^m$. Elements S_i ($i = 1, \ldots, k$) of the partition we call states. We say that an object $u \in U$ belongs to the state S_i if $(\rho_1(u), \ldots, \rho_m(u)) \in S_i$. A state which does not contain objects is called an empty state. Let us notice that the partition (4) induces a natural equivalence relation in U. According to this relation, two objects may by considered as equivalent, if they belong to the same state.

Each continuous condition attribute can be coded by fixing the set of its intermediate values. A coding function $\iota_q : \mathcal{R} \rightarrow \tilde{V}_q = \{1, 2, \ldots, n_q\}$, ($q = 1, \ldots, m$) is defined by the formula

$$\iota_q(t) = \alpha \in \tilde{V}_q \text{ if } t \in \Delta_\alpha^{(q)}, \tag{5}$$

where intervals $\Delta_\alpha^{(q)}$ are defined as in section 2 (see footnote). After coding we obtain the new information system

$$\tilde{\mathcal{J}} = (U, Q, \tilde{V}_1 \times \ldots \times \tilde{V}_m \times V_d, \tilde{\rho}), \tag{6}$$

where $\tilde{\rho} = (\iota_1 \circ \rho_1, \ldots, \iota_m \circ \rho_m, \rho_d)$.

---

[2]In the particular information system

As we stated in section 2, the set of intermediate values for each continuous condition attribute produces the unique partition $S_1, S_2, \ldots, S_k$ of the space $\mathcal{R}^m$. This partition we call a quantization of $\mathcal{R}^m$ generated by the set of intermediate values. We can consider the equivalence relation induced by this partition in U. Let us note that the set of classes $\{X_1, \ldots, X_h\}$ of this relation coincides with the set $C^*_{\tilde{\mathcal{J}}}$ generated by the coded information system (6) ($h \leq k$). That means, that after coding, objects belonging to the one state from the quantization of $\mathcal{R}^m$ have the same values of each condition attribute in $\tilde{\mathcal{J}}$, and also, if objects have the same values of each condition attribute in $\tilde{\mathcal{J}}$, then they belong to the same state of the quantization. Consequently, there exists one–to–one correspondence between the family of the classes $C^*_{\tilde{\mathcal{J}}} = \{X_1, \ldots, X_h\}$ and the family of non–empty states of the quantization. The state which corresponds to class X_i will be denoted by $S(X_i)$.

As we stated in section 2, the domain of the decision attribute d is equal to $V_d = \{1, 2, \ldots, l\}$. Then the class Y_j of the partition $D^*_{\tilde{\mathcal{J}}} = \{Y_1, \ldots, Y_l\}$ corresponds exactly to the value j of the decision attribute. Classes of $D^*_{\tilde{\mathcal{J}}}$ we name categories. Let us note that $D^*_{\tilde{\mathcal{J}}} = D^*_{\mathcal{J}}$. As we stated earlier, from the point of view of accuracy of approximating the categories from D^* by the classes from $C^*_{\tilde{\mathcal{J}}}$, the inclusions of the type $X_i \subset Y_j$ are most desirable. These inclusions mean that all objects belonging to the state $S(X_i)$ correspond to the same value $j \in V_d$ of the decision attribute. In this situation the state $S(X_i)$ will be called the pure state of the j–th category. A state which is not pure and not empty will be called a mixed state. Each pure state S induces a deterministic rule which can be presented in the form

$$\textbf{if} \quad u \in S \quad \textbf{then} \quad d = j. \tag{7}$$

The set of all the rules of the form (7), induced by the pure states, may be treated as a method of classifying new objects from outside the information system. This classification was named in [2] as the natural classification.

Let us think for a moment about choosing a method of attributes coding to obtain a high accuracy of natural classification. It seems, at first, that possibly great number of pure states is most important. This effect is not difficult to obtain. It is sufficient to choose respectively more levels of coding to get the situation in which all classes from $C^*_{\tilde{\mathcal{J}}}$ will be one–elemental. Then all the states will be pure or empty. Unfortunately, the number of the empty states might be too large, and so new objects which fall into the empty states could not be classified.

In order to make an objective evaluation of the usability of the natural classification for classifying new objects, the answer to the following question must be given: 'how often will new objects fall into the pure states'? It is possible to get the answer to the question if some assumptions of the probabilistic nature are made. These assumptions are introduced below.

3.3   A Probabilistic Approach to the Rough Set Theory

In the following, we will denote the probability of an event A by $P(A)$ and the expected value of a random variable X as $\mathbf{E}(X)$.

We assume that the probability p_i of an object occurring in the state S_i, and the probability p_{ij} of an object of j–th category occurring in the state S_i, are known[3] $(i = 1, 2, \ldots, k; \; j = 1, 2, \ldots, l)$. Clearly, $p_i = p_{i1} + p_{i2} + \ldots + p_{il}$. The probability that a new object will be of the j–th category we denote by π_j, and clearly

$$\pi_j = p_{1j} + p_{2j} + \ldots + p_{kj}, \quad j = 1, \ldots, l. \tag{8}$$

The probability of the natural classification of a new object from outside of the information system is equal to the sum of all probabilities p_i over all pure states. This sum is called the quality of classification *a priori* in [2]. Notice that the probability that this classification is correct (that means, we assign to the object this category which it really has) is equal to the sum of p_{ij} over all pure states S_i, where j is the category of the state S_i. This sum is called the correctness of classification *a priori* in [2].

For the particular partition of the condition attribute space the quantities defined above depend on the probabilities p_{ij} as well as on the location of the learning objects (2) in the space $\mathcal{R}^m$. If we take into consideration the expected values of the criteria, then we obtain the new criteria which depend on the probabilities p_{ij} only.

New objects occur as a result of the random sampling, so we can assume that the whole information system is a result of a random process. Then the information system with which we are working on will be only a realization of the more general random information system [2]. On this assumption, the earlier defined criteria become random variables, and it is possible to predict their expected values. These values are relatively easy to compute.

Transition to expected values causes learning objects not to be represented in the condition attribute space by their precise location in the form of coordinates (2), but by estimates of probabilities. The algorithm is still pure–states oriented, but it accepts also mixed states. As a result, the classifier is less sensitive for small changes in the learning sample.

In [2] and [3] we applied the criteria

$$\sum_{i=1}^{k} p_i \left[\left(\sum_{j=1}^{l} (1 - p_i + p_{ij})^N \right) - l(1 - p_i)^N \right] \tag{9}$$

and

$$\sum_{i=1}^{k} \left[\left(\sum_{j=1}^{l} p_{ij} (1 - p_i + p_{ij})^N \right) - p_i (1 - p_i)^N \right]. \tag{10}$$

The criteria (9) and (10) are the expected values of the quality and of the correctness of classification *a priori*, respectively. These criteria are extremely pure–states oriented and may give too many rules for large learning samples with classes that overlap considerable. To solve this problem we can use partition criteria which accept mixed states with a given number of confounding objects.

---

[3] In practice we use some estimates of these probabilities.

Criteria based on mixed states with the predominant category we denote by

$$\mathcal{N}(n_0, n_1, \ldots, n_z), \tag{11}$$

where $\mathcal{N}$ is a symbol of used criteria, and n_i is a minimal number of the predominant category objects if i is a number of confounding objects in the given state $(i = 1, 2, \ldots, z)$. As earlier, the values $n_1, n_2, \ldots, n_z$ in (11) lead us to expect a final form of the classifier, but do not guarantee that it will be realized.

Using the convention (11), the criterion (9) will be $Q(1)$, the criterion (10) will be $C(1)$, and defined in [3] the criteria $\tilde{Q}$ and $\tilde{C}$ will be, respectively, $Q(2)$ and $C(2)$. In section 7 we apply in illustrative examples the criterion $C(3, 5, 10)$.

Now, the quality of classification *a priori* is equal to the sum of the probabilities p_i over all states with the predominant category which satisfies the conditions related to (11). The correctness of classification *a priori* is equal to the sum of all probabilities p_{ij}, where j is the predominant category of the i-th state, over the same set of states. Notice that these characteristics are equal to

$$\sum_{i=1}^{k} p_i \sum_{j=1}^{l} X^{ij}, \tag{12}$$

and

$$\sum_{i=1}^{k} \sum_{j=1}^{l} p_{ij} X^{ij}, \tag{13}$$

respectively, where X^{ij} is a random variable which takes on the value 1 if j is the predominant category of the state S_i, and 0 otherwise.

Now, to find the expected values of (12) and (13) it is sufficient to compute the expected value $\mathbf{E}(X^{ij})$ of the variable X^{ij}. Then

$$Q(n_0, n_1, \ldots, n_z) = \sum_{i=1}^{k} p_i \sum_{j=1}^{l} \mathbf{E}(X^{ij}), \tag{14}$$

and

$$C(n_0, n_1, \ldots, n_z) = \sum_{i=1}^{k} \sum_{j=1}^{l} p_{ij} \mathbf{E}(X^{ij}). \tag{15}$$

A method of computation of $\mathbf{E}(X^{ij})$ depends on the way of interpreting the number of objects

$$N_1, N_2, \ldots, N_l \tag{16}$$

of the same category in the learning sample as fixed or random.

3.4 Criteria for Classification Problems with a Random Number of Objects in the Classes

If we assume that quantities (16) are random, then the random variable X^{ij} defined in last section can be presented as

$$X^{ij} = \sum_{s=0}^{z} \sum_{n=n_s}^{N-s} X_{n,s}^{ij}. \tag{17}$$

In the formula (17) a random variable $X_{n,s}^{ij}$ is equal to 1 if there are, in the state S_i, exactly n objects of the j–th category and s confounding objects. Otherwise $X_{n,s}^{ij}$ is equal to 0.

If a random variable X takes on the values 0 and 1 only, then its expected value $\mathbf{E}(X) = 0 \cdot P\{X = 0\} + 1 \cdot P\{X = 1\}$ is equal to the probability of the event $\{X = 1\}$. In order to calculate the probability $P\{X_{n,s}^{ij} = 1\}$ we will use the Bernoulli's distribution.

Let us assume that a certain experiment is replicated N times independently, and can end in m ways with the probabilities $P_1, P_2, \ldots, P_m$, respectively $(P_1 + P_2 + \ldots + P_m = 1)$. Then the probability of the event: n_1 experiments end in the first way, n_2 experiments end in the second way, etc. $(n_1 + n_2 + \ldots + n_m = N)$ is equal to

$$\frac{N!}{n_1! \, n_2! \, \ldots n_m!} P_1^{n_1} P_2^{n_2} \ldots P_m^{n_m}. \tag{18}$$

We now use the above procedure in the process of creating an information system. We assume that the information system is a realization of N independent replications of the same experiment. The single experiment can give one of the following three results with the probabilities shown in the brackets:

- an object of the j–th category occurs in the state S_i, $\quad (p_{ij})$

- a confounding object occurs in the state S_i, $\quad (p_i - p_{ij} = q_{ij})$

- an object occurs outside of the state S_i, $\quad (1 - p_i = q_i)$.

Therefore, according to (18), we get

$$\mathbf{E}(X_{n,s}^{ij}) = P\{X_{n,s}^{ij} = 1\} = \frac{N!}{n! \, s! \, (N - n - s)!} p_{ij}^n q_{ij}^s q_i^{N-n-s}$$

$$= \frac{N!}{(N-s)! \, s!} q_{ij}^s \frac{(N-s)!}{n! \, (N - n - s)!} p_{ij}^n q_i^{N-n-s}$$

$$= \binom{N}{s} q_{ij}^s \binom{N-s}{n} p_{ij}^n q_i^{N-n-s}.$$

Consequently,

$$\mathbf{E}(X^{ij}) = \sum_{s=0}^{z} \sum_{n=n_s}^{N-s} \mathbf{E}(X_{n,s}^{ij}) = \sum_{s=0}^{z} \binom{N}{s} q_{ij}^s \sum_{n=n_s}^{N-s} \binom{N-s}{n} p_{ij}^n q_i^{N-n-s}$$

$$= \sum_{s=0}^{z} \binom{N}{s} q_{ij}^s \left[(1-q_{ij})^{N-s} - \sum_{n=0}^{n_s-1} \binom{N-s}{n} p_{ij}^n q_i^{N-n-s} \right]$$

$$= \sum_{s=0}^{z} \binom{N}{s} q_{ij}^s \left[(1-q_{ij})^{N-s} - q_i^{N-s} \sum_{n=0}^{n_s-1} \binom{N-s}{n} \left(\frac{p_{ij}}{q_i} \right)^n \right].$$

Using the last formula to (14) and (15) we can easily get formulae for the expected values of the quality and of the correctness of classification *a priori* in the case of a random number of objects in the classes.

3.5 Criteria for Classification Problems with a Fixed Number of Objects in the Classes

In the case of a fixed number of objects in the classes, the expected values of the quality and of the correctness of classification *a priori* will be denoted by small letters. So, we have

$$q(n_0, n_1, \ldots, n_z) = \sum_{i=1}^{k} p_i \sum_{j=1}^{l} \mathbf{E}(X^{ij}), \tag{19}$$

and

$$c(n_0, n_1, \ldots, n_z) = \sum_{i=1}^{k} \sum_{j=1}^{l} p_{ij} \mathbf{E}(X^{ij}), \tag{20}$$

where a random variable X^{ij} is defined as in section 3.3.

After fixing the numbers (16) we can treat the learning objects related to different categories as independently obtained groups. For the particular state S_i and for the particular predominant category j all the objects can be divided into two independent groups consisting of:

(i) N_j objects of predominant category j, which occur in the state S_i with the probability $\bar{p}_{ij} = p_{ij}/\pi_j$,

(ii) $N - N_j$ confounding objects, which occur in the state S_i with the probability $\bar{q}_{ij} = (p_i - p_{ij})/(1 - \pi_j)$,

where π_j are defined by the formula (8).

Now, a random variable X^{ij} defined in section 3.3 can be presented as the sum

$$X^{ij} = \sum_{s=0}^{z} Y_s^{ij}. \tag{21}$$

A random variable Y_s^{ij} in the formula (21) is equal to 1 if there are, in the state S_i, at least n_s objects of the j–th category and exactly s confounding objects. Otherwise Y_s^{ij} is equal to 0.

An event $\{Y_s^{ij} = 1\}$ is the intersection of two independent events:

A_s^{ij} = { in the state S_i there are at least n_s objects of the predominant category j}

B_s^{ij} = { in the state S_i there are exactly s confounding objects }.

Using Bernoulli's distribution we get

$$P(A_s^{ij}) = \sum_{n=n_s}^{N_j} \binom{N_j}{n} \bar{p}_{ij}^n (1 - \bar{p}_{ij})^{N_j - n} = 1 - \sum_{n=0}^{n_s - 1} \binom{N_j}{n} \bar{p}_{ij}^n (1 - \bar{p}_{ij})^{N_j - n},$$

and

$$P(B_s^{ij}) = \binom{N - N_j}{s} \bar{q}_{ij}^s (1 - \bar{q}_{ij})^{N - N_j - s}.$$

Therefore

$$\mathbf{E}(X^{ij}) = \sum_{s=0}^{z} \mathbf{E}(Y_s^{ij}) = \sum_{s=0}^{z} P\{Y_s^{ij} = 1\} =$$

$$\sum_{s=0}^{z} \left[1 - \sum_{n=0}^{n_s - 1} \binom{N_j}{n} \bar{p}_{ij}^n (1 - \bar{p}_{ij})^{N_j - n} \right] \binom{N - N_j}{s} \bar{q}_{ij}^s (1 - \bar{q}_{ij})^{N - N_j - s} =$$

$$(1 - \bar{q}_{ij})^{N - N_j} \times$$

$$\times \sum_{s=0}^{z} \binom{N - N_j}{s} \left(\frac{\bar{q}_{ij}}{1 - \bar{q}_{ij}} \right)^s \left[1 - (1 - \bar{p}_{ij})^{N_j} \sum_{n=0}^{n_s - 1} \binom{N_j}{n} \left(\frac{\bar{p}_{ij}}{1 - \bar{p}_{ij}} \right)^n \right].$$

Putting the last formula to (19) and (20) we get formulae for the expected values of the quality and of the correctness of classification *a priori* in the case of a fixed number of objects in the classes.

4 A Procedure for Assigning Decisions to Elements of the Partition

Let $S_1, S_2, \ldots, S_k$ be an arbitrary partition of the condition attributes space $\mathcal{R}^m$. Let us assume first that the probabilities p_{ij} $(i = 1, 2, \ldots, k; j = 1, 2, \ldots, l)$ of the occurrence of a new object of the i-th category in the state S_i are known. According to the definition of a classifier given in section 2, the decisions $j_i \in V_d$ are assigned without any specified procedure to the partition elements S_i $(i = 1, \ldots, k)$. The probability of the correct classification of a new object by this classifier is equal to

$$\sum_{i=1}^{k} p_{ij_i}. \tag{22}$$

The probability (22) is maximal for the decision j_i which satisfies the condition

$$p_{ij_i} = \max_{j=1}^{l} p_{ij}. \tag{23}$$

From (23) we can conclude that j_i always exists, but may not be unique. Practically we can get only estimators $\hat{p}_{ij}$. In such a case a natural way of constructing the classifier is to assign this decision $j_i \in V_d$ to the partition element S_i, which satisfies the condition

$$\hat{p}_{ij_i} = \max_{j=1}^{l} \hat{p}_{ij}. \tag{24}$$

As earlier, a solution may not be unique. This problem happens quite often when the estimates $\hat{p}_{ij}$ are determined using n_{ij} learning objects of the j-th category from the state S_i. If the numbers of objects in the classes are treated as random, then $\hat{p}_{ij} = n_{ij}/N$. In the case of a fixed number of objects in the classes, and for the known probabilities π_j of the occurrence of a new object of the j-th category, the estimates $\hat{p}_{ij} = \pi_j(n_{ij}/N_j)$. It can happens that a state S_i will be empty. In this case $\hat{p}_{i1} = \hat{p}_{i2} = \ldots = \hat{p}_{il} = 0$. It is also possible that the non–zero solution for (24) will not be unique. In both cases a unique decision is impossible and the classifier may be incomplete. We can solve this problem by a nonparametric estimation of the probabilities p_{ij}. An example of such an estimator is presented in section 7.

5 Auxiliary Criteria

5.1 Criterion $\mathcal{M}$

The considerations in section 4 suggest that the quantity

$$\mathcal{M} = \sum_{i=1}^{k} \max_{j=1}^{l} p_{ij} \tag{25}$$

could be used as a criterion of the condition attributes space partition. However, it is impossible to increase the value of this criterion in the proces of joining the states. Let us denote by S' and S'' such partition elements, that $S = S' \cup S''$ is a new state. If p'_j, p''_j and p_j are the probabilities that an object of the j–th category occurs in the state S', S'' or S, respectively, then $p_j = p'_j + p''_j$.

From the inequality

$$\max_{j=1}^{l}(p'_j + p''_j) \le \max_{j=1}^{l} p'_j + \max_{j=1}^{l} p''_j, \tag{26}$$

we get

$$\mathcal{M}(\ldots, S' \cup S'', \ldots) \le \mathcal{M}(\ldots, S', S'', \ldots). \tag{27}$$

The inequality (27) suggests that an increase of $\mathcal{M}$ can be obtained by the partition of states. This property will be used in section 6.

5.2 Criterion $\mathcal{H}$

As we stated in section 2, in the last stage of the rough classifier generation we can reduce the number of decision rules by performing the permissible joints for the partition elements with the same decision. The auxiliary criterion $\mathcal{H}$ which possesses a property

$$\mathcal{H}(\ldots, S', S'', \ldots) \leq \mathcal{H}(\ldots, S' \cup S'', \ldots), \tag{28}$$

guarantees that the procedure has a tendency to minimize the number of states. Starting from the inequality ${p'_j}^2 + {p''_j}^2 \leq (p'_j + p''_j)^2$, which holds true for non-negative numbers, it is easy to prove that a criterion

$$\mathcal{H} = \sum_{i=1}^{k} \sum_{j=1}^{l} p_{ij}^2 \tag{29}$$

satisfies the inequality (28).

6 Selection of the Preliminary Coding

6.1 Set of All Intermediate Values

Let us take into consideration the information system $\mathcal{J}$ introduced in section 3.2. A set of all intermediate values is determined from the learning sample (2), separately for each condition attribute $q \in \{1, \ldots, m\}$. A method consists in the projection of all values $x_\nu^{(q)}$ on the q–th axis, and in the separation of the objects which belong to different categories. Let us assume that the values of the q–th condition attribute after the projection are given in increasing order

$$\tilde{x}_1^{(q)} < \tilde{x}_2^{(q)} < \ldots < \tilde{x}_{n'_q}^{(q)}, \tag{30}$$

where $n'_q \leq N$, because some of the values may be repeated. Then $\{q\}^* = \{X_1^{(q)}, \ldots, X_{n'_q}^{(q)}\}$ is the partition of the learning objects set for the classes related to the values (30).

The algorithm of selecting the intermediate values is the following:

- if the classes $X_i^{(q)}$ and $X_{i+1}^{(q)}$ are included in the same category, then there are not any intermediate value between the values $\tilde{x}_i^{(q)}$ and $\tilde{x}_{i+1}^{(q)}$ $(1 \leq i \leq n'_q - 1)$,

- if the classes $X_i^{(q)}$ and $X_{i+1}^{(q)}$ are included in the different categories, or at least one of them is not D^*–measurable, then the intermediate value is the arithmetic mean of $\tilde{x}_i^{(q)}$ and $\tilde{x}_{i+1}^{(q)}$ $(1 \leq i \leq n'_q - 1)$.

The intermediate values after arrangement give the sequence $a_1^{(q)} < a_2^{(q)} < \ldots < a_{n_q-1}^{(q)}$, where n_q is the number of levels of the coded attribute q. Figure 1 illustrates the above algorithm.

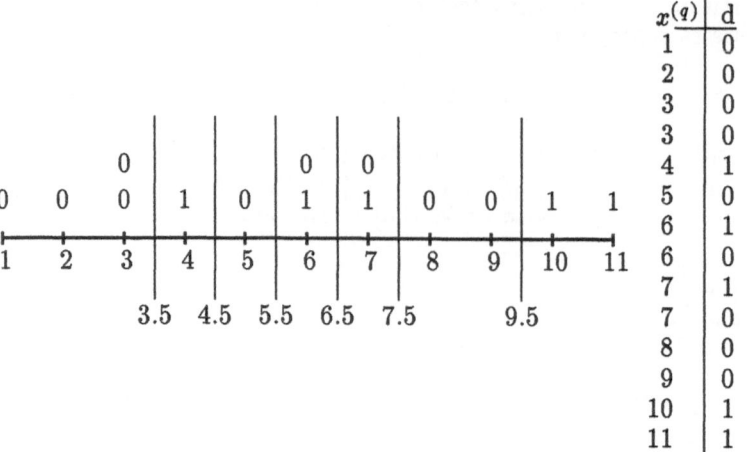

Figure 1: Illustration of the algorithm of selecting the intermediate values

6.2 Selecting the Most Important Intermediate Values

An application of all intermediate values in the first stage of the rough classifier generation might not be efficient in the case of large learning samples. A procedure for selection of the most important intermediate values can solve this problem. We use the criterion $\mathcal{M}$ presented in section 5.1. For each given number of intermediate values the selection process is a stepwise procedure. In each step we select from the set of all avaliable intermediate values the value which results in the greatest increase of $\mathcal{M}$. The optimal number of intermediate values is found empirically.

7 Illustrative Examples

In this section the method of the rough classifier generation will be illustrated with two information systems, which have been used for earlier classifier constructions [4, 5].

All the criteria, applied in the algorithm of the rough classifier generation, use the probabilities p_{ij}. So first, we have to indicate a method of estimating these probabilities.

Let us denote by $f_j(x)$ the probability density function, which determines the distribution of the j-th category objects in the space $\mathcal{R}^m$. Then

$$p_{ij} = \pi_j \int_{S_i} f_j(x), \tag{31}$$

where, as earlier, π_j is the probability that a new object is of the j-th category. We use a kernel method [6] to generate a nonparametric estimate

$$\hat{f}_j(x) = \frac{1}{N_j} \sum_{\nu=1}^{N_j} K(x, x_\nu, h) \tag{32}$$

of the density $f_j(x)$. As the kernel density we apply the normal kernel

$$K(x, \mu, h) = \left(\frac{1}{h\sqrt{2\pi}}\right)^m \frac{1}{s^{(1)} \ldots s^{(m)}} \exp\left[-\frac{1}{2}\sum_{q=1}^{m}\left(\frac{x^{(q)} - \mu^{(q)}}{hs^{(q)}}\right)^2\right], \quad (33)$$

where $s^{(q)}$ denotes the standard deviation of the q-th condition attribute in the given category $(q = 1, 2, \ldots, n)$.

We choose the value of the smoothing parameter h in (33) that maximizes

$$J_j(h) = \prod_{\nu=1}^{N_j} \frac{1}{N_j - 1} \sum_{\substack{\nu'=1 \\ \nu' \neq \nu}}^{N_j} K(x_\nu, x_{\nu'}, h). \quad (34)$$

In the formula (34) the vectors $x_1 = (x_1^{(1)}, \ldots, x_1^{(m)}), \ldots, x_{N_j} = (x_{N_j}^{(1)}, \ldots, x_{N_j}^{(m)})$ represent the objects of the j-th category.

In the case of the random number of objects in the classes, the probabilities π_j in (31) are estimated by $\hat{\pi}_j = N_j/N$. If numbers of objects in the classes are fixed, then the probabilities π_j are treated as known.

The first illustrative example is related to the diagnostic problem [4]. The *rolling bearings* information system consists of 55 objects. The objects are described by 10 continuous condition attributes $S_1, S_2, \ldots, S_{10}$, and one decision attribute d with the domain $V_d = \{0, 1\}$. The primary coding was selected by using the criterion $\mathcal{M}$ with different numbers of intermediate values (Table 1). The process of the elimination of redundant intermediate values (**stage 1**) was based on the criterion $C(3, 5, 10)$. The same criterion was used to join the neighboring elements of the obtained partition (**stage 2**). The assignment of decisions to elements of the partition (**stage 3**) was performed according to the procedure presented in section 4. To reduce a number of rules (**stage 4**) the criterion $\mathcal{H}$ was used. The obtained numbers of rules for different numbers of intermediate values are presented in Table 1. The numbers of errors when the classifier was tested on the learning objects are also given. Basing on the results included in Table 1, we selected the classifier which was generated starting from the 9-elemental set of intermediate values.

The rough classifier for the *rolling bearings* information system has the form

1	if	$S_4 \geq 39.0$					then $d = 0$
2	if	$S_4 < 39.0$	&	$S_9 < 37.25$			then $d = 0$
3	if $15.5 \leq S_4 < 39.0$		&	$S_9 \geq 37.25$	&	$S_7 < 51.5$	then $d = 1$
4	if $15.5 \leq S_4 < 39.0$		&	$S_9 \geq 37.25$	&	$S_7 \geq 51.5$	then $d = 0$
5	if	$S_4 < 15.5$	&	$S_9 \geq 37.25$			then $d = 0$

Table 2 includes characterization of the obtained classifier. In this table we present numbers of objects confirming each rule, the estimates $\hat{p}_i$ of the rules' probabilities, and the estimates $\hat{p}_{ij}/\hat{p}_i$ of the decisions' probabilities for the categories $j \in V_d$.

The structure of the obtained rough classifier is shown in Figure 2.

Table 1: Selection of the number of preliminary intermediate values for the *rolling bearings* information system

number of intermediate values	C(3,5,10) after 2–nd stage	number of rules 3–rd stage	4–th stage	number of errors
1	0.212744	2	2	15
2	0.402817	3	3	5
3	0.570468	4	4	4
4	0.679306	6	5	2
5	0.679306	6	5	2
6	0.718521	6	5	3
7	0.718521	6	5	3
8	0.718521	6	5	3
9*	0.744797	6	5	0
10	0.744797	6	5	0
11	0.744797	6	5	0
12	0.718521	6	5	3

Table 2: Characterization of the decision rules for the *rolling bearings* information system

rule's number	numbers of objects $d = 0$	$d = 1$	estimate of rule's probability	estimates of decisions' probabilities $d = 0$	$d = 1$
1	10	0	0.1729	0.962	0.038
2	20	0	0.2867	0.941	0.059
3	0	21	0.3847	0.139	0.861
4	1	0	0.0402	0.639	0.361
5	3	0	0.1155	0.891	0.109

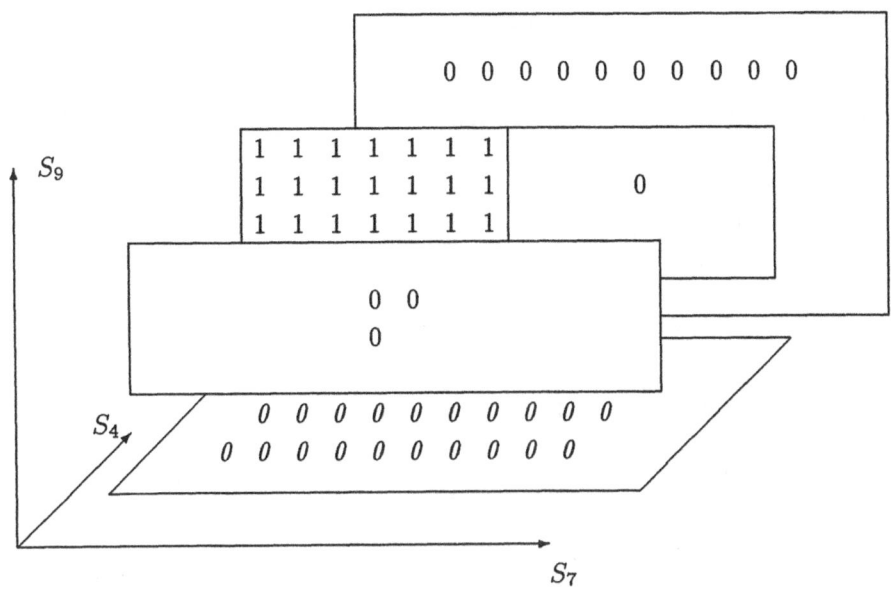

Figure 2: Graphical illustration of the decision rules for the *rolling bearings* information system

The second illustrative example concerns the analysis of the famous *iris* data [5]. This information system consists of 150 objects, which are characterized by 4 condition attributes x_1, x_2, x_3, x_4, and one decision attribute d with the domain $V_d = \{1, 2, 3\}$.

The rough classifier was generated using exactly the same procedure as in the first example. Basing on the results included in Table 3, we selected the 9–elemental set of preliminary intermediate values.

The rough classifier for the *iris* information system has the form

1	if $x_4 \geq 16.5$			then $d = 3$
2	if $x_4 < 16.5$	and	$x_3 < 24.5$	then $d = 1$
3	if $x_4 < 16.5$	and	$24.5 \leq x_3 < 50.5$	then $d = 2$
4	if $x_4 < 16.5$	and	$x_3 \geq 50.5$	then $d = 3$

Table 4 includes characterization of the rough classifier for the *iris* information system. The structure of this classifier is illustrated in Figure 3.

Now, we compare the results obtained for the rough classifiers with those from statistical discriminant analysis [7]. Statistical classifiers have been used for classification purposes for many years. The analysis was performed using the DISCRIM procedure of the SAS System [8]. We chose the linear classifier, which is the most popular parametric discriminant classifier. It assumes that condition attributes within each class have the multivariate normal distribution with equal covariance matrices. We also chose two nonparametric classifiers which, like the rough classifiers, are free of assumptions about any specific form

Table 3: Selection of the number of preliminary intermediate values for the *iris* information system

number of intermediate values	C(3,5,10) after 2–nd stage	number of rules 3–rd stage	4–th stage	number of errors
2	0.470606	4	3	6
3	0.772721	5	4	4
4	0.795846	6	5	4
5	0.854755	7	4	4
6	0.854755	7	4	4
7	0.873561	7	4	4
8	0.882437	7	4	4
9*	0.884892	8	4	4
10	0.871129	9	6	5
11	0.871129	9	6	5
12	0.871129	9	6	5
13	0.871129	9	6	5

Table 4: Characterization of the decision rules for the *iris* information system

rule's number	numbers of objects $d=1$	$d=2$	$d=3$	estimate of rule's probability	estimates of decisions' probabilities $d=1$	$d=2$	$d=3$
1	0	2	46	0.3163	0.000	0.066	0.934
2	50	0	0	0.3334	1.000	0.000	0.000
3	0	47	1	0.3145	0.000	0.960	0.040
4	0	1	3	0.0357	0.000	0.292	0.708

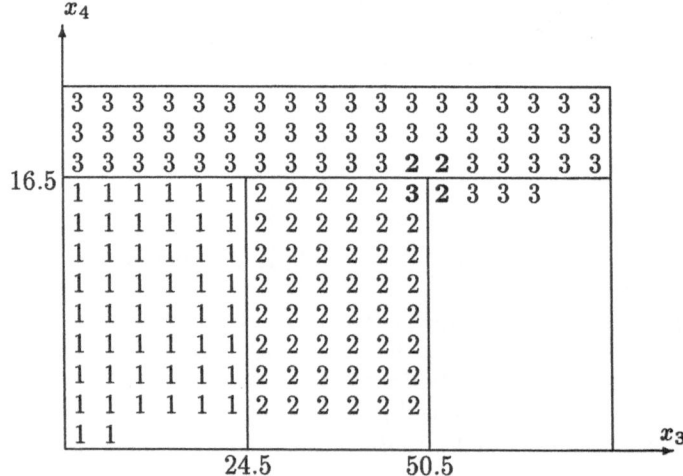

Figure 3: Graphical illustration of the decision rules for the *iris* information system

Table 5: Numbers of misclassified objects obtained by the *leaving–one–out* method

Classifier	*rolling bearings* information system	*iris* information system
rough	6	4
linear	14	3
1–nn	15	5
3–nn	13	5
kernel	15	3

of the probability distribution within the classes. However, with nonparametric discriminant classifiers, learning samples have to be stored, because they are used in classifying new objects from outside the information system. We used the k–th nearest neighbor classifier for $k = 1$ (1–nn) and for $k = 3$ (3–nn), and the kernel classifier with a normal kernel for estimating probability densities.

The accuracy of all used classifiers was evaluated by the *leaving–one–out* method. In accordance with this method, the classifier is generated by using all learning objects with the exclusion of one. Next, this one object is classified. This procedure is repeated until each object has been classified in this way. In Table 5 we included the numbers of misclassified objects obtained by the *leaving–one–out* method with all used classifiers and both information systems. All the classifiers were constructed under the assumption that the numbers of objects in the classes are random (see section 3.4 and section 4).

8 Conclusions

The rough classifiers offer a clearly explained procedure for knowledge discovery which is useful in the classification problems with continuous condition attributes. These classifiers do not need assumptions about the form of the attributes distribution. The knowledge that is involved in the learning sample is expressed in terms of simple logical rules. These rules reflect the structure of the data, and their form coincides with the process of human common reasoning.

The rules can be used to predict decisions for the objects from outside the information system. The validation procedures can be performed easily to estimate the misclassification rate. As with all classifiers, the accuracy of the rough classifiers depends on the structure of data, but frequently it is greater than the accuracy of other classifiers.

The rules generated by the rough classifiers are based on the most important attributes for classification purposes. Redundant attributes are removed automatically. The strength of each rule can be evaluated by the estimate of its probability and by the estimates of decisions probabilities.

The procedure of the rough classifier generation is stable, and rules are not sensitive to small changes in the particular form of the specified elements of the classifier generation algorithm. The presented approach to the classifier construction can be generalized to the mixed case of continuous and discrete condition attributes.

Acknowledgments

This study has been supported by the grant no. 8 S503 033 06 of the Scientific Research Committee (KBN).

References

[1] Z. Pawlak, *Rough Sets: Theoretical Aspects of Reasoning about Data*, Kluwer Academic Publisher, Dordrecht (1991).

[2] A. Lenarcik and Z. Piasta, *Discretization of condition attribute space*, in R. Slowinski, (ed.), *Intelligent Decision Support*, Kluwer Academic Publishers, Dordrecht (1992) pp. 373–389.

[3] A. Lenarcik and Z. Piasta, *Probabilistic approach to decision algorithm generation in the case of continuous condition attributes*, Foundations of Computing and Decision Sciences **vol. 18** 3/4 (1993) pp. 213–223.

[4] R. Nowicki, R. Słowiński and J. Stefanowski, *Analysis of diagnostic symptoms in vibroacoustic diagnostics by means of the rough sets theory* , in R. Slowinski, (ed.), *Intelligent Decision Support*, Kluwer Academic Publishers, Dordrecht (1992) pp. 33–48.

[5] R. A. Fisher, *The use of multiple measurments in taxonomic problems*, Annales of Eugenics **vol. 7** (1936) pp. 179–188.

[6] D. J. Hand, *Kernel Discriminant Analysis*, Research Studies Press, New York (1982).

[7] D. J. Hand, *Discrimination and Classification*, Wiley, New York (1985).

[8] SAS Institute Inc., *SAS/STAT User's Guide, Version 6, Fourth Edition, Volume 1* , Cary, NC: SAS Institute Inc., (1989).

A General Two-Stage Approach to Inducing Rules from Examples

Jerzy Stefanowski

Politechnika Poznańska – Instytut Informatyki
ul. Piotrowo 3a, 60-965 Poznań, Poland

Daniel Vanderpooten

Université Paris Dauphine - LAMSADE
Place du Maréchal De Lattre de Tassigny, 75775 Paris Cedex 16, France

Abstract

A two-stage approach for inducing rules from examples is presented. The first stage consists in a breadth-first exploration which generates all 'relevant' rules. The second stage consists in selecting a subset of these rules so as to produce a 'satisfactory' description. Rough sets concepts may be used in cases of incomplete or inconsistent examples.

1 Introduction

Machine Learning has given rise to a large number of algorithms for inducing generalizations from examples. Considering a set of objects or examples, a generalization consists of a *discriminant* description of each class (or concept). A description of a class is said to be discriminant when it is *complete* (each positive example - i.e. belonging to the class - must be recognized as belonging to the class) and *consistent* (each negative example - i.e. belonging to any of the other classes - cannot be recognized as belonging to the class). Some algorithms provide such descriptions in the form of a decision tree (see ,e.g., [17]) while others provide a set of rules. Rule generation is only considered in this paper.

Many algorithms for inducing rules from examples have been proposed (see, e.g., [13, 14, 3, 7]). They aim at generating a subset of rules which forms a discriminant description and optimizes a *preference criterion* (see [12]). Such a criterion, which should reflect the 'quality' of a description, is usually related with the number of rules or conditions involved in the rules.

A crucial point in these algorithms is the way of performing the search within the space of rules in order to select the required subset. Since explicit characterization and exhaustive exploration of this space lead to combinatorial difficulties, heuristic approaches, avoiding these characterization and exploration steps, are usually implemented. All these algorithms follow the same general *greedy* scheme:

```
begin
    while all the positive examples are not covered do
    begin
        construct a 'best' rule;
        remove the positive examples covered by this rule
    end;
        take the disjunction of these rules as the required description
end
```

(where *'best'* is defined according to the *preference criterion* considered).

As it is well-known in combinatorial optimization, such a *greedy* heuristic strategy (consisting in taking first the best components) may perform rather poorly. Moreover, it should be emphasized in this case that the rule constructed in the above **while** loop is actually not guaranteed to be the *'best'* since it results itself from a heuristic generation process consisting in combining selectors (basic conditions). This process can be performed in a more or less *greedy* fashion: either by progressively choosing *'best'* selectors to form one *'best'* rule (as in the PRISM algorithm [3]) or, less greedily, by generating a limited subset of rules resulting from combinations of *'best'* selectors and selecting one of them as the *'best'* rule (as done when constructing a STAR in the AQ algorithms [13, 12]).

Because of this imbrication of *greedy* heuristics at different levels, the optimality of the resulting description regarding the preference criterion is far from being guaranteed. We suggest an alternative two-stage approach which characterizes and explores, at least partially, the space of rules. This approach should provide better results in terms of the preference criterion considered. Above all, it allows to integrate quite easily various preference criteria. The two stages are:

1. generation of all 'relevant' rules

2. selection of some relevant rules to construct a 'satisfactory' description

The first stage is performed using a *breadth-first* search which generates rules of increasing size. The tests at each step of this search are shown to be quite simple. Several possibilities of controlling the search by incorporating one or several heuristic stopping conditions are discussed. This leads to what we call 'relevant' rules since such heuristic stopping conditions are designed so as to guarantee desirable properties.

The second stage is shown to be equivalent to a well-known combinatorial problem : the *Weighted Set Covering* problem. By considering different types of costs (weights), we show that it is possible to get different types of 'satisfactory' descriptions corresponding to various preference criteria.

Learning systems are often faced with noisy data (see [11, 12, 18]). This can result either from incomplete examples (missing data in the description of the examples), or from inconsistent examples (examples with a same description belonging to different classes). We show that our approach can be easily adapted to both cases. More precisely, we suggest to use rough sets concepts (see, e.g., [15, 16, 21]) which are particularly interesting since they allow to handle these difficulties without introducing additional information.

After introducing some concepts and stating the problem of rule induction (section 2), we present each stage of our approach (section 3). The relevance of this approach, in terms of computational burden and flexibility, is finally discussed (section 4).

2 Definition of The Problem

2.1 Basic Concepts and Notations

Let X be a set of objects or examples partitionned into m classes $X_1, \ldots, X_m$. Each class X_i $(i = 1, \ldots, m)$ is considered independently so as to be described on the basis of its positive examples (objects from X_i) and negative examples (objects from $X \setminus X_i$). In the following, K will represent the concept to be described.

K is either an original class X_i or a subset of X derived from X_i. The second possibility arises when examples are incomplete and/or inconsistent.

In the case of incomplete examples, most of the existing approaches consist in removing or completing these examples (see, e.g., [19, 8]). This results in considering either a subset or a superset of the original class (notice that such completed supersets may give rise to inconsistent examples).

In the case of inconsistent examples, we suggest to resort to rough sets theory which is particularly suited to analyse such examples. One of its advantages is that it does not need any preliminary or additional information about data (like probabilities in probability theory, grades of membership in fuzzy sets theory,...). Moreover, inconsistencies are not corrected but handled by determining for each class X_i its lower approximation $\underline{X_i}$ (corresponding to objects which certainly belong to the class), its upper approximation $\overline{X_i}$ (corresponding to objects which possibly belong to the class) and its boundary (corresponding to objects from $\overline{X_i} - \underline{X_i}$)(see, e.g., [15, 16] for more details). Instead of generalizing the original class, approximations and/or boundary of this class are used as concepts to be described. This leads to *exact* rules when the lower approximation is used and *approximate* rules when the upper approximation or the boundary is used. Rules are certain if they univocally indicate class assignment and possible otherwise. Several induction algorithms based on rough sets have been proposed (see, e.g., [22, 16, 9, 20]).

Let us consider the following concepts and notations:

- a *selector* is an elementary statement representing a basic condition[1] which can be checked for any $x \in X$. Formally, a selector s can be represented as a mapping $s : X \rightarrow \{\text{true, false}\}$.

- a *complex* C, of size q, is a conjunction of q selectors: $C = s_1 \wedge s_2 \wedge \cdots \wedge s_q$. We have: $C(x) = \bigwedge_{i=1}^{q} s_i(x)$. The size of a complex C will be denoted $\text{Size}(C)$.

- the *block* of a complex C, denoted by $[C]$, is the subset of objects which satisfy the conditions represented by C. We have: $[C] = \{x \in X \ / \ C(x) = true\}$.

- considering the concept K to be described, we denote $[C]_K^+ = [C] \cap K$, the set of positive examples covered by C and $[C]_K^- = [C] \cap X \setminus K$, the set of negative examples covered by C.

---

[1]To illustrate this definition, we can refer to the classical attribute-value case, where selectors are in the form $<attribute\ rel\ value>$ where *rel* stands, e.g., for $=$, $\neq$, $\leq$,... or $\in$ and *value* represents a specific value or a set of values

- a *rule* (which partially describes K) is an assertion of the form

$$if \; R(x) = \text{true} \; then \; x \in K$$

where R is a complex $s_1 \wedge s_2 \wedge \cdots \wedge s_q$ which is:

- *partial*: $[R] \cap K \neq \emptyset$,
- *consistent*: $[R] \cap (X \setminus K) = \emptyset$,
- *minimal*: removing any selector s_j from R would result in a complex which is no longer consistent.

Notice that, given a concept K to be described, a rule is fully characterized by its complex. Thus, in the following, we shall identify rules with partial, consistent and minimal complexes.

2.2   Problem Statement

The basic purpose of an induction algorithm consists in constructing discriminant (complete and consistent) descriptions. In our case, a description is a disjunction of rules. As each rule is consistent according to our definition (see definition of a rule - section 2.1), a description which consists of a disjunction of rules is discriminant if it is complete.

Since a very large number of discriminant descriptions are available, machine learning techniques usually aim at generating a *minimal* discriminant description. A discriminant description is minimal if removing any of its rules would result in a description which is no longer complete.

Since there usually still remains a large number of minimal descriptions, additional criteria must be considered. Such criteria are called *preference criteria* in [12] since they should reflect the user's preferences. Classical preference criteria (to be minimized) are:

PC1: the number of rules,

PC2: the number of selectors,

PC3: the difficulty of using the description, ...

The two first criteria deal with the structure of the description. The third one, which is particularly interesting when using descriptions for classifying new objects, is an example of a subjective criterion integrating the user's preferences. For instance, in the attribute-value case, it may happen that some attributes are difficult to evaluate, in which case the user might prefer to avoid these attributes in the description.

A minimal discriminant description which is optimal with respect to a specific preference criterion will be referred to as a *minimum* description. Generating a minimum description is a desirable objective from a theoretical viewpoint. In practice however, this amounts to solving very difficult combinatorial problems. Moreover, imposing strict optimality in terms of the preference criterion considered is often unnecessary since, in many cases, this preference criterion reflects the quality of a description in an approximative way only. We can even accept that some requirements, like completeness of the description, could be relaxed (in practical applications, it may be damaging to impose to cover untypical or even false positive examples). For such reasons, a desirable objective from a practical viewpoint consists in trying to generate a *'satisfactory'* description, i.e., a description which is sufficiently close to the optimal solution and which possibly slightly violates some basic requirements provided that these violations are fully controlled and prevented if required.

Another attitude when considering induction from examples consists in trying to induce all possible knowledge from the data. In this case, we are interested in generating *all* rules. This may produce a very large number of rules, many of which may be weakly established (supported by very few examples and/or very specialized). Thus, it may be relevant to focus on the strongest patterns and generate only all the most 'relevant' rules.

We shall thus distinguish two possible objectives when performing induction from examples:

1. generation of all *'relevant'* rules (or *all* rules)

2. construction of a *'satisfactory'* description (or a *minimum* description)

Similar objectives are also considered in [9] where they are referred to respectively as 'a knowledge acquisition approach' and 'a machine learning approach'.

Both objectives are treated in our approach. We propose a general exploration procedure which allows to get all relevant rules or even all rules (objective 1). When objective 2 is considered, we suggest a two-stage approach which consists first in achieving objective 1 and then in selecting a subset of rules by solving a classical combinatorial problem.

3   The Two-Stage Approach

We now present each stage of our approach.

3.1   Generation of All 'Relevant' Rules

We examine in this section the generation of rules defined as partial, consistent and minimal complexes (see section 2.1).

Considering a candidate complex C, it is partial and consistent if the following relations are satisfied:

$$[C]_K^+ \neq \emptyset \text{ and } [C]_K^- = \emptyset \tag{1}$$

Moreover, considering $C' = C \wedge s_l$ where s_l is a selector, we have:

$$[C']_K^+ = [C]_K^+ \cap [s_l]_K^+ \text{ and similarly } [C']_K^- = [C]_K^- \cap [s_l]_K^- \tag{2}$$

which makes the checking (regarding partialness and consistency) of a candidate complex, derived from another complex by including a new selector, particularly easy. This feature suggests to perform the exploration of the space of rules by considering complexes of increasing size. Such an exploration can be achieved by implementing a simple *breadth-first* search:

```
begin
    for each available selector s do
    begin
        determine [s]⁺_K and [s]⁻_K;
        if [s]⁺_K ≠ ∅ and [s]⁻_K = ∅ then store s as a rule and discard s;
        if [s]⁺_K = ∅ or s satisfies the heuristic stopping condition then discard s
    end;
    form a queue with all the remaining selectors s₁,...,sₙ;

    while the queue is not empty do
    begin
        remove the first complex C from the queue;
        let h be the highest index of the selectors involved in C;
        generate all the complexes C ∧ s_{h+1}, C ∧ s_{h+2},...,C ∧ sₙ;
        let C be the set of these complexes;
        for each C' ∈ C do
        begin
            if [C']⁺_K ≠ ∅ and [C']⁻_K = ∅ then
            begin
                if C' is minimal then store it as a rule;
                C ← C \ {C'}
            end;
            if [C']⁺_K = ∅ or C' satisfies the heuristic stopping condition then C ← C \ {C'}
        end;
        place all the complexes from C at the end of the queue
    end
end
```

The above algorithm is very general and can be improved in many ways to reduce the exploration. These improvements range from general heuristic ideas (e.g., ordering the selectors in decreasing order considering the number of objects covered) to small implementation details (e.g., it is unnecessary to put complexes of the form $C' = C \wedge s_n$ in the queue since they cannot be extended). Other improvements are related to the type of selectors used (in the attribute-value case, when combining selectors to C, all selectors involving an attribute already in C will be discarded).

Regarding *minimality*, it is unnecessary to test it for rules of size 1 and 2. Moreover, taking into consideration the way the exploration is performed, it is sufficient to test the current candidate complex against rules previously generated whose sizes are strictly inferior (but at least 2).

Even if the above algorithm is quite efficient since it rejects a large number of possibilities, its computational complexity is exponential in the worst case. This is one reason why we suggest to incorporate additional *heuristic stopping conditions*. Another reason is that it has been noticed, in practice, that rules which cover a large number of examples and rules of small size are the most interesting. It should be emphasized that, according to the way the search is performed, such rules are generated first. This suggests the following heuristic stopping conditions:

Let C be the complex currently examined,

HSC1: $| [C]⁺_K | < l$, where $| . |$ denotes the cardinality of a set and l is the smallest number of examples that a rule must cover

HSC2: $\mathrm{Size}(C) > m$, where m is the largest acceptable size

Notice that neither HSC1 nor HSC2 guarantees the completeness of the description. This may not be damaging ; it is even instructive to check the objects which are difficult to cover (and possibly present them to the user or an expert). However, when a complete description is required, we should continue the search with complexes which could potentially cover the uncovered examples. It is then possible to design a stopping condition which appears as the conjunction of one of the above **HSC** with the following condition:

HSC3: $[C]_K^+ \subset K'$, where $K' \subset K$ is the subset of objects already covered by rules previously generated

3.2 Construction of a 'Satisfactory' Minimal Description

When a minimal 'satisfactory' description is looked for, we must select a subset of the 'relevant' rules generated at stage 1 to form the description. This selection problem is highly related with the following well-known combinatorial problem referred to as the *Weighted Set Covering Problem* (WSC) :

Instance: A finite set S and a family $\mathcal{S} = \{S_1, \ldots, S_p\}$ of subsets $S_j \subset S$. A cost c_j is associated with each $S_j \in \mathcal{S}$.
A subfamily $\mathcal{S}' = \{S_{j_1}, \ldots, S_{j_m}\}$ of $\mathcal{S}$ such that $\bigcup_{i=1}^m S_{j_i} = S$ is called a *cover* of S. The cost of the cover $\mathcal{S}'$ is $\sum_{i=1}^m c_{j_i}$.

Question: Find a cover with minimum cost.

This problem has been extensively studied in combinatorial optimization, where many exact algorithms (see, e.g., [4, 1, 5]) and approximation algorithms (see, e.g., [6, 10, 2]) are available.

Considering again our initial problem, we have the following relationships. S and $\mathcal{S}$ correspond respectively to the set K of objects and the set of the blocks $[R_j]$, where R_j $(j = 1, \ldots, k)$ are the 'relevant' rules generated at stage 1. c_j is the cost associated with each rule R_j. These costs will be used so as to take into account preference criteria. More precisely, the choice of the values c_j according to the preference criteria introduced in section 2.2 is as follows:

PC1 (minimize the number of rules): $c_j = 1$ $(j = 1, \ldots, k)$

PC2 (minimize the number of selectors): $c_j = \text{Size}(R_j)$ $(j = 1, \ldots, k)$

To illustrate the case of criterion **PC3** (minimize the difficulty of using the description), we consider again the attribute-value case. After having defined a cost α_i of 'using' attribute a_i $(i = 1, \ldots, n)$, we set $c_j = \sum_{i \in I_j} \alpha_i$ where $I_j \subset \{1, \ldots, n\}$ is the subset of indices of attributes used in rule R_j $(j = 1, \ldots, k)$.

Finally, it is also possible to resort to a combination of such criteria or to use them in a lexicographic order. For instance, if we wish to consider in priority criterion **PC1** and then, in case of ties, criterion **PC2**, we just have to set $c_j = M + \text{Size}(R_j)$ $(j = 1, \ldots, k)$ where M is a large number.

4 Conclusions

Unlike classical greedy approaches, our two-stage approach can be tuned in order to guarantee optimality. Indeed, it is sufficient to consider each stage, in its purest form (1. generation of *all* rules - 2. construction of a *minimum* description). This clearly could involve large and even prohibitive computations since each of the above stages has, in its purest form, an exponential complexity in the worst case. However, the first point to be noticed is that our approach can, at least theoretically, guarantee optimality.

Actually, we *do not* suggest to use this approach in its purest form. Considering stage 1, we indicated a series of heuristic stopping conditions designed to restrict the search to the 'relevant' rules, i.e. to the strongest patterns of knowledge. As a result, this also drastically reduces the computational burden. For instance, if we use **HSC2** (which restricts the search to complexes of size at most m), assuming that n selectors are to be combined, the problem considered is polynomial in $O(n^m)$ (where typical values for m are 2, 3 or 4 depending on the size of the problem).

Regarding stage 2, it is possible to resort to an exact or approximation algorithm to solve the Set Covering problem. Considering experimental results reported in [1, 5], exact algorithms can be used with reasonable computational times when the number of objects in each class or concept is up to 400 and the number of candidate rules for this class is up to 4000. Approximation algorithms should be used when faced with large data sets. Computational experiments should be performed to compare our two-stage approach with classical greedy approaches in terms of computational times (which are clearly worse in our case) and in terms of the quality of the resulting description.

As a final remark, we emphasize that an important feature of our approach is its flexibility. Indeed, the two-stage approach can be easily customized to various user's requirements by selecting different types of heuristic stopping conditions (stage 1) and preference criteria (stage 2) (whereas classical greedy induction algorithms are mainly oriented towards the minimization of number of rules - preference criterion **PC1**). The significance of the words 'relevant' and 'satisfactory' is directly related to this variety of possibilities.

References

[1] J.E. Beasley. An algorithm for set covering problem. *European Journal of Operational Research*, 31:85–33, 1987.

[2] J.E. Beasley. A lagrangian heuristic for set-covering problems. *Naval Research Logistics*, 37:151–164, 1990.

[3] J. Cendrowska. PRISM: an algorithm for inducing modular rules. *Int. J. Man-Machine Studies*, 27:349–370, 1987.

[4] N. Christofides and S. Korman. A computational survey of methods for the set covering problem. *Management Science*, 21(5):591–599, 1975.

[5] N. Christofides and J. Paixão. Algorithms for large set covering problems. *Annals of Operations Research*, 43:261–277, 1993.

[6] V. Chvatal. A greedy heuristic for the set-covering problem. *Mathematics of Operations Research*, 24(3):233–235, 1979.

[7] P. Clark and T. Niblett. The CN2 induction algorithm. *Machine Learning*, 3:261–283, 1989.

[8] J.W. Grzymala-Busse. On the unknown attribute values in learning from examples. In *Proc. of the ISMIS'91 6th Int. Symp. on Methodologies for Intelligent Systems*, pages 368–377, 1991.

[9] J.W. Grzymala-Busse. LERS-a system for learning from examples based on rough sets. In R. Słowiński, editor, *Intelligent Decision Support*, pages 3–18. Kluwer Academic Publishers, 1992.

[10] D.S. Hochbaum. Approximation algorithm for the set covering and vertex cover problems. *SIAM J. Comput.*, 11:555–556, 1982.

[11] Y. Kodratoff, M. Manago, and J. Blythe. Generalization and noise. *Int. J. Man-Machine Studies*, 27:181–204, 1987.

[12] R.S. Michalski. A theory and methodology of inductive learning. In R.S. Michalski, J.G. Carbonell, and T.M. Mitchell, editors, *Machine Learning: An Artificial Intelligence Approach*, pages 83–134. Morgan Kaufman, 1983.

[13] R.S. Michalski and R.L. Chilausky. Learning by being told and learning from examples: an experimental comparison of the two methods of knowledge acquisition in the context of developing an expert system for soybean disease diagnosis. *Policy Analysis and Information Systems Journal*, 4(2):125–160, 1980.

[14] R.S. Michalski, I. Mozetic, J. Hong, and N. Lavrac. The multipurpose incremental learning system AQ15 and its testing application to three medical domains. In *Proc. of the 5th Nat. Conf. on Artificial Intelligence AAAI-86, Philadelphia*, pages 1041–1045, 1986.

[15] Z. Pawlak. Rough sets. *Int. J. Computer and Information Sci.*, 11:341–356, 1982.

[16] Z. Pawlak. *Rough Sets - Theoretical Aspects of Reasoning about Data*. Kluwer Academic Publishers, 1991.

[17] J.R. Quinlan. Discovering rules from large collections of examples - a case study. In D. Michie, editor, *Experts Systems in the Microelectronics Age*. Edinburgh University Press, 1979.

[18] J.R. Quinlan. The effect of noise on concept learning. In R.S. Michalski, J.G. Carbonell, and T.M. Mitchell, editors, *Machine Learning: An Artificial Intelligence Approach Vol.II*, pages 83–134. Morgan Kaufman, 1986.

[19] J.R. Quinlan. Unknown attribute values in induction. In *Proc. of the 6th Int. Workshop on Machine Learning*, pages 164–168, 1989.

[20] A. Skowron. Boolean reasoning for decision rules generation. In J. Komorowski and Z.W. Ras, editors, *Methodologies for Intelligent Systems, LN in AI 689*, pages 295–305. Springer Verlag, Berlin, 1993.

[21] R. Słowiński, editor. *Intelligent Decision Support, Handbook of Applications and Advances of the Rough Sets Theory*. Kluwer Academic Publishers, 1992.

[22] S.K.M. Wong and W. Ziarko. On learning and evaluation of decision rules in the context of rough sets. In *Proc. of the ACM SIGART Int. Symp. on Methodologies for Intelligent Systems*, pages 308–324, 1986.

An Incremental Learning Algorithm for Constructing Decision Rules

Ning Shan

Department of Computer Science, University of Regina
Regina, Saskatchewan, Canada S4S 0A2
e-mail : ning@CS.UREGINA.CA

Wojciech Ziarko

Department of Computer Science, University of Regina
Regina, Saskatchewan, Canada S4S 0A2
e-mail : ziarko@CS.UREGINA.CA

Abstract

A number of algorithms and systems for generating the best minimal decision rules from data have been developed based on the theory of rough sets in the past decade. However, these algorithms do not have incremental learning capability. An incremental learning algorithm for computing a set of all minimal decision rules is presented. The algorithm is based on the decision matrix method which can generate all of the minimum decision rules from the training data.

1   Introduction

An inductive learning (learning from examples) system has the ability to automatically generate a knowledge base. A knowledge base is a set of production rules in an **if-then** form. In the standard model of learning from examples, the objective of the learning algorithm is to automatically produce, from a given set of historical data (the training data set), its own knowledge base which will be used to classify future examples (the test data set). It is one of the methods of overcoming the knowledge acquisition "bottle-neck" in the process of encoding knowledge into the decision rules of an expert system.

There are two primary techniques used to represent the induced rules: a decision tree and a set of decision rules. These two methods help human experts understand the solutions to a problem better. Quinlan[8] suggested an inductive algorithm to generate a decision tree based on a statistical theory of information which was initially proposed by Shannon[9]. Pawlak[1], on the other hand, developed a rough sets theory by which a minimal set of decision rules can be obtained.

In the past decade, a number of algorithms and systems for rule extraction from data have been developed based on rough sets theory[1]. Most of them focus on generating the best minimal set of decision rules that is consistent with a given set of training data. However, these algorithms do not have incremental learning capability. By incremental learning capability, we mean that a rule generating algorithm generates a new set of decision rules (or decision tree) without regenerating previous results(rules) when new data objects become available. An incremental learning system builds upon its previous results by gradually expanding and updating its knowledge base while more data becomes available. Such a system is not necessarily incremental in storage and processing costs, e.g., it may need to remember some or all previous examples[7].

An important problem in the application of a machine learning system is the maintenance of the knowledge base in a dynamic environment. It is often necessary to alter the current knowledge base when information on a new object is provided[4]. This paper reports an incremental algorithm for learning decision rules and dynamically adjusting the knowledge base. The presented approach, which is based on the idea of the decision matrix and discernibility matrix defined in previous research works[2,3,6], provides a new way of incrementally learning decision rules.

The paper is organized as follows. Section 2 reviews some elementary notions of rough sets and information systems theory. Section 3 introduces the concept of a decision matrix and some related definitions. The principle of the incremental learning algorithm is presented in Section 4 and concluding remarks in Section 5.

2 Information Systems

This section deals with the concept of information systems as defined in rough sets theory. In the process of data analysis in rough sets theory, the main computational effort is associated with the determination of attribute relationships in information systems. The concept of information system plays a very important role in rough set theory and is adopted by many application systems.

2.1 Information System Model

The basic component of an information system S is a set of objects. It can be conveniently represented by a data table (attribute-value system), the columns of which are labeled by condition and decision attributes. The rows are labeled by objects.

A *decision table* , which is a special case of information system introduced by Pawlak[1], is a finite set of decision rules which specify what decisions (actions) should be taken when certain conditions are satisfied.

Let $S = < OBJ, C, D, \{VAL_a\}_{a \in A} >$ be an information system S, where OBJ is a non-empty set of objects, C is a non-empty set of condition attributes, and D is a non-empty set which contains decision attributes. We have $A = C \cup D$ which is the set of all attributes and $C \cap D = \emptyset$. VAL_a is a domain of an attribute "a" with at least two elements. The elements of VAL_a are called values of attribute a ($a \in A$). Each attribute $a \in A$ can be perceived as a function assigning a value $a(obj) \in VAL_a$ to each object $obj \in OBJ$. Every object which belongs to OBJ is therefore associated with a set of values corresponding to the condition attributes C and decision attributes D.

Table.1 shows an example of an information system. That is, the universe of discourse OBJ consists of eight objects, $OBJ = \{ obj_1, obj_2, ..., obj_8 \}$. Each object is described by set of condition attributes $C = \{$ SIZE, HAIR, EYES, COMPLEXION $\}$, with attribute values $VAL_{size} = \{$ short, tall $\}$, VAL_{hair}

OBJ	C				D
	SIZE	HAIR	EYES	COMPLEXION	CLASSIFICATION
obj_1	short	dark	blue	pale	0
obj_2	tall	dark	brown	matt	1
obj_3	tall	red	blue	pale	0
obj_4	short	blond	blue	matt	1
obj_5	tall	blond	blue	pale	1
obj_6	tall	dark	blue	pale	0
obj_7	tall	blond	brown	matt	1
obj_8	short	dark	brown	matt	1

Table 1: An example of an information system.

$= \{$ dark, red, blond $\}$, $VAL_{eyes} = \{$blue, brown$\}$, and $VAL_{complexion} = \{$ pale, matt $\}$. The set of values $VAL_{classification} = \{ 0, 1 \}$ of the decision attribute D represents the set of concept descriptions which are to be learned based on the attribute values of C. In our terminology, the concept is a subset of objects with a particular value of a decision attribute. All objects belonging to the concept are said to be positive whereas all objects outside the concept are negative.

2.2 Reduction of Decision Rules

The generation of decision rules (knowledge base) is an important aspect of the rough sets methodology. Decision rules can be obtained directly from an information system. Some condition values may be unnecessary in a decision rule produced directly from such a table. Such values can then be dropped to create a simpler rule. The process in which the maximum number of condition attribute values are removed without losing essential information is called *Value Reduction* and the resulting rule is called minimal.

It is possible for one set of attributes to have more than one group of minimal decision rules (covering the target concept). The rule generating process depends much on the sequence in which attributes are processed. Most machine learning algorithms attempt to find the minimal, with respect to inclusion relation, set of such rules covering the target class. The rules in the minimal set can be characterized as[5]:

1. Discriminating between different target concepts;

2. Capturing only essential factors for future classification;

3. Being nonredundant in terms of minimizing the number of rules and their conditions;

4. Matching the maximum number of "training" cases;

5. Resulting in a low error rate in the classification of new cases.

Intuitively, reducing knowledge representation means dropping all dispensable condition attributes and condition attribute values from the information system. In reality, however, it is very difficult to determine which minimal set of decision rules or which attribute reduced table should be used.

3 Decision Matrix

A decision matrix can be used to compute all minimal sets of decision rules and the reduct sets[1] of an information system S. It provides a way to generate the simplest set of decision rules, while preserving all essential information. The approach to generation of rules as presented here is based upon the construction of a number of Boolean functions[2,6] from decision matrices.

Before we define the concept of a decision matrix we will assume some notational conventions. That is, we will assume that all positive and negative objects are separately numbered with subscript i ($i = 1, 2, ...\gamma$) and j ($j = 1, 2, ...\rho$) respectively. To distinguish positive from negative objects we will use superscripts V and $\sim V$, for instance, obj_i^V versus $obj_j^{\sim V}$ for the class "V".

Definition A decision matrix $M(S) = (M_{ij})$ of an information system $S =< OBJ, C \cup D, \{VAL_a\}_{a \in A} >$ is defined as

$$M_{ij} = \{(a, a(obj_i^V)) : a(obj_i^V) \neq a(obj_j^{\sim V})\}$$

The set M_{ij} contains all attribute-value pairs (*attribute, value*) whose values are not identical between obj_i^V and $obj_j^{\sim V}$. In other words, M_{ij} represents the complete information distinguishing obj_i^V from $obj_j^{\sim V}$.

The set of minimal decision rules $|B_i|$ for a given object obj_i^V ($i = 1, 2, ...\gamma$) is obtained by forming the Boolean expression

$$B_i^V = \bigwedge_j \bigvee M_{ij}$$

where $\bigwedge$ and $\bigvee$ are respectively generalized conjunction and disjunction operators.

The Boolean expression called a decision function B_i^V is constructed out of row i of the decision matrix, that is $(M_{i1}, M_{i2}, ... M_{i\rho})$, by formally treating each attribute-value pair occurring in the component M_{ij} as a Boolean variable and then forming a Boolean conjunction of disjunctions of components belonging to each set M_{ij} ($j = 1, 2, ..., \rho$).

The decision rules $|B_i^V|$ are obtained by turning such an expression into disjunctive normal form and using the absorption law of Boolean algebra to simplify it. The conjuncts, or prime implicants of the simplified decision function correspond to the minimal decision rules[2,3,6]. Similarly, by treating the complement of the class "V" as a target concept, a set of decision rules can be computed for each object of the class "$\sim V$" using the same approach. Some of the decision functions obtained from decision matrices given in Fig. 1 and derived from the information contained in Table 1 are presented in *Example 1*.

Once all the decision rule sets $|B_i^V|$ have been computed, a set of all minimal decision rules $RUL(|V_d|)$ for the concept $|V_d|$ corresponding to the decision value V_d ($|V_d| = \{obj \in OBJ : d(obj) = V_d, d \in D, V_d \in VAL_d\}$) is given by

$$RUL(|V_d|) = \bigcup |B_i^V| \quad (i = 1, 2, ...\gamma)$$

i	j OBJ	1 obj_2	2 obj_4	3 obj_5	4 obj_7	5 obj_8
1	obj_1	(S,0)(E,1) (C,0)	(H,0)(C,0)	(S,0)(H,0)	(S,0)(H,0) (E,1)(C,0)	(E,1)(C,0)
2	obj_3	(H,1)(E,1) (C,0)	(S,1)(H,1) (C,0)	(H,1)	(H,1)(E,1) (C,0)	(S,1)(H,1) (E,1)(C,0)
3	obj_6	(E,1)(C,0)	(S,1)(H,0) (C,0)	(H,0)	(H,0)(E,1) (C,0)	(S,1)(E,1) (C,0)

(a) A decision matrix for class '0'

i	j OBJ	1 obj_1	2 obj_3	3 obj_6
1	obj_2	(S,1)(E,2) (C,1)	(H,0)(E,2) (C,1)	(E,2)(C,1)
2	obj_4	(H,2)(C,1)	(S,0)(H,2) (C,1)	(S,0)(H,2) (C,1)
3	obj_5	(S,1)(H,2)	(H,2)	(H,2)
4	obj_7	(S,1)(H,2) (E,2)(C,1)	(H,2)(E,2) (C,1)	(H,2)(E,2) (C,1)
5	obj_8	(E,2)(C,1)	(S,0)(H,0) (E,2)(C,1)	(S,0)(E,2) (C,1)

(b) A decision matrix for class '1'

Figure 1: Decision matrices for Table 1

Example 1.
Fig.1 depicts two decision matrices obtained from the information system given in Table 1. In these decision matrices, S is an abbreviation for "SIZE", H for "HAIR" and so on. $VAL_S = \{0,1\}$ represents $VAL_{size} = \{short, tall\}$, $VAL_H = \{0,1,2\}$ represents $VAL_{hair} = \{dark, red, blond\}$, $VAL_E = \{1,2\}$ represents $VAL_{eyes} = \{blue, brown\}$ and $VAL_C = \{0,1\}$ represents $VAL_{complexion} = \{pale, matt\}$. Each cell (i,j) in a decision matrix is a collection of attribute-value pairs distinguishing row i of the target class from column j of its complement.

Based on these decision matrices we can obtain the following decision functions B_i^0 (i = 1, 2, 3) from the class '0' decision matrix and B_i^1 (i = 1, 2, ...5) from the class '1' decision matrix.

Class '0' decision functions:

$$B_1^0 = ((S,0) \vee (E,1) \vee (C,0)) \wedge ((H,0) \vee (C,0)) \wedge ((S,0) \vee (H,0))$$
$$\wedge ((S,0) \vee (H,0) \vee (E,1) \vee (C,0)) \wedge ((E,1) \vee (C,0))$$
$$= ((S,0) \wedge (C,0)) \vee ((H,0) \wedge (E,1)) \vee ((H,0) \wedge (C,0))$$

$$B_2^0 = ((H,1) \vee (E,1) \vee (C,0)) \wedge ((S,1) \vee (H,1) \vee (C,0))$$
$$\wedge ((H,1)) \wedge ((H,1) \vee (E,1) \vee (C,0)) \wedge ((S,1) \vee (H,1) \vee (E,1) \vee (C,0))$$
$$= (H,1)$$

$$B_3^0 = ((E,1) \vee (C,0)) \wedge ((S,1) \vee (H,0) \vee (C,0) \wedge ((H,0)) \wedge ((H,0) \vee (E,1) \vee (C,0))$$
$$\wedge ((S,1) \vee (E,1) \vee (C,0)) = ((H,0) \wedge (E,1)) \vee ((H,0) \wedge (C,0))$$

Class '1' decision functions:

$$B_1^1 = ((S,1) \vee (E,2) \vee (C,1)) \wedge ((H,0) \vee (E,2) \vee (C,1)) \wedge ((E,2) \vee (C,1))$$
$$= (E,2) \vee (C,1)$$

$$B_2^1 = ((H,2) \vee (C,1)) \wedge ((S,0) \vee (H,2) \vee (C,1)) \wedge ((S,0) \vee (H,2) \vee (C,1))$$
$$= (H,2) \vee (C,1)$$
$$B_3^1 = ((S,1) \vee (H,2)) \wedge ((H,2)) \wedge ((H,2)) = (H,2)$$
$$B_4^1 = ((S,1) \vee (H,2) \vee (E,2) \vee (C,1)) \wedge ((H,2) \vee (E,2) \vee (C,1))$$
$$\wedge((H,2) \vee (E,2) \vee (C,1)) = (H,2) \vee (E,2) \vee (C,1)$$
$$B_5^1 = ((E,2) \vee (C,1)) \wedge ((S,0) \vee (H,0) \vee (E,2) \vee (C,1)) \wedge ((S,0) \vee (E,2) \vee (C,1))$$
$$= (E,2) \vee (C,1)$$

Some example decision rules derived from B_1^0 are:

$$(SIZE = short) \wedge (COMPLEXION = pale) \rightarrow (CLASS =' 0')$$
$$(HAIR = dark) \wedge (EYES = blue) \rightarrow (CLASS =' 0')$$
$$(HAIR = dark) \wedge (COMPLEXION = pale) \rightarrow (CLASS =' 0')$$

The $\bigcup |B_i^0|$ corresponds to all the minimal decision rules RUL for the class '0' of the information system shown in Table 1:

$$(SIZE = short) \wedge (COMPLEXION = pale) \rightarrow (CLASS =' 0')$$
$$(HAIR = dark) \wedge (EYES = blue) \rightarrow (CLASS =' 0')$$
$$(HAIR = dark) \wedge (COMPLEXION = pale) \rightarrow (CLASS =' 0')$$
$$(HAIR = red) \rightarrow (CLASS =' 0')$$

Similarly, $\bigcup |B_i^1|$ represents the set of all minimal rules for the class '1':

$$(EYES = brown) \rightarrow (CLASS =' 1')$$
$$(COMPLEXION = matt) \rightarrow (CLASS =' 1')$$
$$(HAIR = blond) \rightarrow (CLASS =' 1')$$

4   An Incremental Learning Algorithm

An important objective of an incremental learning algorithm is the maintenance of the knowledge base in a dynamic environment. For machine learning problems in which new objects are to be added to an information system S, it is highly beneficial from efficiency point of view to accept objects and modify rules in an incremental fashion, instead of regenerating all the rules already existing in the system. The proposed algorithm computes only the decision rules that are affected by the new objects in a newly organized information system S_{new}.

The learning algorithm presented here processes new objects by modifying current decision matrices and decision rules RUL instead of regenerating a new set of decision rules. Each decision rule set for each information system object is maintained during the process, so that it can be updated during the generation of the set of decision rules. The addition of a new object results in the following incremental learning algorithm (or knowledge base update algorithm):

Process Increment
Step 1. Determine which target concept $|V_d|$ the new object belongs to. If the new object does not belong to any of the current target concepts, then define a new target concept and add it to the set of current target concepts.

i	OBJ		C			D
		SIZE	HAIR	EYES	COMPLEXION	CLASSIFICATION
6	obj_9	tall	dark	brown	pale	1

Table 2: A new object

Next, consider two class decision problem, class "V" equivalent to $|V_d|$ and class "$\sim V$" equivalent to $OBJ - |V_d|$. Let (M_{ij}^V) be the current decision matrix for this problem. If there is only one class then stop processing.

Let us denote the new object as obj_k^V according to convention described in Section 3.

Step 2. Create a new row of decision matrix (M_{kj}^V):

$$(M_{kj}^V) = \{(a, a(obj_k^V)) : a(obj_k^V) \neq a(obj_j^{\sim V}), obj_j^{\sim V} \notin |V_d|\}$$

Step 3. Compute the decision function of obj_k^V

$$B_k^V = \bigwedge_j \bigvee M_{kj}^V$$

and the associated set of decision rules $|B_k^V|$.
Update the current set of decision rules $RUL(|V_d|)$ to become

$$RUL'(|V_d|) = RUL(|V_d|) \cup |B_k^V|$$

Step 4. For each target concept $W_d \neq V_d$, update the current decision matrix (M_{ij}^W) by creating a new column of decision matrix:

$$(M_{ik}^W) = \{(a, a(obj_i^W)) : a(obj_i^W) \neq a(obj_k^{\sim W}), obj_i^W \in |W_d|\}$$

where $obj_k^{\sim W}$ is the new object which belongs to $OBJ - |W_d|$ in this case.

Next, update the current decision functions B_i^W to become $B_i^{W'}$ by computing and simplifying the Boolean expression

$$B_i^{W'} = B_i^W \bigwedge \bigvee M_{ik}^W$$

and then update the rule set by taking the union of the associated rule sets, that is

$$RUL'(|W_d|) = \bigcup |B_i^{W'}|$$

The algorithm offers an approach to incremental learning of all minimal decision rules. Although the algorithm essentially applies to extraction of rules in deterministic cases, it can be extended to non-deterministic cases by constructing rules with decision probabilities using the extended model of rough sets, the Variable Precision Rough Sets model(VPRS)[5].

Example 2.
In Example 1, we obtained all minimal decision rules RUL for the information system shown in Table 1. Now, let's consider adding a new object as shown in Table 2. Suppose that the new object obj_9 belongs to class '1'. To update the knowledge base, we create the following new row in the decision matrix for class '1'

$$M_{6,1}^1 = (S,1)(E,2) \quad M_{6,2}^1 = (H,0)(E,2) \quad M_{6,3}^1 = (E,2)$$

and compute the decision function B_6^1 for the new object:

$$B_6^1 = \quad ((S,1) \vee (E,2)) \wedge ((H,0) \vee (E,2)) \wedge ((E,2)) = (E,2)$$

By adding the rule corresponding to the term (E, 2) to the set of rules obtained in the Example 1 we obtain the following updated set of rules for class '1':

$$(EYES = brown) \rightarrow (CLASS =' 1')$$
$$(COMPLEXION = matt) \rightarrow (CLASS =' 1')$$
$$(HAIR = blond) \rightarrow (CLASS =' 1')$$

To update the rules for class '0', we create a new column in the decision matrix for class '0'

$$M_{1,4}^0 = (S,0)(E,1) \quad M_{2,4}^0 = (H,1)(E,1) \quad M_{3,4}^0 = (E,1)$$

and the we update the decision functions B_i^0 $(i = 1,2,3)$ as derived from Fig.1 (a).

$$B_1^{0'} = \quad B_1^0 \wedge ((S,0) \vee (E,1)) = ((S,0) \wedge (C,0)) \vee ((H,0) \wedge (E,1))$$
$$B_2^{0'} = \quad B_2^0 \wedge ((H,1) \vee (E,1)) = (H,1)$$
$$B_3^{0'} = \quad B_3^0 \wedge ((E,1)) = ((H,0) \wedge (E,1))$$

¿From the above computation, we obtain the new set of minimal decision rules for class '0'.

$$(SIZE = short) \wedge (COMPLEXION = pale) \rightarrow (CLASS =' 0')$$
$$(HAIR = dark) \wedge (EYES = blue) \rightarrow (CLASS =' 0')$$
$$(HAIR = red) \rightarrow (CLASS =' 0')$$

5 Summary and Conclusions

An incremental learning process for constructing a set of all minimal decision rules has been developed. The approach is based upon a decision matrix[6] method stemming from the earlier concept of discernibility matrices[2]. The core of the learning algorithm for generating decision rules offers an improvement over traditional approaches in that it dynamically constructs and improves the decision rules in the learning process. The main computation of decision rules is reduced to the problem of simplification and adaption of a group of associated Boolean expressions. Since the simplification problem can be easily decomposed into a number of disjoint subproblems by independently simplifying parts of the whole formula, the present approach is most suitable for implementation in multiprocessor systems.

334

6 Acknowledgments

The research reported in this paper was supported in part by an operating grant from the Natural Sciences and Engineering Research Council of Canada.

References

[1] Pawlak, Z. *Rough Sets: Theoretical Aspects of Reasoning About Data*, Kluwer Academic Publishers, 1991.

[2] Skowron, A. and Rauszer, C. The Discernibility Matrices and Functions in Information Systems. In Slowinski, R. (ed.) *Intelligent Decision Support: Handbook of Applications and Advances of Rough Sets Theory*, 1992.

[3] Skowron, A., and Suraj, Z. A Rough Set Approach to Real-Time State Identification for Decision Making. *ICS Report 18/93*, Warsaw University of Technology, 1993.

[4] Orlowska, E., and Orlowski, M. Maintenance of Knowledge in Dynamic Information Systems. In Slowinski, R. (ed.) *Intelligent Decision Support: Handbook of Applications and Advances of Rough Sets Theory*, 1992.

[5] Ziarko, W. Variable Precision Rough Set Model. *Journal of Computer and System Sciences*, Vol. 46, No. 1, 1993, pp. 39-59.

[6] Ziarko, W. and Shan, N. A Rough Set-Based Method For Computing All Minimal Deterministic Rules in Attribute-Value Systems. *Technical CS-93-02*, Department of Computer Science, University of Regina,Canada, 1993.

[7] W. M. Shen. Complementary Discrimination Learning with Decision Lists. In *Proceedings of AAAI-92*, San Jose CA. AAAI Press. pp. 153-158.

[8] Quinlan, J. R. Learning Efficient Classification Procedures and Their Application to Chess and Games. In Michalski, R. S., Carbonell, J. G. and Mitchell, T. M. (eds.) *Machine Learning: the Artificial Intelligence Approach*, Palo Alto: Tioga Press. 1983.

[9] Shannon, C. E. A mathematical theory of communication. *Bell System Technical Journal, 4*, pp. 379-423, 1948.

Decision Trees for Decision Tables

Mikhail Moshkov *

Research Institute for Applied Mathematics and Cybernetics
Nizhni Novgorod State University
10, Uljanova St., Nizhni Novgorod, 603005, Russia

Abstract

We investigate decision trees for decision tables. We present some upper and lower bounds on the minimal decision tree depth. These bounds are expressed by some parameters of decision rule systems constructed for decision tables.

Introduction

Information systems [4], [5] and test tables [1] are widely known tools for modeling problems described by some finite systems of functions defined on finite sets.

We consider some problems related to dependencies between attributes in decision tables. They arise when it is necessary to determine the values of some attributes (called decisions) knowing the values of some others (called conditions). We consider the decision algorithms for these problems in the form of decision trees.

We present the relationships between decision trees and decision rule systems investigated in the theory of information systems [6], [7]. In proofs we apply the test theory [2], [3] methods. We prove some lower and upper bounds for the minimal decision tree depth.

1   Basic Definitions and Notations

The concepts of decision table, decision rule and decision tree are defined in this section.

1.1   Decision Tables

Let $\omega = \{0, 1, 2, \ldots\}$ and let $E_k = \{0, \ldots, k-1\}$ for any $k \in \omega \setminus \{0\}$.

A *decision table* is 3-tuple $T = (U, C, D)$, where

a) U - is a non-empty, finite set of objects, called *the universe*,

---

*This work has been done when author visited Institute of Mathematics at Warsaw University. The work was supported by Russian Foundation of Fundamental Researches (grant # 93-012-488). The travel to RSKD'93 was supported by International Science Foundation (grant # 0701).

b) C and D are a non-empty, finite and disjoint sets of *attributes*, i.e. $a : U \to V_a$ for $a \in C \cup D$, where $V_a = \{a(u) : u \in U\}$ is called *the value set* of a.

Attributes from C and D are called *conditions* and *decisions*, respectively. Later on we assume $C = \{c_1, \ldots, c_n\}$ and $D = \{d_1, \ldots, d_p\}$.

With any decision table T we associate the following problem: for any $u \in U$ determine the full information about the values $d_1(u), \ldots, d_p(u)$ knowing only the values $c_1(u), \ldots, c_n(u)$.

The indiscernibility relation [5] $IND(C) = \{(u_1, u_2) \in U^2 : c_i(u_1) = c_i(u_2), i = 1, \ldots, n\}$ defines a partition U into equivalence classes $U_1, \ldots, U_m$.

Let us define a decision table $T^\star = (U^\star, C^\star, D^\star)$:

a) $U^\star = \{U_1, \ldots, U_m\}$;

b) $C^\star = \{c_1^\star, \ldots, c_n^\star\}$ and for any $c_i^\star \in C^\star$, $U_j \in U^\star$ $c_i^\star(U_j) = c_i(u)$ where $u \in U_j$;

c) $D^\star = \{d\}$ and $d(U_j) = \bigcup_{u \in U_j}\{(d_1(u), \ldots, d_p(u))\}$ for any $U_j \in U^\star$.

Let $u \in U_j$. Evidently, the full information about the values $d_1(u), \ldots, d_p(u)$, which we can determine knowing only the values $c_1(u), \ldots, c_n(u)$, consists of the fact $(d_1(u), \ldots, d_p(u)) \in d(U_j)$.

Consequently, the decision tables T and $T^\star$ are equivalent with respect to the decision attributes values determination. Besides, we can to denote all attributes values by numbers from ω.

Now we can to define a concept of simple decision table.

A decision table $T = (U, C, D)$ is called *simple* if it satisfies the following conditions:

a) $|D| = 1$;

b) $V_a \subseteq \omega$ for any $a \in C \cup D$;

c) for any $u_1, u_2 \in U$ such that $u_1 \neq u_2$ there exists an attribute $c_i \in C$ for which $c_i(u_1) \neq c_i(u_2)$.

Let $T = (U, C, D)$ be a simple decision table with $D = \{d\}$. The decision table T is called *non-degenerate* if $|V_d| \geq 2$. We denote by $k(T)$ the minimal number from $\omega \setminus \{0\}$ satisfying the following condition: $V_{c_i} \subseteq E_{k(T)}$ for any $c_i \in C$.

1.2   Decision Rules

Let $T = (U, C, D)$ be a simple decision table with $C = \{c_1, \ldots, c_n\}$ and $D = \{d\}$.

A *decision rule over* T is any expression of the following form:

$$c_{i_1} = \sigma_1 \wedge \ldots \wedge c_{i_m} = \sigma_m \Rightarrow d = \sigma$$

where $c_{i_1}, \ldots, c_{i_m} \in C$, $\sigma_1, \ldots, \sigma_m \in E_{k(T)}$, $\sigma \in V_d$. Let us denote this decision rule by r. The decision rule r is *true in* T if

$$\{u \in U : c_{i_1}(u) = \sigma_1, \ldots, c_{i_m}(u) = \sigma_m\} \subseteq \{u \in U : d(u) = \sigma\}.$$

The expression $c_{i_1} = \sigma_1 \wedge \ldots \wedge c_{i_m} = \sigma_m$ is *the left part of* r and the expression $d = \sigma$ is *the right part of* r. We denote by $h(r)$ the number m.

Let $E(T) = E_{k(T)}^n$ and $E(r, T) = \{(\delta_1, \ldots, \delta_n) \in E(T) : \delta_{i_1} = \sigma_1, \ldots, \delta_{i_m} = \sigma_m\}$.

Let S be a non-empty, finite system (set) of decision rules over T.

The system S is *super complete for T* if $\bigcup_{r \in S} E(r, T) = E(T)$.

The system S is *strong for T* if $E(r_1, T) \cap E(r_2, T) = \emptyset$ for any $r_1, r_2 \in S$ such that $r_1 \neq r_2$.

Let $h(S) = \max\{h(r) : r \in S\}$.

We denote by $RS(T)$ the set of all systems S of decision rules over T satisfying following conditions:

a) S is non-empty, finite system;

b) S is the super complete system for T;

c) S is the strong system for T;

d) any decision rule from S is true in T.

Let $Q(T) = \min\{h(S) : S \in RS(T)\}$.

1.3 Decision Trees

Let $T = (U, C, D)$ be a non-degenerate simple decision table where $C = \{c_1, \ldots, c_n\}$ and $D = \{d\}$.

A *decision tree over* T is a marked finite directed tree which has the following properties:

a) the tree has more than one vertex;

b) any non-leaf vertex is labelled by an attribute from C;

c) exactly $k(T)$ edges are outgoing from any non-leaf vertex and labelled by $0, \ldots, k(T) - 1$;

d) all leaves are labelled by numbers from V_d.

Let Γ be a decision tree over T. A *complete path* in a tree Γ is any sequence $\xi = v_1, e_1, \ldots, v_m, e_m, v_{m+1}$ of vertices and edges of the tree Γ, where v_1 is the root of Γ, v_{m+1} is a leaf of Γ and for $i = 1, \ldots, m$ e_i is outgoing from v_i and incoming into v_{i+1}. We denote by $h(\xi)$ the number m. A *decision rule over* T *associated with a complete path* ξ, denoted by $rule(\xi)$, is an expression equal to

$$c_{i_1} = \sigma_1 \wedge \ldots \wedge c_{i_m} = \sigma_m \Rightarrow d = \sigma$$

where the attribute c_{i_j} is assigned to the vertex v_j, σ_j is the number assigned to the edge e_j for $j = 1, \ldots, m$ and σ is the number assigned to the vertex v_{m+1}.

The decision tree Γ is *true in* T if $rule(\xi)$ is true in T for any $\xi \in PATH(\Gamma)$, where $PATH(\Gamma)$ denotes the set of all complete path in Γ. Let $h(\Gamma) = \max\{h(\xi) : \xi \in PATH(\Gamma)\}$. The value $h(S)$ is called *the depth of* Γ.

We denote by $DT(T)$ the set of all decision trees over T which are true in T. Let $h(T) = \min\{h(\Gamma) : \Gamma \in DT(T)\}$.

One may interpret a decision tree Γ over T as an algorithm for computing the value $d(u)$ from the values $c_i(u)$, $c_i \in C$, for any $u \in U$. This algorithm is correct if and only if $\Gamma \in DT(T)$.

2 Minimal Decision Tree Depth Bounds

In this section for any non-degenerate simple decision table T we present some upper and lower bounds on $h(T)$ expressed by $Q(T)$ and $k(T)$.

2.1 Main result

The parameter $k(T)$ is defined in Subsection 1.1 and the parameter $Q(T)$ is defined in Subsection 1.2.

Theorem 1 *Let T be a non-degenerate simple decision table. Then*

$$Q(T) \le h(T) \le (Q(T))^2 \ln k(T) + 1. \quad \square$$

2.2 Relationships between Decision Trees and Decision Rule Systems

Lemma 1 *Let T be a non-degenerate simple decision table and $\Gamma \in DT(T)$. Then*

$$\{rule(\xi) : \xi \in PATH(\Gamma)\} \in RS(T).$$

Proof. Let $S = \{rule(\xi) : \xi \in PATH(\Gamma)\}$. Taking into account that $\Gamma \in DT(T)$ we get that S is non-empty, finite set and $rule(\xi)$ is true in T for any $\xi \in PATH(\Gamma)$.

Let v be a non-leaf vertex of Γ. Using the fact that Γ is a decision tree over T one can show that the following properties hold:

(i) for any $\delta \in E_{k(T)}$ there exists an edge outgoing from v which is labelled by δ;

(ii) the edges outgoing from v are labelled by pairwise different numbers.

¿From (i) one can show that S is a super complete system for T. Using the property (ii) it is easy to show that S is a strong system for T. Therefore, $S \in RS(T)$. $\square$

2.3 An Algorithm for Constructing Decision Trees

We define an algorithm W for constructing a decision tree $W(T,S) \in DT(T)$ for any non-degenerate simple decision table T and any system $S \in RS(T)$.

Let $T = (U, C, D), C = \{c_1, \ldots, c_n\}$ and $D = \{d\}$. We denote by $DES(T)^*$ the set of all finite words over an alphabet $\{(c_i, \delta) : c_i \in C, \delta \in E_{k(T)}\}$ including the empty word λ. For each $\alpha \in DES(T)^*$ we define a set $E(\alpha, T) \subseteq E(T) = E_{k(T)}^n$ as follows: if $\alpha = \lambda$, then $E(\alpha, T) = E(T)$, otherwise

$$E(\alpha, T) = \{(\delta_1, \ldots, \delta_n) \in E(T) : \delta_{i_1} = \sigma_1, \ldots, \delta_{i_m} = \sigma_m\},$$

where $\alpha = (c_{i_1}, \sigma_1) \ldots (c_{i_m}, \sigma_m)$.

By $S(\alpha)$ we denote the set

$$\{r \in S : E(r, T) \cap E(\alpha, T) \neq \emptyset\},$$

where $\alpha \in DES(T)^*, S \in RS(T)$.

Let us define a function $P_S : DES(T)^* \to \omega \cup \{-1\}$ as follows: $P_S(\alpha) = |S(\alpha)| - 1$ for any $\alpha \in DES(T)^*$.

Now we can describe an algorithm W for computing a decision tree $W(T,S)$ for a given T and S.

Step 1. Construct a tree $W(T,S)$ with of one vertex only labelled by the empty word λ.

Step 2. If there are no vertices in $W(T, S)$ labelled by a word from $DES(T)^*$ then the algorithm stops with the result $W(T, S)$, otherwise choose a vertex v in $W(T, S)$ and a word $\alpha \in DES(T)^*$ such that v is labelled by α.

If $S(\alpha) = \emptyset$ then reconstruct $W(T, S)$ by changing only the label α of v to the minimal number from V_d. Proceed to step 2.

If $S(\alpha) = \{r\}$ for some r with the right part $d = \sigma$ then reconstruct $W(T, S)$ by changing the label of v from α to σ. Proceed to step 2.

If $|S(\alpha)| \geq 2$ then compute $q_i := \max\{P_S(\alpha(c_i, \delta)) : \delta \in E_{k(T)}\}$ for $i = 1, \ldots, n$. Let $i_0 := \min\{k \in \{1, \ldots, n\} : q_k = \min\{q_j : j = 1, \ldots n\}\}$. Reconstruct the tree $W(T, S)$ by changing the label of the vertex v from α to c_{i_0} and by adding a vertex v_δ with the label $\alpha(c_{i_0}, \delta)$ and an edge $e_\delta = (v, v_\delta)$ with the label δ for any $\delta \in E_{k(T)}$. Proceed to step 2.

Lemma 2 *Let T be a non-degenerate simple decision table and $S \in RS(T)$. Then*

$$W(T, S) \in DT(T).$$

Proof. Evidently, $W(T, S)$ is a decision tree over T. For an arbitrary $\xi \in PATH(W(T, S))$ one can prove that $E(rule(\xi), T) = \emptyset$ or there exists a rule $r \in S$ with the following properties: $E(rule(\xi), T) \subseteq E(r, T)$ and the right parts of rules r and $rule(\xi)$ are equal. Taking into account this properties it is easy to show that $rule(\xi)$ is true in T. Thus, $\Gamma \in DT(T)$. $\square$

Lemma 3 *Let T be a non-degenerate simple decision table, $S \in RS(T)$, α, β, $(c_i, \delta) \in DES(T)^*$ and $E(\alpha\beta(c_i, \delta), T) \neq \emptyset$. Then*

$$P_S(\alpha) - P_S(\alpha(c_i, \delta)) \geq P_S(\alpha\beta) - P_S(\alpha\beta(c_i, \delta)).$$

Proof. We denote by $B(\alpha)$ (respectively, by $B(\alpha\beta)$) the set of all rules r from $S(\alpha)$ (respectively, from $S(\alpha\beta)$) with the following property: there is equality $c_i = \sigma$ in the left part of r with $\sigma \neq \delta$. Since $E(\alpha\beta(c_i, \delta), T) \neq \emptyset$ one can prove that $B(\alpha\beta) \subseteq B(\alpha), |B(\alpha)| = P_S(\alpha) - P_S(\alpha(c_i, \delta))$ and $|B(\alpha\beta)| = P_S(\alpha\beta) - P_S(\alpha\beta(c_i, \delta))$. Using these relations it is easy to show that the statement of Lemma holds. $\square$

Proposition 1 *Let T be a non-degenerate simple decision table and $S \in RS(T)$. Then*

$$h(W(T, S)) \quad = \quad 1 \text{ if } h(S) = 1 \text{ and}$$
$$h(W(T, S)) \quad \leq \quad h(S)\ln|S| + 1 \text{ if } h(S) \geq 2.$$

Proof. Let $T = (U, C, D), C = \{c_1, \ldots, c_n\}$ and $D = \{d\}$.

Let $h(S) = 1$. Taking into account that $S \in RS(T)$ one can show that there exists an attribute $c_{i_0} \in C$ for which $S = \{c_{i_0} = \delta \Rightarrow d = \sigma(\delta) : \delta \in E_{k(T)}\}$, where $\sigma(\delta) \in V_d$ for any $\delta \in E_{k(T)}$.

Now we describe how the algorithm W works with T and S as input. After the first step the tree $W(T, S)$ consists exactly one vertex v which is labelled by λ. Taking into account that T is the non-degenerate decision table we have $|S(\lambda)| \geq 2$. Thus, on the second step we compute the value $q_i = \max\{P_S((c_i, \delta)) : \delta \in E_{k(T)}\}$ for $i = 1, \ldots, n$. Evidently, $q_{i_0} = 0$ and $q_i = |S(\lambda)| - 1 \geq 1$ for any $i \in \{1, \ldots, n\} \setminus \{i_0\}$. Hence after the second step the tree $W(T, S)$ consist the vertex v labelled by c_{i_0} and vertices v_δ labelled by

(c_{i_0}, δ) for any $\delta \in E_{k(T)}$. There is an edge e_δ outgoing from v and incoming into v_δ for any $\delta \in E_{k(T)}$. The edge e_δ is labelled by the number δ. Evidently, $|S((c_{i_0}, \delta))| = 1$ for any $\delta \in E_{k(T)}$. Hence when the algorithm W stops we obtain a tree $W(T, S)$ consisting exactly $k(T) + 1$ vertices $v, v_0, \ldots, v_{k(T)-1}$ labelled by $c_{i_0}, \sigma(0), \ldots, \sigma(k(T) - 1)$, respectively. Hence, $h(W(T, S)) = 1$.

Now let $h(S) \geq 2$. Let $\xi = v_1, e_1, \ldots, v_p, e_p, v_{p+1} \in PATH(W(T, S))$ and $p = h(W(T, S))$. If $p = 1$ then the inequality $h(W(T, S)) \leq h(S) \ln |S| + 1$ holds. Assume $p \geq 2$. Let the attribute c_{i_j} be assigned to the vertex v_j and let δ_j be the number assigned to the edge e_j for $j = 1, \ldots, p$. Let us put $\alpha_1 = \lambda$ and $\alpha_{j+1} = (c_{i_1}, \delta_1) \ldots (c_{i_j}, \delta_j)$ for $j = 1, \ldots, p$.

Now we can prove

$$P_S(\alpha_{j+1}) \leq ((h(S) - 1)/h(S)) P_S(\alpha_j) \tag{1}$$

for any $j \in \{1, \ldots, p\}$.

For an arbitrary $i \in \{1, \ldots, n\}$ let σ_i be the minimal number from $E_{k(T)}$ such that

$$P_S(\alpha_j(c_i, \sigma_i)) = \max\{P_S(\alpha_j(c_i, \sigma)) : \sigma \in E_{k(T)}\}. \tag{2}$$

¿From the definition of W we have that i_j is the minimal number from $\{1, \ldots, n\}$ such that

$$P_S(\alpha_j(c_{i_j}, \sigma_{i_j})) = \min\{P_S(\alpha_j(c_i, \sigma_i)) : i = 1, \ldots, n\}. \tag{3}$$

Let $\bar{\sigma} = (\sigma_1, \ldots, \sigma_n)$. ¿From the definition of W we have $|S(\alpha_j)| \geq 2$. Using this inequality and the equality (2) one can show that $E(\alpha_j(c_i, \sigma_i), T) \neq \emptyset$ for $i = 1, \ldots, n$. Hence, $\bar{\sigma} \in E(\alpha_j, T)$. Since S is a super complete system for T we have that there exists a decision rule $r \in S$ with $\bar{\sigma} \in E(r, T)$. Let $c_{t_1} = \sigma_{t_1} \wedge \ldots \wedge c_{t_m} = \sigma_{t_m}$ be the left part of r. Let us denote $\beta = (c_{t_1}, \sigma_{t_1}) \ldots (c_{t_m}, \sigma_{t_m})$. Evidently, $E(\beta, T) = E(r, T)$. Taking into account that S is the strong system for T one can show that $|S(\beta)| = 1$ and $P_S(\beta) = 0$. Hence, $P_S(\alpha_j \beta) \leq 0$. Let

$$
\begin{aligned}
\Sigma = \; &(P_S(\alpha_j) - P_S(\alpha_j(c_{t_1}, \sigma_{t_1}))) + \\
&(P_S(\alpha_j(c_{t_1}, \sigma_{t_1})) - P_S(\alpha_j(c_{t_1}, \sigma_{t_1})(c_{t_2}, \sigma_{t_2}))) + \ldots + \\
&(P_S(\alpha_j(c_{t_1}, \sigma_{t_1}) \ldots (c_{t_{m-1}}, \sigma_{t_{m-1}})) - P_S(\alpha_j(c_{t_1}, \sigma_{t_1}) \ldots (c_{t_m}, \sigma_{t_m}))).
\end{aligned}
$$

Evidently, $\Sigma = P_S(\alpha_j) - P_S(\alpha_j \beta) \geq P_S(\alpha_j)$. Since $\bar{\sigma} \in E(\alpha_j, T)$ and $\bar{\sigma} \in E(r, T) = E(\beta, T)$ we have that $E(\alpha_j \beta, T) \neq \emptyset$. From this observation, Lemma 3, and the equality (3) we have that

$$
\begin{aligned}
\Sigma \leq (P_S(\alpha_j) - P_S(\alpha_j(c_{t_1}, \sigma_{t_1}))) + \ldots + (P_S(\alpha_j) - P_S(\alpha_j(c_{t_m}, \sigma_{t_m}))) \leq \\
m(P_S(\alpha_j) - P_S(\alpha_j(c_{i_j}, \sigma_{i_j}))).
\end{aligned}
$$

Hence,

$$P_S(\alpha_j) \leq \Sigma \leq m(P_S(\alpha_j) - P_S(\alpha_j(c_{i_j}, \sigma_{i_j})))$$

and

$$P_S(\alpha_j(c_{i_j}, \sigma_{i_j})) \leq ((m - 1)/m) P_S(\alpha_j).$$

Now, from the equality (2) we have, that

$$P_S(\alpha_{j+1}) \leq ((m - 1)/m) P_S(\alpha_j).$$

Using this inequality and the evident inequality $m \leq h(S)$ one can show that the inequality (1) holds.

¿From the inequality (1) we have that

$$P_S(\alpha_p) \leq ((h(S) - 1)/h(S))^{p-1} P_S(\lambda).$$

¿From the definition of W follows that $P_S(\alpha_p) \geq 1$. Hence,

$$1 \leq ((h(S) - 1)/h(S))^{p-1} P_S(\lambda)$$

and

$$(1 + 1/(h(S) - 1))^{p-1} \leq P_S(\lambda).$$

Consequently,

$$(p - 1) \ln(1 + 1/(h(S) - 1)) \leq \ln P_S(\lambda).$$

Since, the inequality

$$\ln(1 + 1/t) > 1/(t + 1),$$

is true for any $t \in \omega \setminus \{0\}$, and $h(S) \geq 2$ we have that

$$(p - 1)/h(S) < \ln P_S(\lambda).$$

Hence,

$$h(W(T, S)) = p < h(S) \ln P_S(\lambda) + 1 < h(S) \ln |S| + 1. \quad \square$$

2.4   Proof of Theorem 1

Proof. Let $T = (U, C, D)$, $C = \{c_1, \ldots, c_n\}$ and $D = \{d\}$.

We first prove the inequality

$$h(T) \geq Q(T).$$

Let $\Gamma \in DT(T)$ and $h(\Gamma) = h(T)$. Let $S = \{rule(\xi) : \xi \in PATH(\Gamma)\}$. Applying Lemma 1 we have $S \in RS(T)$. Hence, $h(S) \geq Q(T)$. One can show that $h(\Gamma) = h(S)$. Consequently, $h(T) \geq Q(T)$.

Now we prove the inequality

$$h(T) \leq (Q(T))^2 \ln k(T) + 1.$$

Evidently, $Q(T) \leq n$. Let $S^* \in RS(T)$ and $h(S^*) = Q(T)$. Let $S = \{r \in S^* : E(r, T) \neq \emptyset\}$. Evidently, $S \in RS(T)$ and $h(S) = Q(T)$. ¿From Proposition 1 we have that

$$h(W(T, S)) \leq h(S) \ln |S| + 1.$$

Let us construct an upper bound for the value $|S|$. Taking into account that S is super complete system for T we have that

$$\left| \bigcup_{r \in S} E(r, T) \right| = (k(T))^n.$$

Since S is strong system for T we have

$$E(r_1, T) \cap E(r_2, T) = \emptyset$$

for any different rules $r_1, r_2 \in S$. Let $r \in S$. ¿From the relations $h(r) \leq h(S) = Q(T) \leq n$ and $E(r, T) \neq \emptyset$ it follows that inequality

$$|E(r, T)| \geq (k(T))^{n-Q(T)}$$

holds. Hence,

$$|S| \leq (k(T))^n / (k(T))^{n-Q(T)} = (k(T))^{Q(T)}.$$

Consequently, $h(W(T, S)) \leq (Q(T))^2 \ln k(T) + 1$. Since $W(T, S) \in DT(T)$ we have that $h(T) \leq (Q(T))^2 \ln k(T) + 1$. $\square$

Conclusions

In this paper we present some upper and lower bounds on the minimal decision tree depth. This results have some theoretical interest. Effective approximate algorithms which constructing the decision trees for the simple decision tables are presented in [2], [3].

Acknowledgement.

I am greatly indebted to Professor Andrzej Skowron for stimulating discussion and constructive criticism on an earlier version of this paper.

References

[1] Chegis I.A. and Yablonskii S.V., Logical Methods for Electrical Schemes Testing (in Russian), Trudy MI AN SSSR, 51, 270-360 (1958).

[2] Moshkov M.Ju., On the Conditional Tests (in Russian), Dokl. Akad. Nauk SSSR, 265, No. 3 , 550-552 (1982).

[3] Moshkov M.Ju., Conditional Tests (in Russian), Problemy Cyberneticy, 40, 131-170 (1983).

[4] Pawlak Z., Information Systems - Theoretical Foundations (in Polish), PWN, Warsaw (1981).

[5] Pawlak Z., Rough Sets - Theoretical Aspects of Reasoning about Data, Kluwer Academic Publishers (1991).

[6] Pawlak Z., Skowron A., A Rough Set Approach to Decision Rules Generation, Institute of Computer Science Reports, 23/93, Warsaw University of Technology (1993).

[7] Decision Support by Experience - Applications of the Rough Sets Theory, ed. Slowinski R., Kluwer Academic Publishers (1992).

Fuzzy Reasoning and Rough Sets

T.Y. Lin

Mathematics and Computer Science Department
San Jose State University
San Jose, California 95192 U.S.A.

Abstract

Fuzzy concepts are represented by fuzzy sets, so a fuzzy knowledge is defined to be a collection of fuzzy sets (concepts) which includes two constants, 1 (true) and 0 (false). Abstractly, a logical derivation is a finite series of logical operations acting on a given knowledge. In fuzzy world, logical operations are defined by mathematical operations. So fuzzy logical derivations are mathematical derivations, and vice versa In this paper, the closure of fuzzy reasoning is characterized by **fuzzy rough sets, and by topologies (neighborhood systems)**. A new fuzzy concept FN is derivable from the old knowledge K iff the membership function of FN is continuous in K-topology, or equivalently, iff FN is a rough fuzzy set (concept) of $IND(K)$, or plainly, iff the membership function of FN is a "step" function in the sense that it takes a constant value in each equivalence class of $IND(K)$. A fuzzy set L partitions the universe into equivalence classes; each equivalence class consists of those elements which have the same degree of membership. The indiscernibility relation $IND(K)$ over K is the "intersection" of all the equivalence relations induced by the fuzzy sets in K. The membership function of a fuzzy set is a real valued function, so U can be given the minimal topology such that the membership function of each fuzzy set in K is a continuous function. Such topology is called K-topology.

1 Introduction

In this paper, we study fuzzy reasoning in terms of rough set theory and topology (neighborhood systems). It is well accepted that propositions can be represented as subsets of a given set. "The correspondence between propositions and subsets is useful. The logical notion of conjunction, disjunction, implication and negation can be translated into intersections, union, inclusion and complementation." [7]. So knowledge will be processed via sets instead of propositions. A similar correspondence exits between fuzzy propositions and fuzzy sets. So fuzzy knowledge processing will be expressed in terms of fuzzy set theory.

2 Real World Fuzzy Sets and Admissible Functions

Let U be the universe of discourse, a classical set. A fuzzy set is an ordered pair:

(U, FX)

where $FX : U \longrightarrow M$ maps U into membership space M, where M is a non-negative subset of real numbers and the range of FX has finite supremum. When M contains only the two points 0 and 1, X is a classical set. If the supremum of the range is 1, the fuzzy set is called normal. We can always normalize a fuzzy set by dividing FX by its supremum. Note that (U, FX) is a fuzzy set and FX is a membership function of X. When the context is clear, we will use FX both as the fuzzy set or the membership function, namely,

$$FX = (U, FX)$$

In essence, we identify a fuzzy set with its (unique) membership function. This uniqueness is implicit in the published literature (e.g. [9], [3]). Fuzzy set operations are all defined in terms of membership functions without showing that the operations so defined are independent of the choice of membership functions (if there are more than one choices). However, Kendall did discuss that given a real world fuzzy set, it may have more than one membership functions to represent it; these membership functions are called admissible functions [3]. So we adopt the following convention that a (theoretical/mathematical) fuzzy set is represented uniquely by its membership function in theory, however, in applications, a real world fuzzy set may be represented by more than one theoretical/mathematical fuzzy sets.

3 Fuzzy Knowledge Processing

Let U be a universe of discourse. Following Pawlak[5], a subset X of U is called a concept. Similarly, a fuzzy subset FX is called a fuzzy concept. A user is said to have the fuzzy concept, if FX is available to him. We should like to point out here that in classical set theory, the expression that a user possesses a (classical) set X often assumes that the whole set and all its subsets are available to the user. In knowledge processing, we should stress that this is not a valid assumption. That a user has defined a universe of discourse does not imply that he has gained all the knowledge about that universe. A knowledge K about the universe is said to be complete if the collection K of fuzzy concepts can specify all possible concepts (classical subsets) of U[4]. So the expression that a concept X is given to a user merely means that the characteristic function is available to him.

Example 1. Let Company X has a special Division Y which is devoted to classified projects. The guard at the front gate of Division Y has been instructed about the encoding scheme of company's Badge numbers. So he can identify a member of Division Y by his Badge numbers. However, he has no knowledge about the internal structure or operations of Division Y. This is the situation that the guard has been given the characteristic function of Division Y but nothing else. □

Since every fuzzy set is defined on the universe U, it is an implicit assumption that every user knows the definition of his universe. In terms of membership functions, the assumption implies that the characteristic function of the universe (the characteristic function 1) is available to every user. These constant membership functions (identified as real numbers) are assumed to be a common knowledge to every users; perhaps, they should be called common sense.

A family of fuzzy concepts which includes the characteristic function of the universe (the characteristic function 1) and its complement (the characteristic function 0) is referred to as a fuzzy knowledge about U.

3.1 Formal Fuzzy Knowledge

Knowledge has to be processed, during the processing, its interpretation often becomes obscure. For example in physics, during the derivations of some important mathematical formulas, one may have to pass through some mathematical expressions which have no obvious physical meanings. Nevertheless their meanings are still there, just hidden from our intuition. In fuzzy knowledge processing, we encounter similar situations. We need to introduce a temporary notion, called formal fuzzy set, which has no formal interpretation. We would like to point out here that in this workshop, RSKD'93, Pawlak introduced an elegant notion of soft sets; formal fuzzy sets could be one of his candidates of soft sets. A bounded real valued function, U whose values may be negative, will be interpreted as a membership function of a formal fuzzy set. A collection of formal fuzzy sets which includes the constant functions 1 and 0 is called formal fuzzy knowledge. The family of (genuine) fuzzy sets is a subset of the family of formal fuzzy sets.

Let $K = \{FA_1, FA_2, \ldots, FA_n\}$ be a formal fuzzy knowledge. Then K gives rise to an evaluation map

$$Ev : U \longrightarrow E^n,$$

where E^n is the Cartesian Product of n-copies of reals and Ev is defined by

$$Ev(x) = (FA_1(x), FA_2(x), \ldots, FA_n(x))$$

where x represents an object in U, and each $FA_i(x)$ represents a component of the fuzzy description about x. If the knowledge K is (genuine and) normal, then we can take E^n to be the product of n-copies of $[0, 1]$. The map Ev is an important notion, it defines the indiscernibility relation over K. To explain this, let us recall some general facts about a given map: Let U and V be two classical sets, and $f : U \longrightarrow V$ be a map. Then we can define an equivalence relation as follows:

$$x \approx y \quad \text{iff} \quad f(x) = f(y).$$

It is easy to verify that $\approx$ is an equivalence relation, and will be denoted by R_f (read as equivalence relation associated to the map f). R_f defines a partition on U. Let QU be the quotient set The map $NQ : U \longrightarrow QU$, which maps every element x to its equivalence class $[x]$, is called natural projection. The following proposition follows immediately from the definitions.

Proposition 3.1. There is a "quotient" evaluation map $QEv : QU \longrightarrow E^n$ such that

(1) $Ev(x) = QEv([x])$, where $[x] = NQ(x)$

(2) QEv is one to one.

Note that $Ev(x) = (FA_1(x), FA_2(x), \ldots, FA_n(x))$, and $QEv([x]) = (QFA_1([x]), QFA_2([x]), \ldots, QFA_n([x]))$, where $FA_i(x) = QFA_i([x])$.

3.2 Continuous Formal Fuzzy Knowledge

The essence of fuzzy reasoning is approximation. Mathematician have captured the essence of approximation in terms of "neighborhoods"; they are studied in the theory of topological spaces or Frechet (V) spaces [2], [8]. We will recall some notions of topology here. For a collection K of real valued functions $U \longrightarrow R$, we can impose on U the minimal topology such that all the functions in K are continuous. We will call such minimal topology the K-topology. A formal fuzzy set, whose membership function is continuous under K-topology, is called continuous formal fuzzy concept. QU with quotient topology is called quotient universe. We will identify QU with its image $QEv(QU)$, a subset of Euclidean space. If QU is finite, then QU is discrete and compact. Let $Map(X, R)$ be the set of all functions: $X \longrightarrow R$, and $ConMap(X, R)$ be the set of all continuous bounded real valued functions on X. If X is compact, then $ConMap(X, R)$ is a Banach algebra with sup-norm, further, if X is finite discrete $Map(X, R) = ConMap(X, R)$ [2].

Let $K = \{FA_1, FA_2, \ldots, FA_n\}$ be a formal fuzzy knowledge. The collection $QK = \{QFA_1, QFA_2, \ldots, QFA_n\}$ is called quotient knowledge about the quotient universe QU. Note that QK are "coordinates" for points in $QEv(QU) = QU$. Let $S = \{f1, f2, \ldots, fn\}$ be a given set of real valued functions. Let $P[S]$ be the Polynomial algebra generated by S. The following proposition follows immediately from Stone-Weistrass approximation theorem [2].

Proposition 3.2. If QU is compact, then $P[QK]$ is dense in $ConMap(QU, R)$.

Proposition 3.3. If QU is finite, then $P[K]$ is dense in $ConMap(U, R)$.

Proof: If QU is finite, then $Map(QU, R)$ is isomorphic to $ConMap(U, R)$. To see this, let f be a continuous map in $ConMap(U, R)$. Since $QEv(QU)$ is discrete, f has to be constant on each equivalence class $[x]$, so it induces a "quotient map" $Qf : QU \longrightarrow R$. By similar analysis, $P[K]$ and $P[QK]$ are isomorphic. So the proposition follows from 3.2. $\square$

3.3 Fuzzy Knowledge

Now, we would like to apply the previous work to "genuine" fuzzy knowledge. We will apply the knowledge operator $FX \longrightarrow KO(FX)$ to transform all formal knowledge to normalized fuzzy knowledge, where KO is defined as follows:

Definition 3.5. $(KO(FX))(x) = \max(0, \min(1, FX(x))$.

This equation essentially truncates all function values which are below 0 or above 1. If FX is a multiset (or bag), $KO(FX)$ becomes a Cantor set.

Proposition 3.6. Let FN be a fuzzy concept and S a subset in $ConMap(U, R)$. Then FN is in the closure of $KO(S)$ if and only if FN is in the closure of S.

Proof: The operator KO is continuous on $ConMap(U, R)$. So, $KO(\lim(fi)) = \lim(KO(fi))$. Now if FN is a limiting point of S, then $KO(FN)$ is a limiting point of $KO(S)$. Since FN is a genuine fuzzy concept, $FN = KO(FN)$. So we have proved the proposition. □

The proof implies more than the statement of the proposition. It says that if a "genuine" fuzzy set is close (in the space of formal fuzzy sets) to a set S of formal fuzzy set, then the "genuine" fuzzy set is close (in the space of normalized fuzzy sets) to the "normalized" set of S.

4 Derivable Fuzzy Knowledge

In fuzzy world, fuzzy concepts or propositions are represented by fuzzy sets. Their logical operations are hence represented by fuzzy set operations. Further, the membership functions of fuzzy sets are real valued functions, so fuzzy set operations are defined by mathematical operations of real valued functions. In other words, logical operations of fuzzy concepts are mathematical operations. Abstractly, **a logical/mathematical derivation is a finite series of logical/mathematical operations acting on a given knowledge.** So in fuzzy world , a logical derivation is a special form of mathematical derivation. On the other hand, a mathematical derivation is a special type of logical derivations. So fuzzy reasoning is a series of mathematical operations acting on a collection of known fuzzy concepts(sets). There are two types of mathematical operations, one is the algebraic operations (addition and multiplication), the other is the topological operations (inequality). So the "derived fuzzy knowledge" will be defined by algebraic and topological operations. Let $Der(K)$ denote the closure of fuzzy reasoning; it is the algebraic and topological closure of K, or equivalently it is the topological closure of the polynomial algebra $P[K]$.

Definition 4.1. Let $K = \{FA_1, FA_2 \ldots, FA_n\}$ be a fuzzy knowledge. Let $Der(K)$ be the topological closure of the polynomial algebra $P[K]$. A fuzzy concept FN is said to be derivable from K iff FN belongs $Der(K)$.

Theorem 4.2. A fuzzy concept FN is derivable from K iff its membership function FN is continuous.

Proof: Let FN be continuous. By 3.6, FN is in the topological closure of $P[K]$. So, FN is derivable. Conversely, if FN is not a new knowledge, then it is in the closure of $P[K]$, hence it is a continuous function. A limit of continuous functions (based on sup norm) is continuous. □

Corollary 4.3. The K-topology uniquely determines all derivable knowledge from K.

Example 4.1. Let $U = \{x_1, x_2, x_3, x_4\}$. Let $K = \{FA_1, FA_2\}$ be a knowledge, where $FA_1(x_1) = FA_1(x_2) = 0.5$ and $FA_1(x_3) = 0.75$, $FA_1(x_4) = 0.9$, and $FA_2(x_1) = FA_2(x_2) = FA_2(x_3) = 0.3$ and $FA_2(x_4) = 0.6$. Let G be defined by $G(x_1) = G(x_2) = 0.1$ and $G(x_3) = 0.7$, $G(x_4) = 0.8$. Let H be defined by $H(x_1) = H(x_3) = 0.4$ and $H(x_2) = 0.7$, $H(x_4) = 0.8$. Then G is a continuous function, so is in the $Der(K)$. However, H is not continuous, so it is a new knowledge. The base of K-topology is $\{\{x_1, x_2\}, \{x_3\}, \{x_4\}\}$.

  (1) $G^{-1}(0.1) = \{x_1, x_2\}$, $G^{-1}(0.7) = \{x_3\}$, $G^{-1}(0.8) = \{x_4\}$; they are expressible as union of base, so G is continuous.

  (2) $H^{-1}(0.4) = \{x_1, x_3\}$, $H^{-1}(0.7) = \{x_2\}$, $H^{-1}(0.8) = \{x_4\}$; $\{x_2\}$ can not be expressed as union of base, so H is not continuous. Hence H is a new

knowledge. □

Proposition 4.4. The base of K-topology is the equivalence classes of the evaluation map.

This follows immediately from the meaning of evaluation map.
The K-topology is the Pawlak topology of REv [4]. So we can characterize the derivable set in terms of equivalence relations. We say that the equivalence relation R_1 is coarse than R_2, (or R_2 is finer than R_1) if and only if every equivalence class of R_1 is a union of the equivalence classes of R_2. Let $K = \{R_1, R_2, \ldots, R_n\}$ be a set of equivalence relations. Then $IND(K) = R_1 \cap R_2 \cap \ldots \cap R_n$, the indiscernibility relation over K, is the intersection of the equivalence relations, $R_i, i = 1, 2, \ldots, n$. Each fuzzy set (via its membership function) defines an equivalence relation. So Theorem 4.2 can be rephrase as follows:

Theorem 4.5. L is derivable from $K_1, K_2, \ldots, K_n$ if and only if the equivalence relation R_L is coarser than $IND(K)$ A fuzzy set is called fuzzy rough set on

(U, R) if the membership function is constant on each equivalence class [1].

Corollary 4.6. L is derivable from $K_1, K_2, \ldots, K_n$ if and only if L is fuzzy rough set in $(U, IND(K))$.

Corollary 4.7. The indisernibility relation $IND(K)$ uniquely determines $Der(K)$.

References

[1] Didier Dubois and Henri Prade, Rough fuzzy sets and fuzzy rough sets., Int. Journal of General Systems, pages 191–209, 1990.

[2] John Kelly, General Topology, Van Nostrand, 1955.

[3] Abraham Kandel, Fuzzy Mathematical Techniques with Applications, Addision-Wesley, Reading Massachusetts, 1986

[4] T.Y. Lin, A topological and Fuzzy Rough Sets, Intelligent Decision Support, Kluwer Academic Publishers, Boston, 1992, Chapter 5, Part II. edited by Slowinski.

[5] Z. Pawlak. Rough sets. Theoretical Aspects of Reasoning about Data, Kluwer Academic Publishers, 1991

[6] Z. Pawlak. Hard and soft sets. Proceeding of RSKD'93 in this volume, 1993

[7] Shafer, G., A Mathematical Thoery of Evidence, Princeton University Press, 1976

[8] Sierpenski, *General Topology*, University of Torranto Press, 1960.

[9] Zimmermann, Fuzzy Set Theory –and its Applications, Second Ed., Kluwer Academic Publisher, 1991.

Fuzzy Representations in Rough Set Approximations

Michael Hadjimichael
S.K. Michael Wong
Department of Computer Science, University of Regina
Regina, SK, S4S 0A2, Canada

Abstract

Frequently, knowledge systems represent information crisply. That is, for a given object in the database, and a given property (attribute-value pair), there is no uncertainty whether or not the object has that property. This certainty restricts expressive power. Therefore, we present here an approach to knowledge representation and rough set-based inductive learning using a fuzzy set representation of information. Specifically, we introduce the Fuzzy Property Set model, which is an enhancement of the Property Set model in which each object is represented by a collection of properties. In this fuzzy enhancement, it is possible to denote the degree to which an object has a particular property. Fuzzy rough set upper and lower approximations are defined using this model, as a basis for the inductive learning of concepts. Various similarity and distance measures can then be used to rank objects according their similarity to the upper or lower concept approximations.

1   Introduction

Frequently, our information about the properties describing an object in an information system is imprecise, or unknown. Our goal is to allow expression of this uncertainty in a knowledge representation system, in a way such that inductive learning can take place using the uncertain data. Traditional knowledge representation models (used by systems such as AQ11[2], ID3[7], and their many descendants), describe objects by a fixed set of attributes, such that an object description consists of a tuple of attribute values. This representation is generalized in the Property Set (PS) model so that attribute-value pairs are generalized as *properties*, and each object is then described by some set of properties [1]. As a result, it is no longer necessary for all objects to be described by the same set of attributes. In this paper we further generalize the PS model to the Fuzzy Property Set (FPS) model by specifying the degree to which each property describes each object. This degree may be interpreted in any way. One obvious interpretation would be our certainty that a given object has a given property. Another might be the degree to which an object has a property.

Most work dealing with uncertain, or fuzzy, representations has dealt with extending the definition of relational databases to treat incomplete information and vague queries [6, 11, 3]. The emphasis in such work is relational database applications: how to represent uncertain or partial information, and how to satisfy vague queries. Extended relational algebras and query languages have been developed [6]. In contrast, from a database point of view, inductive learning is concerned with the *creation* of a query, in this case a vague query which must match to the positive examples in the database, or more generally, must order the examples in order of similarity to the query. Other work dealing with the creation of fuzzy rules using inductive learning may be found in [8] and [5].

The traditional table-based knowledge representation consists of a set of objects to be represented, Θ, a set of attributes, AT, a set of values, $VAL = \bigcup_{a \in AT} VAL_a$, and an information function, $f : \Theta \times AT \rightarrow VAL$, defining the information table. Such a representation restricts our representative power in two ways. First, all objects in the universe must be represented by a uniform representation. Specifically, f must be a function with at most one value per attribute, and f must be defined for all elements of $\Theta \times AT$. The consequences of this requirement are that elements in a such a database are restricted to descriptions composed of a uniform set of attributes, i.e. all attributes are defined (meaningful) for all objects. For example, all describable objects must belong to the same category, e.g. *bicycles, animals, diseases, etc*, so that all attributes are defined (meaningful) for all objects. Also, all descriptions must be completely known for each object, and no attribute may have several values at once (for example, a bicycle which is both red and blue). This restriction has been dealt with by the Property Set (PS) model[1], which is reviewed briefly in Section 2. Second, representative power is also restricted by the crisp object representation, i.e. there is no room for the expression of degree in an object's representation. That is, an object either has, or does not have, a property. The purpose of this paper is to present a knowledge representation model, as an extension of the PS model, in which the sets of properties describing an object are fuzzy sets, as introduced by Zadeh[10]. This extension allows us to attach a degree factor in the interval $[0, 1]$ to each property associated with an object. As a result, the object description may be expressed as a fuzzy set membership function defined on the set of *atomic concepts*, which are basic descriptive units previously defined by Hadjimichael and Wong in [1].

Using the fuzzy object descriptions, we define fuzzy versions of the rough set upper and lower approximations of any subset $A \subseteq \Theta$. Traditional upper and lower approximations to A denote sets of objects which *may be* elements of A, and which *are* elements of A. Because fuzzy set membership is not well defined, we propose to use a similarity measure to determine how "close" a fuzzily described object is to a fuzzy upper or lower approximation. Alternately, and perhaps more usefully, the similarity measure may be used to rank many objects according to their closeness to either approximation. The lower approximation may be considered a pessimistic approximation to A, while the upper approximation, by definition more encompassing, may be considered an optimistic approximation to A.

2 The Property Set Model

The property set model was first introduced in [1]. We present some of its basic concepts here. Let $\Theta = \{\theta_1, \theta_2, \ldots, \theta_m\}$ be a subset of objects in the universe, U. Let $\Pi = \{\pi_1, \pi_2, \ldots, \pi_n\}$ be the set of all known *properties* which may be associated with any of the objects. For now, we consider these properties to be simple attribute-value pairs: $\pi = (a, v)$, (for $a \in AT, v \in VAL$). The attribute,

a, is referred to as the *type* of the property. Specify P as the relation *has-property*, such that for any object $\theta \in \Theta$, if θ can be described by the property π, then $(\theta, \pi) \in P$, or equivalently, $_\theta P_\pi$.

For any $\theta \in \Theta$, we denote the *property set* associated by P with θ by:

$$[\theta] = \{\pi \in \Pi \mid (\theta, \pi) \in P\}.$$

Given a set of properties, Π, each $\pi \in \Pi$ is satisfied by some subset of U (its *object set*) defined by:

$$[\pi] = \{\theta \in U \mid (\theta, \pi) \in P\},$$

The property set of the negation of π is those objects not satisfying π:

$$[\hat{\pi}] = \{\theta \in U \mid (\theta, \pi) \notin P\} = U - [\pi].$$

Thus we may use π ($\hat{\pi}$) as a *label* of the subset of objects, $[\pi]$ ($[\hat{\pi}]$). From these property sets, we can construct *atomic sets* $\{[c_i]\}$, which form a partition of U, and their labels $\{c_i\}$ as follows:

$$[c_0] = [\hat{\pi}_1] \cap [\hat{\pi}_2] \cap \ldots \cap [\hat{\pi}_n], \qquad c_0 = \hat{\pi}_1 \wedge \hat{\pi}_2 \wedge \ldots \wedge \hat{\pi}_n$$

$$[c_1] = [\pi_1] \cap [\hat{\pi}_2] \cap \ldots \cap [\hat{\pi}_n], \qquad c_1 = \pi_1 \wedge \hat{\pi}_2 \wedge \ldots \wedge \hat{\pi}_n$$

$$\vdots$$

$$[c_{2^n-1}] = [\pi_1] \cap [\pi_2] \cap \ldots \cap [\pi_n], \qquad c_{2^n-1} = \pi_1 \wedge \pi_2 \wedge \ldots \wedge \pi_n.$$

We refer to these labels as *atomic concepts*. Define $N = 2^n - 1$. These are in fact minterms in standard boolean algebra, and for conciseness we will often write each term without using the conjunctive symbol ($\wedge$), e.g., $c_3 = \pi_1 \pi_2 \hat{\pi}_3 \ldots \hat{\pi}_n$. The set of all atomic concepts is called the *conceptual space* and denoted $\mathcal{C}$. Each atomic concept is in fact a boolean expression labeling an equivalence class, $[c_i]$, in which all objects are indiscernible. That is, every object $\theta \in \Theta$ is labeled exactly by one atomic concept. Thus, there are at most $|\Theta|$ non-empty atomic sets. We may refer to c_i as the *description* of any $\theta \in [c_i]$.

Note that, given any object $\theta \in \Theta$ with properties $[\theta]$, one can easily identify the atomic concept, c_θ, to which θ belongs:

$$c_\theta = \left(\bigwedge_{\pi_i \in [\theta]} \pi_i \right) \wedge \left(\bigwedge_{\pi_j \notin [\theta]} \hat{\pi}_j \right).$$

By its construction, $c_\theta \in \mathcal{C}$.

The collection of properties specified by the PS model implicitly define a table from which rules may be extracted. For example, each object below has a set of properties associated with it:

$$[car_1] = \{(color, red), (speed, fast), (cylinders, 6)\},$$
$$[car_2] = \{(speed, fast), (cylinders, 4), (transmission, manual)\},$$
$$[car_3] = \{(color, red), (transmission, automatic)\},$$
$$[bicycle_1] = \{(color, red)\}.$$

By not explicitly stating the table, any attributes may be associated with each object in the PS model. Each attribute-value pair then specifies a column of the *implicit table*, and the table defines the mapping from atomic concept to decision class (positive or negative). If the expert determines that concept of good cars includes $\{car_1, car_2\}$ (but not $\{car_3, bicycle_1\}$), then we have the implicitly defined table:

object	π_1	π_2	π_3	π_4	π_5	π_6	decision class
car_1	1	1	1	0	0	0	+
car_2	0	1	0	1	1	0	+
car_3	1	0	0	0	0	1	−
$bicycle_1$	1	0	0	0	0	0	−

where $\pi_1 = (color, red)$, $\pi_2 = (speed, fast)$, $\pi_3 = (cylinders, 6)$, $\pi_4 = (cylinders, 4)$, $\pi_5 = (transmission, manual)$, and $\pi_6 = (transmission, auto)$.

3   The Fuzzy Property Set Model

So far, our representation scheme has made the assumption that an object description is crisp, i.e., we can state with complete certainty if a property is a part of an object's description. This is indicated in the implicit table by the appearance of elements from $\{0, 1\}$. We would now like to acknowledge the case when an object description is *fuzzy*. We may wish to specify that some object θ_i has a property π_j with degree α_{ij}. Specifically, a degree of 0 would indicate the absence of a property, degree 1 would indicate presence of a property, degree 0.5 would indicate a lack of knowledge about the presence of a property, etc. Thus, our knowledge representation model must acknowledge the uncertainty of our knowledge.

The implicit table defines the set of coefficients $\{\alpha_{ij}\}$, where α_{ij} denotes the degree to which object θ_i has property π_j. The table now may look like:

object	π_1	π_2	π_3	π_4	π_5	π_6	decision class
car_1	.1	.8	.2	0	0	0	+
car_2	0	.05	0	1	.9	0	+
car_3	.5	0	0	0	0	.25	−
$bicycle_1$	1	0	0	0	0	0	−

Our objective now is to express each object in terms of atomic concepts.

3.1   The Fuzzy Set Object Description

We will now represent every object by a *fuzzy set* [10] drawn from the universe of discourse, defined by C, the set of atomic concepts. We begin by defining a language to manipulate the fuzzy elements describing our knowledge. Our algebra consists of a universe composed of subsets of basic elements, (β, c), defining a fuzzy set and two binary operators and one unary operator defined on those subsets: ∪ (union), ∩ (intersection), and − (negation). The basic element is an ordered pair where c is an atomic concept in C, and β is the degree of membership of that atomic concept in the fuzzy set, so that the fuzzy membership function μ defining a fuzzy set, B, is defined by $\mu_B(c) = \beta$. We interpret $(1, c) = c$ as a positive occurrence of atomic concept c, and $(0, c) = \hat{c}$ as a negative occurrence of c, i.e. $(0, c)$ represents the logical negation of the boolean expression, c.

The operators are defined as fuzzy set operators according to [10]. Therefore, the fuzzy union of two sets, B and C, is given by $\mu_{B \cup C}(x) = \max(\mu_B(x), \mu_C(x))$. The fuzzy intersection of those sets is given by $\mu_{B \cap C}(x) = \min(\mu_B(x), \mu_C(x))$, the fuzzy negation (complement) of set B is given by $\mu_{-B}(x) = 1 - \mu_B(x)$. Fuzzy sets where $\mu_B(x) = \mu_C(x)$ are considered equal.

We abbreviate the set $\{(\beta_0, c_0)\} \cup \{(\beta_1, c_1)\} \cup \ldots \cup \{(\beta_N, c_N)\}$ by $\bigcup_{k=0}^{N} \{(\beta_k, c_k)\}$. We define $\bigcap_{k=0}^{N} \{(\beta_k, c_k)\}$ analogously. From the above definitions it may be shown that:

$$\bigcap_{j=1}^{n} \{ \bigcup_{k=0}^{N} \{(\beta_{kj}, c_k)\}\} = \bigcup_{k=0}^{N} \{ \bigcap_{j=1}^{n} \{(\beta_{kj}, c_k)\}\}. \tag{1}$$

We define the fuzzy set representation of π_j by $\mathcal{I}_j$ (where $\Rightarrow$ denotes logical implication):

$$\mathcal{I}_j = \left(\bigcup_{c_k \Rightarrow \pi_j} \{(1, c_k)\} \right) \cup \left(\bigcup_{c_k \Rightarrow \hat{\pi}_j} \{(0, c_k)\} \right) = \bigcup_{k=0}^{N} \{(p_{jk}, c_k)\} \tag{2}$$

where $p_{kj} = 1$ if $c_k \Rightarrow \pi_j$, and $p_{kj} = 0$ if $c_k \Rightarrow \hat{\pi}_j$.

Define $\{(\alpha, \{(\beta, c)\})\} = \{(\delta, c)\}$ where $\delta = 1 - \alpha + \beta(2\alpha - 1)$. We choose this definition because it allows α to act as the *degree* of negation to apply to the second element in the pair, so that $\alpha = 0$ implies complete negation, while $\alpha = 1$ implies no negation. For example:

$$\{(1, \{(\beta, c)\})\} = \{(\beta, c)\}, \qquad \{(.5, \{(\beta, c)\})\} = \{(.5, c)\},$$

$$\{(0, \{(\beta, c)\})\} = \{(1 - \beta, c)\}.$$

Note that $\alpha = 0.5$ implies that we don't know whether to negate, or not, and the result, $(0.5, c)$ indicates our resulting uncertainty about the presence of atomic concept c. Furthermore, note that for $\alpha = 0$ (complete negation), the result, $(1 - \beta, c)$ corresponds to our definition of fuzzy negation. Then,

$$\{(\alpha, \bigcup_{k=0}^{N} \{(\beta_k, c_k)\})\} = \bigcup_{k=0}^{N} \{(\alpha, \{(\beta_k, c_k)\})\} = \bigcup_{k=0}^{N} \{(\delta_k, c_k)\}, \tag{3}$$

where $\delta_k = 1 - \alpha + \beta_k(2\alpha - 1)$.

In the implicit knowledge table, each $\theta_i \in \Theta$ is expressed as a function of the properties, i.e. each coefficient indicates the degree to which an object belongs to the property set of a particular property. Specifically, each θ_i is located within the intersection of property sets. From this we may express the fuzzy representation of θ_i as ϱ_i:

$$\varrho_i = \{(\alpha_{i1}, \mathcal{I}_1)\} \cap \{(\alpha_{i2}, \mathcal{I}_2)\} \cap \ldots \cap \{(\alpha_{ip}, \mathcal{I}_n)\}$$

$$= \bigcap_{j=1}^{n} \{(\alpha_{ij}, \bigcup_{k=0}^{N} \{(p_{jk}, c_k)\})\} \qquad \text{by (2)}$$

$$= \bigcap_{j=1}^{n} (\bigcup_{k=0}^{N} \{(\delta_{ijk}, c_k)\}) \quad \text{by (3), where } \delta_{ijk} = 1 - \alpha_{ij} + p_{jk}(2\alpha_{ij} - 1)$$

$$= \bigcup_{k=0}^{N} (\bigcap_{j=1}^{n} \{(\delta_{ijk}, c_k)\}) \qquad \text{by (1)}$$

$$\varrho_i = \bigcup_{k=0}^{N} \{(\min_j \{\delta_{ijk}\}, c_k)\} \qquad \text{by definition of } \cap \qquad (4)$$

We now have a description of each object in terms of atomic concepts. This representation may be viewed as a fuzzy set of atomic concepts labeling an object. Therefore, each object $\theta_i \in \Theta$ is described by the membership function, $\mu_{\theta_i}(c_k) = \min_j \{\delta_{ijk}\}$.

This fuzzy representation of objects reduces neatly to the crisp case. In a crisp universe, each object θ is represented by a single atomic concept, namely, c_θ, as demonstrated in Section 2. This corresponds directly to the fuzzy set with the membership function defined by:

$$\mu_\theta(c_i) = \begin{cases} 1.0 & \text{if } c_i = c_\theta \\ 0.0 & \text{otherwise.} \end{cases} \qquad (5)$$

3.2 Upper And Lower Approximations

We use fuzzy operators to define, similarly to [4], the upper approximation of a set A:

$$\overline{A} = \bigcup_{\theta \in A} \varrho. \qquad (6)$$

The lower approximation of A, denoted by $\underline{A}$, may be defined – in analogy to the crisp rough sets case – in terms of upper approximations as follows[4]:

$$\underline{A} = \overline{A} - \overline{\Theta - A} = \overline{A} \cap -(\overline{\Theta - A})$$

$$\underline{A} = \left(\bigcup_{\theta \in A} \varrho \right) \cap - \left(\bigcup_{\theta \in (\Theta - A)} \varrho \right). \qquad (7)$$

Using the definition of ϱ as given in Equation 4, and Equation 6, we may write the fuzzy upper approximation in terms of atomic concepts:

$$\overline{A} = \bigcup_{\theta_i \in A} (\bigcup_{k=0}^{N} \{(\min_j \{\delta_{ijk}\}, c_k)\})$$

$$= \bigcup_{\theta_i \in A} \{(\min_j \{\delta_{ij0}\}, c_0), (\min_j \{\delta_{ij1}\}, c_1), \ldots, (\min_j \{d_{ijN}\}, c_N)\}$$

$$= \bigcup_{\theta_i \in A} \{(\zeta_{i0}, c_0), (\zeta_{i1}, c_1), \ldots, (\zeta_{iN}, c_N)\} \qquad \text{where } \zeta_{ik} = \min_j \{\delta_{ijk}\}$$

Method	Formula
Correlation	$S_{BC} = \dfrac{\mu_B(x_1)\mu_C(x_1)+\cdots+\mu_B(x_M)\mu_C(x_M)}{\sqrt{(\mu_B(x_1)^2+\cdots+\mu_B(x_M)^2)(\mu_C(x_1)^2+\cdots+\mu_C(x_M)^2)}}$
Absolute Distance	$D_{BC} = \|\mu_B(x_1)-\mu_C(x_1)\|+\cdots+\|\mu_B(x_M)-\mu_C(x_M)\|$
Entropy[9]	$S_{BC} = 1-\beta$, where $\beta = H(\frac{1}{2}B+\frac{1}{2}C)-\frac{1}{2}(H(B)+H(C))$, and $H(X) = -\sum_i \mu_X(x_i)\log\mu_X(x_i)$ and $\mu_{\frac{1}{2}B}(x) = \frac{1}{2}\mu_B(x), \mu_{B+C}(x) = \mu_B(x)+\mu_C(x)$.

Table 1: Similarity and Distance Measures

$$\overline{A} = \bigcup_{k=0}^{N}\{(\max_{[\theta_i]\subseteq A}\{\zeta_{ik}\}, c_k)\} \tag{8}$$

From Equations 7 and 8, and the fuzzy definition of set negation ($\mu_{-B}(x) = 1-\mu_B(x)$), we can immediately determine the fuzzy lower approximation:

$$\underline{A} = \left(\bigcup_{k=0}^{N}\{(\max_{\theta_i\in A}\{\zeta_{ik}\}, c_k)\}\right) \cap \left(-\bigcup_{k=0}^{N}\{(\max_{\theta_i\in(\Theta-A)}\{\zeta_{ik}\}, c_k)\}\right)$$

$$= \bigcup_{k=0}^{N}\{(\min(\max_{\theta_i\in A}\{\zeta_{ik}\}, 1-\max_{\theta_i\in(\Theta-A)}\{\zeta_{ik}\}), c_k)\} \tag{9}$$

In the crisp case, each θ is represented by the membership function described in Equation 5. Then, the crisp $\overline{A}$ will consist of the set $\{c_\theta|\ \theta\in A\}$ which corresponds to the crisp description of the upper approximation : $\bigvee_{[\theta]\subseteq A} c_\theta$. It follows from (7) that $\underline{A}$ also reduces neatly to the crisp definition: $\bigvee_{[\theta]\subseteq A} c_\theta$.

3.3 Object Ranking

Now that we have determined a fuzzy set expression for the lower and upper approximations of the desired concept ($A \subseteq \Theta$), to apply the knowledge inherent in these expressions we define a *similarity measure* which will allow us to measure how similar an object $\theta\in U$ is to the lower or upper concept approximation. Table 1 lists some possible similarity (and distance) measures (where B, C are fuzzy sets).

Given two fuzzy approximations of a concept, $\underline{A}$and $\overline{A}$, we may use any of the measures in Table 1 to rank a set of unknown objects according to their similarity to those approximations. The fuzzy upper and lower approximations may be considered as optimistic and pessimistic approximations, respectively, and will yield corresponding optimistic and pessimistic rankings.

4 Conclusion

Traditional table-based knowledge representation systems represent objects crisply. That is, every property either belongs, or does not belong, to an object. The FPS model remedies this problem by representing every object as a fuzzy set of atomic concepts (basic descriptive units). Thus, it is possible to represent the degree to which a property belongs to an object. Rough set upper and lower set approximations are defined using the fuzzy set representation. These approximations define the decision rules, where the upper approximation yields an optimistic rule, and the lower approximation yields a pessimistic rule. Similarity measures defined for fuzzy sets can then be used to rank objects in terms of their similarity to the decision rules. The new degree of freedom resulting from a fuzzy representation gives the resulting system more representational power. Future work on this model would include a in-depth study of the various similarity measures and their relative advantages.

References

[1] M. Hadjimichael, S.K.M. Wong, "Quantifying Inductive Learning Generalization," *submitted for publication*, 1993.

[2] R. S. Michalski, J. B. Larson, "Selection of most representative training examples and incremental generation of VL1 hypothesis: the underlying methodology and the description of programs ESEL and AQ11," *Report No. 867, Department of Computer Science, University of Illinois*, Urbana, Illinois, 1978.

[3] A. Motro, "Accommodating Imprecision in Database Systems: Issues and Solutions," *SIGMOD Record*, **19**, n4, 69–74, 1990,

[4] Z. Pawlak, "Rough Sets," *International Journal of Computer and Information Sciences*, **11**, 341-356, 1984.

[5] X.T. Peng, A. Kandel, "Concepts, Rules, and Fuzzy Reasoning: A Factor Space Approach," *IEEE Trans. Syst., Man, and Cyber.*, **21**, n1, 194–205, 1991.

[6] H. Prade, C. Testemale, "Generalizing Database Relational Algebra for the Treatment of Incomplete or Uncertain Information and Vague Queries," *Information Sciences*, **34**, 115-143, 1984.

[7] J.R. Quinlan, "Learning efficient classification procedures and the application to chess end-games," *Machine Learning, an Artificial Intelligence Approach. (eds. Michalski, Carbonell, Mitchell)*, Tioga Publishing Co., Palo Alto, 1983.

[8] L. Wang, J.M. Mandel, "Generating Fuzzy Rules by Learning from Examples," *IEEE Trans. Syst., Man, and Cyber.*, **2**, n6, 1414–1427, 1992.

[9] S.K.M. Wong, Y. Yao, "A Statistical Similarity Measure," *Proc. 10th Annual International ACM SIGIR Conference on Research and Development in Information Retrieval*, New Orleans, 3-12, 1987.

[10] L. A. Zadeh, "Fuzzy Sets," *Inf. Control*, **8**, 338-353, 1965.

[11] M. Zemankova, A. Kandel, "Implementing Imprecision in Information Systems," *Information Sciences*, **37**, 107-141, 1985.

Trusting an Information Agent*

Hasan M. Jamil†   **Fereidoon Sadri**
Department of Computer Science
Concordia University
1455 de Maisonneuve Boulevard West
Montreal, Quebec, Canada H3G 1M8
e-mail: {jamil, sadri}@cs.concordia.ca

Abstract: While the common kinds of uncertainties in databases (e.g., null values, disjunction, corrupt/missing data, domain mismatch, etc.) have been extensively studied, a relatively unexplored form of uncertainty in databases, called *inaccurate data*, demands due attention. Inaccurate data results when data are contributed by various information agents with some known reliability. Though the data itself is *total* or *complete*, the reliability of the data now depends on the agent's reliability. Several issues of this form of data reliability have been reported recently where the reliability of agents were assumed to be *known* and *static*. In this paper we address the issue of *reliability maintenance* of information agents and take the view that the agent reliability is *dynamic* and is a function of the database knowledge and the agent *evidences* (facts that are observed to be true or false). We propose a method of *quantifying* the level of *trust* (or the agent reliability) that the database system should rest on the agent based on observation, and statistical estimation.

Key words : information agent, evidence, data reliability, database trust.

1   Introduction

While the issue of *incomplete data* has been extensively studied, a different form of uncertainty in data and knowledge-bases, called the *inaccurate data* [4], is relatively unexplored. An inaccurate data is a *complete data* [3], the truth value of which is a probability that depends on the reliabilities of the contributing agents[1] of the data [4]. The reliability of an agent on the other hand is a

---

*This research was supported in part by grants from the Natural Sciences and Engineering Research Council of Canada and the Fonds Pour Formation De Chercheurs Et L'Aide À La Recherche of Quebec.

†This author's research was additionally supported in part by grants from the Canadian Commonwealth Scholarship and Fellowship Plan, and the University of Dhaka, Bangladesh. The author is on leave from the University of Dhaka, Bangladesh.

[1] In IST model [4], Sadri used the term information sources for what we call information agents and thus they both refer to the same entity.

probability *p*, which means that the probability of the data contributed by the agent being true is *p* [4]. Sadri [4] proposed an extended relational model, called the *information source tracking* (IST) model, to represent and manipulate information sources and to calculate the data reliability given the agent reliabilities. The extended relational operations of IST model were shown to be *precise* (sound and complete). An algorithm was also presented that calculates the tuple reliability in the extended model.

In this paper, we view the issue of agent reliability, which ultimately influences the data reliability, from yet another dimension. We take the view that the reliability of an agent is a database *trust* on the agent, which is a function of the database information content and the database knowledge. Hence the trust on an agent changes with database activity. In this paper we will only address the issue of computing time dependent reliability of information agents based on the *observed evidences*.

We organize the rest of the paper as follows. We present the extended IST model in Section 2 and introduce the concept of database trust. We also present a complete set of extended relational operators for the extended model for completeness of the report. Then in Section 3, we present a statistical estimation procedure to compute database trust, and discuss an algorithm for tuple reliability calculation. The algorithm is discussed in detail in [4]. We conclude in Section 4 and discuss future research issues.

2   The Extended IST Model

In this section we will introduce the data model and define the concept of database trust. We adopt the data model proposed in [4] with a simple twist for our purpose and basically keep the same set of extended operators of [4] which is well suited in our model.

From the user's point of view, the database is a classical relational database. However,

- each relation in the database has a special attribute called the *agent* or *source* which is invisible to the users.

- during updates, users are asked to associate with each tuple a set of agents which contributes the tuple.

- in addition to producing answers to user queries, the system also produces the contributing agents of the answer tuples.

- for each answer tuple the system can calculate the probability of the truth value, that is the probability of the answer being true. This probability is a function of the contributing agent reliabilities.

- tuples in a relation are partitioned into two sets, *active*, and *observed*. The active set is further partitioned into two sets called *predict(ed)* or *forecast(ed)* and *true*. The observed set is similarly partitioned into two sets called *fact* and *hoax*. The set of tuples in fact are observed to be true with a data reliability 100% and likewise the tuples in hoax are observed to be false and have a data reliability 0%.

- when a tuple is observed to be true or false in real life, it migrates from the predict set to either fact or hoax set depending on its outcome. Every time a tuple migrates from predict to fact, we add a copy of the pure

SHARE

company	month	price	source		company	month	price	source
IBM	june	200	1 1 0 0					
IBM	june	250	0 0 1 0		IBM	may	200	0 1 0 1
IBM	july	250	0 0 0 1		IBM	april	250	0 0 0 1
AT&T	june	300	0 1 0 1		AT&T	april	280	0 1 0 1
AT&T	june	350	1 0 1 0		IBM	feb	290	0 0 1 1
					AT&T	may	340	1 0 0 0
IBM	may	200	T					
IBM	april	250	T		IBM	april	260	1 1 0 0
AT&T	april	280	T		AT&T	april	290	1 0 1 0
IBM	feb	290	T		AT&T	may	500	0 1 0 1
AT&T	may	340	T		IBM	april	360	0 0 1 0

Left margin labels: *predict* (upper left group), *true* (lower left group).
Right margin labels: *fact* (upper right group), *hoax* (lower right group).
Top labels: Active Relation, Observed Events.

Figure 1: The *Share* relation instance.

tuple (defined shortly) with the special source vector[2] T. The tuples in the observed set are *dead* and do not participate in query processing. They are used only to calculate the agent database trust during query processing.

- the system calculates the data reliability only for the set of tuples in the uncertain part of the database, that is for the tuples in the predict or forecast set. Note that we view each uncertain tuple in the database as a prediction or forecast which a set of agents somehow makes, and the method of prediction is not the concern of the database system.

From the systems point of view, the database is an extended set of relations, with extended relational operators. If, however, the uncertainty component is turned off, the system behaves exactly like a classical relational model. We formally define our extended model as follows:

Let $D = \cup_{i=1}^{k} D_i \cup D_I$ be a finite set of domains, where D_is are classical domains and D_I is a special domain consisting of a set of vectors of the form C^k where k is the number of agents in the database, and $C = \{0, +1, -1, \top\}$, and two special vectors T and F. Let $A = \cup_{i=1}^{\infty} A_i \cup A_I$ be an infinite set of attribute names, where A_is are regular classical attributes, and $A_I = source$ is a special attribute, called the information agent attribute and A_I draws its values from the domain D_I.

Definition 2.1 An *extended relation scheme R* is a set of attributes $\{A_1, \ldots, A_n, A_I\}$. Each attribute A_i has a domain of values D_i, $i = 1, \ldots, n$. The attribute A_I draws its values from the domain D_I. An *extended relation instance* (or just a relation) r on R is a set of tuples such that $r = r_{p(redict)} \cup r_{t(rue)} \cup r_{f(act)} \cup r_{h(oax)} \subseteq D_1 \times \ldots \times D_n \times D_I$, and that r_p, r_t, r_f and r_h are pair-wise disjoint. □

---

[2]Source vectors are discussed in Sections 2.2 and 2.3.

Let t be a tuple in r. Then the projection $t[A_1, \ldots, A_n]$ is called a pure tuple while the projection $t[A_I]$ is called the agent vector. A tuple t in the extended model is often represented by $p@a$, where $p = t[A_1, \ldots, A_n]$ denotes the pure component of the tuple while $a = t[A_I]$ denotes the agent component of it. Let S be the set of database information agents and let each agent $s_k \in S$ be associated with a natural number from 1 to $|S| = n$. Let the k-th projection of the source vector $a = t[A_I]$, denoted $t[A_I]^k$, represents the contribution (will be discussed in detail in Section 2.2) of the k-th agent in tuple t. Then $agrees(s_k, t)$ represents the fact that the tuple t is confirmed by the agent s_k, i.e., $t[A_I]^k = a_k = +1$.

Definition 2.2 Let r_i be an extended relation on scheme R_i, and let $i = 1, \ldots, n$. Let $\mathbf{D}$ be a database such that $r_i \in \mathbf{D}$, $i = 1, \ldots, n$. Now if r_{i_p}, r_{i_t}, r_{i_f}, and r_{i_h} denotes the predict, true, fact and hoax sets of the relations r_is, then $\mathbf{D}_p = \cup_{i=1}^n r_{i_p}$, $\mathbf{D}_t = \cup_{i=1}^n r_{i_t}$, $\mathbf{D}_f = \cup_{i=1}^n r_{i_f}$ and $\mathbf{D}_h = \cup_{i=1}^n r_{i_h}$ denotes respectively the predict, true, fact and hoax sets of the database $\mathbf{D}$, and $\mathbf{D} = \mathbf{D}_p \cup \mathbf{D}_t \cup \mathbf{D}_f \cup \mathbf{D}_h$. □

2.1 Database Trust

How people trust another entity in real world is extremely hard to explain and understand. It is often based on faith, observation, statistics, acquaintance, intuition, etc. For automated systems and any application to be considered useful, we need to have a quantitative notion of trust which may be based on observations, tests, evidences and possibly heuristics. Since an exact quantification of trust is believed to be impossible, we have to resort to an approximation, and thus we must also accommodate a method of trust revision. Trust revision is also necessary because of the simple reason that trust on an entity may change with time, say for example, based on new evidences, observations and knowledge. We take the view that the trust or reliability of agents can be conveniently expressed as a (range) probability, which will indicate the level of confidence we can have on an agent. In the following two definitions we formally define the notion of evidence and trust.

Definition 2.3 Let r be a relation on scheme R, and let the database $\mathbf{D}$ contain only relation[3] r. The evidence corresponding to an agent α, denoted η_α, is a function of $\mathbf{D}$ such that

$$\eta_\alpha : \mathbf{D} \to 2^{\mathbf{D}}$$

where, $\eta_\alpha(\mathbf{D}) = \{t \mid t = p@a \in \mathbf{D}$ and $agrees(\alpha, t)\}$[4]. Let η_α^u, η_α^+, and η_α^- denote three partitions of η_α corresponding to the set of uncertain, positive and negative evidences of agent α, such that $\eta_\alpha^u : \mathbf{D} \to 2^{\mathbf{D}_p}$, $\eta_\alpha^+ : \mathbf{D} \to 2^{\mathbf{D}_f}$, and $\eta_\alpha^- : \mathbf{D} \to 2^{\mathbf{D}_h}$, where, $\eta_\alpha^u(\mathbf{D}) = \{t \mid t = p@a \in \mathbf{D}_p$ and $agrees(\alpha, t)\}$. Similarly for $\eta_\alpha^+(\mathbf{D})$ and $\eta_\alpha^-(\mathbf{D})$. Hence an agent's total database evidence is given by $\eta_\alpha(\mathbf{D}) = \eta_\alpha^u(\mathbf{D}) \cup \eta_\alpha^+(\mathbf{D}) \cup \eta_\alpha^-(\mathbf{D})$. □

Definition 2.4 The *database trust* τ on an agent α, denoted τ_α, is a real interval between 0 and 1 (exclusive) and is a function of the database and the evidence of α. Formally,

$$\tau_\alpha : \mathbf{D} \times \eta_\alpha \to [0, 1] \qquad \qquad □$$

---

[3] We can assume so without loss of any generality.
[4] Note that η_α returns the set of tuples that are contributed by the agent α.

2.2 Interpretation of Source Vectors

Consider a pure tuple t in r. The source vectors corresponding to t identify information sources that are contributing (positively or negatively) to the pure tuple t. Note that there can be more than one source vector associated with a pure tuple t in a relation, i.e., $t@u_1, \ldots, t@u_p$, $p \geq 1$ can be in r. We will make this concept precise by introducing the *expression* corresponding to a pure tuple t as follows.

First, consider the case where there is a single (extended) tuple $t@u \in r$, where $u = (a_1 \cdots a_k)$. We denote the set of information sources by $S = \{s_1, \ldots, s_k\}$, where $k = |S|$. The sources $S^+ = \{s_i | a_i = +1 \text{ or } a_i = \top\}$ are contributing positively to the pure tuple t, while the sources $S^- = \{s_i | a_i = -1 \text{ or } a_i = \top\}$ are contributing negatively. Note that the case of inconsistent informations agent, $a_i = \top$, is treated as the agent s_i is contributing positively as well as negatively to the corresponding information. We also associate with each information source s_i a Boolean variable f_i. The *expression corresponding to t with respect to u*, denoted $e(t@u)$, is written as

$$e(t@u) = \bigwedge_{s_i \in S^+} f_i \bigwedge_{s_j \in S^-} \neg f_j$$

Note that $e(u) = false$ if $a_i = \top$ for at least one $i, 1 \leq i \leq k$. Now, consider the case where $t@u_1, \ldots, t@u_p$ are all the tuples with the pure part t in r, which we write as $t@x \in r$, where $x = \{u_1, \ldots, u_p\}$. The *expression corresponding to t with respect to x* (expression corresponding to t for short), is written as

$$e(t) = e(t@x) = \bigvee_{i=1}^{p} e(t@u_i)$$

We can regard the expression corresponding to a tuple $t \in r$ as a propositional logic expression, where $f_1, \ldots, f_k$ represents Boolean variables. A truth assignment $f_i = true$ is interpreted as "information source s_i is correct", while $f_i = false$ indicates that source s_i is incorrect. The truth value of $e(t)$ is a function of the truth values of $f_1, \ldots, f_k$, and indicates whether t is a valid tuple, i.e., $e(t) = true$, or an invalid tuple, i.e., $e(t) = false$.

2.3 Source Vector Manipulation

The extended operators in IST uses the information source vector operations *s-conjunction*, *s-disjunction*, and *s-negation* as described below. We observe that the information source constants $\{0, -1, +1, \top\}$ form a lattice of the form $0 \prec +1 \prec \top$, and $0 \prec -1 \prec \top$. The bottom element, 0, can be regarded as designating *under specification*, and the top element, $\top$, designating *over specification* or *inconsistency*.

Given two source vectors $v = (a_1 \cdots a_k)$ and $w = (b_1 \cdots b_k)$, their conjunction, called the *s-conjunction*, $u = v \overset{s}{\wedge} w$ is a source vector $u = (c_1 \cdots c_k)$, such that each c_i, $1 \leq i \leq k$ is the *least-upper bound* of a_i and b_i in v and w respectively, i.e., $c_i = \overline{lub}(a_i, b_i)$, $1 \leq i \leq k$. The conjunction of two sets of source vectors x and y is performed as $x \overset{s}{\wedge} y = \{v \overset{s}{\wedge} w | v \in x \text{ and } w \in y\}$. The disjunction of two sets of source vectors x and y, written $x \overset{s}{\vee} y$, is their union, i.e., $x \overset{s}{\vee} y = x \cup y$. The negation of a source vector $v = (a_1 \cdots a_k)$, written $\overset{s}{\neg} v$, is defined as follows.

Let u_i denote the source vector $(b_1 \cdots b_k)$ where $b_i = +1$ and $b_j = 0$, for $j \neq i$, and similarly let w_i denote the source vector $(b_1 \cdots b_k)$ where $b_i = -1$ and $b_j = 0$, for $j \neq i$, then $\overset{s}{\neg} v = \{u_i | a_i = -1 \text{ or } a_i = \top\} \cup \{w_i | a_i = +1 \text{ or } a_i = \top\}$. The negation of a set of source vectors $x = \{v_1, \ldots, v_m\}$ is performed as $\overset{s}{\neg} x = (\overset{s}{\neg} v_1) \overset{s}{\wedge} (\overset{s}{\neg} v_2) \overset{s}{\wedge} \ldots \overset{s}{\wedge} (\overset{s}{\neg} v_m)$. The cases where one or both operands are the special source vectors T or F, are handled in the obvious way. Namely, $F \overset{s}{\wedge} v = F$ for all vectors v, and $T \overset{s}{\wedge} v = v$ for all vectors $v \neq F$. The following theorem follows.

Theorem 2.1 Let $z = x \overset{s}{\wedge} y$, $z = x \overset{s}{\vee} y$, or $z = \overset{s}{\neg} x$. Then $e(z) = e(x) \wedge e(y)$, $e(z) = e(x) \vee e(y)$, or $e(z) = \neg e(x)$ respectively. $\qquad\square$

2.4 Extended Relational Algebra Operations

Here we summarize extended relational algebra operations. Interested readers are referred to [4] for a detailed discussion. We shall note that the source attribute S is not visible to users, and can not be referenced. Selection, projection and union are defined the same way as for regular relations.

$$\sigma_C(r) = \{t@u | t@u \in r, \text{ and } t \text{ satisfies condition } C\}$$
$$\Pi_X(r) = \{t[X]@u | t@u \in r\}$$
$$r \cup s = \{t@u | t@u \in r \text{ or } t@u \in s\}$$
$$r - s = \{t@x | (t@x \in r \text{ and } \neg \exists y\ t@y \in s)\} \cup \{t@x | (t@y \in r \text{ and}$$
$$t@z \in s \text{ and } x = y \overset{s}{\wedge} (\overset{s}{\neg} (z))\}$$
$$r \times s = \{t_1 \bullet t_2 @ (u_1 \overset{s}{\wedge} u_2) | t_1 @ u_1 \in r \text{ and } t_2 @ u_2 \in s\}$$

Note that an implicit union operation takes place for source vectors in the selection, projection and union operations, while s-disjunction and s-negations of source vectors are used respectively for Cartesian product and set difference operations above. Sadri [5] proved that the operations are sound and complete.

3 Computing τ_α

We take the view that the development of a satisfactory trust function is beyond the scope of this paper and is a research issue by itself. So, in this section we are merely interested in a function for trust calculation for database agents that makes use of the observed evidences in the database and gives us an acceptable result. It may be noted here that the choice of a trust function is independent of the reliability calculation of the tuples. Users are free to choose any function of their choice that better models their environment or has better precision.

We present a function based on standard statistical estimation based on the concept of *statistical evidence*. Let the cardinality of the total evidence, i.e., $|\eta_\alpha(\mathbf{D})|$, denote the total number of tuple contribution of an agent α. Let $\eta_\alpha(\mathbf{D})$ also denote the population P of α, whereas $|\eta_\alpha(\mathbf{D})|$ denotes the size N of population P. Similarly, the positive, negative and uncertain contributions of an agent α can be defined as $|\eta_\alpha^+(\mathbf{D})|$, $|\eta_\alpha^-(\mathbf{D})|$ and $|\eta_\alpha^u(\mathbf{D})|$ respectively.

The database observed partition corresponding to an agent α can be thought of as a sample S of size n randomly drawn from the finite population P of size

N of α. If the proportion[5] of facts and hoax is p and q respectively in the population (i.e., $p+q=1$), then our goal is to estimate p on the population N to some degree of accuracy and confidence. If p is the proportion of facts in $\mathbf{D}$ then the confidence limits for p are given by $F \pm z_c \sigma_p \sqrt{(N-n)/(N-1)}$ [1], where F denotes the proportion of facts in the sample S of size n. z_c is called the *confidence coefficient* that corresponds to a confidence level of the estimate, and can be obtained from the standard chart for z_c.

If the sample size $n \geq 30$, and we use the sample variance $\sqrt{pq}$ for the population variance σ_p then the trust for an agent is given by

$$\tau_\alpha = F \pm z_c \sqrt{\frac{pq}{n}} \sqrt{\frac{N-n}{N-1}}$$

$$= \frac{|\eta_\alpha^+(\mathbf{D})|}{(|\eta_\alpha^+(\mathbf{D})| + |\eta_\alpha^-(\mathbf{D})|)} \pm z_c \sqrt{\frac{\frac{|\eta_\alpha^+(\mathbf{D})|}{|\eta_\alpha^+(\mathbf{D})| + |\eta_\alpha^-(\mathbf{D})|} \times \frac{|\eta_\alpha^-(\mathbf{D})|}{|\eta_\alpha^+(\mathbf{D})| + |\eta_\alpha^-(\mathbf{D})|}}{|\eta_\alpha^+(\mathbf{D})| + |\eta_\alpha^-(\mathbf{D})|}} \times$$

$$\sqrt{\frac{|\eta_\alpha(\mathbf{D})| - (|\eta_\alpha^+(\mathbf{D})| + |\eta_\alpha^-(\mathbf{D})|)}{|\eta_\alpha(\mathbf{D})| - 1}}$$

This is a standard estimation formula that assumes a normal distribution. The following theorem formalizes the correctness of the trust function τ_α.

Theorem 3.1 *Let N be the population of an agent α, and n be a sample size of the observed evidences of α. If p and q are the proportions of positive and negative observed evidences of α and $n \geq 30$, then the trust F computed by the function τ_α is correct within $z_c \sqrt{\frac{pq}{n}} \sqrt{\frac{N-n}{N-1}}$ with confidence c.* □

If the sample size is less than 30, instead of z_c, we should use the t distribution. A formula using t_c can be easily derived and is not presented here. However, we assume that the database is large and the population of any agent is also large. It can be shown that t_c and z_c are practically the same for large samples, i.e., $n \geq 30$.

3.1 Tuple Reliability Calculation Algorithm

Consider an expression for a tuple $t@x$ (from Section 2.2)

$$e(t@x) = \bigvee_{i=1}^{p} e(t@u_i)$$

This expression is in disjunctive form where each $e(t@u_i)$ is a conjunct. Convert this expression into *disjunctive normal form*, i.e.,

$$e(t@x) = \bigvee_{i=1}^{q} e(t@v_i)$$

where each $e(t@v_i)$ is a conjunct in which all variables $f_1, \ldots, f_k$ (may be negated) appear. Note that the disjunctive normal form of a Boolean expression

---

[5]Note that neither the facts nor the hoax cardinality can be equal to the sample size n. In those cases the database trust τ_α is undefined.

is unique (up to a permutation of conjuncts). Then reliability of t, denoted $re(t)$, is given by

$$re(t) = re(t@v_1) + \cdots + re(t@v_q)$$

Example 3.1 Consider the *Share* relation of Figure 1. Let the database agents be s_1 = forbes, s_2 = linden, s_3 = johnson and s_4 = smith. Note that the vector (1100) in the predict tuple t =<IBM,june,200>@(1100) means that the agents forbes and linden confirms the tuple t, and so on. For the given *Share* instance, we can calculate the trust of the agents for a confidence of 95% as follows: $\tau_{forbes} = 0.33 \pm 0.38$ $\eta_{linden} = 0.5 \pm 0.3$, $\tau_{johnson} = 0.33 \pm 0.38$ and $\tau_{smith} = 0.8 \pm 0.2$. Note that the large margin of error is due to the fact that the number of observed tuples are very small (i.e., less than 30). Use of a t distribution will improve the picture slightly in this case. However, as we have assumed, that in real life the number of tuples in a relation will be very large and thus the margin of error will be very low.

Now consider the query $\Pi_{Month,Price}(\sigma_{Company="IBM" \wedge Month>april}(share))$. The set of tuples in the relation *Share* that qualify is $\{< \text{june}, 200 > @(1100),$ $< \text{june}, 250 > @(0010),\ \ < \text{july}, 250 > @(0001), < \text{may}, 200 > @(T)\}$. The tuple reliability computed by the reliability algorithm will be 16.5%, 33%, 80% and 100% respectively (ignoring the confidence limits for simplicity). □

We will not discuss complex queries involving multiple relations and multiple tuples in a relation with different source vectors for the sake of brevity. Interested readers will be able to readily notice that using the extended operators, the source vectors in the answer tuples can be manipulated to obtain source vector expressions, and then from which the tuple reliability can be calculated using the given algorithm.

4 Conclusions and Further Research Issues

We have presented an extended relational model for the management of inaccurate data [4] and shown that the tuple (or data) reliability can be obtained from the information agent's reliabilities, called the *trusts*. We have assumed that the trust on an agent may change with database activity, and presented an estimator function τ_α that estimates the trust of an agent α based on the evidences of the agent.

The trust function τ_α presented in this paper computes a probability of the form $p \pm e$, where p is the probability that a property θ – i.e., the proportion of *facts*, is true in the population P – i.e., the database. For useful purposes, it is essential either to reduce the error margin e, or to be able to find a *maximum likelihood* of the probability p within the error limit, and thus giving us a point probability.

The maximum likelihood estimation can be viewed as a *smoother* function that uses database knowledge and experience about an agent and estimates it's trust. To be able to do so, the database system must accumulate information about the performance of the agents, their behavior, and organize the information as database knowledge. In other words, the database system must have a learning component that views the database information agents as performance elements and observes their performance and possible behavior patterns. The smoother component of the database will use the knowledge learned by the learning system with a goal to reduce the error limit in the estimate, and possibly improve on the estimate itself. At a more formal level, we may modify the estimator formula for τ_α as follows:

$$\tau_\alpha = F\gamma_\alpha \pm z_c\sqrt{\frac{pq}{n}}\sqrt{\frac{N-n}{N-1}}\psi_\alpha$$

where, in absence of any knowledge, or if the learning system is off line, we assume $\gamma_\alpha = 1$, and $\psi_\alpha = 1$. The objective of the learning component thus is to help determine the correction factors γ_α and ψ_α for each agent α in the database by discovering interesting rules.

One immediate extension to this idea can be the estimation of the trust of an agent when the information are taxonomical (discrete or continuous). For example, if an agent asserts that John has fever, while another agent says John has typhoid, and we observe that in reality John has typhoid, then we say that the second source is more reliable than the first. In [2], we propose a method to estimate the agent reliability based on context dependent similarity measure and the expertise of agents. In another work [7], we extend the basic IST model to accommodate reliability of sources based on their expertise.

There are of course other open issues like how does the reliability of an agent is affected in a relation r when a *relevant* tuple in another relation s becomes true? This is assuming that an agent has different reliability in different relations [7]. Or is it possible to model some kind of dependencies or relationships of the reliability of agents in different *contexts* (relations) and how these dependencies should be taken into account during query processing? Is it then possible to allow the users to specify different dependency modes between relations either in the query specification or at the database schema level? These are some of the issues we seek to investigate in our future research.

References

[1] Cochran, W. G.; "Sampling Techniques"; *John Wiley & Sons, NY*; 1977.

[2] Jamil, H. M. and Sadri, F.; "Recognizing Credible Experts in Inaccurate Databases"; *Manuscript*; 1993.

[3] Maier, D.; "The Theory of Relational Databases"; *Computer Science Press*; 1983.

[4] Sadri, F.; "Reliability of Answers to Queries in Relational Databases"; *IEEE Transactions on Knowledge and Data Engineering*; Vol 3, No 2, pp 245-251; 1991.

[5] Sadri, F.; "Modeling Uncertainty in Databases"; *IEEE 7th International Conference on Data Engineering*; pp 122-131; 1991.

[6] Sadri, F.; "Integrity Constraints in the Information Source Tracking Method."; *To appear in IEEE Transactions on Knowledge and Data Engineering.*

[7] Shiri, N. and Jamil, H. M.; "Uncertainty as a Function of Expertise[6]"; *Proceedings of the Workshop on Incompleteness and Uncertainty in Information Systems, Montreal, Quebec*; October, 1993; pp 121-132.

---

[6] An extended version of the paper is to appear in the Springer-Verlag Lecture Notes in Computer Science Series.

Handling Various Types of Uncertainty in the Rough Set Approach

Roman Słowiński and Jerzy Stefanowski

Institute of Computing Science,
Technical University of Poznań,
60-965 Poznań, Poland

Abstract

The paper refers to problems of handling various types of uncertainty in the rough set approach to analysis of information systems. Besides ambiguity resulting from a limited discernibility of objects, we consider uncertainty caused by: discretization of quantitative attributes, imprecise descriptors, unknown descriptors, or multiple descriptors. A special way of modelling the first three types of uncertainty using fuzzy sets, boils them down to the fourth type, i.e. multiple descriptors. So, the generalization of the rough set approach consists in handling the case of multiple descriptors.

1 Introduction

Rough set theory has been proven to be an effective tool for managing uncertainty in information systems (also called decision tables or knowledge representation systems). The source of uncertainty is, however, specific in this case. It results from ambiguity caused by a limited discernibility of objects by values of attributes. In particular, objects having the same values of condition attributes may belong to different decision classes. This creates inconsistencies in the decision table preventing a precise (certain) description of the decision classes in terms of the condition attributes. It is assumed, however, that all data in the information system are crisp, i.e. for each pair [*object, attribute*], there is known a precise and unique value called descriptor.

In fact, descriptors may also be uncertain because of many reasons. So, we can speak about different types of uncertainty coming from specific sources. Considering information systems, besides the ambiguity, one can have to deal with uncertainty coming from the following sources:

(i) discretization of quantitative attributes,
(ii) imprecise descriptors,
(iii) unknown (missing) descriptors,
(iv) multiple descriptors.

Uncertainty of type (i) is an essential issue in data pre-processing for the rough set analysis. Attributes creating the information system are divided, in general, into qualitative and quantitative ones. An original domain of a quantitative attribute is usually a subset of a real line (interval) while the domain of a qualitative attribute is a finite set of qualitative terms, usually of a low cardinality. In practice, values of quantitative attributes are rarely directly used in the rough set analysis. Instead, prior to the analysis, they are interpreted in qualitative terms, e.g. low, medium, high, very high, etc. So, the original domain (interval) is divided into few subintervals corresponding to the qualitative terms. Bounds of these subintervals are established according to norms, conventions, traditions existing in the field of a given application. It must be noticed, however, that such a definition is more or less arbitrary and may influence the results of the rough set analysis (see [11],[7]). Thus, the arbitrariness involves uncertainty of type (i) and should be taken into account in the analysis.

Uncertainty of type (ii) appears when instead of a precise value of a quantitative attribute for a given object (i.e. a single descriptor) a subinterval of possible values is known. For instance, the statement "the temperature is between 36°C and 37°C" may result from an imprecise measurement of the attribute value.

Uncertainty of type (iii) refers to an unknown (missing) value of the descriptor for pair [object, attribute].

Uncertainty of type (iv) occurs when instead of a single value of a descriptor for pair [object, attribute], a finite set of attribute values is known (i.e. the object is described by a multiple descriptor).

Although all these types of uncertainty are often met together in real-life applications, they are not handled in the classical model of rough sets (see [9]). A review of literature shows that uncertainty of type (iii) has been discussed in [6]. The first attempt at handling uncertainty of types (i) and (iii) together was described by the authors in [13]. It is also known a generalization of the rough set approach allowing for a definition of discretization with overlapping bounds of subintervals [12]. However, no attempt is known at handling all the four types of uncertainty together in the rough set approach.

This is precisely the aim of this paper. The uncertainty coming from discretization, imprecise and unknown descriptors will be modelled by fuzzy sets in a way which transforms these types of uncertainty to the case of multiple descriptors with different degrees of possibility. Thus, the generalization of the rough set theory has to concern this case only.

Modelling of uncertainty of type (i-iii) by means of fuzzy sets is discussed in the next section. Section 3 contains the generalization of the rough set theory for handling the case of multiple descriptors. Conclusions are drawn in the final section.

2 The use of fuzzy sets for modelling uncertainty of type (i), (ii) and (iii)

The methodology of handling the three types of uncertainty starts with the problem of modelling uncertainty of type (ii), i.e. the discretization of quantitative attributes.

Let us notice that original values of these attributes are usually interpreted in linguistic terms corresponding to different levels of original values, like low temperature, normal temperature, ... , high temperature or low cost, ..., high cost, etc.

Thus, the quantitative attributes are interpreted as linguistic variables, according to fuzzy set theory, with values equal to the terms like low, medium, high etc. These values can be modelled by fuzzy subintervals on a real interval (an original domain of the attribute). Informally speaking, the fuzzy subinterval corresponding to a given value of the linguistic variable is a set of original values of the attribute belonging to the given value of the linguistic variable with some degrees of possibility (membership degrees).

We do not assume any restrictions of the form of fuzzy subintervals. For instance, the analyst (expert creating the information system) may prefer LR-fuzzy numbers [3].

As a consequence of uncertainty in the definition of subintervals, the fuzzy subintervals have overlapping bounds with decreasing membership degrees in these zones. An example of the definition of fuzzy subintervals for a linguistic variable taking values *low, medium* or *high* is given in Fig. 1.

We assume that the analyst is able to define the discretization by the fuzzy subintervals for each quantitative attribute. In case of certainty, the consecutive intervals have common bounds and uniform distribution of membership degrees equal to 1 over each subinterval. While defining the fuzzy subintervals, the analyst could also be supported by methods of fuzzy grouping (e.g. see [1] or [14]).

In result of overlapping bounds of the fuzzy subintervals, an original value of the attribute may belong with a non-zero degree of possibility to more than one fuzzy interval.

Below we are presenting the way of calculating the membership degree of an original value of the discretized attribute to a linguistic value.

Let U be a set of objects in the information system; $x \in U$ is an object; Q is a set of attributes in the system; $q_i \in Q$ is an attribute.

Let $q_i(x)$ denote an original value of quantitative attribute q_i for object x; V_i denotes the original domain of quantitative attribute q_i, i.e. a real interval; $\widetilde{v_{ih}}$ – is a h–th fuzzy subinterval defined on V_i, corresponding to a linguistic term v_{ih}, $h = 1, \ldots, m_i$, where m_i is a number of different linguistic terms for attribute q_i; $\mathcal{F}(\widetilde{v_{ih}})$ is a family of all fuzzy subintervals $\widetilde{v_{ih}}$ defined for attribute q_i and covering the whole domain V_i, i.e. $\{\forall q_i(x) \in V_i \; \exists \text{ such } \widetilde{v_{ih}} \in \mathcal{F}(\widetilde{v_{ih}}) \text{ that } q_i(x) \in \widetilde{v_{ih}}\}$.

The original value q_i may be either crisp or imprecise. In the latter case, it is an imprecise descriptor and represents uncertainty of type (ii). An imprecise descriptor corresponds to a subinterval of possible values with a distribution of degrees of possibility for them. So, it can be modelled by fuzzy subinterval, e.g. $\widetilde{q_i(x)}$.

To evaluate the membership of $\widetilde{q_i(x)}$ or $q_i(x)$ to fuzzy subintervals $\widetilde{v_{ih}}$ we are using the consistency measure for two fuzzy sets introduced by Zadeh [17]. For fuzzy subintervals $\widetilde{v_{ih}}$ and $\widetilde{q_i(x)}$ it is defined as:

$$\pi(\widetilde{q_i(x)}, \widetilde{v_{ih}}) = \sup_{q_i(x) \in V_i} \left\{ \min \left[\mu_{\widetilde{q_i(x)}}(q_i(x)), \mu_{\widetilde{v_{ih}}}(q_i(x)) \right] \right\}$$

For $q_i(x)$ it reduces to:

$$\pi(q_i(x), \widetilde{v_{ih}}) = \sup_{q_i(x) \in V_i} \left\{ \min \left[\mu_{q_i(x)}(q_i(x)), \mu_{\widetilde{v_{ih}}}(q_i(x)) \right] \right\} = \mu_{\widetilde{v_{ih}}}(q_i(x))$$

A graphical illustration of the above operation for two exemplary values $\widetilde{q}_i$ and $q_i(x)$ is presented in Fig. 1.

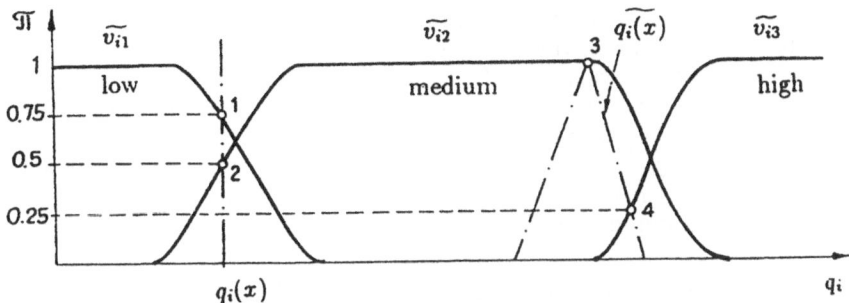

Fig. 1. Graphical illustration of calculation of $\pi(\widetilde{q_i(x)}, \widetilde{v_{ih}})$ and $\pi(q_i(x), \widetilde{v_{ih}})$

It can be seen that in the case of precise value $q_i(x)$, membership degrees to fuzzy subintervals $\widetilde{v_{i1}}$ and $\widetilde{v_{i2}}$ are equal to 0.75 and 0.5, respectively, and refer to intersection points no. 1 and 2. Similarly, for fuzzy subinterval $\widetilde{q}_i$, membership degrees to $\widetilde{v_{i2}}$ and $\widetilde{v_{i3}}$ are equal to 1 and 0.25 (points no. 3 and 4), respectively.

As the original value of the quantitative attribute may belong to one or two (even more in case of $\widetilde{q}_i$) consecutive intervals, each pair [*object, attribute*] may be associated with one or two linguistic terms having some degrees of possibility. Thus, the description of objects by original descriptors is substituted by multiple descriptors and boils down to the case of multiple descriptors (uncertainty of type (iv)).

In case of unknown (missing) values of descriptors (uncertainty of type (iii)), we assume that the analyst is able to define a subset of possible values containing a "true" value of the attribute with corresponding degrees of possibility (maybe all equal each other). Thus, it is again the case of multiple descriptors. While defining these subsets the analyst can use techniques developed in inductive learning field for handling missing values of attributes (cf. [8]). According to them, unknown values of the attributes can be determined basing on known values of other attributes; replaced by the most common or likely values; or even replaced by all values from the domain of this attribute.

So, the modelling of all three types of uncertainty (i-iii) leads to the case of multiple descriptors. Thus, the generalization of the rough set approach should essentially consists in handling this case only .

3 Generalization of the rough set theory for handling multiple descriptors

3.1 Introductory remarks

Let V_i denote a finite set of linguistic terms for attribute q_i. If attribute q_i has originaly been quantitative, than it has been transformed into linguistic variables with fuzzy subintervals $\widetilde{v_{ih}}$ (cf. section 2); each subinterval corresponds to a linguistic term denoted by v_{ih}. If attribute q_i has been qualitative, however, the qualitative terms can also be denoted by v_{ih}. So, V_i is a "linguistic" domain of attribute q_i; $v_{ih} \in V_i$, h=1, ..., m_i where m_i is a cardinality of V_i.

By a multiple descriptor for object $x \in U$ and attribute q_i ($i = 1, \ldots, n$; n is a number of considered attributes) we understand:

$$MDes(x, q_i) = \{(v_{ih}, \pi_{ih}(x)) : v_{ih} \in V_i \text{ and } \pi_{ih}(x) > 0\}$$

where:

$$\pi_{ih}(x) = \begin{cases} \pi(\widetilde{q_i(x)}, \widetilde{v_{ih}}) & \text{if descriptor } \widetilde{q_i(x)} \text{ is quantitative but} \\ & \text{imprecise and } \widetilde{v_{ih}} \text{ is a fuzzy subinterval} \\ & \text{corresponding to linguistic term } v_{ih}, \\ \pi(q_i(x), \widetilde{v_{ih}}) & \text{if descriptor } q_i(x) \text{ is quantitative but} \\ & \text{crisp and } \widetilde{v_{ih}} \text{ as above,} \\ \pi(q_i(x), v_{ih}) & \text{if descriptor } q_i(x) \text{ is qualitative and} \\ & v_{ih} \text{ is also a qualitative term} \end{cases}$$

Let us notice that in the two first cases, $\pi_{ih} \in [0, 1]$ while in the third one, $\pi_{ih} = 1$ if $q_{ih}(x) = v_{ih}$ and $\pi_{ih} = 0$, otherwise.

Thus, a generalized information system with multiple descriptors is 4-tuple $\tilde{S}_{MDes} =< U, Q, V, \tilde{\varrho}_{MDes} >$ such that for each $q_i \in Q$, $x \in U : \tilde{\varrho}_{MDes}(x, q_i) = MDes(x, q_i)$.

Any object in $\tilde{S}_{MDes}$ may be described by multiple descriptors. If it is the case, such an object could be represented by several univocal vectors of attributes coming from combinations of possible descriptors. Thus, each object x described by multiple descriptors could be subdivided into a set of objects corresponding to these vectors. Objects resulting from this subdivision will be called *sub-objects*.

If x^j denotes a sub-object coming from x, $j = 1, \ldots, p$; (p is the number of possible combinations of descriptors), x^j is described by a vector of single descriptors $Des(x^j, q_i) = (v_{ih}, \pi_{ih}(x^j))$ where $(v_{ih}, \pi_{ih}(x^j)) \in MDes(x, q_i)$ and $\pi_{ih}(x^j)$ is a degree of possibility assigned to term v_{ih} for sub-object (combination) x^j.

Each sub-object x^j is associated with a degree of possibility of its realization $\pi(x^j)$ resulting from aggregation of $\pi_{ih}(x^j)$, using a t-norm operator. In the present paper we suggest to choose Yager's parametrized t-norm [16] defined as

$$\pi(x^j) = 1 - min\{1, [\sum_{i=1}^{n} (1 - \pi_{ih}(x^j))^l]^{1/l}\}$$

Depending on value l, Yager's t–norm covers a wide range of possible conjunctive operators (see [4]). In particular, for $l \longrightarrow \infty$:

$$\pi(x^j) = min\{\pi_{1h}(x^j), \pi_{2h}(x^j), \ldots, \pi_{nh}(x^j)\}$$

In order to express a relative degree of possibility for sub-object x^j (denotation $\eta(x^j)$) we will take into account the number of sub-objects associated with the original object x:

$$\eta(x^j) = \frac{\pi(x^j)}{\sum_{k=1}^p \pi(x^k)}$$

The coefficient $\eta(x^j)$ can be understood as a "part" of original object x characterized by a given combination of single descriptors.

We assume that the sub-objects inherit values of decision attributes assigned to the original object. In the present study we do not assume any uncertainty for decision attributes.

Subdividing the original object into sub-objects leads to the generalized information system. By generalized information system we understand the 5-tuple $\tilde{S} = < U', \eta, Q, V, \tilde{\varrho} >$ where U' is a finite set of sub-objects ($x' \in U'$); η is a finite set of degrees of possibility for objects from U', i.e. the set of $\eta(x')$; Q is a finite set of attributes; $V = \bigcup_{i: q_i \in Q} V_i$; $\tilde{\varrho}$ is a generalized information function such that for each object $x' \in U'$ and $q_i \in Q$: $\tilde{\varrho}(x', q_i) = (v_{ih}, \pi_{ih}(x'))$.

In particular, an original object described by single descriptors corresponds to one sub-object with degree of possibility equal to 1.

We will show that all operations of the rough set approach can be performed in generalized information system $\tilde{S}$ in the same way as in the classical approach. In comparison with the classical approach, however, we have to consider the degrees of possibilities.

3.2 The generalized indiscernibility relation

Sub-object $x' \in U'$ is possibly indiscernible with sub-object $y' \in U'$ in $\tilde{S}$ (denotation $x' \widetilde{IND}_P y'$) with respect to a subset of attributes $P \subseteq Q$ iff $q_i(x') = q_i(y')$ for every $q_i \in P$; where $q_i(x')$ is a linguistic value of attribute q_i for object x'.

The generalized indiscernibility relation is defined basing on the equality of attribute values (like in the classical approach). However, as the degree of possibility is associated with each attribute value, we have also to define the degree of possibility for indiscernibility between objects.

If sub-objects x' and y' are possibly indiscernible, they can create a possible P–elementary set. The P–elementary set is described by the same combination of attribute values as sub- objects x' and y'. New degrees of possibility are assigned to these values of attributes in its description. Let us assume that attribute $q_i \in P$ has value $v_{ih} = q_i(x') = q_i(y')$. Then, the degree of possibility assigned to the value v_{ih} appearing in the description of the P–elementary set results from using Yager's t–norm for $l \longrightarrow \infty$ and is equal to:

$$\pi_{ih}(X'_P) = 1 - min\{1, [(1 - \pi_{ih}(x'))^l + (1 - \pi_{ih}(y'))^l]^{1/l}\}$$

where X'_P denotes the P–elementary set composed of x' and y'.

372

The cardinality of the possible P–elementary set X'_P is equal to the sum of degrees of possibility of realization of sub-objects belonging to the P–elementary set:

$$card(X'_P) = \sum_{x' \in X'_p} \eta(x')$$

3.3 Generalized approximations of a set and a classification

Let $U'|\widetilde{IND}_P$ be a family of all possible equivalence classes of the generalized indiscernibility relation induced by subset $P \subseteq Q$ on U'.

For any subset $Y \subset U'$, we define a generalized P–lower and P- -upper approximation of Y with respect to $P \subseteq Q$ (denotation $\tilde{\underline{P}}(Y)$ and $\tilde{\overline{P}}(Y)$) as follows:

$$\tilde{\underline{P}}(Y) = \bigcup X'_P : \{X'_P \in \widetilde{IND}_P \text{ and } X'_P \subseteq Y\};$$
$$\tilde{\overline{P}}(Y) = \bigcup X'_P : \{X'_P \in \widetilde{IND}_P \text{ and } X'_P \cap Y \neq \emptyset\};$$
$$\widetilde{Bn}_P(Y) = \tilde{\overline{P}}(Y) - \tilde{\underline{P}}(Y)$$

$\widetilde{Bn}_P(Y)$ is called a generalized P-boundary of Y. Cardinality of the lower generalized approximation of Y is equal to:

$$card(\tilde{\underline{P}}(Y)) = \sum_{X'_P \subseteq \tilde{\underline{P}}(Y)} card(X'_P) = \sum_{x' \in \tilde{\underline{P}}(Y)} \eta(x')$$

The cardinality of generalized P–upper approximation and P-boundary is defined in the similar way.

With every subset $Y \subset U'$ we associate number

$$\alpha_{\tilde{P}}(Y) = card(\tilde{\underline{P}}(Y))/card(\tilde{\overline{P}}(Y))$$

called accuracy of the generalized approximation of Y.

Let $\mathcal{Y} = \{Y_1, Y_2, \ldots, Y_m\}$ be a classification of U' in the generalized information system $\tilde{S}$. By the P–lower (P–upper) generalized approximation of $\mathcal{Y}$ in $\tilde{S}$ we understand the sets $\tilde{\underline{P}}(\mathcal{Y}) = \{\tilde{\underline{P}}(Y_1), \tilde{\underline{P}}(Y_2), \ldots, \tilde{\underline{P}}(Y_m)\}$ and $\tilde{\overline{P}}(\mathcal{Y}) = \{\tilde{\overline{P}}(Y_1), \tilde{\overline{P}}(Y_2), \ldots, \tilde{\overline{P}}(Y_m)\}$, respectively.

The coefficient

$$\gamma_{\tilde{P}}(\mathcal{Y}) = \frac{\sum_{i=1}^m (card\tilde{\underline{P}}(Y_i))}{card(U')}$$

defines the quality of the generalized approximation of classification $\mathcal{Y}$. Cardinality of U' is equal to cardinality of U.

3.4 Reduction of attributes

The minimal subset $R \subseteq P \subseteq Q$ such that $\gamma_{\tilde{R}}(\mathcal{Y}) = \gamma_{\tilde{P}}(\mathcal{Y})$ is called the generalized Y-reduct of $\overline{P}$ (in short the generalized reduct) and is denoted by $R\widetilde{ED}_{\mathcal{Y}}(P)$. If system $\tilde{S}$ contains more than one generalized reduct, their intersection is called a core, i.e. $C\widetilde{ORE}_{\mathcal{Y}}(P) = \bigcap R\widetilde{ED}_{\mathcal{Y}}(P)$.

Reducing attributes is performed analogously to the classical approach. Removing particular attribute from system $\tilde{S}$ we check whether the quality of classification decreases. It must be, however, accompanied by modification of the degrees of possibility for attribute values in elementary sets if the removal of some attributes causes a clustering of several elementary sets into a new one. This modification is performed in the same way as described in section 3.2. Thus, the degree of possibility assigned to the value of attribute in the newly created elementary set results from the use of the t-norm over degrees for elementary sets clustered together. The cardinality of the new created elementary set is the sum of degrees of possibility for sub-objects belonging to it.

3.5 Decision rules

The generalized information system $\tilde{S}$ may be identified with the generalized decision table $\widetilde{DT} = < U', \eta, C \cup D, V, \tilde{\varrho} >$ where $U', \eta, V, \tilde{\varrho}$ are defined as for $\tilde{S}$ assuming that C refers to Q and denotes condition attributes. Values of decision attributes D are uniquely defined. In the following, we consider one decision attribute d only. A decision table with more than one decision attribute can always be transformed to a decision table with one attribute only by a simple coding.

Let $B \subseteq C$ in $\widetilde{DT}$, $V_B = \bigcup_{i:q_i \in B} V_i$. Expressions of the form $[(q_i = v_{ih}), \pi_{ih}]$ are called generalized elementary conditions defined on B and V_B (π_{ih} is a degree of possibility that attribute q_i in the generalized conditions has value v_{ih}; it is defined on the basis of subobjects in U' satisfying the condition $(q_i = v_{ih})$).

A conjunction of the generalized elementary conditions $[(q_i = v_{ih}), \pi_{ih}]$ for $q_i \in B$ and only one value v_{ih} per each attribute q_{ih}, is denoted by $[\widetilde{r_B}]$ denote the set of sub-objects in U' satisfying $\widetilde{r_B}$.

A resultant possibility for conjunction of conditions $(q_i = v_{ih})$ is calculated using the Yeager's t-norm over $\pi_{ih}(x')$ for all $x' \in [\widetilde{r_B}]$ and for all v_{ih} appearing in $\widetilde{r_B}$; This conjunction is denoted by r_B, its resultant possibility by π_B; and $[r_B] = [\widetilde{r_B}]$

For decision attribute d, the elementary decision is of form $(d = v)$ where $v \in V_d$. By r_d we understand the disjunction of elementary decisions, i.e. $(d = v_1) \vee (d = v_2) \vee \ldots \vee (d = v_s)$ where $v_1, v_2, \ldots v_s \in V_d$. Let $[r_d]$ be a set of sub-objects in U' satisfying expression r_d.

The expression $r_B \Rightarrow r_d$ is called generalized decision rule rd in $\widetilde{DT}$. The rule is true iff $[r_B] \subseteq [r_d]$. If r_d consists of one elementary decision only, the decision rule is deterministic otherwise it is nondeterministic. Each rule $rd : r_B \Rightarrow r_d$ (deterministic or not) is associated with resultant possibility $\pi_{rd} = \pi_B$

3.6 Classification support for new objects

The classification of a new object consists in assigning the object described by values of condition attributes to one of predefined decision classes.

As the description of the classified new object may be imprecise or missing, it is transformed to the case of multiple descriptors. Thus, the classified object (denoted as x) is substituted by sub-objects x'.

The process of classification support is done by matching the object's description (descriptors of sub-objects) to generalized decision rules. For every decision rule rd one can calculate the degree of possible matching for sub-object x' and the rule. As in the classical fuzzy reasoning approach (cf. [2], [5], [10]), we suggest to define this degree as a the Yager's t–norm for $l \longrightarrow \infty$, i.e.

$$\pi(x', rd) = min(\pi_{1h}(x'), \pi_{2h}(x'), \ldots, \pi_{rh}(x'), \pi_{rd})$$

where $\pi_{ih}(x')$ denotes the degree of possibility for sub-object x' to take value v_{ih} for attribute q_i, while v_{ih} is represented in the condition part r_b of rule rd.

Every rule rd with $\pi(x', rd) > \tau$ (where τ is a certain non-zero discernibility threshold) is characterized as possibly matched with x' and should be considered in classification support for x'. Moreover, every rule rd is described by the parameter called strength of the rule, i.e. $S(rd)$. It corresponds to the number of sub-objects in $\tilde{S}$ satisfying condition part of rule rd. Formally, if $[r_B]$ is the set of sub-objects satisfying r_B then :

$$S(rd) = \sum_{y' \in [r_B]} \eta(y')$$

In the case of a non-deterministic rule, it is necessary to calculate the strength for each possible decision separately.

Thus, in classification support we present to the DM the set of possible matched rules with their $\pi(x', rd)$ and $S(rd)$ coefficients. In this process we consider all sub-objects x' coming from classified original object x.

If one wants to know the degree of membership of the classified object to given decision classes or even perform classification automatically, we suggest to use the special operators $\pi_{x'}(D_j)$ showing the degree of possibility that sub-object x' belongs to decision class D_j ($j = 1, 2, \ldots, s; s$ is $card(V_d)$). Using fuzzy reasoning principles we can define several possible operators. Below, some proposals are presented:

(i) Max–min composition (classical operator in fuzzy reasoning)

$$\pi_{x'}(D_j) = \max_{rd \in \mathcal{R}_j} \{min(\pi_{1h}(x'), \pi_{2h}(x'), \ldots, \pi_{rh}(x'), \pi_{rd})\}$$

where $\mathcal{R}_j$ is the set of rules indicating class D_j.

(ii) Average weighted sum

$$\pi_{x'}(D_j) = \frac{\sum_{rd \in \mathcal{R}_j} \pi(x', rd) \cdot S(rd)}{\sum_{rd \in \mathcal{R}'} \pi(x', rd) \cdot S(rd)}$$

where $\mathcal{R}'$ denotes the set of all considered rules. These coefficients are calculated for sub-objects x' and then summed up in appropriate decision classes forming $\pi_x(D_j)$. For other proposals of operators see [15].

The classification procedure is as follows : object x possibly belongs to class D_j with the degree $\pi_x(D_j)$.

4 Conclusions

In the present paper a new methodology for coupling various types of uncertainty with the rough set approach has been introduced. The new proposal starts from modelling uncertainty referring to the discretization of quantitative attributes and imprecise or unknown descriptors using fuzzy set concept. All three types of uncertainty have been transformed to the case of multiple descriptors and the generalization of the classical rough set approach is concerning, in fact, this case only. The idea of using sub-objects instead of the original object described by multiple descriptors has allowed to keep a concordance with the classical approach. In particular, the new proposal reduces itself to the classical model when data creating the information system are complete and precise and there is no ambiguity in the discretization of quantitative attributes.

5 Acknowledgments

This research has been supported by KBN grant no. 8 0570 91 01/P2 and IC 1010 CRIT Project V/92.

References

[1] Bezdek, J.C. Pattern Recognition with Fuzzy Objective Function Algorithm. Plenum Press, New York, 1981.

[2] Czogala, E., Pedrycz, W. Identification and control problems in fuzzy systems. In: Zimmermann H.J., Zadeh L.A., Gaines B.R. (eds.), Fuzzy Sets and Decision Analysis, North–Holland, Amsterdam, 1984,pp 447–466.

[3] Dubois,D., Prade, H. Teorie des Possibilites. Masson, Paris, 1985.

[4] Dubois,D., Prade, H. Criteria aggregation and ranking of alternatives in the framework of fuzzy set theory, TIMS/Studies in the Management Sciences 1984 vol 20, pp. 209-240.

[5] Hruschka, H.(1988): Use of fuzzy relations in rule– based decision support systems for business planning problems. European Journal of Operational Research 1988 vol. 34, pp 326–335.

[6] Grzymala–Busse, J.W. On the unknown attribute values in learning from examples. In: Ras Z.W., Zemankowa M. (eds.) Proc. of Methodologies for Intelligent Systems. Spinger Verlag 1991, pp 368- -377 (Lecture notes in AI no. 542).

[7] Nowicki R., Slowinski R., Stefanowski J. Rough set analysis of diagnostic capacity of vibroacoustic symptoms. Computers and Mathematics with Applications, 1992, vol. 24, no. 7, pp. 109-123.

[8] Quinlan J.R. Unknown attribute values in induction. In: Proc. 6th Int. Workshop on Machine Learning, Morgan Kaufmann, San Mateo C.A. 1987, pp. 31-37.

[9] Pawlak Z. Rough sets. Some Aspects of Reasoning About Knowledge. Kluwer Academic Publishers, Dordrecht, 1991.

[10] Pedrycz W. Numerical and applicational aspects of fuzzy relational equations. Fuzzy Sets and Systems, 1983, vol. 11, pp 1– 18.

[11] Slowinski K., Slowinski R. Sensitivity analysis of rough classification. International Journal of Man–Machine Studies, 1990, vol.32, pp.693-705.

[12] Slowinski R. Rough sets with strict and weak indiscernibility relations. In: Proc. IEEE Int. Conf. on Fuzzy Systems, San Diego, CA, March 8–12, 1992, IEEE Catalog no.92CH3073-4, 1992, pp 695–702.

[13] Slowinski R., Stefanowski J. Rough classification in incomplete information systems. Mathematical and Comput. Modelling, 1989, vol. 12, no. 10/11, pp 1347–1357.

[14] Sugeno,M.,Yasukawa,T. A fuzzy-logic-based approach to qualitative modeling. IEEE Transactions on fuzzy systems, 1993, vol. 1, no. 1, pp. 7-31.

[15] Tanaka H., Ishibuchi H., Shigenoga T. Fuzzy inference system based on rough sets and its application to medical diagnosis. In: Slowinski R. Intelligent Decision Support. Handbook of Applications and Advances on Rough Sets. Kluwer Academic Publishers, Dordrecht 1992.

[16] Yager, R.R. Some procedures for selecting operators for fuzzy operations. Technical Report RRY-79-05, Iona College, New Rochelle, N.Y. 1979.

[17] Zadeh L.A. Fuzzy sets as a basis for theory of possibility. Fuzzy Sets and Systems, 1978, vol. 1, pp 3–28.

Intelligent Image Filtering Using Rough Sets

Zbigniew M. WOJCIK
Smart Machines,
13703 Morningbluff Drive,
San Antonio, TX 78216, USA

The paper presents a class of novel, high-quality image filters which are based on the rough sets and which both effectively remove noise and enhance edges. Current filtering techniques do not do both effectively: some enhance edges but do not remove noise sufficiently, and most filters blur edges and small image details when removing noise. Many filtering techniques lose the shape details because of statistical averaging or sorting gray levels within a window. The novel methodology presented in this paper uses the upper approximation to check good continuation of the window center with templates distributed uniformly around the center. A non-statistical variance between the center of a window and pixels of window templates is used as the measure of good continuation. The minimum value of this semi-variance is found to get the most homogeneous template. The average or median of this most homogeneous template is then used as the gray level of the window center and is assigned to the pixel gray level in the filtered image. In addition, adaptation of template shape to the region shape in the image is accomplished. Several variations of the technique have been constructed on the top of other filters.

A typical problem with low-pass filtering is its inability to distinguish between the noise and tiny image elements such as sharp edges and corners. Noise occupies the highest spatial frequencies. Sharp edges and corners involve the highest spatial image frequencies as well. Low-pass filtering attenuates high spatial frequencies in both noise and sharp edges and thus blurs the edges and corners as a side effect.

We use the upper approximation of the rough set [3,10] to detect the existence of a good continuation of window center with a window template and then use parameters of the template with this good continuation as parameters of the window center. The upper approximation follows the region in the direction of highest homogeneity with the window center. Such anisotropic processing complies with the Gestalt law of good continuation of region. Use of the rotating template [5,6,7], combined with the rough sets [3,8,10,11], finds the optimal continuation of a window center with a surrounding region (i.e., the best match for the window center in its neighborhood as far as gray level is concerned).

The philosophy behind the formalities of the rough sets is to devise an operation to consider the optimal computer approximation of an object in question (e.g., a pixel) represented by data, by defining the two following quantitative or qualitative sets: a) the greatest definable set of elements contained by the data representing the object; and b) the smallest definable set of elements (including symbols) containing the data representing the object.

The rough set is defined on an image approximation space $K = (I, R)$ composed of image I (treated as a universe) and an equivalence relation R. A rough set approximating a set X of data (e.g., pixels) selected from the image I is a pair of subsets $\underline{R}X$, $\overline{R}X$ [3]:

$$\underline{R}X = \{x \in I : [x]_R \subseteq X\} \tag{1}$$

$$\overline{R}X = \{x \in I : [x]_R \bigcap X \neq O\} \tag{2}$$

where: $X \in I$; $\underline{R}X$, the lower approximation of X by R, is the union of all partitions of I which are entirely included in X; $\overline{R}X$, the upper approximation of X by R, is the union of these partitions of I where at least one element is a member of X; O is the empty set. $\underline{R}X$ is entirely included in $\overline{R}X$. The difference $\overline{R}X$ - $\underline{R}X$ is the roughness of approximation of X by R.

The rough set specified above assumes the existence of an equivalence relation R that takes noise X apart from image I. The relation R can be described as follows: "pixels x_1 and x_2 are in relation R if each of them is in a selected range of frequency or statistical parameters for noise." $\underline{R}X$ is the set of pixels that is definitely noise. $\overline{R}X - \underline{R}X$ is the set of pixels that may or may not be noise (i.e., is only roughly noise). Subset $I - \overline{R}X$ is definitely not noise.

The above application of the rough set provides an equivalence relation that is fixed for the entire image. One noise pixel creates an equivalence class of noise pixels because it determines a noise range of statistical or frequency parameters bounded by a plus-minus measurement error. It describes noise globally, not locally. Experience, however, shows that noise is a nonlinear local image property. Consequently, a rough element that provides a more efficient local noise removal than global rough sets is defined below.

Our modified approximation space is the pair (W, h). The universe W is the set of pixel gray levels in a window. The equivalence relation defined for the rough sets is extended to a homogeneity detection operation $h=max_n(\frac{1}{var_n})$, where var_n is the sum of the differences of the gray levels of the window center with the pixels of a template n defined in the window.

The lower and upper approximations $\underline{h}W$ and $\overline{h}W$ are elements, and not sets as $\underline{R}X$ and $\overline{R}X$. Thanks to this improvement, each element is easily adjustable to the local noise level.

The upper approximation $\overline{h}W$ of a window center is the median or mean gray level of the template which is most homogeneous (least contrasting) with the window center. The template i carrying $\overline{h}W$ indicates good continuation with the region which the window center belongs to. The upper approximation is thus definable by h on all templates of W surrounding the center. The template i selected as possessing the least contrast against the center is used for image filtering and edge enhancement. The operation $\overline{h}$ is designed to find this greatest set of elements adjacent to each other and contained in a template (e.g., all pixels of the template i) that is most homogeneous with the center, and to represent the window center by the mean or median of this greatest set:

$$\overline{h}W = \{mean(template(i)) \bigcup median(template(i)) :$$

$$i = min_n(var_n(W)) \bigcap template(i)\}, \qquad (3)$$

where $\{1, ...n, ...N\}$ are the template subscripts in the window W; i is the subscript of the selected template; N is the number of window templates; Q is a threshold; and the equivalence class $[X, Y]_{\underline{e}} = min_n(var_n(W)) > Q$.

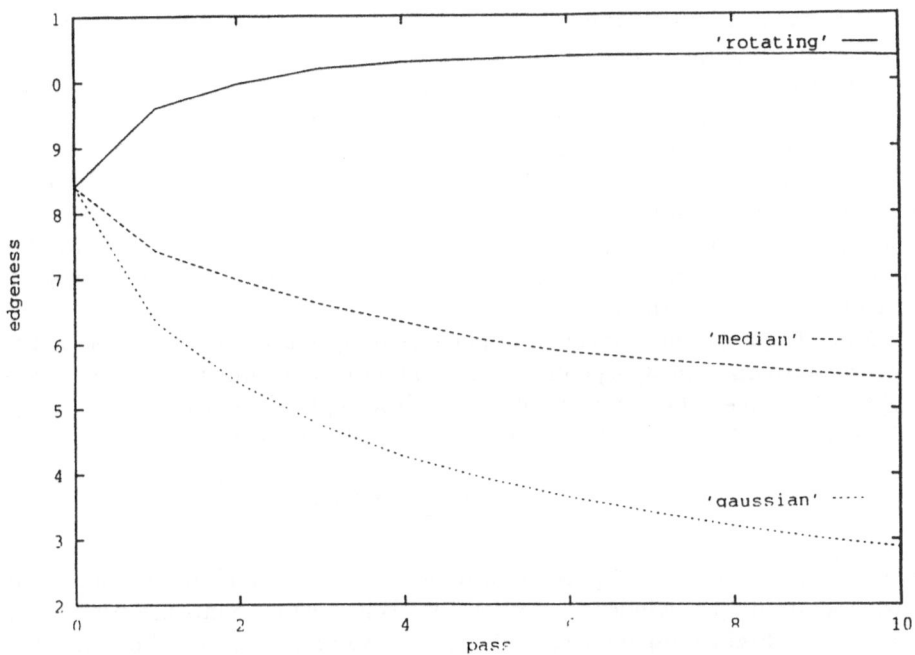

Fig. 1. *Average edgeness of pixels shown in Fig. 3 computed for the image presented in Fig. 2 as a function of the number of passes by the following three filters: a) the rotating template; b) the median filter; c) the Gaussian (or Fourier) filter. The pass 0 stands for the average edgeness (contrast at edges) of the original image*

Using Eq.(3), i is computed first by finding window template of the smallest non-statistical variance var with respect to window center. Then, a rough inference is made about the entire i by extracting all its components (pixels).

Then, a rough inference about an object (template) i is made using a term $\bigcap template(i)$ by extracting all elements (pixels) of i. The subscript i is indicated using the predecessor $i = min_n(var_n(W))$. Then, all these inferred components of i are used to compute a mean or median to be used as this upper approximation $\overline{h}W$.

The most homogeneous pixels make the greatest set in the window, because in most cases, regions occupying greatest image areas are about uniform in values of some parameters, e.g., in grey level. Regions are greatest sets of pixels contained by objects and locally by windows. Basically, only noise and edge pixels are different from their surroundings.

Similarly, our lower approximation defines edges by the least (smallest) set of pixels in the window, because only edge pixels and noise are expected to be very different compared to most pixels in the window. At the same time, edges are the least information (smallest set of pixels) that contain (represent) image objects.

The upper approximation $\overline{h}W$ enforces the Gestalt law of *good continuation* of region for high-quality noise removal purposes. The upper approximation has the wonderful advantage of enhancing (and not blurring) edges while detecting disturbances or noise and while filtering. All other well-known filters (e.g., Fourier or Gaussian filters and median filters) blur edges (compare Fig. 1).

The most important feature of our improvement to the rough sets theory is that the lower and upper approximations $\underline{h}W$ and $\overline{h}W$ are elements or values, and not sets as needed by original concepts $\underline{R}X$ and $\overline{R}X$. Thanks to this improvement, each operation $\overline{h}$ or $\underline{h}$ is easily adjustable to the local noise level or to the local strength of edges.

More formally, our rotating-template technique using the concept of the upper approximation [3] depends on the calculation of a non-statistical variance $r_n(X,Y)$ between the window center gray level $v(X,Y)$ and pixels $v_n(X_i,Y_i)$ of the neighborhoods (templates) $1,..n,...N$ in the window:

$$r_n(X,Y) = \frac{\sum_{k=1}^{K}(v(X,Y) - v_n(X_k,Y_k))^2}{K} \tag{4}$$

where K is the number of pixels in a template n. All templates are uniformly disposed around the window center. All pixels in each template are adjacent to each other. Eight tempates are sufficient, twelve or sixteen may be used. The window center may or may not belong to each of the templates.

For edge-enhancing image filtering, a much simpler non-statistical variance will be exploited:

$$r_n(X,Y) = \sum_{k=1}^{K}|v(X,Y) - v_n(X_k,Y_k)|. \tag{5}$$

The sample variance would is more time consuming and would select a wrong template. We find the template of the minimum contrast with respect to the center because the center location is given with high accuracy and we associate the measure of the homogeneity (i.e., reverse of our non-statistical variance) with the center. We are not looking for the template whose pixel intensities vary the least inside the entire template, because this variation can only be assigned to the entire template (or to a template pixel selected at random) and not to any specific pixel of the template.

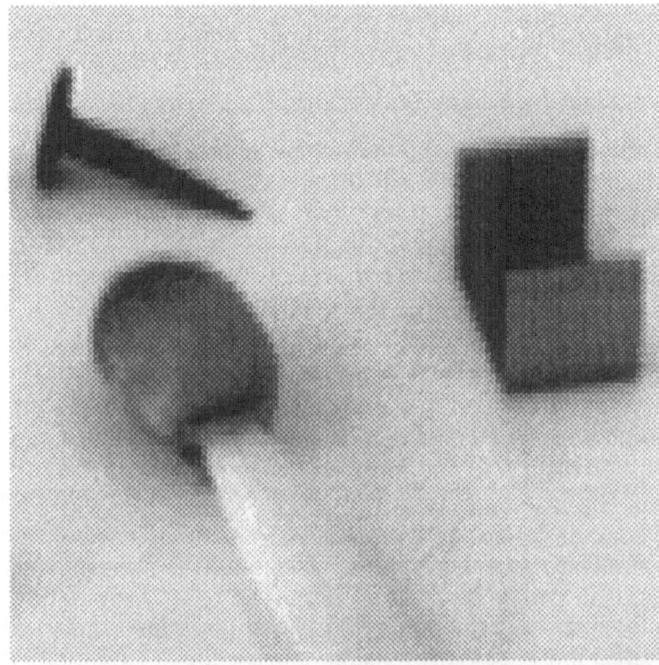

Fig. 2. An input image of dimensions 128×128 pixels processed by some of the techniques discussed in this paper

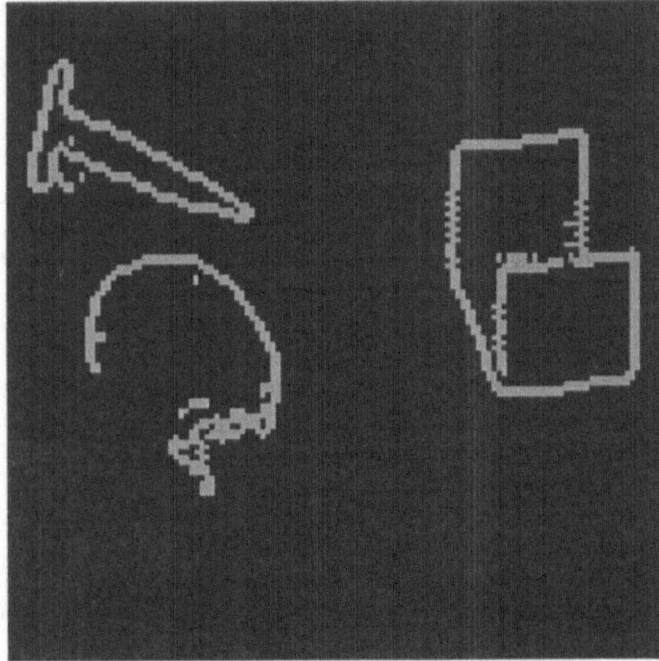

Fig. 3. Double edges of the objects in the above image detected by our novel technique. These double edges have been used for the evaluation of the edge blurring / enhancement level during filtering

Region and edge pixels cannot be localized precisely using sample variance, and thus edges filtered cannot be sharp. Selection of a template with the smallest sample variance of pixels inside it, but with no reasonable way to tell which specific pixel of this template inherits average or median of this template, causes edge blurring.

The template (neighborhood) t_m of the minimum non-statistical variance is selected:

$$t_m = min_n(r_n(X,Y)) \tag{6}$$

and the average or median of this neighborhood is substituted for the pixel gray level $v(X,Y)$ to obtain the enhanced image. The enhancement of edges is achieved by taking, as the window center, the median or average from the template located at the region the most homogeneous with the center. The level of the enhancement is controlled by the mean or median found in the most similar adjacent template. Use of the median or mean from the best adjacent template assures that the value assigned to the window center never makes the results of filtering worse than in the input image.

The upper approximation $\overline{h}W$ of a window center is the median or mean gray level of the template which is most homogeneous with the window center. This definition complies with (2): the mean or median indicates belongs to image I and the equivalence class $i = min_n(var_n(W))$ indicates the greatest set of pixels contained by a $template(i)$ most homogeneous with the window center, and thus by a region. This equivalence class intersects with the region. The upper approximation is definable by h on all templates of W surrounding the center. Because we consider only a window, the operation h finds the greatest set of elements contained not in the entire region, but locally in a template (i.e., the template pixels most homogeneous with the center), and then represents the center by its mean or median. The center thus takes parameters of the region, and not of noise. The upper approximation enforces thus the Gestalt law of good continuation of region for high-quality noise removal purposes.

We do not use in here the full rough sets, but only its upper approximation $\overline{h}W)$ (i.e., without the lower approximation). This is sufficient for this application, because all elements $\overline{h}W)$ filter image and enhance the edges. In Fig. 1 the strength of edges resulting from the image filtering algorithms used by our technique goes up with each pass through the filter; edgeness returned by other approaches (such as Fourier filtering, convolutions or median filters) goes down for the same edge pixels. At the same time, randomly generated impulsive gray level noise is entirely eliminated when using our technique.

It should be noted that another current technique, which enhances edges by averaging a few window pixels that are the most homogeneous with the window center [4], provides stronger edge enhancement than our technique. However, its removal of the impulsive noise is weaker (see Figs. 3.a,b).

The median hybrid filter (which is a variation of a rotating template technique devised by Wojcik and published in 1976 [5] and 1977 [6]) considers four window sub-regions W_N, W_E, W_S, W_W. The average gray level in each of the sub-regions is computed separately, and then the median of the computed averages is selected as the gray level $v'(X, Y)$ of the window center:

$$v'(X, Y) = med(W_N, W_E, W_S, W_W). \tag{7}$$

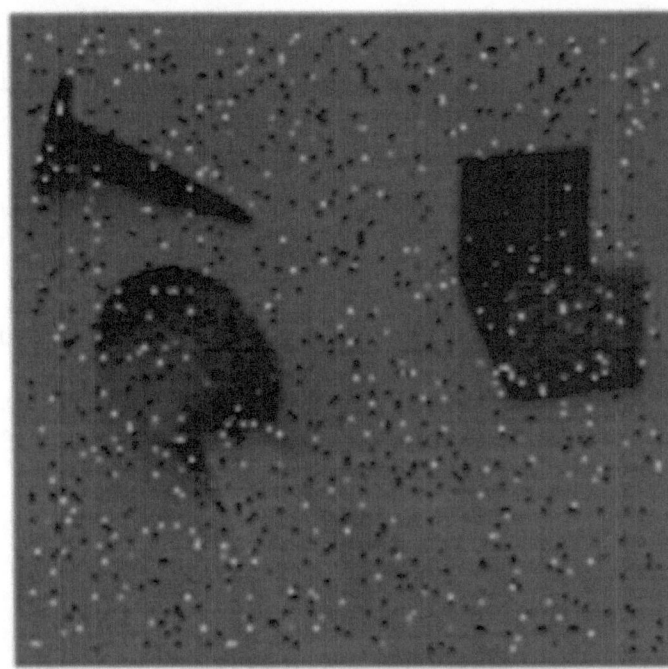

Fig. 4. The input image corrupted by the 2% noise. The noise gray level was generated randomly

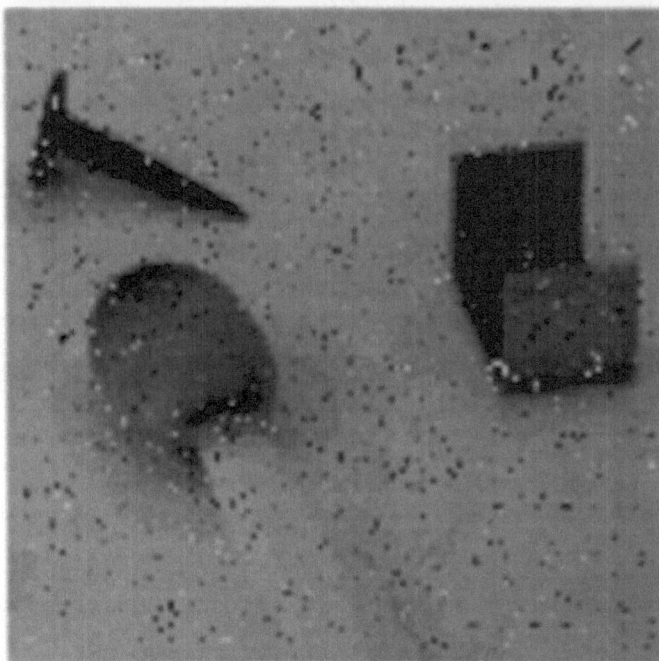

Fig. 5. Insufficient attenuation of noise by the technique enhancing edges by averaging the window pixels most homogeneous with the window center: A
mean of eight pixels most homogeneous
with the 5 × 5 window center substitutes for the center gray level

The median computed in this way selects one of two window sub-regions located on the edge. This decision is not the best, because it leads to edge blurring: the edge pixels are averaged across a smaller sub-region around the boundary.

Order statistics filters, called also *L-filters*, are generalizations of the median filters. They consider some of the ordered gray levels of a window. The median filter takes the $(\mid W_k \mid DIV\,2 + 1)$–th element of the sorted list of the window gray levels. Another order statistics filter, the midpoint filter, takes the average of the first (smallest) element and the last (greatest) element of the sorted list of window gray levels.

The α–trimmed mean takes the average of the gray levels of the range between the $\alpha N+1$ -th element and the $N - \alpha N$-th element (inclusive) in the sorted list, where $N = \mid W_i \mid$. The 0-trimmed filter (for $\alpha = 0$) is the mean filter. Up to the fraction 2α of $\mid W_i \mid$ window pixels, the noise pixels can be removed from the window. Edge pixels get blurred if the pixels of the other region are not fully involved in the $2\alpha N$ of pixels trimmed off.

The modified trimmed mean (MTM) filter excludes window pixels $v_i(y, x)$ which differ by more than an assumed threshold Q from the center gray level $v(y, x)$ or from the mean $\overline{W}_k$:

$$v'(y, x) = \frac{\sum_{i \in W_k} a_i v_i(y, x)}{\sum_{i \in W_k} a_i} \qquad (8)$$

where:

$$a_i = 1, \qquad if \qquad \mid v_i(y, x) - ref \mid \le Q;$$
$$a_i = 0, \quad otherwise, \qquad\qquad\qquad\qquad (9)$$

where ref is either gray level $v_k(y, x)$ of the center or the mean $\overline{W}_k$ and $v'(y, x)$ is the window center gray level in the filtered image.

The MTM does not specify what to do if the selected threshold Q is so small that no pixels qualify to the mean (8). We suggest that the center should be classified as noise in such a case. To remove the noise detected, the mean (or median) of the window pixels excluding the center or median can be computed.

The arbitrarily selected threshold Q can also err in the other direction and be too large on other image fragments. If Q is too large, then MTM becomes a Gaussian filter with strong edge blurring. An improvement is to take only a few window samples or pixels which are most homogeneous with the center (or with the window mean) and to use the mean of the selected pixels as the center gray level. Such a filter enhances edges very well.

The MTM filter, in selecting pixels which are most homogeneous with the center but not necessarily adjacent to each other, is susceptible to impulsive noise. The susceptibility of the MTM filter to noise can be explained by the fact that a good continuation of the window center (expressed by upper approximation) is not checked necessarily in the continuous region, but also in noise pixels dispersed randomly around the center.

One remedy is to check good continuation of the window center gray level against continuous regions around the center, as our new rough technique does. Assignment of higher weights to pixels less distant from the window center when computing the mean of the most homogeneous template increases the attenuation of noise. A further remedy is to recognize the impulsive noise, also using the rotating-template technique, and to compute the median in case of noise. A third technique is to find the good continuation through pixels lying on a straight line that crosses the window center and the neighboring pixel most similar to the center.

The filter selecting pixels most homogeneous with the mean blurs edges. This is because the average of these pixels converges to the mean, and the Gaussian filter blurs edges.

Another trimmed filter (published in 1978 [2]) measures variability inside each window neighborhood (sub-region), and then replaces the center with the mean of the least variable neighborhood. This is a later version of the rotating-template technique (published in 1976 [6] and in 1977 [7]). The main difference is that the regular trimmed filters do not measure the variability of sub-regions with respect to the window center, but with respect to the mean of the sub-region. Statistical variance is used as the measure of the variability. The rotating-template technique does not use the statistical variance; this is less time consuming, leads to edge enhancement and avoids blurring. The trimmed filters, in selecting a neighborhood of minimum statistical variability, blur edges in the presence of noise. Furthermore, noise located in the object interior disturbs selection of the proper neighborhood. Thin lines are blurred as well by the trimmed filters in cases when the line is thinner than the dimension of the neighborhood.

The filters adapting the sample to the window contents are well known in the literature. The median hybrid filters blur edges because the median prefers a subregion located on an edge in cases when the center is located on the edge. The trimmed filters blur edges because both the most and the least homogeneous neighboring pixels are removed from the sample containing pixels located on the edge, and these are partly blurred. Our technique averaging the neighboring pixels most homogeneous with the window center enhances the edges. This edge enhancement is stronger compared to the edge enhancement produced by our rotating template technique based on the rough sets, but, it does not sufficiently attenuate all the noise pixels because a good continuation of neighboring pixels with the window center is not checked. The neighboring pixels of similar gray levels can be separated from the center by regions of different gray levels; as a result, a center representing noise is not attenuated is some cases.

In general, only the filtering technique presented in this paper is effective at both attenuating noise and enhancing edges. Several filters have been constructed and tested using our novel methodology with the rough sets. All versions attenuate noise and enhance any statistical edge pixels; none shows the effects of blurring. This novel technique can be built of the top of a variety of non-linear filters.

Finally, this paper shows a new area of applications of the rough sets: not only for the evaluation of results after main processing of data, but during processing, to actively receive best results. The upper approximation can represent the results most wanted.

References

1. R.M. Haralick, L.G. Shapiro, *Computer and Robot Vision*, vol. I, Addison Wesley, 1992.

2. M.Nagao, T. Matsuyama, "Edge preserving smoothing," *Proc. Fourth Int. Conf. Pattern Recognition*, Kyoto, Japan, pp. 518-520, 1978.

3. Z. Pawlak, "Rough sets," *International Journal of Information and Computer Sciences*, vol. 11, 5, pp. 341-356, 1982.

4. A. Rosenfeld, A.C. Kak, *Digital Picture Processing*, Acad. Press, 1982.

5. Z.M. Wojcik, "Automatic Detection of Semiconductor Mask Defects," *Microelectronics and Reliability*, v.15, Pergamon press, pp585-593. 1976.

6. Z.M. Wojcik, "A system for an automatic detection of defects of semiconductor masks and PC boards," *Electron Technology*, Institute of Electron Technology, Warsaw, vol. 10, no. 4, pp95-108, 1977.

7. Z.M. Wojcik, "A Natural Approach to Image Processing and Pattern Recognition: Rotating Neighborhood Technique, Self-Adapting Threshold, Segmentation and Shape Recognition," *Pattern Recognition*, vol.18, no.5, pp299-326, 1985.

8. Z.M. Wójcik, "Rough Approximation of Shapes in Pattern Recognition," *Computer Vision, Graphics and Image Processing*, 40, pp228-249, 1987.

9. Z.M. Wójcik, B.E. Wójcik, "Rough Grammar for Efficient and Fault Tolerant Computing on a Distributed Architecture," *IEEE Trans. on Software Engineering*, vol.17, no.7, pp652-668, 1991.

10. Z.M. Wojcik, Rough Sets For Intelligent Image Filtering," *Proceeding of the International Workshop on Rough Sets and Knowledge Discovery (RSKD-93)*, Banff, Alberta, Canada, October 13-15, 1993, pp399-410.

11. Z.M. Wojcik, "Edge Detector Free of the Detection/Localization Tradeoff Using Rough Sets," *Proceeding of the International Workshop on Rough Sets and Knowledge Discovery (RSKD-93)*, Banff, Alberta, Canada, October 13-15, 1993, pp421-438.

12. A.C. Bovik, T.S. Huang, D.C. Munson, "A generalization of median filtering using linear combinations of order statistics," *IEEE Trans. on ASSP*, vol. ASSP-31, no. 6, pp.1342-1349, 1983.

Multilayer Knowledge Base System for Speaker-Independent Recognition of Isolated Words

Andrzej Czyzewski, Andrzej Kaczmarek
Sound Engineering Department, Technical University of Gdansk
Gdansk, Poland

1 Introduction

The aim of the presented research was to elaborate and test the speaker-independent system for the man-machine voice interfacing using small vocabulary (digits). Speaker-independent recognition of digits may be applied practically, among others in telecommunication for the dialing by voice. The mentioned assumptions caused the necessity to consider technologically applicable and economically optimized concepts only. Thus, extensive search for the theoretical background and relevant technologies was performed at the initial stage of the investigations. Resulting speech recognition system implements the combined methods of time-domain signal feature extraction, of neural network learning procedures and of fuzzy logic decision rules. All mentioned procedures tested at the software model stage are fully supported by the new hardware solutions in the domain of signal processing. More detailed analysis of the elaborated system reveals its multi-layer nature, hence it applies the domain-dependent knowledge base to acquire and to reorder data in such a way that they become separable and it uses learning algorithms to acquire knowledge enabling final object classifications.

2 Feature Vector Extraction Module (FVEM)

The time-domain processing of speech signal proven to be suitable to the task of feature vector acquisition. The input speech signal is split to 1000-bit segments to be used to parameter calculations. The total energy of samples and lowest relative amplitude of signal are to be found. Subsequently, the number of local time-envelope peaks are determined on the basis of the following relationship:

$$p_i - p_{i-1} > k \text{ or } p_i - p_{i+1} > k \tag{1}$$

where p_i is the number i sample and k is the threshold value selected arbitrarily by the operator.

The determination of word boundaries is achieved on the basis of an assessment of the average amplitude of signal and of the number of envelope peaks related to each segment. The determined values are compared to the predefined thresholds and the decision is made as to the significance of the individual sample segments in the received sample stream. The word beginning and ending segment are discerned using this procedure. Finally, the resulting sample sequence corresponding to the isolated word is subdivided into certain number of sets consisting of the equal number of samples. As the number of these sets is always constant (6 sets was used in practice), thus such a procedure may serve as some kind of linear time scaling method applied to all received word patterns. The proposed procedures have been verified practically, revealing low dependency of the results on the additive noise presence. The last mentioned feature is not guaranteed when the signal zero crossing density is used to the determination of word boundaries [1].

The Feature Vector includes also two more elements, namely the relative amplitude midpoint value p_A and the relative amplitude peaks midpoint coefficient p_W. These values have been defined as follows:

$$p_A = \frac{\sum_i i\, A(i)}{\sum_i A(i)} \qquad p_M = \frac{\sum_i i\, M(i)}{\sum_i M(i)} \qquad (2,3)$$

where: i - number of segments,
   A(i) - relative average amplitude for segment i,
   M(i) - number of local peaks for segment i.

Thus, the Feature Vector for each spoken word is to be represented by $2 * 6 + 4 = 16$ parameters. These are: total energy and number of envelope peaks for each segment, the values defined by the relationships (2), (3), the smallest amplitude value and the global energy value.

3 Statistical Validation Module (SVM)

Feature Vectors corresponding to received words are stored in the reference memory. The resulting sets have to be separable in order to enable the effective recognition of words. Hence, the statistical approach is needed allowing for the evaluation of significance level of differences between the elements belonging to the sets. The Behrens-Fisher statistics was found suitable to the evaluation of "discernibility" of individual elements. This statistics was defined on the basis of the following relationship:

$$V = \frac{\overline{X} - \overline{Y}}{\sqrt{S_1^2/n + S_2^2/m}} \tag{4}$$

where:

$$\overline{X} = \frac{1}{n} \sum_{i=1}^{n} X_i, \qquad S_1^2 = \frac{1}{n-1} \sum_{i=1}^{n} (X_i - \overline{X})^2$$

- are estimators of the average value and of the variance for the test $X_1,...,X_n$ and $\overline{Y}$, S_2^2 - are analogous parameters related to the test $Y_1,.....Y_m$.

Using this statistics in the form of the significance level table it is possible to determine which ones elements should be acquired and added to the knowledge acquisition system and which ones should be rejected because of being not applicable to further recognition procedures.

4 Neural Network Learning System (NNLS)

The program written in C language for the NeXT workstation allows for the defining optional perceptron structures. The number of layers and neurons in each layer can be selected by the operator. The hyperbolic tangent was used as a transfer function for each neuron. Hence, neuron output states are determined by the values of the following function:

$$y = th \left(\sum_i w_i x_i + b_i \right) \tag{5}$$

where: x_i - input signals,

w_i - i-th synapse weights,

The modified by the authors back propagation algorithm [2] was used in the perceptron learning procedure. The neural network state is determined by the status vector:

$$\overline{S} = [w_1, w_2, ..., w_p, b_1, b_2, ...,b_r] \tag{6}$$

where: p - number of synaptical connections, r - number of neurons,
   w_i - weight of the i-th connection, b_j - bias of the j-th neuron.

Denoting Y_{ijk} as the state of i-th output while the j-th element of k-th set is present at the perceptron input one can obtain:

$$Y_{ijk} = f (\overline{S}) \tag{7}$$

The total output error value may be calculated using the next relationship:

$$E = \sum_{k=1}^{K} \sum_{j=1}^{j_k} \sum_{i=1}^{n} (Y_{ijk} - Z_{ik})^2 \tag{8}$$

where: K -   number of sets,
   j_k -   number of k-th set elements,
   n -   number of outputs,
   Z_{ik} - the desired state of i-th output for k-th set.

   In order to minimize the error rate   the error gradient is calculated with regard to all elements of the vector $\overline{S}$, where $E=E(\overline{S})$:

$$\text{grad } E = \left[\frac{\partial E}{\partial w_1} , \frac{\partial E}{\partial w_2} ,..., \frac{\partial E}{\partial w_p} , \frac{\partial E}{\partial b_1} , \frac{\partial E}{\partial b_2} ,..., \frac{\partial E}{\partial b_r} \right] \tag{9}$$

   Practically, instead of computing partial derivatives the following quotients are to be found:

$$\frac{\Delta E}{\Delta w_i} ; \frac{\Delta E}{\Delta b_j} \qquad i = 1, ..., p; \quad j = 1, ..., r \tag{10}$$

At first, increments $\Delta w_1,..,\Delta w_p$, $\Delta b_1,...,\Delta b_r$ are all set equal to a small number Δ, for example to $\Delta = 10^{-4}$. Further, these increments are multiplied by the coefficient equal to 0.9 in each iteration step. Correspondingly, the need is fulfilled to estimate the gradient more precisely during the approaching the end of this value computations. Subsequently, the new state of the network is found, such that the following term is fulfilled:

$$E (\overline{S}_n^j) < E (\overline{S}_o^j) \tag{11}$$

where: $\overline{S}_o^j$ - an output status vector,

   $\overline{S}_n^j$ - the consecutive output status vector.

It is also assumed that:

$$\overline{S}_n{}^j = \overline{S}_n(j) = \overline{S}_p - \overline{grad}\ E\ (step)\ \ j \qquad (12)$$

where: step - certain small value equal to Δ at the training beginning,

j - variable to be described below.

The coefficient j in the relationship (12) is an integer number varying accordingly to the following rule:

$$\underset{j>1}{\bigvee}\ \underset{i<j}{\bigwedge}\ \{E\ [\overline{S}_n(i)] > E\ [\overline{S}_n(i+1)]\} \cap \{E\ [\overline{S}_n(j)] < E\ [\overline{S}_n(j+1)]\} \qquad (13)$$

The smallest number j fulfilling the above relationship (13) is used to the calculation of the final status vector $\overline{S}_n$ for a given iteration step. The result j = 1 is equivalent to the reaching the local error minimum, thus it is necessary to increase the Δ value, so that the next iteration step based on the revised gradient calculation result is allowing to escape from the minimum zone. Hence, it is possible to resume error minimization procedure starting far from the minimum zone. As results from above, there is a need to keep the allowed Δ values within certain range: $\Delta \in (\Delta_{min}, \Delta_{max})$.

5 Fuzzy Logic Decision Block (FLDB)

The neural network is generating vectors on its output, such as: "0110100000" etc. Consequently, the rule system is needed allowing for making proper decisions as to the belonging of each recognized word representation to one of defined reference knowledge base. Thus, triple decision making procedure was elaborated allowing to compare each kind of decision system effectiveness:

1* simple decision rule based on one-bit threshold quantization of output neuron signal which is determined by the neuron transfer function value. as in the relationship (5). The obtained output state vector $\overline{Y} = [Y_1, ..., Y_p]$ is then based on the following rule:

$$Y_r = \begin{cases} 1 \text{ for } y_r > 0 \\ \\ 0 \text{ for } y_r \le 0 \end{cases} \qquad (14)$$

where: y_r - are individual net output values,

Y_r - $\overline{Y}$ vector elements for r = 1,...,p; p - number of output neurons.

In the case of the above rule implementation there is a probability to not find the matching pattern in the reference sets, thus the result of recognition is none, in such a case.

2* typical decision rule implementing the Euclidean distance definition:

$$e_w(\overline{Y},\overline{Y}_w) = \left\{ \sum_{r=1}^{r} (Y_r - Y_{w,r})^2 \right\}^{1/2} \tag{15}$$

where: Y_r - r-th parameter of the examined vector $\overline{Y}$

$Y_{w,r}$ - r-th parameter of reference vector $\overline{Y}_w$

In this case the decision consists in searching for such w for which the distance e_w is lowest, thus a result of recognition is always available.

3* based on fuzzy logic analysis of the knowledge base through the implementation of the following rule set:

if $(Y_1=0$ AND $Y_2=1$ AND $Y_3=0$ AND $...Y_{10}=0)$ then "one" $\qquad(16)$
if $(Y_1=0$ AND $Y_2=0$ AND $Y_3=1$ AND $...Y_{10}=0)$ then "two"

....

if $(Y_1=0$ AND $Y_2=0$ AND $Y_3=0$ AND $...Y_{10}=1)$ then "zero"

Each of the above rules is returning certain minimum value (the μ-cut product) [3] chosen from all computed membership function values. These values are calculated using arguments representing individual net output states.

The process of building up the knowledge base is consisted of two phases in such a case. The first of them is the perceptron training procedure. This phase has its natural limitations related to the saturation phenomenon, what means that the neural net becomes not capable to effectively acquire more pattern data until it is not redefined bigger. Hence, the second training phase is started basing on the fuzzy set knowledge acquisition system important for both: strengthening the decision rule and optimizing the neural net capacity.

Fuzzy knowledge base is built up with regard to the assumption that set boundaries might be described by the simple trapezoid membership functions. This assumption is justified in the current technology solutions offering the integrated fuzzy processors usually implementing triangular, trapezoid or bell-type membership functions [4].

Hence, the neural net training procedure was limited to 3 speakers (2 males and 1 female) pronouncing ten digits. The 7 more speakers voices (6 males and 1 female) were used to build up the fuzzy sets. The data for fuzzy knowledge base were acquired from the neural net outputs during the recognition tests performed with the participation of all 10 speakers. The obtained in such a way

collections of net responses were subjected to the further processing in order
to obtain the fuzzy sets with trapezoid boundary functions. The boundary
functions are related to the estimated probability density function chosen to
describe these sets.

The membership function parameters a and b may be found using the elements
acquired in the tests. Computing of 2nd and of 4th order central moments are
based on the following relationships:

$$M_2 = \int_{-\infty}^{+\infty} x^2\, p(x)dx = A\, a^3 \left(\frac{2}{3} - \frac{a}{2b} \right) \tag{17}$$

$$M_4 = \int_{-\infty}^{+\infty} x^4\, p(x)dx = A\, a^5 \left(\frac{2}{5} - \frac{a}{3b} \right) \tag{18}$$

The membership function center value A was calculated assuming that:

$$\int_{-\infty}^{+\infty} p(x) = 1 \tag{19}$$

thus it is equal to:

$$A = \frac{b}{2ab-a^2} \tag{20}$$

The fuzzy sets obtained using this method proven not to be disjoint ones,
however the proper decision rule (16) allows to qualify every pattern to one of
these sets during any recognition test. The decision is made on the basis of
calculation of the degree of element membership to each set [3]. The rule is
firing for which the maximum value was assigned during the computations. One
can notice that in such a case the fuzzy AND definition is used during the
processing of rules (16), such as that:

$$\mu(x_1 \text{ AND } x_2) = \min \{ \mu(x_1), \mu(x_2) \} \tag{21}$$

Hence, NNLS response vector is qualified as belonging to the particular set
for which the fuzzy rule is giving the highest result, even "in the worst
case". The described FLDB module is generating results of word recognition
using all mentioned decision making methods 1*, 2* and 3*. Consequently, it
allows to compare the accuracy of each method.

6 Results and Conclusions

The results of recognition of 10 digits pronounced by seven new speakers (5 males and 2 females unfamiliar to the system) are presented in the Tab. 1.

Table 1 Comparison of recognition results

classification rule	accurate results	wrong results	result unknown
1*	61	8	1
2*	64	6	-
3*	68	2	-

The obtained results allow the authors' to consider the possibility of the practical implementation of the elaborated system to the modern electronic hardware processing circuitry. The FVEM/SVM block may be implemented to the low cost Motorola DSP processors [5]. The NNLS module was conceived in such a way that it is applicable to the ANL silicon-based neural network processors [6] and the FLDB (decision system 3*) matches the ANL fuzzy logic microcontrollers architecture [4].

As it was proven by the results, it was possible to implement the multilayer knowledge representation in the system consisting of the statistical preprocessing module, of the learning connectionist algorithm and of the fuzzy rule-based decision block.

References

1. Wasson D. A, Donaldson R. W. Speech amplitude and zero crossing for automated identification of human speaker. IEEE Trans. ASSP-23, 1975; 4
2. Czyzewski A, Kaczmarek A, Kostek B. A Method of Recognition of Parameterized Binary Representations of Audio Signals. In: 94th AES Convention, Berlin, 1993
3. Kacprzyk J, Fedrizzi M. Studies in Fuzziness. Fuzzy Regression Analysis. Springer-Verlag, Stuttgart, 1992
4. American Neural Logix. NLX 230 Fuzzy Microcontroller Application Note. Sanford, U.S.A., 1992
5. Motorola. MC68HCZ1 DSP Processor Application Note, 1992
6. American Neural Logix. NLX 420 Neural Processor Application Note. Sanford, U.S.A. 1992

Image Segmentation Based on the Indiscernibility Relation

Simon Shek Yuen Lau*

Department of Computer Science, University of Regina,
Regina, Saskatchewan, Canada S4S 0A2

Abstract

In this paper, the concepts of indiscernibility relation and approximation space are applied in image segmentation. Specifically, objects can be segmented providing that they are defined to be the connected components with similar gray level; the final segmental image is formed after the region fusion process using the statistical criteria. Then, a generalized method that generates the contour of the objects using the definition of upper and lower approximations is discussed. Thinned image could also be generated from the segmental image.

1   Introduction

1.1   Image Segmentation

Image segmentation is a process to decompose an image into non-overlapping regions. There are three main segmentation approaches including thresholding, edge detection and region growing.

In general, thresholding techniques are classified into three main categories namely global, optimal and local thresholding. Global thresholding method partitions the image histogram by using a single threshold. Local thresholding approach subdivides the image into subimages and selects a threshold for each subimage. Optimal thresholding method chooses threshold value with respect to the optimization process involving some given criteria [1].

Edge detection is also an important method for image segmentation because edges frequently represent a transition area from one homogeneous region to another. Given an image, the objective of edge detection is to generate a binary image having the same size as that of the original image, where each pixel is classified as either an edge or non-edge pixel.

Unlike edge detection that aims at locating the boundaries which separates the various regions in an image, region growing method partitions the image into homogeneous connected regions. Adjacent regions are merged if the larger merged regions satisfy the homogeneity criterion. Generally, region growing is useful when the histogram of the image does not have sharp valleys but it is very computationally expensive. Moreover, merging might take place incorrectly when a real region boundary is weak due to the illumination effects [1].

---

*Current correspondence address: 1A, 14/F, Humbert Street, Mei Foo Sun Chuen, Kowloon, Hong Kong

Using the rough set theory, the image segmentation technique discussed here is generally region-based. It uses new statistical criteria for merging adjacent regions and segments the noisy image correctly.

1.2 Rough Sets

Let U be a non-empty finite set called universe and R be a binary relation over U, known as indiscernibility relation; R is assumed to be an equivalence relation. An ordered pair $A = (U, R)$ is referred to as an approximation space. For any element $x \in U$, $[x]_R$ is the equivalence class of R containing x.

Let $X \subseteq U$ and the upper and lower approximations of X are defined as

$$\overline{R}X = \{x \in U | [x]_R \cap X \neq \emptyset\} \tag{1}$$

and

$$\underline{R}X = \{x \in U | [x]_R \subseteq X\}. \tag{2}$$

The set

$$BN(X) = \overline{R}X - \underline{R}X \tag{3}$$

is known as the boundary of X [3].

2 Binary Image Labelling

Definition 2.1 *Neighbourhood*

1. *4-Neighbourhood*

   The 4-nearest neighbours of a given pixel are immediately above, below, to its left and to its right.

2. *8-neighbourhood*

   The 8-nearest neighbours of a given pixel are 4-neighbours along with 4 pixels on the diagonals.

Definition 2.2 *Connectivity*

If for any region S belonging to the image and for any pixels $A, B \in S$, there exists a set of pixels $A = A_1, A_2, ..., A_{t-1}, A_t = B$ such that $A_j \in S$ where $j = 1, ..., t$, S is said to be

1. *4-connected if A_i, A_{i+1} are 4-neighbours,*

2. *8-connected if A_i, A_{i+1} are 8-neighbours.*

Define an equivalence relation R_1 as "has the same intensity level as". Then R_1 will partition U (the set of all pixels in the image) into many equivalence classes. Each equivalence class (connected region) is either background or object.

By defining an increment intensity level mapping function in which the difference of the gray level of region S_{i+1} and S_i is equal to one stepsize, the objects can be identified in the binary image (Fig. 1 (a) -(b)).

Algorithm 2.3 *Binary Image Labelling*[1]

1. *Scan the image from left to right, top to bottom.*

2. *Use depth first search (DFS) to find the objects (pixels) satisfying R_1.*

   (a) *The intensity level of the seed pixel is either black or white.*

   (b) *The equivalence class (region) can be found by searching a set of all connected pixels having the same intensity level with the seed pixel.*

3. *Assign the region number to each equivalence class.*

4. *Assign the brightness to each equivalence class for visualizing a change in pixel intensity level.*

3   Gray-Scale Image Segmentation

In this section, a region-oriented image segmentation algorithm will be proposed. Specifically, regions S_k formed satisfy the equivalence relation R_2[2] which is defined as [2]

$$|f(i) - f(j)| \leq \zeta \tag{4}$$

where $f(i)$ is the intensity level at seed pixel $i \in S_k$; pixel $j \in S_k$ and ζ is an integer.

Here, ζ can be determined by the peak of the difference histogram (Fig. 4) which shows the frequency of the average of the absolute gray level differences between a pixel and its 4-neighbours [4]. In the difference histogram, the high peak on the left is due to the homogeneous region of the image and the edges between regions result in the small peak on the right.

Algorithm 3.1 *Region-Based Image Segmentation*[3]

1. *Scan the image from left to right, top to bottom.*

2. *Find ζ from the high peak of difference histogram.*

3. *Use DFS to find the pixels satisfying R_2.*

   (a) *The gray level of the starting pixel $i \in U$ is $f(i)$.*

   (b) *DFS is used to find the 4-connected region S_k such that all searched pixel gray levels are within the range of $[f(i) - \zeta, f(i) + \zeta]$.*

4. *Assign the region number to each equivalence class.*

5. *Assign the brightness to each equivalence class for identifying the regions by using the 4-colour mapping function such that no two adjacent 4-connected regions have the same gray level.*

After one pass of algorithm 3.1, noise might be segmented. In the next section, the region fusion process will be discussed to solve this problem.

---

[1] Input: binary image; Output: segmental image.

[2] R_2 is an equivalence relation based on the connected components of the image partition.

[3] Input: Original gray-scale image; Output: segmental (labelled) image.

4   Region Fusion Process

Region fusion process is used to merge two adjacent regions S_i, S_j based on the statistical criteria. Precisely, another indiscernibility relation R_3 is defined to fuse two adjacent regions providing that their mean gray levels satisfy equation 4.

Mathematically,

$$|M(i) - M(j)| \leq \zeta \tag{5}$$

where

$$M(i) = \frac{\sum_{k=1}^{N} f(k)}{N} \tag{6}$$

and $f(k)$ is the intensity level of pixel $k \in S_i$; N is the number of pixels in S_i.

With reference to the local histogram of the two regions, if the variance s^2 of this histogram is such that $s^2 > \beta$ where β is a certain threshold value, it is of bimodal type and the edges exist. Thus no merging is performed.

Here,

$$s^2 = \frac{\sum_{i=1}^{N}(f(i) - \overline{f})^2}{N - 1}, \tag{7}$$

where $\overline{f}$ is the mean gray level of two adjacent regions; $f(i)$ is the intensity level and N is the total number of pixels of two adjacent regions.

Moreover, if no rejection occurs in the hypothesis testing, the regions will be merged. For the small sample size (N_i, $N_j < 30$), the $t-test$ will be performed with the given level of significance α and the test statistic t is given by

$$t = \frac{(\overline{f_i} - \overline{f_j}) - \zeta}{\sqrt{s_p^2(\frac{1}{N_i} + \frac{1}{N_j})}} \tag{8}$$

where

$$s_p^2 = \frac{(N_i - 1)s_i^2 + (N_j - 1)s_j^2}{N_i + N_j - 2}, \tag{9}$$

$\overline{f_i}$, s_i^2 and N_i are the mean gray level, variance and the number of pixels in region S_i.

For large sample size, the $z-test$ will be used and z is written as

$$z = \frac{(\overline{f_i} - \overline{f_j}) - \zeta}{\sqrt{\frac{s_i^2}{N_i} + \frac{s_j^2}{N_j}}}. \tag{10}$$

This fusion process is repeated by incrementing ζ and is terminated when either certain region numbers have been obtained or ζ is increased to certain threshold value γ which can be determined from the valley of the difference histogram (Fig. 4).

5 Contour Formation and Thinning

The classical contour tracing algorithms applied to binary images usually locate a pixel belonging to the contour by scanning an image from left to right, top to bottom and use either clockwise or anti-clockwise traversal of the boundary to trace the contour (a boundary is defined as a set of pixels and a contour is defined as an orderly sequence of pixels; both terms will be used interchangeably) [2]. On the other hand, the conventional thinning algorithms usually eliminate points or layers of outline from the object until all the lines or curves are one pixel wide [2]. The collection of such lines or curves is called skeletons.

The concepts of rough set theory can be served for the purpose of contour and skeleton generation. Mrozek and Plonka have introduced such algorithms which are suitable for binary images [2]. Using the segmental image, a generalized version of contour generation method and a new thinning algorithm will be given in the following subsections.

5.1 Contour Generation based on the Segmental Image

The segmental image (Fig. 2 (a) - (b)) formed in section 4 can be viewed as a universe U of pixels having region numbers. Then, the universe is subdivided into many equivalence classes by a 2×2 mask [2]. For each object X which is equivalent to each equivalence class (connected region) in approximation space A (segmental image), the lower and upper approximations of X (denoted by $\underline{P}X$ and $\overline{P}X$) based on the partition could be found and the contour of X is obtained by using the definition of boundary $BN(X)$. The width of contour is equal to the mask size.

Disjointed contour might occur and this can be solved by labelling any one of two adjacent masks as contour providing that these two adjacent mask contents belong to two different object interiors.

Algorithm 5.1 *Contour formation*[4]

1. *For any pixel $x_i \in U$ and any subset $X \subseteq U$, x_i is certainly in X when $x_i \in \underline{P}X$ and x_i is possibly in X when $x_i \in \overline{P}X$.*

2. *Find $\underline{P}X$ and $\overline{P}X$.*

3. *Compute $BN(X) = \overline{P}X - \underline{P}X$ which is the contour.*

4. *Check disjointed contour.*

It should be noticed that the contour generation technique discussed here produces distorted contours compared with classical methods. Besides, unlike the classical contour tracing algorithms, the proposed technique is unable to produce an orderly list of contour elements. In other words, it is impossible to obtain the information about the coordinates of consecutive pixels. Nevertheless, one additional pass of algorithm 2.3 with the contour image (Fig. 3 (a)), this kind of information can still be yielded. It should also be noticed that the suggested approach is suitable for implementation in parallel hardware for fast processing [2].

---

[4]Input: segmental image with pixels having region numbers; Output: contour image.

5.2 Thinning based on the Segmental Image

Based on the segmental image, two types of masks, 1 × 2 horizontal and 2 × 1 vertical masks, partition the universe U (of pixels with region numbers) into many equivalence classes. The boundary of objects X (connected region of the segmental image) can be found by using the definition of lower and upper approximations based on the partition.

A more efficient way to locate the boundary is to slide the masks all over the entire image. If the mask contains different region numbers, it should be labelled as boundary. Otherwise it is the interior of object.

The thinning algorithm is summarized as follows:

Algorithm 5.2 *Thinning from segmental image*[5]

1. *Slide the 1 × 2 horizontal and 2 × 1 vertical masks all over the image.*

2. *Label the mask as boundary of X if the mask has different region numbers.*

3. *Obtain the thinned image.*

The suggested thinning algorithm is faster than the old approaches and produces minimal but slightly distorted skeletons. If the information about the orderly list of skeletons is required, an additional utilization of algorithm 2.3 with the thinned image (Fig. 3 (b)) will fulfill this purpose. Again, it seems that this skeleton generation method can be implemented efficiently in parallel hardware [2].

6 Concluding Remarks

In conclusion, the image segmentation technique based on the indiscernibility relation is introduced and the final segmental image can also be obtained by performing the region fusion process iteratively. Using the definition of boundary $BN(X)$, the contour image is obtained from the segmented image. The thinned image can also be formed from the segmental image and is a single pixel wide in the skeleton.

References

[1] R. C. Gonzalez and R. E. Woods, **Digital Image Processing**. New York: Addision-Wesley, 1992.

[2] A. Mrozek and L. Plonka, "Rough Sets in Image Analysis", **Foundations of Computing and Decision Sciences**, vol. 18, no. 3-4, pp. 259-273, 1993.

[3] Z. Pawlak, "Rough Sets", **International Journal of Computer and Information Science**, vol. 11, no. 5, pp. 341-356, 1982.

[5] Input: segmental image with pixels having region numbers; Output: thinned image.

[4] M. Pietikainen and D. Harwood, "Edge Information in Colour Images based on Histogram of Differences", **Proceedings of Eighth International Conference on Pattern Recognition**. Washington: IEEE Computer Society, October 27-31, Paris, France, pp. 594-596, 1986.

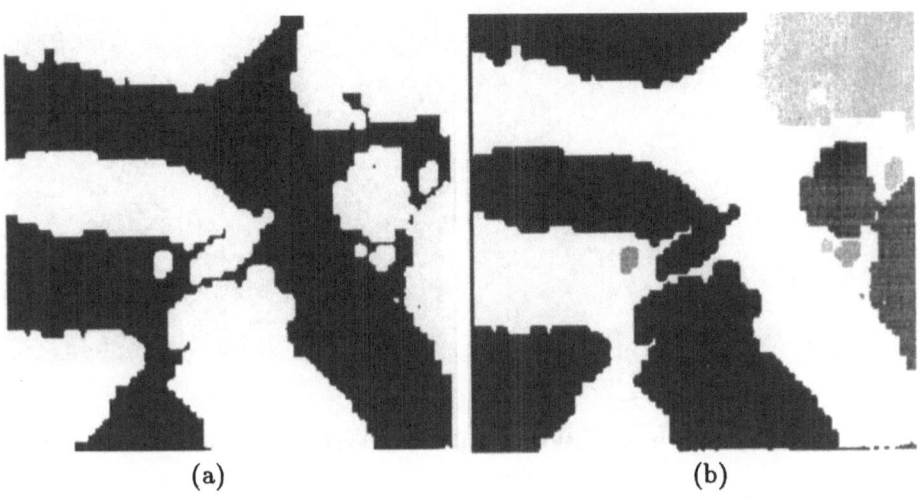

Figure 1: (a) original binary image (b) segmented binary image

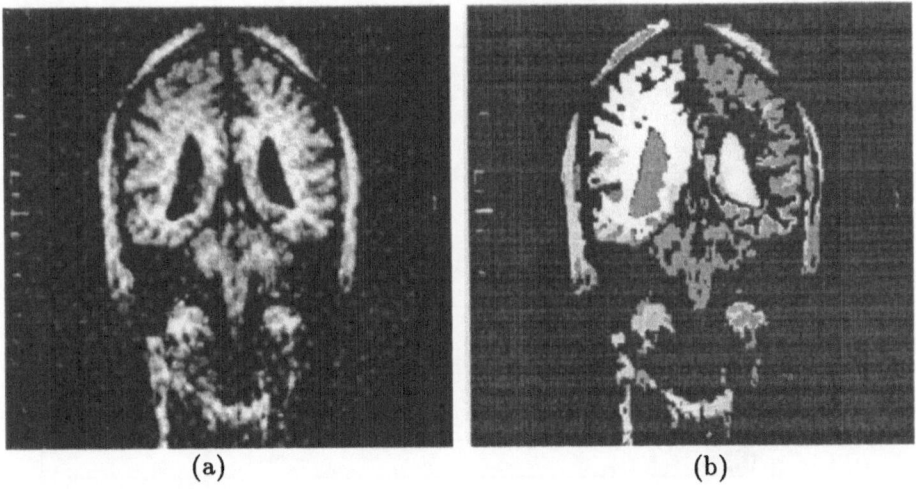

Figure 2: (a) original MRI coronal scan (b) segmented MRI coronal scan using 4-colour mapping function

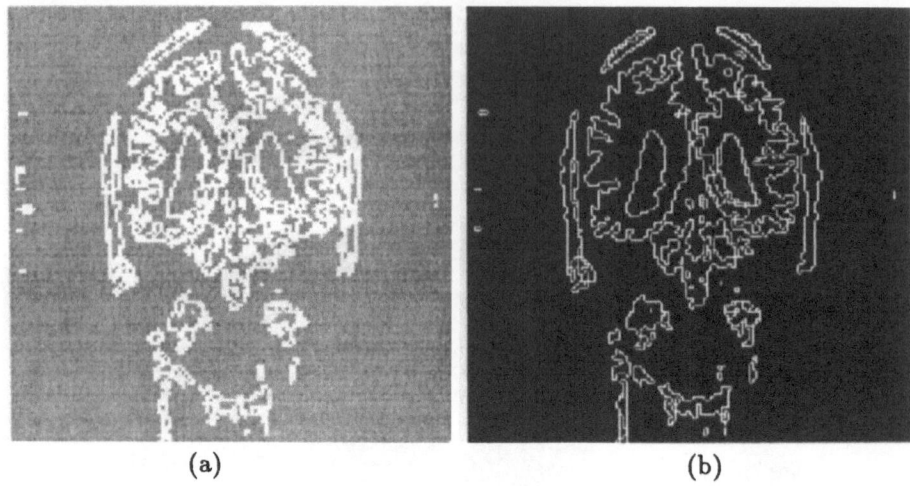

(a)   (b)

Figure 3: (a) contour information of MRI coronal scan (b) thinned MRI coronal scan

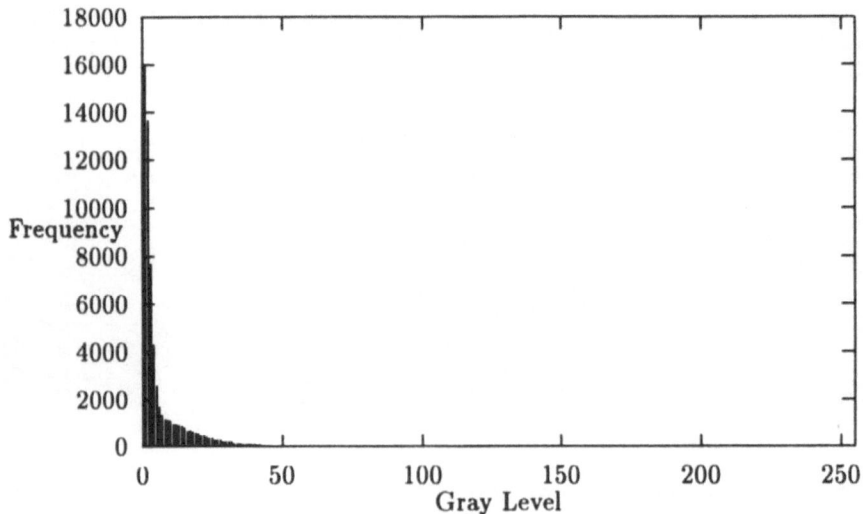

Figure 4: difference histogram of original MRI coronal scan

Accurate Edge Detection Using Rough Sets

Zbigniew M. WOJCIK
Smart Machines,
13703 Morningbluff Drive,
San Antonio, TX 78216, USA

The paper presents a novel application of the rough sets for a high-accuracy edge detection producing edges with uniform thickness of one pixel. The edge detector does not blur edges, and provides a desired signal-to-noise ratio within a single iteration.

This edge detector uses primarily the concept of contrast (reinforced by the rough set concepts) and direct adjacency of neighboring regions. A gradient is used to attenuate noise and not for edge localization. A Gaussian filter is not used, to avoid its characteristic deformations of edge shape.

Our universe is the set of pixel gray levels in a window. We modify the equivalence relation to select only one element at a time from the window, but we apply the lower approximation (and rough set) membership operation for all windows in the image. The equivalence relation defined for the modified rough sets uses a non-statistical variance operation, which is the difference (contrast) of the window center gray level with a template (e.g., with another window pixel). Results of edge detection are presented and advantages over other edge detectors are discussed.

There are two conflicting requirements for an edge detector: to localize edges accurately and to suppress noise and disturbances. All current techniques detect noise with edges if edges must be detected with high accuracy, or accuracy in localization of edges is reduced if total elimination of noise is required. This is the so-called "detection/localization tradeoff". A Gaussian filter, especially, causes some edge pixels to be dislocated when noise is to be discarded. Our technique which uses the rough sets does not sacrifice edge detection accuracy for higher signal-to-noise (edge-to-noise) ratio.

We control the signal-to-noise ratio (while keeping the edge detection accuracy at the maximum) by making a logical product of the edges detected by our operator and the edges detected by a gradient with a threshold. By reducing the threshold value, more noise pixels and more small-contrast edge pixels are admitted to the edges. Because our edge detector is set permanently to the minimum threshold (i.e., to 1), many noise pixels in the background and in the regions could be detected as the edges. A gradient (e.g., approximated by Sobel operator) with a threshold then attenuates noise efficiently inside the regions. The blocking effect by the contrast of the opposite sign (usually stronger than noise) blocks noise effectively to the distance of one half-window diameter from edges. We apply the gradient with threshold only to the edge pixels. This results in a specialized filtering of edge pixels only, without processing all regions.

Our remedy to the noise removal/edge localization tradeoff problem and to the ridge problem of the gradient is to compute contrast as edgeness in the direction of the strongest change of the image intensity for each pixel. We introduce the reverse of the Gestalt law of *good continuation* of region: the *worst continuation*. In fact, both good and bad continuations draw the attention of human vision. Our rotating template technique [2,3] combined with the rough sets [1,4] is the methodology used here to find and compute the highest change of image intensity.

Fig. 1. Input image taken by a CCD camera

The rough set involves: a) the greatest definable set of elements contained by the data representing the object (e.g., a smooth region fragment contained in a window), so-called upper approximation; and b) the smallest definable set of elements containing the data representing the object (e.g., edges), so-called lower approximation. We use only the lower approximation for edge detection.

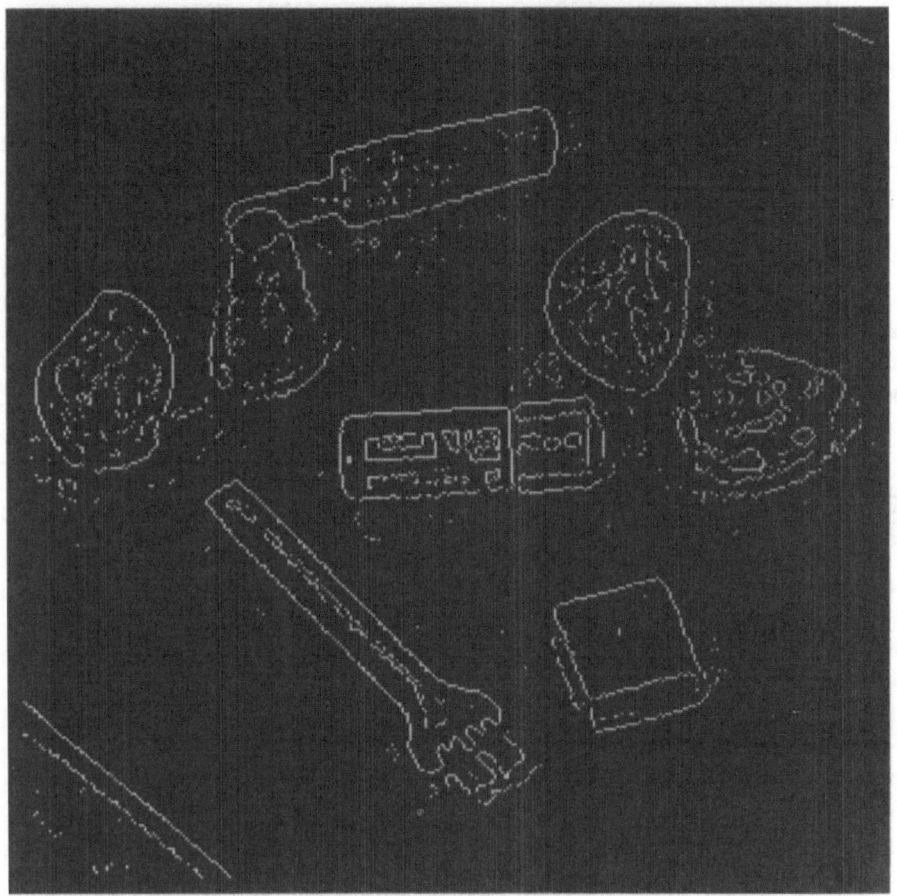

Fig. 2. Edges detected using our new edge detector which incorporates three edge components: contrast, adjacency of the neighboring region, and intensity gradient for edge filtering

Let $K = (I, R)$ be an image approximation space composed of image I (treated as a universe) and an equivalence relation R. A rough set approximating an object X represented by a set of elements (e.g., pixels) selected from the image I is a pair of subsets $\underline{R}X$, $\overline{R}X$ [1]:

$$\underline{R}X = \{x \in I : [x]_R \subseteq X\} \tag{1}$$

$$\overline{R}X = \{x \in I : [x]_R \bigcap X \neq O\} \tag{2}$$

where X is the set of pixels representing edges, $X \subseteq I$; $\underline{R}X$, the lower approximation of X by R, is the union of all partitions of I which are entirely included in X; $[x]_R$ is an equivalence class; $\overline{R}X$, the upper approximation of X by R, is the union of those partitions of I where at least one element is a member of X; and O is the empty set. $\underline{R}X$ is entirely included in $\overline{R}X$. The difference $\overline{R}X - \underline{R}X$ is the roughness of the approximation of X by R.

The rough set specified above assumes the existence of an equivalence relation R that takes edges X apart from image I. The relation R can be described as follows: "pixels x_1 and x_2 are in relation R, if each of these two pixels is in a selected range of parameters for the edge." $\underline{R}X$ is the set of pixels that are definitely edges. $\overline{R}X - \underline{R}X$ is the set of pixels that may or may not be edges (i.e., represent edges only roughly). Subset $I - \overline{R}X$ definitely does not represent edges.

The above application of the rough set provides an equivalence relation R (e.g., an edge detector based on the gradient and a threshold) that is fixed for the entire image. One edge pixel creates an equivalence class of edge pixels in the image because it determines a range of parameters specific to edge bounded by a plus-minus measurement error. It describes edges globally, not locally. Experience, however, shows that edgeness is a nonlinear local image property. Consequently, a rough element that provides a more efficient local noise edge detection than global rough sets is defined below.

Our modified approximation space is the pair (W, e). The universe W is the set of pixel gray levels in a window with center at (X, Y), and thus our edge detector is local. The equivalence relation defined for the modified rough set (rather, a rough element) will use a non-statistical variance operation $e = var_n(W)$, which is the sum of the differences of the gray levels of the window center with the pixels of a template n defined in the window $W(X, Y)$. Thus, our equivalence relation admits no more than one element, i.e., pixel of the maximum non-statistical variance, to its equivalence class. Our lower approximation $\underline{e}W$ of W defined by e is the maximum non-statistical variance of the window center of coordinates X, Y, if the maximum contrast, representing the worst continuation of the window template n with the window center, exceeds a threshold Q:

$$\underline{e}W = \{e(X, Y) \in W : \quad e(X, Y) = (max_n(var_n(W)) > Q) \subseteq W\} \qquad (3)$$

where $\{1, ...n, ...N\}$ are the template subscripts in the window W; N is the number of window templates; Q is a threshold; and the equivalence class $[X, Y]_{\underline{e}}$ $= (max_n(var_n(W)) > Q)$. Using (3), the template n of $max_n(var_n(W))$ is selected and then this $max_n(var_n(W))$ is assigned to the edgeness (lower approximation $\underline{e}W$) if it exceeds Q. The lower approximation determines a maximum level of contrast to serve as the "worst continuation of the window center" which detects edges and prevents their blurring. The contrast $\underline{e}W$ is a quantitative measure of our novel law of *worst continuation*. Note that through incorporating a psychological law of human perception (or its reverse), our edge detector becomes more intelligent.

The most important feature of our improvement to the rough sets theory is that the lower approximation $\underline{e}W$ is an element, and not a set as needed by original concept $\underline{R}X$. Thanks to this improvement, each operation $\underline{e}$ is easily adjustable to the local noise level or to the local strength of edges. The rough set is created by all elements $\underline{e}W$ in I. Note, that we do not use in here the full rough sets, but only its lower approximation $\underline{e}W$).

More formally, our rotating-template technique using the lower approximation depends on the calculation of a non-statistical variance $r_n(X, Y)$ between the window center gray level $v(X, Y)$ and pixels $v_n(X_i, Y_i)$ of the neighborhoods (templates) $1, ..n, ...N$ in the window:

$$r_n(X, Y) = \sum_{i=1}^{I} (v(X, Y) - v_n(X_i, Y_i)).$$ (4)

where I is the number of pixels in a template n.

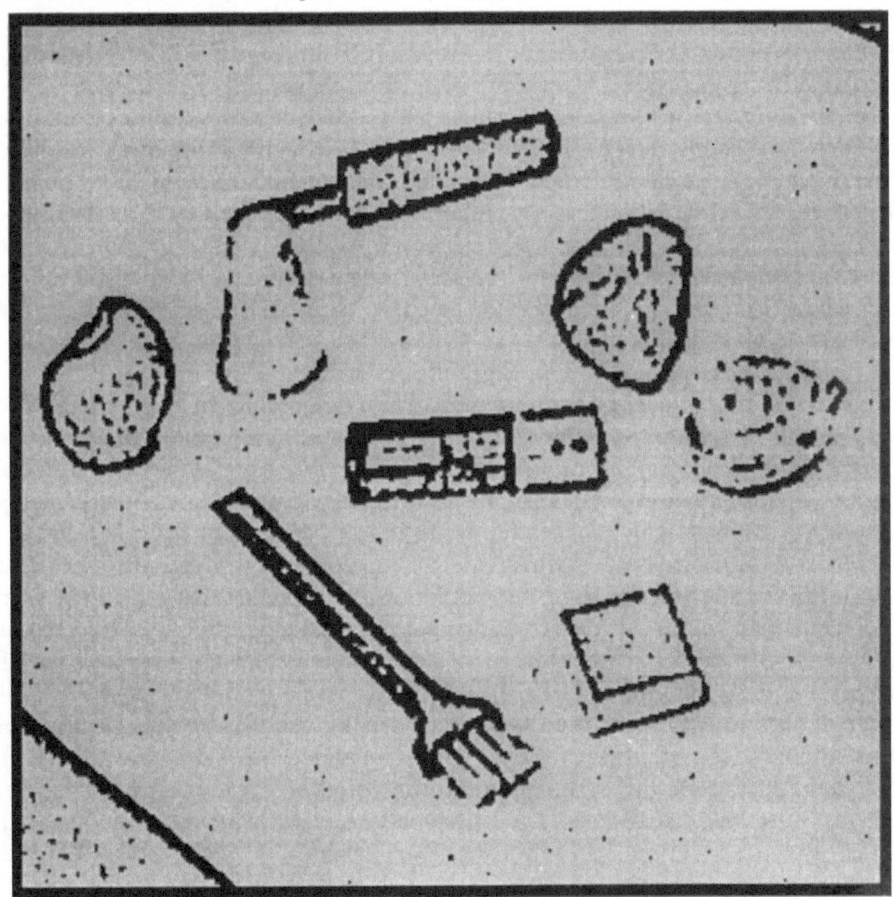

Fig. 3. Edges detected by the Laplacian of Gaussian operator

The sample variance (not used here) is more time consuming and would select a wrong template. We are not looking for the template whose pixel intensities vary the most inside the entire template, because this variation can only be assigned to the entire template (or to a template pixel selected at random) and not to any specific pixel of the template. Contour pixels cannot be localized precisely using the statistical (sample) variance, and thus edges detected cannot be sharp. There is no way to say which specific pixel should be assigned the sample variance as edgeness.

To detect delimits of regions as edges, both positive and negative contrasts $r_n(X, Y)$ are determined using (4) independently for each pixel. A maximum value of positive contrast and a maximum value (in module) of negative contrast are found independently for the pixel. These two maximum contrasts are used as positive and negative edgenesses correspondingly. The positive contrast is set to 0 if its value is smaller than the absolute value of the negative contrast, and vice-versa. A well-known effect of blocking in a neural net (known also in the psychology of human vision) is exploited in this way to attenuate noise that is close to edges. The algorithm computing the blocked contrasts considers only one pixel per one template, so, instead of the sum specified in Eq.(4), only a single term is incorporated, which is less time consuming.

In the next step pixels are detected at a positive contrast level exceeding a threshold and giving the set of edge pixels $\underline{e}W$. An absolute minimum threshold value equal to 1 can be selected. These thresholded pixels must have a pixel of negative contrast as a direct neighbor. The set of pixels $\underline{e}W$ determines the delimit of positive contrast and represents the edges of regions of positive contrast against the background. So, only edgeness directly adjacent to the edgeness of the opposite sign creates the edges. Edges of negative contrast are detected in a similar way.

The pixel contrast against background (or against adjacent objects) is assumed to be the main edge component. Most high-contrast pixels which do not represent edges are eliminated by the absence of adjacency of the negative contrast (the second edge component). Very thick edges are eliminated because most of these high-contrast pixels are not directly adjacent to the neighboring region.

Most low-contrast edges which might be created by noise are discarded because of the low level of their intensity gradient. The intensity gradient used for edge filtering is the third edge component. Fig. 2 presents edges detected as the non-zero borders between positive and negative contrast intersected with the pixel intensity gradient (a filter) that is above some gradient threshold. This gradient threshold is more than two times smaller than the threshold used for thresholding of the contours obtained with the aid of the Sobel operator (Fig.4). The contrast threshold at the minimum is equal to 1 (because any smaller contrast threshold, e.g., equal to 0, detects edges at all pixels of any image). Sobel operator produces edges of a variable thickness. The time complexity of our simplest edge detector based on the rough sets without edge filtering is the same as the complexity of the Sobel operator; we compute 8 differences in pixel gray levels while the Sobel operator uses 6 differences and calculates a square root.

The high-quality Laplacian of Gaussian [5] operator reduces noise, but produces edges of variable thickness (see Fig. 3). The edges of variable thickness need thinning. However, the thinning process disturbs edges, slightly changing the shape of the edge and introducing false forks. These distortions need additional processing. Also, the Laplacian of Gaussian operator represents thin objects as single thick edges. After thinning, which is obligatory with the Laplacian of Gaussian operator, all information is lost as to the thickness of all thin objects.

Our edge-detection technique based on the rough sets has a few main advantages over currently-used methods: a) it eliminates fluctuations of noise around edges; b) it receives the best edge localization within one iteration (because it does not blur edges); and c) is rotation invariant.

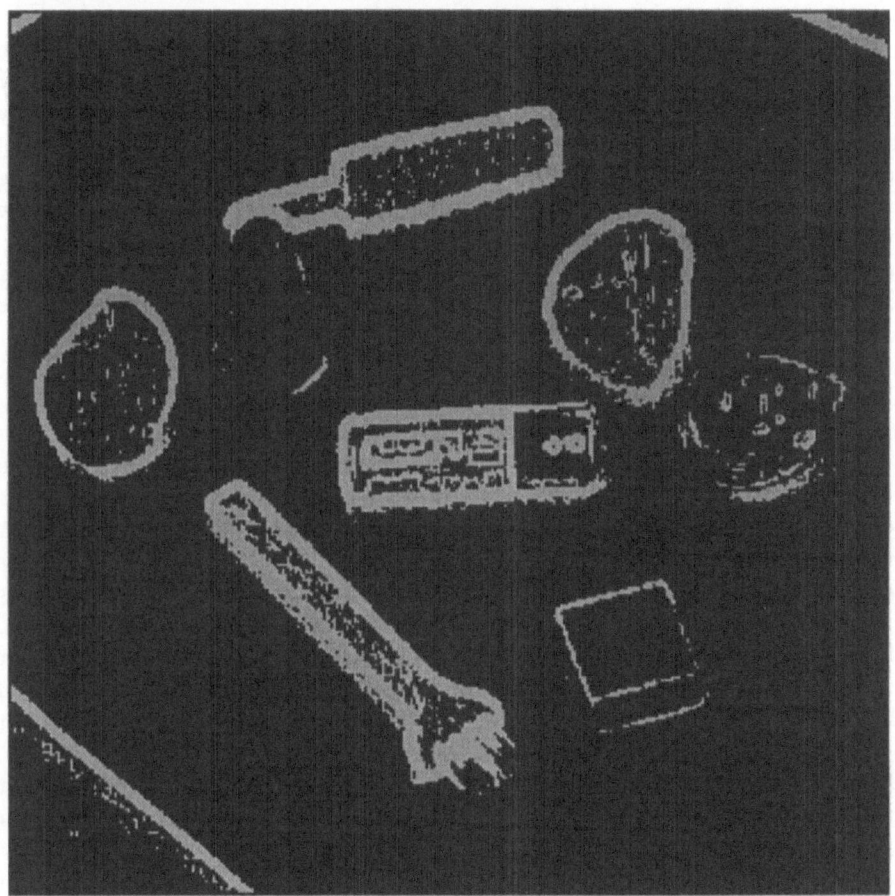

Fig. 4. Edges detected by the Sobel operator

All edge detectors involving Gaussian, Fourier, or median filters have problems with the correct localization of edges. Corrections are time consuming or erroneous. Our edge detector localizes edges exactly where they are in the image without any additional iterations. Instead of Gaussian or median filters, we use a gradient filter that hardly alters localization of edges at all.

The computation of the regular gradient considers intensity changes near to the window center at fixed window locations (symmetrical to vertical and horizontal axes passing the window center). The change in intensity returned by the gradient operator may be insignificant for sharp corners because the highest change in the window gray levels is ignored. The edge detector presented in this paper involves the largest changes in intensities of pixels more distant from the window center, thus ignoring small fluctuations inside the edges and considering more stabilized highest changes in intensities of pixels more distant from the window center. The regular gradient is used for edge filtering only, not for precise edge localization. A Gaussian filter is not used at all. This makes our edges very accurate and there is no need to perform time-consuming computations improving edge localization.

Contrasts computed near the edges, if added to the image, enhance the image at the edges. The same contrasts at the edges block all small intensity changes, including noise, smaller than the changes of the intensities caused by the edges. This effect of blocking very efficiently eliminates small fluctuations of noise around the edges. Hence, our technique incurs a very high signal-to-noise ratio at distances very close to edges, making the edges very clear. Small noise fluctuations, distant from the edges by more than by half of window diameter, are attenuated by accepting only the intensity gradient component exceeding some threshold (i.e., by our edge filter). The gradient is basically large at the edges and small at noise. Unfortunately, the gradient intensity spreads over several pixels around the contour giving thick edges at high contrast contours. This spread out has been reduced to one pixel by using another edge component: the direct adjacency of other neighboring region at the edge pixel.

The next advantage of our edge detector is its sub-pixel accuracy exactness in edge localization. This exactness is caused by its production of edges as the delimits of positive or negative contrast. These delimits are one pixel thick because the direct adjacency of the other contrast is checked. The contours detected by gradient and Laplacian operators are ambiguous because the contours are of variable thickness, and time-consuming thinning distorts the shape of the edges. Using the gradient, it is hard to determine whether a contour pixel belongs to an object interior, its edge, or its background. Shade and shading are out of control at the edges, producing high values of gradients at distances of more than one pixel from the edge and yielding the thick contours. Our edge detector produces much less ambiguous edges because gradient is not used for detection of contour limits, but to attenuate noise located at higher distances from the real edges.

Finally, this paper shows a new area of applications of the rough sets: not only for the evaluation of results after main processing of data, but during processing, to actively receive best results. The lower approximation can represent the results most wanted.

References

1. Z. Pawlak, "Rough sets," *International Journal of Information and Computer Sciences*, vol. 11, 5, pp. 341-356, 1982.

2. Z.M. Wojcik, "Automatic Detection of Semiconductor Mask Defects," *Microelectronics and Reliability*, Vol. 15, Pergamon press, 1976, pp. 585-593.

3. Z.M. Wojcik, "A Natural Approach to Image Processing and Pattern Recognition: Rotating Neighborhood Technique, Self-Adapting Threshold, Segmentation and Shape Recognition," *Pattern Recognition*, Vol.18, No. 5, 1985, pp. 299-326.

4. Z.M. Wojcik, "Edge Detector Free of the Detection/Localization Tradeoff Using Rough Sets," *Proceeding of the International Workshop on Rough Sets and Knowledge Discovery (RSKD-93)*,Banff, Alberta, Canada, October 13-15, 1993, pp421-438.

5. R.M. Haralick, L.G. Shapiro, *Computer and Robot Vision*, vol. I, Addison Wesley, 1992.

Rough Classification of Pneumonia Patients using a Clinical Database

Grace I. Paterson, M.Sc., ISP

Coordinator, Medical Informatics, Faculty of Medicine, Dalhousie University
Halifax, Nova Scotia, Canada B3H 4H7

Abstract

This study used the original model of rough sets [1] for data analysis of objective clinical findings from pneumonia patients. Pawlak's rough classification algorithm [2] was used to find the reduct, which is a logical construct of the most information-preserving findings from a decision table. The condition attributes were the clinical findings that were used by a hospital information system, MedisGroups, as independent variables in the disease severity scoring algorithm for Bacterial Lung Infection or Other Lung Infection diseases. The International Classification of Diseases (ICD) code on the patient's medical record was used as the decision attribute. The condition attributes not included in the reduct are considered superfluous with respect to the decision attribute. Six of the twenty-five condition attributes formed the reduct.

Some diseases, such as pneumonia, do not have a gold standard for validating a diagnosis. Iliad, an expert system based on Bayes' Theorem, was chosen for evaluation of the rough classification results. The same subset of condition attributes appeared in both the rough sets logical classifier and Iliad's probabilistic classifier.

In addition, a machine learning system, LERS (Learning from Examples based on Rough Sets), was used to induce rules from the decision table.

1 Introduction

A rough set represents a new mathematical approach to vagueness and uncertainty. Data analysis, data reduction, approximate classification, machine learning, and discovery of patterns in data are functions performed by a rough sets analysis [3].

A minimal subset of attributes is sought that has the same discriminating power between types of pneumonia as the set of all attributes. The International Classification of Diseases, 9th edition, Clinical Manifestations (ICD) codes classify patients in medical record keeping. There are over twenty ICD codes that indicate the patient has pneumonia. The ICD classification scheme is used for reimbursement and comparative studies between hospitals.

1.1 Rough Set Theory

Rough sets is a set theory that classifies objects into sets based on attributes of the objects. Zdislaw Pawlak introduced rough sets in a 1982 paper [2]. The rough sets methodology is based on the premise that lowering the degree of precision in data makes the data patterns more visible [4].

Rough sets was one of the first nonstatistical methodologies for data analysis. It extends classical set theory by incorporating into the set model the notion of classification information as an indiscernibility relation [3]. It uses the notion of an information system for representing classifications. Knowledge can be understood as the ability to classify objects from available information.

A decision table is an information system, DT=(U,C,D,V,f). U is a finite set of objects and its elements are called examples of DT. C is the set of condition attributes, D is the set of decision attributes, V is a set of attribute values, and f is a function which describes an element x in terms of its attribute values. C and D are disjoint sets.

The preliminary notions of indiscernibility relation, approximation space, lower approximation, upper approximation, boundary, and rough set are described elsewhere [5].

2 MICD Information System

The information system for the ICD classification is described as a decision table, MICD=(U,C,D,V,f). Let $C \cup D = A$. Two objects belong to the same equivalence class, X_i, if they have the same attribute values for set A. The family of equivalence classes is F.

Let us consider MICD where,
$U=\{x_1,\ldots,x_{67}\}$, $C=\{c_1,\ldots,c_{25}\}$, $D=\{icd\}$,
$V_c =\{0,1\}$, $V_{icd} = \{482.0, 482.1, 482.2, 482.3, 482.4, 486.0\}$
$F=\{X_1,\ldots,X_6\}$, $X_1=\{x_1,x_{64},x_{66}\}$, $X_2 = \{x_2,x_3\}$,
$X_3 = \{x_{16},x_{18},x_{20}\}$, $X_4=\{x_8,x_{17},x_{19}\}$, $X_5 = \{x_{65},x_{67}\}$,
$X_6 = \{x_4,\ldots,x_7,x_9,\ldots,x_{15},x_{21},\ldots,x_{63}\}$.

2.1 Elements of MICD

Three sets of clinical summaries from the hospital information system, Medis-Groups, were used in this study: 1) all pneumonia cases treated by the Department of Family Medicine at the Camp Hill Medical Centre in a 6-month period; 2) all pneumonia cases treated at the Camp Hill Medical Centre over a 2-year period where the patient was not over 65 and there were no complications or comorbidity; 3) all patients treated during a 6-month period who had fever, lethargy, and sputum culture findings.

The age restriction was used in set two because pneumonia is one of the most serious infections in elderly persons. These patients often may not present with either fever or cough, and underlying pulmonary or cardiac disease may confound their radiological studies [6]. In set three there were three records selected that did not have an ICD diagnostic code indicating pneumonia. A further audit confirmed that the patients showed pneumonia-like findings but did not have pneumonia. These three records were not used in the MICD information system.

2.2 Condition Attributes of MICD

MedisGroups is a medical illness severity grouping system which provides a completely objective hospital database [7]. A disease-specific scoring algorithm, based on stepwise logistic regression, computes probability of death from the values recorded in the clinical summaries. It should be noted that for an abnormal clinical finding to be considered for the MedisGroups scoring algorithm it had to occur in at least 1% of the comparative hospital database sample. The 25 condition attributes were identified as negative or positive predictors in the probability of death calculation for Bacterial Lung Infection and Other Lung Infection disease groups.

Field	MedisGroups Clinical Finding	Cases
A	Albumin Low (<30 gm/l)	9
B	Alk Phos High (>200 u/l)	2
C	Bands % High (>.20 rate)	33
D	BUN High (>10.9 mmol/l)	8
E	Cachexia	3
F	Cancer	2
G	Coma/Stupor	4
H	Curr Med Immunosuppressive	4
I	Glucose High (>13.8 mmol/l)	9
J	Hematocrit Low (<30)	7
K	Infiltrate	35
L	Lethargy	9
M	Ph Low (<7.35)	7
N	Pleural Effusion	6
O	Pulse High (>129)	4
P	PO2 Low (<75.0)	26
Q	PCO2 High (>45)	7
R	Respirations High (>24)	30
S	SGOT High (>80 IU/l)	6
T	Sodium Low (<130 mEq/l)	6
U	Sputum Culture Positive	13
V	Systolic Blood Pressure Low (<90)	8
W	Temperature High (>38.2 Celsius)	35
X	White Blood Count High (>17.0)	25
Y	White Blood Count Low (<5.0)	6

2.3 Decision Attribute of MICD

The decision attribute is the ICD diagnosis code. The etiologic agent identified by the sputum culture is used to assign the ICD code for pneumonia due to bacteria. The sputum culture was not available for fifty-four of the sixty-seven records used in the study, so these were coded as Pneumonia, Organism Unspecified. Of the sixteen sputum cultures found in the original sample of seventy records, eight were correctly coded, five were incorrectly coded, two were coded under non-pneumonia disease codes, and one was not coded. Medical records personnel concurred that 38% of the sample that had a sputum culture finding required recoding.

3   Rough Sets Data Analysis

3.1   Approximate Classification

The concept of rough classification addresses the problem of finding the description of each class in terms of the data available for each object of the class. The process requires checking whether the set of attributes is dependent or independent, finding reducts for each class, and computing the quality and accuracy of the classification as attributes are removed [2].

The steps for generating the lower and upper approximation spaces are [1]:

- Classify U based on the values for the set of conditions $C = \{C_1, \ldots, C_{25}\}$. Let A⊆C and let $A^* = \{X_1, \ldots, X_n\}$. The elementary set X_i includes all the objects for which the values of the subset of condition attributes are the same and is also referred to as an elementary set of MICD. The resultant classes are referred to as a family of indiscernible relations, IND(A), approximated or characterized by the partition A^*.

- Partition U based on the values of the decision attribute D={ICD}. The resultant partitions are referred to by set $B^* = \{Y_1, \ldots, Y_m\}$. The resultant classes are referred to as a family of indiscernible relations, IND(B), approximated or characterized by the partition B^*.

- Find the lower approximation of the set Y_j. We check A^* to see which elementary sets are entirely in Y_j to build the lower approximation $\underline{A}(Y_j)$. The lower approximation is the positive region of the partition B^* and denoted as $POS_A(B*) = \cup \underline{A}(Y_j)$ for every $Y_j \epsilon B^*$.

- Find the upper approximation of the set Y_j. We check A^* to see which elementary sets are partially in Y_j to build the upper approximation $\overline{A}(Y_j)$. The collection of all objects which can be classified with certainty on the basis of available information as not belonging to the set Y_j is called the negative region, or the exterior of Y_j, and this is denoted as $EXT_A(B*) = \cup \overline{A}(Y_j)$ for every $Y_j \epsilon B^*$.

- Find the boundary region of the set Y_j. The boundary area is the set of objects whose membership cannot be determined with certainty and is denoted as $BND_A(B*) = \cup(\overline{A}(Y_j) - \underline{A}(Y_j))$ for every $Y_j \epsilon B^*$.

3.2   Quality and Accuracy Measurements

Let $F = \{X_1, \ldots, X_n\}$, $X_i \subseteq U$, be a classification of U induced by the attributes, A⊆C∪D. The quality of approximation of classification F by set A of attributes expresses the ratio of all A-correctly classified objects to all objects in the system [8]. If the quality measure is 1 then the information system is deterministic, if less than 1 it is roughly deterministic, and if 0 it is totally non-deterministic.

$$\lambda_A(F) = |\underline{A}F| / |U|$$

The accuracy of approximation of F by set A of attributes is a measure of vagueness and captures how accurately the set X_i is definable in F based on knowledge A.

$$\alpha_A(F) = |\underline{A}F| / |\overline{A}F|$$

3.3 Data Reduction

The information system is reduced by identifying those objects that have identical attribute values and collapsing them together. Condition attributes are checked to see whether they are dependent or independent with respect to the decision, and dependent attributes are removed as they are superfluous. A relative reduct, RED, is a maximal independent set of condition attributes with respect to the decision attribute. In general, more than one reduct of condition attributes can be identified and this stems from the fact that the order in which we check the conditions determines the final sets of independent conditions [9].

If we remove an attribute, p_i, from RED then we obtain a set of attributes RED-$\{p_i\}$. The quality of the approximation without p_i is a roughly superfluous measure given as

$$\varepsilon = \lambda_D(RED) - \lambda_D(RED - \{p_i\}).$$

3.4 Machine Learning

The machine learning system looks for regularities in the examples, finally inducing a set of rules in the following format

$$(C_1, v_1)\&(C_2, v_2)\& \ldots \&(C_M, v_m) \Longrightarrow (D, d).$$

The system LERS (Learning from Examples based on Rough Sets), developed by Jerzy Grzymala-Busse, was used for rule induction [10].

3.5 Data Evaluation

Iliad is the expert system that was used in the data evaluation. Iliad is designed to draw conclusions from incomplete information, as it is based on Bayes' Theorem which revises existing prior probabilities based on new information. The issues that relate to the development of good rules in the rough sets approach are similar in some ways to issues associated with statistical approaches to classification. According to Szladow and Ziarko, the main issue in the statistical approach to classification is the construction of a probabilistic classifier which would approximate the theoretically optimal Bayes' classification rule [4].

Iliad identifies both dependent and independent attributes through a series of nested disease frames. This study drops the attributes from the original set of 25 condition attributes in decreasing order by the likelihood ratio, as identified in the Pneumonia Disease frame and Hospital Acquired Pneumonia Disease frame of Iliad, version 4.1 [11]. The attributes are dropped from the reduct, RED, in decreasing order by the roughly superfluous measure, ε.

4 Application of Rough Sets Methods

4.1 Decision Classes and Attribute Frequencies

The 67 objects in MICD were partitioned by the ICD code as follows:

Class	ICD	Cases	Diagnosis Description	Group
Y_1	482.0	3	P. due to Klebsiella	Bacterial
Y_2	482.1	2	P. due to Pseudomonas	Bacterial
Y_3	482.2	3	P. due to Haemophilus Influenzae	Bacterial
Y_4	482.3	3	P. due to Streptococcus	Bacterial
Y_5	482.4	2	P. due to Staphylococcus	Bacterial
Y_6	486	54	Pneumnonia, Organism Unspecified	Other

4.2 Independent, Dependent, Superfluous, and Reduct

- Collapse those objects with the same condition and decision attributes into the same elementary set. This results in a reduced information system composed of 61 elementary sets of the 67 objects. The information system is fully definable, as the upper and lower approximations of MICD are the same. Y_1 through Y_5 are described by 1-element sets, and Y_6 is described by 44 1-element sets, 3 2-elements sets, and 1 4-element set.

- Remove superfluous attributes by checking whether the number of elementary sets remains the same before and after elimination of these attributes. The non-superfluous attributes are the reduct. Numerous reducts were identified. This stems from the fact that the order in which we check the attributes determines the final set of non-superfluous attributes.

- Find the independent set of condition attributes with respect to the decision attribute, ICD. There are two reducts, {C,L,R,U,W,X} and {K,L,R,U,W,X}. The collection of all reducts is 7 of the 25 condition attributes in MICD.

Class	ICD	Cases	$\underline{A}X$	$\overline{A}X$	Qual.	Accu.	Sets
X_1	482.0	3	3	3	1.00	1.00	3
X_2	482.1	2	2	2	1.00	1.00	2
X_3	482.2	3	3	3	1.00	1.00	3
X_4	482.3	3	3	3	1.00	1.00	3
X_5	482.4	2	2	2	1.00	1.00	2
X_6	486	54	54	54	1.00	1.00	48

4.3 Drop According to ε-superfluous

As each attribute is removed one at a time from the reduct, we obtain the roughly superfluous measure, ε-superfluous, for the classification F. This measure of how much the accuracy changes without an attribute ranges from .67 up to 1.00.

Drop	Attributes	Quality	Accuracy	Sets
0. None	CLRUWX	1.00	1.00	29
1. L	CRUWX	.97	.94	25
2. C	RUWX	.87	.73	15
3. W	RUX	.81	.58	8
4. X	RU	.81	.50	2
5. R	U	.81	.45	2

4.4 Drop According to Iliad's Likelihood Ratios

Iliad supplies a likelihood ratio for each clinical finding associated with pneumonia. These clinical findings are dropped from the set of 25 condition attributes
in decreasing order of their likelihood ratio. Since the Pneumonia disease frame
is nested within Iliad's Hospital Acquired Pneumonia disease frame, we first
drop the 7 clinical findings identified in the Pneumonia disease frame, before
dropping the 4 clinical findings identified in the Hospital Acquired Pneumonia
disease frame. There are 14 condition attributes that Iliad did not associate
with pneumonia, as shown in the attribute set that remains after all pneumonia-
associated clinical findings are dropped from MICD.

Drop	Attributes	Qual	Accu	Sets
0. None	ABCDEFGHIJKLMNOPQRSTUVWXY	1.00	1.00	61
1. P	ABCDEFGHIJKLMNOQRSTUVWXY	1.00	1.00	55
2. R	ABCDEFGHIJKLMNOQSTUVWXY	.97	.94	50
3. L	ABCDEFGHIJKMNOQSTUVWXY	.97	.94	49
4. W	ABCDEFGHIJKMNOQSTUVXY	.96	.91	43
5. C	ABDEFGHIJKMNOQSTUVXY	.96	.91	37
6. X	ABDEFGHIJKMNOQSTUVY	.94	.89	30
7. K	ABDEFGHIJMNOQSTUVY	.94	.89	30
8. H	ABDEFGIJMNOQSTUVY	.94	.89	29
9. F	ABDEGIJMNOQSTUVY	.94	.89	29
10. D	ABEGIJMNOQSTUVY	.94	.89	28
11. U	ABEGIJMNOQSTVY	.43	.21	26

4.5 Decision Rules Generated using LERS

The LEM2 algorithm in the LERS program was used to generate decision rules.
In this study, these rules were used for checking data quality. A further analysis
is required to determine how these decision rules can best be used for decision
support applications.

5 Discussion

The rough sets approach discovered a logical classifier that was contained in
the probabilistic classifier for pneumonia disease in the Bayesian-based Iliad
expert system. This study shows that the quality of the classification can
be maintained by less than one quarter of the attributes used as predictors
of mortality for pneumonia cases. Rough sets methods can be used to identify
data elements which do not make a meaningful contribution to disease labelling,
and can help us deal with information overload by eliminating superfluous
information.

It has been shown that individualized reports to physicians detailing their
practice patterns with respect to pneumonia patients leads to fewer hospital
resources and no compromise in outcomes for patients [12]. The identification
of local practice patterns and the generation of decision rules based on these
patterns could facilitate medical education in a hospital setting.

References

[1] Pawlak Z., Wong S.K.M., Ziarko W., Rough Sets: Probabilistic Versus Deterministic Approach, **International Journal of Man-Machine Studies** (1988), 29, pp. 81-85.

[2] Pawlak Z., Rough Classification, **International Journal of Man-Machine Studies** (1984) 20, pp. 469-83.

[3] Ziarko W., Analysis of Uncertain Information in the Framework of Variable Precision Rough Sets, **Foundations of Computing and Decision Sciences** (1993), 18(3-4), pp. 381-396.

[4] Szladow A., Ziarko W., Rough Sets: Working with Imperfect Data, **AI Expert** (1993), 8(7), pp. 36-39.

[5] Ziarko W. (ed.), **Proceedings of the International Workshop on Rough Sets and Knowledge Discovery RSKD '93**, (1993), Banff, Alberta.

[6] Fagon J.-Y., Chastre J., Hance A.J., Domart Y., Trouillet J.-L., Gibert C., Evaluation of Clinical Judgment in the Identification and Treatment of Nosocomial Pneumonia in Ventilated Patients, **Chest**, (1993), 103(2), pp. 547-553.

[7] MedisGroups Scoring Algorithm: A Technical Description, **MediQual Systems** (1993).

[8] Pawlak Z., Rough Classification of Patients after Highly Selective Vagotomy for Duodenal Ulcer, **International Journal of Man-Machine Studies**, (1986), 24, pp. 413-433.

[9] Hashemi R.R., Jeolovsek F.R., Razzaghi M., Developmental Toxicity Risk Assessment: A Rough Sets Approach, **Methods of Information in Medicine**, (1993), 32, pp. 47-54.

[10] Grzymala-Busse J., LERS–A System for Learning from Examples Based on Rough Sets, **Intelligent Decision Support: Handbook of Applications and Advances of the Rough Sets Theory**, Roman Slowinski (ed.), Kluwer Academic Publishers, (1992), pp. 3-18.

[11] **Iliad User's Manual Version 4.1**, (1992), Applied Informatics Inc., Salt Lake City, Utah.

[12] Johnson C.C., Martin M., Epstein S.M., Lee J.D., The Effect of a Physician Education Program on Hospital Length of Stay and Total Patient Charges, **The Journal of the South Carolina Medical Association**, (1993), June, pp. 293-301.

Rough Sets Approach to Analysis of Data of Diagnostic Peritoneal Lavage Applied for Multiple Injuries Patients.

Krzysztof SŁOWIŃSKI and El Sanossy SHARIF
Dept. of Surgery, F. Raszeja Mem. Hospital
60-833 Poznań, Poland

Abstract

Three kinds of information systems containing 80 patiens with multiple injuries, who had diagnostic peritoneal lavage, are analysed with the concept of rough sets. Twenty three attributes are used to describe these patients. Twenty of them concern: anamnesis, description of general condition, state of consciousness, and kind of injuries. Three last attributes define classification of patients according to three clinical problems.

Using the rough sets methodology implemented in the microcomputer program RoughDAS, the information systems are reduced so as to get the minimum subsets of attributes ensuring an acceptable quality of the classification. The relationship between these attributes and three classifications is shown by the decision algorithms. Analysis of these algorithms leads to the concrete clinical conclusions.

1 Introduction

The data describing 80 patients with multiple injuries were analysed using the method based on the rough sets theory [4,5]. The patients were subjected to diagnostic peritoneal lavage (DPL) in order to exclude or confirm the occurrence of intraabdominal injuries.

The examination was carried out in the following way [2] : in local anaesthesia, the skin was incised below the navel, to a length of 2-3 centimeters along the medial line, and the abdominal integuments were uncovered. Through the incision, a catheter on guide was introduced and placed in the peritoneal cavity. A dose of 1000 ccm of Ringer liquid, warmed to the temperature of 37 degrees C, with the addition of 20 ccm of 8,4% Natrium bicarbonicum was transfused through the catheter. In the case of children, the amount of liquid was 20 ccm per 1 kg of weight.

At the end of the transfusion, the empty bottle together with the transfusion set was turned over and placed on the floor, which caused the reverse free flow of liquid from the abdominal cavity by force of the column of liquid.

The test was considered positive - confirming the occurrence of intraabdominal trauma - if one of the following was observed in the drained liquid [3] :

- aspiration of blood or bloody content
- obtainment of the intensely plethoric liquid
- over 50 x 10^9 /l erythrocytes
- over 0,3 x 10^9 /l leucocytes
- considerably increased concentration of bilirubin or amylase (at least double the amount of blood serum)
- the presence of bacteria.

2 Analysis of experience - rough sets methodology

Three information systems (A, B and C) were created for the needs of the analysis of the experience with DPL application in   multiple injuries. Those systems described patients by means of 20 attributes checked in the hospital surgery before DPL is executed. The attributes are:

a1 - age
a2 - sex
a3 - cause of accident
a4 - other victims
a5 - pulse
a6 - arterial pressure
a7 - skin (paleness)
a8 - abdominal pain
a9 - muscular defense of abdominal integuments
a10 - Blumberg sign
a11 - peristalsis
a12 - state of consciousness
a13 - presence of chest bruises
a14 - rib fracture
a15 - pneumothorax
a16 - pleural haematoma
a17 - bruises of limbs
a18 - fracture of long bones
a19 - amputation of limb after injury
a20 - alcohol odour from mouth

The feature of the three information systems is that some of the attributes are common for 2 or 3 of them (Table 1.) [1]. This corresponds to clinical practice in which we make decisions based on the consideration of only those attributes that intuitively seem to be the most crucial.

This paper presents the attempt to find cause and effect the relationship between the attributes of the three information systems and the following clinical problems (classifications):

1. The period of time from the admission to the hospital to the execution of DPL
2. DPL result (positive or negative)
3. The result of treatment as the basis for future prognoses.

Table 1. Information systems.

Information system	Attributes	Classifications		
A	a1, a2, a3, a4, a5, a6, a7, a12, a13, a17, a20	1	2	3
B	a1, a2, a3, a4,a5 a6, a7, a8, a9, a10, a11, a12 a20	1	2	3
C	a1, a2, a3, a4, a5, a6, a7, a12, a14, a15, a16, a18, a19, a20	1	2	3

For the analysis of each of the three systems, the RoughDAS computer system [6] was used in order to obtain the smallest possible set of attributes remaining in the closest causal dependence with the classification. The most crucial attributes (conditional attributes) served subsequently for the derivation of decision algorithms for particular classification (decision attributes).

From the twenty attributes describing patients before peritoneal lavage, only three have the real value: age, pulse and arterial blood pressure. The remaining attributes are qualitative. In clinical practice, the exact values of the quantitative attributes are most often interpreted in qualitative term, e.g. age - "young", "middle-aged", "elderly", pulse/pressure - "high", "low". Therefore, the application of such a classification leads to the division of the domain of a given attribute within the specified range of real numbers into several value intervals.

The qualitative attributes assume digital values in the form of definitions established in the clinical practice. Both the value intervals of quantitative attributes and clinical definitions of qualitative attributes were described by means of the numerical code (0, 1, 2, 3, 4, ...), thus creating a new domain for a given attribute. The transition from the domain of real and digital numbers to the domain of the code was carried out through the so-called norms based on the clinical practice. The normalized values of attributes describing patients before they undergo peritoneal lavage is shown below, in Table 2.

Table 2. Values of attributes normalised according to the adopted code.

Number	Name of attribute	Code 0	Code 1	Code 2	Code 3	Code 4
a1	age (years)	3 - 18	19 -40	> 40	-	-
a2	sex	F	M	-	-	-
a3	cause of accident	traffic	fall from height	blunt blow in abdomen	stabbed wound	unknown
a4	other victims of the same accident	none	present	-	-	-
a5	pulse (n/min)	≤ 100	≥ 100	-	-	-

a6	arterial pressure (mmHg)	> 100	≤ 100	-	-	-
a7	skin	normal	pale	-	-	-
a8	abdominal pain	absent	present	-	-	-
a9	muscular defense	absent	present	-	-	-
a10	Blumberg sign	absent	present	-	-	-
a11	peristalsis	present	absent	-	-	-
a12	state of consciousness	conscious	consciousness blurred	unconscious	-	-
a13	chest bruise	absent	present	-	-	-
a14	rib fracture	absent	single	multiple	-	-
a15	pneumo thorax	abstent	present	-	-	-
a16	pleural haematoma	absent	present	-	-	-
a17	bruises of limbs	absent	present	-	-	-
a18	fracture of long bones	absent	single	multiple	-	-
a19	limb amputation after injury	absent	present	-	-	-
a20	alcohol	imperceptible	perceptible	intoxination	-	-

Table 3. presents the way of coding the values of adopted classifications.

Table 3. Coded values of classifications.

No	Name	Code			
		0	1	2	3
1	Time from admission to DPL	≤ 30 min	31 - 120 min	121 - 300 min	> 300 min
2	DPL result	0 negative		1 positive	
3	Result of treatment	0 lived		1 died	

3 The Results

Using the microcomputer program RoughDAS, the information systems were reduced so as to get the minimum subsets of important attributes, ensuring an acceptable quality of the classification - ≥ 0,700.

The following results were obtained (Table 4.).

Table 4. Distribution of important attributes of the three information systems in the three classifications.

Information system	Clsssification / Important attributes		
	1	2	3
A a1 a2 a3 a4 a5 a6 a7 a12 a13 a17 a20	a1 a3 a5 a7 a12 a17	a1 a3 a4 a5 a12	a3 a5 a7 a12 a17
B a1 a2 a3 a4 a5 a6 a7 a8 a9 a10 a11 a12 a20	a1 a3 a4 a5 a7 a8 a12	a1 a3 a4 a5 a12	a1 a2 a3 a7 a12
C a1 a2 a3 a4 a5 a6 a7 a12 a14 a15 a16 a18 a19 a20	a1 a3 a5 a7 a12 a18	a1 a3 a4 a5 a12	a3 a7 a12 a18

The crucial attributes influencing the time of DPL completion were:
- age
- cause of accident
- pulse frequency
- paleness of the skin
- state of consciousness

Attributes of the closest cause-and-effect relation to the DPL result were:
- age
- cause of accident
- other victims
- pulse frequency
- state of consciousness

Finally, the attributes of the greatest prognostic significance with regard to the results of the treatment were:
- cause of accident
- paleness of the skin
- state of consciousness.

In RoughDAS system the obtained essential attributes served subsequently as conditional attributes for the creation of decision algorithms, from which several conclusions arise that prove to be useful in the clinical practice. These algorithms were presented on the 2nd International Workshop on Rough Sets and Knowledge Discovery in Banff, Alberta, Canada, in October, 12-15, 1993 (Tutorials and System Demonstrations).

4 Conclusions

1. Patients expected to obtain positive result of DPL (young, with the pulse above 100/min, after the fall from height or blunt blow in the abdomen) should have it done as soon as possible, disregarding the values of other essential attributes.

2. Unfavourable prognosis in multiple injuries concerns elderly, unconscious patients, and when the reason of the injury is unknown. DPL should be carried out as soon as possible. The prognosis is better for younger, conscious patients from traffic accidents.

3. The decision algorithms representing the present-day experience with peritoneal lavage may serve as the basis for the creation of a decision support system aiding the treatment of next patients after multiple injuries. Such a system could be employed to help hospital doctors who first deal with such patients.

The obtained results and conclusions demonstrate the suitability of the rough sets theory to analyse clinical problems connected with treatment of patients after multiple injuries.

References

[1] El Sanossy Sharif, The Analysis of Experience with Diagnostic Peritoneal Lavage in Multiple Injuries (in Polish), Ph.D. dissertation, Medical Academy, Poznań 1993.

[2] Fibak J., Technique of Diagnostic Peritoneal Lavage (in Polish), The Polish Medical Weekly 1985; 40: 231-234.

[3] Kolasiński J., Experience in the Use of Diagnostic Peritoneal Lavage (in Polish) Polish Surgical Review, 1984; 56: 611-614.

[4] Pawlak Z., Rough Sets. Theoretical Aspects of Reasoning about Data, Kluwer Academic Publishers, 1991.

[5] Słowiński K., El. Sanossy Sharif, Rough Sets Analysis of Experience in Surgical Practice, Proceedings of International Workshop "Rough Set State of the Art and Perspectives", Poznań -Kiekrz, September 2 - 4, 1992.

[6] Słowiński R., Stefanowski J., "RoughDAS and RoughClass Software Implementation of the Rough Sets Approach", in R. Słowiński (ed.) "Intelligent Decision Support - Handbook of Applications and Advances of the Rough Sets Theory", Kluwer Academic Press, 1992, p.445 - 456.

NEURAL NETWORKS AND ROUGH SETS - COMPARISON AND COMBINATION FOR CLASSIFICATION OF HISTOLOGICAL PICTURES

Jacek JELONEK, Krzysztof KRAWIEC, Roman SŁOWIŃSKI,
Jerzy STEFANOWSKI, Janusz SZYMAŚ*

Institute of Computing Science
Technical University of Poznań
PL-60-965 Poznań, Poland

*Departament of Pathology
University School of Medicine in Poznań
PL-60-355 Poznań, Poland

Abstract

Learning neural networks using large sets of data often appears to be very complex task. Well-known backpropagation algorithm for the learning of non-linear layered networks requires a lot of floating-point computation. The learning time is proportional to (among others) the size of the input vectors, so any reasonable reduction of the redundant information on the input is welcome. Rough set approach to reduction of the input data to a neural network is presented in this paper. Over two hundred records describing microscopic slides of 7 classes of brain tumours constitute considered data set.

1 Introduction

Artificial neural networks (or simply neural networks, NN) constitute one of the most promising branches in the Artificial Intelligence field. Huge number of publications, describing both theory and practice, related to this issue have appeared in recent years. NN are used in pattern recognition, classification, control, prediction and many other fields.

Generally speaking, what made them so popular is, that NN tested on many data sets, in both classification and reclassification tests, are inclined to show better results than other methods. This improvement in comparison with other tools is usually not very large, but remarkable. However, "no rose without a thorn": to achieve such a good result, a huge amount of the computation time is often required. Learning algorithms for NN are usually very complex and require even millions of iteration steps to meet the convergence criterion. This concerns the popular backpropagation algorithm, used in this paper to learn two- and three-layer non-linear networks, as well.

Hence, it may be understood that there is tendency in many of the recent NN-research to focus on pre-processing of the information used for learning and testing [2]. Data representation should fulfil at least two conditions at the same time: to be, firstly - suitable for a given kind of the network, and secondly - concise. The latter condition constitutes the issue this paper is focused on.

We tried to use rough set theory (RS), a well-suited tool for analysing and reducing the information systems describing object classification, to make the original data set used in this paper brief. Its ability to extract reducts of attributes and the core from the original description vector has been here exploited. In this way, the minimal representation of knowledge has been used.

To obtain credible results cross validation (CV) method was used for learning and testing. The approach has been slightly modified: like in common CV, the entire set of examples has been divided ten times into learning and testing samples in proportion 9:1. Each division has been done randomly, but *with respect to the percentage shares of the classes in the entire set of examples*. Thus, every test set includes *exactly* the same number of cases: 26, i.e. more than 10% from the whole set of 216 examples (some cases occur in more than one test set). In consequence, the sum of cardinalities of all the testing sets is bigger than in "normal" CV and amounts to 10×26=260.

Other popular method for testing learning systems is leaving-one-out (LOO). However, due to very long learning time, it was impossible to use it in this case. One can treat CV as some kind of generalization of LOO: its accuracy is comparable, while the time-consumption may be even many times smaller (especially for large data sets; see [10]).

2. Microscopic images of brain tumours and their description

The pattern recognition problem considered in this paper concerns recognition of medical images. Our goal is computer aided recognition of the microscopic pictures

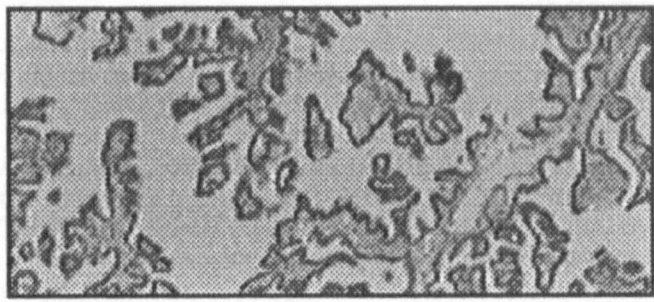

Fig. 1: (White-black) reproduction of an exemplary brain tumour slide

of brain tumours. NN-based decision support system has been implemented to this end.

In cytological images, used mostly in medical image recognition, cells are usually well visible on the background, what is very helpful during the image

428

fragmentation and automatic feature extraction [5]. This is not the case in histological images, which we have focused on. There is no background, cells (the correct and the pathological ones) are filling the whole image. Fig. 1 presents example of the image of microscopic slide of brain tumour.

The surface of the microscopic section amounts usually to several square centimeters, what gives from several hundred to several thousand observation fields (depending on the magnification factor of the microscope: approximately from 100 to 1000 times). Furthermore, the image is very complex: includes often (besides the correct and the pathological cells) parts of vessels, calc tuff or haemorrhage. Besides the shape of particular cells the structure of the tissue is important as well.

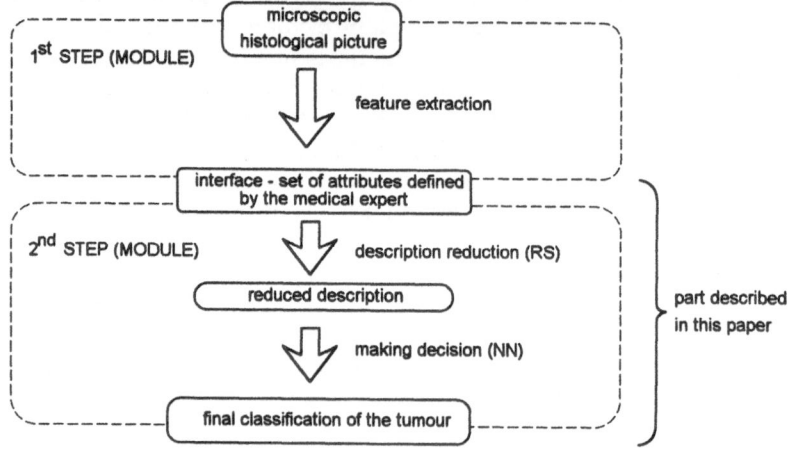

Fig. 2: Structure of the entire recognition system for histological images

From huge quantity of information carried by a histological picture in its original form (photograph, bitmap), only a small fraction is important for making the decision. The exploitation of human expert's knowledge was the natural way to select this relevant data.

We decided for two-step solution: the entire image recognition system should consist of two modules. The task of the former should be the feature extraction and of the latter one - making the decision. The paper is focused on the latter step. Figure 2 represents the structure of the system.

Interface between both the modules has been created in the following way. The specialist defined a set of 26 features, each one represented by a tree-structure, faithfully reflecting the nature of the histological image. Every bifurcation in a feature-tree corresponds to picking out some concrete value (leave) or some subset of values (remaining tree nodes) for this feature. Process of assigning the value to the feature starts in the root of the feature-tree and ends in one of its leaves (more exactly, in this one, which corresponds to this value). For every feature-tree there is a corresponding 0-1 vector. Choice of the leave from the tree sets the related vector element to 1, whereas others are equal to 0. Only one leave in every feature-tree may be chosen by the expert.

All the 26 feature-vectors are then linked together building the final image descriptor. It constitutes a 0-1 vector as well, and its length is equal to the sum of lengths of all the 26 feature vectors. There are finally 155 basic attributes; in other words: a 0-1 vector of length 155. The idea is illustrated in Figure 3.

Description vector constitutes an interface between the feature extraction module and the decision making module. However, as it will come out in the further part of the paper, this reduced (in comparison to the original picture) representation is still too large for reasonable NN-application.

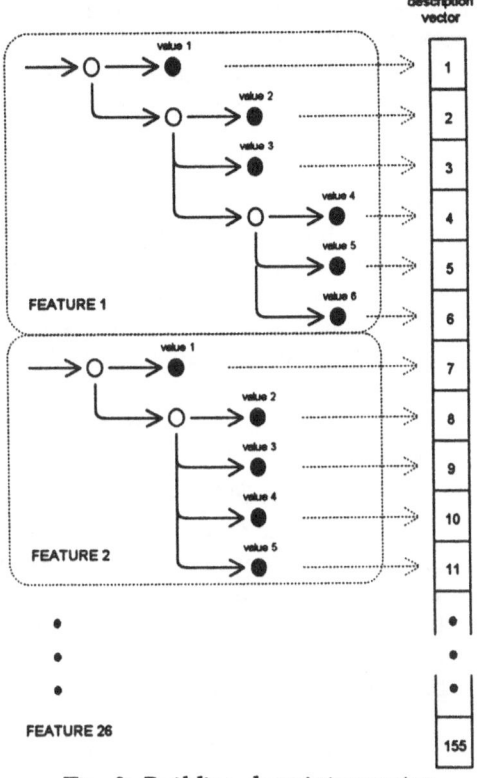

Fig. 3: Building descriptor vector

3. Data set

The data have been collected by Janusz Szymaś from Departament of Pathology of Universiry School of Medicine in Poznań. The expert selected (from a larger data base) 216 cases (images) representing 7 classes of brain cancer. To avoid the suspicions of simplifying the task, all the seven classes have been chosen from the same group of cancers (astrocytic tumours), so the pictures are relatively similar (especially for a layman). Table 4 shows the distribution of the classes (their absolute cardinalities and percentage shares).

Class No.	1	2	3	4	5	6	7
No. of cases in class	54	12	15	22	82	14	17
Percentage share	25.0	5.6	6.9	10.2	38.0	6.5	7.9

Table 4: Distribution among the classes (the smallest and the biggest marked)

The significant dispersion of the class sizes makes the problem naturally more involved. On the other hand, this state of the art quite well reflects the reality (i.e. the occurrence frequencies of cases belonging to particular classes in practice).

4. Neural Networks used in research

From among plenty of known kinds of NN and theirs learning methods, a non-linear neural network and a backpropagation algorithm have been chosen in the described research. This proved approach almost always appears to be effective

430

and, besides, is relatively easy to implement. The parameters and properties of the networks have been assumed as follows (details in, e.g., [3]):

- Sigmoidal transfer function, i.e. defined by the following formula, has been used:

$$\varphi(e) = \frac{1}{1 + \exp(-e)}$$

where:

e - excitation, equal to scalar product of the weight vector and the input vector

- Weight correction in the backpropagation algorithm depends on the current state of the network only (especially on the committed error). No inertia has been implemented; in other words, the momentum factor is equal to 0. Thus correction for the ith weight of neuron in the jth step of learning is defined as follows:

$$\Delta w_i^j = \alpha\left(z^j - y^j\right)x_i^j y^j\left(1 - y^j\right)$$

where:

x_i^j - state of the ith input of the neuron in the jth step

y^j - output value of the neuron in the jth step

z^j - desired output value of the neuron in the jth step

- Coefficient α (influences the convergence step) remains constant during the learning; however, some test have been carried out using many different values of this parameter;
- MSE (Medium Square Error) has been used to calculate the global error of the network;
- Every tested network has 7 outputs: as many as the number of classes represented in the set of examples; desired outputs are represented by 0-1 vectors of length 7 (coding: "1 from 7");
- The convergence criterion for the learning algorithm has been defined in the following way. The basis was the difference between the desired and the computed output value of the units in the output layer. The convergence threshold was set to 0.25. Learning algorithm met the convergence criterion if, during the learning of one epoch (entire learning set), all of the output units fulfilled this condition.

5. Experimental results before the reduction

The amount of computation during learning the NN is proportional to the number of connections in the network and, in consequence, to the size of the input vector. In the case of the original, not reduced input vector, there are 155 connections (weights) linking every unit in the hidden layer with all of input vector elements. This makes the tests very expensive as a matter of both computer memory and time.

Due to these restrictions relatively small number of units in the hidden layer has been chosen (30) and only one full 10-fold cross validation test for $\alpha=3.25$ has been carried out. The final true-ratio achieved (i.e. the percentage of properly classified cases) was **86.15%**.

6. Reduction method

Reduction of the image description vector has been carried out in two steps:

1) First step was based on suggestions of the medical expert. Set of attributes has been divided into six groups and some order of importance among these groups has been proposed. Then few possibilities (combinations) of including and non-including of individual groups were considered. One of them gave very good result: reduction by over 50% (only 87 attributes) without decreasing the quality of classification (in terms of RS theory).

2) The second step of reduction was based directly on the RS theory. The set of 87 attributes, resulting from the previous step, has been used as input data for the RoughDAS system [7]. The trial of computation of the core has failed: it appeared to be empty. This result suggested us, that there are many exclusive reducts in the set of attributes. Thus, few of the reducts were computed and the smallest of them, including only 17 attributes has been chosen for the further work. Of course, there was no decrease of the quality of classification as well.

Thus, overall reduction factor obtained through this reduction achieved almost 90% (from 155 to 17) and the quality of classification has been conserved at the same time.

7. Experimental results after the reduction

Due to almost 10-times reduction of the attributes' set size, it was possible to carry out more tests as in the case of the not reduced one. Both two- and three-layer networks were tested, using different values of coefficient α (from 0.5 to 4.5 with step 0.5). Due to lack of formal methods for estimating the number of units (neurons) in the hidden layer, rough number has been assumed: 17 in the case of the two-layer network, 17 and 12 in three-layer network.

Table 5 presents the results of the reclassification obtained using two- and three-layer networks (in percents). In both cases the best result is indicated.

α	0.5	1.0	1.5	2.0	2.5	3.0	3.5	4.0	4.5
17-17-7	85.00	85.00	85.38	85.76	84.61	85.38	83.07	85.38	83.46
17-17-12-7	88.07	84.61	85.00	86.53	83.84	85.38	83.07	83.07	86.15

Table 5: Results of the reclassification using reduced set of attributes

8. Reclassification using other methods

Probabilistic decision tree (PDT): These tests have been carried out using our own implementation of decision tree algorithm, based on the original ID3 [6]. The point of the extension is the reduction of the tree, so called pre-prunning, described by and dependent on some coefficients (system Assistant86, see [1]).

Following values for the parameters have been assumed:

- minimal weight of examples in a node: 0.0
- sufficient values of class frequency: 1.0
- suitability of attribute: 0.0
- minimal values for class frequency for the nondeterministic decision: 0.7

Rough Sets: Standard cross validation and our implementation (systems RoughDAS and RoughClass, see [7]) of the "nearest rule" method [8,9] have been used. Following values for parameters have been assumed (for details, see [9]):

- number of neighbours: 1
- distance for the nominal attributes: 0.5
- compensation ratio: 1
- veto-thresholds: 2
- weights of all the attributes: 1
- all the attributes are nominal
- looking for nearest rules according to the L_p method

Table 6 shows the comparison of reclassification results obtained by particular methods. Note, that slightly different CV techniques have been used for NNs and

	Method	Reclassification
Before reduction:	NN 155-30-7	86.15%
After reduction:	PDT	84.26%
	RS	83.79%
	NN 17-17-7	85.76%
	NN 17-17-12-7	88.07%

Table 6: The comparison of the reclassification results achieved by individual methods (see text for details)

other methods, so the performance comparison is only approximate.

9. Conclusions and discussion

Described example shows the importance of data pre-processing in learning systems. There are at least three profits of used approach:

1) Smart reduction of description vector decreases considerably the learning time. Computation for both not-reduced (155-30-7) and reduced (17-17-7) description vectors were executed on the same computer, namely on PC 486DX2 (66MHz). Average time necessary to teach network for each of 10 cross validation learning sets amounted to, respectively, over four hours and less than half an hour (reduction factor about 10 times). Decrease of the classification ability was at the same time very small (0.39%, see Tab. 6). Moreover, time required for this reduction was very small in comparison to this needed for learning the NNs.

2) Reduction of time-consumption mentioned above allowed to make use of the three-layer networks, what was completely impossible (from a rational point of view) in case of not reduced vector. Non-linear NN should have at least three layers to be able to learn successfully every classification task. Described research provides some kind of experimental proof for this statement: adding hidden layer resulted with increment of the classification ability by over 2.3% (see Tab. 6).

3) As it has been mentioned in the Introduction, NNs are inclined to give better results than the other methods (improvement by 3.8% in comparison to PDT and by 5.6% in comparison to RS). Thus, their ability for better generalization and extrapolation has been corroborated in this way.

References

[1] Cestnik B., Kononenko I., Bratko I: Assistan86 a knowledge - elicitation toll for sophisticated users. In: Bratko I.,Lavrac N. (eds.) Progress in Machine Learning, Sigma Press, Wilmshow 1987, pp. 31-45.

[2] Cherkasky V., Lari-Najafi H.: Data Representation for Diagnostic Neural Networks, IEEE Expert, October 1992, pp. 43-53

[3] Freeman J. A., Skapura D. M.: Neural Networks. Algorithms, Applications and Programming Techniques, Addison-Wesley 1991

[4] Jelonek J., Krawiec K.: Application of Neural Networks for Support of the Learning Process of Advisory Systems, Master's Thesis, Technical University of Poznań, 1993

[5] Moallemi C.: Classifying cells for cancer diagnosis using neural networks, IEEE Expert, December 1991, p. 8

[6] Quinlan J.R.: Learning efficient classification procedures and their application to chess and games. In: Michalski R.S, Carbonell J.G., Mitchell T.M. (eds.): Machine learning. An Artificial Intelligence Approach, vol 1. Morgan Kaufmann, San Mateo C.A. 1983, pp 461-482.

[7] Slowinski R., Stefanowski, J.: "RoughDAS" and "RoughClass" software implementations of the rough sets approach. In: R. Słowiński (ed.), Intelligent Decision Support - Handbook of Applications and Advances of the Rough Set Theory. Kluwer Academic Publishers, Dordrecht/Boston/London, 1992, pp. 445-456.

[8] Slowinski R.: Rough set learning of preferential attitude in mult-criteria decision making. In: J. Komorowski, Z. W. Ras (eds.), Methodologies for Intelligent Systems, LNAI 689, Springer-Verlag, Berlin, pp. 642-651.

[9] Stefanowski J.: Classification and Decision Supporting based on Rough Set Theory. Foundations of Computing and Decision Sciences, Vol. 18 No. 3-4 (1993), pp. 371-380.

[10] Weiss S. M., Kapouleas I.: An empirical comparison of pattern recognition, neural nets and machine learning classification methods. In: Proceedings Int. Joint Conf. on AI 1989 (ISCAI-89), pp. 781-787

Towards a Parallel Rough Sets Computer

Mieczyslaw Muraszkiewicz

Institute for Computer and Information Engineering, Ltd.
02-793 Warsaw ul. Lokajskiego 16/22, Poland

Henryk Rybinski

Institute for Computer and Information Engineering, Ltd.
02-793 Warsaw ul. Lokajskiego 16/22, Poland

Abstract

A proposal of a parallel computing structure for implementing basic Rough Sets Theory operators as definability, indiscernibility, upper and lower approximation is given. This structure takes a form of a SIMD computer based on cellular arrays which are rectangular matrices and vectors composed of primitive processors.

Keywords: Rough sets, cellular arrays, SIMD machines, rough sets operators

1   Introduction

The Rough Sets Theory (RST) whose foundations and exemplary applications are presented in [8] is a methodology which has demonstrated its usefulness in the context of the various cognitive science processes. In particular, RST has provided an array of tools which turned out to be especially adequate for conceptualization, organization, classification and analysis of the various types of data, especially, when dealing with inexact, uncertain or vague knowledge and when discovering hidden patterns and regularities in applications related to information systems and AI.

On the other hand, all the RST actual applications and prototypes have been implemented on conventional serial computers (sort of von Neumann SISD machines according to the Flynn classification [2]), although a lot of inherent parallelism occurs in the RST algorithms. Hence, a problem addressed in this paper is to establish a certain background for constructing a parallel computing structure, a kind of Parallel Rough Sets Computer (PRSComp), which might be able to perform basic rough sets operations, in particular, those that reduce the redundancy of knowledge, if any. Such a computer has to be equipped with facilities which, *inter alia*, allow us to calculate two fundamental rough sets concepts - a reduct and a core.

Before starting our considerations we need to fix basic notations dealing with matrices. Let $A_{(m,n)}$ be a rectangular matrix composed of m rows and n columns. The set of its column numbers $\{1, 2, \ldots, n\}$ is labelled by *Col*. The matrix element $a_{i,j}, 1 < i < m, 1 < j < n$, occurs in row i and column j, i.e.

$$A_{(m,n)} = \begin{vmatrix} a_{11} & a_{12} & \cdots & a_{1n} \\ a_{21} & a_{22} & \cdots & a_{2n} \\ & & & \\ a_{m1} & a_{m2} & \cdots & a_{mn} \end{vmatrix}$$

We shall also deal with vectors which are particular cases of matrices, i.e.

$$B_{(p)} = \begin{vmatrix} b_1 & b_2 & \cdots & b_p \end{vmatrix}$$

The i-th row of a matrix $A_{m,n}$ can be considered as a vector and is denoted by $A_{i,*}$. We assume that each vector $A_{i,*}$ is given a unique identificator (it might be the matrix row number where the vector comes from) what allows to distinguish vectors even though their respective elements are identical. By binary matrices (vectors) we understand the matrices (vectors) whose all elements take values from the set $\{0, 1\}$. The vectors whose all elements are O's, i.e. $|0\ 0 \ldots 0|$ are called zero-vectors and are marked by 0. If we write $B_p = C_p$ we understand that $b_1 = c_1,\ b_2 = c_2, \ldots, b_p = c_p$.

2 Cellular Arrays

Let us briefly present a structure and functions of a cellular array which is proposed to handle RST notions. More detailed information on cellular networks for processing nonnumeric information is given in [4]. A network of identical elements, called cells, which are organized so that they form a rectangular homogeneous and regular array is referred to as CA (Cellular Array). Fig.1 displays the CA structure wherein one can distinguish $m_* n$ cells arranged in m rows and n columns. The figure includes some registers that will be presented below. Boxes represent cells, lines denote cells' interconnections. Each cell can be connected to its east, south, west and north neighbors, and the cell around the edges of the array are connected to either auxiliary registers which lie outside the array or to fixed external signals.

A cell is assumed to be able to perform the following operations: (1) store one character; (2) set up its status - either transparent or opaque; (3) compare two characters, matching included; (4) move a character to its south neighbor; (5) interchange two characters from the adjacent cells in a column; (6) read-out a character from its memory; (7) write a character into its memory; (8) transfer a bit from its east input to its west output, if a transparent status is set up. A particular operation to be performed is determined by a control signal delivered to the cell from an external control unit (not shown in Fig.1). All the cells are supposed to be supplied with the same control signal, thus they execute the same operation at a time. In other words, CA works as a SIMD machine.

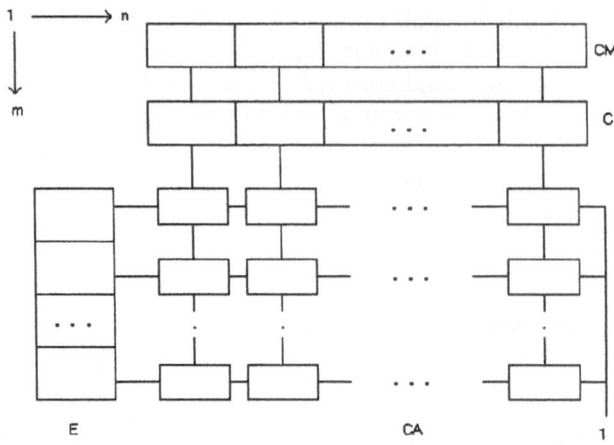

Fig.1

Since the CA is made up of $m * n$ cells and each cell is assumed to be a primitive associative processor that can store in its memory one character, the matrix $A_{m,n}$ may be stored and processed in the array due to a straight mapping between the topology of CA and the layout of the matrix $A_{m,n}$. Once the matrix $A_{m,n}$ is stored in a cellular array we denote it $A[m,n]$; the element a_{ij} is symbolized by $a[i,j]$. Sometimes it is convenient to consider the vector $A_{(i,*)}$ as a word; in this case it is marked as $\underline{a}_i$. Similarly, for the vector $C_{(n)}$ we use the notation $C[n]$ and when it is considered as a word we write $\underline{c}$.

Different registers can be connected to CA. A register can be regarded as a one-column or one-row array. The former is called a vertical register while the latter is referred to as horizontal one. Note, that a word (vector) is the contents of a register. In the sequel a word from the register X will be denoted by x. Now, let us present some registers which are used with CA (cf. Fig.1):

- *column mask register CM* (horizontal) which is used to inhibit the execution of operations in some columns. CM contains a binary vector. The meaning of its elements is as follows: if $cm[j] = 0$ then the j-th column of the $A[m,n]$ matrix is excluded from processing; if $cm[j] = 1$ the j-th column participate in the processing. Later on we shall use the set $\overline{MASK} = \{j|cm[j] = 1, j = 1, \ldots, m\}$

- *comperand register C* (horizontal). We assume that a word from the array can be read-out to C, and vice versa. Physically, the stage output of both C and CM registers are bussed vertically along columns to all rows of the array;

- *word selection register* E (vertical) where the result of comparison of words is injected. It may happen that the register E plays the role of the characteristic register which contains a characteristic vector.

Now, we shall describe a procedure that allows us to compare simultaneously a word kept in the C register with all the words stored in the CA rows.

Given a matrix $A[m,n]$ stored in CA, a vector $C[n]$ stored in the register C and a mask kept in the CM register. One wants to select the words that hold the condition $(c) = \underline{a}_i$ with respect to the mask $\overline{MASK} \subseteq Col$, $i = 1, \ldots, m$, i.e. for each $j \in \overline{MASK} \subseteq Col$ $c[i,j] = a[i,j]$. By a couple we understand a pair $(c[j], a[i,j])$, $i = 1, \ldots, m$; $j = 1, \ldots, n$. Physically, the couple $(c[j], a[i,j])$ is available in the cell whose coordinates are i, j since $a[i,j]$ is stored in this cell and $c[j]$ is delivered also to this cell by means of a vertical bus from the C register.

Routine EXTCOMP $(A[m,n], C[n], E[m])$

(a) Set up $\overline{MASK}$. All the masked couples are consider as transparent and labelled by "t". They are excluded from processing.

(b) A word selection vector $E[m]$ is set up so that the word $00 \ldots 0$ is written into it.

(c) Within each non-transparent couple matching involving couple's elements is performed. Matching is done in parallel in all the couples. If $c[j] = a[i,j]$ then a couple is considered as transparent and labelled by "t" and the couples cell becomes horizontally transparent for incoming signals; otherwise it is called opaque and marked with "o" and cannot transmit any horizontal incoming signals.

(d) A constant signal fixed at 1 at the right edge of CA, (cf. Fig.2) is generated and transmitted horizontally through all the transparent cells. If all the cells in the i-th row are transparent this signal injects 1 to $e[i]$. If at least one cell in a row is opaque nothing is injected to the corresponding position of the E register. Thus, for $i = 1, \ldots, m$:

$$e[i] = \begin{cases} 1, & \text{if } \underline{c} = \underline{a}_i \quad \text{with respect to } \overline{MASK} \\ 0, & \text{otherwise.} \end{cases}$$

It is worth mentioning that the proposed method exhibits associative features and belong to the class of fully parallel algorithms (parallel-by-character, parallel-by-word). One can notice that EXTCOMP can be easily modified to cover other types of comparison $(>, \geq, <, \leq, , \neq)$ [4].

3 Rough Set Notions by Matrices

In this Section we shall show how some basic RST notions can be expressed in terms of matrices and vectors. We assume here that one is familiar with Rough Sets Theory [7, 8], therefore, we feel there is no need to recall its fundamental concepts.

Given a matrix $A_{(m,n)}$ we can take into account the so called *matrix universe* that is the set U composed of vectors being the rows of the matrix. Hence,

$$U = \{A_{i,*} | i = 1, 2, \ldots, m\}$$

It has to be noted that even if two or more vectors have identical respective elements they are considered as distinct items since they have different identificators. Let $X \subseteq U$. We say that $B_m(X))$ is a *characteristic vector* of X against $A_{(m,n)}$ if

$$b_1(X) = \begin{cases} 1 & \text{for } i \text{ such that } A_{(i,*)} \subseteq X \\ 0 & \text{otherwise.} \end{cases}$$

We can also talk about the set of matrix rows determined by a characteristic vector. Given a matrix $A_{(m,n)}$ and a characteristic vector $C_{(m)}(Y)$, it follows form the above that Y is given as

$$Y = \{A_{(i,*)} | c_i(Y) = 1, i = 1, 2, \ldots, m\}.$$

The operation of determining Y from its characteristic vector $C_{(m)}(Y)$ is to be referred to as $SET(C_{(m)}(Y))$.

Let U be defined as above for the matrix $A_{(m,n)}$. We recall that the set of its column numbers $\{1, 2, \ldots, n\}$ is labelled by it Col. With every subset of columns $R \subseteq Col$, a binary relation $IND(R)$, *called an indiscernibility relation* is associated and defined as follows:

$$IND(R) = \{(A_{(i,*)}, A_{(j,*)}) \in U | \text{ forevery } k \in R, a_{i,k} = a_{j,k}; i = 1, \ldots, m;$$
$$j = 1, \ldots, n\}.$$

It should be noted that $IND(R)$ is an equivalence relation. The matrix rows satisfying the relation $IND(R)$ are indiscernible by columns whose numbers are from R. For simplicity, if it does not cause confusion, we shall identify R and the corresponding relation $IND(R)$. We shall refer to the R relation as the relation over the matrix $A_{(m,n)}$.

Now, we define some auxiliary operation on matrices and vectors.

(a) Given binary vectors $C_{(p)}$ and $D_{(p)}$. The positional sum of binary vectors is a binary vector $B_{(p)}$ such that

$$B_{(p)} = C_{(p)} + D_{(p)} \Leftrightarrow b_{(i)} = \begin{cases} 0 & \text{if } c_i = 0 \text{ and } d_i = 0 \\ 1 & \text{otherwise.} \end{cases}$$

(b) Given binary vectors $C_{(p)}$ and $D_{(p)}$. The *positional product* of binary vectors is a binary vector $B_{(p)}$ such that

$$B_{(p)} = C_{(p)} * D_{(p)} \Leftrightarrow b_i = \begin{cases} 0 & \text{if } c_i = 0 \text{ or } d_i = 0 \\ 1 & \text{otherwise.} \end{cases}$$

(c) Given a matrix $A_{(m,n)}$, the set of its column numbers $R \subseteq Col$, an indiscernibility relation $IND(R)$ over this matrix and a vector $C_{(n)}$. The *parallel comparison* (of the vector with all the rows of the matrix) is a binary vector $B_{(m)}$ such that, for $i = 1, 2, \ldots, m$

$$B_{(m)} = A_{(m,n)} \top_R C_{(n)} \Leftrightarrow b_i = \begin{cases} 1 & \text{if } DA_{(i,*)} R C_{(n)} \\ 0 & \text{otherwise.} \end{cases}$$

Having defined basic notions and operations on matrices and vectors we can determine the operations corresponding to Pawlak's rough set concepts.

Basic category
Given a matrix $A_{(m,n)}$, indiscernibility relation $IND(R)$ over this matrix and a vector $A_{(i,*)}$, $1 \leq i \leq m$. We say that a *basic category* generated by $A_{(i,*)}$ over the matrix $A_{(m,n)}$, called $BCAT(A_{(i,*)})$, is a subset of the matrix rows obtained in the following way
$$BCAT(A_{(i,*)}) = SET(A_{(m,n)} \top_R A_{(i,*)}).$$

Having $BCAT$ operation at one's disposal it is easy to determine all the basic categories within the matrix $A_{(m,n)}$. It can be done by performing a sequence

$$BCAT(A_{(1,*)}), BCAT(A_{(2,*)}), \ldots, BCAT(A_{(m,*)}).$$

Upper approximation
Let $X \subseteq U$, where U is the universe of $A_{(m,n)}$ and $IND(R)$ be an indiscernibility relation over U. The characteristic vector of X is $B_{(m)}(X)$. The definition of the *R-upper approximation of X* says

$$\overline{R}X = \{BCAT(A_{(i,*)}) | BCAT(A_{(i,*)}) \cap X \neq \emptyset\}$$

The procedure to calculate RX is as follows.

Procedure_Upper_Approximation

1. Generate the characteristic vector of X against $A_{(m,n)}$, i.e. to calculate $B_{(m)}(X)$.

2. Determine all the basic categories and to generate their characteristic vectors against $A_{(m,n)}$

$$B_{(m)}(BCAT(A_{(1,*)})), B_{(m)}(BCAT(A_{(2,*)})), \ldots, B_{(m)}(BCAT(A_{(m,*)}))$$

3. Calculate the following positional products $P_{(m)}(i), i = 1, 2, \ldots, m$

$$P_{(m)}(1) = B_{(m)}(X) * B_{(m)}(BCAT(A_{(1,*)}))$$

$$P_{(m)}(2) = B_{(m)}(X) * B_{(m)}(BCAT(A_{(2,*)}))$$

$$\ldots$$

$$P_{(m)}(m) = B_{(m)}(X) * B_{(m)}(BCAT(A_{(m,*)}))$$

4. Calculate the positional sum of all the basic categories characteristic vectors such that the corresponding $P_{(m)}(i)$ vectors are not zero-vectors. We shall use a shorthand notation

$$B_{(m)}(BCAT(A_{(i,*)}))/P_{(m)}(i) = \begin{cases} B_{(m)}(BCAT(A_{(i,*)})), & \text{if } P_{(m)}(i) \neq 0 \\ 0 & \text{otherwise} \end{cases}$$

The result is a characteristic vector of the set being the upper approximation of X

$$\begin{aligned} B_{(m)}(\overline{R}X) \quad = \quad & B_{(m)}(BCAT(A_{(1,*)}))/P_{(m)}(1) + \\ & B_{(m)}(BCAT(A_{(2,*)}))/P_{(m)}(2) + \\ & \dots + \\ & B_{(m)}(BCAT(A_{(m,*)}))/P_{(m)}(m) \end{aligned}$$

5. Determine the R-upper approximation of X

$$\overline{R}X = SET(B_{(m)}(\overline{R}X)).$$

$\square$

Lower Approximation
The definition of the *R-lower approximation of X* says

$$\underline{R}X = \{BCAT(A_{(i,*)})|BCAT(A_{(i,*)}) \subseteq X\}$$

The procedure to calculate the RX is as follows.

Procedure_Low_Approximation

1. Generate the characteristic vector of X against $A_{(m,n)}$, i.e. to calculate $B_{(m)}(X)$.

2. Determine all the basic categories and to generate their characteristic vectors against $A_{(m,n)}$

$$B_{(m)}(BCAT(A_{(1,*)})), B_{(m)}(BCAT(A_{(2,*)})), \dots, B_{(m)}(BCAT(A_{(m,*)}))$$

3. Calculate the following positional sums $S_{(m)}(i), i = 1, 2, \dots, m$

$$S_{(m)}(1) = B_{(m)}(X) + B_{(m)}(BCAT(A_{(1,*)}))$$

$$S_{(m)}(2) = B_{(m)}(X) + B_{(m)}(BCAT(A_{(2,*)}))$$

$$\dots$$

$$S_{(m)}(3) = B_{(m)}(X) + B_{(m)}(BCAT(A_{(m,*)}))$$

4. Calculate the positional sum of all the basic categories characteristic vectors such that they are equal to the corresponding $S_{(m)}(i)$ vectors. The result is a characteristic vector of the set being the R-lower approximation of X

$$
\begin{aligned}
B_{(m)}(\underline{R}X) = \ & B_{(m)}(BCAT(A_{(1,*)}))S_{(m)}(1) + \\
& B_{(m)}(BCAT(A_{(2,*)}))S_{(m)}(2) + \\
& \ldots + \\
& B_{(m)}(BCAT(A_{(m,*)}))S_{(m)}(m)
\end{aligned}
$$

5. Determine the R-lower approximation of X

$$
\underline{R}X = SET(B_{(m)}(\underline{R}X)).
$$

□

Definability

Given the matrix $A_{(m,n)}$ and an indiscernibility relation $IND(R)$ over the matrix universe U. Let $X \subseteq U$ be a set. We say that the set X is *definable* in $A_{(m,n)}$ with respect to R if $\underline{R}X = \overline{R}X$.

Procedure_Definability

1. Calculate $\underline{R}X$ by executing the **Procedure_Low_Approximation**

2. Calculate $\overline{R}X$ by executing the **Procedure_Upper_Approximation**

3. if $\underline{R}X = \overline{R}X$ then **X is definable** otherwise X **is not definable** □

Dispensability

A column $j \in R \subseteq Col$ is dispensable in R if

$$
IND(R) = IND(R - \{j\})
$$

otherwise j is indispensable in R, where $IND(R)$ be an indiscernibility relation over U.

Procedure Dispensability

1. Set up the row index $i = 1$.

2. Calculate $B_{(m)} = A_{(m,n)} \top_R A_{(i,n)}$

3. Calculate $C_{(m)} = A_{(m,n)} \top_{R-\{j\}} A_{(i,n)}$

4. if $B_{(m)} \neq C_{(m)}$ then **{j} is indispensable, stop** otherwise go to p.5

5. if $i < m$ then increase i by 1 and go to p.2 otherwise **{j} is dispensable,**

□

Let us remind that $R \subseteq Col$ is *independent* if every column from R is indispensable in R. A set $R \subseteq Col$ is called a *reduct* in Col if R is independent in Col and $IND(R) = IND(\overline{C}ol)$. The set of all independent columns in Col is called the *core* of Col. Needless to argue that on the basis of the above dispensability procedure one can establish procedures to calculate reducts and cores which are central notions of the Rough Set Theory [8].

4 Implementation of the RST Operators

For the sake of simplicity and lucidity we limit ourselves to the matrices and vectors composed of entries being characters, i.e. for the matrix $A_{(m,n)}$ all the elements a_{ij} are characters rather than strings of characters.

Routine BasicCAT$(A[m, n], i, E[m])$ /* *Basic category* */
/* The E register contains the characteristic vector that indicates the words belonging to the basic category generated by $\underline{a_i}$ */

$\overline{MASK}$

$C[n] := \underline{a_i}$

$EXTCOMP(A[m, n], C[n], E[m])$

Routine UpperAPPROX $(A[m, n], B[m], C[m])$ /* *Upper approximation* */
/* $B[m]$ stores the characteristic vector of the set X */
/* $C[m]$ the characteristic vector of the upper approximation of X */

for $i = 1$ to m $BasicCAT(A[m, n], i, E_i[m])$

for $i = 1$ to m $E_i[m] := E_i[m] * B[m]$; $C[m] := 0$

for $i = 1$ to m if $E_i[m] \neq 0$ then $C[m] := C[m] + E_i[m]$

Routine LowerAPPROX$(A[m, n], B[m], C[m])$ hfill /* *Lower approx.* */

/* $B[m]$ stores the characteristic vector of the set X */
/* $C[m]$ characteristic vector of the upper approximation of X */

for $i = 1$ to m $BasicCAT(A[m, n], i, E_i)$

for $i = 1$ to m $S_i[m] := E_i[m] + B[m]$; $C[m] := 0$

for $i = 1$ to m if $E_i[m] = S_i[m]$ then $C[m] := C[m] + E_i[m]$

RoutineDef $(A[m, n], B[m])$ /* *Definability* */

/* $B[m]$ stores the characteristic vector of the set X */

UpperAPPROX $(A[m, n], B[m], C[m])$
LowerAPPROX $(A[m, n], B[m], C'[m])$
if $C[m] = C'[m]$ then *the set X is definable*

Routine Indispensable$(A[m, n], j)$ /* *Indispensability* */
/* j indicates the column number to be checked out */

for $i = 1$ to m
begin
   $\overline{MASK}$
   BasicCAT $(A[m, n], i, B[m])$

$\overline{MASK} - \{j\})$
BasicCAT $(A[m,n], i, C[m])$
if $B[m] \neq C[m]$ then $\{j\}$ is **indispensable**
end

It has to be stressed that the routines presented above are supposed to be implemented by the appropriate use of the registers co-operating with the CA rather than by a software program. All the operations executed at the array and register levels are performed in parallel.

5 Final Remarks

The objective of this paper was to set up a methodology for the Parallel Rough Sets Computer design which in practical terms means that we were supposed to propose a fully parallel method for implementing basic Rough Sets Theory notions. To this end, we used the cellular arrays which offer homogeneous computing structures working in parallel. The arrays are main building blocks of the proposed PRSComp architecture.

References

[1] E.F. Codd, "Relational Completeness of Data Base Sublanguages", in: R.Rustin, **Courant Computer Science Symposium 6** - Data Base Systems, Prentice- Hall Inc., 1972, pp.65-98.

[2] M.J. Flynn, "Some Computer Organizations and their Effectivness", **IEEE Trans. on Comp.**, 9 (1972) pp.948-960.

[3] D. Maier, The Theory of Relational Databases, Computer Science Press Inc., 1983.

[4] M. Muraszkiewicz, Sieci komorkowe do przetwarzania danych nienumerycznych, Prace IINTE, no.52, 1984.

[5] M. Muraszkiewicz, "Cellular Array Architecture for Relational Database Implementation", **Future Generations Computer Systems**, 4(1988) pp.31-38.

[6] M. Muraszkiewicz, H. Rybinski, Parallel Implementation of Basic Rough Sets Notions in Cellular Arrays, Bulletin of PAS, Tech. Sciences, 2(1992), pp.165-177.

[7] Z. Pawlak, Systemy informacyjne, WNT, Warszawa, 1983

[8] Z. Pawlak, Rough sets: Theoretical aspects of reasoning about data, Kluwer, 1991.

Learning Conceptual Design Rules: A Rough Sets Approach

Tomasz Arciszewski

Department of Systems Engineering, George Mason University
Fairfax, VA 22030, USA

Wojciech Ziarko

Department of Computer Science, University of Regina
Regina, Saskatchewan, Canada S4S 0A2

Tariq L. Khan

Department of Civil Engineering, Wayne State University
Detroit, MI 48202, USA

Abstract

The paper presents the results of a feasibility study conducted in the area of learning conceptual design rules governing the selection of wind bracing components in steel skeleton structures of tall buildings. The study's objectives were to compare decision rules produced by different learning systems using the same body of examples, and to formally verify these rules using the overall empirical error rate. The study was conducted using two learning systems, both based on the theory of rough sets: 1) System ROUGH which usually produces a large number of complex deterministic rules, 2) System DataLogic which can generate probabilistic rules, relatively simple and much fewer in number than in the case of ROUGH. All experiments were conducted using a collection of 374 examples of minimum weight (optimal) design of wind bracings in steel skeleton structures of tall buildings. The examples were prepared under identical design assumptions for a three bay skeleton structure of a tall building. They were produced using SODA, a computer software package for the analysis, design and optimization of steel structures. The paper gives a description of the learning experiments performed. It also provides a comparison of decision rules produced by DataLogic and Rough, and an analysis of empirical error rates obtained for the various collection of examples for ROUGH.

1 Introduction

Conceptual design of wind bracings in steel skeleton structures of tall buildings is usually understood as a process of selecting various structural components, such as rigid frames, vertical or horizontal trusses, etc., which will be used together in a wind bracing in a given design case[2]. This process is still poorly understood, and there is little knowledge available, which could be used by a designer to make optimal decisions in conceptual design. The manual acquisition of conceptual design knowledge is in this case very difficult, if not impossible, because of the complexity of the structural problems involved and

Attribute Value	1	2	3	4	5
Number of Stories	6	12	18	24	30
Bay Length	20	30			
Wind Intensity	Low	High			
Static Character of Joints	Rigid	Hinge	Mixed		
Number of Bays Occupied by Bracing	1	2	3		
Number of Vertical Trusses	0	1	2	3	
Number of Horizontal Trusses	0	1	2	3	
Steel Unit Weight	Low	Medium	High		

Table 1: Knowledge Representation Space

secrecy surrounding details of the design of tall buildings. For these reasons, the automated knowledge acquisition, based on the use of machine learning and learning from examples of optimal minimum weight designs, is an attractive approach to acquiring design knowledge and to improve the present state of the art in the designing of wind bracings in tall buildings. Design knowledge is understood here as a system of relationships among various groups of attributes describing a given wind bracing. These relationships are decision rules which could be used to guide the designer in the conceptual design to make correct decisions regarding the configuration of a wind bracing.

In th paper, the results of a feasibility study are reported. The study was conducted using two learning systems, both based on the theory of rough sets, and its objective was to compare decision rules produced by both systems using the same body of examples, and to formally verify these rules using the overall empirical error rate.

2   Knowledge Representation

Knowledge representation used in the feasibility study contains three classes of nominal attributes and their values which describe wind bracings in the steel skeleton structures of the tall buildings[1]. The attributes were developed for the most common three-bay skeleton structures. The first class can be considered as a description of the building for which a given bracing is designed and is called "design requirements". The second class is a description of the wind bracing structural system. These two classes of attributes constitute together a collection of independent attributes. The third class of attributes contains in our case only one dependent attribute which is called "Unit Steel Weight". This attribute provides an evaluation of the unit steel weight of a given wind bracing for the design case considered. All attributes and their values are given in the Table 1.

The class of design requirements contains three attributes: 1. Number of stories, 2. Bay length, and 3. Wind intensity. The first two attributes are self-explanatory, while the third attribute identifies the location of the building with respect to the wind zones and it has two values for low and high wind intensity zones respectively.

The description of the wind bracing structural system is based on four attributes: 1. Static character of joints, 2. Number of bays occupied by bracing, 3. Number of vertical trusses, and 4. Number of horizontal trusses. The first attribute describes the joints in bracing in terms of their ability to carry bending moments and has such values as rigid, pinned, or mixed. The second attribute describes the width of bracing in terms of the number of bays entirely occupied by the bracing. The last two attributes identify the existence and number of vertical and horizontal trusses in the bracing respectively.

The dependent attribute "Unit Steel Weight", identifies the relative unit weight of the wind bracing structural system. For individual building heights unit weights are considered and normalized. The unit weights in three ranges [0, 0.33], [0.34, 0.66], and [0.67, 1] are considered low, medium, and high, respectively.

3   Knowledge Acquisition Tools

Two knowledge acquisition tools from REDUCT Systems, Inc. were used in the experiments described. Both tools are based on the theory of rough sets[3]. The tools are PC-based and they are aimed at analysis and modeling of inter-attribute relationships in attribute-value systems, which are also called information systems. The tools have been developed as a result of research on machine learning applications of the rough sets methodology[5]. They accept a two dimensional table in an attribute-value format whose rows represent objects of interest (e.g. cases of different design solutions for wind bracings) in terms of attribute values. The user can subsequently analyze the dependency between a selected group of "condition" attributes and a "decision" attribute. The condition attributes usually reflect some important features of the objects whereas the decision attribute typically represents an outcome of the interest, the unit steel weight of the wind bracing in our case. The dependency analysis is done entirely automatically by the system. The dependency can be either functional or probabilistic in nature. The result of the analysis is a collection of simple logical expressions in the form of minimized production rules i.e.: If <condition> then <decision>, which have probability p added in the case of DataLogic system producing probabilistic rules. The simplicity and the "strength" of the rules expressed as number of matching table rows are usually proportional to the degree of the relationship existing between condition attributes and the decision attribute. Although, because of poor quality of data it many happen that not all the identified rules are strong or useful, the system presents the user with a collection of potentially valuable discovered logical patterns which, otherwise, left unnoticed. The discovered "rules" are subject to further improvement and verification, and can be treated as machine-generated hypotheses about properties of population of all potential objects belonging to a specific domain.

4   Knowledge Acquisition

The experiments with learning tools have been conducted using the collection of 376 examples of optimal, minimum weight designs of wind bracings in steel

Learning System	336 examples	374 examples
ROUGH	41	49
DataLogic	3	4

Table 2: Comparison of Number of Decision Rules

skeleton structures of tall buildings. Individual examples represented various types of wind bracings in the height range of 6 to 30 stories, and all wind bracings were designed under the identical assumptions for the same three-bay skeleton structure of a tall building. All examples were prepared using SODA, a computer software system for the analysis, design, and optimization of steel structures.

Two learning systems were used as knowledge acquisition tools, which are described in the Section 3, "Knowledge Acquisition Tools". Both learning systems were used to produce decision rules from two collections of examples. The first collection contained 336 examples, while the second one - 374 examples. The first collection was prepared in the Civil Engineering Department at Wayne State University during the last two years, while the second one was created adding to the available examples another 38 examples, which were developed as a part of the research reported in this paper.

Two experiments were conducted with each learning using both collections of examples. The comparison of the numbers of decision rules obtained in individual cases is given in Table 2.

In terms of the number of decision rules, there is a significant difference between results obtained using ROUGH and DataLogic. The first system produces only deterministic rules, and therefore a large number of such rules is necessary to deal with a complex engineering problem. DataLogic, however, has an ability to produce probabilistic rules, which are valid only for the majority of examples, but are much simpler and easier to interpret than deterministic rules. For example, when decision rules for the determination of the normalized steel unit weight are considered for the attribute nominal value **HIGH**, the following results were obtained:

ROUGH System:
Unit Steel Weight (Attribute H) = **HIGH**
if:
Attribute B = 2 and
Attribute D = 1 or D =3
Attribute A = 1 or A =5
Attribute E = 1 or E = 2 or E=3

DataLogic System:
Unit Steel Weight (Attribute H) = **HIGH**
if:
Attribute A = 1 and
Attribute F = 1

The interpretation of the first decision rule is quite complex. The second rule is valid only in 68% of cases considered, but its engineering interpretation is quite simple: in the case of a 6-story skeleton structure with wind bracing in the form of a rigid frame, the heigh steel unit weight should be expected.

At present, the available results are insufficient to identify all engineering advantages and disadvantages of the deterministic and probabilistic decision rules. However, our initial experience indicates, that both types are useful for the decision making purposes. The probabilistic decision rules could be particularly useful when the time factor is involved and only "rough classification" is sufficient.

5 Knowledge Verification

Knowledge produced as the result of all four experiments has been verified using the overall empirical error rate as an estimator of the actual error rate for the entire population of examples. This error rate was found particularly appropriate for the engineering applications of machine learning[1], and it provides the most global evaluation of the knowledge produced. The overall error rates were calculated using the "Leave-One-Out" resampling method, in accordance to the technique described in [4] for the decision rules produced by ROUGH. The error rate was 4.5% for 336 examples, and 13.3% for all 374 examples considered.

In the case of experiments reported, the error rates were significantly worse for the larger collection of examples, and this result was unexpected. However, the close examination of examples revealed, that the collection of 38 examples prepared as a part of our research, and which were added to an existing collection of examples, contained several incorrect examples. These examples affected the quality of the decision rules produced, and resulted in the relatively poor error rates.

6 Conclusions

The conducted feasibility study demonstrated the applicability of the rough sets-based learning systems to learning conceptual design rules. The domain in which experiments were conducted is particularly complex and it is still poorly understood. However, the results of learning in the form of decision rules are acceptable for the domain experts, and the formal verification of the obtained knowledge indicates that the rough sets-based learning of design rules should be useful for a large class of design problems. Much more research should be conducted to study the deterministic versus probabilistic decision rules in the context of engineering, and this work is planned.

7 Acknowledgments

The research reported in this paper was supported in part by an operating grant from Natural Sciences and Engineering Research Council of Canada. The permission to use the knowledge acquisition tools from Reduct Systems Inc., Regina, Canada, is gratefully acknowledged.

References

[1] Arciszewski T., Bloedorn E., Michalski R.S., Wnek J., *Machine Learning of Design Rules: A Case Study in the Automated Acquisition of Design Rules for Wind Bracings in Tall Buildings*, The ASCE *Journal of Computing in Civil Engineering*, in print.

[2] Mustafa M., Arciszewski T., *Inductive Learning of Wind Bracing Design for Tall Buildings*, Chapter, in the book *Knowledge Acquisition in Civil Engineering*, edited by T. Arciszewski and L. Rossman, American Society of Civil Engineers, 1992.

[3] Pawlak Z., *Rough Sets*, International Journal of Computer and Information Sciences, Academic press Limited, Vol. 5, No. 11, 1982.

[4] Weiss S.M., Kulikowski, C.A., *Computer Systems that Learn: Classification and Prediction Methods from Statistics, Neural Nets, Machine Learning, and Expert Systems*, Morgan Kaufman Publishers, 1991.

[5] Ziarko W., *Data Analysis and Case-Based Expert System Development Tool ROUGH*, Proceedings of Case-Based Reasoning Workship, Pensacola Beach, Florida, 1989.

Intelligent Control System Implementation to the Pipe Organ Instrument [1]

Bozena Kostek

Sound Engineering Department, Technical University of Gdansk
Gdansk, Poland

Abstract

The main mechanism differences between mechanic and electrical control of pipe organs were reviewed. It was shown that the mechanism features influenced the acquired pipe sound quality. A review of computer modeling methods applied to the verification of experiments results was presented. The methods of knowledge acquisition employed to the musical signals were shown. The intelligent control system of the pipe organ was proposed and its conceptual background was shortly presented. Some conclusions concerning the implementation of artificial intelligence methods in musical signal domain were derived.

1 Introduction

As most of pipe organs is built nowadays with an electrical action, thus there is a need to design the organ control system in such a way that it would allow for playing with musical articulation. Effective use of such an instrument requires controllers that transform the musicians' artistic intention into parameters of the nonlinear servo system. Contrarily to the mechanical tracker actions, an electromagnetic valve being the main part of an electric control reacts always in the same way, namely equally fast opens and closes the flow of the air [1]. Thus, the organists cannot obtain the desired musical effects and consequently, in musicians' opinion even the best tuned organs are hardly to compare to classic pipe instruments having the mechanical tracker action. That is the reason for paradoxical situations when the newly built organs with an electrical action have to be rebuilt to the mechanically controlled ones.

2 Problem Description

Traditional, mechanical control systems of organs allow for the use of subtle techniques of playing defined by the musicians as the articulation. The mechanical tracker action provides the simplest form of the organ control systems (Figure 1).

[1]Research N 8 S503 028 06 sponsored by the Committee for Scientific Research, Warsaw, Poland

451

The key (1) being depressed, rises the back end and lift the vertical sticker (2), then in turn the bridge (3) pulls the tracker (4). The last one opens a pallet (5) and the wind is admitted to groove (6) for the note concerned.

From both the performers' and the audience viewpoint this is the only control system that allows for the use of musical techniques, called by musicians the articulation. In practice, the musical articulation might be shortly described as the way of how the key was depressed. The resulting sounds patterns differ from each other in cases of slow and fast depressing a key.

That is why, the starting point of this research was the fact that the articulation phenomena proven to be wide recognized feature among musicians, however its influence on the parameters of the pipe organ sound was not fully explained before.

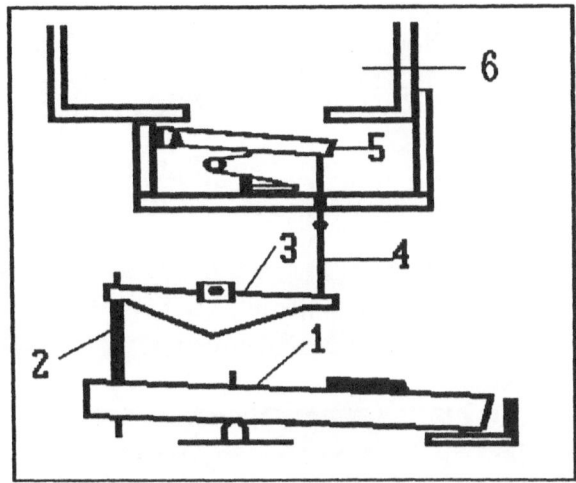

Figure 1 Block diagram of the main mechanisms of mechanical tracker action.

3 Analysis of the Pipe Organ Sound

Basing on the recent research performed by the author, many conclusions were drawn out concerning the articulation phenomena in the pipe sound [1], [2]. Main parameters determining these phenomena were discovered basing on the complex computer analysis of the pipe sound of instruments belonging to different historical epochs. These analyses employed a variety of software tools such as time-domain and spectral as well as sonagraph and LPC (Linear Predictive Coding) analyses. An exemplary time-domain analysis of the pipe organ sound is shown in Figure 2. Additionally, a computer model based on the analytical description of sound rise in pipes was designed and then carefully examined [3]. Moreover, in order to examine the articulation phenomena more precisely, the computer model of an electrical equivalent network of an organ action was built and examined on the basis of the acoustic-electrical analogy [3]. Also, practical work was carried out in the domain of the pipe organ control [1]. However, a new type of an electronic pipe organ control system was not fully conceived, yet.

a.
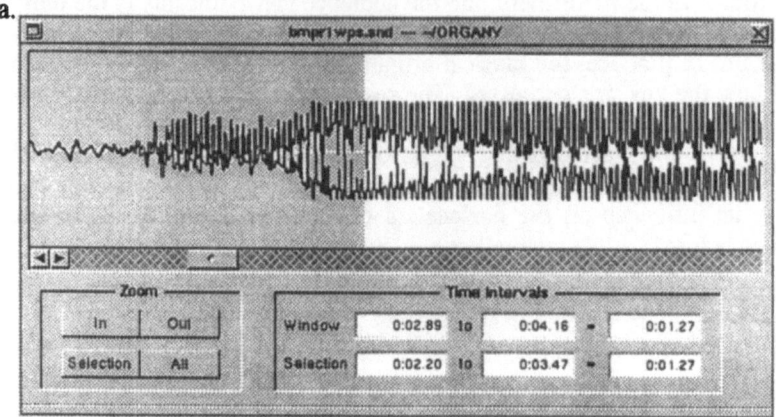

b.
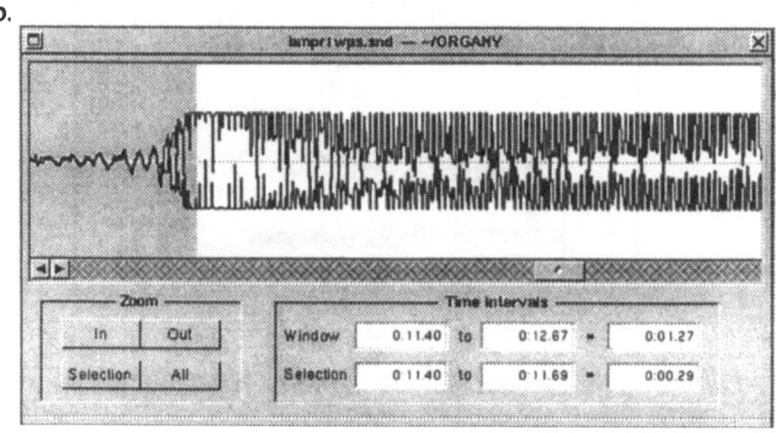

Figure 2 Time-domain analysis of the pipe organ sound:
a. the case of slow depressing a key,
b. the case of fast depressing a key.

4 Knowledge Acquisition

The subtlety of playing on the organ using musical articulation however visible in the computer analysis of a pipe sound needs more complex examination. A learning algorithm seems to be an appropriate tool for this study. An implementation of the neural network may be used first in the knowledge acquisition process.

The task to acquire knowledge on transient states of musical signal demands building patterns of the musical articulation in the pipe sound, at first. A block diagram shown in Figure 3 illustrates all stages of this process. First, a variety of pipe sounds should be acquired from different organs having mechanical tracker actions and stored in the computer hard disk. As the articulation phenomena occur mostly at the sound attack transients, thus the steady state and the ending transient of the sound might be cut off. Subsequently, the feature vector extraction should take place in order to diminish the stream of the input data. The feature extraction using time- or frequency-domain description of the transient signal such as speed of time-envelope rising or the presence of overblown phenomenon and others may represent a few parameters that are to form input data of the learning system.

The next step is the neural net training process with the back propagation algorithm implemented (Figure 4). However, human reference decisions are needed in this process. At the output of the neural network the reference indices of the musical articulation are to be obtained. The task to be solved next is to recognize the articulation features in the parameterized fragments of pipe organ music. Properly trained neural net can assist human decision during the analysis of organ sound.

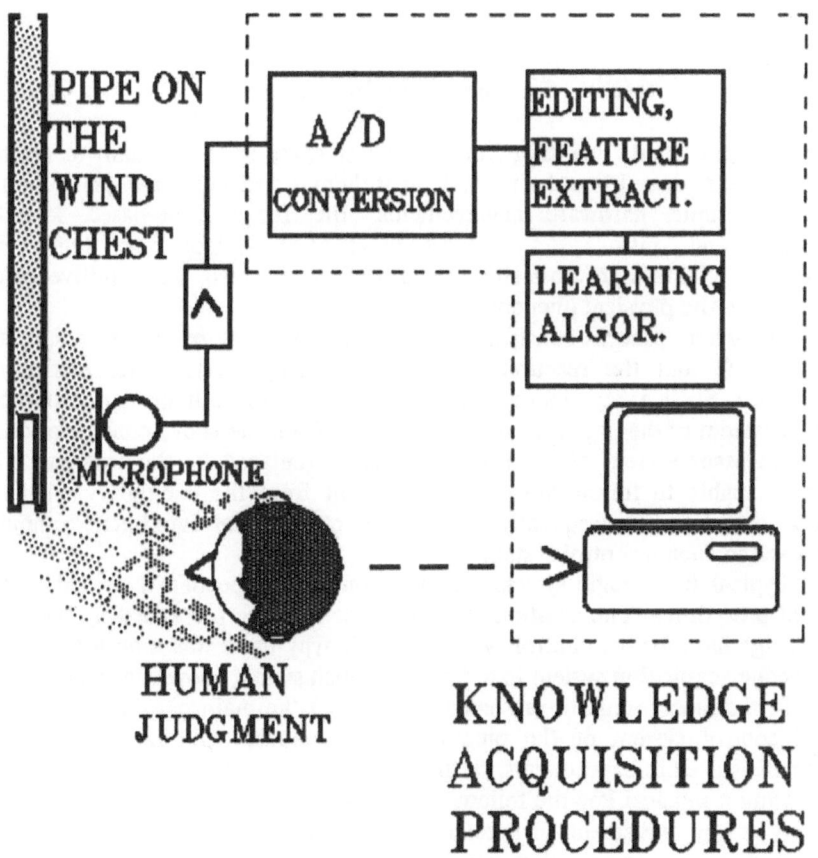

Figure 3 Block diagram of the musical sound acquisition and analyzing system.

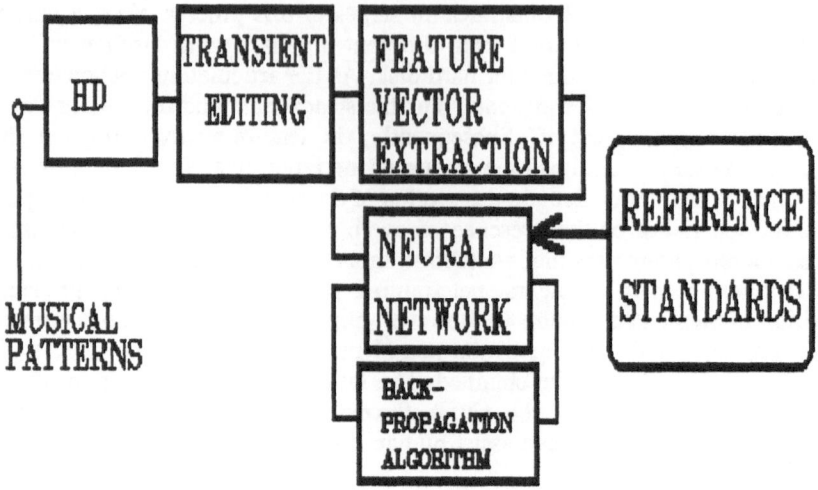

Figure 4   Neural network training phase.

5 Fuzzy Control of the Valve

New technical trends resulting from the latest study in the domain of electronic control were reviewed in order to implement them to the pipe organ [4]. Among the latest electronic hardware achievements, the fuzzy logic-based knowledge acquisition and control system seems to be an adequate tool. Fuzzy logic being a technically viable and cost-effective discipline is also an intuitive way of approaching the physical phenomena.

The whole process consisting of depressing the key by the musician, sound rise in pipe and the reaction of the valve escapes any exact mathematical description. Such a description might form a basis to built up a microprocessor control system of the organ. However, as results from the above considerations, the microprocessor system of the organ should be replaced by the learning control system capable to follow non-linearities learnt from the exemplary entries and related decisions. Consequently, some kind of artificial intelligence should be employed in such a control system.

Typical fuzzy logic systems use the domain-independent knowledge for the control procedures. The creation of fuzzy rules must be preceeded by building up knowledge base for the control system. That is why there was a need to built up a knowledge acquisition system in order to establish such a knowledge base.

In the block diagram presented in Figure 5 the main parts of a fuzzy logic-based control system of the pipe organ are shown. The modern synthesizer keyboard is used in experiments. In this particular case when examining the way of depressing a musical key the following parameters can be observed: either time or velocity of key movement, or acceleration. The MIDI keyboard ability to generate MIDI code including so called velocity parameter is exploited. A sensor under the keyboard picks up the signal correlated to the way of depressing the musical key and in the same time transforms it into the system input signal. The information from the sensor is processed and is encoded in the MIDI stream of data. An 8-bit word is used to express the velocity value in the MIDI standard.

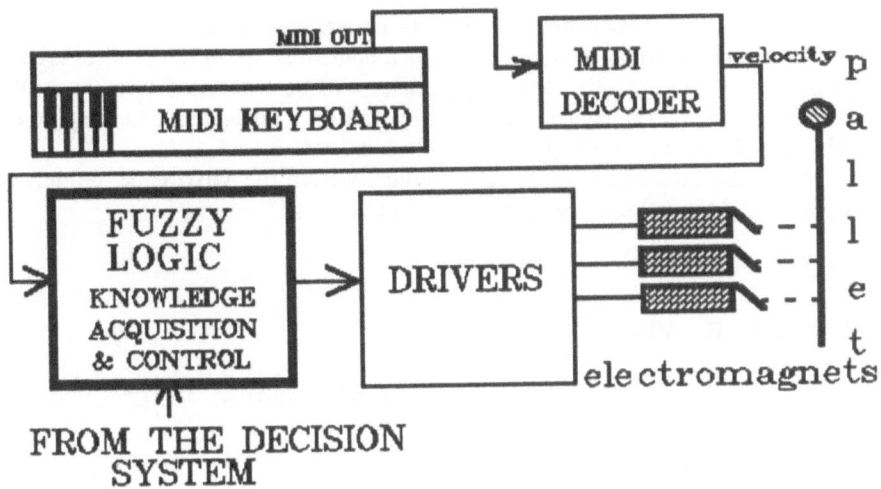

Figure 5 Fuzzy logic based control system of the pipe organ.

The information related to the musical key number may be also essential because of the dependence existing between the size of the pipe and the articulation features. Traditional, mechanical organs enable the articulation mostly in low tones. The sound rise in large pipes may be slow or fast, so it is possible to hear the differences in the articulated sounds. Small pipes are excited by the wind blow very quickly and always speak in the same way.

The above information, namely concerning the key number and velocity is to be decoded by the computer through the special MIDI decoding procedure. The obtained values are periodically transmitted to the fuzzy logic control system derived to control the electromagnetic valve according to the rules reflecting the non-linearity of the control task. Transistor drivers are used to amplify the electromagnets current. As it is shown in the Figure 5, three electromagnets are applied to drive the pallet of each big pipe. According to the rules of the fuzzy system, individual electromagnets are switched on in the sequence defined by the fuzzy rule system.

The main problem faced during the building up the control system is the selection of its rules. Only people having so called "musical ear" can easily detect the articulation phenomena and the artistic musical performance escapes any formal mathematical description. Hence, the idea that occurs when looking at the problem is to use the human judgment to define each kind of the articulation feature. In such a case, the knowledge base is built according to the semantic description, for example the expressions such as: slow, medium and high speed of

456

rise of sound are to be employed. Then, the selection of the the numerical ranges corresponding to the above definitions should take place in the fuzzy control system. Such numerical expression of the semantic description might be set experimentally and may serve as the initial tuning of the whole control system. Final tuning is to be made experimentally with the assistance of the sound analyzing tools.

The fuzzy logic procedures are used to determine the desired system output states. These signals are subsequently sent as a control states to the electromagnetic stepping valve. Subsequently, any keying rates will be translated into the way of opening the valve, and in consequence into the building air pressure in the pipe that is decisive to the rising sound quality.

Two parameters being extracted periodically from the MIDI code, namely the key number and the velocity create two fuzzy inputs:

INPUTS:

KEY_NUMBER; VELOCITY,

and outputs are associated with the current sequence in the individual electromagnet coils:

OUTPUTS:

SLOW_SEQUENCE; MEDIUM_SEQUENCE; FAST_SEQUENCE.

The fuzzifiers may be named as follows:

FUZZIFIERS:

for KEY_NUMBER: - ELIGIBLE
                - NONELIGIBLE

for VELOCITY: - SLOW
              - MEDIUM
              - FAST

The inputs and fuzzifiers are producing terms that are used in the following exemplary rules:

EXEMPLARY RULES:

if KEY_NUMBER is ELIGIBLE and VELOCITY is SLOW then SLOW_SEQUENCE

if KEY_NUMBER is ELIGIBLE and VELOCITY is MEDIUM then MEDIUM_SEQUENCE if KEY_NUMBER is ELIGIBLE and VELOCITY is FAST then FAST_SEQUENCE

..................................etc.

Each rule is producing a number which is calculated from the cross section of the input value with the membership functions. The rule is winning that is having the highest value assigned during the calculations. In this case membership functions corresponding to the VELOCITY employed in the fuzzy controller are triangular [4]. These are common principles of the fuzzy logic-based processing systems, applied to pipe organ control.

6 Conclusions

It seems that through the use of the mentioned techniques, the new approach to the musical instruments control may be found, namely a knowledge discovery approach widely used in the artificial intelligence systems. As many interesting sounds and musical effects occur on the verge of chaos, operating on this border requires refined techniques. Such approaches as rough sets and fuzzy logic supporting neural networks show a considerable promise for the identification and control of nonlinear dynamic systems, to which most of the musical instruments belong to.

This kind of approach to the musical instruments may give measures for understanding the perception of musical complexity and might result in practical conclusions and solutions in the domain of musical instruments control.

References

1. Kostek B, Czyzewski A: Articulation features in the digitally controlled pipe organ. In: Proc. 90th Audio Eng. Soc. Conv., Preprint 3023, Paris, 1991, 1-20, J. Audio Eng. Soc. 1991; 39, N. 5 (Abstr) : 440
2. Kostek B, Czyzewski A: Computer Modelling of the Pipe Organ Valve Action. In: Proc. 92nd Audio Eng. Soc. Conv., Preprint 3266, Vienna, 1992, 1-18, J. Audio Eng. Soc., 1992; 40, N. 5 (Abstr) : 382
3. Kostek B: Untersuchungen an Orgeltrakturen unter dem Aspekt musikalischer Artikulierung. In: FORTSCHRITTE DER AKUSTIK, Teil A, DAGA '92, Berlin, 1992 pp 245-248
4. American Neural Logix. NLX 230 Fuzzy Microcontroller Application Note, Sanford, U.S.A. 1992

An Implementation of Decomposition Algorithm and its Application in Information Systems Analysis and Logic Synthesis

Tadeusz Łuba, Robert Lasocki

Institute of Telecommunications, Warsaw University of Technology
Warsaw, Poland

Janusz Rybnik

AT&T Polska
Warsaw, Poland

Abstract

In this paper we consider the problem of decomposition of information and logic systems and its implementation using decision and truth tables, respectively. The main reason behind using the described method is its economic representation of knowledge in information systems, knowledge base, data base and in all the other applications of information storing systems. Another potentially very promising area of application of decomposition is logic systems designing. This is because the novel hardware building blocks impose limitations on the size of circuits that can be implemented with them. The decomposition method has been implemented as a set of tools including reduction of attributes as well as functional decomposition. The experimental results show that the method is very efficient.

1   Introduction

Avoiding data redundancy is an important problem in the implementation of information and logic systems. At present, the problem is over-come by minimizing the number of attributes and removing redundant decision rules. A similar problem arises in logic synthesis where circuit behavior is described by truth tables which are in fact decision tables with two valued attributes, where condition attributes are the input variables, and decision attributes are the output variables of the circuit. In the practical application of Boolean algebra the key problem is to represent Boolean functions by formulas which are as simple as possible. One approach to this simplification is to minimize the number of variables appearing in the truth table explicitly. Then the optimization concerns the so called product terms and relies on the minimization of their number. The above problem strictly corresponds to the problem of decision algorithms optimization.

This article presents a new approach based on decomposing a given system into smaller sub-systems. It is shown that a decomposed system (e.g. decision table) is superior to a monolithic one, specially with respect to memory space required to store data. In the logic synthesis problems, particularly in the field of programmable multi-block logic devices, the decompositional implementation is not a choice but a real necessity [1], [8], [9].

2 Decomposition Theory in Respect with Information Systems

2.1 Preliminary Notions

By an information system we mean a sequence $S =< U, A, V, f >$, where U is a set of objects, A is a set of attributes, V is a set of values of the attributes from A and f is a function which describes an element x in terms of its attribute values i.e.

$$f : U \times A \longrightarrow V \text{ and}$$

$$\bigwedge x \in U, \bigwedge a \in A \quad f(x, a) \in V_a$$

where V_a is a set of possible values of attribute a.

An information system is usually represented by its function f as data table with rows corresponding to objects and columns corresponding to attributes. A special class of information systems, called decision tables (DT) is used as a kind of description which specifies what decisions should be made when some conditions are satisfied.

Let $S =< U, A, V, f >$ be an information system and $C, D \subset A$ two subsets of attributes such that $C \cap D = \emptyset$ and $C \cup D = A$, called condition and decision attributes respectively. Information system S with specified condition and decision attributes will be called a decision table, and will be denoted by $DT =< U, C, D, V, f >$.

Every information system $S =< U, A, V, f >$ generates a partition Π_S and every attribute a generates a partition Π_a that represents the equivalence classes of binary relation IND on U defined as follows:

Let $B \subseteq A, \ x, y \in U$

$$(x, y) \in IND(B) \qquad \text{iff } f(x, a) = f(y, a) \text{ for every } a \in B$$

If we denote the equivalence classes of $IND(B)$ as Π_B, then

$$\Pi_B = \prod_{a \in B} \Pi_a$$

where $\prod$ denotes the product of partitions.

Using the above notion of partition generated by a set of attributes we can introduce a functional relation between disjoint subsets C, D of A.

We say that D functionally depends on C (in symbols $C \Longrightarrow D$) iff Π_C is not greater than Π_D (i.e. $\Pi_C \leq \Pi_D$).

2.2   Decomposition of a Decision Table

Many problems related to decision making are of the following nature: given a decision table – find the minimal decision algorithm associated with the table. In machine learning the idea of simplifying the instance space is well known and relies on selecting the most representative examples from the set of all examples before rule learning.

Another approach to reduction of instance space may be based on the technique called decomposition, which compresses sets of examples, attributes, and attribute-value tuples. The main idea is to decompose a decision table into subsystems in such a way that the complete DT can always be recovered by means of a sequential operations. Decomposition influences the possible storage savings or other considerations.

Basically the need for decomposition arises very naturally in the case of functional dependencies. The meaning of the dependency relation is as follows: holding the condition $C \implies D$ assures that if a pair of objects cannot be distinguished by means of the attributes belonging to the set C, then it cannot be distinguished by the attributes from the set D, in other words the values of the attributes from the set D are determined by the values of the attributes from the set C.

Functional decomposition may lead to a complex structure in which the global description is broken down sequentially into smaller and smaller subtables and at each step of the process the data associated with the attributes being resolved should be regenerable from the several data collections defined. Such a structure is called a multi-stage decomposition.

Let F be a function representing functional dependency $D = F(C)$, where C is the set of condition attributes and D is the set of decision attributes.

Let A, B be the subsets of C such that $C = A \cup B$ and $A \cap B = \emptyset$. We say that there is a functional decomposition of F iff

$$F(C) = H(A, G(B)) = H(A, g)$$

where G and H denote functional dependencies: $G(B) = g$ and $H(A, g) = D$.

In other words we try to find a function H depending on the attributes of the set A as well as on the decision of a function G depending on the set B. The decisions of the function H are identical with the decisions of F.

As the data tables are usually stored in computer memory we are usually interested in fictitious attributes with minimum number of values. In searching the attributes of set A ensuring the minimum number of values for variable g we use a test based on a quotient partition.

Let τ and ρ be partitions on a set S, and $\tau \geq \rho$. Then $\tau | \rho$ is the quotient partition of τ over ρ, whose elements are the blocks of ρ and whose blocks are those of τ.

The minimum number of values of fictitious attribute g, sufficient to represent the function F in the form $F = H(A, G(B))$ is equal to the number of elements in the largest block of the quotient partition $P(A) | P_F$.

Having estimated the sets of attributes with respect to fictitious attribute g, we formulate the main problem in the following theorem.

Theorem 2.1 *Functions G and H represent a functional decomposition of function F i.e. $F = H(A, G(B))$ iff there exists a partition $\Pi_G \geq P(B)$ such* *that*

$$P(A) \cdot \Pi_G \leq P(D) \tag{1}$$

where all the partitions are over the set of objects and the number of values of component G is equal to the number of blocks (i.e. equivalence classes) of partition Π_G.

The structure of the decomposed function is shown in the Fig. 1. The procedure of making a final decision is as follows: a supplementary decision is made on the basis of the attributes' subset B and then taking into consideration both the supplementary decision and the attributes subset A, the final decision is made, which is equal to the corresponding value of the function.

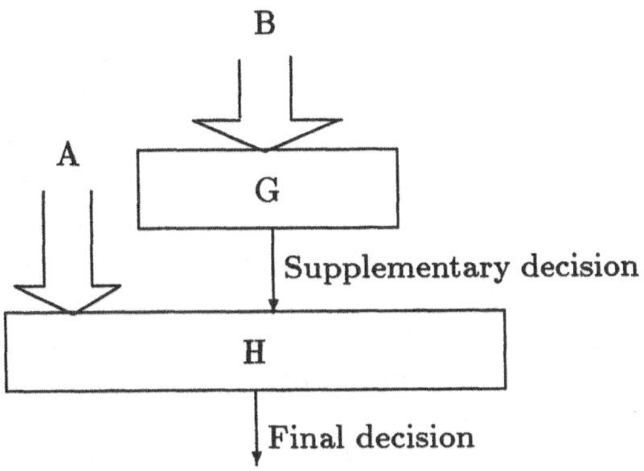

Fig. 1 Two-stage realization of a decision table

In the theorem the partition Π_G represents component G, and the product of partitions $P(A)$ and Π_G corresponds to H. The decision tables of the resulting components can be easily obtained from these partitions and the gain of the whole process arises from the fact that the two components (i.e. tables G and H) generally require less memory space than the non-decomposed table.

The main task in decomposition process is to find a subset of attributes for component G which, when applied as supplementary decision for component H will generate final decision F, i.e. to find $P(B)$, such that there exists $\Pi_G \geq P(B)$ that satisfies condition (1) in Theorem 2.1. To solve this problem, consider a subset of condition attributes, B, and an m-block partition $P(B) = (B_1; B_2; \ldots; B_m)$ generated by this subset.

A relation of compatibility of partition blocks will be used to verify whether or not partition $P(B)$ is suitable for functional decomposition.

Two blocks $B_i, B_j \in P(B)$ are compatible if and only if partition Π'_G obtained from partition $P(B)$ by merging blocks B_i and B_j into a single block B'_{ij} satisfies condition (1) in Theorem 2.1, i.e., iff

$$P(A) \cdot \Pi'_G \leq P_D$$

A subset of n partition blocks, $\mathcal{B} = \{B_{i_1}, B_{i_2}, \ldots, B_{i_n}\}$, where $B_{i_j} \in P(B)$, is a class of compatible blocks for partition $P(B)$ iff all blocks in $\mathcal{B}$ are pairwise compatible.

A compatible class is called Maximal Compatible Class (MCC) iff it cannot be properly covered by any other compatible class.

So the set $M = \{MCC_1, \ldots, MCC_r\}$ of all Maximal Compatible Classes can be formed from the set of all compatible pairs (B_i, B_j), which in this case can be interpreted as arcs of a graph $G = (\mathbf{B}, COM)$, where elements of **B** represent its vertices, COM represents the compatibility relation and where two vertices are connected by an arc iff B_i and B_j are compatible i.e. $(B_i, B_j) \in COM$. In such a formulation the procedure for computing the MCCs can be summarized as follows:

Let S_j be the set containing all the blocks B_i for which B_j and B_i are compatible and $i < j$.

a) A compatible list (CC-list) is initiated with one set containing the first block as its only element.

b) If S_j is an empty set, a new class consisting of one block B_j is added to the CC-list before moving to the next S. Since block B_j is in conflict with blocks B_1 to B_{j-1}, it is placed in a one element set.

c) If S_j is not empty, its intersection with every member CC of the current CC-list, $S_j \cap CC$ is calculated. If the intersection is empty, the sets are not changed, otherwise a new class is created by adding to the intersection an one element set B_j.

The next step of calculating of Π_G is only a process of selecting only a subset of MCCs that cover the set of all blocks of P_G i.e. $\mathbf{B} = \{B_1, ..., B_m\}$. This procedure is based on the following observation. As for each $MCC_i \in M$, where $MCC_i = \{B_{i_1}, B_{i_2}, \ldots, B_{i_k}\}$, a partition

$$\Pi = \{\{B_{i_1}, B_{i_2}, \ldots, B_{i_k}\}, \{B_{i_{k+1}}\}, \ldots, \{B_{i_m}\}\}$$

satisfies the inequality $P(A) \cdot \Pi \leq P_D$, then the partition Π_G satisfying the same inequality i.e. $P(A) \cdot \Pi_G \leq P_D$ and having the minimum number of blocks can be found by solving the following cover problem:

$$\bigcup MCC_j = \mathbf{B} \text{ and } k = \min.$$

The minimal k ensures the minimum number of blocks of partition Π_G. In other words we try to find a subset of MCCs such that their union results in the set **B**.

We will describe a selection $MIN(M) = \{MCC_{i_1}, MCC_{i_2}, \ldots, MCC_{i_r}\}$ of all MCCs in the form of a binary matrix M for which an element m_{ij} $(i = 1, \ldots, r = CARD(\mathbf{B}), j = 1, \ldots, t = CARD(M))$ is defined as follows

$$m_{ij} = \begin{cases} 1, & \text{if } x_j \in C_i \\ 0, & \text{otherwise} \end{cases}$$

Thus, the M matrix is a 0-1 matrix determined by the MCCs and the problem transforms to the classical Boolean matrix covering problem, often called the Unate Covering problem [5], where the goal is to select an optimal set L of MCCs corresponding to columns of M. Here a "column covering" L means that every row of M contains a "1" in some column which appears in L. More precisely, a column cover of binary matrix is defined as a set L of columns such that for every i:

$$\sum_{j \in L} m_{ij} \geq 1$$

Cover L of M is in one-to-one correspondence with the selected subset of MCCs such that their union forms the set $\mathbf{B}$.

The $MIN(M)$ represents partition $\Pi_G = \{\beta_1, \ldots, \beta_k\}$ in the following way: $\beta = \{B_{i_1}, B_{i_2}, \ldots, B_{i_q}\}$ is a block of Π_G if and only if $\beta \subseteq MCC$ and there is no β' such that $\beta \cap \beta' \neq \emptyset$. Thus blocks of Π_G can be created from MCC by eliminating the repeated elements of B in the minimal cover $MIN(M)$. The final Π_G is a result of the union of objects forming a set of blocks included in any one block of Π_G.

3 Implementation and Experimental Results

The decomposition method has been implemented within the PLA-based Synthesis System (PLASS), a modular environment integrating our own tools and providing interface to third party tools. Originally it was intended to manage logic synthesis processes, however, the flexibility of our methods allows for its application in information systems analysis as well. In fact it proved to be very efficient in this case.

At present the system contains two tools:

1. *Functional Decomposer* implementing decomposition of decision tables based on the theory given in section 2.2, and decomposition of truth tables [3].

2. *Argument/Attribute Minimizer* implementing minimization of the set of attributes and input variables based on unate complement concept [4].

Table 1 the presents results of our method applied to Information Analysis examples. Performance parameter shows the data compression factor achieved by decomposing the original decision table into two smaller decision tables. In the case of the example House the decomposition process was preceded by the attribute minimizer which substantially reduced the attributes of the original table.

Table 1

Name	Performance	Rows/Columns
MISEX2	94%	100x43
RD84	32%	256x12
MISEX3	88%	2103x12
ALU4	83%	1547x22
9SYM	46%	87x10
Z4	71%	128x11
RD73	37%	141x9
House	41%	231x17

Table 2 presents the results of decomposition applied to Logic Synthesis examples. Profit rate shows the silicon area saved by decomposing original truth table into two smaller truth tables. In all the examples the decomposition is followed by a minimization procedure which directly leads to physical structures.

The described method has also been implemented in a prototype decomposition program dedicated to FPGA-based logic synthesis [6]. The input to the

Table 2

Name	Original area	Area after decomposition	Profit rate
z9sym	1045	475	54%
rd84	1620	660	59%
life	798	369	54%
rd53	234	180	23%
test4	4830	3524	27%
z4	720	556	23%
adr4	3360	1585	53%

program is a truth table and the output is a network of n-input m-output cells, each realizing an n-variable function of m outputs. However the numbers n, m can be fixed arbitrarily, in the present version we assumed $2 \leq n \leq 5$ and $1 \leq m \leq 2$ as it covers all the existing FPGA cells. Table 3. shows the results of decomposition of the benchmark circuits into five-input two-output cells, which is in fact the decomposition aimed at the Xilinx Logic Blocks. The comparison of our results with the other published results shows that the proposed method does not suffer because of its universality but, in fact, provides better solutions in many cases.

Table 3

Name	Our method	Sasao [7]	mis-pga (new)	HYDRA [1]	ASYL [8]	Chortle [2]	TRADE [9]
rd84	5	11	10	27	17	35	8
rd73	4	6	6	13	30	16	5
misex1	7	22	11	8	13	11	14
z4	3	5	5	4	4	3	4
5xp1	8	18	18	21	24	24	11
sao2	11	–	28	36	36	27	27
9sym	4	7	7	33	8	51	6

4 Conclusions

A new method that permits reduction of space requirements for information storing and logic systems, based on functional decomposition, has been presented. The method is general in the sense that many kinds of information storing systems and all kinds of Boolean functions can be processed. The conceptual layer of the method and its core are very general. They can be applied to many decomposition problems in knowledge representation, data base and logic systems and especially to the problems where the nominal data cannot be reduced to the quantitative data without substantial loss of information. In the case of logic synthesis the presented procedure is universal, i.e., it can be applied to completely or incompletely specified, binary or multiple-valued Boolean functions and any decomposition topology making it suitable for various implementation styles including PLAs and FPGAs. The input and output routines and the analysis of the problem are only to be tuned to a particular problem. The preliminary experimental results obtained from the software implementation of the method show that the method is very efficient.

References

[1] D. Filo, J.C. Yang, F. Mailhot, and G.D. Micheli, Technology Mapping for a Two-Output RAM-based Field-Programmable Gate Array. Proc. European Conference on Design Automation, pp. 534–538, 1991.

[2] R. Francis, J. Rose, Z. Vranesic, Chortle-crf: Fast Technology Mapping Look-up Table-Based FPGAs. Proc. 28-th ACM/IEEE Design Automation Conf., pp. 227–233, 1991.

[3] T. Luba, R. Lasocki, Decomposition of multiple-valued boolean functions. Journal of Applied Mathematics and Computer Science, vol. 4, No.1., WSI Zielona Góra, 1994.

[4] T. Luba, J. Rybnik, Algorithm of Elimination of Attributes and Arguments Based on Unate Complement Concept. Bull. Polish Acad. Sci., vol. 40, No. 3. pp. 313–322, 1992.

[5] T. Luba, J. Rybnik, Rough Sets and Some Aspects in Logic Synthesis. In Intelligent Decision Support – Handbook of Application and Advances of the Rough Sets Theory, R. Słowiński (ed), Kluwer Academic Publishers, 1992.

[6] T. Luba, H. Selvaraj, A. Kraśniewski, A New Approach to FPGA-based Logic Synthesis. Workshop on Design Methodologies for Microelectronics and Signal Processing, Gliwice – Cracow, pp. 135–142, 1993.

[7] T. Sasao, Logic Synthesis and Optimization. Kluwer Academic Publishers, 1993.

[8] P. Sicard, M. Crastes, K. Sakouti, G. Saucier, Automatic synthesis of boolean functions on Xilinx and Actel Programmable devices. Proc. Euro ASIC '91. pp. 142–145, 1991.

[9] W. Wan, M.A. Perkowski, A New Approach to the Decomposition of Incompletely Specified Multi-Output Function Based on Graph Coloring and Local Transformations and Its Application to FPGA Mapping. Proc. European Design Automation Conf., pp. 230–235, 1992.

ESEP: An Expert System for Environmental Protection

Jerzy W. Grzymala-Busse
Department of Electrical Engineering and Computer Science, University of Kansas
Lawrence, KS 66045, U. S. A.

Abstract

An expert system called ESEP (Expert System for Environmental Protection) was developed to enhance facility compliance under Sections 311, 312, and 313 of the Emergency Planning and Community Right to Know Act. The transfer of knowledge from knowledge sources, such as state Right-to-Know Program experts and data bases, into the knowledge base of ESEP was done in part directly, in the form of interviews, and in part indirectly, by using machine learning. The machine learning system LERS (Learning from Examples based on Rough Sets) used in the project was forced to handle uncertainty because input data had missing values and inconsistencies. The tool used to deal with inconsistencies was rough set theory, developed by Z. Pawlak in the early 80's. The system LERS is implemented in C and runs on VAX 9000. On the other hand, the system ESEP is implemented in C and runs on any PC.

1 Introduction

The expert system described in this work and called ESEP (Expert System for Environmental Protection) has been built as a result of a two-year project funded by the U. S. Environmental Protection Agency. In 1986 Congress passed the Emergency Planning and Community Right to Know Act as Title III of the Superfund Amendments and Reauthorization Act (SARA). Under Title III of SARA, facilities are required to report extremely hazardous substances they store and accidental releases of some chemicals. This information is provided to the Local Emergency Planning Committees (LEPCs). The system ESEP was developed to enhance facility compliance under Sections 311, 312, and 313 of Title III and to assist Local Emergency Planning Committees in community-response planning. The main objective of the project was to develop a system based on information obtained from three counties: Douglas, Sedgwick, and Wyandotte in the state of Kansas.

2 Knowledge Acquisition

The most important stage in building an expert system is knowledge acquisition—the process of transferring knowledge from human experts, data bases, textbooks, manuals and so on into the knowledge base [1].

The basic source of knowledge in the project was the Kansas Right-to-Know Program developed by the Kansas Department of Health and Environment. A number of data bases, state- or nation-wide, were reviewed from the viewpoint of their usefulness for knowledge acquisition for the expert system ESEP. The crucial criterion for data base selection was the presence of attributes that may be useful for identification of noncomplying facilities.

An example of the set of attributes with their values, describing Section 313 of Title III of SARA, is given below:

Annual-Sales-in-Millions-of-Dollars: Don't-Know, <1, 1–9, 10–49, >50,

Flammable-or-Combustible-Storage-Tanks: Don't-Know, No, Yes,

Floor-Space-in-Thousands-of-Square-Feet: Don't-Know, <10, 10–100, >100,

Number-of-Employees: <10, 10–49, 50–99, >100,

RCRA-Defined-Hazardous-Waste: Don't-Know, Yes,

RCRA-Permit-for-Hazardous-Waste: Don't-Know, No, Yes,

SIC-Code-for-Products: Don't-Know, 14,..., 59,

SIC-Code-for-Purchases: Don't-Know, 50, 51,

Spraying-or-Dipping-of-Flammable-Materials: Don't-Know, No,

Use-of-Ammonium-Nitrate: Don't-Know, Yes,

Use-of-Compressed-Gases: Don't-Know, No, Sometimes,

Use-of-Flammable-Liquids: Don't-Know, No,

Use-of-Liquefied-Gases: Don't-Know, No, Yes,

Use-of-Materials-Dangerous-when-Wet: Don't-Know, No,

Use-of-Materials-with-Material-Safety-Data-Sheet: Don't-Know, No,

Use-of-Spontaneously-Combustible-Materials: Don't-Know, No, Regularly,
Sometimes.

Although more than twenty data bases owned by state and federal governmental agencies were investigated, most of them were not useful because they contained only partial information. It was difficult to identify the same companies from different data bases (e.g., different agencies use different identification codes for companies), there were different dates of last update of data bases, and—last but not least—in some cases data base owners were uncooperative. Another problem was that access to data bases containing only data about filers under Title III has not been sufficient—learning is efficient if it is done from not only positive examples but also from negative examples (characteristics of companies that do not need to comply under Title III).

The first useful decision table was compiled from Emergency Planning Surveys developed and collected by an LEPC member in Wyandotte County. The next useful source of knowledge was two enforcement experts in the Kansas-Right-to-Know Program. The knowledge in the form of rules was acquired from the experts by interviewing.

The next source of knowledge was a facility survey created specially for this purpose. These surveys were mailed to a random sample of 800 facilities within the three counties. Unfortunately, less than one hundred responded.

468

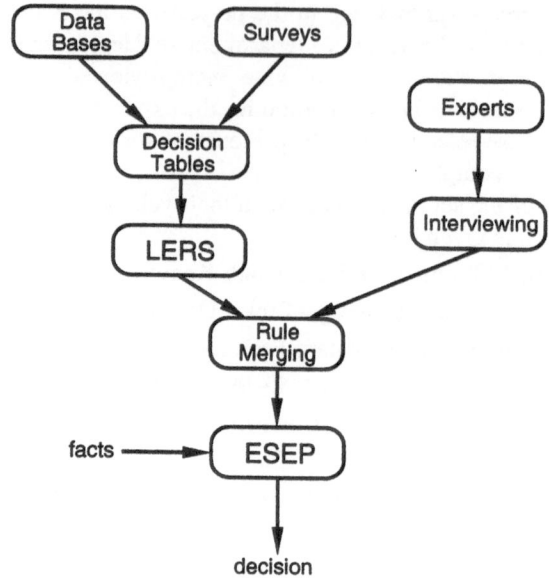

Figure 1. Knowledge Acquisition for ESEP

The data base FINDS (Facilities-INDex System), maintained by the U. S. Environmental Protection Agency, was eventually used for cross-referencing.

Decision tables, in the format of the input data file for the machine learning system LERS (Learning from Examples based on Rough Sets), were created from data bases and surveys. Rule sets induced from decision tables by the system LERS and rule sets obtained from interviewing experts were verified and merged together before being put into the expert system ESEP; see Figure 1.

3 Machine Learning System LERS

The machine learning system looks for regularities in a data set, finally inducing a set of rules of the following format:

if (attribute_1, value_1) **and** ⋯ **and** (attribute_n, value_n) **then** (decision, value).

System LERS [2] finds a minimal description of a concept described by positive examples while at the same time excluding from the description of the concept the remaining, negative examples. Rules, induced by LERS, are more general than information contained in the original decision table representing input data, since— in general—more new examples may be correctly classified by rules than may be matched with examples from the original decision table.

An example of the very simple decision table is presented in Table 1. The decision table from Table 1 has nine examples, named *A, B,..., F*.

The variable *Name* from Table 1 is not an actual attribute. Attributes are variables *RCRA-Waste-Permit*, *SIC-Products*, *SIC-Purchase*, and *Ammonium-Nitrate-Use*. A decision is variable 313-*Filer*. Table 1 is presented here only for

Table 1

Name	RCRA- Waste-Permit	SIC- Products	SIC- Purchase	Ammonium- Nitrate-Use	313-Filer
A	No	48	50	No	No
B	Yes	48	50	No	Yes
C	No	48	50	Yes	Yes
D	No	48	51	Yes	Yes
E	Yes	20	50	No	Yes
F	Yes	20	50	No	No

illustration. The actual decision tables will have many more variables and examples. The current version of system LERS can handle about one hundred attributes and a few thousand examples.

System LERS may work with imperfect data, i.e., with uncertainty in the input decision table [1, 3]. There are two kinds of uncertainty in decision tables: missing values of attributes or inconsistent examples. Missing attribute values are caused by lack of information or *don't care* values. The latter case happens when we do not care what the attribute value is. Two examples are inconsistent when they are characterized by the values of all attributes, but they belong to two different concepts. A decision table with at least one pair of inconsistent examples is called *inconsistent*. Table 1 is an example of the inconsistent decision table. Indeed, examples *E* and *F* are inconsistent, because the corresponding values of all attributes: *RCRA-Waste-Permit*, *SIC-Products*, *SIC-Purchase*, and *Ammonium-Nitrate-Use* are identical, yet the values of the decision are different, *Yes* and *No*, respectively.

LERS handles inconsistencies using rough set theory [4, 5]. Let U denote the set of all examples of the decision table and let P denote a nonempty subset of the set Q of all variables, i.e., attributes and decisions. Obviously, set P defines an equivalence relation $\wp$ on U, where two examples x and y from U belong to the same equivalence class of $\wp$ if and only if both x and y are characterized by the same values of each attribute from P. The set of all equivalence classes of $\wp$ will be denoted U/P. In the example of Table 1, for $P = \{RCRA\text{-}Waste\text{-}Permit, SIC\text{-}Products\}$,

$$U/P = \{\{A, C, D\}, \{B\}, \{E, F\}\},$$

where $U = \{A, B, C, D, E, F\}$.

Equivalence classes of $\wp$ are called *elementary sets of* P. Any finite union of elementary sets of P is called a *definable set in* P. Let X be any subset of U. In general, X is not a definable set in P. However, set X may be approximated by two definable sets in P, the first one is called a *lower approximation of* X *in* P, denoted by $\underline{P}X$ and defined as follows

$$\cup\{Y \in U/P \mid Y \subseteq X \}.$$

The second set is called an *upper approximation of* X *in* P, denoted by $\bar{P}X$ and defined as follows

$$\cup \{ Y \in U/P \mid Y \cap X \neq \emptyset \}.$$

The lower approximation of X in A is the greatest definable set in P, contained in X. The upper approximation of X in P is the least definable set in P containing X. A *rough set of* X is the family of all subsets of U having the same lower and the same upper approximations of X.

For any concept X, described by the decision with fixed value, the system LERS induces *certain rules* from the set $\underline{A}X$ of positive examples and set $U - \underline{A}X$ as the set of negative examples, where A is the set of all attributes. Similarly,

possible rules are induced from the set $\bar{A}X$ of positive examples and set $U - \bar{A}X$ as the set of negative examples.

For decision table from Table 1, set $X = \{A, F\}$ describes the concept: decision 313-*Filer* has value *No*, and for $P = \{RCRA\text{-}Waste\text{-}Permit, SIC\text{-}Products, SIC\text{-}Purchase, Ammonium\text{-}Nitrate\text{-}Use\}$,

$$U/P = \{\{A\}, \{B\}, \{C\}, \{D\}, \{E, F\}\},$$

$$\underline{P}X = \{A\},$$

and

$$\bar{P}X = \{A, E, F\}.$$

Let x be in U. We say that x is *certainly in* X if and only if $x \in \underline{P}X$, and that x is *possibly in* X if and only if $x \in \bar{P}X$. Our terminology originates from the fact that we want to decide if x is in X on the basis of a definable set in A rather than on the basis of X. This means that we deal with $\underline{P}X$ and $\bar{P}X$ instead of X. Since $\underline{P}X \subseteq X \subseteq \bar{P}X$, if x is in $\underline{P}X$, it is certainly in X. On the other hand, if x is in $\bar{P}X$, it is possibly in X.

A *quality of lower approximation of* X *by* P is equal to

$$\frac{|\underline{P}X|}{|U|},$$

where for a set Z, $|Z|$ denotes the cardinality of Z. Thus, the quality of lower approximation of X by P in S is the ratio of the number of all certainly classified examples by attributes from P as being in X to the number of all examples of the system. It is a kind of relative frequency. Note that quality of lower approximation is a *belief function* according to Dempster-Shafer theory [6]. In our example, the quality of lower approximation of $X = \{A, F\}$ by $P = \{RCRA\text{-}Waste\text{-}Permit, SIC\text{-}Products, SIC\text{-}Purchase, Ammonium\text{-}Nitrate\text{-}Use\}$ is equal to

$$\frac{|\{A\}|}{|U|} = \frac{1}{6} = 0.166667.$$

A quality of upper approximation of X by P is equal to

$$\frac{|\bar{P}X|}{|U|} \cdot$$

The *quality of upper approximation of* X *by* P is the ratio of the number of all possibly classified examples by attributes from P as being in X to the number of all examples of the system. Therefore, it is again a kind of relative frequency. The quality of upper approximation is a *plausibility function* from the Dempster-Shafer theory viewpoint. Rough set theory is objective—for given decision table, qualities of corresponding approximations are computed. On the other hand, Dempster-Shafer theory is subjective—it is assumed that values of belief (or plausibility) are given by an expert. In our example, the quality of upper approximation of $X = \{A, F\}$ by $P = \{RCRA\text{-}Waste\text{-}Permit, SIC\text{-}Products, SIC\text{-}Purchase, Ammonium\text{-}Nitrate\text{-}Use\}$ is equal to

$$\frac{|\{A, E, F\}|}{|U|} = \frac{3}{6} = 0.5.$$

The main advantage of rough set theory is that it does not need any preliminary or additional information about data (like probability in probability theory, grade of membership in fuzzy set theory, etc.) [3]. In rough set theory approach inconsistencies are not removed from consideration. Instead, lower and upper approximations of the concept are computed. On the basis of these approximations, LERS computes two corresponding sets of rules: certain and possible [3].

The following rules are induced by running the program LERS for the input data file presented in Table 2:

Certain rules:

(RCRA-Waste-Permit, No) & (Ammonium-Nitrate-Use, No) -> (313-Filer, No),

(Ammonium-Nitrate-Use, Yes) -> (313-Filer, Yes),

(RCRA-Waste-Permit, Yes) & (SIC-Products, 48) -> (313-Filer, Yes),

and possible rules that are not certain:

(SIC-Products, 20) -> (313-Filer, No) with rough measure 0.5,

(RCRA-Waste-Permit, Yes) -> (313-Filer, Yes) with rough measure 0.666667.

Every rule induced by LERS is accompanied by its rough measure. The rough measure may be interpreted as the conditional probability that the rule correctly classifies examples from the concept when given is the set of all examples described by the rule. A *rough measure of the rule describing concept* X is equal to

$$\frac{|X \cap Y|}{|Y|},$$

where X is the concept and Y is the set of all examples described by the rule. The rough measure of the rule describing concept X is the ratio of the number of all examples from the concept X correctly described by the rule to the number of all examples described by the rule. Thus, it is a kind of relative frequency, that may be interpreted as a conditional probability $P(X| Y)$. Obviously, the rough measure of a

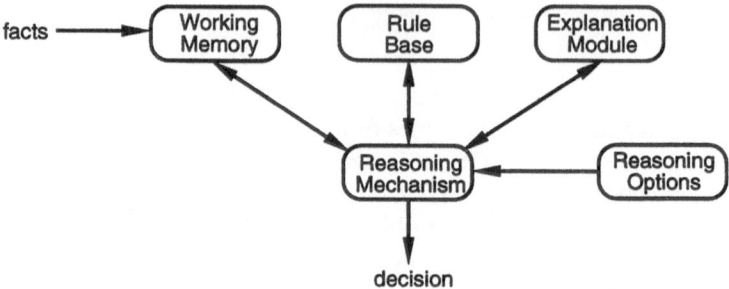

Figure 2. Structure of ESEP

certain rule is equal to 1. The higher rough measure for a possible rule the more reliable rule is. In our example, for the concept $X = \{A, F\}$ and possible rule

$$(\text{SIC-Products}, 20) \rightarrow (313\text{-Filer}, \text{No})$$

set $Y = \{E, F\}$, and rough measure is equal to

$$\frac{|\{A, F\} \cap \{E, F\}|}{|\{E, F\}|} = \frac{|\{F\}|}{|\{E, F\}|} = \frac{1}{2} = 0.5.$$

Table 1 is just an example of the decision table, describing the method; with actual data the set of rules would be more complicated. However, the principle remains.

4 System ESEP

The expert system ESEP, developed in the project, has the following components: a rule base, a working memory, a reasoning mechanism, and an explanation module; see Figure 2. The rule base is a file containing knowledge, in the form of rules, describing conditions identifying a facility as either a potential candidate for compliance with the Title III requirements or as one free from this duty. The working memory is represented by a part of the system that, when activated, asks the user for values of all attributes characterizing facilities. The reasoning mechanism of ESEP is simple and efficient since no chaining of rules is necessary—every decision is made in one step. The explanation module is based on a special file with explanations, accompanying a rule file.

The system ESEP is universal: it may be loaded with any kind of rule file in the format of a rules set induced by LERS (for example, such rule files may correspond to different sections of Title III of SARA).

In general, it is possible that a few rules match known facts describing a given facility. Even more, rules may indicate conflicting decisions. In this case ESEP warns the user that more than one solution is possible and informs him/her which solution is most likely as well (the corresponding rule has the highest rough measure). It is possible to run ESEP in a way that only rules reliable enough—those with rough measures greater than some given threshold—will be activated. Another possibility is that no decision is produced by ESEP because no one single rule may be activated with the given facts. If this is so, a solution is to use one of the special options of ESEP: matching rules with given facts *less one fact, two facts*, or *three facts*. If one of these three options is selected, say *less one fact*, than ESEP tries to match rules with given facts plus an arbitrary fact. Thus, if the rule is

$$(A_1, v_1) \,\&\, (A_2, v_2) \,\&\, (A_3, v_3) \to (D, w)$$

and only two facts, say (A_1, v_1) and (A_2, v_2) are given, the rule will be activated and the system will inform the user that the decision may have value w provided that the additional fact, (A_3, v_3), is known. This option increases dramatically the number of rules that may be used. At the same time, the user must select the solution on the basis of a guess: which missing fact is the most likely.

5 Concluding Remarks

The pollution of the environment, including releases of toxic chemicals, and potential danger created by storage of hazardous substances in excessive amounts have been subjects of concern on the local, state, and national level. It is extremely important to provide sufficient information to Emergency Response personnel at all levels. The expert system ESEP has been developed with this need in mind. Technically—as a computer program—the system is mature; it is robust, field-tested, and works reliably. However, its use is limited because its knowledge base, the crucial part of any expert system, is not yet finished. In order to improve the system, additional effort is required in the area of knowledge acquisition. Nevertheless, this should not be considered a fault because an expert system is never completely finished; there is always a room for improvement.

The other conclusion is that the role of surveys in the process of knowledge acquisition should not be underestimated—in this project it was the main source of knowledge.

References

1. Grzymala-Busse J. W. Managing Uncertainty in Expert Systems. Kluwer Academic Publishers, Dordrecht, The Netherlands, 1991.
2. Grzymala-Busse J. W. LERS—A system for learning from examples based on rough sets. In: Slowinski R. (ed.), Intelligent Decision Support Handbook of Applications and Advances of the Rough Sets Theory. Kluwer Academic Publishers, Dordrecht, The Netherlands, 1992, pp. 3–18.
3. Grzymala-Busse J. W. Knowledge acquisition under uncertainty—a rough set approach. Journal of Intelligent & Robotic Systems, 1988; 1:3–16.
4. Pawlak Z. Rough sets. Int. J. Computer and Information Sci., 1982; 11:341–356.
5. Pawlak Z. Rough Sets: Theoretical Aspects of Reasoning about Data. Kluwer Academic Publishers, Dordrecht, The Netherlands, 1991.
6. Shafer G. A Mathematical Theory of Evidence. Princeton University Press, Princeton, New Jersey, 1976.

Author Index

Published in 1990–92

AI and Cognitive Science '89, Dublin City
University, Eire, 14–15 September 1989
Alan F. Smeaton and Gabriel McDermott (Eds.)

**Specification and Verification of Concurrent
Systems,** University of Stirling, Scotland,
6–8 July 1988
C. Rattray (Ed.)

Semantics for Concurrency, Proceedings of the
International BCS-FACS Workshop, Sponsored
by Logic for IT (S.E.R.C.), University of
Leicester, UK, 23–25 July 1990
M. Z. Kwiatkowska, M. W. Shields and
R. M. Thomas (Eds.)

Functional Programming, Glasgow 1989
Proceedings of the 1989 Glasgow Workshop,
Fraserburgh, Scotland, 21–23 August 1989
Kei Davis and John Hughes (Eds.)

Persistent Object Systems, Proceedings of the
Third International Workshop, Newcastle,
Australia, 10–13 January 1989
John Rosenberg and David Koch (Eds.)

Z User Workshop, Oxford 1989, Proceedings of
the Fourth Annual Z User Meeting, Oxford,
15 December 1989
J. E. Nicholls (Ed.)

**Formal Methods for Trustworthy Computer
Systems (FM89),** Halifax, Canada,
23–27 July 1989
Dan Craigen (Editor) and Karen Summerskill
(Assistant Editor)

Security and Persistence, Proceedings of the
International Workshop on Computer
Architectures to Support Security and Persistence
of Information, Bremen, West Germany,
8–11 May 1990
John Rosenberg and J. Leslie Keedy (Eds.)

**Women into Computing: Selected Papers
1988–1990**
Gillian Lovegrove and Barbara Segal (Eds.)

3rd Refinement Workshop (organised by
BCS-FACS, and sponsored by IBM UK
Laboratories, Hursley Park and the Programming
Research Group, University of Oxford),
Hursley Park, 9–11 January 1990
Carroll Morgan and J. C. P. Woodcock (Eds.)

Designing Correct Circuits, Workshop jointly
organised by the Universities of Oxford and
Glasgow, Oxford, 26–28 September 1990
Geraint Jones and Mary Sheeran (Eds.)

Functional Programming, Glasgow 1990
Proceedings of the 1990 Glasgow Workshop on
Functional Programming, Ullapool, Scotland,
13–15 August 1990
Simon L. Peyton Jones, Graham Hutton and
Carsten Kehler Holst (Eds.)

4th Refinement Workshop, Proceedings of the
4th Refinement Workshop, organised by BCS-
FACS, Cambridge, 9–11 January 1991
Joseph M. Morris and Roger C. Shaw (Eds.)

AI and Cognitive Science '90, University of
Ulster at Jordanstown, 20–21 September 1990
Michael F. McTear and Norman Creaney (Eds.)

Software Re-use, Utrecht 1989, Proceedings of
the Software Re-use Workshop, Utrecht,
The Netherlands, 23–24 November 1989
Liesbeth Dusink and Patrick Hall (Eds.)

Z User Workshop, 1990, Proceedings of the Fifth
Annual Z User Meeting, Oxford,
17–18 December 1990
J.E. Nicholls (Ed.)

IV Higher Order Workshop, Banff 1990
Proceedings of the IV Higher Order Workshop,
Banff, Alberta, Canada, 10–14 September 1990
Graham Birtwistle (Ed.)

ALPUK91, Proceedings of the 3rd UK
Annual Conference on Logic Programming,
Edinburgh, 10–12 April 1991
Geraint A.Wiggins, Chris Mellish and
Tim Duncan (Eds.)

Specifications of Database Systems
International Workshop on Specifications of
Database Systems, Glasgow, 3–5 July 1991
David J. Harper and Moira C. Norrie (Eds.)

**7th UK Computer and Telecommunications
Performance Engineering Workshop**
Edinburgh, 22–23 July 1991
J. Hillston, P.J.B. King and R.J. Pooley (Eds.)

Logic Program Synthesis and Transformation
Proceedings of LOPSTR 91, International
Workshop on Logic Program Synthesis and
Transformation, University of Manchester,
4–5 July 1991
T.P. Clement and K.-K. Lau (Eds.)

Declarative Programming, Sasbachwalden 1991
PHOENIX Seminar and Workshop on Declarative
Programming, Sasbachwalden, Black Forest,
Germany, 18–22 November 1991
John Darlington and Roland Dietrich (Eds.)

Building Interactive Systems:
Architectures and Tools
Philip Gray and Roger Took (Eds.)

Functional Programming, Glasgow 1991
Proceedings of the 1991 Glasgow Workshop on
Functional Programming, Portree, Isle of Skye,
12–14 August 1991
Rogardt Heldal, Carsten Kehler Holst and
Philip Wadler (Eds.)

Object Orientation in Z
Susan Stepney, Rosalind Barden and
David Cooper (Eds.)

Code Generation – Concepts, Tools, Techniques
Proceedings of the International Workshop on Code
Generation, Dagstuhl, Germany, 20–24 May 1991
Robert Giegerich and Susan L. Graham (Eds.)

Z User Workshop, York 1991, Proceedings of the
Sixth Annual Z User Meeting, York,
16–17 December 1991
J.E. Nicholls (Ed.)

Formal Aspects of Measurement
Proceedings of the BCS-FACS Workshop on
Formal Aspects of Measurement, South Bank
University, London, 5 May 1991
Tim Denvir, Ros Herman and R.W. Whitty (Eds.)

AI and Cognitive Science '91
University College, Cork, 19–20 September 1991
Humphrey Sorensen (Ed.)

5th Refinement Workshop, Proceedings of the 5th
Refinement Workshop, organised by BCS-FACS,
London, 8–10 January 1992
Cliff B. Jones, Roger C. Shaw and
Tim Denvir (Eds.)

Algebraic Methodology and Software
Technology (AMAST'91)
Proceedings of the Second International Conference
on Algebraic Methodology and Software
Technology, Iowa City, USA, 22–25 May 1991
M. Nivat, C. Rattray, T. Rus and G. Scollo (Eds.)

ALPUK92, Proceedings of the 4th UK
Conference on Logic Programming,
London, 30 March–1 April 1992
Krysia Broda (Ed.)

Logic Program Synthesis and Transformation
Proceedings of LOPSTR 92, International
Workshop on Logic Program Synthesis and
Transformation, University of Manchester,
2–3 July 1992
Kung-Kiu Lau and Tim Clement (Eds.)

NAPAW 92, Proceedings of the First North
American Process Algebra Workshop, Stony Brook,
New York, USA, 28 August 1992
S. Purushothaman and Amy Zwarico (Eds.)

First International Workshop on Larch
Proceedings of the First International Workshop on
Larch, Dedham, Massachusetts, USA,
13–15 July1992
Ursula Martin and Jeannette M. Wing (Eds.)

Persistent Object Systems
Proceedings of the Fifth International Workshop on
Persistent Object Systems, San Miniato (Pisa),
Italy, 1–4 September 1992
Antonio Albano and Ron Morrison (Eds.)

Formal Methods in Databases and Software
Engineering, Proceedings of the Workshop on
Formal Methods in Databases and Software
Engineering, Montreal, Canada, 15–16 May 1992
V.S. Alagar, Laks V.S. Lakshmanan and
F. Sadri (Eds.)

Modelling Database Dynamics
Selected Papers from the Fourth International
Workshop on Foundations of Models and
Languages for Data and Objects,
Volkse, Germany, 19–22 October 1992
Udo W. Lipeck and Bernhard Thalheim (Eds.)